THE
LIRI VALLEY

Happy Birthday
to Moe
June 2/04
with Love
from
Grace

MARK ZUEHLKE

THE LIRI VALLEY

CANADA'S WORLD WAR II BREAKTHROUGH TO ROME

Douglas & McIntyre
Vancouver/Toronto/Berkeley

This book was published originally by Stoddart Publishing.

Douglas & McIntyre
2323 Quebec Street, Suite 201
Vancouver, British Columbia
Canada V5T 4S7
www.douglas-mcintyre.com

National Library of Canada Cataloguing in Publication Data
Zuehlke, Mark
    The Liri Valley: Canada's World War II breakthrough to Rome / Mark Zuehlke.

    Includes bibliographical references and index.
    ISBN 1-55365-013-1

    1. World War, 1939-1945—Campaigns—Italy—Liri River Valley.
2. Canada. Canadian Army—History—World War, 1939–1945. I. Title.
D763.I82L57 2003   940.54'21562   C2003-910549-0

Library of Congress Cataloging-in-Publication data is available.

Cover design by Peter Cocking
Cover photograph by Strathy Smith, NAC, PA-169121
Part title photograph by Daniel Crack
Interior design and typesetting by Kinetics Design & Illustration
Printed and bound in Canada by Friesens
Printed on acid-free paper
Distributed in the U.S. by Publishers Group West

The publisher gratefully acknowledges the financial support of the Canada Council for the Arts, the British Columbia Arts Council, and the Government of Canada through the Book Publishing Industry Development Program (BPIDP) for its publishing activities.

*War, which used to be cruel and magnificent,
has now become cruel and squalid.*

— Winston Churchill

*Of what use is decisive victory in battle
if we bleed to death as a result of it?*

— Liddell Hart

*Hey, Willy. You're going back
in a box if you don't watch out.*

— Sergeant Bill Worton, Seaforth Highlanders of Canada

CONTENTS

FOUR / The Pursuit

PREFACE

Since publication of *Ortona: Canada's Epic World War II Battle* in 1999, I have been blessed with ever more contacts within the small community of the remaining Canadian veterans of the World War II Italian Campaign. As was true of that first work in what is now to be a trilogy on this long, brutal, and costly campaign, this book would not have been possible without their contribution. It is their ability and willingness to reach back across the span of almost a lifetime to recount often painful wartime experiences that enriches the pages here. In letters, personal interviews, e-mail correspondence, and telephone calls, they provided the vivid details that — sifted together with the official records, regimental war diaries and official histories, autobiographies and biographies, and other archival materials — enabled depiction of the combat experienced by Canadians in the Liri Valley in the spring of 1944.

There is a school of thought in the study of military history that advocates the belief that veteran memories, filtered as they are by the span of time, are suspect. Accordingly, the only fact that can be relied upon is that provided by the official records and histories —

particularly where veteran memory contradicts such sources. Yet anyone delving into the official histories will find that the record is quite often muddled and contradicted by the accounts filed by soldiers at the time and by the many day-to-day records contained in the regimental war diaries. The "fog of war" becomes particularly thick during the furtive, desperate days when a great battle is under way and often the paperwork that ultimately becomes the basis for the official record is not completed until days or weeks after the event. Often, too, officers stationed well back of the fighting lines wrote these records with only passing consultation with the men who had been in combat.

So where is truth? The official record or the memories of the veterans? Each writer plunging into the writing of military history ultimately develops a personal, somewhat unscientific, process for filtering information. Mine involved using a fair degree of gut instinct and cross-checking supposed facts wherever possible. When two or three veterans said the same thing and this contradicted the official record, it seemed to me logical that these old soldiers, who had been there when the bullets and shrapnel were flying around them, were most likely telling the story truthfully. It should be particularly noted that I have yet to find a veteran who showered himself in glory and heroism. Most are modest to a fault about their own role in events.

For those caught in its maw, war is a terrifying and intensely mind-focusing experience. Sensations are heightened as the adrenaline courses through the body and memories were so deeply seared into the mind of many veterans that they will never be forgotten. It has been a source of amazement to me to discuss the fighting in the Liri Valley with a veteran and have him provide a precise time reference down to the virtual minute at which something pivotal occurred. Go back to the official war diaries and the veteran's time reference is seldom out and, if so, by no more than a minute or two.

I found that where a veteran was unsure of something, or simply could not remember, he invariably informed me of the fact. "I don't remember the details of this event" was a fairly common response to my oral or written questions. Often a battle had been so intense and prolonged that the events became a jumble or, as they often stated, "a blur." Yet through this haze of time, many incidents were starkly illuminated in their descriptions. Pierre Potvin's horrific, yet self-effacingly humorous, account of his suffering multiple wounds on the edge of the Hitler Line. Tony Kingsmill standing next to his experimental bridge at the Gari River and watching a flow of terribly injured young Indian soldiers stream past on their way to the rear. Tankers, like David Kinloch, seeing friends and comrades perish inside the burning wreckage of Sherman tanks. Those are the types of memories reflected in this book.

Finally, it should be noted that the many stories regarding the experiences of individual veterans related here normally align closely with the official accounts. Where there is discrepancy, I have endeavoured to verify details with other veterans or other historical source material. Seldom have I found a veteran in error and normally this was limited to mixing up dates and precise locations. Usually I have been able to locate sufficient other accounts by veterans or source material to enable the creation of an accurate depiction of events. Where the official record and that of veterans conflicted dramatically, I have more often trusted the veteran accounts. They lived the battle, buried comrades in its aftermath, and carried the scars of the physical and emotional wounds suffered there for the rest of their lives.

ACKNOWLEDGEMENTS

The veterans who contributed to this book are listed in the bibliography and it is to all of them that I owe the greatest thanks. I would, however, like to single out a few for specific recognition. Without Tony Poulin's meticulous translation of letters and accounts written by Pierre Potvin, that soldier's incredible ordeal before the Hitler Line would not be included here. Strome Galloway was always gracious and quick to respond to my queries on many topics. Victor Bulger, John Dougan, Stan Kanik, David Kinloch, Charles Prieur, and Frederick Ritchie were equally helpful and patient. Bill Worton served as a guide to other veterans in Vancouver. In a lengthy written account of his experiences, Donald Reid provided many details about the rear-area operations of a tank regiment that greatly broadened my understanding of armoured operations in Italy. Unfortunately, space limits did not allow inclusion of much of his material, but it is now deposited at the Museum of the Regiments in Calgary and will be a boon to other researchers.

The Battle of the Liri Valley was the first corps-scale engagement fought by Canadians in World War II. In its wake, military personnel generated many thousands of pages of reports, analyses, and accounts. The archivists and contacts in the regimental associations who helped me ferret out much of this valuable information are too numerous to mention all by name. Special thanks, however, to Tony Walters of the Rocky Mountain Rangers and Howard Hisdal of the British Columbia Dragoons. Thanks also to Dr. Steve Harris and others at the Department of National Defence, Directorate of History and Heritage, staff at the National Archives of Canada, Debbie Lindsey at the Canadian Broadcasting Corporation's Radio Archives, Chris Petter and the two Terrys at the University of Victoria's Special Collections, and Benoit Cameron at Royal Military College's Massey Library.

In Italy, Oreste Schiano di Zenise of Naples helped greatly with initial logistics and it was unfortunate that a communication glitch foiled our attempts to actually meet in Cassino. Federico Lamberti reorganized his business schedule to show me around Cassino and described many aspects of the battle that I had not previously encountered. The staff at Cassino's La Pace hotel went out of their way to provide a friendly environment to a Canadian researcher who spoke terrible Italian and was always asking another question about how to get somewhere or other or needing to send another e-mail.

Dr. Bill McAndrew supplied many useful contacts and information on various aspects of the Italian campaign. Alex McQuarrie in Ottawa helped greatly with enabling me to contact both Italians and Canadian veterans. He also hosted a great dinner with Strome Galloway and Tony Poulin for company. Major Michael Boire, now a professor at Royal Military College, offered valuable advice on what to look for during my battlefield tour.

I am privileged to once more have Elizabeth McLean as my manuscript editor and to work again with Don Bastian and Jim Gifford at Stoddart. Literary agent Carolyn Swayze continues to work her magic on the contractual and financial side of keeping this writer's career viable. I am blessed to have the companionship and support, both at home and, happily, also this time in Italy, of Frances Backhouse.

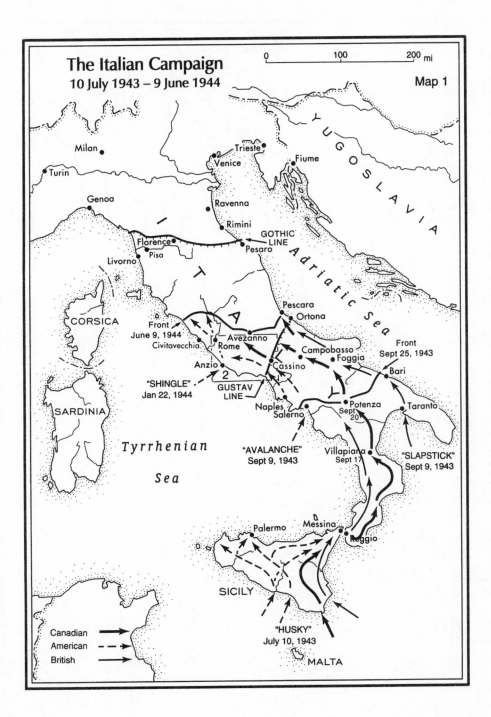

The Italian Campaign
10 July 1943 – 9 June 1944

Map 1

0   100   200 mi

MILAN •

Trieste
Venice
Fiume

Turin

Genoa

YUGOSLAVIA

Ravenna

Rimini

GOTHIC
LINE

Florence •
Pisa
Pesaro

Livorno

Adriatic Sea

CORSICA

Front
June 9, 1944
Avezanno
Civitavecchia
Rome

Pescara
Ortona

Anzio
Cassino

Campobasso
Foggia

Front
Sept 25, 1943

Bari

"SHINGLE"
Jan 22, 1944

GUSTAV
LINE

Naples
Salerno

Potenza
Sept
20

Taranto

SARDINIA

Tyrrhenian

Sea

"AVALANCHE"
Sept 9, 1943

Villapiana
Sept 17

"SLAPSTICK"
Sept 9, 1943

Palermo

Messina

Reggio

SICILY

Canadian
American
British

"HUSKY"
July 10, 1943

MALTA

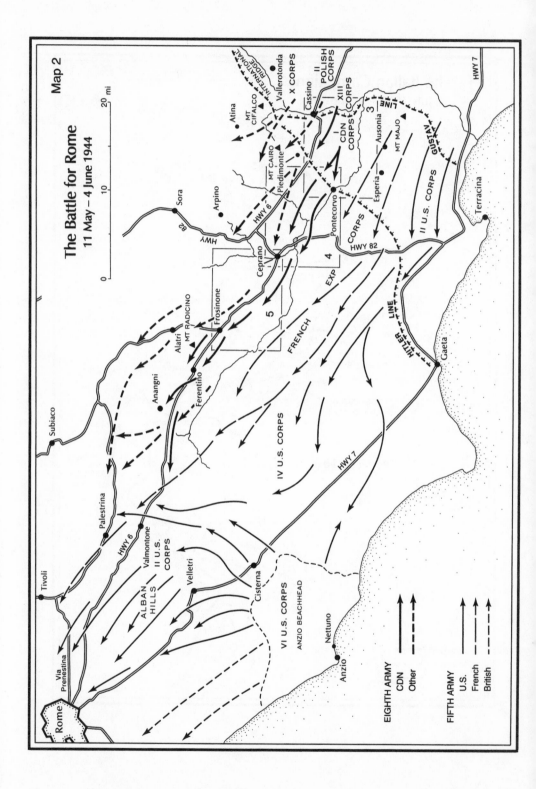

Map 2

The Battle for Rome
11 May – 4 June 1944

EIGHTH ARMY
CDN
Other

FIFTH ARMY
U.S.
French
British

Rome
Tivoli
Via Prenestina
Subiaco
Palestrina
HWY 6
ALBAN HILLS
Valmontone
II U.S. CORPS
Velletri
Anangni
Ferentino
Alatri
MT RADICINO
Frosinone
Cisterna
ANZIO BEACHHEAD
VI U.S. CORPS
Nettuno
Anzio
IV U.S. CORPS
HWY 7
5
FRENCH
EXP CORPS
4
Ceprano
HWY 82
Pontecorvo
HWY 6
HWY 82
Sora
Arpino
Piedimonte
MT CAIRO
MT CIFALCO
Atina
INTERNATIONAL BRIGADE
X CORPS
Vallerotonda
Cassino
II POLISH CORPS
XIII CORPS
CDN CORPS
1
3
Ausonia
MT MAJO
Esperia
GUSTAV LINE
II U.S. CORPS
HITLER LINE
Gaeta
Terracina
HWY 7

0   10   20 mi

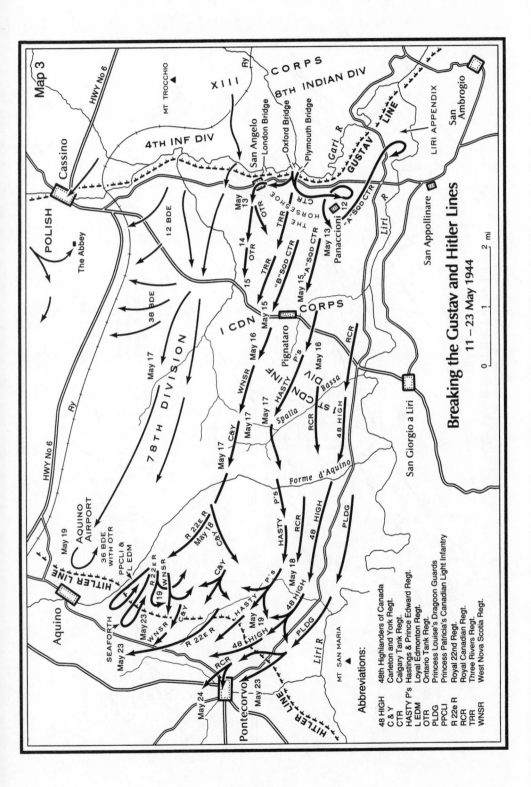

Map 3

Breaking the Gustav and Hitler Lines
11 – 23 May 1944

Abbreviations:

48 HIGH	48th Highlanders of Canada
C & Y	Carleton and York Regt.
CTR	Calgary Tank Regt.
HASTY P's	Hastings & Prince Edward Regt.
L EDM	Loyal Edmonton Regt.
OTR	Ontario Tank Regt.
PLDG	Princess Louise's Dragoon Guards
PPCLI	Princess Patricia's Canadian Light Infantry
R 22e R	Royal 22nd Regt.
RCR	Royal Canadian Regt.
TRR	Three Rivers Regt.
WNSR	West Nova Scotia Regt.

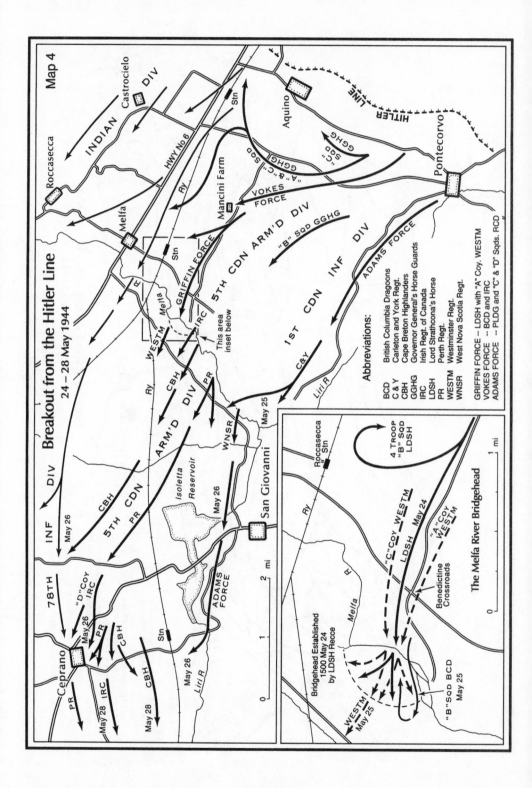

Map 4

Breakout from the Hitler Line
24–28 May 1944

Abbreviations:

BCD	British Columbia Dragoons
C & Y	Carleton and York Regt.
CBH	Cape Breton Highlanders
GGHG	Governor General's Horse Guards
IRC	Irish Regt. of Canada
LDSH	Lord Strathcona's Horse
PR	Perth Regt.
WESTM	Westminster Regt.
WNSR	West Nova Scotia Regt.

GRIFFIN FORCE -- LDSH with "A" Coy. WESTM
VOKES FORCE -- BCD and IRC
ADAMS FORCE -- PLDG and "C" & "D" Sqds. RCD

The Melfa River Bridgehead

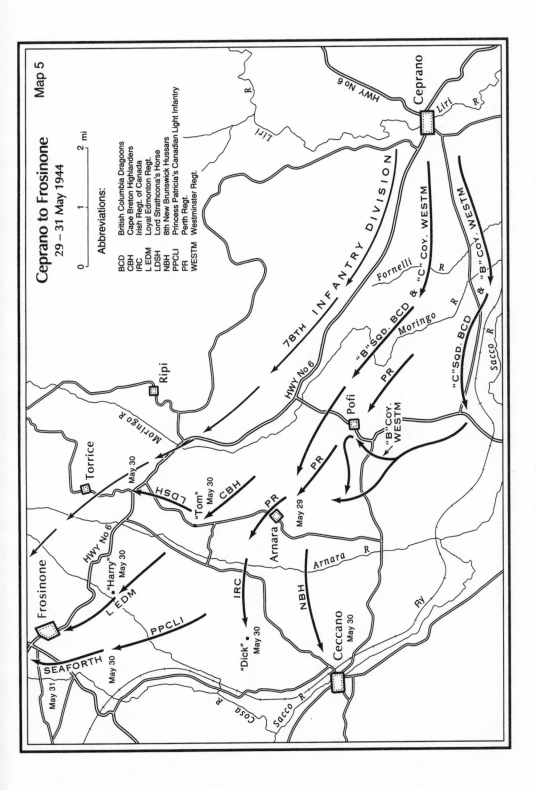

Map 5

Ceprano to Frosinone
29 – 31 May 1944

Abbreviations:

BCD — British Columbia Dragoons
CBH — Cape Breton Highlanders
IRC — Irish Regt. of Canada
L EDM — Loyal Edmonton Regt.
LDSH — Lord Strathcona's Horse
NBH — 8th New Brunswick Hussars
PPCLI — Princess Patricia's Canadian Light Infantry
PR — Perth Regt.
WESTM — Westminster Regt.

0   1   2 mi

Ceprano

Liri R
Liri R
HWY No 6

78TH INFANTRY DIVISION

Fornelli

"B" SQD. BCD & "C" COY. WESTM

"C" SQD. BCD & "B" COY. WESTM

Moringo

R
R
Sacco R

PR

Pofi

"B" COY. WESTM

HWY No 6

Ripi

Moringo R

Torrice
May 30

LDSH
"Tom"
May 30

CBH
May 30

PR
May 29

PR

Arnara

Arnara R

IRC

NBH

HWY No 6
"Harry"
May 30

L EDM

Frosinone

PPCLI

SEAFORTH
May 30

May 31

"Dick"
May 30

Ceccano
May 30

Cosa R

Sacco R

Ry

INTRODUCTION

THE ROAD TO
THE LIRI VALLEY

On July 10, 1943, some 26,000 Canadians landed on the beaches at Pachino, the southernmost point of Sicily. The Canadians were part of a massive invasion force mounted by two armies — the United States Seventh Army and the British Eighth Army. In one day, the invasion force established a solid toehold inside the Axis's much vaunted Fortress Europe. First Canadian Infantry Division and 1st Canadian Army Tank Brigade served in the British Eighth Army alongside not just British troops but also New Zealanders, South Africans, Indians, and Poles. However, the Canadians were new to this army, which had recently won the long, bitter North African campaign. While Eighth Army had fought in the desert wastelands, these Canadians had languished along with 465,000 of their compatriots in Britain.

First, the Canadians had waited to repel a German invasion that never came. Then they had waited for the Allied invasion of Western Europe, which often seemed as illusory as Hitler's never-launched invasion of Britain — Operation Sea Lion. They trained, they drank, they went sightseeing, they fell in love and married British women, they fathered children. What they did not do was fight. Except for one dreadful day on August 19, 1942, when a largely Canadian force landed at Dieppe, France, and was cut to pieces on the beaches, leaving 907 Canadians dead and 1,946 as prisoners of war after surrendering.

After Dieppe, it would have been understandable if Canadians had been content to have their soldiers spared the inevitable costs of battle. But public opinion clamoured all the louder for its army to fight. The government shared this sentiment, as did most of Canada's military leaders. Pressure was brought to bear to commit Canadians to the Sicily venture. Britain, somewhat reluctantly, acceded.

The campaign in Sicily was over in thirty-eight days. During those days, Canadians marched 130 miles, fought several small, fierce engagements, and took 2,310 casualties. Of these, 562 died and most were buried in a Canadians-only cemetery outside the village of Agira in Sicily's sun-scorched interior. Originally, it had been expected that after Sicily the Canadians would return to Britain, but new plans were afoot. British Prime Minister Winston Churchill believed Sicily could serve as the launching point for a greater venture, the invasion of Italy. In Italy, he argued, the Allies would find Fortress Europe's soft underbelly. It might even be possible to drive right up the Italian boot and plunge into Austria, bringing a swift conclusion to the war.

When, on September 3, Eighth Army invaded Italy by crossing the Strait of Messina, Canadian troops led the way. The Italian army, already bloodied and beaten by its defeats in North Africa and Sicily, collapsed. On September 8, Italy surrendered, but German divisions rushed in to fill the gap and the rapid advance up the Italian boot that Churchill had envisioned deteriorated into a blood-soaked slog. Eighth Army followed dusty roads up the eastern coast between the Apennine Mountains and the Adriatic Sea. On the west, the American Fifth Army advanced north from Salerno up the Tyrrhenian coast. Progress for both was slow, as the German opposition proved cunningly deployed and tenaciously offered.

In November, both armies tried to crack through stiffening German resistance centred on two great defensive lines. To the west, the Americans hammered into the Gustav Line. To the east, Eighth Army tackled the Bernhard Line. Rome was the prize each army sought and, with the rains of winter rapidly approaching, all involved knew time was running out. The Americans made virtually no headway, their attacks broken against the solid defensive wall of the Gustav Line, which was anchored by the incredible defensive bastion of Monte Cassino.

Eighth Army battered a crossing over the Sangro River, forcing the Germans to fall back a few miles to the Moro River. Here the Canadians took the lead, fighting a vicious slugging match against the elite 90th Panzer Grenadier and 1st Parachute divisions. From December 6 to January 4, the battle raged. The Moro River, Villa Rogatti, San Leonardo, Casa Berardi, Cider Crossroads, The Gully, and Ortona became battle honours for the regiments engaged at each place. The eight-day street battle between the German paratroops and the Loyal Edmonton Regiment, the Seaforth Highlanders of Canada, and the Three Rivers Tank Regiment was one of the most intense and costly battles ever fought by Canadian soldiers. At month's end, 2,339 Canadians were casualties and 502 of these had been killed.

Even as this great battle was playing out in the mud and rain, more Canadians were arriving to join the war in Italy. No longer did the government believe a single infantry division and an armoured brigade represented sufficient Canadian participation in the Italian campaign. The fall of 1943 had been spent lobbying for British agreement to an expanded Canadian role. In November, I Canadian Corps was formed and brought into the strength of Eighth Army. In late winter, the corps would become fully operational, comprising veterans of the 1st Canadian Infantry Division and the 1st Canadian Armoured Brigade, as well as the newly arrived 5th Canadian Armoured Division. By the end of 1943, about 75,000 Canadians were in Italy, including the many support personnel necessary to keep an entire corps operational.

With the approach of spring, the Allies desperately sought to find a way to break the deadly impasse in which they had been mired for months, as on either side of the Apennine Mountains each army had fruitlessly attempted to sever the heavily fortified German lines. The Canadians had spent a bitter winter just north of Ortona engaged in costly but futile patrols and probing attacks without purpose. General Harold Alexander, Deputy Supreme Commander Mediterranean, decided the only solution was to break through the Gustav Line on the western coast. To do so, he would require the combined strength of his two armies. Plans were developed to shift the majority of Eighth Army west in time for a massive assault across the width of the Gustav Line from Monte Cassino to the sea.

Operation Diadem would be launched on May 11, 1944. I Canadian Corps was to play a leading role in determining the offensive's success or failure by breaking out of the German defences and driving up the fertile Liri Valley, which formed the southern gateway to Rome. So, with the first hint of spring, the Canadians started marching west toward the Liri Valley and a new battle, the first test of their ability to fight as a corps. This is the story of that terrible test of arms.

ONE

PRELUDE TO OPERATION DIADEM

1

MILITARY SINS

The hulking, bombed-out ruin of the Benedictine Abbey of Monte Cassino glared menacingly toward International Ridge. Huddled inside the rock-walled enclosure of his sangar shelter, Sergeant Ron Hurley knew that if he could see the shattered abbey that clearly, the Germans manning observation posts inside the rubble and equipped with binoculars and spotting scopes could probably see him. Or would, if he were foolish enough to stand up or move out into the open on the rocky spine. So, like everyone else in the Westminster Regiment that had moved onto International Ridge on April 15, 1944, Hurley kept out of sight during daylight hours. When darkness cloaked the ridge, the men emerged from their slit trenches, sangars, and fortified farm buildings to eat, relieve themselves, and attempt to intercept German patrols probing the Canadian lines for weak points. It was miserable work in a godforsaken place that Hurley thought had damned all to recommend it.

If International Ridge served some essential tactical role in threatening the German Gustav Line, which stood just sixty miles short of the prize of Rome and which had foiled Allied attempts to reach the capital throughout the long, bitter winter months, nobody had bothered to tell Hurley. The ridge's name derived from the endless parade of national units drawn from either the U.S. Fifth Army or the British Eighth Army to man the position since its capture in the winter of 1944. Fierce French Goumiers from Morocco, Free Italians, Americans, Poles, New Zealanders, British, and now Welsh Paratroopers currently serving alongside the Canadians had all done hard duty on the 9,000-yard ridgeline. Nobody even thought of advancing forward from here any more. The job was just to hang on, keep Jerry from taking it back, and hope your unit would soon be relieved so the tedious and dangerous task could be handed off to some other poor wretch wearing a different national shoulder patch.

It helped not at all, of course, that the ridge was under German observation from dominant points far closer than the five-miles-distant abbey. Right in front of the ridge stood Monte Cifalco. Separating ridge and mountain was a narrow valley, through which a tributary of the Rapido River ran. Monte Cifalco, at 3,173 feet, was 1,300 feet higher than Hurley's position, so the German observers on its broad summit could see the Canadians on International Ridge without fear of being seen. Then there was the massive 5,000-foot-high, pyramid-shaped summit of Monte Cairo rising behind Monte Cassino that was being used by the Germans to observe the entire battle front from the eastern mountains to those in the west.

The instantaneous response to virtually any movement was a cluster of mortar bombs the Canadians called stonks, or a burst of machine-gun fire, or a couple of rounds from a sniper rifle. When the mortar rounds struck the ridge's rocky spine, they threw a deadly ring of metal shrapnel and bits of the rock chipped by the explosion out of the ridge's stony surface. Anyone nearby who was not well down in a slit trench or inside the sangars was likely to be badly wounded or killed. The ridge's impenetrable rocky spine had largely resisted any attempts to dig slit trenches, so Indian and New Zealand troops had introduced the sangars to the ridge — rough, circular enclosures ringed by stoutly built rock walls.

Like those who had come before them, the Canadians spent the days with their heads down, fighting boredom more than the Germans. Once in a while, however, some officer threw a monkey wrench into this logical and established routine by demanding daylight movement. Which was the case this afternoon. Hurley's platoon commander had called him into the command post and said, "You're an athlete. Go back and get the major."

Hurley was aghast. "What do you mean, go back? We're not supposed to be moving anywhere in daylight."

The lieutenant laughed grimly. "I want you to go back and get the major and guide him up. He wants to see things." Hurley knew there was no point arguing further. His platoon leader was also right in picking Hurley for the job of fetching 'C' Company's commander, for it was true that he was an athlete. Indeed, he was one of the Canadian army's top track-and-field competitors, a winner of many Allied service meets in Canada, England, and Italy. As a boy growing up in Penticton, British Columbia, Hurley had often hitchhiked up and down the Okanagan Valley from one little community to another to compete in track-and-field events that paid out first-place prizes of twenty-five cents. His family had been hard hit by the Depression and the coin prizes were almost as welcome to Hurley as the sheer joy he derived from competition. His athletic skills were immediately recognized when he enlisted and Hurley became a favourite of senior officers, who expected him to add laurels to the reputation of their regiments, brigades, and divisions while at the same time winning them sizeable betting returns. So successful was he in fulfilling both these objectives that the wiry, tough sergeant was almost held back in England when the Westminsters deployed to Italy so that he could serve the rest of the war as a poster boy of Canadian athletic prowess. But Hurley had raised a hellish stink and threatened to not compete. Finally, he was packed off to the regiment that brought him eventually to International Ridge and a race that he must run for his very life on a sunny April afternoon.

Headquarters was two and a half miles to the rear. In between lay a narrow steep-sided gully that was thickly wooded in the bottom, where a wooden footbridge crossed a small stream. The upper slopes of the gorge were nakedly exposed, with a rough mule track switching up out of the trees to either rim. Hurley hightailed out of the company position down the slope, dodging boulders, and short-cutting the switchbacks wherever possible. About halfway from the gully's edge to the trees, Hurley heard the whistle of incoming mortar rounds and knew Jerry had him spotted. There was no cover, nothing to do but to try outrunning the stonk. With explosions going off in his wake and shrapnel whistling past, Hurley threw himself into the cover of the trees and slithered off on a radical tangent to avoid the next mortar volley.

The Germans held fire. As Hurley warily approached the tree line on the opposite side of the gully, he knew they were probably waiting for him to emerge from the woods en route to the top, but there was nothing he could do beyond running like hell once he broke cover. That seemed to work because the mortars stayed silent, he topped the ridge, ducked into the cover of some thickets of scrub brush, and made his way without further incident to the cluster of houses known as Vallerotonda, which served as the Westminster headquarters.[1]

Vallerotonda was also under German observation, so the staff there was as confined to the protective cover of the heavy stonewalled buildings as the line companies in their sangars. All supplies had to be brought up from the rear at night by trucks driving with headlights turned off, then unloaded at headquarters and strapped onto mules for the trip up to the front. Knowing this procedure was under way, the Germans routinely illuminated the village with flares and then mortared the exposed resupply outfits. Surprisingly, this tactic proved ineffective and the only casualties so far had been a couple of mules that had had to be destroyed after suffering severe shrapnel wounds.

Because of the daytime hazard, the headquarters staff were going a bit stir-crazy. Westminster commander Lieutenant Colonel Gordon Corbould found an accordion somewhere and spent afternoons squeezing and keying away in an enthusiastic, if untalented, attempt to master the instrument. Meanwhile, the Military Police sergeant had become seemingly obsessed with improving his marksmanship. Each lull in accordion playing was punctuated with the sharp cracks of his pistol firing. HQ staff hotly debated whether the braying of the mules at night was preferable to the daily accordion entertainment.[2]

Hurley puffed his way into HQ and was dumbfounded when Major Ian Douglas looked up at him and said, "What are you doing here?"

"You ordered me back. Don't you remember?"

"Oh yes, you're going to take me to the line, aren't you?" Douglas said. Hurley replied that was what he was there for and asked permission to get something to eat while the major got ready. Digging thankfully into a pot of stew simmering on a stove, he favourably compared the fare to the bully beef and hardtack that was the standard, repetitive diet of the line companies. Ammunition and water had priority on the nightly supply runs. In between mouthfuls, Hurley explained to the major that they must cross the gully before dark, as the Germans had infiltrated a patrol in there the previous night and might repeat the stunt. Douglas decided to detail a section of HQ troops to accompany them through the gully bottom. This meant more people tagging along than Hurley would have liked. There was no way to move quickly or quietly with five or six men in tow who didn't know the ground and were loaded down with guns and equipment that clinked and jingled noisily with every step.

They made it to the gully edge without incident, however, and the approaching dusk probably hid them from most of the German observation points. But about a hundred yards away on the overlooking slope of Monte Cifalco was a shell-pounded house suspected of being an enemy observation post. Hurley pointed the structure out to Douglas and suggested they crawl across the open ground to the tree line. He set off with Douglas immediately behind and the others following in a line. When Hurley was nearly to the trees, a burst of machine-gun fire zipped past his ear from directly behind. "Goddamn it," Douglas said. "I slipped." Looking around, Hurley saw that the major had dropped his Thompson submachine gun and the weapon had loosed off a burst. Douglas shrugged apologetically, then said, "Okay, that's enough of that. Go down the hill." With all need for stealth scuttled by the major's inadvertent fire, Hurley scrambled down through the trees, reaching the footbridge in the rapidly descending darkness. Finding no Germans about, Douglas released the headquarters section and the two men prepared to continue the trip alone.

Hurley urged haste. He wanted to get out of the gully and across the open ground of International Ridge before the moon started lighting things up. They clambered slowly up the steep slope with Hurley moderating his pace to accommodate the major, whom Hurley respected and was genuinely fond of, despite this crazy mission he had been dragooned into. He knew the man was older than he and not in such good condition. Although Douglas had served in the New Westminster militia before the war, he had also been a school principal rather than a young athlete like Hurley. Finally, a hand tapped his shoulder. "Sergeant Hurley, we got to rest for a moment."

Despite the heaviness with which Douglas was puffing, Hurley demurred. "We can't stay here for too long, sir."

Douglas slumped onto a rock. "Just sit down here for a minute."

Hurley wasn't going to sit down; he was getting nervous. "We got to keep going." The major looked up and asked Hurley's age. Twenty, the sergeant responded. "You're twenty, I'm thirty-nine. What the hell am I doing here? You should be in charge of this company and I should be back home smoking my goddamned pipe," Douglas said with a weary chuckle. Then he heaved himself up. The two men climbed the slope and soon reached the forward positions, where they spent an uneventful night.[3]

◆ ◆ ◆

In addition to the Westminsters, the three regiments of 11th Canadian Infantry Brigade were rotating duty, so the four regiments served with two on the ridge and two nearby in reserve. Every night, the regiments in the line sent patrols into the no man's land between their lines and those of the alpine warfare–trained German 5th Mountain Division troops. The purpose of these patrols was always the same — to capture enemy prisoners for intelligence purposes and to intercept enemy patrols trying to penetrate Canadian lines. Having left Britain for Italy on November 8, 1943, as part of 5th Canadian Armoured Division, the regiments on International Ridge were still wet behind the ears.

Many of the young Canadians not only lacked combat experience, but were also new to mountain environments. Although the Westminsters were a Vancouver-based militia regiment, a good proportion of its men came not from British Columbia, where some experience of rugged terrain might be expected, but from the prairies, particularly Saskatchewan. The Perth Regiment had been raised in the gently rolling Ontario farm country of southern Ontario, the Irish Regiment of Canada hailed from the streets of Toronto, and most Cape Breton Highlanders had seldom seen, let alone hiked, steep mountains.

Perth Regiment Private Stan Scislowski, a twenty-year-old from Windsor, Ontario, saw himself and his fellow Perths as "a bunch of young, still inexperienced infantrymen, almost all of whom had never seen or climbed anything higher than the hills around Collingwood." Still, he believed these "flatland dwelling Perths" were as up to the job of duty on International Ridge as any Allied regiment before them. Although the Germans were far more aggressive in their patrolling and even launched infrequent assaults against sections of the Canadian line, they were always driven off relatively easily by heavy rifle and machine-gun fire backed up by a hail of Type 36 grenades.[4] Generally known as the "pineapple" because the metal case was ribbed into eighty sections that exploded into individual shrapnel chunks, the Type 36 had proved itself one of the war's most deadly grenades. The Canadians on International Ridge used it enthusiastically at night because the position of the thrower remained unrevealed, whereas the muzzle flash from a rifle or machine gun immediately betrayed the shooter's location.

This combination of intensive fire and increasing combat experience bore particular fruit on the nights of April 27 and 28. Just before midnight on April 27, a German patrol probed the section of line held by 'D' Company of the Cape Breton Highlanders. The wily company commander let the small patrol move unmolested past his hidden men rather than wipe them out. This led the Germans to believe the line was only lightly defended. The following evening, 'D' Company's perimeter was pounded by a heavy mortar bombardment that lightly wounded three men. From their sangars, the thirty men of No. 18 Platoon, watched a German officer meticulously position two platoons in line abreast for an attack. When he finished, the officer shouted, "Surrender, Canada, we have you completely surrounded!" The Canadians responded with a string of shouted profanities and a shower of about thirty grenades, followed immediately by every man opening fire with his Lee Enfield rifle, Thompson submachine gun, or Bren light machine gun. The Germans fled screaming with fear, abandoning their dead and wounded on the slope. In the morning, German stretcher-bearers came forward under the protection of Red Cross flags and were allowed to evacuate their dead and wounded.[5]

On May 5, regiments of the 12th South African (Motor) Brigade replaced the Canadian regiments on International Ridge. They marched out under the cover of darkness to rendezvous with trucks that transported them to positions about thirty miles north of Naples and well to the rear of the front lines. Total casualties suffered by 11 CIB on International Ridge numbered about 125 men.

No sooner had 11 CIB's regiments reached their rest positions than the men realized a major operation was teeing up. The entire rear area was choked with supplies and a multitude of infantry, armoured, and artillery units. Included in their number were all the divisions and brigades of I Canadian Corps, brought over from the Adriatic coast. On May 7, 5th Canadian Armoured Division's commander, Major General Bert Hoffmeister, inspected the Westminsters' company lines. He paid scrupulous attention to the state of the men's equipment and the effectiveness of their concealment of the Bren carriers and White scout cars that gave the regiment its motorized mobility. The following day, British Eighth Army commander General Sir Oliver Leese himself visited, impressing many of the men with his casually informal style and manner of dress. And every day, the Westminsters spent many hours engaged in intensive training. The battalion's war diarist, anticipating a major attack to break through the German Gustav Line, wrote, "The days of static warfare are over and in a short time we should be operating in our normal role of a Motor Battalion."[6]

◆ ◆ ◆

Since the failure of the major offensive of November and December 1943, the U.S. Fifth Army and the Eighth Army on their respective coasts had deadlocked before the virtually impregnable, well-entrenched, and heavily defended German lines. Rome remained as far out of reach as ever and the entire offensive Allied plan for Italy was reduced to tatters as the two armies stagnated amid battlefield conditions that increasingly mirrored those of the Western Front trenches of World War I.

In the west, Fifth Army, under General Mark Clark, had faltered early in its attempts to crack the German Winter Line — an advance section of the Gustav Line defensive network — in November. Horrendous casualties had been suffered just to force the Germans back a few miles to the Gustav Line proper, against which the offensive quickly crumbled. Hoping to relieve pressure on the divisions trying to crack the Gustav Line, VI U.S. Corps, a combined American-

British amphibious force of almost 50,000 men, landed at Anzio on January 22, 1944, sixty miles to the rear of the Gustav Line and less than thirty miles southwest of Rome. With half his total force of 100,000 men ashore and facing virtually no opposition, U.S. General John P. Lucas dithered on the beaches rather than pushing inland.

General Harold Alexander, Deputy Supreme Commander Mediterranean, had intended that the Anzio force push boldly toward the Alban Hills and cut the German Tenth Army's lines of communication back to Rome. This would force Tenth Army to withdraw from the Gustav Line, give up Rome, and fall back to the defensive line running across Italy from Pisa to Rimini, code-named the Gothic Line. Lucas, however, never intended to carry out this ambitious scheme. Instead, he had been instructed by his direct superior, General Mark Clark, to "seize and secure a beachhead" and advance slowly toward the Alban Hills. Clark further cautioned that he should move out from the beachhead only if German resistance remained weak. The Fifth Army commander fully expected that divisions drawn from the enemy at the Gustav Line would quickly counterattack the beachhead. The more Germans were diverted in this way, the better his chances of breaking through the Gustav Line and driving north to Rome while at the same time relieving the Anzio beachhead.

Lucas's opportunity for bold action lasted three days and he spent those, as Clark had directed, solidifying his grip on a small beachhead. Meanwhile, the Germans moved to contain the divisions ashore at Anzio, but not in the way anticipated by the Americans. Rather than drawing Tenth Army divisions from the Gustav Line, Commander-in-Chief Southwest Generalfeldmarschall Albert Kesselring rushed reinforcements south from Fourteenth Army stationed in northern Italy. By January 25, a ring of 70,000 men from eight divisions hemmed in a beachhead only seven miles deep and sixteen miles wide. A belated breakout attempt achieved only heavy casualties. On February 2, Lucas, having received intelligence reports that the Germans were mounting a major attack to wipe out the beachhead, ordered his divisional commanders to dig in and hold.[7]

The feared counterattack fell on February 16 at the direct order of Adolf Hitler, in the form of a single regimental thrust on a narrow front by the Infantry Demonstration Regiment. Dubbing the Anzio beachhead "the Abscess," the Führer was determined that it should be pinched out of existence. Kesselring was not surprised when the attack failed, because the assigned regiment was a home defence unit with no combat experience. Kesselring tried again on February 29 with a stronger force drawn from the LXXVI Panzer Corps, consisting of the 114th Light Infantry, 362nd Infantry, 26th Panzer, and Hermann Göring divisions.

The day before the attack, Kesselring visited the troops and almost cancelled the operation. Heavy rain had transformed the battle-ground into sloppy mud and so obscured visibility that Kesselring could barely imagine the men moving forward, much less fighting. "But the units detailed for the operation were so full of confidence that in deference to their wishes I let it stand," he later wrote. The assault quickly faltered and was abandoned on March 1.[8] The Anzio beachhead was secure, but it was also contained.

Fifth Army, meanwhile, had tried throughout late January and into February to batter its way past the Gustav Line around the small town of Cassino in what were soon designated the first and second battles of Cassino. Before becoming the focus of battle, Cassino had been a minor service town for Liri Valley farmers with a population of about 25,000 people. Most fled east into the Apennines as the fighting approached, rendering Cassino a ghost town by the time the battle moved into the streets. Gains here and elsewhere along the Gustav Line were insignificant, but cost 12,400 Allied battle casualties.[9]

◆ ◆ ◆

Another casualty had been the abbey on Monte Cassino, destroyed by a massive Allied bombing raid. The Christian monk, and later beatified saint, Benedict founded Monte Cassino in A.D. 529. By the time of his death on March 21, 547, it had become the spiritual seat of the Benedictine Order, from which monks began dispersing throughout Christendom to establish monasteries. Benedict's original abbey had been destroyed in about 580 by Langobards. Rebuilt in 717, it was again razed in 883 by Saracens and not reconstructed until the mid-tenth century. In the eleventh century, the abbey's reconstruction was accelerated, employing master craftsmen and artists brought in from every corner of Italy. The final structure, built entirely from white travertine stone, was in the shape of an irregular quadrilateral 210 metres long and up to 150 metres wide. It covered almost seven acres. By 1087, most of the features that contributed to its splendour were complete. The basilica was grandly decorated with mosaics, marble, and woodcarvings, and the great bronze-sheeted central door engraved with the names of churches and monasteries founded by the Benedictines was installed. In 1349, an earthquake heavily damaged this incarnation of the monastery. Work began immediately to restore the structure perfectly. Throughout the ensuing centuries, more works of art were added to the monastery and the rebuilding of various sections heightened its grandeur.

Equally impressive were the large library and archive. Here, during the European Dark Ages, the monks had gathered and transcribed many literary works that might otherwise have been lost. These included the *Varrone de Lingua Latina*, the oldest known work on grammar, along with writings by Virgil, Homer, Cicero, Ovid, and other ancient Greek and Roman writers. Approximately 10,000 hand-lettered parchment scrolls were gathered here.[10]

On February 16, 239 Allied bombers, attacking over the course of four hours in eight consecutive waves, dumped on the abbey 453.5 tons of bombs, including 66.5 tons of incendiary bombs intended to set fires. The magnificent basilica and all the other buildings inside the stout outer walls were reduced to rubble. Between 1,000 and 2,000 refugees, many from as far away as Naples, had taken shelter in the cellars. They had come to Monte Cassino believing the abbey would be protected as one of Christendom's most sacred shrines. At least 230 died in the bombing.[11]

Neither the bombings nor the heavy artillery barrages that followed succeeded in breaching the walls, which were a standard width of three metres thick set upon a slightly wider base.[12] As a tactical defence base, the rubble of the abbey served as well as the undamaged structure would have. Ironically, however, the Germans had not occupied the abbey to this point, although elements of the 1st Parachute Division were dug in all around it, so that the abbey was integrated by default into their defensive network. Once the devastating bombardment ended, the paratroops quickly transformed the ruins into a pivotal anchor in their line.[13]

Although virtually all the artwork that adorned the structure itself was destroyed, the removable works of art and the vast holdings of the library and archive had been removed to the safety of the Vatican. General der Infanterie Frido von Senger und Etterlein, who commanded the Germans' Cassino sector, had used his soldiers and trucks to rescue the artifacts. By a strange twist of fate, Senger — a Rhodes scholar and devout Catholic — had, as a young man, joined a lay group committed to Benedictine philosophy. Well aware of the abbey's treasures, Senger also knew that the critical phase of the battle for Rome must inevitably be fought at Cassino and in the Liri Valley, which the abbey overlooked. Monte Cassino would therefore be a scene of fierce fighting.[14] Accordingly, he had evacuated the treasures during the months of October and November, and by December 5 the process was complete.[15]

The destruction of the abbey was to have broken the German defences on Monte Cassino and permitted the newly arrived Eighth Army New Zealand and Indian divisions to capture both the mountain and town. On February 24, however, rain poured down relentlessly and continued to March 15, the Ides of March. During this time, the wet and chilled Commonwealth troops could only cling grimly to their start lines and wait for the rains to relent. In the mountains, rain often turned to snow and the threat of frostbite loomed for soldiers unable to build fires or find shelter.[16]

At 0830 hours on March 15, 455 Allied bombers consisting of 164 Liberators, 114 B-17 Flying Fortresses, 105 Marauders, and 72 Mitchells pulverized the ancient town of Cassino with more than 1,000 tons of bombs dropped over three and a half hours. While most hit the target, 43 planes that drifted off course bombed nearby Venafro, Pozzuoli, and other small hamlets, along with several Allied positions, leaving 96 Allied soldiers and 140 Italian civilians dead in their wake. Cassino was devastated. Every building was badly damaged or reduced to a pile of rubble.[17] Immediately after the planes departed, an artillery barrage fired by 890 guns hammered Cassino with 195,969 shells.[18] Inside the town, 160 of 2nd Battalion, 3rd Parachute Regiment's 300 men lay dead, wounded, or entombed alive in the rubble. Most of those trapped perished, as there was no opportunity in the ensuing fighting for the Germans to rescue them. The remainder of the paratroopers, however, emerged from the ruins with arms at the ready and moved methodically to their positions.[19]

A vicious battle ensued as 2nd New Zealand Division fought

amid the rubble, often hand to hand, against the determined German defenders, while regiments of 4th Indian Division vainly attempted to climb Monte Cassino and capture the summit and abbey. The battle seesawed back and forth, with the Germans losing ground and then regaining it in bloody counterattacks, until March 24 when the offensive was finally called off. A total of 881 men in 2nd New Zealand Division had been killed and 1,080 in 4th Indian Division. A blizzard swept the slopes of Monte Cassino as the Indian units withdrew and the British 78th Infantry Division secured the small dent they had shoved into the Gustav Line. The German defenders had also paid a fearful price. The parachute battalions could only field 40 to 120 fit men apiece, when normal battalion strength was about 800. Major General F.S. Tuker wrote that the battle would be remembered as one of the great "military sins" of history. It had been folly to throw the Indians and New Zealanders against a "mountain position which had for centuries defied attack from the south and which in 1944 was not only the strongest position in Italy, but was held by the pick of the German troops in that theatre of war."[20]

♦ ♦ ♦

The participation of the New Zealand, Indian, and British 78th Infantry divisions in the disastrous Third Battle of Cassino marked the beginning of Alexander's transfer of Eighth Army divisions from the Adriatic. Only a thin screening force would be left behind. Once the majority of Eighth Army was moved, Alexander intended that the Fifth and Eighth armies would jointly shatter the Gustav Line and charge up the narrow Liri Valley to Rome. Alexander recognized this was the only strategy left that might break the Italian campaign deadlock.[21]

Sir Harold Rupert Leofric George Alexander, third son of the Fourth Lord of Caledon, was no military neophyte. He had entered Sandhurst at nineteen, desiring nothing more in life than to be a professional soldier. At fifty-three, he was a World War I veteran who had won the Military Cross during the Battle of Loos in 1915 when his company of 2nd Battalion Irish Guards had captured Chalk Pit Wood. During the bitter third phase of the disastrous Battle of the Somme, he won the Distinguished Service Order for his valour and became 2nd Battalion's commander at the age of twenty-six. Following the war, Alexander spent two years fighting with the White Russians against the Bolsheviks in Latvia and then participated in two Imperial frontier campaigns defending the Empire in the far-off lands of Loe Agra and Mohmand. At the disaster of Dunkirk in May 1940, he had been promoted to command of I Corps, which he successfully evacuated from the beaches despite having received permission from Churchill to surrender. Alexander went on to demonstrate exemplary tactical skill in Burma against the Japanese and had established a good reputation for competence in his position in the Mediterranean theatre. His one major personality flaw was a tendency to attempt to gain cooperation of subordinates through persuasion rather than imposition of his leadership. This trait fostered an atmosphere in which his army commanders, particularly Clark, a self-confessed anglophobe, felt free to substitute their own plans for Alexander's.[22]

In late March 1944, Alexander started drafting his plan for a May offensive called Operation Diadem. This time he was determined that the two armies under his command would march to a unified drum and that his commanding generals would follow orders to the letter. Guiding his thoughts was the belief that the rugged Italian terrain and strongly constructed and manned German defensive lines could be only penetrated if the Allies enjoyed a three-to-one superiority of infantry. Unfortunately, intelligence estimates of German strength tallied against Allied strength in Italy gave him an infantry superiority of only one-and-one-quarter times.

Furthermore, Kesselring undoubtedly expected the next Allied move would be directed against the Gustav Line.[23] It was impossible for the Allies to mount a true surprise attack against the Germans, all of which combined to render any offensive a desperate gamble. Failure could well stalemate Allied operations in Italy until events in northern Europe or elsewhere forced a German withdrawal.

Even a May offensive was terribly late, because it had been agreed that Operation Overlord — the amphibious invasion of northern Europe — and the supporting Operation Anvil invasion on southern France's Mediterranean coastline would have priority in 1944. Operations in Italy would take a back seat. The two armies in Italy would be third in line for supplies, reinforcements, air asset allocations, amphibious landing equipment, and would also have at least two American divisions leeched off for Operation Anvil.

The failure to breach the Gustav Line earlier in the winter jeopardized this latter invasion, something that greatly displeased the Combined Chiefs of Staff in London. Their early planning had assumed that by May 1944, Rome would have fallen and the Germans in Italy would be digging in behind the Gothic Line between Pisa and Rimini. The length of this line, running across the wide northern region of Italy, was such that it would require all German divisions currently in Italy to remain in place to prevent a breaching offensive by the Allies. With Kesselring's divisions thus tied up, there would be little possibility that any could be shifted to southern France to repel the invading forces.

The Combined Chiefs of Staff considered abandoning Operation Anvil entirely. However, they also believed this would increase the risk of the forthcoming invasion of northern France being thrown back into the sea, as German divisions in southern France would be free to move north against the invasion beaches. Finally, on April 19, it was agreed that Operation Anvil "should be cancelled as an operation but retained as a threat."[24] It was hoped that demonstrations by naval vessels off the coast of southern France would suffice to keep German divisions tied down on this front waiting for an invasion that would probably never come. Cancellation of Operation Anvil meant that an all-out offensive in Italy now became the second priority, after Operation Overlord, for Allied operations on the Western Front. The chiefs instructed Alexander's newly appointed superior, General Sir Henry Maitland Wilson, to plan for the "best possible use of the amphibious lift remaining to you either in support of operations in Italy, or in order to take advantage of opportunities arising in the south of France or elsewhere."[25]

Alexander assumed that this meant Italy would be given great priority in terms of resources and possibly even amphibious equipment. The reality was that Overlord was sucking up most available assets, virtually all amphibious landing craft, and that the Americans still remained wedded to the idea of mounting Operation Anvil as soon as practicable. No matter what other eventuality might arise, they were determined that this invasion would come before the end of summer 1944, assuming that Operation Overlord succeeded.[26] Soon realizing he would not receive a major influx of fresh divisions or have the strategic option of carrying out another amphibious landing in the German rear, Alexander knew he must concentrate his forces before the Gustav Line. Whether the offensive succeeded would depend on the strategy he employed in striking the line.

On April 2, Alexander summoned Clark and Leese to his headquarters in Caserta and explained his battle plan for Operation Diadem. Eighth Army was to break through the Gustav Line and what the Allies persisted in calling the Adolf Hitler Line, known to be situated a few miles back from the Gustav Line, with the village of Pontecorvo hinging its western flank and Aquino the eastern. Recently, the Germans had realized the line might be breached in the forthcoming fighting and renamed it the Senger Riegel (Senger Line), after the German commander of the Monte Cassino sector. The Allies, recognizing the propaganda value that could be derived from smashing a line named after the Führer, continued to use the old identifier. If the Gustav Line fell, the defenders could hastily retreat into the Hitler Line's prepared defensive positions, contain the Allied advance, and then counterattack to regain the Gustav position.

Alexander was determined that the Hitler Line would fall as quickly as the Gustav Line and that once Eighth Army was through both, it would dash up the Liri Valley via Highway 6 to Valmontone on Rome's southern outskirts. Meanwhile the Fifth Army would secure the Ausoni Mountains and protect the Eighth Army's left flank by driving along the eastern flank of the mountains into the Liri Valley via the village of Esperia. The VI U.S. Corps would break out of the Anzio beachhead and advance toward Valmontone, and link up with Eighth Army at the gates of Rome. Alexander expected all preparations for the offensive to be in place by May 3 or, at the latest, May 5.

A paramount consideration for Alexander was that the timing of the offensive benefit the launching of Operation Overlord, which, he understood, would happen at the end of May. If the Liri Valley operation began fifteen to twenty-one days ahead of Operation Overlord, Alexander believed he could take Rome and mangle the Germans in Italy before the Allies hit the beaches in northern Europe. This would leave Kesselring nothing to send north and threatened with losing Italy entirely unless he himself were reinforced.

An offensive in early May also coincided nicely with the phases of the moon, which was to be full on May 8. Movement of troops in the Italian campaign generally occurred at night, so Alexander thought it advantageous to have the light of a strong moon to guide the troops. For all these reasons, Alexander, Clark, and Leese agreed that the offensive should start on May 10.

Date set, the next problem was to determine the timing of each action. Alexander's original thought had been to have Lucas lead with the breakout from Anzio to sever German communications between Rome and Cassino. After some discussion, he abandoned this idea because the Germans containing the Anzio beachhead had strong mobile reserves that could block such a breakout before it could reach Highway 6. Alexander suspected too that Kesselring would be expecting the first blow to come from Anzio, so striking elsewhere might gain a modicum of surprise. Finally, Alexander decided that Eighth Army and Fifth Army would attack simultaneously and that the Anzio force would be ready to jump off four days later.[27]

Alexander told Leese and Clark that the "attack will continue until seriously checked or until a pause is essential to regroup. At that stage all the enemy's resources should have been drawn in, and we hope the enemy's troops guarding the beachhead will have been drawn on and weakened. This will be the moment to strike from Anzio — under the full protection of the air. If this flank is successful and gets as far as Valmontone it may well be decisive and lead to the destruction of all the German forces between the bridgehead and the main battle front."[28] Such an eventuality would enable the encirclement and ultimate destruction or capture of the majority of the German Tenth Army and parts of the Fourteenth Army. This would be far more strategically beneficial than simply driving the Germans beyond Rome. An envelopment of Tenth Army alone could well eliminate Kesselring's ability to effectively defend Italy.[29]

Such a strategic windfall would materialize only if the Eighth and Fifth armies broke through the Gustav Line with devastating and rapid force, sending the defending Tenth Army reeling as the Allies controlled the flow of battle. Quoting Lord Horatio Nelson, Alexander said, "Only numbers can annihilate."[30] That he had numerical superiority in men and arms was undisputed, but still he would go into battle with nowhere near his desired three-to-one ratio.

For the Gustav Line attack, Fifth Army had 170,000 troops organized into two corps, each fielding seven divisions equipped with

600 artillery guns and 300 tanks. Eighth Army had an authorized strength of 300,000 men, but there were critical shortages and the divisions were collectively about 21,000 men short.[31] Many of the divisions, particularly those in X Corps that had born the brunt of the Third Battle of Cassino, were exhausted from months of unrelieved combat. Alexander estimated that he had twenty-eight divisions to Kesselring's twenty-three. Berlin rated nineteen of these divisions with a total strength of 412,000 men, as being capable of mounting sustained defensive actions. This included the fourteen divisions currently holding the Gustav Line and the ring around the Anzio beachhead. Tenth Army had nine divisions on the Gustav Line, while Fourteenth Army had five divisions at Anzio.

Kesselring, for his part, was intensely gloomy about his manpower strength. That some of his divisions were seriously understrength was rammed home during a visit to the headquarters of the 29th Panzer Grenadier Division. Its commander, Generalmajor Walter Fries, was one of Kesselring's best and not given to histrionics. Yet no sooner had Kesselring walked into his office than Fries launched into a "tirade spiced with recriminations of his intolerable situation. He complained that his depleted companies were faced by two Allied divisions that were frequently relieved; that an Allied division had almost double his strength, on the top of which they had twice the number of guns and a quite fantastic supply of ammunition in the ratio of ten to one."

Jokingly, Kesselring told his Prussian comrade that he understood Prussians "never asked how strong the enemy was, but only where he was." He praised Fries and his men while also cautioning him to have confidence in the wisdom of his superiors and that then "all would be well."

Bravado aside, Kesselring knew Fries's fears were valid. His divisions were understrength, outnumbered, and outgunned. He also knew that Alexander could not "be satisfied for much longer with the slow and costly way the Allied front was edging forward."[32]

Kesselring discounted any offensive's being launched on the Adriatic front. Instead, he later wrote, the "Garigliano with its mountain spurs beyond Cassino and the Anzio beachhead had to be envisaged as battle-fronts, supplemented perhaps by feint or diversionary landings north of Rome in the region of Civitavecchia and by airborne landings in the valley of Frosinone. I calculated that the American Fifth and British Eighth Armies would open the offensive by launching a broad and deep attack against the right wing of our Tenth Army across the Majo, Petrella, and Monte Cassino massif, with a connecting inward movement into the valley of the Liri."

In his directive simply entitled *Defence*, Kesselring set out clearly how the defensive battle should be fought. He was convinced the Gustav Line could be held as long as Monte Majo in the Aurunci Mountains on the right and Monte Cassino on the left were held. With 1st Parachute Division on Monte Cassino, Kesselring was convinced this pivot point would hold. Monte Majo he left thinly occupied, as he saw no real threat of an attack there. The situation at Anzio, he believed, was excellent. Only if the point where the lines of the Tenth and Fourteenth armies met were breached did the Allies in the beachhead stand any chance of breaking out. "All in all," Kesselring concluded, "I could await coming events calmly, as we had done all we could in every field to meet the major offensive expected."[33]

◆ ◆ ◆

Alexander had been apprised of an intelligence intercept by Ultra — the code-breaking operation that was reading much of German signals traffic — that the Germans knew the attack was coming and that his armies also faced some of Germany's top divisions. An April report sent from Italy to Berlin graded the divisions on a four-tier scale that ranged from a high rating of "capable of offensive action" to a low of "fit for static defence only." The 1st Parachute Division and 29th Panzer Grenadiers were top rated. Eight other divisions earned second ratings, eight a third rating that deemed them capable of mounting mobile defences, and only four were bottom-ranked.[34]

No similar rating had been made of Alexander's divisions, but he had a number of fresh ones and even a new corps that had almost no battle experience. Clark's Fifth Army had just received the American 85th and 88th divisions, made up of raw recruits with little training. Eighth Army had an equally unknown commodity in the form of I Canadian Corps, which was to play a major role in its plan for Operation Diadem. Once the Gustav Line was breached, the two divisions of I Canadian Corps would lead the drive up Highway 6.[35] Yet only one of the two divisions in I Canadian Corps had previous experience in major offensive operations. That division — 1st Canadian Infantry Division — would lead for only the first phase of the advance, driving forward to close on and break through the Hitler Line. Once the Hitler Line was severed, the advance would fall to the largely untested 5th Canadian Armoured Division. Whether the Canadian troops or their commanders were sufficiently trained and competent to carry off their starring role was very much unknown to either Alexander or Leese. Certainly its performance to date had done little to instill confidence in either the abilities of its soldiers or that of its seemingly ever-changing and bickering leadership.

2

THE UNWANTED CANADIANS

Even as the Allies had marched across Sicily in July 1943, Canada's Minister of National Defence Colonel James Layton Ralston had proposed that the nation play a greater role in the Mediterranean. A World War I veteran, Ralston had personally argued his case during a meeting with First Canadian Army commander Lieutenant General Andrew McNaughton in London on August 5, 1943. Fielding a Canadian corps in Italy, he said, would provide battlefield training to an essential nucleus of corps level officers. It would also increase the number of soldiers of all ranks with combat experience preparatory to the northern European invasion. Equally important, it would raise the morale of the divisions languishing in Britain and civilian morale at home because both would see an army that was fighting rather than just endlessly waiting and training.

McNaughton's response was chilly. He had objected to sending any Canadians to the Mediterranean and believed that sending even more would jeopardize the nation's ability to field its own army-sized force in the main European invasion. Still, if Ottawa endorsed the idea, and as long as the Combined Chiefs of Staff assured Canada that the divisions serving in Italy would be transferred back to England before the invasion began, McNaughton told Ralston he could implement the plan. During the meeting, however, it had become obvious that Ralston did not see the return of the divisions to Britain as essential. Sensing that his dream of having all Canadian soldiers overseas serving in one unified army was dying at Ralston's hand, McNaughton said, "If the Canadian Government decided upon dispersion, then it would be wise to put someone in control who believed in it."[1]

Ralston next raised the matter with British Prime Minister Winston Churchill just before the Quadrant conference of western leaders opened on August 11 at Quebec City's Château Frontenac. Gaining Churchill's support prior to this meeting was essential because the intent of the conference was to finalize planning for the invasion of northern Europe. If the Canadian divisions in Britain were detailed to specific roles in the invasion, it might prove impossible for Ralston to have I Canadian Corps and an additional division reassigned to service in Italy. Churchill was sympathetic and promised to ensure that the Combined Chiefs of Staff duly considered the request. When the meeting wrapped up on August 24, however, Churchill advised Ralston that he should not count on approval. To maintain Operation Overlord's required divisional strength, it would be necessary to exchange any division sent to Italy with one withdrawn from that theatre. If another Canadian division were deployed to Italy, then a matching British division must be repatriated. The implication was clear. Any Canadian division sent to Italy would not be returned for the invasion. Yet Ralston urged Churchill to press on with Canada's request, effectively endorsing the very dispersion of Canadian strength that McNaughton had warned Ralston against at the beginning of the month.

On August 31, Churchill cabled the Chiefs of Staff in London following a meeting that day with the Canadian War Committee in Ottawa. "A strong desire was expressed that a second Canadian Division should be dispatched to the Mediterranean area as soon as possible," Churchill wrote. He ended the cable saying, "Pray let me know as soon as possible what can be done."[2]

The Chiefs of Staff responded on September 14 by telling McNaughton that there was insufficient shipping available to move an entire division and a corps element to Italy while meeting commitments for bringing U.S. divisions from America to Britain for the invasion. Churchill supported this conclusion with a September 19 cable to Prime Minister William Lyon Mackenzie King, in which he concluded that sending a Canadian division to Italy would disturb plans for the invasion without fulfilling any valid military goal. King responded on September 30 by sending the Canadian High Commissioner in London, Vincent Massey, to ask Churchill if the decision might not be reconsidered. Churchill reluctantly agreed to have another try at persuading the Chiefs of Staff to support the idea.

Churchill's intervention worked. On October 7, the Chiefs of Staff advised McNaughton that deployment of a Canadian corps could be facilitated through a straight exchange of British divisions and corps sections in Italy for those of the Canadians. If the Canadians wished, Britain would repatriate XXX Corps headquarters and all corps troops along with the 7th Armoured Division in exchange for the 5th Canadian Armoured Division and headquarters and support troops of I Canadian Corps, commanded by Lieutenant General Henry Duncan Graham Crerar. But there was a caveat. Because of restricted shipping availability, the Canadians must leave behind their heavy equipment, such as tanks, armoured cars, artillery, trucks, and Jeeps. The returning British would do the same so that the equipment could simply be traded. Urged on by Ralston, the Canadian War Committee endorsed the proposal on October 12.

The decision finally made, plans for what was dubbed Operation Timberwolf rapidly proceeded. General Alexander, Deputy Supreme Commander Mediterranean, was immediately informed that he would receive a new division and a corps headquarters unit under which all the Canadians in Italy could be grouped. Alexander was dumbfounded. He fired a cable back to London saying: "The proposed move of the Canadian Armoured Division has come as a complete surprise to me. We already have as much armour in the Mediterranean as we can usefully employ in Italy. I should have preferred another Canadian Infantry Division. I shall be grateful if I can be consulted in future before matters of such importance are agreed upon. These decisions upset my order of battle which in turn affect my plans for battle."

Despite Alexander's resistance, sailing schedules were soon in place to move 25,000 Canadian troops on October 25, another 10,000 in November, 4,000 in December, and such numbers as might be required in January to create a "balanced Corps." This corps would be composed of 1st Canadian Infantry Division, 5th Canadian Armoured Division, 1st Canadian Armoured Brigade, an Army Group Royal Artillery, and supporting hospital and rear-echelon units. The 5th Division would leave behind all its major equipment, the troops carrying only their personal arms in accordance with the agreement reached between the Canadian government and the Chiefs of Staff.[3]

♦ ♦ ♦

As the Canadian soldiers in England prepared to board ships bound for Italy, Crerar and an advance headquarters composed of about thirty officers and non-commissioned officers flew into Algiers on October 24. Fifty-five-year-old Crerar, who went by the first name of Harry, was a graduate of Royal Military College and had served as an artillery officer in World War I. He ended that war as a lieutenant colonel in charge of Canadian Corps' counter-battery operations. In 1940, he had been appointed Chief of the Canadian General Staff and in December 1941 was given command of I Canadian Corps in Britain. Crerar enthusiastically supported bringing that unit to Italy and knew he had to move quickly to have things ready for its imminent arrival.[4] Like Ralston, Crerar was a fire-breather, intent on getting Canadian troops into the thick of battle at every possible opportunity.

As Canada's Chief of General Staff, he had led the charge in convincing King to accede to Britain's request that men be sent to bolster the weak Imperial defences of Hong Kong, despite the fact that Britain had no intention of reinforcing the garrison itself. The subsequent loss of the entire force of 1,975 men of the Royal Rifles of Canada and the Winnipeg Grenadiers when Hong Kong's governor surrendered to the Japanese on Christmas Day, 1941, had failed to dampen his martial ardour. Next he had lobbied successfully for the use of Canadian troops in the Dieppe raid and subsequently defended the operation as costly but worthwhile because of the lessons the Allies had learned. After Dieppe, Crerar continued to work tirelessly to undermine McNaughton's efforts to keep all the Canadians together. Crerar joined Ralston at every opportunity in advocating the need for Canada to commit troops to fighting on some front in order to cement the nation's Imperial ties and maintain political support at home for the war effort.[5]

Pausing only a few days in Algiers, Crerar moved his corps head-quarters advance staff to Sicily, intent on getting the corps operational as quickly as was humanly and logistically possible. There was no time to lose, for on the evening of October 27, a twenty-five–ship convoy had sailed from Britain jammed with the majority of 5th Canadian Armoured Division and the rest of Crerar's corps staff. The convoy was scheduled to arrive in Naples and other Mediterranean ports on November 8.

Awaiting the arrival of 5 CAD was also its new commander, Major General Guy Simonds, a forty-year-old who had led 1st Canadian Infantry Division across Sicily and up the toe of Italy in the first weeks of September. Hospitalized since then by a serious bout of jaundice, he had just returned to command when McNaughton decided Simonds should take over the soon-to-arrive armoured division, so he could gain experience commanding a combined tank and infantry division. Simonds had a good reputation with McNaughton. As well, he was a protege of General Bernard Law Montgomery, who, in late 1943, still commanded Eighth Army. Simonds had also served under Eighth Army corps commander Lieutenant General Sir Oliver Leese and earned that man's respect. About the Canadians in the Sicily campaign, Leese wrote, "They have been very well com-manded by Simonds, who is young and forceful." Montgomery added that "he will be a 1st Class DIV. Commander in due course."[6]

Before taking over 1 CID, Simonds had served as Brigadier General Staff under Crerar in Britain. He blamed Crerar for allowing the remounting of the Dieppe raid after its initial cancellation. The entire fiasco could have been prevented, he believed, if Crerar had exerted his authority as the senior Canadian commander and objected to Canadian units being committed to a badly planned oper-ation. Simonds also despised the way in which Crerar worked to undercut McNaughton at every turn. The result was that Simonds not only did not like Crerar; he also deeply distrusted him.[7]

When Crerar arrived in Italy, Simonds was still attempting to interpret what he thought must be an underlying explanation for his lateral transfer to command another division. Furthermore, he had only been informed of his nemesis's arrival by a signal from McNaughton mere days before Crerar landed in Algiers. At first blush, he believed the transfer was tantamount to a demotion, but when he took that complaint to Montgomery, his mentor assured him that leading an armoured division was a requisite step for attaining corps command. This, Montgomery said, was McNaughton's purpose. That mollified Simonds somewhat, until he learned that 5 CAD would march to war with the heavy equipment left behind by the departing British 7th Armoured Division.[8]

Simonds was furious. The equipment of the renowned Desert Rats dated back to the North African campaign. Most of the tanks, artillery, trucks, and Jeeps being left behind for the Canadians were so dilapidated as to be almost beyond repair. Serious shortages of all types of heavy armaments and transport in the Mediterranean theatre meant there was scant chance that the newly arrived division could beg, borrow, or steal equipment from other sources.[9]

It was, therefore, an agitated Simonds who icily received Crerar in his command caravan at the Canadian base in Campobasso on October 30. Within minutes of the older officer's arrival, the two men exchanged harsh words. Crerar was shocked by Simonds's outspoken, nearly insubordinate manner. He also was little impressed by Simonds's acquired British mannerisms and his informal dress, which included wearing a tanker's black beret identical to Montgomery's trademark beret. For his part, Simonds thought Crerar was completely puffed up with his own sense of self-importance. As for Crerar's formal conception of how corps command should be organized and administered, Simonds believed it hopelessly out of step with the way Eighth Army operated in the field. Eighth Army and the Canadians who served in it were little given to paperwork. Even attack orders were generally delivered orally, with no written record created. Much of the reason for this stemmed from the army's polyglot of nations gathered into one large formation. Montgomery had found that confusion was limited by less paperwork. Now here was Crerar in Simonds's caravan, which he kept scanning with a covetous eye because of its clever design, obvious comforts, and organization, spouting the virtues of vast amounts of written reports and orders that must be maintained on a daily basis and duly filed to corps headquarters. The meeting ended badly.

Crerar left the meeting convinced that Simonds had become too British for his own good. That Simonds had always had great affection for all things English was well known throughout Canadian military circles. Eighth Army's informality promoted cohesion of divisions without regard for national distinctions. This sat well with Simonds but was anathema to Crerar, who was not only charged with creating a distinct Canadian corps but was determined that its character and operational style would conform to the doctrine accepted by Canadian army regulations. In Italy, Crerar was surrounded by young Canadian officers who had been battle-seasoned in a hard campaign fought in a tactical landscape that bore no resemblance to his World War I terrain. Crerar quickly understood that his subordinates resented the prospect of being ordered about by an officer lacking infantry or armoured combat experience who could only hark back to service as an artillery officer to guide his field decisions. Bringing these young Turks to heel, Crerar decided, was going to be an essential task that he must fulfill quickly if his corps were to be clearly and distinctly Canadian.[10]

♦ ♦ ♦

It was soon evident that Crerar faced an uphill struggle. Montgomery did little to hide his lack of faith in Crerar. The seeds of his negativity had been sown long before, when Crerar was among a group of officers attending a study week led by Montgomery in Tripoli in February 1943. The purpose of the week had been for senior generals to analyze traditional Allied battle doctrine in light of the experiences learned in the desert battles of North Africa. Montgomery had been disappointed with almost all of the commanders who attended, but singled Crerar out for specific criticism in a letter to the Chief of the Imperial General Staff, Field Marshal Sir Alan Brooke. "Harry Crerar told me he had never handled an Armoured Division," Montgomery wrote. "It is probably one of the first things he will have to do in battle; he should learn how to handle armour in peace training. My Corps Commanders have to be able to handle any types of formations."[11] He added, "I am really very fond of him, [but] I don't think he has any idea of how to handle a Corps in battle."[12]

Montgomery's opinion of Crerar remained unchanged and he was acutely aware that the Canadian general had never commanded even a regiment or brigade in the field. Montgomery suggested Crerar take over command of 1st Canadian Infantry Division for a few weeks. This would serve two useful purposes. First, it would give Crerar badly needed combat experience. Second, Major General Chris Vokes, who had been leading 1 CID in Simonds's absence and had not had any leave since the invasion of Sicily, could get a few weeks' rest and recreation in Cairo. Meanwhile, I Canadian Corps headquarters could assemble in Sicily to sort out its operational structure and 5th Canadian Armoured Division could carry out some training exercises near Naples before being moved into an operational role. After a few weeks commanding 1 CID, Crerar could assume command of his corps, which would be temporarily composed of the Canadian infantry division and one or two experienced British divisions, until he was comfortable in the role of corps commander. At that time, 5th Canadian Armoured Division could come under Crerar's command in exchange for the British units.[13]

Crerar rejected the proposal out of hand, insisting that Vokes needed no time off and that his job was to bring all Canadian units in Italy together under a Canadian corps command. He established a corps headquarters in the sumptuous San Domenico Palace Hotel in the northeastern Sicilian resort town of Taormina and signalled Montgomery early in November that he would fly into Foggia air-field, some forty miles east of Campobasso, to see him at Eighth Army headquarters in the nearby village of Lucera. Montgomery's temper snapped and he called to his office Canadian Liaison Officer Major Richard Malone, who was assigned to Eighth Army HQ to ensure smooth relations between the British command and the Canadians. Malone, Montgomery said, was to go to Foggia and tell Crerar that he would meet with the corps commander when it was his desire to do so and not before. Meanwhile, Crerar was to remain in Taormina until summoned.

Malone, caught between the proverbial rock and a hard place, set off for Foggia. Having served under Crerar when he was Chief of the Canadian General Staff, Malone knew the lieutenant general was fix-ated on administrative detail and observance of correct military procedure and protocol. Being rebuffed on the edge of a broken-down airstrip by a mere major was going to infuriate Crerar. As he approached Crerar's airplane, Malone was still trying to find some diplomatic way to communicate Montgomery's directive.

Crerar barely acknowledged Malone's formal salute. "Where is the staff car?" he snapped. Malone signalled the driver to bring it for-ward. Crerar jumped into the back and slammed the door. Realizing he was relegated to sitting beside the driver, Malone walked around to the front and got in. Crerar stiffly directed Malone to take him to Montgomery. A few minutes after they cleared the airfield, Malone told the driver to pull over and go for a stroll and cigarette. Then he turned slowly to Crerar and said, "Harry, Monty says he won't see you and I don't know how to tell you any other way." Obviously stunned at this news, Crerar sat silent for several minutes. Finally, he said, "Well, what do I do now?"

Malone advised him to forget Montgomery and instead informally visit Vokes at 1 CID, so he would still have some legitimate justification for making the flight from Sicily. Then he should return to Taormina and await a summons from Montgomery. Crerar agreed and Malone hoped the integration of I Canadian Corps into Eighth Army's operational structure would proceed more smoothly.[14]

His hopes were dashed when Crerar, a stickler for proper dress and protocol, expressed his disapproval of Eighth Army's dress codes. Here too, the Canadian officers took their cues from Montgomery and the veteran officers of the North African campaign, who favoured sweaters worn over bush shirts or under open-neck battle dress. Their men were even less given to formality, cobbling together whatever manner of dress proved most comfortable in current weather and battle conditions. In Sicily, they wore shorts. At Ortona they wore whatever might keep them warm and somewhat dry in the unending torrents of rain. Canadian drivers had also picked up the British custom of painting names of girlfriends and satiric slogans on trucks and tanks. Some tanks sported paintings of well-endowed, mostly naked women.

This was all too much for Crerar. He issued a directive in late November to all Canadian commanders, whether yet under his command or not, that as senior Canadian officer he did not approve of any of this and everyone was now to be correctly dressed and all the artwork was to be stripped from vehicles. Malone thought the directive absurd. He was amused to see that Crerar ended the directive with the statement that the soldiers "were to remember that they must uphold the reputation of the Canadian Army in appearance."[15] Soon the directive became a source of jokes throughout Eighth Army and few Canadian commanders made any attempt to implement the orders while Crerar was still in Sicily.

Crerar quickly exacerbated matters by issuing a sixteen-page movement order that was to be implemented to bring I Canadian Corps from Sicily to the mainland. The order contained map traces, start lines for each movement phase, a detailed order of march for each unit, provost marshalling points and feeding arrangements en route, and other details that complied perfectly with Staff College requirements. Unfortunately for Crerar, rather than confining the order's distribution to his officers in the corps, he distributed it to virtually everyone of higher level rank in the Eighth Army for information purposes. The order, Malone noted, was soon "almost a collector's item, passed around in amazement that so much paper was required by the new corps to move a few HQ vehicles about."[16]

◆ ◆ ◆

Meanwhile, Simonds had relinquished command of 1 CID permanently to Vokes and moved to Naples to meet 5th Canadian Armoured Division. While Vokes had led 1 CID and 1st Canadian Armoured Brigade into the December battle for the Moro River and Ortona, Simonds had spent the remainder of 1943 consolidating his armoured division and trying to conduct various training schemes.

The problem of properly equipping the division plagued Simonds's efforts. As he had predicted, most of the equipment left behind by 7th Armoured Division needed to be replaced. Worsening the situation was the fact that the British division had swapped what decent equipment it had in its inventory for wrecks cast off by other veteran British divisions. There was also a chronic shortage of parts and tools.[17]

Like most of 5 CAD, the Westminster Regiment had expected that in Italy they would eventually reunite with the shiny new equipment they had been given in Britain, but they never saw any of it again. Nobody had bothered to tell anyone in the lower ranks that the equipment had been left behind as part of the price of the division's admission to the Mediterranean theatre. The regiment's transport ship landed first in Algiers, where the men transferred to a train and trundled over to Philippeville. Here, heavily weighed down with packs holding all their kit, they had to board another boat by clambering like monkeys up huge rope-net ladders strung along its sides. The ship sailed into Naples the next day, where the men disembarked and, as no transport was in sight, marched uphill from the noisy and bomb-battered port area through the squalid slums into the countryside. Eventually, some trucks showed up and carried them to a fig orchard, where they slept outside for two days until moving to the village of Avellino and barracking in a school. It was in Avellino that Private Dan Nikiforuk and the regiment's other drivers were introduced to their armoured cars and Bren carriers courtesy of the Desert Rats. The men were told their own vehicles had been lost at sea when the enemy had sunk the ship carrying them.[18]

When the Lord Strathcona's Horse Regiment was finally consolidated near Naples in mid-December, it still lacked any tanks with which to equip its squadrons.[19] Simonds had taken one look at his ramshackle collection of diesel-powered Sherman tanks that mounted ineffectual six- or even two-pounder British-made guns and decided to accept a proposal that the Canadians be equipped with new tanks. These were scheduled to arrive soon in North Africa and were fitted with Chrysler gasoline engines and 75-millimetre guns. This would necessitate a serious delay in equipping his armoured regiments and training them for combat conditions in Italy, but he had to accept that. The regiments were also desperately short of trucks, Bren carriers, and Jeeps. Mechanics started cannibalizing two or three trucks of different makes for sufficient parts to create one functioning vehicle.[20]

The Westminsters' Nikiforuk was allotted a White scout car that was perforated with bullet and rust holes. When he started the vehicle — a lightly armoured truck capable of carrying about twelve infantrymen — it sputtered and coughed, as if running out of fuel, despite having full tanks. He finally pulled the fuel tanks and discovered a large quantity of sand sloshing around and fouling the gas lines. That difficulty repaired, the armoured car proved serviceable, but it was still subject to a variety of haphazard and unexpected mechanical problems that Nikiforuk knew were symptomatic of a vehicle that had long outrun its serviceable life. He worried about how the machine would perform when the regiment moved into the rigorous world of combat.

Nikiforuk knew trucks. The twenty-one-year-old had been driving heavy trucks over the rough roads of Saskatchewan for years, eking out a living through the Depression. He hauled mostly fuel then.

When war broke out and construction of airports began under the British Commonwealth Air Training Plan scheme, Nikiforuk shifted gravel for runways to the bases going up at Estevan, North Battleford, and other small Saskatchewan towns. On February 10, 1942, he drove into Saskatoon and enlisted, stating his specialization as a driver. Motorized vehicles were still enough of a novelty in Canada before the war that the army was chronically short of men who arrived already trained and experienced in driving anything, but truck drivers were particularly in demand.

Nikiforuk reasonably expected to be assigned in this capacity to the Army Service Corps, but the army decided he should be an infantryman instead. It sent him off to the Westminster Regiment in Britain, where he slogged about on foot until the Westminsters were designated as a motorized unit shortly before being shipped to Italy. Such regiments used White scout cars or Bren carriers to advance into the thick of an engagement, jumped out, and then fought on foot as regular infantry. Nikiforuk was the driver for No. 4 Platoon of 'A' Company. He would drive the vehicle into battle, then get out and fight alongside everyone else.

The cars offered dubious protection to the soldiers during the advance. Their fronts had relatively heavy steel plates set on an angle to deflect enemy shot, and dropdown shields to protect the driver while providing a narrow slot for him to see through. This front armour could repel most small-arms fire, but the sides and rear of the vehicles offered no protection against even a rifle slug. The men assigned to the armoured cars were no more impressed with them than were those Westminsters in the scout platoons who were given Bren carriers for transport. These tracked vehicles carried six men and their equipment. They were open-topped and the sides came up only to about waist height, leaving the men inside exposed to enemy fire. The scouts quickly learned that the Bren was best utilized as a motorized mule. It usually carried their equipment while they walked alongside, rather than clustering inside its exposed interior.

◆ ◆ ◆

Simonds, wondering how any of the stuff he had been allotted would hold up in battle, was determined to get better equipment first. Learning that I Canadian Corps in Sicily was to receive a shipment of

3,350 Canadian-built vehicles fresh from the factory, Simonds asked that these all be allotted to his combat troops. Crerar shot back that this was impossible, for it would provide the British with an excuse to delay formation of the corps due to lack of vehicles.

The sniping between Crerar and Simonds escalated throughout December. Matters soon took on the appearance of the ridiculous as Crerar sent a major to measure Simonds's caravan in detail so that he could have a replica constructed for his own use. Simonds gave the major fifteen minutes to clear off. When the major reported back, Crerar fired off a letter to Simonds accusing him of committing "an indirect act, on your part, of personal discourtesy to me." The letter went on to say that "the much more important effect of this episode is that it tends to indicate that your nerves are over-stretched and that impulse, rather than considered judgement, may begin to affect your decisions. Should this, indeed, be the situation, I would be extremely worried, for you are now reaching a position in the Army when balance is becoming even more important to your future than brilliance."[21]

Simonds was technically not even under Crerar's command yet, for 5 CAD was drawing on 2nd Echelon headquarters in Naples for equipment and supply and was to take direction from its commander. Simonds was also receiving orders directly from Montgomery. But Crerar kept issuing vast barrages of written orders to both Simonds and Vokes that called for immediate responses. Directed by Crerar to submit copies of virtually all reports and orders the division issued, Simonds responded frostily with a signal to Crerar that 5 CAD was not under his command. Montgomery, hearing of the conflict, backed him by sending Malone to Taormina to deliver instructions that Crerar leave Simonds alone.

When Malone entered the corps's anteroom outside the officers' mess, he was delighted to meet an old friend who was serving as a brigadier in the Medical Corps. Dr. Fred Van Nostrand told Malone he now acted as the chief psychiatric advisor to the Canadian Army. Asked what brought him to Sicily, the doctor whispered that Crerar had summoned him from London to certify that Simonds was insane. The next day, he was to travel to Naples and examine Simonds. Over dinner, Crerar insisted that Simonds was suffering a nervous breakdown and responding to Crerar's signals with insane replies. When

Malone delivered Montgomery's message to Crerar after dinner, the general offered no reply.

Malone gave Van Nostrand a lift in his plane to Simonds's HQ the next morning and it was arranged that the three of them should dine together that evening. During dinner, Malone found Simonds "his usual alert, rather crisp and formal self." After discussing the state of the division's training, he told the doctor and Malone frankly that Crerar was "quite bonkers." He added that the corps commander belonged in an institution and had lately taken to "sending insane signals all over the place."

Before turning in for the night, Malone asked Van Nostrand what he planned to do now that each commander was certain the other was mad. Van Nostrand smiled and threw his hands up in the air. "I am going back to London as fast as I can get there. This isn't a problem for me."[22]

Crerar was not done. In a long letter to Montgomery on December 17, he extolled Simonds's military brilliance and said he had "a first-class military mind." Having offered praise, Crerar proceeded to write that Simonds was "highly 'tensed up'" and "resents any control or direction on my part — a responsibility which is now mine concerning certain 'Canadian business' and later, when the Canadian Corps is functioning operationally, in the widest possible manner." While Simonds, he said, "has all the military brilliance for higher command in the field, with his tense mentality, under further strain through increased rank and responsibility, he might go 'off the deep end' very disastrously indeed."[23]

Montgomery, preparing to return to Britain to take direct command of Operation Overlord, responded with surprising civility that he had "the highest opinion of Simonds. . . . Briefly my views are that Simonds is a first class soldier. After a period with an armoured division he will be suitable for a corps. He will be a very valuable officer in the Canadian Forces as you have no one else with his experience; he must be handled carefully, and be trained on. Vokes is not even in the same parish. I am trying hard to teach him but he will never be anything more than 'a good plain cook.' I do not, of course, know what has taken place between you and Simonds. He is directly under my command for training and so on, but of course would deal with you on purely Canadian matters. If you have been sending him any instructions or directions on training he might possibly ignore them! He gets that from me — verbally. I suggest you discuss it with me when you visit Eighth Army. Come whenever you like."[24]

Montgomery's relatively light tone to Crerar was obviously intended to defuse the situation between Crerar and Simonds, but he was also deeply concerned about the friction between the two Canadian generals. In a letter to Field Marshal Brooke on December 28, he offered extensive suggestions on how matters throughout the European and Italian theatres should be organized. In his fourth point, Montgomery wrote: "The more I think of Harry Crerar the more I am convinced that he is quite unfit to command an army in the field at present. He has much to learn and he will have many shocks before he has learnt it properly. He has already (from Sicily) started to have rows with Canadian generals under me; he wants a lot of teaching; I taught him about training; Oliver Leese will now have to teach him the practical side of war."[25] Three days later, Montgomery bid farewell to the Eighth Army and left for Britain.

◆ ◆ ◆

In Britain, changes were under way as McNaughton, who had led First Canadian Army overseas since September 1939, resigned, having lost the confidence of both the British Chiefs of Staff and the Canadian War Committee, particularly Ralston. His resistance to the breakup of the army for the Italian operation had heightened tensions between himself and Ottawa. Although he enjoyed the quiet support of Prime Minister King, this proved insufficient. On Boxing Day 1943, he flew home to Canada in the wake of a resignation tendered just before it became obvious Ottawa was about to fire him. Lieutenant General Kenneth Stuart was made acting commander of First Canadian Army, but his was only a caretaker role. Ottawa's intention was that the command would go to Crerar once he completed another couple of months as corps commander in Italy.

That Crerar's tenure in Italy was to be short was not revealed to his divisional commanders. Following Montgomery's departure and the promotion of Leese to command of Eighth Army, 1 CID commander Major General Chris Vokes was led to ponder the future of his division. Although he would miss Montgomery, Vokes believed Leese a competent replacement. Leese, he wrote, "had experience in all lower echelons of command and was very likely to require a similar experience in the corps commanders of the Eighth Army." The tall, forty-nine-year-old general had been twice severely wounded while serving with the Coldstream Guards during World War I and had commanded XXX Corps since September 1942. Vokes found him cheerful, "a complete extrovert with a ribald sense of humour. His favourite form of dress was khaki plus-fours, a khaki shirt and a woolen pullover, topped by the red-banded general's hat worn by all general officers in the British Army. At all times he attired himself for personal comfort and never to the regulation pattern."

Leese's style of dress and personality stood completely at odds with that of Crerar. Vokes observed that "Crerar was meticulous in his observance of the clothing regulations. If he was improperly dressed I'm quite sure he felt naked. If he had a sense of humour it was never in evidence. I think he was inclined to look on the Canadian generals of the younger generation, like myself, as ignorant upstarts who in spite of considerable operational experience really knew nothing."

Vokes envisioned Leese and Crerar clashing sharply and worried that "mutual antagonism" would lead to I Canadian Corps's not having "much of an operational future." He also thought that Crerar had a lot to learn before he should be entrusted with commanding a corps in battle. Crerar, he wrote, "had outstanding administrative and organizational ability and was a disciplinarian, but there was all the difference in the world between the make believe training in England and the real thing in Italy with the lives of men at stake." He added that he "did not view with much enthusiasm the prospect of serving under a corps commander and his staff all totally inexperienced in battle."[26]

While concerned about Crerar's battlefield command abilities, he was equally uncertain of the wisdom of the entire Canadian corps concept. "The permanent grouping of the two divisions in a Canadian Corps was our national policy, but it did not accord with British operational doctrine. British army commanders regarded field divisions as their tactical pawns of manoeuvre. He could concentrate divisions for an attack at a place and time of his choosing or disperse them in defence." This meant that the grouping of divisions by corps "was a purely temporary one and the number and type of the divisions under operational command in any army corps was usually a gauge of the army commander's confidence in its corps commander's capability and field experience. It was rare to have the number of divisions exceed six in an army corps. It was usually three to four."[27]

First Canadian Corps, however, had only two divisions — the two Canadian divisions in Italy. And it was unlikely that, given Crerar's inexperience, any other Commonwealth or British divisions in Eighth Army were to be assigned to the corps until Leese considered its commander sufficiently competent. In a letter to his wife, Leese wrote: "I am having a big problem with Canadian commanders. Harry Crerar is here — & of course knows nothing of military matters in the field — but is presumably the commander designate of the Canadian Army in England. So I have to teach Crerar for a time — and then change again to another totally inexperienced commander." Montgomery had done nothing in the latter part of 1943 to teach Crerar anything, Leese remarked. Now he was stalling at returning Crerar to Britain to take command of First Canadian Army in the wake of McNaughton's resignation.[28]

◆ ◆ ◆

While the squabbling at high command continued, 5th Canadian Armoured Division pulled up stakes near Naples on November 15 and set off on a long march across the Apennines to the Adriatic. Its destination was the town of Altamura, twenty-eight miles southwest of Bari. Simonds was glad to be gone from Naples, wanting to "get the troops away from this sort of suburban 'built up' area" which "was a very poor training area, the squalid slums are depressing and constitute a very bad atmosphere in which to condition troops."[29] The division left Naples with many of its trucks towed by others. Along the way, increasing numbers had to be abandoned because of breakdowns. Drivers soon discovered on the steep mountain grades that their brakes were often barely capable of keeping a fully loaded truck from running out of control. Three weeks after the journey was completed, 11th Canadian Infantry Brigade's Royal Electrical and Mechanical Engineers (REME) were still recovering broken-down vehicles that had been abandoned.[30]

Shortly after Simonds and 5 CAD settled into the new bivouac at Altamura, Crerar and his corps establishment moved from Sicily to set up shop in the same area. Crerar was actively pressing Leese for the corps and its divisions to be assigned an active combat role. But

Leese kept assigning segments of the Canadian divisions to tasks that threatened to spread them across Italy, which added nothing to their training and kept them away from combat. Four of Crerar's artillery regiments were shunted back to Salerno to operate a transit camp for the divisions preparing to invade Anzio. Two days after complying with this order, Crerar was told to dispatch 1,700 men for refugee control duties in Brindisi and Bari. He complied by sending the Royal Canadian Dragoons and more artillerymen.

Crerar complained directly to Alexander, who replied that it was "in no sense derogatory to ask fighting troops to carry out such duties when for any reason they cannot be employed on the battle-front."[31] Soon, however, Crerar convinced Leese to allow I Canadian Corps to take over command of its two divisions and begin operations in the field by the end of January.

Not all of 5 CAD's regiments were out of the line during January. As an armoured division, 5 CAD's operational structure divided it into several distinct elements. One was the 5th Canadian Armoured Brigade, composed of the Lord Strathcona's Horse, 8th Princess Louise New Brunswick Hussars, and British Columbia Dragoons. These were all tank regiments, largely still awaiting their tanks. Also awaiting armoured vehicles was the reconnaissance regiment, the Governor General's Horse Guards. The motorized Westminster Regiment was continuing to equip itself with vehicles to fulfill its mobile role. Collectively, these units provided 5 CAD with its mobile armoured component. The division also included the 11th Canadian Infantry Brigade, with three regiments: the Perth Regiment, the Cape Breton Highlanders, and the Irish Regiment of Canada. These regiments were intended to support the armoured brigade in combat operations.

As the infantry brigade was not hampered by the lack of tanks and also less affected by the shortages of trucks and other vehicles, Simonds requested in early January that 11 CIB be sent forward "to get its first experience of contact with the enemy." On January 4, he advised its commander, thirty-four-year-old Brigadier George Kitching, that 11 CIB would relieve 1 CID's 3rd Canadian Infantry Brigade on the front lines north of Ortona. The brigade's diarist wrote, "The intention is to 'break us in easily.' We shall soon see whether it is 'easy' or not."[32]

3

BAPTISM
OF FIRE

Just before dark on January 12, Perth Regiment Private Stan Scislowski marched with the rest of 'D' Company through the eerie ruins of Ortona. The entire regiment was strung out in a long slender thread snaking its way single file through the town. A number of troops from the Loyal Edmonton Regiment stood watching from the doorways of the few scattered houses that remained more or less intact. Along with the Seaforth Highlanders of Canada, the Edmontons had spent eight December days fighting, often hand-to-hand, with men of the elite 1st Parachute Division for possession of the town. They were still bloodied, exhausted, and all too glad to see somebody else manning the Canadian front-line positions.

Two days earlier, Scislowski and his mates in No. 18 Platoon had listened with a mixture of trepidation and anticipation as Captain Sam Ridge explained that the opposing line was still held by the paratroopers. "These guys you're going up against are fanatics," he said, "and their greatest wish is to die for their Führer." Ridge smiled. "And it's your duty to see that their wishes come true." Scislowski and the others responded with a rousing cheer.[1]

A few of the men were still feeling cocky. One, referring to 1st Canadian Infantry Division's red identification sleeve patches, joked loudly to a clutch of Edmontons: "Okay, you red patch bastards, you can get your lily-white asses to hell out of here, because you're looking at real soldiers now. We'll show you what the hell fightin's all about!"[2] Within hours of 11th Canadian Infantry Brigade's arrival, the story of the derogatory remark made by the Perth in Ortona had raced through the entire ranks of 1 CID. Royal Canadian Regiment Acting Lieutenant Colonel Strome Galloway laughed when he heard the story. "We'll show you red patch bastards how it's done," he muttered. "I doubt it." Galloway knew that Brigadier George Kitching, whom he had served with in the RCR prior to the Sicily invasion, commanded the brigade. Another old RCR hand, Lieutenant Colonel Bobby Clark, led the Irish Regiment. Galloway expected the new infantry brigade would soon learn the harsh reality of combat.[3]

Major General Chris Vokes told Kitching that his task was to "build up a detailed picture of the enemy defence on the brigade's front. This was to be obtained by forward observation during daylight and by intensive patrolling at night."[4] Between the Canadian and German lines was the riverbed of the Riccio River, which remained dry despite the heavy rains and occasional snow that had fallen in past weeks. The enemy positions on the opposing bank were well concealed, as were those of the Canadians. Everyone lived underground in slit trenches, shell craters, root cellars, or behind the stout walls of shell-battered farmhouses and outbuildings. Within a couple of days of the brigade's getting settled into their soggy slit trenches, Vokes summoned Kitching for another meeting.

Kitching and Vokes were physical opposites — Vokes a big, burly, rough-hewn man with a loud, profane, bullying manner; Kitching slender, soft-spoken, and possessed of English public–school manners. Yet the two had become fast friends during their service in Sicily and had spent some rollicking leave times in May 1943 prior to the launch of Operation Husky, drinking and carousing through Cairo's finer hotels and watering holes. Vokes gravely told Kitching his instructions were changed and, on January 17, 11 CIB would attempt to seize the plateau on the northern shore of the Riccio, which overlooked the lower reaches of the Arielli River. Its capture, Vokes said, "would be a valuable territorial gain."[5]

Possibly more important, the attack would fulfill a directive from theatre commander General Harold Alexander for Eighth Army to maintain pressure on the Adriatic front to keep German divisions from being shifted westward where they might interfere with the forthcoming Anzio landings. Accordingly, V Corps commander Lieutenant General Charles Allfrey — under whose command 1 CID continued to serve until I Canadian Corps reached operational status at month's end — decided the newly arrived brigade should be blooded.

Vokes opposed the operation and tried hard to get the attack order rescinded. Having just brought 1 CID through a month of hellish battles during which he had repeatedly squandered his reserves and devastated his regiments through ill-conceived one-battalion assaults against heavily entrenched German positions, Vokes knew the hard way the folly of such ventures. He thought the major strategic goal behind this order was based on a far-fetched premise. How could a brigade-sized attack on the Adriatic divert enemy attention away from Cassino? This would work only, he later wrote, if "the enemy believed it to herald a renewal of the Eighth Army offensive. The Germans were not military incompetents. They knew full well . . . any attack mounted on the Adriatic front in the prevailing mud had to be a very limited operation. Furthermore they were fully aware it had little or no prospect of success against organized defence."

Allfrey told Vokes to get on with the attack precisely because of its "diversionary connotations." Then, incredibly, Allfrey emphasized that Vokes ensure the brigade did not suffer heavy casualties. How, Vokes wondered, can "I prevent heavy casualties in an operation in which they would inevitably be so?" What did Allfrey consider heavy casualties, anyway? "How will I know if casualties have become heavy?" Vokes knew from the December fighting that it was impossible to get accurate casualty reports in "the heat of action. Such reports are often exaggerated and very inaccurate. Once infantry is committed to an assault there is no way to avoid casualties, whether they be 'heavy' or 'light,' if the attack is to be pressed home. It is only possible for the assaulting troops to count heads when the fighting dies down, usually at night." Vokes decided that "it would be impossible for me to assess the degree of casualties suffered by the 11th Brigade until the end of the day's fighting."

The fact that 11 CIB was a green outfit ensured heavy casualties. Vokes considered the brigade "well trained and eager for combat, but this would be their first battle, their baptism of fire. They would be forced to assault, as inexperienced troops, in the worst possible going conditions." And they faced the 1st German Parachute Division, which "all ranks of the 1st Canadian Division regarded with respect. I doubted whether any other infantry brigade in the whole Eighth Army, no matter how battle seasoned, could succeed in the task given to the 11th Brigade. It was asking too much as it could only result in very heavy casualties with no hope of success."[6]

Vokes, however, had his orders and he passed the task to Kitching, leaving the details to a man he knew to be a competent, battle-experienced officer. Kitching's men might be green, but their commander was not. While Vokes stood back and gave Kitching operational freedom, Allfrey stepped in and interfered. Allfrey had an idea about how to bring the attack off successfully and made sure Kitching planned his deployments accordingly. Allfrey's plan was to direct all available artillery in the corps ahead of a single attacking battalion. Once that battalion followed this sheet of shrapnel and blasted through to its objective, another battalion would advance, protected by a second wave of corps artillery, and then the third battalion would receive identical support. Allfrey was convinced the paratroops would be stunned by the massive bombardment and so disorganized that 11 CIB could charge through and gain the objective. This scheme meant that Kitching's leading battalion would have to operate without support from the brigade's other battalions for several hours, until the guns could institute a new firing plan.

Although Kitching thought "it might be better to disperse the enemy's counter fire by attacking with two battalions," he did not voice his opinion, and he agreed to Allfrey's proposed course without complaint. He thought that perhaps Allfrey was right in arguing that "the overwhelming fire support of sixteen artillery regiments would neutralize the enemy during that critical period when our leading companies would close with him."[7] Kitching was also confident that the tank support provided by the Three Rivers Regiment, which he had fought alongside in Sicily with excellent results, would ensure the attacking battalion had a good shot at taking its objective.

As earlier planned, Kitching gave the Perth Regiment the task of leading the way, for he thought the battalion "deserved a slight boost." The battalion had been recruited mainly in southwestern Ontario with the men drawn off farms and from small towns. They marched in a regiment with a Scottish tradition, which normally served to infuse immediate esprit de corps throughout the ranks. But there was little ethnic harmony within the regiment itself, as most of the men traced their lineage back to all corners of Europe rather than to Scotland. They did not, Kitching thought, have "the 'glamour' of the Irish Regiment with its green 'Cawbeen' or of the Cape Breton Highlanders with their heavy Gaelic content." Leading the brigade's first major attack, he reasoned, would send the message to these men that their battalion was as highly regarded as the others under his command and would bind the men more tightly together.[8] The battalion and company officers in the three battalions were briefed on Sunday, January 16.

While Kitching was setting out the specific company tasks to his line commanders, the Perth's 'D' Company attended its first church parade in a front-line area. Private Stan Scislowski, a Polish-Canadian conscript, was amazed to see the company's entire complement of just over 100 men made to line up "elbow to elbow out in the clear, within sniper shot of the enemy lines," to sing hymns and listen to a sermon. Here they were, less than half a mile from the Germans, trying to sing "Abide With Me" or "What a Friend We Have in Jesus" with "ears cocked for the rustle of an incoming shell or the last second flutter of a mortar bomb on its downward flight." Ordering such a church parade in the front lines, Scislowski thought, "had to be by far the stupidest order of the many stupid orders I'd had to obey since I took on the uniform." He expected that at any moment a couple of mortar bombs were going to drop smack in the middle of them all and reduce everyone "to ratshit."[9] Amazingly, however, the Germans held their fire and let the service conclude and the men dispersed unmolested.

Back in the company lines, Scislowski and the rest of 'D' Company gathered around Captain Sam Ridge and learned they were going into the attack the next morning. Scislowski remembered hanging "on his every word, knowing there'd be no more pretending. From here on in everything would be for real." Like most of the men around him, Scislowski was excited, more so than he had ever been during the pep talk preceding a football game because he knew "a man could get himself killed in this particular kind of game."[10]

Ridge, whom the men called Sammy, said intelligence estimated they faced only a couple of platoons and, even though these were paratroopers, they were unlikely to hold up against the planned heavy artillery barrage and a battalion assault supported by tanks. 'A' and 'C' companies would lead off behind the creeping artillery barrage at 0530 hours.[11] As this barrage moved forward in a series of designated lifts that eventually would roll over the defending Germans, the Perths would advance close behind its protective cover. The Perths' line of attack would follow a rough track that crossed a fork in the Riccio River at two fords lying about 250 yards apart. Across the river, the track climbed steeply for half a mile to a junction where the Tollo Road came in from the west to meet Highway 16, which ran parallel to the Adriatic coast. This road junction, on top of the opposing ridge, was the Perths' main objective. Once the junction and a blown bridge that crossed a gully 500 yards north of it were secure, the Cape Breton Highlanders would come forward to capture the high ground between the Tollo Road and Highway 16. Finally, both battalions would push forward in line to secure a position on the south bank of the Arielli River.[12]

The array of promised artillery designated to support the brigade was impressive. In addition to the creeping barrage, artillery would fire set concentrations against known defensive positions, and conduct counterfire to force the German artillerymen to keep their heads down throughout the advance. It would also lay down smokescreens to shield the advancing troops from observation by German machine-gun troops and Forward Observation Officers, who might otherwise call down direct artillery or mortar fire on the men. All the guns of 1st Canadian and 8th Indian divisions, as well as 1st Army Group Royal Artillery, would participate. This meant that one heavy 7.2-inch gun regiment, five medium 5.5-inch gun regiments, and nine field regiments would dedicate their guns to the operation. Each of the 25-pounder artillery pieces in the field regiments would have 400 rounds available, while the mediums could fire up to 300 rounds. Also pitching in would be the thirty-two 4.2-inch mortars of 1 CID's Saskatoon Light Infantry support group.[13] On the left flank, the brigade's own support group, an element of the Princess Louise

Fusiliers, would shower indirect arcing fire from its 50-calibre Vickers machine guns on a small bridge crossing the Riccio. This would prevent German engineers from laying charges on the bridge and blowing it. Once the line companies took the assigned objectives, tanks and Bren carriers could use the bridge to bring up antitank weapons and other heavy support equipment.[14] Beginning on Sunday, which was a clear sunny day, four Kittyhawk and twelve light-bomber squadrons started strafing and bombing targets along the Tollo Road. On Monday, the air squadrons were to return and subject the Arielli River positions to similar treatment.[15]

Scislowski went to bed Sunday night with a swarm of contradictory thoughts and emotions swirling through his head. Mostly he envisioned himself heroically acting as "a one-man army charging into the heart of the enemy positions, bludgeoning and bayoneting my way through a swarm of defenders." This gallantry brought him next to "standing before the King at Buckingham Palace as he pinned the coveted Victoria Cross on my tunic." Such thoughts were sobered, however, by thoughts of home, his mother, brother and sisters, the teachers, who, like his family, had been regularly writing to him and sending parcels. What would they all think of him now? As the night wore on, fear crept in and he tried hard not to dwell on thoughts that he might not be alive at day's end or that he might lose a leg, an arm, "or even get my nuts shot off." Finally, he cast off these morbid thoughts and fell into a slumber that was all too abruptly ended when a sergeant nudged him awake at 0400 hours.[16]

In the hour before the attack, Scislowski suddenly was struck by acute incontinence, as were many of the others in his company. Bladders and bowels had to be relieved three or four times before the orders to move up to the start line came down to them. As Scislowski adjusted his battle pack, checked the bolt of his rifle to make sure it worked smoothly, and ensured his two Type 36 grenades were properly fused, he noticed his platoon mate, Joe Gallant, sitting by a snow fence staring off into space. In his mid-thirties, Gallant was the oldest man in the platoon and was consequently nicknamed Pop. The man looked poorly, as he had for four or five days. Gallant had tried repeatedly to get permission to see the dentist because he said his teeth were hurting. The Medical Officer, suspecting cowardice, refused to send him to the rear for a checkup. Finally, Gallant told his friends one evening that he was going to be dead before noon if he went on this attack. Now as the men fell out on the road and started moving toward the start point, Gallant reminded Scislowski despairingly that he "was as good as dead." Scislowski replied, "Aw, come off that, Joe! Quit your worrying. You're going to be okay."[17]

◆ ◆ ◆

At precisely 0530 hours on January 17, the artillery barrage opened and the Perths went forward. It was a gloomy day with such a low ceiling that the promised air support was unable to fly.[18] As the battalion reserve, 'D' Company remained at the start line. 'A' Company, under command of Captain Jack Kennedy, and 'C' Company, commanded by Major Robert MacDougall, led the assault with 'A' on the right and 'C' on the left. 'C' Company's lead platoon quickly forded the dry stream but then ran face on into heavy machine-gun and rifle fire from positions held by the paratroopers' 3rd Battalion. The weight of this fire was increased with deadly effect when well-sited mortar and artillery fire unchecked by the Allied counter-barrage caught the second wave of the company struggling through the mud in the second ford. 'A' Company was stopped by even more withering fire that pinned it down in the narrow valley bottom and sent many of the men crawling for shelter into abandoned German slit trenches.

The most accurate and deadly fire directed at 'C' Company came from a large white-painted stone house 200 yards up the hillside. MacDougall and Lieutenant Laurent Rochon gathered six men and attempted to storm it, with MacDougall in the lead waving his revolver to urge the men forward. In seconds, bullets cut down the entire small force.[19] MacDougall, Rochon, and two of the men were killed instantly. The four others were wounded, but the heavy fire from the house prevented any attempt by the Perths to recover them from the open ground where they lay. All were eventually taken prisoner.

On the right, 'A' Company's Kennedy desperately tried to get his men going again by sending a platoon led by Lieutenant Alfred Clements out to the right to circle behind two machine-gun posts that were pinning down the company. Within seconds of setting out, Clements and five of his men were cut down by two other machine guns hidden directly in the line of their advance.[20]

About this time, many of the Perths were wondering about the

whereabouts of the Three Rivers tanks that should have been providing close support. So was Kitching. From his observation post, he
could see that one tank had struck a mine and lost a track and a
bogie wheel, but that "none of the others in the squadron had any
intention of trying to cross the Riccio to go to the aid of the infantry."
Angrily he sent for the commander, Lieutenant Colonel E. Leslie
Booth. When a major showed up in his stead, Kitching instructed the
officer "to give the infantry all possible support by crossing the
Riccio and getting into the fight." Soon the tanks of 'A' Squadron's
No. 1 and No. 2 Troops began pressing forward.[21] Minutes later,
Corporal R. Bower of No. 1 Troop had two fingers sliced off when his
hatch was blown closed by an exploding mortar round. The tankers
began pouring heavy fire with their main 75-millimetre guns and
machine guns against "known enemy machine gun positions and
possible tank, anti-tank, and other positions in and around the various buildings along the line of advance and on the objective."[22]

The fire had no apparent effect on the opposing paratroopers, who
kept blasting away at the infantry. 'A' and 'C' companies remained
pinned down. At 0700 hours, because 'C' Company had made the
most gains, 'D' Company was ordered to advance to this company's
left at a point where the ridge was lower and might be more easily
assaulted. 'D' Company had no sooner jumped off from the ditch
where they had been sheltering than a heavy mortar barrage
pounded down on top of the men. Gallant, who had been certain he
was going to his death, was the only fatality. A large fragment ripped
into the back of his head, killing him instantly. The platoon's radio,
which he carried, was also knocked out. Scislowski and the others
hit the dirt. Chunks of half-frozen earth struck Scislowski's face as he
looked desperately around for a shell hole or ditch to take cover in.
Other cowering Perths filled every good position. Finally, he found
the slight depression left by the track of a German tank and crawled
into the meagre refuge it afforded.

When the mortaring suddenly lifted, Ridge ordered the men forward again. Crouching, they moved warily up a small depression
toward the Riccio valley. Behind them, two Three Rivers tanks rolled
up to the rim of the valley and opened up with their machine guns.
Scislowski's No. 18 Platoon veered to the right to take cover in three
rubble heaps that had once been a farmhouse and its outbuildings.

Just as they reached the protection of the ruins, heavy machine-gun and mortar fire forced them to huddle out of sight among the piles of masonry, broken timbers, and chunks of stone. When the gunfire slackened, the platoon leapfrogged seventy-five yards forward with bullets tearing up the dirt around their legs to another ditch and hunkered down, barely able to offer any counterfire against the storm of German bullets and mortar rounds invited by the slightest movement.

Scislowski was exhausted. Adrenaline and sheer heart-pumping terror had shaken him to the core. Although he was proud he had not fled in panic or otherwise disgraced himself, the young private realized that about all that had kept him going was his determination to not let his friends down or be outdone by them. He was also damned sure that "our glorious attack wasn't going at all well, otherwise we should have been on our objective by this time."[23]

◆ ◆ ◆

In fact, the attack was foundering and all Kitching's attempts to breathe new life into the advance failed. At 1245 hours, he had sent the Cape Breton Highlanders toward a draw on the right of the Perths to get into the Riccio river bottom behind the cover of a smokescreen. The battalion was thirty-five yards from the Riccio when a mortar barrage reached through the smoke with uncanny accuracy, along with machine guns firing from houses on either side of the gully. The fire ripped into the advancing troops. For two hours, the two leading companies were helplessly pinned down, unable to go forward or to retreat. Kitching ordered Highlanders commander Lieutenant Colonel Jim Weir to hold back his remaining companies for fear of their becoming similarly trapped.[24]

The two companies pinned in the gully were taking heavy casualties. Every time a man moved, he attracted intense fire. Major W.W. Ogilvie commanding 'D' Company was wounded, but Company Sergeant Major M.A. O'Grady crawled to the ditch in which the stricken officer lay and dragged him back to protection. Three men were killed instantly by an exploding mortar round. In 'C' Company, lieutenants H.W. Carn and D.C. Johnson were wounded minutes after the company stopped. Throughout the hours of their ordeal in the gully, stretcher-bearer teams crawled back and forth between the trapped soldiers offering what aid they could. They also courageously managed to evacuate a few of the more badly wounded by dragging them back up the gully to the rear despite the continuous fire.[25]

Kitching was having a terrible time trying to follow events. All communication with the forward companies of both the Perths and Highlanders had been lost within minutes of their going into action. Highlanders commander Weir, who was in a trench dug well forward on the slope, provided his only real link to the action. From the trench, Weir could see quite well over the entire Riccio front. He also had a telephone cable link back to Kitching's headquarters. Weir's position was hardly a good observation post, though, as it had been spotted and was subject to gunfire every time anything appeared above the trench rim. To give Kitching an idea of the situation, Weir held up his phone while raising the antennae of a radio set and let the brigadier hear the bullets striking around it.

From Kitching's position, it was impossible to see. "Smoke, dust and debris all floated slowly back towards our positions masking all accurate observation from the crest of our ridge," he later wrote. When the Highlanders' attack collapsed and a renewed attempt at 1600 hours by the Perths' 'D' Company was stopped in its tracks, Kitching accepted the inevitable and gave the order for the two battalions to withdraw at nightfall.[26]

There was nothing dignified about the retreat. The Perths came back in small straggling groups. They were exhausted and badly shocked by the day's fearful fighting and the loss of so many men. Kitching started organizing another attack for the morning but received word shortly from Vokes that the offensive was to be abandoned. The two battalions had lost enough men to clearly surpass Allfrey's heavy casualty proviso. In all, 8 officers and 177 other ranks had been killed or wounded. The Perths were hardest hit: 3 officers and 44 men killed, 62 wounded, and one officer and 27 men taken prisoner. The Highlanders lost 13 men killed and 3 officers and 30 men wounded. The other 22 killed or wounded were mostly from the Irish Regiment, which had waited in forward positions subject to German artillery or mortar fire, but had not been committed to the attack. Some Three Rivers tank crewmen were also among the casualties. Nothing had been gained and the Germans lost only 27 men killed and another 36 wounded.

Commander-in-Chief Southwest Generalfeldmarschall Albert

Kesselring was so buoyed by the botched attack that in a telephone conversation on January 19 he told Tenth Army Commander Generaloberst Heinrich von Vietinghoff that the relief of 1 CID by elements of 5th Canadian Armoured Division was good news for the paratroops. "We need not be afraid that anything will happen there; they are unseasoned troops and we can easily cope with them."

The Tenth Army commander answered cautiously, "They all want to show their wares."

Kesselring scoffed: "The trial runs of green troops are nothing famous."[27]

◆ ◆ ◆

Eleven CIB's trial run had not only been costly; it also contributed little to building a bond between the men of 5 CAD and the more veteran Canadians alongside whom they were to serve. During the night of their withdrawal, the Perths had failed to let the Three Rivers' 'A' Squadron tankers know they were leaving. Morning found the tankers sitting on the rim of the Riccio River valley with nary an infantryman around to provide protection. They quickly rumbled back to a defence position inside the perimeter held by the Loyal Edmonton Regiment, who, along with the other two battalions of 2nd Canadian Infantry Brigade, had replaced 11 CIB in the front line.[28]

For their part, the 1 CID battalions that watched the men of 11 CIB straggle past on the way to the rear remembered the bold, derisive jests of only five days earlier. The men got their own back with sharp digs about the "Mighty Maroon Machine," derived from the maroon identity patch each 5 CAD soldier wore on his sleeve. "Look at the Mighty Maroon Machine," some of the men yelled, "marching bravely away from battle." Rumours swept through 1 CID that the Perths had fled the field, many throwing aside their weapons in their panicked flight.[29]

Even Vokes, who had known from the outset that the attack was doomed to failure, could not resist attending a Perth roll call to offer some backhanded praise from the back of his Jeep and then scold the men loudly for letting themselves be pinned down. Scislowski had admired Vokes to this moment and thought most of 11 CIB had felt the same. Now he was disdainful, for the private knew in his heart that if they had kept pushing forward the entire battalion would only have died in vain. One soldier directly behind Scislowski said loudly, "Give me a fuckin' Bren and I'll show you, you bastard, what it's like to be pinned down!" Obviously Vokes heard, for his face turned red. Abruptly stopping his speech, Vokes tapped his driver on the shoulder and directed him to roar off without saying another word.[30] Vokes, for his part, decided that he would not approve of the Canadians' taking any further part in Eighth Army offensive actions on the Adriatic front until spring came and the ground dried out. Until that happened, he felt, "General MUD allied himself with the defence," which handed the Germans an overwhelming tactical advantage.[31]

◆ ◆ ◆

On the same day that Kesselring and von Vietinghoff congratulated each other on stemming the 11 CIB attack, Vokes accepted a suggestion by Allfrey that he finally take a long overdue leave. Vokes thought it a good time to go, as his division should be engaged in nothing more than patrolling operations until it was brought under I Canadian Corps control at month's end. He left for Cairo in the last week of January, leaving the division in the capable hands of Brigadier Bert Hoffmeister. This would give the young officer, who had risen rapidly through the ranks since coming ashore at Sicily as a mere major, some valuable divisional command experience. It was rumoured that he was slated to take over 5th Canadian Armoured Division in the spring. Simonds had relinquished command of this division to Major General Eedson L.M. (Tommy) Burns on January 11 when he was posted to Britain to assume command of 2nd Canadian Corps because its commander had been returned to Canada due to ill health. Hoffmeister's rumoured promotion rested on the probability that Burns would be given command of I Canadian Corps once Crerar was deemed to have gained enough battlefield experience in Italy to warrant command of the First Canadian Army. That hand-off would have to happen sometime in the next couple of months to allow sufficient time for Crerar to settle into his new command before the northern European invasion got under way.[32]

Unknown to Vokes and without notifying the Canadian corps commander, Allfrey ordered Hoffmeister to carry out a limited attack on January 30, just one day before 1 CID was to move from Allfrey's command to that of Crerar. Again the primary purpose was stated as being to prevent the Germans from shifting Adriatic front units to the Anzio beaches or to Cassino. Hoffmeister complied without question or opposition. He handed the task to 1st Canadian Infantry Brigade commander Brigadier Dan Spry. It was decided that only one battalion should make the attack, the Hastings and Prince Edward Regiment, commanded by Lieutenant Colonel A.A. (Bert) Kennedy. Because a holding attack, as this form of offensive was called, often resulted in heavy casualties, Allfrey insisted that both Hoffmeister and Spry should keep its real purpose from the troops so as not to weaken their morale. The officers should, he said, rationalize the operation as intended to secure a forward base that would allow more aggressive patrolling to determine the strength and precise whereabouts of the German paratroops.

The attack would advance along a road running from Villa Grande north across a level plain known as the Piana di Moregine toward the village of Tollo. Supporting the Hasty P's would be squadrons drawn from the Calgary Tanks of the 1st Canadian Armoured Brigade. At 1600 hours on January 30, the Hasty P's advanced behind a heavy artillery barrage with the tanks slogging through the mud in support. Just as Kennedy radioed back that his men were closing on the objective, a fierce counter-barrage shattered 'B' Company, and 'D' Company was brought up abruptly by heavy machine-gun fire. Despite heavy casualties, the two companies kept trying to advance for two hours to no avail and finally were forced to withdraw to a position 300 yards back from their assigned objective. They suffered fifteen dead and thirty-three wounded.

The following day, they tried again at 1330 hours, with 'A' Company on the left and 'B' Company on the right, advancing across the open field under cover of a smokescreen. Teller antitank mines disabled two of six Calgary Tanks in support. The other four emerged out of the smoke just fifty yards from the objective and took the defending paratroopers entirely by surprise. Although the Germans rallied quickly, managing to knock out two Shermans with 75-millimetre fire from three dug-in antitank guns, the Calgary troopers won the shootout by destroying the enemy weapons. This success was nullified when heavy mortar, machine-gun, and rifle fire cut down so many of the Hasty P's that they were reduced first from platoons to sections, and finally to just two or three men acting in independent groups. Kennedy could only order a general withdrawal. Lacking infantry support, the two remaining tanks also pulled back. The day's butcher bill for the Hasty P's was nine killed and thirty-four wounded.[33] Lieutenant Colonel Cyril Neroutsos, commander of the Calgary Tanks, and an old Three Rivers Regiment veteran of the prewar Canadian armoured corps, was infuriated. In two days, he had lost four tanks and fifteen crewmen in an operation he had opposed from the outset as employing tanks in a completely ineffective manner.[34]

Vokes returned late on the evening of January 31 and immediately learned of the failed attack. He had found the peaceful atmosphere of Cairo got on his nerves and was "eager to get back to the war in Italy, even to the misery of the Italian winter." Having come back expecting his regiments to be in good condition, perhaps even a bit rested up, Vokes was angered that Allfrey would order such an attack in his absence when he had explicitly stated that no further offensive actions were to be undertaken by 1 CID. "What grieved me most," he later wrote, "about this second senseless attack was the loss to the Hastings of 90 all ranks, killed, wounded or missing. It was too big a price to pay for an attack staged in the impossible conditions of ground and weather which prevailed. I wondered," he added, "when the senior Allied command in Italy would realize the futility of attacks in the mud of an Italian winter."[35]

The attack by the Hasty P's was, however, the last offensive mounted by 1 CID on the Adriatic front. On the evening of January 31, the division shifted from Allfrey's command to Crerar's. For the next ten to twelve weeks, the newly formed corps and its divisions endured a bleak, cold, and wet time in trenches that came increasingly to mirror in their construction those of World War I, as slit trenches were linked together and deepened.

Shortly after Crerar assumed command, he toured the front lines to get a better appreciation of the conditions in which his men lived and operated. Captain Don Smith of the Carleton and York Regiment was sitting on the edge of his slit trench eating lunch out of his mess tin when he saw a small, older officer standing a few feet away. The man wore the typical Tommy piss-pot–shaped steel helmet of British and Commonwealth troops and a leather jerkin that covered his badges of rank. Standing behind him was the regiment's commander, Lieutenant Colonel Dick Danby. Smith put down his mess tin, slowly stood up, and saluted the two men. In a soft, friendly way, Crerar chatted with Smith for a few moments about conditions and the state of his men. He congratulated Smith, who had been awarded the Military Cross for his bravery during the January 4 battle for Point 59, just north of Ortona.

When the older officer and Danby walked off, Smith wondered who he was and why he and the commander were wandering the lines with nobody else in their company. Soon after the two departed, his company commander, Major Burt Kennedy, walked over and asked if Smith had seen Lieutenant General Crerar and the colonel. Smith said, "I guess I did. Who is General Crerar?" Kennedy told him Crerar was the new General Officer in Command of I Canadian Corps. Smith was impressed and thought Crerar, unlike some of the officers, such as Vokes, was very Canadian in his mannerisms rather than mimicking the Eighth Army British brass in both their speech and dress.[36]

The same day, Crerar showed up at the Royal Canadian Regiment's battalion headquarters. Galloway walked out with him onto the frozen mud to look toward the front lines. Behind the two men stood the shattered house in which the RCR headquarters was located; ahead lay the trenches in which the men were hunkered. The surrounding olive grove trees and vineyards were splintered and ripped asunder by weeks of artillery fire, shell craters were full of half-frozen water, a bitter grey sky hung overhead. Leaning on his walking stick, Crerar shifted his gaze over the scene. "Why, it's just like Passchendaele," he muttered. "Just like Passchendaele." Galloway had never heard about Passchendaele, but he listened politely as Crerar spoke with a faraway look in his eyes of "the mud of Flanders, the rainfall in the Ypres Salient, the misery of trench warfare." Then Crerar left, returning in Galloway's mind "to his comfy caravan ten miles behind the line, well out of even long distance artillery fire, and left us to the mud of Italy, the rainfall in the Ortona Salient and the misery of position warfare as we knew it."[37]

4

FRUSTRATED
AMBITIONS

Since arriving in the Mediterranean theatre, I Canadian Corps commander Lieutenant General Harry Crerar had single-mindedly laboured to bring all Canadian soldiers serving in Italy under a common corps banner. This purpose, advanced and defended at every turn with his usual tactless manner, had brought Crerar into conflict with the former Eighth Army commander, General Bernard Montgomery, its current commander General Sir Oliver Leese, and General Harold Alexander, Deputy Supreme Commander Mediterranean.

On the evening of January 31, 1944, Crerar's ambition appeared realized as I Canadian Corps became operational in the field for the first time. Within four days, a series of orders shifted most of the approximately 75,000 Canadians in Italy to his command. On February 9, however, Crerar realized an entirely dedicated Canadian corps would not come into being when Leese advised him that the 3,700 tankers of 1st Canadian Armoured Brigade would not be assigned to the Canadian corps after all. Instead, 1 CAB was attached to the British XIII Corps.[1]

Since the invasion of Sicily, 1st Canadian Infantry Division and 1 CAB had mutually supported each other during countless operations.

Eighth Army, however, tended to treat armoured brigades as quasi-independent entities that operated outside normal corps organizational structures. The reason for this was that there were fewer armoured brigades in the Eighth Army than infantry divisions, so the tankers served as fire brigades, shifting rapidly from one infantry support role to another as the combat situation dictated. That the British wanted to maintain this flexibility, despite Crerar's all-Canadian plan, was apparent. It was one of the reasons Montgomery had argued against the formation of an additional corps organized on national lines. Coincidentally, however, acrimony between two senior Canadian commanders provided an alternative justification for Leese's decision that deflected blame away from the British, while ensuring that Eighth Army retained armoured brigade flexibility.

The culprit who somewhat unwittingly scuttled Crerar's all-Canadian corps was Major General Chris Vokes. Throughout the December and January fighting on the Ortona front, Vokes had been critical of 1 CAB's commander Brigadier Bob Wyman. In late January, Vokes made it known to anyone of equivalent rank or higher that he would welcome the opportunity to never work with Wyman and his brigade again. Wyman, he said, was "a bull-headed guy, a little lord unto himself."[2]

He was not alone in his complaints about the performance of Wyman's three armoured regiments. Brigadier George Kitching, commander of 11th Canadian Infantry Brigade, had been sharply critical of Wyman's handling of the Three Rivers Regiment during the disastrous January 17 attack. Kitching picked up a rumour after the battle that Wyman had orally ordered Lieutenant Colonel Leslie Booth to keep his tanks far enough back from the front-line action to ensure they did not become engaged in a "dog fight" with German armour or antitank guns. Kitching thought this order undoubtedly explained why the tanks had not come down into the Riccio valley but instead had lurked on the southern rim doing little more than acting as close support artillery. Apparently, he reasoned, Wyman considered infantry expendable, but not tanks. Had he known this to be the case, Kitching would have "never agreed to put in the attack."[3]

Both Kitching and Vokes directed their attacks toward Wyman personally. Neither had any disrespect for the ability of the 1 CAB tankers, who had proved themselves in many battles. The tankers had fought hard and well in the horrific mud, tangled vineyards, and debris-strewn town streets that had so hampered tank operations during the December fighting. Vokes, however, was convinced that as long as Wyman led the armoured brigade, it would fail to march to orders that he issued, despite the fact that he was the senior officer.

Just over two weeks after 1 CAB had been sent into the wilderness, Vokes came to regret his denunciations of the Canadian tank brigade. On February 27, Wyman left Italy to assume command of the 2nd Canadian Armoured Brigade. Command of 1 CAB went to Brigadier Bill Murphy, who, Vokes knew, was a "first class" officer.[4] Murphy was a likeable, easy-going Irishman who quickly proved himself popular to the tankers under his command. Vokes wished he could take back his earlier statements, but the damage was irreparable and the Canadian armoured brigade would seldom fight alongside Canadian infantry during the rest of the Italian campaign.

◆ ◆ ◆

Throughout February, Vokes had little time to dwell on the impact of his actions with regard to 1 CAB. For Crerar was determined to make the corps — the first Canadian corps under a Canadian commander to be in contact with the Germans — operate by the book. Vokes was buried under a continuous deluge of written instructions setting out training and administrative details that would previously have warranted only a quick telephone call. Vokes thought the obsession with paper "verged on the stupid." But he also knew there was no alternative but to comply with Crerar's demands and "hope that time and battle experience would produce a saner and more practical outlook."

Having never previously served under Crerar, Vokes was unimpressed by the man's attitude toward his subordinates. The infantry division commander found he could get along well enough with Crerar only so long as he offered no arguments. "No amount of argument could budge him from a pre-conceived idea, even though it had been found unworkable or unreasonable in contemporary practice. His whole outlook on tactics was influenced by his experience as a junior officer of artillery in the Great War. He believed the tactical methods of attack employed in Italy were wrong and should be brought in line with those used in France and Flanders in World War I."[5]

Crerar's apparent obsession with the muddy stalemate north of

Ortona, which the older general kept comparing to the Western Front, alarmed Vokes. When he tried telling Crerar that neither the Germans nor the Allies considered this anything more than a temporary stalemate caused by the weather, which in the spring would again allow a campaign of movement, Crerar was dubious. During a February 11 study period held in Lanciano, some nine miles south of Ortona, Crerar delivered to Leese, his staff, and the other British corps commanders a long lecture entitled "The Principles of Effective Fire Support in the 'Break-in' Battle." He told them that "in this theatre conditions and circumstances have faced us once more with the tactical problems and conditions which typified the last Great War." Crerar emphasized how the same combined artillery and infantry tactics that had been used on the Western Front, particularly at Vimy Ridge, could, despite the winter morass that currently engulfed them, be employed to break through the German defences and restore the campaign of movement.[6] His comments, Vokes noticed, "were heard in stony silence by that battle-experienced galaxy." Vokes came away thinking that Crerar had done himself no good with Leese by treating him like some inexperienced junior officer who had never seen previous combat.[7]

To prove his point, however, Crerar hammered out a plan whereby 1 CID would capture the village of Tollo through the application of the tactical techniques he had described at Lanciano. Vokes was relieved when this scheme came to naught because V British Corps replaced I Canadian Corps in the line on March 7. The Canadians withdrew to the village of Larino, forty-five miles southeast of Ortona. Two days later, Crerar received orders to proceed immediately to Britain for promotion to the command of First Canadian Army. Royal Canadian Regiment second-in-command Major Strome Galloway thought the presence of Crerar during the winter of 1944 was somehow fitting. It seemed, he later wrote, "as though Flanders Fields had come to Italy bringing the same old mud, the same old boredom, the same old wounds and death by day and night, the same old rum ration, and as an extra, an elderly general whose mind went back to Passchendaele." With the spring, it was equally fitting that this general should fade quietly away, leaving behind little trace of his having passed.[8]

◆ ◆ ◆

Soon after Crerar's departure, many officers and other ranks were transferred to Britain. Distributed through all layers of First Canadian Army, from its headquarters down to individual rifle platoons, these combat veterans were expected to stiffen the backbone of this untried army when it received its baptism of fire during the northern European invasion. Acting Lieutenant General Guy Simonds had, of course, already returned to Britain to command 2nd Canadian Army Corps. He personally asked for Brigadier Kitching, who left his command of 11 CIB and returned to Britain on March 1. Promoted to acting major general, Kitching assumed command of 4th Canadian Armoured Division. Only thirty-four, he became the youngest Canadian general officer.[9] First CID's artillery commander, Brigadier Bill Matthews, and its engineering commander, Lieutenant Colonel Geoff Walsh, left. Two battalion commanders, Three Rivers Regiment's Lieutenant Colonel Leslie Booth and Loyal Edmonton Regiment's Lieutenant Colonel Jim Jefferson, headed off to brigade commands in Britain. Major Herschell A. Smith of the Ontario Tank Regiment and Major Ned Amy from the Calgary Tank Regiment also departed.

As had been rumoured, Tommy Burns was promoted to Acting Lieutenant General and given command of I Canadian Corps. Fifth Canadian Armoured Division went to Bert Hoffmeister, promoted from brigadier to acting major general. At thirty-seven this made him, after Kitching, the second youngest Canadian divisional commander.[10] Crerar told Hoffmeister of his promotion shortly before departing Italy. A radio signal from Crerar had asked Hoffmeister to meet him at a particular map reference within a couple of hours. The map reference turned out to be the centre of a bridge and, as Hoffmeister pulled up at one side, Crerar drove up to the other end. Both men walked from their Jeeps to the centre of the bridge. Hoffmeister saluted and then shook Crerar's proffered hand. The two officers perched side by side on the bridge railing and Crerar asked, "How would you like to take over command of the 5th Canadian Armoured Division?"

Hoffmeister's reply was immediate. "I would, sir. When do I take over?" Crerar seemed surprised by Hoffmeister's self-assured manner, but the young officer was confident he could handle the job. The command was Hoffmeister's, Crerar said, effective immediately. Then he warned Hoffmeister that the Canadians would soon take part in a major offensive "that was going to be *the* big battle in Italy up to that point." The timetable for this attack, Crerar said, was still classified, but Hoffmeister should know he "didn't have long to get ready for it." Hoffmeister knew the 11th Canadian Infantry Brigade required rebuilding after the January 17 debacle. That would be his most pressing immediate task.

Meeting over, Hoffmeister drove back to 2nd Canadian Infantry Brigade and arranged for his belongings to be moved to 5 CAD head-quarters. Although he was eager to take up the job of commanding 5 CAD, it was hard for him to leave his infantry brigade. Hoffmeister had worked his way up through the brigade from an initial posting as a major in its headquarters in December 1941. In October 1942, he had been promoted to Lieutenant Colonel and taken command of the Seaforth Highlanders of Canada, the Vancouver militia regiment he had joined at the age of eleven. He led that regiment across Sicily and into Italy until being promoted to brigadier and commander of 2 CIB in September 1943.[11]

Hoffmeister's promotion necessitated a reorganization of brigade command within 1 CID. Vokes shifted 3rd Canadian Infantry Brigade's Brigadier Graeme Gibson over to command 2 CIB and promoted Lieutenant Colonel Paul Bernatchez, commander of the Royal 22e Regiment, to brigadier and commander of 3 CIB. Meanwhile, the interchange of officers between Britain and Italy flowed both ways as brigadiers Bill Ziegler and Eric Snow arrived to command respectively 1 CID's artillery regiments and 11 CIB. The parachuting of battalion- and brigade-level commanders from Britain was controversial and a source of complaint for many seasoned Italian campaign officers denied promotion as a result. The fact that officers such as Snow and Ziegler had no previous combat experience often weakened their credibility.[12]

One officer who was left particularly embittered by his failure to be given permanent command of a regiment was Major Strome Galloway, who at the end of December had been commanding the Royal Canadian Regiment. Galloway's courage and leadership ability were highly respected within the RCR and 1st Canadian Infantry Brigade, of which the regiment was part. The brigade's commander, Brigadier Dan Spry, and Galloway had served together and were also friends. Spry had been promoted to brigadier during the December battle and after two more senior officers had been lost to wounds or sickness, RCR command had fallen to Galloway. He had been hoping to be confirmed as the regiment's commander, but in early January Lieutenant Colonel Bill Mathers, who had been wounded by a sniper during the December fighting, was returned to the regiment and resumed command. Galloway went from acting lieutenant colonel back to major and became Mathers's second-in-command.[13]

A small, blond man, Mathers was a Permanent Force officer and a spit-and-polish commander. During the height of the fighting before Ortona, he had, among other bizarre orders, demanded that everyone in the regiment find time to shave each morning and to keep their uniforms neat and tidy despite the muddy conditions and almost constant enemy shelling.[14] Mathers was also given to bullying and continued to be unpopular among the RCR officers and other ranks alike. When Mathers returned to the regiment, Galloway went to see Spry. Noted for his Boy Scout politeness and gentlemanly manners, Spry told his friend: "You know, Strome, you can't expect to command the battalion. You are not a Permanent Force officer. They have their post-war careers to think of. So they've got to have battalion command. So Mathers has got to have it."[15]

To Galloway, this was yet another example of something he considered all too prevalent in the Canadian army — a determination by the Permanent Force officers to put their careers ahead of winning the war. The twenty-nine-year-old officer had been a newspaper reporter prior to the war, but had served in the militia through most of the 1930s and in war found he loved the army life. When peace returned, Galloway hoped to continue in the service, but was finding his ambitions hampered because he was militia rather than Permanent Force. He and other militia officers commented to each other, "There's nothing you can do about it. The Permanent Force Protection Society will always look after its own first and bugger the results." Galloway believed the results were too often the elevation to senior rank of officers who were incompetent, unimaginative, and given to needlessly squandering men's lives.[16]

◆ ◆ ◆

Burns had little time for this reluctance on the part of Italian front officers to trust those who had not proven themselves in either Sicily or Italy. He saw a disturbing tendency among officers in Italy to "assume that the history of modern warfare had begun on July 10, 1943, and that only the lessons which had been learned after that date had any relevance to the way the war in Italy ought to be fought."[17] When, as 5 CAD commander, Burns had reported to Crerar, the corps commander had told him, "This war is so much like the last one, it's not even funny."

Burns agreed that the Ortona battlefield was certainly reminiscent of Flanders and that battles such as the one fought in January by 11th CIB were depressingly similar to those that had been fought on the Somme River. But he thought the modern trappings of war made it very different from that of World War I. The modern infantryman, Burns later wrote, had artillery support, "which he could call for by radio and which came promptly, he could also call for bombing from aircraft hovering over the battlefront, and within minutes see the bombs fall. His own armament included many more machine guns and mortars; and tanks backed him up or preceded him. When infantry, tankmen, gunners and airmen had got to know one another through training together as a team, and when they were put into battle with the advantages of surprise and a concentration of superior force, victories could be won without paying such a high price in soldiers' blood."[18] There would be no more Sommes or Passchendaeles, he believed.

Like Crerar, Burns was a veteran of World War I. Born in Montreal in 1897, he had entered Royal Military College in 1914 and remained there until his eighteenth birthday in June 1915. Commissioned as a lieutenant in the Royal Canadian Engineers, he went overseas as a signals officer and was posted to the 11th Canadian Infantry Brigade of the 4th Canadian Division in August 1916. He served with the brigade for eighteen months, was wounded twice, and awarded the Military Cross after personally repairing and laying signal cables while under enemy fire. On April 1, 1920, he joined the Permanent Force as a Royal Canadian Engineers captain and soon established a reputation as not only a capable peacetime officer but also an original military thinker. When World War II broke out, he seemed well positioned to rise to high command.[19]

The appointment of Burns to command the Canadian corps was welcomed by Leese. "I think he will be good," Leese wrote. "I will be glad to get rid of Harry and get Burns installed & to get down to some degree of permanency."[20] Burns thought Leese an eccentric. Soon after his promotion, Burns called on Leese and ended up discussing important issues of command while his superior bathed naked in a large tub of water. While not as prudish as Crerar, Burns was still offended and shocked.[21]

Burns had been surprised by his own promotion, as Vokes had the modern combat experience he lacked. However, Crerar, like Montgomery, believed that Vokes had reached his ceiling as a divisional commander so had recommended Burns instead. Vokes's impulsive womanizing, his caustic tongue, and the endless stream of profanities that punctuated his every sentence had regularly offended Crerar. Some said that Vokes was the inspiration behind a quip that if the words "fuck" and "frontal" were removed from military jargon, the entire Canadian army would be left both speechless and incapable of attack.[22]

Vokes told no one whether he was disappointed at not getting corps command. Hoffmeister, probably one of his closest and oldest friends in Italy, heard not a word of complaint from Vokes on the matter.[23] Vokes had known Burns for years, having been taught by him as a Royal Military College cadet twenty-two years earlier. While he admired Burns for his intelligence, Vokes was uncomfortable in the man's company. "His manner," Vokes thought, "was shy, introverted and humourless. He seemed most unfriendly and distrustful." Vokes wondered if this was because of his own "more extensive experience in operational command" and a fear that he might consequently "prove difficult to handle. For old times sake I determined to tread warily and give him my loyal support."[24]

Burns's introverted ways and the fact that he was, at forty-seven, the oldest Canadian active field officer did little to inspire officers who didn't know him. Throughout the corps, Burns quickly won the nicknames of Laughing Boy and Smiling Sunray. The latter was derived from the radio protocol that designated any commander Sunray within his unit, but both referred derisively to the fact that Burns appeared perpetually grim and unsmiling. Vokes thought Burns's habit of constantly acting "like a funeral director" made it hard for his subordinates to remain cheerful and so the grim business of war seemed even grimmer after Burns took command.[25]

Galloway was particularly struck by Burns's humourless demeanour when the general visited RCR headquarters. Burns sported a black armoured corps beret, worn perfectly level above his eyebrows. At the moment of Burns's arrival, Galloway was delivering a sand-table demonstration lecture to the other RCR officers, so he decided to have a little fun at the general's expense. Snapping off a salute, he said, "Galloway here, Sir. I am just giving a talk on infantry-cum-tanks and I'm saying, 'The only trouble is, Sir, the tanks never come.'" Laughter broke out in the room, lifted, checked, then trailed off as Burns fixed Galloway with a long, dour stare before departing without so much as a word.[26]

Within days of taking over corps command, Burns travelled to the Cassino front so he could get some idea of the lay of the land in which the Canadians must soon fight. He became an observer of the bloody Third Battle for Cassino, which raged from March 15 to 24. Burns and a group of other senior Eighth Army officers had a spectacular view from a ridge on 1,400-foot-high Monte Trocchio, immediately southwest of Cassino. From this lofty perch, the officers watched the New Zealanders attack the ruined town and the Indians assault the Benedictine Abbey. Despite the advantage of their position, "little could be seen except the shellbursts, ragged smokescreens and perhaps an occasional tank. The infantry were invisible, except for a few figures now and then. But it was clear, from what we could see and the reports that came in belatedly, that in spite of the most gallant efforts the German position on the heights below the monastery was holding firm." Burns believed that so long as the abbey remained in German hands, any advance up the Liri Valley, on the axis of the road to Rome, "could hardly be achieved."[27] Burns returned to the corps knowing the Canadians must soon carry out this advance. Time was short. He would have less than six weeks to prepare before leading the corps into its biggest battle. He urged Hoffmeister and Vokes to step up training and quickly make whatever organizational changes were required.

◆ ◆ ◆

While Vokes had a fairly well-oiled and experienced team, Hoffmeister faced a challenge to build an efficient division capable of carrying out a major offensive operation. His major problem, as he had suspected, would be putting 11 CIB back on its feet. Shortly after taking command, he called the entire division out for an inspection and made a point of checking every rifle, Bren gun, tank, artillery piece, and man's kit. He found the armoured regiments, which had been spared the terrible combat experience through which 11 CIB had passed, all well turned out. But the infantry was another matter entirely. The weapons in the brigade were filthy, the men generally sullen.[28] The brigade could not be trusted in heavy combat.

Hoffmeister planned to restore morale by holding several divisional-level training exercises that would entail 11 CIB's operating as an integral part of a strong, powerful armoured division. This way, the soldiers of the Perth, Irish, and Cape Breton regiments would come to understand that the January 17 battle had been exceptional and that nothing like it would happen to them again.

First, though, Hoffmeister ran the brigade through some smaller company-level exercises so he could "meet each company of the brigade in the field." He made a point of being present as each company was led through a set-piece attack in which the men went in behind a live artillery barrage to seize a designated objective. Hoffmeister found "it took a lot of coaxing to get those shocked troops up to the point where they would get close to the barrage, just before the lift, and then it was up and at 'em again." To push them on, he elected to get right up front with the leading platoons. Before they went in to the mock attack, he would give them a lecture, telling them "how important it was to keep right up to the shell bursts, that the first shells were all forward and there was absolutely no danger in keeping up." After one such lecture, he started forward with a company of Cape Breton Highlanders only to have one of the first artillery rounds strike behind his group. Hoffmeister and everyone around him hit the dirt. Lying there with shrapnel flying overhead, Hoffmeister could see the men looking over at him "as if to say, 'OK wise guy, what have you got to say about this?'"[29]

After the company-level exercises, Hoffmeister led the brigade through battalion-sized exercises, then brigade exercises, and finally launched a divisional exercise "to let them see first hand the formation of which they were a part." Through this exercise, he believed, the brigade came to realize "the fact that there were these hundreds of tanks there to support them, an SP [self-propelled gun] regiment. We had tractor-drawn guns, we had the Westminster motor battalion, the Governor General's Horse Guards — the armoured recce regiment. The punch, the club this division had, was just tremendous, and no person, private soldier, NCO, or officer could fail to be impressed by this." Hoffmeister thought the exercise achieved its purpose for every battalion in the brigade except the Perth Regiment, where morale remained dangerously low.

After consulting with both the brigade's new commander, Eric Snow, and the Perth commander, and receiving no satisfactory explanation for the problem or how to solve it, Hoffmeister decided to get to the heart of the matter himself. He issued an order that, at 0900 hours the next morning, two men of no rank higher than lance corporal would be drawn from each of the battalion's platoons and would report to him directly. The men were ushered into a room and sat down in front of their major general. Hoffmeister told them there was a great danger in "going into a battle with this lack of confidence and the poor morale that existed in the Perth Regiment." He was going to sit there with them until somebody explained what the root of the problem was. "I don't have the names of any of you men," he said, "and don't want to know your names. Nothing you say here is being recorded. This is for my information and my information only, so that I in turn may take the necessary action to get this unit in shape to fight." Then he sat down and looked at the men, who sat looking back. The minutes passed slowly. Nobody moved or spoke. After a long time, Hoffmeister said quietly, "Men, I'm serious when I say we're going to stay here until I get the answers, and that there is no way in which you're going to be implicated, and your lives and the lives of your comrades depend on it."

Hesitantly, the men started talking, with Hoffmeister gently prodding them with questions. It emerged that there were four Perth officers who had performed poorly during the January 17 battle and as a result had jeopardized lives. The men told Hoffmeister they "had absolutely no confidence in them and were very reluctant to go into battle with them. That was the reason for the low morale in the regiment." Hoffmeister dismissed the men, returned to his headquarters, and told Snow to "dispose of these officers forthwith."[30] No sooner had these officers been dispatched for assignment to other non-combat duties than the morale of the Perths improved remarkably. When the order came for I Canadian Corps to prepare for a major movement to the western coast of Italy preparatory to the launch of Operation Diadem, Hoffmeister thought his division ready to fight.

5

DECEPTIONS

On April 18, 1944, Canadian radio operators started systematically going off the air. By day's end, not a single radio at I Canadian Corps headquarters in Raviscanina on the eastern Adriatic or at the headquarters of 5th Canadian Armoured Division at Castilnuova near Lucera was broadcasting. First Canadian Infantry Division, still in the line north of Ortona, maintained normal radio traffic. A cloak of silence settled over all the other units, effectively concealing the whereabouts of about 27,000 men who constituted the combined strength of the corps headquarters and its support elements and most of 5 CAD. Only the whereabouts of 11th Canadian Infantry Brigade and the attached Westminster Regiment, already deployed on International Ridge before Monte Cassino, remained known to German intelligence. At the same time the Canadian signallers were signing off the Eighth Army radio net, 36th U.S. Infantry Division ceased broadcasting on the Fifth Army system.[1]

Cessation of radio traffic by I Canadian Corps and its armoured division was so decisive and complete that the unusual silence could not help but be detected by the German Tenth Army's intelligence staff. The message was clear — the Canadians must be on the move, for radio silence was a normal precursor to major movements of Allied formations. But where were they going? To the Liri Valley to participate in the inevitable offensive there? Or somewhere else? Four days later, German intelligence officers thought they had at least a partial answer when radio traffic started emanating from what appeared to be a newly established I Canadian Corps headquarters at Baronissi on the west coast, five miles north of Salerno. A few hours later, 5th Canadian Armoured Division HQ radios started broadcasting out of a site at nearby San Cipriano. Even more revealing, the missing U.S. infantry division was soon broadcasting from within the Canadian Corps wireless net. This implied that the American division was now attached to the Canadian Corps for some unknown future operation.[2]

On the same day these radio operations were detected, 1st Canadian Infantry Division radios went silent and the division withdrew covertly from the front line to the Campobasso area. On April 28, however, German intelligence began picking up radio intercepts from what appeared to be 1 CID's HQ now established at Nocera, ten miles from Salerno. Soon radio messages, some coded, some broadcast in the clear, were being regularly intercepted.[3]

These messages revealed that 1 CID, supported by two regiments of 5 CAD, was engaged in an exercise code-named Wilderness along a ten-mile section of coast just north of Ogliastro Marina. Ogliastro was situated on a promontory forming the southern coastal boundary of the Gulf of Salerno. With the support of Royal Navy transport and combat ships and elements of the Desert Air Force, it appeared that the Canadians were practising an opposed amphibious landing. The exercise, started on April 28, was scheduled to terminate on May 3, with an actual mock assault against beaches on May 2.

Maps were pulled from drawers and the terrain surrounding Ogliastro was subjected to intense scrutiny by German intelligence. The topographical profile of this area was then carefully compared to coastal sections of the Tyrrhenian Sea still under German control. The resemblance between Ogliastro and the area immediately to the north of the German-controlled port Civitavecchia was striking. Even more so when the presence in the mock assault of a notional airfield just north of Ogliastro was revealed by messages regarding that target's capture. At Tarquinia, just a few miles north and inland of

△ The many German guns dug into the Hitler Line enjoyed excellent fields of fire, as was the case for this one knocked out during the May 23 fighting.
— ALEXANDER MACKENZIE STIRTON, NAC, PA-189925

▷ Famous for his consistently grim demeanour, Lieutenant General Tommy Burns failed to win the confidence of his divisional commanders, his corps staff, or Eighth Army general staff and its commander General Sir Oliver Leese during his handling of the Liri Valley offensive. — C.E. NYE, NAC, PA 134181

▽ One of the Panzerturms that devastated the supporting British tank regiments during the main assault on the Hitler Line. This one was dug into the rubble of a building, rendering all but its heavily armoured turret impervious to Allied fire.
— C.E. NYE, NAC, PA-130200

▷ Canadian
artillery pounds
the Liri River area
near Pontecorvo.
— W.H. AGNEW,
NAC, PA-115146

◁ Lance bombardiers
D. Sacobie and
W. Harvey of the
Canadian Light
Anti-Aircraft
Regiment examine
a disabled German
self-propelled gun
on the Hitler Line.
— W.H. AGNEW,
NAC, PA-130346

▷ A direct hit from
a British Churchill
tank tore the
88-millimetre gun
(foreground) right
out of this German
Mark IV tank during
the fighting in front
of Pontecorvo.
— C.E. NYE,
NAC, PA-130340

◁ Both sides paid a grim price in the failed attack by 2nd Canadian Infantry Brigade against the Hitler Line on May 23. Here, a dugout overrun by the Princess Patricia's Canadian Light Infantry is crowded with German dead.
— W.H. AGNEW,
NAC, PA-163658

▷ A Canadian soldier blinded in the fighting is guided back to the Casualty Clearing Section.
— STRATHY SMITH,
NAC, PA-136311

◁ A Three Rivers Regiment tank moves through woods in front of the Hitler Line en route to support the advance by Royal 22e Regiment.
— PHOTOGRAPHER UNKNOWN,
NAC, PA-204153

△Lieutenant W.H. Salter and Gunner J. Misckow of Royal Canadian Artillery's 4th Anti-tank Regiment examine two captured German Nebelwerfers knocked out by the regiment on May 24.
— STRATHY SMITH, NAC, PA-169111

▷Royal Canadian Regiment Lieutenant W. Smith (left) and one of his platoon sergeants, F.G. White, in Pontecorvo shortly after its capture.
— C.E. NYE, NAC, PA-144722

▽Pontecorvo, like most towns in the eastern Liri Valley, was mostly destroyed in the fighting. German dead were found scattered throughout the rubble.
— C.E. NYE, NAC, PA-144721

▷ A Cape Breton Highlander trudges past a dead German soldier during the march from the Hitler Line to the Melfa River.
— STRATHY SMITH, NAC, PA-135904

◁ A heavily camouflaged Governor General's Horse Guard armoured car moves out from the Hitler Line toward the Melfa River.
— STRATHY SMITH, NAC, PA-137999

▷ After the collapse of the Hitler Line, some surrendered prisoners eagerly offered information on German dispositions. Here, a German prisoner briefs a Canadian Intelligence Officer in a Liri Valley grain field.
— STRATHY SMITH, NAC, PA-114915

◁ Two B.C. Dragoon tanks from 'C' Squadron knocked out during the disastrous attempt to break open the bridgehead across the Melfa River. In the foreground is a knocked-out Bren carrier.
— C.E. NYE, NAC, PA-143903

▷ Honey tanks of Lieutenant Edward J. Perkins's reconnaissance troop at Benedictine Crossing immediately prior to the advance to establish a bridgehead across the Melfa River.
— PHOTOGRAPHER UNKNOWN, NAC, PA-204157

◁ A bridging tank, called a Scissors bridge, moves into position. In the foreground is a destroyed Stuart tank from a reconnaissance troop.
— ALEXANDER MACKENZIE STIRTON, NAC, PA-201347

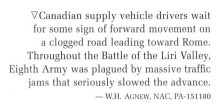

▽Canadian supply vehicle drivers wait
for some sign of forward movement on
a clogged road leading toward Rome.
Throughout the Battle of the Liri Valley,
Eighth Army was plagued by massive traffic
jams that seriously slowed the advance.
— W.H. AGNEW, NAC, PA-151180

△Major John Mahony
of the Westminster
Regiment would win
the Victoria Cross for
his leadership during
the heroic stand
by the Westminsters
and the Strathcona's
reconnaissance troop
at the Melfa River.
— PHOTOGRAPHER
UNKNOWN, NAC, PA-140089

△Possibly taken in Frosinone. Canadian troops run
down the street of a town during the final days of
I Canadian Corps's advance on Rome.
— ALEXANDER MACKENZIE STIRTON, NAC, PA-141699

◁Westminster Regiment Private Dan Nikiforuk (left)
and Private Bill Paticho in Caserta shortly before the
Battle of the Liri Valley. — PHOTO COURTESY OF DAN NIKIFORUK

▷ A provisional cemetery somewhere near Pontecorvo for Canadians killed during the Liri Valley fighting.
— C.E. NYE, NAC, PA-115143

◁ Two young boys and their pet dog enjoy the Royal Canadian Regiment pipe and drum band practice prior to the band's unofficial trip into Rome.
— C.E. NYE, NAC, PA-152153

▷ Members of the Royal 22e Regiment meet Pope Pius XII at the Vatican on July 3, 1944.
— DND PHOTO, NAC, PA-166069

Civitavecchia, there was an airstrip that corresponded with the map reference being used by the Canadians to represent the notional air-field. As Civitavecchia was just forty-five miles northwest of Rome, it could well be the target for a forthcoming amphibious invasion intended to outflank both the German Tenth and Fourteenth armies. A successful landing that far north by two Canadian divisions sup-ported by an armoured brigade and an American infantry division could prove disastrous.[4]

Such an invasion also matched Commander-in-Chief Southwest Generalfeldmarschall Albert Kesselring's personal fears. Kesselring was convinced that the Allies would attempt a spring amphibious invasion at either Civitavecchia or Leghorn "to force a decision more cheaply by landings" than by launching a single-front offensive to break through the Gustav Line in the Liri Valley. Kesselring knew that the divisions he had in Italy were too extended to successfully counter a well-coordinated invasion "by superior land, sea, and air forces." The defending Germans had no major coastal defence fortifi-cations and could not mount a defence in depth against any landing force. The best he could offer was a thin screen of defence right at the beach. If that defence were breached, the Germans would be hard pressed to contain any aggressive advance.[5]

Knowing he must immediately throw any invasion force into the sea or face defeat, Kesselring moved the 90th Panzer Grenadier Division to guard the coast from the Anzio beachhead north to the southern bank of the Tiber River and the 29th Panzer Grenadier Division to the Civitavecchia area. The 3rd Panzer Grenadier and 26th Panzer Grenadier divisions were put on readiness either to respond to an offensive in the Liri Valley or to move rapidly to reinforce whichever coastal section was struck by an amphibious landing.[6]

Through the top secret Ultra operation, which had broken the codes used by Germany's Enigma encryption machines, Deputy Supreme Commander Mediterranean General Harold Alexander's staff happily read decoded German high-command messages that showed Kesselring doing virtually nothing to reinforce the Gustav Line at Cassino. Instead, he was actually drawing divisions away to meet the potential threat of a Canadian invasion fleet. Since the German air force in Italy, Luftflotte 2, was barely able to conduct any daytime aerial reconnaissance flights over Allied lines, Kesselring was operating almost blind.[7] His only relatively reliable means of determining the whereabouts and activities of the enemy was through wireless transmission intercepts, reports from patrols penetrating the Allied front lines, and sightings made by the many observation posts that were monitoring activities in the Liri Valley from the surrounding heights. With the exception of 11 CIB on International Ridge, the Canadians had disappeared from the front lines. It was consequently easy for Kesselring to accept at face value the radio traffic emanating from the Salerno area.

There was no invasion force. The only Canadians in the Salerno area were 37 officers and 191 men operating sixty-one radio sets from the confines of sixty signal trucks.[8] The messages they sent back and forth and up the communication line to Eighth Army headquarters were drawn from a carefully written script drafted over a two-month period by Alexander's intelligence staff. Alexander knew Kesselring was obsessed with amphibious attacks and so had ordered a scenario created that would feed on his fearful preoccupations. Dubbed Nunton, the scheme was an elaborate ruse intended to mislead Kesselring and his staff about the true location of I Canadian Corps, which was being carefully safeguarded by an equally elaborate exercise in concealment.[9] Keeping I Canadian Corps's whereabouts hidden was vital to ensuring Alexander's bluff was not exposed.[10]

◆ ◆ ◆

Under cover of darkness on May 1, Lieutenant Patrick Harrison directed the four guns of 'F' Troop in 'C' Battery of the Royal Canadian Horse Artillery into a thicket of trees. These hid its new gun position situated just behind the crest of a hill looking toward Monte Cassino. Digging in was relatively easy, because the position had previously been occupied by a gun troop of the British 78th Division. The British left behind nine gun pits — four for upper register firing and five for lower register firing. The pits designed for upper register firing were steep ramps, so that the gun wheels could be run up the ramp, the trail lines anchored at the bottom, and a 45-degree angle attained that could bring plunging fire down on targets inside ravines or behind hills.

Since landing in Sicily, Harrison had never fired an upper register mission and didn't anticipate doing so now. He ordered his crews to set their 25-pounder field guns up in the best of the existing, basically level, lower register pits and to empty the trailers and trucks of their ammunition. Then most of the unit's vehicles were taken to the rear where they could be well hidden. The men sweated in the humid, warm spring night digging hides near the guns in which to stash the ammunition and to improve the gun pits. Once the guns were in place and the ammunition stowed, camouflage netting was installed to help conceal their presence. Telephone lines were soon strung, linking Harrison's troop command post to all the guns, and radio communication was established to the battery headquarters. Before sunrise, Harrison's gun troop was ready to carry out any firing missions that came its way. Not that the gunnery officer expected anything this morning. The Canadian gunners were supposed to lie low so their presence in the Liri Valley would remain unknown to the Germans.

In the growing dawn light, Harrison walked fifty yards up the hill into the ruins of the little hamlet of San Michelle. There, about 7,000 yards to the northwest, he saw for the first time the shattered hulking form of the Abbey of Monte Cassino, with Monte Cairo rising up massively behind. The two features were partially screened by smoke, and as Harrison looked on more smoke shells burst, adding further to the concealing fog intended to prevent German observation units from seeing the Allied activity in the valley bottom. In front of Monte Cassino, the town of Cassino appeared to have been laid waste by the fighting and the more devastating artillery and aerial bombardments.

A thick, greasy grey-black fog blanketed the valley to the west of his position.[11] This was the product of a massive Eighth Army–wide smoke-generation operation. Throughout the army's positions, hundreds of fuel barrels were kept replenished with a slow-burning oil mixture that cloaked the ground in a turgidly churning cloud that limited visibility in the low-lying parts of the valley to about 200 yards.[12] In I Canadian Corps's sector alone, 2,250 of the barrels officially identified as either No. 24 or No. 38 Smoke Canisters were employed, with between forty and eighty generators installed at each designated Emission Point.[13] The putrid stench of these fires mingled with the reek of death that seemed to hang over the valley and emanated particularly strongly from the wreckage of Cassino. How many bodies lay unburied among the town's ruins was beyond imagining. The twenty-four-year-old former bank clerk who had enlisted in Winnipeg on March 15, 1940, just two days before his twentieth birthday, walked back to his gun position thinking that the entire scene he had just looked upon was about the grimmest and most darkly depressing he had ever witnessed.[14]

He had little time to dwell on this, however, as the gun troops of 'C' Battery RCHA had been attached to the 77th Field Regiment of the Royal Artillery. Soon Harrison and the other officers of the battery were receiving firing coordinates and timing schedules for a smoke shoot that would be laid down that night to obscure the movement of supply columns coming up to replenish the front-line units with ammunition, food, and other necessary supplies. Without the artillery-created smokescreen, the columns would have been nakedly exposed under moonlight or German star shell and illumination flare fire. Although the German artillery was heavily outgunned by a ratio of about four guns to one, the Allies had little idea where the German batteries were hiding and could not silence them. Therefore, they tried to blind the spotters so they would be unable to direct their artillery, mortar, and Nebelwerfer fire. Called "cigarettes," these smokescreen artillery missions were to be part of Harrison's nightly ritual until the big offensive to cross the Gari River got under way.

While 'C' Battery prepared for its first "cigarette" mission, 'A' and 'B' batteries settled into the new positions they had occupied on the night of May 1 inside leafy olive groves. By dawn, a large network of camouflage nets that rendered the eight guns virtually invisible a few yards away had supplemented this naturally excellent cover. The grove was situated behind Monte Trocchio, where Major George Browne quickly established an observation point called Whiskey. From its position on the leading edge of a razor-backed ridge jutting out on the plain to the southwest of Cassino, Browne could observe the fall of shot from the two batteries and make corrections as needed. Hard to hide in, the spot was in constant danger of attracting enemy fire if the observing officer was detected. Browne alternated with Captain F.P.O. (Paddy) Leask on this hazardous duty. Supporting their efforts was Lieutenant Norm Cram, kept busy most nights and often during the day crawling along the telephone line running from

Whiskey back to the Regimental Command Post to repair breaks created by the frequent enemy shelling and mortaring.[15]

During their first day in the new position, the gunners of 'A' and 'B' batteries spent several hours carefully sawing through the trunks of the trees standing directly in front of the guns. When the trees were nearly severed, they were secured in place by lines tied to untouched adjacent trees. This procedure was under way at many Eighth Army gun positions, so that when the major barrage that would precede the assault on the Gustav Line began, the trees could be dropped flat on the ground. This would ensure the trees would neither hamper the line of fire when the guns were swung to new firing coordinates nor be set ablaze by the muzzle blasts emanating from the rapidly firing weapons. Lance Sergeant Victor Bulger of 'B' Battery's 'D' Troop didn't like this scheme of removing the trees. From the front of the grove, through the haze created by the oil-burning barrels scattered around their position, they could see the vague outline of Monte Cassino and Monte Cairo. Bulger thought that when the trees were pulled aside, the Germans would see them manning their guns and they would be in for a hell of a lot of counter-battery fire.

Although the men were under strict orders to avoid unnecessary daytime movement that might betray the artillery presence to the Germans, the twenty-two-year-old from Cobourg soon set off on a pressing family mission. His older brother Jim had married in England and his bride Marjorie had written to see if Victor might be able to ship her any olive oil, impossible to get in wartime Britain. Bulger had learned there was a large cask of the oil stored in the attic of the Battery Office's building. Rustling up a jar with a screw-top lid, Bulger slipped over to the house and asked Battery Sergeant Major "Badgy" Williams if he could take some oil. Distracted by the paperwork scattered across his desk, Williams said only, "Make sure you don't spill any." Bulger climbed the rickety ladder to the attic and was soon happily filling his jar. Just before it was full, however, he accidentally tipped the cask too far and a wave of oil boiled out, missed the jar, and rushed down the wall. He quickly righted the barrel and completed filling the jar. Descending the ladder, Bulger was horrified to see oil seeping down the wall and dripping all over Williams's desk and papers while the sergeant desperately tried to drag his desk out of the way. "I knew I shouldn't have let you go up there," Williams moaned. "Look at the bloody mess you've made." Bulger offered hasty apologies and beat a quick retreat back to his gun position, where he packaged up the jar of oil and sent it by army mail to his sister-in-law. He was pleased to hear a few weeks later that it had arrived unscathed, which was more than could be said for the sergeant's papers.[16]

One thing Bulger noticed about their new position was the prevalence of mosquitoes. This raised concern about the risk of malaria among everyone who had been through the Sicily invasion, where the disease had infected many.[17] The Canadian Medical Corps doctors obviously shared this concern, for no sooner were the troops in position than Mepadrine antimalarial tablets were issued throughout I Canadian Corps. As a result of the daily pills, only thirty-one new cases a week were reported, which was a ratio of infection of only 6 per 10,000 men. At the same time, however, some men in 1st Canadian Infantry Division were coming down with either recurrences of malaria or the first symptoms of malarial infections contracted during operations the previous autumn in southern Italy. This resulted in several hundred hospitalizations for malaria, with the outbreak peaking in mid-April but lingering still when the division moved into the Liri Valley.[18] A couple of days after taking up the new position, Sergeant Jack Wilkes was struck with malarial fevers and hospitalized. Bulger was promoted to Acting Sergeant and put in charge of Wilkes's gun crew.

Soon after his promotion, Bulger walked over to a deep well near the olive grove intending to get some water. Looking into the depths, he saw something shining on the surface. Striking a couple of matches, he dropped them into the well to see what was down there. From the depths came a sharp roaring sound and Bulger instinctively leapt back just in time to avoid a ball of flame that shot up out of the well. Bulger's commander came running over and said he had dumped a gallon of gas into the well to kill the mosquitoes breeding in it. He explained that the gas should be less polluting than oil, but Bulger failed to see how the water could still be drinkable. He was grateful not to have been burned by the "silly bugger's" stunt. The troop now had another problem. The well was the only source of fresh water on the site that could be reached during daylight without risk of being seen. Denied this source, they were reliant on the water trucked in each night. Supply runs bringing in water were few, however, as ammunition and food had priority. Finding time during the night to refill water bottles at the nearest stream was difficult, since the men were usually manning the guns for "cigarette" shoots or offloading and storing ammunition.[19]

Every third night, the gunners fired a "cigarette." For up to six hours at a time, the 25-pounders hammered Monte Cairo and Monte Cassino with an endless concentration of smoke shells. The hours of firing put strain on the gun barrels and mechanisms and Lieutenant Harrison made a point during each shoot to rotate one gun at a time out of the line to allow it to cool down. One night, the guns had been firing for three hours at a rate of three to four rounds per minute. Just as Harrison was about to order No. 3 gun to take a rest, its loader shoved in another round, which exploded prematurely when it contacted the beginning of the rifling. The blast threw the loader backwards, his arm and hand nearly torn off in several places. Harrison quickly had the gun crew find a board. He then secured the man's arm to the board by wrapping it in two shell dressings. After giving him a shot of morphine, Harrison loaded the gunner into a Jeep and raced him to the Medical Officer's station. The MO told Harrison his quick response had saved the soldier from losing his arm or even any fingers.

On nights when the battery was off the firing line, Harrison would meet Army Service Corps trucks coming up with ammunition. 'C' Battery, like other Eighth Army artillery units, was stockpiling ammunition all over its battery site in preparation for the offensive barrage. To reach his battery, the truckers had to cross a road junction that the Germans had accurately registered with their guns and routinely subjected to nightly bouts of harassing fire. Harrison would wait in the darkness on his side of the crossroads until he heard the sound of the trucks grinding up the dusty, rough road. The vehicles travelled without lights, so their pace was slow. When they finally hove into view Harrison waved them hurriedly through the crossroads and guided them to the gun position. Somehow their timing was always fortunate, for the crossroads were never fired on when one of these convoys was passing through, but several times it was plastered with shellfire only moments before or after.

Once the trucks arrived at the position, everyone worked madly to get the shells out of the trucks and into safe hides where they would be less likely to detonate if the position took enemy fire. With each ammunition delivery, the task of finding a safe place for the shells became more difficult. Soon 'C' Battery had 22,000 rounds of high explosive and 8,000 rounds of smoke in its overflowing position.

Knowing there were more than 1,000 guns arrayed across the breadth of the Liri Valley in preparation for the big barrage, Harrison understood why the position was known as Gun Alley.[20] And in front of, behind, and on all sides of Gun Alley gathered thousands of infantry, tanks, antitank guns, reconnaissance vehicles, engineering units with their bridging equipment, and countless other men and equipment. Harrison was amazed to think the Germans were apparently unaware that just a few hundred yards from their front line an army assembled. That it remained largely hidden from the Germans was testimony to the effectiveness of the smokescreens and other camouflaging methods.

◆ ◆ ◆

The strategists developing the offensive against the Gustav Line knew its success or failure hinged on how well the intelligence deceptions and the camouflaging effort prevented the Germans from anticipating the timing, location, and strength of the attack mustering before the Gari River. The dispersion of the Panzer Grenadier divisions away from the Liri Valley to guard the coast confirmed that the deception was working despite the immense logistical and engineering challenges required to screen the divisions massing right under German noses. The resourcefulness and thoroughness of the specially trained and deployed camouflaging teams awed Alexander, who had set the entire operation into action. In one section that was impossible to hide from observation posts on Monte Cassino, engineers erected a one-mile-long vertical wood and canvas screen covered in camouflage. This screen made it impossible for the Germans to monitor traffic using a road running from the rear to the headquarters of the Eighth Army's 3rd Carpathian Division, which was part of II Polish Corps.

In XIII Corps's sector, engineers silently worked through the night to cut new tracks by hand through the thick woods between their forward positions and the banks of the Gari River. These tracks would be essential for allowing the infantry divisions and supporting tanks to get up to the river on the day of the assault. As each dawn approached, the engineers meticulously covered their handiwork with brush. When armoured formations, such as 1st Canadian Armoured Brigade, tasked with supporting 8th Indian Division in its river crossing, moved up from rear positions, their movement was concealed by positioning dummy tanks and vehicles constructed of plywood in the abandoned position. So effective was the concealment of the Fifth Army's Corps Expéditionnaire Français moving into position on the Eighth Army's left flank to face the Garigliano River that, in a radius of only 4,000 yards, twenty battalions, five artillery batteries, and two divisional headquarters were hidden. Intercepted German intelligence reports revealed that they believed this area occupied by only one French division and that the rest of the corps was still well back.

Alexander knew, however, that the greatest feat of all was the concealment of the entire Canadian Corps.[21] Even 5 CAD, forming up near Vitulazio about thirty miles south of the Liri Valley, undertook an extensive camouflaging effort. Major General Bert Hoffmeister issued a directive to all ranks cautioning that: "It is of paramount importance that the camouflage policy in this area be such that there is no disclosure of concentration and even more important that the type of our formation is not made known to the enemy.

"The element of surprise must be preserved and to this end emphasis is therefore placed on concealment rather than dispersion. Siting and concealment will therefore be such that to the casual observer the extent of the concentration is not apparent." To ensure the camouflaging was effective, officers from the camouflage units flew over the division's positions. The officer in charge reported back to Hoffmeister that the division's camouflaging activity "was the finest effort of its kind I have seen."[22]

Eager to ensure a good view of the impending Liri Valley battlefield, Lieutenant General Tommy Burns had an observation post established on Monte Trocchio. The post was carefully constructed so that it mimicked a natural part of the rocky hillside, and a covered approach was created so that Burns and his staff members could come and go without fear of being observed. Huge amounts of ammunition, stores, and equipment were being pooled within the corps perimeter to allow rapid resupply of the attacking units in the midst of the battle. Corps staff tasked with camouflaging this matériel decided at the outset that it would be impossible to adequately conceal large supply depots so close to the enemy observation points. Their solution was to distribute supplies in the roadside ditches and shadowed edges of groves of trees and thickets of brush. When these small caches were covered with foliage-garnished camouflage netting, they were rendered virtually invisible.[23]

Burns was confident that I Canadian Corps was ready for the coming offensive, although 1 CID's infantry battalions were still undergoing infantry-cum-tank tactical training with a regiment of British armour that was to support their advance. This training was scheduled to continue to the last moment before the division moved toward battle. That movement would not happen until the British XIII Corps broke the Gustav Line and opened the way for the Canadians to charge up the Liri Valley.

◆ ◆ ◆

On May 5, Alexander issued his final operation order that defined the intention of the forthcoming engagement. The Allies in Italy were "to destroy the right wing of the German Tenth Army; to drive what remains of it and the German Fourteenth Army north of Rome; and to pursue the enemy to the Rimini-Pisa line, inflicting the maximum losses on him in the process."[24] This objective would be achieved by the combined might of the Fifth and Eighth armies overwhelming the German defensive line stretching from Cassino to the coast. The II U.S. Corps commanded by General Geoffrey Keyes would drive up the coastline, with the Corps Expéditionnaire Français under Marshal Alphonse-Pierre Juin pushing through the mountains on the American right. These mountains formed the southwestern flank of the Liri Valley, which ran roughly in a northwesterly line from Cassino almost to Rome. The British XIII Corps commanded by Lieutenant General Sir Sydney Kirkman would provide the offensive's main thrust by breaking into the valley and opening a breach through which I Canadian Corps could advance. On the XIII Corps's right, the II Polish Corps commanded by General Wladyslaw Anders would storm Monte Cassino and then Monte Cairo.

That was Phase One. The second phase would see 1st Canadian Infantry Division sever the Hitler Line so that 5th Canadian Armoured

Division could pass through and undertake a rapid advance toward Rome by travelling across the good tank country that intelligence believed the valley provided. Meanwhile, the U.S. Fifth Army would fight its way toward Anzio, enabling Major General Lucian Truscott, who now commanded VI Corps, to break out of the encircled beachhead. With VI Corps on the loose, Alexander hoped that Phase Three would have the American corps establish a blocking position in the Alban Hills south of Rome at Valmontone, into which the advancing Eighth Army would drive the remnants of the German Tenth and Fourteenth armies. Alexander's plan was for Truscott's Americans to play the anvil to Leese's Eighth Army hammer. If it worked, Alexander was confident he could smash the majority of the German divisions in Italy.[25]

While Operation Diadem was similar in many respects to the failed offensives conducted previously against the Gustav Line, a number of factors worked in its favour. Most significant was the sheer preponderance of massed force. Second, Alexander's deception and camouflage operations had largely hidden the presence of XIII Corps and I Canadian Corps. Finally, the campaign had until now been fought in the middle of dreadful winter conditions. This time, there should be little mud to mire the advancing troops and the long-range forecast called for the skies to remain largely sunny and clear throughout the month.

While spirits were running high among the British and Canadian troops preparing for the offensive, U.S. General Mark Clark was less enthusiastic. Clark thought the obstacles the Eighth Army faced in the Liri Valley were the same ones that the Americans had failed to crack. In fact, he felt the Germans had only had more time to strengthen their two major defensive lines there to make them more impregnable than ever. But Clark's major point of disagreement with Alexander regarded Phase Three. Clark had little interest in seeing Truscott's corps driving toward Valmontone. He thought Alexander's hammer-anvil plan was too simplistic and doomed to failure. There were many, albeit poor, roads leading out of the Liri Valley to the north and east. A blocking force at Valmontone would cut only the major routes following Highway 6 toward Rome, leaving many routes by which the Germans could escape. If the Americans concentrated their efforts on fighting through the Alban Hills to Valmontone, Clark also believed they might be denied the honour of liberating Rome. The British might get there first.

"I know factually," he confided to his diary, "that there are interests brewing for the Eighth Army to take Rome, and I might as well let Alexander know now that if he attempts any thing of that kind he will have another all-out battle on his hands, namely, with me." Clark decided he would try to be in Rome before the opening of the invasion of northern Europe, which was scheduled for the end of May. The Americans, Clark said, "not only wanted the honour of capturing Rome, but we felt that we more than deserved it. Nothing was going to stop us on our push toward the Italian capital."26

While Clark was telling Truscott to keep VI Corps ready during the breakout for a switch in the line of advance away from Valmontone toward Rome, Eighth Army commander General Sir Oliver Leese was enthusiastically briefing his Canadian generals on the tasks expected of I Canadian Corps. Leese's meandering lecture utterly baffled Burns, who turned to Major General Chris Vokes and said, "What the hell is he talking about?"

"Our attack on the Hitler Line, sir," Vokes whispered.

"Then why the hell doesn't he say so instead of prancing about waving his hands like a whore in heat?"27 Vokes had no answer.

Luckily Leese appeared not to have overheard Burns, for he remained confident in the new corps commander. "The Canadians under Burns," he wrote, "are developing into a fine Corps. He is an excellent commander and will, I feel sure, do well in battle."28

Burns dourly dogged Leese around the corps, listening to the general give the sort of upbeat pep talks to selected formations of officers that Montgomery had made common coin in the Eighth Army. Leese's message, Burns thought, was always the same. "Eighth Army, together with the Fifth, was about to deliver a terrific blow against the enemy, and if we all did our utmost we could expect to drive him out of Italy, and perhaps, together with the Allied forces on other fronts, win final victory in 1944."

Heartening troops before battle with promises "that a shining victory could be won by their bravery and constancy is a proven technique," Burns realized. But he wondered "what the effect might be if, in fact, final victory in Italy and the whole Western theatre should *not* be won in 1944."29

◆ ◆ ◆

Even if the forthcoming attack delivered "a shining victory," Burns knew that his divisions would inevitably absorb heavy casualties breaking through the Hitler Line and driving the Germans back toward Rome. Yet the corps was desperately ill prepared to replace casualties at the rate that could normally be expected from any major offensive operation.

On May 5, Burns travelled to Naples to see Brigadier Ted Weeks, who was in charge of the corps's rear-echelon unit. Weeks delivered the bad news that a draft of reinforcements expected in mid-June had been reduced to only 250 men and that there was an insufficient number of reinforcements currently in the holding unit to replace probable casualties.[30] Burns expected that the Canadians faced two months of "intense wastage rates, which amounts to about 325 men in the case of infantry battalions and proportionately less in the case of other arms." At best, the corps would be out of reinforcements by mid-July "and no further reinforcements to speak of can be expected before that date, due to priorities in the other theatre."[31] The invasion of northern Europe was taking priority over everything and I Canadian Corps was largely left to fend for itself in keeping its units operational.

Although there were about 75,000 Canadians in the Italian theatre, fewer than 20,000 served on the sharp end of the infantry and tank regiments. Behind them was a giant wedge of manpower necessary to keep those front-line troops in the field. The generally accepted wisdom was that it took three to four men in the rear to keep one man engaged directly in combat. While the men in the rear were normally less exposed to enemy fire, they were not immune from casualties. Truck drivers had to move supplies up to the front and their vehicles drew German artillery and mortar fire. Drivers were routinely killed or wounded as a result. The artillery gunners were regularly targeted by German fire. Ambulance drivers and stretcher-bearers shared the hazards with front-line troops, often suffering a proportionately higher casualty rate as they exposed themselves to fire in order to rescue wounded from the battlefield.

German action was not the only cause of casualties. In an environment where men constantly carried firearms, handled ammunition, travelled in vehicles on bad roads, and worked in harsh conditions, accidents were common and injuries often no less severe than combat wounds. Men died or were permanently maimed by such accidents. Poor hygiene, diet, and living in perpetually harsh out-door conditions increased the rates of illness and disease. The cumulative result of all these perils was that the normal strength of all units was seldom maintained. Every unit was short of manpower.

In the front-line units, the situation had been severe since the Canadians landed in Sicily. Within days of the first battles, it was common for infantry companies that were supposed to number about 125 men to go into action only 75 to 80 strong.[32] When companies were broken down into their platoon strengths and the platoons into section strengths, the picture appeared even darker to the individual soldier. Private Dan Nikiforuk of the Westminster Regiment drove an armoured car that was supposed to hold twelve men, but he seldom had more than four or five riding in the vehicle. It did nothing to boost his morale to know that, instead of having the mutual fire sup-port that a dozen men could lay down, his section would be lucky to fight with half that number.[33]

Burns knew that the best way he could keep enough men in the front was to reduce losses to avoidable causes, particularly disease. To underscore the importance of preventing manpower losses, he prepared a special briefing of his brigadiers that focused on the rein-forcement issue. After describing the problem, he outlined how the corps might have to strip down or eliminate some services that were less important to operations than combat units, such as "postal sorting, kit disposal." Losses due to illness, he wrote, "are a direct indication of the efficiency of the unit and its command in these mat-ters." Medical Officers would do their part in prevention, but "nothing they can say or do will be effective unless the CO takes proper disciplinary measures to enforce the hygienic regulations, and sees that his officers all follow out his directions."

An equally critical cause of loss, Burns wrote, was battle exhaus-tion. "It has often been observed that the incidence of this type of disability varies directly with the state of discipline, training and man-management in the unit. Basically, the cause is the inability of the man to control his fear, and while most men are afraid, they over-come it by the example of others and by the feeling that they are safer, better off and happier while enjoying the respect of their fellows in their section, platoon or regiment. Esprit de corps can only be high where discipline, training and man-management are good."[34]

Once men were diagnosed with battle exhaustion, however, they seldom proved able to be returned to front-line combat units. The men and officers there generally didn't trust such men. All too often they quickly relapsed and had to be evacuated. To retain these men in some semblance of a worthwhile role, I Canadian Corps had created a Pioneer Company where "personnel who, by reason of nervous instability, are temporarily unfit to take their place in the line" were "employed on strenuous manual labour." The purpose of this unit, strikingly akin to an ongoing field punishment detail, Burns said, was to prevent exhausted men being able to "escape to the Base, much less to the UK." The Pioneer Company service, he hoped, would "recondition them physically and mentally so that they will be able to return to fighting units, though it is realized this may not be possible in many cases."

Burns had little sympathy for battle-exhaustion cases. "I personally feel that men who fail to do their duty in the way these men have, should be under certain disabilities in relation to the man who continues to risk his life in the front line, or do his duty wherever he may be placed. For one thing, I think it must be made clear to these 'psychiatrics' that they may not expect to leave the theatre here during hostilities, and that those remaining in the unit at the close of hostilities will be the last (except prisoners) to return to CANADA."

If men are to be treated this way, he warned, so too must be the officers who succumbed to battle exhaustion. "At present, a certain number of officers are dealt with by adverse report, generally to the effect that the officer is unfit to lead men in a fighting unit. I presume that this procedure is only resorted to when it has been found impossible to make the officer do his duty after repeated and vigorous admonition and reproof. It must be made thoroughly clear to all officers that to be sent back in this way is a great disgrace. It might be more just if any officer so found unfit were stripped of his command and obliged to serve in the ranks in this theatre. If standards are strict for men, they must be more than strict for officers. But present regulations do not permit this. The trouble is that it is not fair to the men under him that an inefficient officer should continue to serve as such, and at the moment I do not see any entirely satisfactory answer to this problem."

Burns ended his briefing paper with a veiled threat to the brigadiers. "If any unit shows a high rate of wastage from these avoidable causes, it means that it will eventually be under strength and there will be no more reinforcements for it, and it will represent from all points of view, a weakness in the formation concerned. The remedy in such cases is obvious."[35]

A growing intolerance for diagnosing men with battle exhaustion and then according them appropriate psychiatric care developed within the corps's medical service. The corps's medical director, Brigadier Emmet McCusker, issued orders directing that any battle-exhaustion cases appearing in a medical unit were to be held "until personally examined by the commander of a Field Ambulance." Psychiatrists were prohibited from intervening in such cases and the service's neuropsychiatric unit was removed from the forward Field Ambulance, where it could quickly offer psychiatric treatment, and assigned to the corps maintenance area.

Unit psychiatrist Major Arthur Manning Doyle thought McCusker "appeared to believe that [exhaustion casualties] could all be prevented by discipline; that they were due partly to bad leadership on the part of officers and partly to laxity" by Medical Officers.[36] Despite Doyle's objections, the Canadian medical approach to treating battle-exhaustion cases in the forthcoming battle would provide only token and belated psychiatric care, an approach that differed from the one Doyle had developed and implemented during his time as the 1st Canadian Infantry Division's psychiatric officer. He thought the new, more intolerant approach unlikely to succeed in returning affected men back to their regiments.

◆ ◆ ◆

Believing he had done everything possible to address the reinforcement crisis, Burns began planning his offensive operation. He and Vokes visited the corps observation post on Monte Trocchio and it served to remind both officers of the difficult obstacles the Canadians must overcome. Because of the greater height of Monte Cassino and Monte Cairo, Vokes felt he could almost reach out and touch the features, even though they stood more than three miles away. "Their overwhelming dominance of the scene gave me an uneasy feeling that enemy eyes could see through my concealment," he later wrote. "At any moment, I expected to become a target for enemy fire."

The floor of the Liri Valley appeared undulating and was, in the Gari River region directly below him, overgrown by the usual vineyards and olive groves that typified the terrain through which the Canadians had fought since the Sicily invasion. Near the Liri River on the left-hand flank of the valley, farms were interspersed with scrub forest. Monte Cassino and Monte Cairo bordered the right-hand side. Highway 6 and the Naples-Rome mainline railroad skirted along the foot of the right-hand mountain range and disappeared into the distant haze that obscured the towns of Aquino and Pontecorvo, which were Vokes's marking points for the Hitler Line. The highway passed directly through the rubble of Cassino and, running out of the town, the Gari River followed a winding course to its confluence with the Liri River, where the river was renamed the Garigliano. Along the Gari's course, two piles of rubble marked the remains of San Angelo and Panaccioni. The former stood directly astride the Gustav Line and overlooked the Gari River from a low-lying ridge. Panaccioni held another height of land several hundred feet back from the river. Although he carefully studied the heavy brush bordering the German side of the Gari River, Vokes saw no enemy movement. It was hard to believe they were actually down there in strength, waiting for the inevitable attack.

Vokes was "over-awed by the task which faced the Eighth Army in breaking into the Liri Valley. From his observation posts sited on Monte Cassino and Monte Cairo the enemy could see any attempt by assaulting troops to cross the Gari River, and thus bring down a murderous artillery fire on them. The same applied to any movement in the valley. His possession of that ground gave him a tremendous tactical advantage." The divisional commander experienced a "feeling of relief" that the "1st Division was not taking part in the initial assault. It was bound to be a difficult and bloody operation.[37]

TWO

THE GUSTAV LINE

6

A JUST AND
RIGHTEOUS CAUSE

The picture that Eighth Army's intelligence officers were developing of the Gustav Line confirmed that the planned breakthrough would prove costly. Since November 1943, the Germans had been feverishly constructing strong fortifications immediately behind the Gari River. The fast-flowing river drained from the northerly mountains through Cassino. In its upper reaches, it was known as the Rapido River, but became the Gari from south of Cassino to the river's confluence with the Liri River.

The Gari averaged a width of forty to sixty feet and a depth of six to eight feet. Its combined depth, width, and swiftness rendered the river a natural antitank trench that would be difficult to bridge. On either side, but particularly on the eastern bank from which the Allies would attack, the approach was flat with open grain fields stretching back from it for several hundred yards. Because the fighting had overrun the Cassino area in late fall 1943, many of the fields remained unplanted, but had been deeply ploughed, leaving the soil broken and soft. The river was running high, and the ground close to its shores was soggy from seepage. A couple of hundred yards from the western bank, a low ridge covered in thick scrub provided the Germans with complete domination of the ground on either side of the river. The banks rising up from the water were also steeply cut.

The Germans had dug in "well-prepared infantry, antitank and field gun positions sited in depth up to about 4,000 yards or approximately as far back as Pignataro." These fortifications were numerous along the western ridge, particularly in the vicinity of the village of San Angelo. The emphasis, however, was on machine-gun and mortar positions in the forward areas, with field and medium artillery pits located further back. There were few antitank positions. The Germans had put little effort into countering a tank attack because their engineers were confident that the river posed a sufficient obstacle to bar Allied tanks from crossing. As the defences had already withstood two major offensives launched by the U.S. Fifth Army, intercepted German reports expressed confidence that the line would again hold.[1]

In November 1943, Adolf Hitler, taking a personal interest in the construction of the Gustav Line, had accelerated the flow of materials necessary to strengthen its defences. He also authorized construction of a series of fallback or switch positions behind the main line, of which the Hitler Line was of primary importance.[2] With the Anzio landings in January, Hitler had decided it was inappropriate for this main switch line to continue bearing the official name Führer Riegel (Führer Switch Line). On January 23, Tenth Army headquarters was notified that its name was now Senger Riegel.[3]

While the switch lines were vital components of the German defence in depth, primary construction focused on strengthening the Gustav Line. Here, 100 steel shelters were buried in the ground — effectively providing a steel inner lining for large dugouts. These positions were virtually impervious to artillery fire and could each protect about a dozen men. Seventy-six armoured pillboxes, weighing three tons apiece, were also dug into the ground.[4] Steel cylindrical cells, the pillboxes were seven feet deep and six feet in diameter. Only the top thirty inches, constructed of five-inch-thick armour, protruded out of the ground with a gun slit cut into the side facing the line of the enemy advance. Known by the Germans as "armoured crabs" because of their appearance when being towed into position on a set of removable wheels, the pillboxes sheltered a two-man heavy-machine-gun crew.[5] Nothing short of a direct artillery hit could harm this fortification.

All along the line, a vast system of concrete pillboxes was constructed. Many contained sleeping quarters for twenty to thirty men, while others were only big enough to protect a single soldier manning a light machine gun. The large pillboxes were interconnected by underground tunnels and linked directly to an open system of firing trenches, which the infantry would be able to man once the Allied artillery ceased firing. Existing buildings were tied into the defensive line. Many farmhouses and buildings in villages had inner shelters built at ground level to provide protection from artillery fire. These shelters had walls and roofs constructed of heavy logs that were reinforced with thick layers of crushed stone.

On the eastern side of the river and on the western bank running right up to the German main defensive lines, thousands of mines were buried. At least 24,000 had been planted immediately in front of the Gustav Line. Most common was the Schümine, a small, pressure-triggered device with sufficient charge to sever or mangle the foot of the person engaging it. S-mines were equally common. These mines were released when someone stepped on a trigger plate or inadvertently pulled a tripwire that engaged the trigger, causing a small charge to be thrown up to waist height where it exploded. Loaded with steel pellets, an S-mine usually caused massive multiple injuries to the groin and stomach area. Often these antipersonnel mines were constructed with a wooden casing that rendered them virtually impossible to locate with mine-detection equipment. Teller antitank mines powerful enough to blow the track off a tank or destroy a Jeep or truck were scattered through the minefields, particularly on roads or pathways that would tempt vehicle traffic. Thick fields of barbed wire were strung across the minefields and immediately behind them. And just back of the wire were the first rows of machine-gun positions, sited so they could provide a curtain of interlocking fire across the entire width of the front.

While the defences on the Gustav Line were impressive, German tactical doctrine never relied solely on a statically manned defensive line. The German divisions, particularly the Panzer Grenadier divisions, were trained to counterattack constantly to keep the Allies off balance and deny them the ability to consolidate gains won. No sooner would an Allied company seize a position from the Germans than it would face a series of determined counterattacks, often heavily supported by mortar and artillery fire. The German infantryman's task "is above all to send out reconnaissance parties and patrols to ensure the safety of the heavy weapons, to take part in close-quarters fighting, and to conduct counter-attacks," read one German divisional report.[6]

The XIII Corps infantry divisions and the supporting tank brigades were well briefed on the fortifications they faced and the German tactics doctrine. On May 11, the Three Rivers Tank Regiment war diarist cited a report detailing the forward Gustav Line defences and summarizing the locations and defensive works of each of the two switch lines that lay between the Gustav Line and the Hitler Line. Of particular note were intelligence estimates that the Germans had placed immediately behind the second switch line 120 field guns, 48 medium artillery pieces, and nine to twelve heavy 17-centimetre guns. It was also estimated that a battalion of tanks and an assault gun battalion were concentrated here, so either or both could quickly intercept any armoured breakthrough.[7]

Three Rivers' Intelligence Officer and consequently the regiment's war diarist, Lieutenant Horace Dugald Beach, was so enthusiastic about the quality of information that the Allies had on the German defences that he thought the attack plan far too conservative. Instead, he argued in the regiment's official diary that an armoured-infantry flying column could explode out of the shattered Gustav Line and be "manning the ADOLF HITLER Line behind the Boche, in a minimum of 2 hours from zero hour of the push-off." However, he concluded sadly, "that possible method has not entered into the planning notes or Ops Orders."

"Nevertheless," he added, "a more carefully considered or assiduously prepared plan has seldom been worked out. Perhaps only a Second Front would have more bumph. For almost a month all units and formations down to [battalions] have been planning, holding numerous information and discussion groups, making extensive recces of the ground east of the Gari and training for his own special task. Practically every officer knows all [roads] and [tracks] leading up to and possible crossings of the Gari, all such knowledge gleaned at night."[8]

With virtually uncontested air superiority over the battleground, Allied aerial reconnaissance had taken thousands of photographs of the countryside. Beach sorted through more than a thousand photos pertaining to the regiment's assigned area of operation. One series of photos was overlain with definitions of how well the ground would serve for tank movement. Roads were classified as to their quality and even the narrowest track was subjected to categorization. As the day of the attack approached, more photos were passed to Beach, showing overprints of the enemy positions and their believed strengths. A colour map was produced that graded soil conditions from the Gari River up the Liri Valley to Ceprano. This enabled Beach to brief the tankers on how the terrain would respond to tank traffic and how particular ground would respond to rain. Never had the Eighth Army been so well prepared and briefed for an attack and the spirits of the tankers in the Three Rivers Regiment ran high as a result.[9]

On May 7, the 1st Canadian Armoured Brigade issued Operations Order No. 1, detailing the role the three Canadian tank battalions would play in the forthcoming attack, code-named Honker. XIII Corps would attack with two of its infantry divisions up front — the British 4th Division supported by the 26th British Armoured Brigade on the right, and the 8th Indian Division backed by 1 CAB on the left. The British 78th Division would be in reserve. The role for 1 CAB was to assist the 8th Indian Division in crossing the Gari River, securing a bridgehead, and seizing and then holding the San Angelo "Horseshoe" position as a preliminary to operations against the Adolf Hitler Line. The San Angelo Horseshoe described a series of rises along the ridgeline that loosely formed the shape of a horseshoe, with San Angelo anchoring the northern flank. The 17th Brigade and Ontario Tank Regiment on the right and the 19th Brigade and Calgary Tank Regiment on the left would lead the 8th Indian attack against this feature. Three troops of Three Rivers Tanks would support the crossing with direct fire while the rest of the regiment remained in reserve.[10] Half of the regiment's reconnaissance troop, which manned the light Stuart tanks, was assigned to accompany the Calgary regiment and the other half to follow the Ontario regiment. Corporal Gwilym Jones's patrol of two Stuarts would work with the Ontario regiment.[11]

In the early evening of May 10, the Three Rivers tankers assembled in a large shack for a movie. Also present were many troops from the 8th Indian Division, with which they had been training for the past month. The film was *Bataan*, starring John Wayne and Humphrey Bogart. Jones, a twenty-three-year-old American who had enlisted in the Canadian Army in 1940, was soon laughing at the "stupidity of the producers and technical advisers in making such a film." In one scene, Bogart stood and threw a grenade at a bridge. "It flew about half a mile through the air, landed in the middle of the bridge, and blew up the entire bridge — it just disintegrated." The soldiers were so amused that they immediately started issuing wireless calls back to the supply depot for someone to "Send us up some of those Humphrey Bogart grenades."[12]

Preparations continued the next day for the attack and at 1800 hours on May 11, two messages were read aloud to all Eighth Army regiments. The first was from Sir Oliver Leese. "Our plan is worked out in every detail — we attack in great strength, with large numbers of tanks and guns, supported by a powerful American Air Force and our own Desert Air Force," the message read. "Let us live up to our great traditions and give news of fresh achievements. . . . I say to you all — Into action, with the light of battle in your eyes. Let every man do his duty throughout the fight and the day is ours!"

General Alexander's message was longer, but no less a rallying cry. "From the East and the West, from the North and the South, blows are about to fall which will result in the final destruction of the Nazis and bring freedom once again to Europe, and hasten peace for us all. To us in Italy, has been given the honour to strike the first blow.

"We are going to destroy the German Armies in Italy. The fighting will be hard, bitter, and perhaps long, but you are warriors and soldiers of the highest order, who for more than a year have known victory. You have courage, determination and skill. You will be supported by overwhelming air forces, and in guns and tanks we far outnumber the Germans. No armies have ever entered battle before with a more just and righteous cause.

"So with God's help and blessing, we take the field — confident of victory."[13]

As darkness settled over the valley, the tankers ate a tense dinner and then climbed into their tanks. The three squadrons of Three

Rivers Tanks that were to provide direct fire support to the 8th Indian Division crossing the river started their Sherman tank engines. The moment the Calgary and Ontario regiments moved to the riverbank and began crossing the Gari on bridges that were to be hastily erected by the engineers, these squadrons would concentrate on the eastern bank and fire their 75-millimetre main guns against visible enemy targets. The moon would not rise for several hours yet and the normal thick fog that settled into the valley virtually every spring night was building. Beach wrote, "it was very dark out; everyone waited, not anxiously, nor with fear. It was like a boxer feels before he enters the ring — just a certain tension."[14]

◆ ◆ ◆

While the tankers and infantrymen waited for the signal to attack, the Allied artillerymen stood by their guns awaiting orders to commence the most powerful barrage ever delivered by Western forces. Alexander's trump card, the ace he counted on to drive this fourth attack through the Gustav Line, was an overwhelming weight of Allied firepower. At 2300 hours, 1,060 guns would open fire in support of the XIII Corps and II Polish Corps attack. Another 494 guns would support the Fifth U.S. Army divisions in their attack.[15] The bombardment would begin with a forty-minute counter-battery program directed at known and suspected German artillery and mortar positions. Once this program ended, the guns would switch to a slow-moving creeping barrage to cover the infantry crossing the Gari River.[16] The scheduled artillery barrage was to be the climactic moment in a combined air-artillery operation that had been planned to destroy the German ability to effectively counter the offensive.

Primary responsibility for the operation's success had originally relied on an elaborate and intensive tactical bombing program begun on February 18 and continued with unrelenting intensity to May 11. While the artillery was only to provide the short-term suppression and destruction of immediate German targets threatening the crossing infantry and tank units, by the date of the attack the Allied air force was to have rendered it impossible for Kesselring to "maintain and operate his forces in Central Italy."[17] Officially dubbed Operation Strangle, the operation by the U.S. Strategic Air Force and the Desert Air Force had been the largest "interdiction" operation ever. British

Air Marshal Sir John Cotesworth Slessor, Commander-in-Chief Royal Air Force Middle East, supported by his immediate superior, Lieutenant General Ira C. Eaker, Commander-in-Chief Mediterranean Allied Air Forces, had confidently predicted that air power alone would cripple the German army in Italy. In a mid-April Ultra intercept, Tenth Army's daily consumption of vital supplies had been reported at 120 tons of ammunition, 200 cubic metres of gas, and 50 cubic metres of diesel.[18] A week before this intercept, Eaker promised that "when our ground forces move northward it will, in fact, be following up a German withdrawal made necessary by his inadequate supply."[19]

Between March 19 and May 11, about 65,000 sorties were flown and 33,000 tons of bombs dropped. Every form of bombing aircraft was implemented. Heavy bombers, such as B-17 Flying Fortresses, hammered the major rail marshalling areas in key cities from Rimini to Milan to Pisa. More then two-thirds of the sorties were directed against Italy's rail network and repair facilities. Fighter-bombers, such as Typhoons, and Spitfire and Mustang P-41 fighters hunted for trains to strafe and bomb. The Typhoons also struck small road and rail bridges with rockets and light bombs.

Operation Strangle did put great stress on Kesselring's supply network. He had also been compelled to transfer many of his trucks to other German operational theatres because OKW (Supreme Command of the Armed Forces) in Berlin believed he could rely primarily on the Italian rail system. Kesselring complained at the end of April that systematic air strikes were causing the "increasing destruction of railway supply routes." He drafted Italian prisoners-of-war and impressed male civilians to repair the damage. "If operations are to be carried out, the Italian railways must remain in working order," Kesselring warned OKW.[20] Kesselring, however, made alternative arrangements to compensate for lost railroad efficiency. At his order, German troops commandeered vast numbers of Italian civilian vehicles, ranging from heavy trucks to the smallest models of cars. All were utilized to move supplies and men as needed. By April, tonnage moved by road increased to 12,000 tons from only 4,500 tons in December. Moving mostly at night, these vehicles were also immune from air attack.[21]

Despite the railroad damage, Operation Strangle failed to stop

German supplies reaching front-line divisions. In fact, largely due to the lull in fighting along the entire Italian front between March and May, German reserves had actually increased, so that by May 11, Tenth Army was in better shape than it had been at the beginning of the operation. On March 15, Tenth Army's total ammunition supplies on hand had been 16,891 metric tonnes. On May 11, the total was 18,102 metric tonnes.[22] Total ammunition stocks in Italy were higher than those held in any other German theatre and there were enough rations to feed the troops for at least two weeks.[23]

Well apprised of these reports through Ultra intercepts, Slessor admitted by mid-April that Operation Strangle alone could force neither a German withdrawal nor seriously hamper Kesselring's ability to resupply his armies. The simple fact was that the Italian rail system was too efficient and developed to cripple beyond repair. Intelligence estimates showed that the rail system was capable of delivering to the front a daily quota of about 80,000 tons of supplies. The German front-line troops in Italy required only about 5,500 tons per day. Before the Tenth and Fourteenth armies could be forced to withdraw due to lack of supplies, almost 90 percent of the rail system would have to be knocked out of action.[24]

Slessor conceded that Kesselring was able "to keep up his reserves of supplies to a level that will enable him to put up a very stiff resistance when the attack comes. That may be inevitable, but it is unfortunate."[25] With the failure of Operation Strangle, it was now up to the army to either win or lose the battle. Air support would be available to the attacking units, but the implementation of aerial bombardment and strafing in a close-support role was still in its developmental stages and its effectiveness was limited.

◆ ◆ ◆

The attack did, however, have the advantage of complete surprise. Kesselring and his subordinate generals had misjudged the Allied schedule, believing the attack would come much later in May. Because of the complex deception plan and camouflaging operations, German intelligence still held that I Canadian Corps was concentrated near Salerno and thought that XIII Corps headquarters was still based in Termoli on the Adriatic coast. They had also seriously underestimated the front-line strength of II Polish Corps and the

Corps Expéditionnaire Français. Continuing to credit the threat of a Canadian amphibious landing at Civitavecchia, Kesselring wrote of his unit dispositions on May 11, "I feel that we have done all that is humanly possible."[26] General der Infanterie Frido von Senger und Etterlein, commanding the XIV Panzer Corps, was in Germany to be decorated by Hitler. Before he had left, von Senger advised his staff that nothing would happen before May 20. Tenth Army commander Generaloberst Heinrich von Vietinghoff told Kesselring during a telephone conversation on May 11 at 0905 hours: "There is nothing special going on. Yesterday I called at the HQ of the two corps. Both commanders told me they did not yet have the impression that anything was going on."

The previous day, Tenth Army Chief of Staff Generalmajor Friedrich (Fritz) Wentzell had chatted at length with Oberst Beelitz, Kesselring's acting chief of staff. "To my great pleasure everything is quiet," Wentzell said. "Only I do not know what is going on. Things are becoming ever more uncertain." He later added that, "I think it not impossible that things are going on of which we have no idea." Wentzell, a highly experienced staff officer, was more uneasy than most of the high command in Italy.[27] So confident was von Vietinghoff that the offensive would not come for some weeks that he spent much of May 11 preparing to depart the next day for a period of leave in Germany.

Not only were the Germans not expecting an attack but they had also concentrated their forces along the Cassino front in expectation that any major thrust would be directed against the Abbey of Monte Cassino rather than into the Liri Valley. As a result, the German dispositions behind the Gari River were both weak and poorly organized. Holding a one-mile line west of Cassino was 1st Parachute Division's Machine Gun Battalion. West of this unit, responsibility for defending the Gari River all the way to its junction with the Liri River rested on two battalions of the 576th Panzer Grenadier Regiment and two battalions of the 115th Panzer Grenadier Regiment, which had been detached from its parent, 15th Panzer Grenadier Division.[28]

As was true for the entire German army in the spring of 1944, the divisions in Italy were drastically understrength. One Canadian intelligence report estimated the average company in the 115th Panzer Grenadier Regiment was only about sixty men per company or roughly half strength.[29] This state of depletion was typical. A battalion of the 576th Panzer Grenadier Regiment was not only weak in numbers, but also considered of relatively low quality, composed of many foreigners drafted into service from nations conquered by Germany. Such troops were generally, and understandably, unreliable, prone to using any opportunity to surrender.

Morale was also an issue. Although the core of the Panzer Grenadier, and the parachute divisions in particular, consisted of hardened veterans, these soldiers were increasingly skeptical about the chances of a German victory or even their own survival.[30] Feldwebel Fritz Illi, a platoon commander in 6th Company, 2nd Battalion, 3rd Regiment of the 1st Parachute Division, knew the war was lost by the time his division transferred to the Cassino front after the Battle of Ortona. Illi believed the December 1943 fighting had convinced virtually every paratrooper involved that Germany could not continue to "fight the whole world." Yet each man kept his silence about this because "the tolerance for defeatism in the regiment was absolutely zero." Discipline remained strong. The men, Illi thought, "fought on for our country, for our honour, and for each other."[31]

Other divisions voiced their cynicism sardonically through song. A popular piece of doggerel among the troops of 362nd Infantry Division, commanded by General Heinz Greiner, who were involved in containing the Anzio beachhead, aptly captured the fears of many German veterans. Translated, the chorus went: "This Division of Greiner/Gets chopped ever finer/Till roll call's a one-liner/Which simply reads Greiner."[32]

This did not mean that the German army in Italy was verging on collapse or wallowing in defeatism. Its soldiers continued to resist with tenacity and skill, despite the weakened unit strengths and a general belief that the war was ultimately lost. Elite divisions proved particularly capable of quickly reorganizing and putting up stout resistance no matter how heavy their losses. For this reason, Eighth Army intelligence staff recognized that the regiments manning the Gustav sector that was about to be hit by two of XIII Corps's divisions could be expected to mount a fierce defence, even though they were meeting the attack with slightly less than the strength of a single division. It was also recognized that the preponderance of machine guns deployed by the Panzer Grenadier regiments and the

1st Parachute Machine Gun Battalion gave the Germans a formidable superiority in automatic weapon firepower, further strengthened by their extremely strong defensive positions.

Despite these advantages, General der Gebirgetruppen Valentin Feuerstein, commander of the heavily drawn-down German divisions of the LI Mountain Corps that controlled the mountainous region east of the Liri Valley entrance over to the Adriatic shore, thought the entire Gustav Line too thinly manned. The sixty-year-old veteran, anticipating the forthcoming offensive, pleaded with Kesselring on May 10 for a withdrawal to the Senger Line. Such a withdrawal would allow creation of a mobile reserve, something at present entirely lacking. Everything was out front; there was no depth, no ability to shift a division to contain a breakthrough. Kesselring refused, citing Hitler's order that all positions everywhere, no matter how vulnerable or impossible, must be held to the bitter end.[33]

At 2300 hours on May 11, time for discussion and adjustment of forces abruptly and unexpectedly ceased. For one German soldier in the line, who was listening to the familiar sounds of a patrol coming in and a mess party bringing up hot food, it was "as if a light had been switched on. There was a blaze of flame down the valley . . . and then ear-splitting screaming, whizzing, exploding, banging and crashing . . . I squeezed into the narrow cover-hold. Splinters buzzed over me; stones and clods of earth whirled through the air. The ground trembled under the force of the blasts."[34] Germans all down the line dived desperately into their steel and concrete shelters as explosive blasts and flying shrapnel devastated an already scarred landscape.

◆ ◆ ◆

As darkness fell on May 11, Lance Sergeant Victor Bulger and the other gunners of the Royal Canadian Horse Artillery's 'B' Battery, 'D' Troop, had sawed through the last remaining fibres of the trees fronting their gun position and dropped them to the ground to clear their field of fire. Some lights had been used to help finalize the aiming of the guns and, just as the lights were turned off, Bulger heard the whistle of incoming shells. The gunners dived into their slit trenches as about twenty-five German rounds exploded all around them.[35] Two shells scored direct hits on the well-dug-in regimental headquarters, but failed to cause any damage, as the previous day a work party had strengthened the roof with heavy timbers and a sheet of metal. Nobody was wounded and the guns remained unscathed.[36] A few minutes later, precisely at Zero Hour, Bulger and the other gunners fired their 25-pounders. Bulger thought it seemed as if "the guns almost split the sky and the noise of those thousands of shells sounded like freight trains as they travelled overhead." The men were firing five rounds per minute at first. Then, following the prepared plan, they gradually slacked off to three rounds a minute. "The sky was lit up for as far as we could see with the constant flashes," Bulger later wrote, "and flares could be seen in the distance."[37]

Thirty-year-old Peter Stursberg, Canadian Broadcasting Corporation correspondent, recorded his impressions. "The night is lit by the flashes of the guns. It's just as though hundreds of arc lights were flickering and sputtering in the valley and behind the mountains too. The white flames bring the hills out in black relief. . . . Sometimes it's so bright that I can see the CBC engineer, Lloyd Moore, bending over our equipment recording this. . . . It's an amazing and terrifying sight and yet thrilling. I don't know how to describe it properly in words, and I think it is easier for you to picture it by listening." He held the microphone up and for several seconds Moore's recording device captured the incessant booming of the guns. "There are guns in front of us," Stursberg then explained. "They're the ones that make the sharp cracks — and guns behind us — if you listen carefully you'll hear the whoosh of their shells going over our heads."[38]

At the headquarters of the Royal Canadian Regiment, Major Strome Galloway joined the rest of the regimental staff on the verandah of the house they occupied. Although their position was almost sixty miles away from the gun lines, the flashing of the weapons lit the sky so brightly that when Galloway opened a newspaper he found it easy to read the small print.[39]

So, too, did Lieutenant Patrick Harrison of the RCHA's 'C' Battery, 'F' Troop. With little to do once his four guns went into action according to the fire plan worked out earlier, Harrison stood outside his command post and read the paper "just to be able to say I did it." Harrison believed the counter-battery bombardment that the Allied gunners were laying down must be devastating the enemy, for it was estimated that a hundred guns were firing for every German gun deployed along the Gustav Line. The men worked the guns feverishly, maintaining a steady, unrelenting rhythm of three shells per minute until, at 2340 hours, the order to cease fire was given.[40]

Like the other gun crews, Bulger's had no time to rest. Another firing program, scheduled to begin in fifty-five minutes, would directly support the attacking divisions with a combination of high-explosive and smoke shells. He and his men spent the time between shoots quickly checking and servicing their gun, piling the empty shell casings out of the way, and bringing fresh ammunition to hand. There was no thought of sleep. Men wiped blood away from ears battered by the tremendous concussion and wadded cotton batting back into them or wrapped their heads in heavy cloths to provide some scant protection.[41] At 0035 hours on May 12, the guns resumed firing. They would continue to fire with only brief pauses throughout the night and on through the rest of the day. By day's end, the RCHA alone had fired 10,248 rounds — its largest firing scheme to date.[42]

Journalist Stursberg visited one of the British medium gun emplacements during the firing program of May 11–12 and recorded his impressions for later broadcast. Around the Gari River, he said, lay "a nightmare land that shakes and trembles as though pounded by a sledgehammer and the sounds of the fearful rushing noises that might be the angel of death on wings. At no time in the war has the Eighth Army had so many guns. And the Eighth Army is very fond of artillery. Remember the barrage at El Alamein, the hundreds of thousands of shells that were fired during the battle of the Moro River? Well, they are small shoots now." The gunners of the medium battery, Stursberg said, would fire more shells in these two days than were fired during all of the previous Italian campaign. "They are tired, these gunners. Their eyes red-rimmed from the dust and smoke and the lack of sleep. . . . But the shells that the gunners are firing are breaking up the Gustav Line. . . . That bloody little creek which is no more than forty feet wide," he declared, "was the main ditch before the German defenses." The battle, he said, was all but won.[43]

The radio correspondent's prediction was premature, for the battle raged on, its outcome very much in the balance.

7

AN UNHOLY
BALLS-UP

Fifteen minutes after the barrage ceased at 2355 hours, the 8th Indian Division and the British 4th Division closed on the eastern bank of the Gari River. The men staggered across the spongy ground under the weight of their battle gear and the assault boats they were to use to cross the fast-moving stream. Within minutes of the leading companies' launching their fragile flat-bottomed craft into the river, things went badly wrong. The current proved stronger than had been experienced during rehearsals on other streams. Many boats were dragged far downriver and units became hopelessly jumbled. This difficulty was only partially addressed when those troops managing to cross in the right sector ran ropes back to the opposite shore so that other boats could be pulled across.[1]

Frantically paddling troops often overbalanced, causing their boats to flip or swamp. Machine-gun fire slashed boats to pieces or rendered them adrift when the men aboard were all killed or wounded. Most of the men who ended up in the water drowned as their eighty-pound equipment loads dragged them like stones to the river bottom.[2] A terrific number of boats were lost. By dawn, one brigade of British 4th Division had only five of its forty assigned boats still afloat.[3]

Although the thick mist so blinded the Indian and British infantry that they were unable to see the defenders, the Germans were largely unaffected. Following a predetermined firing plan, they saturated the river and its banks with automatic weapons fire and mortar rounds. The massive artillery barrage had failed to suppress the German machine-gunners and riflemen.[4] They were there in force and suffering no apparent shortage of ammunition. The dead quickly piled up on the riverbank, mingling with the badly rotted corpses of American and German soldiers never recovered or buried after a failed assault on January 20, 1944, by the 36th U.S. Infantry Division, in which 1,681 men were killed or wounded in a fruitless forty-eight-hour battle.[5]

When the artillery began the scheduled creeping barrage which the infantry was to advance behind at a rate of 100 yards every six minutes, the Indian regiments were unable to follow. German small-arms fire never slackened, even when the artillery fire crawled over the weapon pits and pillboxes on the ridge. The Indians could only start frantically digging in on the river's western bank. Those companies that did try to fight their way up to the ridgeline and capture San Angelo simply disappeared into the fog, many never to be seen again. Battalion commanders lost all radio communication with these companies, since most of the sets they had carried across the river either broke down or were knocked out. When the company and platoon commanders tried to indicate their positions by firing flares, the fog swallowed the bright light. Some resorted to having men shout traditional war cries so the company commander would know where platoons were. The few platoons and sections that did close on the ridge were mired in minefields or hung up in the tangles of barbed wire the artillery had failed to blast out of the way.

In the first twenty-four hours, the 8th Indian Division had been scheduled to complete three tasks. First, establish a bridgehead; second, expand that bridgehead to a depth of about 2,000 yards; and, finally, clear any opposition from San Angelo and consolidate its hold on the Horseshoe. Once this was achieved, British 78th Division, currently in reserve, would pass through and broaden XIII Corps's grip on the western shore. Then I Canadian Corps could sweep through and crack into the Hitler Line.

By dawn, the attack was in a shambles, with the twenty-four-hour schedule thrown completely out the window. The two divisions held only precarious beachheads on the river edge and desperately needed armoured support just to hold on.[6] For the tankers of the Ontario and Calgary regiments waiting to cross the river, it was possible to read the perilous state of things from the sound of the battle that drifted back from the western shore. While the crack of British Lee Enfield rifles and the slow thudding fire of Bren guns could be heard, the sound that threatened to drown out all else was the sheet-tearing rip of German MG42 light machine guns that could loose up to 1,200 rounds a minute.

At the earliest, the bridges were now scheduled to be up after 0830 hours. Until then, the Canadians could only fidget impatiently in their Shermans while men they had worked with in the past fought and died a few hundred feet away.[7] Lieutenant Al Cawsey of the Calgary Regiment's 'C' Squadron was to have led his troop across a bridge code-named Cardiff in British 4th Infantry's sector, north of San Angelo. However, at about 0300 hours, construction of this bridge had been abandoned because the site was subject to withering small-arms fire. The entire squadron consequently shifted a few hundred yards left to where Oxford Bridge was being built in 8th Indian Division's sector, about three-quarters of a mile south of San Angelo. Hearing their wait would be at least another half-hour and being well sheltered from German fire by an interposing hill, Cawsey and his crew took advantage of the time to eat a quick breakfast and even have a shave and wash. While they were busy with their ablutions, the men followed the battle's progress on the tank radio set. Directly across the river from their position, the 3rd Punjabi Regiment was having a very tough time. Many casualties had been suffered, including Major Sujohn Singh, who was reported killed. Cawsey had worked previously with the major, and the two had become friends.

◆ ◆ ◆

The Canadian tankers had first fought alongside the 8th Indian Division in the mountains west of Ortona. Upon learning that they would support the Indian attack on the Gustav Line, everyone had been delighted. Most of the battalions were composed of either Punjabi or Gurkha troops, equally known for their steady bravery and fierce combat skills. The language barrier proved only a minor problem, since Indian and Canadian troops could usually communicate with each other in pidgin Italian and all the Indian officers spoke English. During combat training, the tankers taught the infantry to indicate where they wanted the tank's main gun or machine guns directed by firing a burst of tracer fire from their light machine guns into the target area.

Like many of the tankers, twenty-five-year-old Major Frederick Ritchie, who commanded 'B' Squadron of the Calgary Regiment, was both amused by and fond of the Indian division's commander, Major General Dudley Russell, known as "Pasha" Russell by almost everyone in his division and consequently by the Canadian tankers. Russell had a large, walrus moustache, wore sandals instead of combat boots, and carried a shepherd's crook that he used to point out things that caught his attention. He seemed to be fluent in every Indian dialect spoken by his troops and often paused to chat with privates or corporals, apparently taking into account their interpretation of developments as much as that provided by his officers. Ritchie knew the major general spent many hours every night reading all patrol or after-action reports filed to the divisional staff, but he frequently showed up in the forward areas by 0900 hours to see things for himself. He was, Ritchie thought, one of the last of the breed of old India officers who knew well how to lead Indian troops and bring out the best of their exceptional fighting abilities.

Russell and his officers were at pains to consult the tankers in the same way they did their own troops. Ritchie never heard an 8th Indian officer tell a tanker, "You are under my command. I order you to do such and such." Instead, the common line was "I say, what can you do for us here?" The Canadians would then discuss the matter with the infantry officers and quickly work out a plan that best got the job done. Ritchie thought the Indian division's approach resulted from its senior staff's being very experienced soldiers and passing that experience down to every level of command. It seemed a refreshing change from the way the tankers had generally been treated by officers in 1st Canadian Infantry Division, who often seemed to think they knew more about tank tactics than did the tankers.

If the Indian troops were having a hell of a time across the Gari, Ritchie knew it was not for lack of valour, determination, or ability.

They needed support, plain and simple.[8] But the fog was blinding the artillery gunners from doing more than shelling selected grids. It also prevented the Three Rivers Regiment squadrons from providing the promised direct fire support against specified targets.* And the engineers were having a harder time than expected installing the bridges. If they failed to complete the task, every tanker knew the infantry divisions on the other side could be destroyed. That would mean the failure of the entire offensive.[9]

♦ ♦ ♦

In the shelter of a small copse a few miles back from the Gari River, Captain H.A. Kingsmill was orchestrating the last details required to undertake launching an innovative new form of bridging that he and his staff had invented over the past few weeks. Twenty-four-year-old Tony Kingsmill was an officer of the Royal Canadian Electrical and Mechanical Engineers. He commanded the Calgary Tank Regiment's RCEME 61 Light Aid Detachment. A native of Toronto and a graduate of the University of Toronto's engineering program, he had trained as a chemical engineer but had also studied mechanical engineering. Using sheer eyeball engineering methods, Kingsmill and his team had designed a mobile bridge that could be driven into position already fully constructed.

The decision to build a new type of bridge had developed out of a shortage of normal bridging materials for the offensive. Calgary Tanks commander Lieutenant Colonel Cyril H. Neroutsos had been deeply concerned when the XIII Corps planning for the offensive allowed construction of just one bridge in his sector — Oxford. Neroutsos told Major General Russell that being dependent on only one bridge would seriously hinder the ability of the tankers to adequately support the 8th Indian Division attack. Russell agreed, but the two officers could think of no immediate solution.

---

*There is disagreement about whether the Three Rivers Regiment actually did provide fire support as planned or not. In a narrative written on May 24, 1944, 1 CAB commander Brigadier Bill Murphy reported that the Three Rivers Regiment fired 250 high-explosive shells. But the regiment's war diary entry for May 12, 1944, says the night was so dark that the troops could undertake no effective shooting. Veteran reports indicate there was some firing, but none comment on whether they fired blind or at visible targets.

When they discussed the matter with some of their staff officers, the 8th's Lieutenant Colonel Schoolhouse asked, "Well, why can't we build a Bailey bridge and push it across the damned river? It's only a couple hundred yards wide." Neroutsos and Russell thought the idea humorous at first blush, but the more the Canadian lieutenant colonel pondered the scheme the more practicable it seemed.[10]

Meanwhile, the Calgary Tanks technical adjutant, Captain Bert Linnel, told Kingsmill that nobody could figure out how to position a 30-ton Bailey bridge over the Gari River because the area was so terribly exposed to German fire. Making such an attempt in the conventional manner, Linnel said, would be suicide for the engineers. When Linnel told Kingsmill about the crazy tank-bridge idea, he agreed it was foolish. Then the two men shrugged and decided to take a good hard look at a Bailey bridge.

Kingsmill later wrote: "After a few hours of looking and measuring, it became obvious that to have a Bailey bridge on top of a Sherman tank, it would be necessary to remove the turret. Eventually, we conceived the idea of welding a launching ramp with the four rocking rollers to the turret ring that rotates the turret. The launching ramp beam was twenty feet long, which would be strong enough to carry a 30-ton Bailey bridge. By welding the beam to the turret ring we could rotate the beam 90 degrees so that it was parallel to the tank. This meant we could drive the turretless tank with the launching beam down a normal road."[11]

Kingsmill realized that one tank alone would not suffice, since there was no way to control the bridge's launching or positioning from the tank it was mounted on. The solution was to tie the back end of the bridge to a second tank and have the first tank drive into the river with the bridge on top of it. The rear tank would then push the bridge across the river by sliding it along the carrier tank's installed roller system. Kingsmill and Linnel decided the idea was feasible, but it needed testing.

Enlisting the help of a platoon of Royal Sikh Engineers commanded by Captain Cyril Howe, Kingsmill rustled up four Calgary tanks. Along with the tanks came four drivers and a wireless operator, Trooper Ian Seymour of Calgary. After several days of planning, the team mounted a bridge on a turretless tank and, using a mechanism that could be released by pulling a single pin, hooked it to a rear tank. The release mechanism allowed for speed and simplicity because the operation would be conducted under enemy fire. The engineers successfully launched the prototype over a large hole dug in a field. Kingsmill reported to Neroutsos that the idea was practical, but more trials showed that the pin release could be prone to problems. A simpler method for releasing the rear tank from the bridge was just to wrap plastic explosive around the fitting and blow it apart once the bridge was in place. On May 5, a test launch was conducted across a river with Russell and his staff present. While not entirely successful, the bridge was included in the overall battle plan. Kingsmill was told he had six days to get everything ready to go, as the launch must take place on the night of May 11–12.

Up to now, Kingsmill had been approaching the whole thing in quite theoretical terms. He had given no thought to where the bridge should actually be launched and had little direct battlefield experience. Howe, however, had built many a bridge under fire and said he knew what kind of site to look for. The two men slipped down to the Gari River in the middle of the night under a full moon. Holding the end of a measuring tape in his mouth, Howe swam into the river and was soon being swept away by the strong current. Clinging to his end of the tape and to Howe's clothes, Kingsmill ran along the shore trying to keep up with Howe. About 100 yards downstream, the engineer managed to return to shore. The river, they decided, was somewhere between sixty and eighty yards wide and where they stood made as good a launching point as any.[12]

Russell, meanwhile, was having second thoughts and asked Neroutsos if he wanted to abandon the scheme. Neroutsos replied that he still believed in it and was intending that the bridge — named Plymouth — would carry most of his traffic. One squadron would cross on Oxford, he said; the rest of the regiment would use Plymouth. Neroutsos ordered the creation of two duplicate bridge systems, each served by its own engineering platoon. For the launch, Trooper George MacLean from Sydney Mines, Nova Scotia, was selected as the carrier driver and Seymour as the radio operator.[13]

On the night of May 11, the four bridging tanks and trucks carrying the two engineering platoons and parts for the still unassembled bridge slowly crept down a narrow, white-taped corridor toward the Gari River crossing point. Visibility increasingly worsened as fog and what seemed to be smoke fired by German artillery obscured the landscape. The trucks carrying the first platoon's bridging material strayed off the narrow track and overturned one after the other into a ditch. Meanwhile, Kingsmill, Seymour, and MacLean, riding in the first platoon's carrier, got lost when MacLean wandered to the left of the track. Soon the carrier's tracks were entangled in long strips of white marking tape and Kingsmill realized the tank had torn up a great length of the left-hand marker line, a development that could result in the whole convoy's going astray. He ordered a halt and sent Seymour back on foot to locate the other tanks and alert them to the situation.

Stumbling across the rough ground in the dark, Seymour ran back to where the track was and, following the right-hand marking tape, searched for the remainder of the two engineering platoons. He came across several overturned trucks and a couple of Military Police checkpoints. The MPs had no idea where the other tanks were. Realizing the entire operation was in a mess, Seymour headed back to fetch Kingsmill.

By the time he reached the spot where the tank had left the track, the Germans were pounding the area with Nebelwerfer fire. Seymour crept cross-country, trying to follow the tank's path, but he was forced time and again to dive for cover as another stonk of Moaning Minnie rockets shrieked down and exploded. Seymour realized he was completely disoriented and huddled in a hole, trying to figure out what to do next.

Luckily, Kingsmill realized that Seymour must be lost and told MacLean to rev the tank engines loudly to attract the trooper's attention. Seymour immediately ran toward the tank. The Germans, too, heard the motors and intensively mortared the area. Zigzagging through the exploding rounds, Seymour reached the tank and scrambled inside. He told Kingsmill that he had seen no sign of the other tanks.

Kingsmill climbed out of the tank and guided the carrier driver to back up the way they had come to the track. The party then rumbled forward and, much to Kingsmill's relief, found the other three tanks in position near the river. The second bridging platoon came up a few minutes later with its bridging material intact. Kingsmill ordered the engineers to immediately assemble the Bailey bridge so it could be mounted onto the carrier tank. By now, the operation was badly behind schedule.[14]

At the riverbank, it was almost impossible for the bridging party to work. The smoke was so dense that Kingsmill could see nothing more than three feet away. With the Allied artillery firing relentlessly and the Germans replying with their own guns and mortars, the noise was so loud that he could not make himself heard even when he was yelling in a man's ear. As dawn broke, the fog kept their position obscured, making it possible to continue.[15] Kingsmill's ears were ringing and he was half terrified. All around the launch site, wounded infantrymen were making their way toward the rear. Kingsmill felt sick watching "all those poor kids streaming back, many of them holding each other up, blood pouring out of terrible wounds. The whole operation seemed nothing but a disaster."[16]

Things went from bad to worse. Despite the arrival of a smoke-generating team that was trying to keep the launching team's activity concealed, the fog was burning off in the hot sunshine and visibility was up to about 200 yards. Time was definitely running out. The launching party set out, Kingsmill walking alongside the slow-moving carrier tank. As the tanks advanced, Kingsmill talked to the two drivers by radio. About halfway to the river, he climbed into the front tank to escape the German shelling. When the carrier was about fifteen feet from the river's edge, Kingsmill ordered MacLean to stop and told the rear tank to start pushing the bridge forward. The bridge started going out like a drawbridge over the river. When it was about halfway across the water, Kingsmill noticed the carrier tank "was sinking into the mud and the bank of the river was starting to cave in due to the tremendous weight of the rig."

He shouted into his radio for the drivers to go full speed ahead and the carrier tank slammed into the water, wallowed a short distance through the muddy river bottom, and then bogged down completely. The bridge dropped into place with such a large crash that Kingsmill feared it must have broken, but then he realized that "miraculously it was in one piece and was over the river."[17]

Although Plymouth Bridge was across the river, it still rested on top of the mired carrier tank. This left the bridge canted like a teeter-totter, with the carrier tank serving as the balance point. While the end on the south bank of the river was resting on the ground, the bridge was three feet in the air above the northern bank.[18]

Kingsmill bailed out and made his way to shore. Meanwhile, the tank was flooding, leaving Seymour standing in waist-deep water. Just as Seymour thought he had better go down to make sure the driver wasn't trapped, the hatch over the driver's seat opened and MacLean popped to the surface and swam to shore. Seymour climbed out of the tank, grabbed the steel frame of the bridge's understructure and with his body half in the water crawled hand over hand to the shoreline. The two men clambered up the bank, dripping wet and quickly growing cold in the chill dawn air. As they approached, the pusher tank was blown free and Kingsmill radioed Neroutsos that the bridge was ready for use.[19] The time was 0950 hours.[20] Seconds after Kingsmill gave his report, he saw three shadowy figures suddenly burst from a nearby thicket of rushes, run past some engineers, and charge across the bridge before anyone could issue a challenge. From the outline of their helmets, Kingsmill realized the figures were German infantry who must have been trapped on the wrong side of the river by the attack and had now escaped toward the German lines.[21]

◆ ◆ ◆

Elsewhere along the Gari River, two other engineering units had experienced an equally difficult time getting their bridges into place. Three main bridges were to have been constructed during the night: Cardiff to the north of San Angelo, Oxford about three-quarters of a mile south of San Angelo, and Plymouth about a quarter of a mile farther south of Oxford. It had also been planned for engineers to establish eleven raft operations during the first night to ferry additional men and supplies across the river to support the initial assault forces. The following night, a fourth bridge called London was to be constructed on the site of a demolished bridge immediately south of San Angelo. Most of the work on the bridges and raft systems was carried out by engineers of the two infantry divisions, with some support provided by the smaller Canadian engineering elements attached to 1st Canadian Armoured Brigade.

The engineers working on Oxford were badly hampered by the fog, smoke, and direct fire from German machine-gun positions. But they were able to persevere despite heavy casualties, and at 0830 hours Oxford was ready to handle traffic.[22] Ontario Tank Regiment Shermans started lumbering from their sheltered positions toward the bridge. Also manoeuvring down a taped track toward the bridge was Corporal Gwilym Jones in one of the Three Rivers Regiment reconnaissance squadron's Stuarts, which were lightly armoured tanks, nicknamed Honeys, that mounted a 37-millimetre gun and three .30-calibre Browning machine guns. When the lead Stuart entered a small depression, it bottomed out on a Teller antitank mine that ripped a hole in the tank's underside. The blast tore off the driver's legs. Jones saw a panicked trooper jump out of the tank turret and land outside the taped pathway. As he hit the ground, a mine went off under his feet, killing him instantly. The reconnaissance squadron was stuck in place until the engineers could come up with a tractor to pull the badly damaged tank out of the way. Then the three remaining Stuarts moved on within the dubious safety of the marked path, which was supposed to have been free of mines.[23]

◆ ◆ ◆

Twenty minutes after Oxford Bridge was opened, two troops of Ontario Tank Regiment's 'B' Squadron rolled off into a wide strip of open, boggy ground. Although the squadron's original orders were to advance directly from the river to a road that ran from San Apollinare through San Angelo to Cassino, no route had been cleared of mines over the ground lying between the river and the road. Consequently, 'B' Squadron's commander ordered the tanks south toward the Plymouth crossing where the road neared the river and a crossing should be more easily effected. A few minutes later, No. 4 Troop's three tanks linked up with some 8th Indian infantry and supported their efforts to clear several German machine-gun positions that were barring their advance. The 75-millimetre main gun and .30-calibre Browning machine-gun fire from the tanks quickly silenced the German machine-gunners.

No sooner was this done than the squadron received orders to stop moving toward Plymouth and instead cut across to the San Apollinare–San Angelo lateral road. Once on the road, it was to move north and help the Gurkhas of the 1st Frontier Force Regiment to clear the village. Then it was to move north of San Angelo to support the 1st Royal Fusiliers Regiment, which was "having an extremely sticky time." Although the squadron managed to cross the open ground without encountering any German antitank mines, eight of its tanks mired in the soft ground and were disabled. While the crews of the bogged-down tanks and men from the regiment's engineering platoon tried to extract them from the mud, the remaining eight tanks pressed on and became heavily engaged on the approaches to San Angelo.[24]

'C' Squadron by now was to have crossed Oxford and come up to support 'B' Squadron. Because Cardiff Bridge had had to be abandoned, however, the Ontario Regiment's crossing schedule was delayed to allow the Calgary Tanks' 'C' Squadron to use Oxford and move to support 3rd Punjabi Regiment, engaged in the Plymouth bridge area. Leading the advance of 'C' Squadron was Corporal Bill McWithey, with Lieutenant Al Cawsey, his troop commander, directly behind. A hundred yards before the bridge, the ground turned extremely muddy and McWithey's tank got stuck. No engineers were available to help extract the tank and the line of Canadian tanks was drawing heavy fire from German artillery, mortars, and machine guns.

Cawsey knew he had to act quickly, because if the tanks failed to get over Oxford the Punjabi soldiers were likely to lose their tenuous hold on the bridgehead and be wiped out. Despite the risk of mines, he directed his tank out of the marked pathway and started inching around McWithey's tank. Cawsey's co-driver, Trooper Price, walked ahead of the tank, looking for telltale signs of mines. In this way, the tank was able to straddle three mines without triggering any. Once back on the track in front of McWithey's tank, Price hooked the tow cable mounted on the rear of Cawsey's Sherman to the stuck tank and pulled it clear. The two then proceeded to Oxford and crossed it, but the rest of the squadron could not immediately follow as the track was now too chewed up for further use without repairs.[25] Instead, 'C' Squadron of the Ontario Regiment moved to the support of the regiment's 'B' Squadron. Half of this squadron bogged down in the same field that had trapped so many tanks of Calgary's 'C' Squadron.[26]

The first thing Cawsey saw after the two tanks came off the bridge were the many rotting corpses of American soldiers scattered through the brush and hanging on barbed-wire obstacles. The tanks turned hard left and followed the river south toward the Punjabi regiment. Soon Cawsey came across a company of Punjabi troops. He saw one soldier, wielding a bayonet on the end of his rifle, clearing a German machine-gun position single-handedly. When the man finished his bloody task, he ran over to Cawsey's tank and told him where the company's officer was located. Then the small soldier ran off over a hill, bayonet at the ready, conducting a one-man charge. Cawsey found the officer, the company adjutant. The wounded officer explained that of the eighty men in the company who had crossed the river, only ten were still alive and he was the only surviving officer. His battalion had been virtually eliminated. The man told Cawsey that the tanks would have to operate without support, as he had nothing left to give. Cawsey raised his squadron commander, Major Don Taylor, on the radio and reported. Taylor told him there was no point in his sitting there, so they should try for the original squadron objective of Panaccioni. The rest of 'C' Squadron would join Cawsey and McWithey there when it managed to get across Oxford.

The moment the two tanks left the infantry position, McWithey radioed Cawsey that there was a German 75-millimetre self-propelled gun manoeuvring into a firing position against them. Immediately spotting the enemy vehicle, Cawsey directed his main gun on it and his gunner scored a direct hit with the first round. The German crew bailed out and started running away, but McWithey cut them down with machine-gun fire. A few yards further along, Cawsey's tank almost collided with another self-propelled gun sitting astride a sunken track. As his tank was too close to fire its gun at the vehicle, Cawsey popped out of the turret hatch and threw a grenade into the enemy's open cupola. Then McWithey hit it with a main gun round. One crewman piled out with his hands up. With no infantry to take him prisoner, Cawsey motioned for him to jump on the back of the tank and stay there. Minutes later, the two tanks were caught in an artillery barrage and the German started trying to climb inside the tank while Cawsey, fearing the man might be armed with a grenade or pistol, tried to keep him out. The matter was resolved when Cawsey ducked down inside the cupola and McWithey shot the German off the tank with his machine gun. Immediately, another German self-propelled gun appeared about 250 yards off. Cawsey's gunner scored another direct hit and knocked the weapon out of action. A few minutes later, they overran and destroyed a 75-millimetre antitank gun.

They were now on a small hill south of Panaccioni, still lacking any infantry support, and Cawsey was worried about running out of ammunition. He radioed back to Taylor for instructions. Taylor said Oxford had been temporarily knocked out of action and the squadron would not reach the two tanks for several more hours. Cawsey and McWithey should hunker down and call in artillery that would be put at their disposal against any German concentrations they spotted. Cawsey set about the task enthusiastically, wondering if he might not be able to bring down the might of the entire Eighth Army artillery if he liked.[27]

◆ ◆ ◆

The first tank to follow the German infantrymen across Plymouth Bridge was that of Calgary Regiment's 'A' Squadron, No. 1 Troop commander Lieutenant Al Wells. As his tank rumbled up the angled bridge and crossed the pivot point where it still rested on the carrier tank, the Bailey bridge tipped forward, allowing Wells's tank to move off without difficulty. When the tank exited the bridge, the release of the tank's weight tottered it back to rest on the south shore. Next across was the troop corporal's tank and then troop Sergeant Rolly Marchant started over. Inside Marchant's tank was Trooper Stan Kanik, the Sherman's gunner.

Raised on a Saskatchewan homestead, Kanik had enlisted in June 1941 at the age of seventeen. He had volunteered for the armoured corps and in early 1942 arrived in England and was detailed to the Calgary regiment as a gunner. This was exactly the position Kanik had wanted. He always said a gunner is "in the best place to be in a tank because you are in charge of the gun." By comparison, being a tank driver, the co-driver, or even the radio operator–loader "was boring" and these positions all required you "to depend on somebody else for your life and safety." That somebody else was the gunner. From Kanik's perspective, the commander sitting in the upper cupola of the turret was mainly along for the ride. If Kanik waited for the commander to find enemy targets for him, their gunnery would be too slow and they would all wind up dead or at least have the tank shot out from under them.

Now, as Kanik's tank reached the balance point on the bridge, he was surprised not to feel it starting to drop down toward the northern shore as the others had. Instead the bridge stayed angled upward and suddenly the tank rolled off the end and dropped three feet to crash onto the ground. Everyone was jostled around inside but nobody was hurt. However, when Kanik checked the electrical system that automatically traversed the turret, he discovered it had shorted out. This was not a big problem, since the turret could still be traversed with a hand-cranked wheel, which he normally used anyway for fine-tuning his aim on a target. He still wondered why the bridge had failed to seesaw.

Behind Kanik, the driver of Lieutenant Jim Quinn's tank had moved onto the edge of the bridge before Marchant's tank had cleared. The thirty-ton weight of the tank pinned the bridge to the southern bank. Once Marchant's tank dropped off the other end, Quinn's tank rolled across it and the bridge functioned just as it had for the first two tanks.

As the tanks rolled forward, Kanik could see through his viewing telescope that the driver was running the tracks over the bodies of dead Indian soldiers scattered thickly on the ground around them. Heavy machine-gun fire was coming from an embankment about 150 yards away. The Indian troops were holding only the narrowest of beachheads.[28]

Small-arms fire was slapping against the tank. Through the telescope, Kanik could see ahead for about 500 yards into the gloomy darkness and across an arc of about three degrees, so he kept swivelling the turret back and forth to increase his ability to locate enemy targets. Following the line of some German tracer fire back to what he figured was a trench system, Kanik raked the position with his machine gun. Then, after making a quick calculation on the range to the target and figuring how long it would take a shell to get there, he told the loader to put a round of delay-fuse high explosive in the main gun with the fuse set for 1.2 seconds. He cracked off the shot so it was travelling about ten yards above the ground. When the round was almost directly over the German trench, the fuse burned out and the shell ignited, spraying the trench with deadly splinters of shrapnel.

Delay-fuse rounds were the tank's best infantry-killer because an airburst over infantry in the open was devastating when it was on target. The same rounds were also highly effective against an enemy inside a building. When a delay-fuse round struck a building, the shell could penetrate the wall and then travel as far as fifteen more feet into the interior rooms before exploding. A normal contact-fuse round would explode against the outside of the wall and usually cause little or no harm to anyone inside. But as the Shermans were not fitted with the ranging gear that most German tanks carried, the Canadian gunners had to do the sighting and range calculations entirely in their heads. Most had difficulty attaining any accuracy with the delay-fuse shells, so seldom used them. Kanik was an exception. Possessing a quick mind for mathematical and spatial problems, he was quite deadly with the shells. Unfortunately, the shells were expensive and consequently only five were issued to each tank per day. Kanik, however, found it easy to get the other gunners to trade delay-fuse rounds for normal high-explosive or armour-piercing rounds.

Once No. 1 Troop had shot up the local area with machine-gun and shellfire for a few minutes, Wells ordered a move toward the San Apollinare–San Angelo lateral road. This was about a thousand yards west of the river and marked where the Argyll and Sutherland Highlanders Regiment was supposed to be waiting to marry up with 'A' Squadron of the Calgary Tanks. Quinn was unable to raise anyone from the infantry regiment on his radio, nor could he see any friendly troops who were still alive. Most of the Germans, seemingly scattered in slit trenches all over the place, stopped firing and went to ground at the approach of the tanks. Quinn stuck with Wells's troop because his own troop was reported stranded on the other side of the river when a German artillery shell damaged Plymouth Bridge right after Quinn's tank crossed. The bridge was temporarily out of action until repairs could be effected.[29]

Kingsmill, MacLean, and Seymour were on that task. Joining the driver and radio operator of the spare carrier tank, they roared back to the initial bridge construction site. Loading the necessary bridge replacement parts and some Indian sappers aboard, they returned to the bridge, made a somewhat perilous crossing with the carrier tank, and started unloading bridge parts. When the parts were about half unloaded, a German machine gun suddenly brought the men under fire and a sapper standing next to Seymour was shot in the stomach. The sapper "emitted a loud, hideous groan and folded to earth, like a discarded accordion." Seymour was spattered with blood and bits of flesh, and several bits of shrapnel struck him in the face but barely penetrated.[30] The same burst of fire raked the tank and steel bridge parts, chipping off a spray of hundreds of tiny pieces of metal shrapnel. Kingsmill's back was riddled with bits of shrapnel, his shirt torn to shreds. The officer was loaded into a Jeep ambulance and evacuated.[31]

His injuries proved to be only flesh wounds that were easily mended, but Kingsmill was so exhausted by the days spent constructing the bridge and the experience of its launch that he was held for three weeks at 14th General Canadian Hospital in Caserta for recuperation.[32] He was awarded the Military Cross, while MacLean was awarded the Military Medal, and Seymour was Mentioned in Despatches. The Calgary Tank Regiment unofficially renamed the bridge Kingsmill Bridge in the engineer's honour.[33]

◆ ◆ ◆

While the struggle to keep the bridge open raged, the four Calgary tanks that had crossed earlier took up position in the early afternoon in some brush on the outskirts of Panaccioni. After camouflaging their tanks with branches, the troopers set about observing enemy activity inside the village. They noticed that a large building about 300 yards to the left was the scene of much coming and going. Quinn believed it a headquarters and possibly also a field dressing station. To the northeast of their position, he saw concentrations of German infantry and tracked vehicles moving toward San Angelo. Establishing radio contact back to the regimental headquarters, Quinn called artillery fire down on the force advancing toward San Angelo and soon several of the vehicles were burning and some infantry lay scattered along the roadside, obviously dead.

Since the Argylls were still missing and the tankers therefore had no infantry protection, they were carefully refraining from firing for fear of betraying their presence and bringing a swift German reaction. Now, however, a section of German infantry with weapons slung casually on their shoulders marched across their immediate front. Several of the soldiers spotted the tanks hunkered in the wood and waved and grinned at what they obviously presumed was a Panzer unit. Then a few of the men paused, did a visible double take, and Quinn knew the game was up. As one, the four tanks opened up with all their machine guns, cutting down most of the section before it could react. Quinn quickly allocated each tank an area of the enemy positions they could see in and around Panaccioni and they started shooting up everything in sight with their machine guns and main 75-millimetre cannon.

The German response was instantaneous. Mortar and artillery fire fell on the wood and infantry was soon closing in, hitting the tanks with largely harmless small-weapons fire. Quinn had pounded the large building he thought was a headquarters with cannon fire, but now he saw someone standing just back of a top-floor window. The figure was looking through a pair of binoculars and Quinn assumed he was directing the increasingly threatening artillery fire. He ordered his gunner to put a round of high explosive through the window and that part of the building disintegrated.

While the four Calgary tanks were causing a lot of damage and enemy casualties, Quinn was also acutely aware that they were terribly vulnerable. It had to be increasingly obvious to the Germans that the tankers were alone and that the still missing Argylls were unlikely to reach them any time soon. He contacted the regimental headquarters to get instructions and at 1900 hours was ordered to withdraw back to the San Apollinare–San Angelo lateral road, where it was believed the Argyll Regiment was now dug in. However, when the tankers reached the position, they found no sign of the Argylls so they settled down to await developments.[34]

◆ ◆ ◆

On the opposite side of Panaccioni, Lieutenant Al Cawsey and Sergeant Bill McWithey had been reinforced by 'C' Squadron commander Major Don Taylor and a few other tanks of the squadron that had crossed on the repaired Plymouth Bridge. From its position, 'C' Squadron was able to subject targets in the little village to damage similar to that wrought by Quinn and his 'A' Squadron group.

But as it grew dark, Taylor ordered the squadron to fall back to the lines of the 3rd Punjabi Regiment at the Gari River so it could be refuelled and supplied with ammunition. Quinn and the three tanks of No. 1 Troop, having given up trying to find the Argylls in the area of the lateral road, fell back and joined Taylor's squadron's position a few hours later. The badly depleted infantry threw a perimeter circle around the tanks, but things were still so tense that Cawsey and the other tankers could not afford to stand down from their machines. They slept in the tanks, each man taking a two-hour shift on guard while the others tried to sleep in their cramped quarters. Everyone expected the Germans to counterattack and the position was subject to persistent shelling and small-arms fire throughout the night. It was the first time Cawsey had ever spent a night in his Sherman — an experience he hoped not to repeat.

Shortly before dawn on May 13, Major Gudari Singh of the Punjabi regiment came over to Cawsey's tank and asked him to move it up the hill a short distance because he expected the Germans would launch a counterattack against the position from that direction at first light. Cawsey told his driver to fire up the tank and move to the new position. With dawn rapidly approaching, Cawsey sat up in the turret cupola looking through his binoculars for signs of German activity. Suddenly he felt as if "someone had tried to stick a red hot needle" through him. He fell to the floor of the tank and then realized he had been hit in the back under the left shoulder blade by a fragment from either an artillery shell or mortar bomb. Blood was running from his mouth. He radioed Taylor and reported his condition. Taylor told him to hand the tank command over to his gunner and have him drive it to the river so Cawsey could be evacuated. Meanwhile, Major Gudari Singh had climbed into the tank and jabbed Cawsey with a shot of morphine, so he was feeling quite mellow by the time the tank reached the riverbank. He was loaded into an ambulance, taken to the Regimental Aid Post for immediate treatment, and then evacuated to a rear hospital at Caserta.

♦ ♦ ♦

By dawn on May 13, despite the fact that the Ontario Tank Regiment, the 1st Frontier Force Regiment, and the 1st Royal Fusiliers had established a strong position extending from the bank of the Gari River into the outskirts of San Angelo, XIII Corps's beachhead remained tenuous. It was also evident that the Tenth Army was doing everything it could to stiffen the resistance with reinforcements. The lack of any bridges in the British 4th Division sector of the line between San Angelo and Cassino meant the division had fought without armoured support for more than thirty-six hours. Casualties were high and its brigades were still checked on the riverbank.

On XIII Corps's right, II Polish Corps had been cut to pieces during its assault on Monte Cassino. On the left flank, the French corps had made only modest gains and was behind schedule. Eighth Army headquarters engineering officer General Sir William Jackson found it "impossible to stifle the desperate feeling that the whole affair had grossly miscarried or, in soldier's language, was 'an unholy balls-up.'"[35]

The tragic losses inflicted on the Poles were of particular concern. The Poles had suffered 4,000 casualties during the night attack and by dawn on May 12 most of the corps' divisions had been forced to withdraw to the initial start lines.[36] Although the Polish attack had been courageously determined, it was cut apart by well-emplaced German machine-gun positions and also ran afoul of a wide swath of minefields that were unknown to Eighth Army intelligence staff.

Because of the curious history of the Polish Corps, its losses would be hard to replace. In September 1939, when Germany and Russia had agreed to divide Poland between themselves, with Russia taking the eastern half of the nation and Germany the western portion, about 1.7 million Polish men, women, and children were forcibly deported to the Soviet Union. A small number of Poles, including many soldiers and airmen of the shattered Polish Army, managed to escape the German-Russian invading forces via Romania and France to Britain. In London, these refugees formed a government-in-exile with Wladyslaw Rackiewicz as president and Wladyslaw Sikorski as prime minister. With the German invasion of Russia in June 1941, the Free Poles were forced by Britain to reach an accommodation with Joseph Stalin's dictatorship and it was agreed that a Polish Army would be recruited from the Poles detained in the Soviet Union. Major General Wladyslaw Anders, a detainee, was given command. In December 1941, after the Russians had failed to properly equip, train, or even feed the neophyte army, Stalin agreed to allow six divisions totalling 25,000 men to leave for the Middle East. In the summer of 1942, more Poles had been allowed to join their comrades.

Arriving in Palestine, the Poles had been placed under British command and armed, trained, and organized as Commonwealth troops. Transferred to North Africa, the new Polish unit was designated II Polish Corps. It consisted initially of the 3rd Carpathian Rifle Division and the 5th Kresowa Infantry Division. Integrated into this strength was the Independent Carpathian Rifle Brigade, which had been formed from Free Poles in Britain. Because the Polish divisions were understrength and suffered chronic manpower shortages due to the lack of any assured source for new recruits, the divisions had only two brigades rather than the standard Commonwealth formula that called for three brigades to a division. In Italy, the corps reinforced itself with Poles who had been impressed into the German army and then surrendered to the Allies. After being vetted to ensure they were not actually pro-Nazi volunteers, the men hastily exchanged German field grey for Commonwealth khaki and returned to the front.

The Poles fought not just to defeat Germany, but also to convince the Western Allies that they deserved political support to create an independent democratic monarchy after the war was over.[37] Other soldiers in the Eighth Army generally considered them brave to a fault, often forsaking such defensive measures as digging slit trenches because that would slow down their effort to close on and destroy the Germans. Such heroics unnecessarily increased casualties.

A minor contribution to the Polish attack's failure had resulted from a mix-up between a Forward Observation Officer party of the Royal Canadian Horse Artillery and the Polish troops it was to support on a forward slope of Monte Cassino known as Point 593. The RCHA FOO party, commanded by Captain Peter Newell, joined a brigade of the 3rd Carpathian Division prior to the beginning of the counter-battery barrage at 2300 hours on May 11. Newell, his signaller Tim Helmsley, and Gunner J. Romanica, who was fluent in Polish and present as an interpreter, climbed the steep slope to a house at Point 593 that was being used by the Poles as a brigade headquarters. En route, Romanica was wounded and evacuated, so Newell and Helmsley had to try communicating as best they could through a Polish soldier who spoke very poor English.

The brigade headquarters was about a thousand yards from the abbey, separated from it by only a narrow gully. Helmsley was aware that the building must be exposed to direct German observation from positions in and around the abbey. By the time they arrived, the Poles were already putting in an attack across the gully against the abbey and the two men worked quickly to set up their No. 18 radio set. They then tried to establish communications with a base camp further down the hill manned by the other half of the RCHA FOO party. The base camp element had a more powerful No. 19 set that would provide a link through to the regimental headquarters, which would in turn direct artillery concentrations against the targets called in by Helmsley.

Just as Helmsley started talking to the base camp to check his radio signal strength, "a terrific barrage came down around the house." When the fire died down, he tried again and immediately another concentration of enemy fire hammered down outside the house. When this firing eased, Helmsley again tried to establish contact with the base camp but two Polish soldiers jammed a gun into his ribs and ordered him outside, where they forced him to lie down beside the house. Helmsley then heard the Poles smashing the radio set to pieces. Whenever he tried to get up, the men forced him back down. Finally one told him in fractured English that they believed he was a spy, for every time he spoke into the radio German artillery shelled the position. Helmsley was made to lie outside the house until late afternoon when he heard a lot of orders being shouted and suddenly Polish troops ran up the hill to man positions around the house in preparation to meet a German counterattack coming down from the abbey.

While Helmsley was being taken outside the house, a Polish major had approached Newell with a pistol in his hand and, holding it to the officer's head, marched him to the front of the house. The major accused Newell in English of "being a German dressed in Canadian uniform." He was told to sit quietly in a corner of the house or he would be shot.

When the counterattack threat arose at about 1600 hours on May 12, Newell took advantage of the momentary confusion to slip out of the house, round up Helmsley, and escape to the RCHA base camp. The Polish troops were soon streaming past as the German paratroopers successfully launched the counterattack and drove them off Point 593. Newell was furious with the Poles and believed that the brigade in question was badly trained and that Point 593 could have been held if they had just allowed him and Helmsley to have called in the artillery that could have broken up the attack.[38]

◆ ◆ ◆

Lieutenant Colonel John Buchan, Lord Tweedsmuir, returned at midday on May 12 from the Polish headquarters where he had been serving as liaison to report to Leese on the casualties suffered by II Polish Corps. He found Leese outside his villa headquarters standing in the soft Italian spring sunlight amid a small field of wild blue cornflowers that shimmered in the gentle breeze. Seeing Buchan's expression, Leese raised a hand and said quietly, "Stop." The tall officer, who was often to be found tending the plants around the villa, then said, "Let's pick some cornflowers." Finally, when the two men had finished gathering large bouquets, Leese said, "Right. Now tell me about the casualties."[39]

After receiving Buchan's report, Leese drove to the Polish headquarters to consult with General Wladyslaw Anders. He found Anders distraught. *"Ah, mon Général,"* Anders said. *"Tout est perdu, tout est perdu."*

"Ah, mon Général," Leese snapped back. "Nothing is fucking *perdu."*[40]

Anders soon rallied and offered to immediately put in another attack, but Leese declined the offer. At best, the Poles had one more all-out attack in them and Leese decided to hold off further offensive action against the abbey until XIII Corps had reached its objectives in the Liri Valley and slightly turned the German defences on Monte Cassino. Then, with I Canadian Corps pushing through XIII Corps and the French making further inroads in the mountains to the south of the valley, the German position on Monte Cassino would be sufficiently perilous that it might fall.[41] The success of the entire offensive now depended on XIII Corps cracking the Gustav Line open.

8

A Most
Satisfactory Day

Dawn on May 13 found Commander-in-Chief Southwest General-feldmarschall Albert Kesselring grappling with a confused picture of the battle situation developing along the Gustav Line. His primary problem was lack of information coming back from the headquarters of either Tenth or Fourteenth armies. Both had been struck shortly after daylight on May 12 by pinpoint-accurate bombing raids that caused considerable damage. Devastating bombing raids that continued throughout much of the day had similarly paralyzed Kesselring's Army Group headquarters. The first raid against Kesselring's head-quarters north of Rome and Tenth Army headquarters near Avezzano was carried out by heavy bombers of the U.S. Strategic Air Force that en route "paraded low along the battle front" as a morale booster for the soldiers engaged in the fighting. A total of 375 tons of bombs hit the two headquarters during this raid.[1] Tenth Army Chief of Staff Generalmajor Fritz Wentzell saw the bombers coming in against the Avezzano headquarters at 0900 hours. The staff had sufficient warning that almost everyone reached the air-raid shelters before the bombs fell, so German casualties were slight. Civilian casualties, however, were reportedly heavy and damage to buildings throughout the village was extensive. Although the Germans quickly re-established radio and telephone communications, "conditions in the village no longer favoured quiet and intensive work on the part of the staff." Therefore, the headquarters moved later that day to Castel Massimo near Frosinone where XIV Panzer Corps headquarters was located and "there was room enough, and we had the advantage of being in the immediate vicinity of Corps HQs."[2]

The aerial raids against the German high command headquarters had been made possible by Ultra intercepts that had identified the precise location of each headquarters several weeks before the launch of Operation Diadem, giving Allied intelligence staff plenty of time to set up the raids.[3] When Kesselring visited both the Tenth and Fourteenth headquarters by plane shortly after the raids, he discovered that both "had almost ceased to function." While the German high command struggled to return the various headquarters to operational status, Kesselring ruefully reflected that the Allies had outfoxed him and that his "fears of an airborne landing or a fresh invasion had no substance; the movement and use of strategic reserves had therefore become less hazardous."[4]

Kesselring acted quickly on May 13 to start shifting some reserves toward the Liri Valley. That morning he received a message, duly recorded by Ultra, from General der Infanterie Gustav von Zangen, stationed in Lombardy, that the newly established 278th Division had reached a level of fitness and organization sufficient to allow it to undertake limited offensive action. Kesselring issued immediate orders for the division, which was maintaining a coastal defensive position to prevent an Allied amphibious invasion there, to move to the Liri Valley. Still fretful about the potential threat of amphibious operations behind his forward armies, Kesselring ordered an untrained reserve division to take over defence of the Lombardy coast. Kesselring and his staff persisted in expecting General Harold Alexander, Deputy Supreme Commander Mediterranean, to show some strategic subtlety by launching attacks in their rear. It was hard for them to imagine that after three previous failures to break through the Gustav Line with frontal assaults, the Allies were once again resorting to a battering-ram approach.[5]

The sheer Allied weight of firepower was, however, opening

cracks. The incessant aerial operations undertaken by their air forces seriously hampered German efforts to shift reinforcements to the Gustav Line. On May 12, a record number of 2,991 sorties were flown. Yet, although these raids disrupted movement of reinforcements and supplies by day, they failed to isolate the battlefield. Enough road and rail bridges or hastily constructed emergency river crossings remained intact to allow reinforcements and supplies to come forward at night.[6]

In fact, I Canadian Corps intelligence reports at the end of May 12 revealed that the 1st Parachute Division was utilizing four separate crossings at the Melfa River that had replaced a destroyed Highway 6 bridge. Aerial reconnaissance detected the presence of many small supply dumps hidden in buildings and caves bordering the highway that stretched from Ceprano south to the battle front. Most of these positions were either too small or too fortified to be easily destroyed or damaged by bombing. The 15th Panzer Grenadier Division was feeding troops and supplies through San Giovanni and then following a roundabout route running south of the Liri River and back to the northern side of the river over a still-standing bridge at Pontecorvo. From here, the Panzer Grenadiers could either link into Highway 6 north of Aquino or use a series of narrow local farm tracks cutting through the fields between Pontecorvo and Pignataro, believed to be serving as a forward assembly area for feeding men into the Gustav Line.[7]

Despite having been caught by surprise, the forward troops and commands responded quickly to meet the offensive. On the day the offensive began, LI Mountain Corps commander General der Gebirgetruppen Valentin Feuerstein was in the process of taking over responsibility for the section of Gustav Line directly facing XIII Corps. As soon as Feuerstein realized the attack was in earnest, he ordered his alarm units, consisting of a company from each of the 5th Mountain Division and the 114th Jäger Division, to move from the northern mountain area into the Liri Valley. Next, he formed a mobile reserve near Aquino on Highway 6 to back up the front-line units and intercept any deep penetrations Eighth Army might achieve.

Later in the day, Feuerstein realized the bridgehead 8th Indian Division had established rendered the situation more critical. He issued a demand that Tenth Army release one regiment of the 90th

Panzer Grenadier Division as a strategic reserve that could, if necessary, be immediately deployed. Tenth Army commander Generaloberst Heinrich von Vietinghoff demurred. He had positioned the 90th around Frosinone, fearing that its airfield might be attacked by an airborne force of Allied paratroopers. By day's end, von Vietinghoff grudgingly placed the 90th's 200th Panzer Grenadier Regiment under Feuerstein's authority, but only Kesselring could authorize its forward deployment. All three commanders remained optimistic, believing still on May 13 that the Eighth Army offensive could be thrown back.[8]

♦ ♦ ♦

The two small clusters of Canadian tankers of the Ontario and Calgary regiments on the western side of the Gari River had spent a tense night waiting for counterattacks that never materialized. Nobody had slept and, with an impenetrable fog blanketing the ground at dawn, they remained at their stations inside the Shermans. Lieutenant Jim Quinn noted that the crews in the Calgary tanks were exhausted. There had been little opportunity for sleep from the night of May 10–11 when the regiment had moved to its forward assembly areas, to this grey, dreary morning.[9] In 'A' Squadron's No. 1 Troop tank, Trooper Stan Kanik wolfed a tin of cold rations and then, like everyone else in the tanks, urinated out of the emergency escape hole built into the bottom of the tank rather than risk going outside. Periodically, German small-arms fire rattled against the tank's armoured hide and occasional mortar and artillery rounds exploding nearby rocked the Sherman from side to side. Close explosions were followed by the sound of shrapnel clattering against the tank. Peering through his viewing telescope, Kanik could see no enemy targets moving in the fog. There was nothing to do but sit there until it lifted sufficiently to allow the attack to resume.[10]

At least Quinn and No. 1 Troop commander Lieutenant Al Wells had now learned by radio the fate of the missing Argyll and Sutherland Highlanders infantry battalion they were supposed to have been supporting the previous day. During the initial attack on the night of May 11–12, the Argylls had been thrown back from the western bank of the river. A devastating rain of artillery shells, mortar bombs, and machine-gun fire had slaughtered those who had managed to paddle their assault boats across. The few who survived had been left huddling in the water along the muddy bank. Repeated attempts to reinforce these men were repulsed and by day's end most of the battalion's boats had been sunk or lost in the current. Many Argylls had drowned. While the men clinging to the riverbank had seen the four Calgary tanks successfully cross Plymouth Bridge and move across the ground in front of their position, they lacked a functioning radio set and had been unable to signal their location to the tankers. So they had watched forlornly as the tanks headed west toward the battalion objective of Panaccioni. During the night of May 12–13, however, the Argylls had launched another assault across the river and this time had managed to establish a viable beachhead. Soon after dawn, they linked up with the Calgary Tanks' 'A' Squadron.[11]

Having just crossed the Gari River, Calgary Tanks' 'B' Squadron commander Major Frederick Ritchie stared at a passing landscape reminiscent of World War I battlefields. Shellfire had shattered or splintered the trees and German slit trenches were everywhere. Enemy artillery and mortar fire kept hammering down, so his crew had all the hatches closed up tight, limiting their vision.[12] Ritchie's orders were to support the 6th (Royal) Battalion, Frontier Force Rifles (RFFR), in an attack on a ridge 1,000 yards north of Panaccioni. If this attack succeeded, 'B' Squadron and the RFFR would then advance toward the village in an effort to effect its capture.[13] Ritchie directed the tanks to a predesignated position near the spot where the RFFR commander, Colonel Green, was supposed to have established a headquarters in a small dugout. Ritchie had worked with Green during the pre-offensive training operations.

Once the tanks were all well sheltered behind a bank bordering the San Apollinare–San Angelo lateral road, Ritchie set off on foot to find the infantry colonel. As he walked through some bush and started down an embankment toward the dugout, a German soldier suddenly materialized out of the fog. The two men, both frightened witless, stared at each other for several long moments before the German dashed off. Ritchie cursed himself for not having had the presence of mind to draw his pistol and shoot the Jerry, but his infantry training had entirely vaporized the instant the man appeared. A sudden volley of incoming artillery, however, wiped thoughts of the encounter from his mind and he rushed on to the safety of Green's headquarters. He was beginning to worry that the heavy German fire and the fact that the only infantry he had so far seen had been the German soldier indicated that the RFFR had failed to get over the river.

Bursting into the rough bunker that was supposed to be the battalion's headquarters, Ritchie was relieved to find Green and his batman calmly sitting on the dirt floor sharing some tea and cake. Green looked up and smiled. "Good boy, Fred," he said. "Come and have some cake." Then, while Ritchie sat down and took the proffered piece of cake and mug of tea, Green described the situation. Sitting there, Ritchie felt that the officer's calm and his ability to offer up refreshments while shells were exploding directly outside the entrance made "the whole crazy situation even more like a dream." This was certainly not the normal battlefield experience.

Snack finished, the two men set off to find Green's brigadier in order to finalize arrangements for the attack. They found the brigadier sitting in a huge shell crater with several other British officers. "Shrapnel was whistling everywhere and the noise made it hard to concentrate." But the officers were calmly chatting away as if they were attending a cricket match. Ritchie found "it doubly hard because a poor little sepoy was half buried under the ground I was sitting on." He was even more jangled when the sepoy and another man who was completely buried came to life, wriggled out from under the dirt covering them, then staggered off into the fog. Unmindful of the distraction, the brigadier finished his briefing and Ritchie accompanied Green back to the RFFR positions.[14]

♦ ♦ ♦

At 1000 hours, the fog finally lifted and the Calgary and Ontario tanks went into the attack in support of their respective infantry battalions. The Calgary tankers struck toward Panaccioni and the Ontario Regiment picked up its drive toward San Angelo. The Ontarios' 'C' Squadron pressed forward with ten tanks aiding the 1st Frontier Force Regiment attack on a cemetery about 1,000 yards southwest of the village.[15] Italian cemeteries were favourite German defensive strongpoints because they were "surrounded by high and substantial walls. These were normally lined on the inside by small, but very strongly built, family mausoleums. The whole structure provided excellent protection from shellfire. Added to this the little mausoleums made comfortable sleeping quarters and cooking fires could be lighted in them at night without being observed by [Allied] ground troops. In the Sicilian campaign and the early part of the Italian campaign it had been an Eighth Army order that churches and cemeteries should not be shelled. However, this order had to be cancelled."[16]

In fact, church steeples were now considered fair game the moment a tank moved within range of one. The Canadians had found that almost invariably the Germans used the steeples as observation posts or machine-gun positions, manning them for as long as possible and often inflicting heavy casualties on infantry that had no means of bringing effective fire against the stoutly walled structures. Calgary Trooper Stan Kanik, the only Roman Catholic gunner in his squadron, had made gunning for steeples a specialty. Some of the other men felt uneasy about shooting up the churches, so Kanik had told them back in Sicily, "Let me do the churches. It's no sin to me. I do the churches." Without a second thought, he had been knocking down steeples and sometimes entire churches ever since.[17]

The San Angelo attack was heavily supported by a five-minute-long artillery concentration by seven field regiments that pounded the village and cemetery.[18] When the concentration lifted, 'C' Squadron and the Frontier Force Regiment Gurkhas fought their way through a series of machine-gun and sniper posts. Then the infantry broke into the cemetery and cleared it in fierce fighting. With this objective captured, the way was now open for an attack on San Angelo itself.

A tiny village of only about 200 souls, San Angelo stood hard on the edge of the ridge dominating the Gari River. Its buildings were all badly damaged by the months of shellfire directed against it, and the Germans had transformed the rubble into defensive strongpoints. Two troops of Ontario's 'B' Squadron were tasked with carrying out the attack, scheduled for 1200 hours. The squadron's line of approach along the San Apollinare–San Angelo lateral, however, had been blocked when the Germans blew a bridge crossing a creek that drained into the Gari River. An attempt by one tank to cross the creek on a bed of rubble that had been pushed into it left the tank badly stuck. Requests for a Bailey bridge and an engineering party to install it went unanswered. Finally, one troop swung to the right, crawling along the edge of the ridge. From this party, a tank commanded by Corporal Lawrence Toye from Englewood, Ontario, managed to cross the creek and advance on the village.[19]

The delay in getting armour forward had forced the two attacking Gurkha companies to go to ground in shell holes fronting the village. As Toye's tank came up with machine guns blazing, the infantry came out of their hides and charged behind it into San Angelo. Above ground, the village had been reduced to a continuous pile of rubble that led to its being nicknamed the Second Cassino. Shell craters overlapped each other so closely that it was almost impossible to tell where one ended and another began. But the Germans were inside the village in force and had dug fighting pits into the cellars and even under the cellar foundations.[20] Toye's tank lumbered forward, clawing its way over rubble heaps until he spotted a German Mark IV tank hidden in a rubble-clogged basement. Swinging the Sherman's 75-millimetre gun onto the target, Toye's crew knocked it out with a well-placed armour-piercing shell. By 1300 hours, the village was slowly being cleared, and a few minutes later another 'B' Squadron tank, commanded by Sergeant John Stobbart, crossed the creek and entered the town.[21]

Toye was out of main-gun ammunition, so he let Stobbart lead, the two tanks advancing toward a still-standing house being used as an enemy strongpoint. The tank sergeant blasted the house with a volley of high explosive until the building collapsed. Stobbart thought it unlikely that the gunfire had killed any Germans, for they were all down in the cellar. Now, however, they were sealed inside as Stobbart hammered every cellar entry point he could see and closed them up. At 1800 hours, a bridge was finally in place across the creek and the rest of 'B' Squadron rushed toward San Angelo. Minutes before they entered the village, Toye reported by radio that San Angelo was now clear of German troops.[22] Four days later, Toye told CBC Radio correspondent Peter Stursberg that the entombed Germans would probably still be alive.[23]

By nightfall, the Ontario tanks had pushed forward elements of 'B' Squadron in support of Gurkha companies about a thousand yards west of San Angelo. This was the deepest penetration so far achieved against the Gustav Line during the initial two days of the offensive.[24] It was becoming obvious to the regimental command that the Germans were totally unprepared to offer a defence in the San Angelo sector against a combined tank and infantry attack. The tank squadrons had encountered surprisingly few antitank defences and there were very few antitank mines in the minefields. Although Toye had engaged and destroyed a tank in the village itself, from the way it was dug in, the Mark IV was positioned with a mind to fighting infantry rather than opposing tanks. Bill Murphy, 1st Canadian Armoured Brigade's commanding brigadier, realized the absence of enemy antitank units allowed the Canadian armour to play "havoc with enemy infantry strong points and inflict severe casualties on the defenders."[25]

◆ ◆ ◆

While the Ontario Tank Regiment and the Gurkha battalions were capturing San Angelo and widening the bridgehead there, the Calgary Regiment fought a stiff battle for control of Panaccioni. 'B' Squadron kicked off first in support of the RFFR drive to the north of the village. When the infantry neared the crest of the ridge, heavy machine-gun fire from some buildings along the ridgeline forced the Indian troops to take cover. Just as trained, the infantry pinpointed the German positions by firing a stream of tracers from their Bren guns against the walls of the houses containing enemy machine guns. Ritchie and the other tankers blasted the buildings and other targets marked out by the infantry with high-explosive shells. As the tanks began to close on the ridgeline, however, a hidden antitank gun struck one of the Shermans with an armour-piercing shot and killed Lieutenant Harry Emerson and two crewmen. The driver and co-driver managed to escape and crawled back to the safety of the river.[26] The gun swung and snapped a round that narrowly missed Ritchie's turret but struck a small stone building his tank was partially sheltering behind. Ritchie's driver hammered the Sherman into reverse and backed into cover without waiting for instructions from his commander. Well concealed from the antitank gun's position, the rest of the squadron saturated the ridgeline with high-explosive fire and a few minutes later the infantry rushed it, only to find that the Germans had fled.[27]

With the first objective secured at 1200 hours, 'C' Squadron attacked in support of the 3rd Punjabi Regiment toward a road junction 200 yards northwest of the village. The tankers and infantry were soon slogging their way forward in the face of intense opposition from German machine guns and antitank fire. Despite heavy casualties, the infantry pressed on, with the tanks following warily because of the antitank opposition. When the tanks were approaching the road junction, two German self-propelled guns were spotted and quickly knocked out by the advancing Shermans. Seconds later, another self-propelled gun moved into the open and struck Lieutenant Al Abram's tank with an armour-piercing round that killed Abram and one of his crewmen. Return fire from the Canadian tanks destroyed this gun before it could bear on a new target.[28] After one hour of fierce fighting, the road junction was secure. From the ridge-line, the tankers could see that the road they were on ran back into the German lines as far as Pignataro, no more than two miles away. Streaming out of this village was a long line of German transport vehicles heading west up the Liri Valley.[29]

At 1730 hours, two troops of 'B' squadron and two RFFR companies attacked Panaccioni immediately on the heels of a ten-minute artillery concentration. Initial stiff resistance from sniper and machine-gun positions on the edge of town was swept aside. When the infantry and tanks entered the village, opposition unexpectedly collapsed. The 2nd Battalion, 576th Panzer Grenadier Regiment headquarters was captured en masse. In all, about 130 prisoners were taken. At the end of the day, the Calgary Regiment's war diarist happily recorded that "it was estimated almost the complete second battalion of 576 Regiment was wiped out."[30]

◆ ◆ ◆

As the XIII Corps infantry battalions and attached squadrons of the Calgary and Ontario regiments consolidated their gains in the closing darkness of May 13, it was evident that Eighth Army's grip on the western shore of the Gari River was solidifying. The bridgehead had been extended to an average depth of 500 yards and was held continuously for a length of 3,000 yards. Although the Germans continued to shell the bridges crossing the river, their accuracy was poor because the previous excellent observation points they had enjoyed on the overlooking ridgeline had all been captured. A good stream of supplies was brought over the bridges to resupply the forward units. Throughout 1st Canadian Armoured Brigade, morale ran high.[31]

Because of the persistent German harassing fire, however, supplies were being brought up to the forward tank formations by open-topped Stuart tanks whose side armour offered some protection to the resupply crews. A shortage of space inside the Stuarts meant that ammunition and fuel had priority. Consumption of both by the tankers engaged in combat was heavy. A report to 1st Canadian Armoured Brigade filed at 1800 hours on May 13 stated that the two tank regiments had expended 1,555 high-explosive rounds and 50 armour-piercing rounds during the day. On the night of May 12–13, the Stuarts resupplying the Ontario Tank Regiment brought up more than 1,200 gallons of gas, 900 75-millimetre shells, and 20,000 rounds for the .30-calibre Brownings. The Calgary Tank Regiment received 500 gallons of fuel, 900 main-gun rounds, and 50,000 Browning rounds. Ammunition and fuel was being consumed almost as quickly as it could be moved across the river, so stockpiles were not increasing.

Soon concern was being expressed by staff at 1 CAB headquarters that available reserves could not compensate for the loss of both tanks and crews. The Three Rivers Regiment's Stuart tank that had been destroyed early on May 12 when it bottomed on an antitank mine could be neither replaced nor repaired. There were no fresh Stuarts in the reserve unit's holding area and no parts for these tanks would be available until the end of June. For now, it was also impossible to provide sufficient Shermans to enable each squadron to retain its full strength of fourteen tanks. This owed not to tanks's being destroyed or damaged by enemy fire, but rather to the number of Shermans bogged down on the west side of the Gari River that could not be reached because of the threat enemy fire posed to recovery crews. Until these tanks could be recovered, they had to be replaced by Shermans held in the reinforcement pool, and there was now a danger that too few tanks remained to make up for losses in the heavy fighting expected over the next few days.

No complete tank crews were to be found in the reinforcement pool either. There remained only nine gunners and nine co-drivers, so any casualties to other members of the crews could not be covered. This shortage again resulted from losses of tanks to the mud, as the crews were required to remain with the bogged-down Shermans in order to protect them if necessary and to work at getting them unstuck. Headquarters staff of 1 CAB put out a desperate plea for more personnel, and soon seven officers and eighty-seven other ranks had been rounded up from rear-area units, sufficient to fully crew eighteen tanks. A recovery team was also dispatched from the Brigade Workshop to help with repairing and freeing the disabled tanks.

With the priority for resupply going to ammunition and fuel, steps were taken to ensure the tank squadrons were also adequately supplied with food. Major Roberts of the brigade's Army Service Corps company decided the best way to prevent shortages was to adopt a new practice of issuing a full compo-ration every three days rather than daily. The previous daily ration issue had resulted in the packs's being broken into equal amounts that were shared between a squadron troop's three tanks. Now each tank crew would receive an entire compo-ration from which it could draw meals for three days. Roberts also told 1 CAB staff that he would try to arrange regular direct draws of fresh meat from the refrigerator cars, for the increasingly warm weather was causing much spoilage.[32]

In the front lines, not everyone was thrilled to receive a full compo-ration kit, and fresh meat remained an extraordinarily rare sight when the regiments were engaged in a prolonged battle. Kanik continually groused about the standardized compo-ration, which consisted of a bar of concentrated chocolate; portions of tea, sugar, and condensed milk; hardtack biscuits; a package of boiled sweets; ten cigarettes; tins of corned beef (bully beef); tins of meat and vegetable stew; two small tins of fruit; and a box of matches. The kit came with a cooker stand that would hold a mess tin of water or a can of stew. A cake composed of methyl alcohol was placed under the tin and then ignited. The heat source would quickly bring the contents in the mess tin to a boil. Six heat cakes were included in the ration box.[33]

To Kanik, drawing from the compo-ration meant an endlessly repetitive diet of tired and stringy tinned mutton and limp, flavourless vegetables. Only the bully beef ration had any bite to it. He never understood why Canada, with about 300,000 men in khaki, couldn't come up with its own ration kits that contained food Canadians would want to eat. He thought a lot about food like bacon, eggs, salmon, and sardines. Kanik loved sardines, which he hadn't tasted since going overseas.

After months of the same dull food, Canadian tankers were highly adept at scrounging around the countryside at every opportunity for non-regulation food. Each tank tended to have one man who was a particularly good scrounger. Kanik was the star scrounger in his crew. Part of the reason for this was that he received a monthly supply of about a thousand cigarettes from the women's auxiliary of his Saskatchewan hometown. Not a smoker, he sold the cigarettes each month for about $18. This meant that he always had cash and never even tapped into his soldier's pay. That all went home and into a bank account, so he would have a decent grubstake when the war ended. The cash from the cigarettes was useful for buying eggs, fruit, and vegetables from Italian farmers. And, of course, food was often found in abandoned fields and inside empty or destroyed farmhouses and other homes, where no one was around to accept his money. Wine was plentiful and most tanks carried a good supply squirrelled away carefully in the extremely cramped quarters.

In addition to the seventy-six shells for the .75-millimetre gun and boxes containing thousands of rounds of .30-calibre for the Browning machine guns, every corner of available space was normally filled to the brim. Rations, personal kit, water, a supply of tools and odd bits and pieces of parts to replace the things that most commonly broke down on the tank were stored in whatever manner best suited a particular crew. There was also a mandatory supply of bulky smoke bombs for the external launcher that almost nobody ever used, because doing so exposed the person manning the launcher to enemy fire. Every man also had to find room for his personal weapons. Kanik carried a .38-calibre revolver and a Thompson submachine gun. Unless he was well to the rear, the Thompson and the revolver went with him whenever he was outside the tank, even when doing maintenance or small repairs.

As well, each tank carried a Bren light machine gun with several boxes of .303 ammunition. This was for anti-aircraft use and replaced the .50-calibre machine gun that had been originally mounted on the turret and was to have been manned by the tank commander. Within the first days of moving off the beaches in Sicily, these guns were constantly becoming entangled in the wires used in vineyards to support grapes, so had been removed. It was rare to see a tank anywhere in the Eighth Army equipped with its regulation .50-calibre.[34]

◆ ◆ ◆

Tank crews were endlessly ingenious at figuring out new ways to squeeze more stuff into the narrowly limited amount of space. They were also adept at developing means to up the armour-protection quotient of the Shermans, such as by draping spare tracks over the tank's front glacis. Although the Sherman M4 was the standard tank used by Canadian and American forces, as well as by most British armoured regiments, it was not a popular machine with tank crews. It was undergunned compared with most of the German tanks it had to fight, and with a frontal thickness of 75 millimetres was more thinly armoured.

German Panzerkampf-Wagen V Panther and Panzerkampf-Wagen VI Tiger tanks, which had been appearing in the Italian theatre since January 1944, were virtually impervious to Sherman shots that struck the front. The Panther boasted 120-millimetre-thick frontal armour, and the Tiger 100 millimetres. Only a hit against select portions of the side armour or against the rear was generally effective. Meanwhile, a Tiger's 88-millimetre gun could easily punch through a Sherman's frontal armour at a range of 3,000 yards, while the Panther's lighter 75-millimetre gun would penetrate a Sherman's front at a range of 1,000 yards. The Sherman gunner might, if lucky enough to get that close for the shot, pierce the front of an enemy tank at 500 yards.[35]

Another fundamental problem with the Sherman was that most models, including those used by the Canadians, burned gasoline rather than diesel, which the German tanks used. If an enemy shell penetrated a gasoline-fuelled tank's engine compartment or crew compartment, the tank normally went up in flames so quickly that escape was impossible. Death by burning was all too common. Furthermore, the way the shells were stored on both sides of the tank just inside the armoured skin also posed a grave hazard. When a German shell pierced the compartment, it would often break some of the shell casings open and strew cordite and propellant everywhere, which would ignite in an instant high-temperature flame.[36] Both German and Allied soldiers called the Sherman the Ronson Burner, after the cigarette lighter of the same name. The Germans also nicknamed it the Tommy Cooker.

Canadian Shermans were generally fitted with five eight-cylinder Chrysler engines and had a top speed of about twenty-nine miles per hour. By comparison, the Tiger could muster no more than twenty-three miles per hour and was ponderous in turning, while the Panther had a surprising top speed of thirty-four miles per hour and proved a match for the relatively agile Sherman in cross-country manoeuvrability. This made the Panther a frighteningly effective opponent, while it was sometimes possible to outmanoeuvre the sluggish Tiger. Even the common Panzerkampf-Wagen IV, which Allied forces called the Mark IV, had a slightly more powerful 75-millimetre gun, 80 millimetres of frontal armour, and a top speed of twenty-six miles per hour that made it a good match against the Sherman in a shootout.[37]

The only significant advantage that the Sherman crews had going for them was their numerical superiority in almost every battlefield in which they opposed the Germans. In May 1944, Allied forces in Italy had a total of 3,036 tanks at their disposal. Between the armoured brigade of 5th Canadian Armoured Division and the tanks of 25th Army Tank Brigade that were to be tasked with supporting 1st Canadian Infantry Division, the corps's tank strength was between 350 and 400.[38] For its part, 1st Canadian Armoured Brigade, as was true of all Commonwealth tank brigades, mustered 194 Sherman medium tanks and 43 Stuart light tanks. As of April 1944, the total number of German tanks in Italy was 403, of which only 310 were serviceable.[39] Few of these tanks were actually deployed on the Gustav Line battle front. On May 5, Ultra intercepts reported that the Tenth and Fourteenth armies had available 18 Mark IIIs mounted with 5-centimetre guns, 47 Mark IIIs with .75-millimetre guns, 160 Mark IVs, 58 Panthers, and 43 Tigers. None of these tanks was at that time deployed on the front line and nearly 100 of these 326 tanks were so far back that they could not be brought forward in time to have any effect on the battle for Rome. Another 50 were with the Hermann Göring Division that was pointlessly guarding the Leghorn coast. Forty more of these tanks were estimated by Ultra staff to be completely out of the line for undetermined reasons, such as needing repair. This left, at most, 136 tanks to cover the entire Gustav Line front.[40]

◆ ◆ ◆

By the evening of May 13, the situation had improved vastly for XIII Corps. For the past twenty-four hours, Royal Engineers of the British

4th Division had been struggling to get a bridge across in their sector. Although 80 of the 200 sappers were killed or wounded, by nightfall the division's reserve infantry brigade was crossing the bridge. More important, three squadrons of tanks from the 17th Regiment of the 21st Lancers Brigade got over. This secured XIII Corps's right flank between Cassino and San Angelo. XIII Corps commander Lieutenant General Sir Sydney Kirkman declared May 13 a "most satisfactory day." He ordered three more bridges built over the Gari River immediately, and "gingered up Russell to go faster tomorrow." He also warned the commander of the British 78th Infantry Division, his reserve division, to be prepared to cross the river the next day to strike northwest between the 4th and 8th divisions, with an eye to getting in behind Monte Cassino and threatening that bastion from the rear.[41]

On the left flank of the 8th Indian Division, the Corps Expéditionnaire Français had captured the critical Monte Majo in the Aurunci Mountains and had inflicted about 5,000 casualties on the Germans in two days of fighting that had left the 71st Infantry Division badly mauled and disorganized. The 94th Infantry Division, also trying to stave off the French advance, was reportedly starting to fray and might soon break entirely. If these two divisions collapsed, it would open the way for a rapid advance by the French corps along the extreme southern edge of the Liri Valley to the Hitler Line.[42]

The progression of the fighting on May 14 would determine whether the Gustav Line shattered quickly or collapsed only after a drawn-out slugging match. What had looked to be an "unholy balls-up" the previous day now offered the promise of an imminent breakthrough. Echoing the words of then British I Corps commander Sir Douglas Haig, when his line had been broken during the First Battle of Ypres in World War I, Kirkman reflected that: "Things are never as bad or as good as they appear in the first reports."[43]

9

ONE COULD NOT
AFFORD TO GRIEVE

In the last hours of May 13, Lieutenant Colonel L. Fernand Caron held an Orders Group with the officers of the Three Rivers Regiment. Known throughout the regiment by the nickname La Buche, which means either "immovable log" or "blockhead," Caron had started the war as a sergeant in the Régiment de Châteauguay. By 1940, he was the youngest lieutenant at Officers' Training school and followed this up by graduating top of his class at the British Defence College course on Tactics. At the age of twenty-five, when Lieutenant Colonel E. Leslie Booth was promoted to brigadier in early 1944 and transferred to command of 4th Armoured Brigade in Britain, Caron took command of the Three Rivers Regiment. He was noted for possessing an uncanny ability to clearly visualize the forward terrain even though he was back at regimental headquarters. Caron had advised many a squadron commander that his reported map grid location was incorrect. The lieutenant colonel was invariably right.[1]

During the Orders Group, Caron explained that all three squadrons plus the regimental headquarters unit would cross Oxford Bridge before first light and join the battle action. 'C' Squadron was to support a battalion of 21st Indian Brigade in an attack designed to break out from the Gustav Line and cut the road running between Pignataro and Cassino. The start line would be situated halfway between San Angelo and Panaccioni, approximately 1,500 yards west of the Gari River. Once the first wave reached its objective, the remaining squadrons would come forward in support of other 21st Indian Brigade battalions.

This attack would cut directly through the series of low hills known as the San Angelo Horseshoe. The arms of the Horseshoe terminated at San Angelo and Panaccioni respectively, while the centre of the curve brushed across the Cassino-Pignataro road at a point lying almost precisely between the two villages. Tightly spaced and tall-growing vineyards, broken by dense, scrubby oak groves, dominated the ground. Narrow ravines and sunken roads isolated the hills from each other and these roads formed natural defensive trenches for the Germans. The Horseshoe held what was considered some of the roughest ground in the Liri Valley. It was ideal terrain for defence.[2]

The attack plan called for a slow, methodical advance aimed at wearing the Germans down, rather than cracking through their defences to encircle and destroy the forward units. This caution frustrated Three Rivers Lieutenant Horace Dugald Beach, who felt that it typified everything wrong with the offensive against the Gustav Line. The twenty-five-year-old Intelligence Officer from Ernfold, Saskatchewan, had run a farm for three years before entering the University of Saskatchewan in 1940. The following year he had joined the Canadian Officers' Training Corps, entered active service in 1942, and was shipped overseas that December. Fall of 1943 saw him assigned to the Three Rivers Regiment and in January 1944 he was appointed the regiment's Intelligence Officer. Beach believed that Eighth Army had a far too ponderous offensive approach and that this resulted from the line troops' being insufficiently trained in mounting aggressive attacks.

He also contended that the persistent fog that blanketed the valley each morning blinded the Germans as much as it did the Allies. Beach suggested that the brigade's three regiments open up "the bloody tanks, put on the sirens, and just roll ahead." In this way, he said, the Germans would be overwhelmed before they could react because they had few tanks or antitank guns deployed forward that could engage or slow such an armoured juggernaut. Caron patiently heard the young officer out and then went back to outlining XIII Corps headquarters' plan. Beach had not really believed his idea would be adopted. It was not the way of Eighth Army or General Sir Oliver Leese to ever take a chance. He did, however, feel better for having spoken his mind and appreciated that Caron was willing to let his officers do so.[3]

'C' Squadron crossed Oxford Bridge at 0100 hours on May 14, followed by 'B' Squadron at 0400, and 'A' Squadron and the regimental headquarters tanks at 0500. Although control of the bridgehead was considered firmly in XIII Corps's hands, Beach found this hard to believe as the headquarters unit formed up for its crossing. "It was an eerie feeling," he wrote, "to move along, and visibility nil, due to fog and heavy smoke screens laid to cover the bridges. There were several halts; finally up to the bridge and our tank drivers took them over. Still dark, shells bursting all over, mortars, more lethal crumps, machine gun bullets whining through the air. At last we halted, tight into the side of a little road with steep banks on either side."[4]

At the same time Beach was moving out from Oxford, 'C' Squadron attacked. The infantry and tanks groped forward through the thick fog, which reduced visibility to little more than twenty yards. The tankers had trouble maintaining contact with the virtually invisible infantry that snaked off into ravines and disappeared into dense vineyards. Deep pockets of mud mired some of the tanks and the Shermans encountered unexpectedly heavy antitank defences.

Headway slowed to a crawl and the Punjabi troops took heavy casualties. As the morning wore on, the tanks pressed 500 or more yards ahead of the infantry, ultimately breaking through to Point 66, the first objective, alone. Just short of the objective, 'C' Squadron commander Captain A.E. Wood's Sherman took a direct hit from a high-explosive shell. Not knowing what kind of shell had struck the tank and fearful it might at any second catch fire, or in tanker parlance "brew up," the crew bailed out. When it became apparent that the explosion had failed to crack the armour, the men jumped back in. Discovering that his radio had been disabled by the blast, Wood switched to another tank. Behind the tankers, the infantry went to ground every time they encountered machine-gun, mortar, or sniper opposition and their advance soon petered out, leaving 'C' Squadron dangerously isolated and forcing it to withdraw.[5] Twice more the tanks surged ahead to the objective, but each time the infantry failed to follow and the squadron had to retreat. Although possession of Point 66 continued to change hands, it was obvious to the tankers that the German defenders were absorbing heavy casualties. With each advance, the tanks were able to knock out more defensive positions, particularly after the fog lifted in the late morning. Still, the seesaw battle continued with no sign of a breakthrough.[6]

Three 'C' Squadrons tanks were stuck, two had been knocked out by antitank mines, and one destroyed by an armour-piercing round fired by an antitank gun. The crew of this tank had managed to escape without injury, but Sergeant McKinnon was killed when a mine knocked out his tank, and two of his crewmen were wounded.[7] More tanks might have been knocked out by antitank fire, but when Caron learned that a 'C' Squadron troop was planning to advance across some ground that on the maps looked particularly exposed he provided outside assistance. "I think the Germans are going to take a shot at them as they go across the valley," he told Beach. "I think we'll throw a little smoke down there." An artillery smoke concentration soon blanketed the little valley and the troop crossed without incident. Its commander radioed back that he had been very happy to see the smoke and had ordered his men "to beetle right across fast as you can."[8]

Finally at 1730 hours, 'B' Squadron passed through 'C' Squadron with the Royal West Kent Regiment, relieving the Punjabi regiment. These fresh units proved too strong for the now exhausted German defenders, and the tanks and infantry quickly crashed through Point 66 and 500 yards beyond. During this advance, they were engaged by two .75-millimetre antitank guns that were both quickly knocked out by the tanks. When the tankers raked several trench lines with machine-gun fire, many of the soldiers manning the position threw down their arms and surrendered.

Shortly after the prisoners were taken, Captain Wood returned to the regimental headquarters and handed Beach a sheet of paper he had confiscated from a surrendered German sergeant. Beach excitedly realized the paper was a sketch map detailing the locations of mines within a field the Germans had laid on May 1 near Ceprano. He immediately sent the map up the line and was pleased to see the details come back a few days later as part of an intelligence summary update issued by army headquarters.[9] It was a refreshing change to see something that had been captured at the regimental level given credence by the higher-ups, while Beach was often hard pressed to really use the plentiful stream of data that flowed his way from on high. The information on enemy dispositions, strengths, weapons, and tactics seldom referred to what lay immediately in front of the regiment's tanks and he had to sift through everything in search of useful grains. Then he had to package that information into an easily digested form that would be useful to the usually harried and often exhausted squadron leaders and troop commanders.[10]

In mid-afternoon of May 14, however, Beach had received some news from 1st Canadian Armoured Brigade headquarters that was easily digested by everyone in the regiment when he passed it over the radio net. The second front had been opened! A vast Allied armada was landing troops at two locations in France, one at Marseilles and the other at Dieppe. As soon as he relayed the news, Beach could hear the excited chatter on the radio net and the regiment's morale surged. Beach credited 'B' Squadron's breakout from Point 66 as resulting from this great morale boost.[11]

♦ ♦ ♦

News of the second front opening spread throughout XIII Corps as the day went on, energizing everyone. On the corps's far left flank, 'A' Squadron of the Calgary Tank Regiment was so buoyed that it slammed fiercely into the Germans holding a position known as the Liri Appendix. They met only scattered opposition from a relatively small force of German infantry trying to hold this salient, which extended from Panaccioni into a finger of land bordered to the south by the Liri River and to the east by the Gari River. Whenever the infantry were held up by machine-gun positions, the tankers rolled up and the Germans manning the guns immediately surrendered before the Shermans had to fire. After only six hours' fighting, the Appendix was clear. 'A' Squadron and the Argyll and Sutherland Highlanders formed a line bordering the Liri River and extending north to Panaccioni, thus securing XIII Corps's left flank.[12]

Meanwhile, the Ontario Tank Regiment had faced a stiffer fight pushing out of San Angelo with the Royal Fusiliers and the Royal

Gurkha Rifles. The objective was a point midway between the village and the Cassino-Pignataro lateral road. 'C' Squadron was just pushing off when tanks from the British 26th Armoured Brigade passed through its rear area, causing confusion and congestion. By the time the traffic jam cleared, the attack was late. The infantry and tanks met strong opposition from German infantry and antitank guns, the latter positioned within the thin cover of some hedgerows. The Shermans hammered the exposed weapons with high-explosive shells and left in their wake a string of wrecked guns, while suffering no losses.[13]

'B' Squadron and the Gurkhas had banged directly into a determined German counterattack. An antitank round hit one Sherman and it burst into flames. At 1030 hours, about fifty German infantrymen were observed forming up around some farmhouses to join the counterattack that threatened to drive the Gurkhas back. The Forward Observation Officer for the supporting artillery regiment, who was riding along in one of the tanks, directed an artillery concentration on the German position. When the concentration came in, however, some rounds landed among the Gurkhas, who hastily retreated. Minutes later, the tank in which the FOO was riding was knocked out by antitank gun fire. The situation became badly confused and 'B' Squadron was ordered to withdraw to where the Gurkhas were digging in to fend off the German counterattack. While the other tank troops in the squadron pulled back, Lieutenant R. Mulcaster's troop failed to hear the order and held firm. As the Germans closed on his position, Mulcaster, who had just erroneously been reported as killed, established radio communication with the artillery regiment and the supposedly dead officer called down effective fire that broke the counterattack.

The rest of 'B' Squadron, the Gurkhas, 'C' Squadron, and the Royal Fusiliers renewed the attack and, despite one 'C' Squadron tank being knocked out by a German Mark IV tank, succeeded in capturing the objective by 1200 hours. Eight German antitank guns, one self-propelled gun, and the Mark IV tank were all destroyed. By 1700 hours, the Ontario tanks and 17th Indian Brigade regiments were well west of San Angelo and in a strong position to drive toward the Cassino-Pignataro lateral road in the morning.[14]

With the onset of evening, the Canadian tankers were dismayed to hear that the news of a second front being opened in France had been nothing more than an unfounded rumour. Lieutenant Beach described the initial report as "The Ballox of the day. . . . A big let down."[15]

◆ ◆ ◆

For Tenth Army Chief of Staff Generalmajor Fritz Wentzell, May 14 had been a day fraught with disappointment. He realized that "hope of recovering our positions in the Gustav Line had to be abandoned when, on the third day of the offensive, 14th May, the vital sector of the Gustav position from Cassino to the sea, was lost." Field Marshal Kesselring was less disturbed by events. He told Wentzell that, if required, the "enemy offensive could be stopped on a line somewhat farther back; for example on the Senger [Hitler] Line, or in the Melfa sector, somewhat after the manner in which it had occurred in the Sangro battle." There, the severed Sangro River line had been reformed first on the Moro River and then again rebuilt on the Arielli River. That position had held throughout the winter of 1943–44. Kesselring told Wentzell that if that success could be repeated "by and large, the basis of our winter position would have been retained."[16] There was, of course, a major difference between the earlier situation and that currently faced. The fighting from the Sangro River to the Arielli River had taken place from November to December and, with the New Year winter rains, had effectively drowned in mud any possibility of immediate large-scale offensive action by Eighth Army. Leese's army could now expect six months of good campaigning weather, rendering Kesselring's comparison between the two situations an exercise in optimistic delusion.

So strong was his belief that things were not as desperate as his army commanders were reporting that Kesselring refused to consider a withdrawal to the Senger Line. Since Monte Cassino held firm and much of the ruined town itself was in German hands, he believed the offensive could still be checked if the line between Cassino and the sea were stiffened. Should this happy outcome be realized, Kesselring knew the paratroopers could hold Monte Cassino indefinitely against any attacking force Eighth Army cared to deploy. Everything hinged on preventing the current offensive into the Liri Valley from successfully turning 1st Parachute Division's right flank. Kesselring ordered the 26th Panzer Grenadiers forward to reinforce the German forces fighting in the Liri Valley, and the reserves of 94th Infantry Division to deploy in the Aurunci Mountains to blunt the French Corps's advance.[17]

An intelligence summary prepared at the end of May 14 by I Canadian Corps staff gloomily reported that German resistance from Cassino to Pignataro had strengthened despite the regiment's losing more than 200 men taken prisoner there. "This definitely indicates the arrival of fresh troops, but who they are is not known at this time," the report stated. Aerial observation suggested the reinforcements were regiments of the 90th Panzer Grenadier Division, but intelligence staff also believed the new troops could as easily represent a polyglot of units formed into an "ad hoc battle group." The intelligence report went on to state: "The interesting thing about today's fighting has been the series of counterattacks mounted by the enemy and the noticeable increase in the number of tanks forward." Intelligence staff noted that the Ontario Tank Regiment operations for the day had faced the most determined counterattacks on the whole front "and progress continued only against stiff resistance. Although these attacks have slowed down the advance, they had probably also provided the enemy the opportunity to carry out a certain amount of re-grouping and to establish a more defined main line of resistance."[18]

◆ ◆ ◆

May 15 dawned to the standard Liri Valley fog, but by 0700 hours it had lifted and warm sunshine washed over the lush landscape. At first, only the soft call of mourning doves and nightingale song was heard. Then small knots of men in khaki, hunched forward as if moving into a wind, walked out of their previous night's positions. Behind them, scattered in twos and threes, came the dull green Shermans. Moments later, the snap of rifles, chatter of machine guns, and thump of guns drowned out the natural sounds. Another day of battle began.

In the Calgary Regiment's sector, 'B' Squadron and the Royal Frontier Force Rifles headed toward Pignataro, passing through a squadron of Three Rivers Regiment at a crossroads about a thousand yards east of the village. German resistance was light and the advance proceeded more quickly than anticipated.

On 'B' Squadron's left, 'A' Squadron supported the Argyll and Sutherland Highlanders' advance to a line parallel to Pignataro that extended south to the Liri River.[19] Shortly after the squadron moved off, No. 1 Troop encountered a small cluster of houses only recently evacuated by the Germans. The tankers paused to check the buildings and Trooper Stan Kanik warily entered a large house, where he found stacks of German supplies tightly packed from floor to ceiling. To his delight, there was a large stock of food — all sorts of wonderful food. Quickly Kanik loaded up on tins of Danish butter, pickled herrings, pumpernickel bread, and beer. Soon every extra inch of space in the already cramped quarters of the tank was bursting with a cornucopia of delicious-looking German rations. There were even boxes of German food and beer strapped on the outside of the tank. Then Kanik and the other tankers in No. 1 Troop rejoined the advance.[20]

Lieutenant Jim Quinn's troop led. Following one bound behind was Lieutenant Al Wells's No. 1 Troop with Wells in the lead, Sergeant Rolly Marchant's tank immediately behind, and the corporal's tank bringing up the rear. Passing through a vineyard, the corporal's Sherman pushed through a row of vines and long strands of supporting wire tangled in its tracks and trailed out behind. When the wire twisted around the track sprockets, the tank was disabled. It was soon obvious that only a recovery crew armed with a blowtorch could cut the wire out of the tracks and render the tank operational.[21]

Wells and Marchant carried on alone, hurrying to catch up to Quinn's troop. So far, except for mechanical problems, 'A' Squadron's advance had gone well. At about 1430 hours, the tankers and the Argylls approached the Cassino-Pignataro lateral road and were bracketed by heavy artillery and mortar fire. They pressed on regardless, the infantrymen using the cover of the many vineyards and small gullies to conceal themselves from enemy observation. As Quinn's troop rolled out on a height of ground, the lieutenant spotted an armoured vehicle moving through the trees on a ridge about a hundred yards back of the western side of the road. Quinn ordered his troop to drop down into a depression next to the road. In front of the troop was a deep ditch and what looked like a pillbox. As the infantry had yet to come forward, Quinn dismounted and conducted a brief reconnaissance to ensure that the tanks could safely cross the ditch and that the pillbox was clear of Germans. He could hear the grinding sound of an armoured vehicle moving about on the ridge-line but was unable to see it.[22]

Meanwhile, No. 1 Troop crossed the road and pressed up onto the ridge. From his position behind the gun in Marchant's tank, Kanik was surprised at how many dead infantrymen and burned-out German trucks and guns were scattered along the roadside. He could also see very alive grey figures dashing about in the woods, but they were always gone before he had time to bring the machine gun to bear on them. So far, there had been no signs of operational enemy tanks or antitank guns.

Kanik peered through the telescope. He was a bit nervous because they were well ahead of the infantry. That was safe enough if the opposition was only infantry with small arms, but if an antitank gun was lurking about they could be in deep trouble. Suddenly there was a hellishly loud boom inside the tank. The air seemed to fill with a million little splinters and Kanik could feel them piercing virtually every inch of his flesh except his eyes, which were still glued to the telescope sights. It was over in a second. Sitting back from the tele-scope, Kanik saw that he was completely covered in blood. Marchant was down on the deck and looked dead. There was a hole in the tank right behind where Kanik was sitting. One of the loader-operator's arms was a real mess. It dawned on Kanik that the shell had pene-trated the tank and then shattered into shrapnel rather than exploding. Instinctively, Kanik bailed out of the tank, knowing it might start burning at any moment. As he hit the ground, a German machine gun opened up, kicking up bullets around him. Kanik crawled quickly into a shell hole. He was in a field of two-foot high wheat with red poppies laced through it. He knew he was badly wounded or perhaps even dying. A German machine-gunner was trying to finish him off.

Another explosion drew his attention forward and Kanik watched in horror as Wells's tank blew up. The stools that the tank com-mander and gunner sat on in the turret both shot out of the tank and flew about 150 feet straight up into the air. He figured everyone inside had probably been incinerated, as smoke was boiling out of the Sherman.

Behind him, he could see the driver, co-driver, and loader-operator of his own tank bailing out. Just then, another shell hammered into the turret and shrapnel sprayed everywhere. He lost sight of the loader-operator, but saw the co-driver and driver scramble clear and into cover. Seeing some brush nearby, Kanik wriggled through the wheat to the better protection it offered. He was still bleeding profusely, particularly from his chest, face, and legs. The brush was the leading edge of a small wood and Kanik moved carefully through this, looking for help. After a while, he heard some voices speaking English and found a group of tankers that included Major Don Taylor, the 'C' Squadron commander.

Kanik stumbled up and said, "Sir, Wells's tank exploded and everybody's killed. Our tank was hit but it didn't burn. Can you send someone to see what happened to the four other guys?" Just then, Wells's co-driver emerged from the wood and Kanik was amazed to see that he was completely unhurt. "Send somebody to see what happened to the other three guys," he said.

Taylor replied that he couldn't send anyone right now, as the squadron was fending off a German counterattack. Once that was dealt with, he would send help. Kanik worried that would be too late for the more badly wounded. He turned to the co-driver and said, "Come on, we got to get those guys." The co-driver looked anxious. "No, no, Stan," he said, "we got the ambulance coming."[23]

In fact, an ambulance Jeep carrying Regimental Medical Officer Captain Sidenberg was on the way. Within minutes of Kanik delivering his report to Taylor, the ambulance had set out from regimental headquarters toward the position where No. 1 Troop had been knocked out. Unfortunately, at 1530 hours, the Jeep struck a mine and both Sidenberg and his driver were wounded. Shortly thereafter, Taylor dispatched a rescue team to the knocked-out tanks. They found that only Wells and his loader-operator had been killed in the explosion. Wells's gunner, Trooper Tony Szeler, was seriously wounded. The driver and co-driver miraculously were uninjured, as the tank had not burned. In Kanik's tank, Marchant was dead and the loader-operator had lost an arm, but would survive.[24]

Kanik crudely patched himself up and then he and the co-driver walked a mile back to regimental HQ. He felt badly shaken and was still bleeding heavily from an array of surface wounds. The men reached headquarters just as a Jeep ambulance was leaving for the rear with some other wounded tankers. Kanik was loaded on board. When they got back to the Regimental Aid Post, a doctor told him to lie down on a bunk. After giving him a shot of morphine, the doctor said he would be okay and that he would not be operated on at the RAP. He drifted off to sleep, only awakening at 1100 hours the next day to find he was in a hospital in Caserta. The operating room staff had already removed much shrapnel from his wounds and there was a padre standing next to him, as if the man had somehow instinctively known Kanik would awaken that very moment. The padre said, "Write your parents today."

He remained in hospital for a week, spending hours plucking bits of shrapnel out of his chest and legs with tweezers. When he ran a hand over his chest, Kanik could feel dozens of metal pieces that felt like glass weeping off his flesh. Throughout that week, Kanik often thought back to the events of the day when his tank was knocked out and every time was reminded that his crew had never had a chance to eat any of those German rations.[25]

Despite the loss of No. 1 Troop, 'A' Squadron succeeded in holding the objective against the German counterattack. By day's end, the Argylls and the Calgary tankers were well dug in and the position secure. On their right flank, 'B' Squadron and the Royal Frontier Force Rifles reached the outskirts of Pignataro at 1730 hours. While the tankers shelled the town and called artillery concentrations down on it, two companies of the RFFR worked around the southern side of Pignataro and fought their way in. They then set about clearing it in house-to-house fighting that resulted in heavy German casualties and many prisoners. At 2300 hours, the rubble heap that had been Pignataro was reported cleared of the enemy. The RFFR and 'B' Squadron tanks consolidated their hold on both it and a crossroads just to the north.[26]

◆ ◆ ◆

On the northern flank of the Calgary Tank Regiment, the Three Rivers Regiment pushed toward the Cassino-Pignataro lateral road with 'A' Squadron leading. No. 1 and No. 4 troops under command of Captain F.W. Simard were up front, with No. 2 and No. 3 troops under Captain D.C. Whiteford in reserve. Resistance was scattered but occasionally fierce. Mud continued to be a problem and two tanks became stuck.

When Sergeant J. Leslie dismounted from his tank to conduct a reconnaissance on foot, he was killed. Then an armour-piercing round struck Lieutenant J.M. O'Dell's tank and it burst into flames. Remarkably, the crew managed to escape unharmed.

At 1400 hours, 'B' Squadron passed through 'A' Squadron and took over. As the tanks followed a sunken road, the tankers heard armour-piercing shot constantly hissing overhead, but because of the road depth their Shermans were below the line of fire and the shot passed harmlessly over them. At 1730 hours, the squadron was on the secondary objective about 300 yards short of the Cassino-Pignataro lateral road. Lieutenant Colonel Fernand Caron decided to throw all the battle squadrons forward on the heels of a ten-minute artillery barrage with 'B' left, 'C' right, and 'A' centre. Lacking infantry support, the tanks would advance at full speed. When the attack slammed forward, German opposition collapsed. A few minutes later, the tanks severed the road.[27]

North of the Three Rivers Regiment, the Ontario Regiment and the Frontier Force Regiment tried to capture another segment of the lateral road. Two troops from 'A' Squadron and two infantry companies led. On the right was 'B' Company; on the left, 'A' Company. All the tanks were delayed when an antitank gun blocked the only route that could be used to get through some rough, overgrown ground. A detailed attack had to be worked out between tankers and infantry to knock the gun out. The gun and crew were subsequently destroyed and six prisoners taken when the infantry overran machine guns protecting the antitank gun. The advance resumed, with the troop supporting 'A' Company fighting its way through numerous machine-gun and sniper positions. As the tanks approached the objective, they managed to surprise and knock out three antitank guns, including one in a heavily fortified house.[28]

During the sharp engagement to seize the lateral road, the Germans attempted a counterattack. At Three Rivers Regiment HQ, Lieutenant Beach heard the Ontario tankers reporting excitedly that Germans were forming on their left. This gave him pause, since the Ontario left was also Three Rivers' right flank and the counterattack could pose a hazard to that regiment as well. He reported the radio traffic to Caron, who called for a concentration by two artillery regiments on the cited position. When the shells started falling, the Ontario headquarters was instantly on the radio demanding the concentration be stopped. Beach reported that his regiment had requested the concentration, but he would stop it forthwith. The Ontario staff officer told Beach curtly that Three Rivers was "not, repeat not, to interfere with their show, and not to bring down arty unless they asked for it. However, five minutes later, it came over the air that the enemy counter-attack had been broken up by arty fire." Beach felt rather smug about the whole incident.[29]

As the Three Rivers' fighting squadrons settled in for the night on the ridge paralleling the Cassino-Pignataro lateral, the reconnaissance squadron started bringing fresh ammunition and fuel supplies forward in its Stuart tanks. The wisdom of not deploying trucks for resupply purposes was brought home to Corporal Gwilym Jones when his Stuart was suddenly struck in the side by a German shell as it approached the slope leading up to the ridgeline. Everyone bailed out fast, with Jones diving headfirst to the ground and somersaulting into some rocks. Seeing the tank undamaged, Jones limped painfully back to it and they carried on.

Around them, the infantry was moving up to join the tank squadrons, and to the north, battle sounds could be heard, indicating that British 78th Division was making hard headway along the southern slope of Monte Cassino against still-determined resistance. On the way back from the resupply run, Jones saw an infantry officer lying on the ground with wounds in both his legs. He climbed out, picked the man up and loaded him into the tank. As he tried to inject morphine into him, Jones inadvertently jammed the hypodermic needle into his own thumb. On the way back to the rear, Jones held the wounded man in his arms to cushion him from the rough ride while struggling himself to remain awake. The tiredness accruing from days without adequate sleep combined with the morphine to make him feel like a zombie.[30]

♦ ♦ ♦

Everyone was exhausted. Beach noted that the battle in the latter hours of May 15 seemed to be running out of steam, "as if both sides had spent their strength and just had to pause and get their breath. It had been a terrific slogging match. Not only tough on the nerves, but practically no sleep, completely worn out men, and officers in particular."[31] Between the heavy casualties suffered by XIII Corps and the supporting armoured brigades and the exhaustion of those men who were still combat ready, it was obvious the corps, particularly 8th Indian Division and British 4th Division, had pretty much shot its bolt.

Eighth Army commander General Sir Oliver Leese had been seeking the perfect moment to order I Canadian Corps to pass through XIII Corps. The trick was to identify not only when XIII Corps was played out, but also to anticipate the point at which the German battalions in the front lines were reeling from a combination of exhaustion and heavy casualties. If he struck before Kesselring decided to funnel significant reinforcements into the front line to shore up the defence, the Canadians could crack through with such force that they would not be stopped.

The current situation was hardly propitious. True, 8th Indian Division had decisively broken the Gustav Line from San Angelo south to the Liri River. The German defenders in that sector were disorganized and so reduced by casualties and men surrendered that their ability to resist was negligible. Yet, in the sector between San Angelo and Cassino, the British 4th and 78th divisions were making slow headway, often intermingled and mired in congestion as units from each tried to advance along the same few functional roads or tracks. German resistance in this sector remained tenacious. Was this the moment to play his trump card by sending I Canadian Corps forward? Or should he wait for the divisions on XIII Corps's right flank to wear down the Germans there further? Leese decided to play the Canadian card now.

His decision was prompted by the realization that if he could drive far enough forward into the Liri Valley, the Germans' possession of Monte Cassino and Monte Cairo would be outflanked. Further, the unrelenting grip the German paratroopers had inside a fragment of Cassino's ruins must then be withdrawn or left surrounded. Leese contacted Lieutenant General Tommy Burns on the evening of May 14 and ordered I Canadian Corps forward. Burns's first task would be to advance from the Cassino-Pignataro lateral road to the Hitler Line.[32]

Anticipating the order, Burns was more than ready for action. In the initial planning for the Canadian role in Operation Diadem, two scenarios had been envisioned. The first was that XIII Corps would rapidly break through the Gustav and Hitler lines. At this point, I Canadian Corps would pass through and race directly up Highway 6 toward Rome. This was the "pie-in-the-sky" scenario. More realistically, both Burns and Leese had developed an alternative scenario whereby heavy opposition slowed XIII Corps and a breakthrough seemed in question. At this point, the Canadians would come up on XIII Corps's left flank and advance up the valley on a front paralleling the other corps. It was this strategy that Burns was to initiate.[33]

The Canadians were to relieve 8th Indian Division and advance westward on a front extending from just north of Pignataro south to the Liri River. To their right, 78th Division would continue its drive forward with its right flank anchored hard against the base of the northern mountains. The 1st Canadian Infantry Division would lead the Canadian Corps's drive, while 5th Canadian Armoured Division remained in readiness to assume the lead once the Hitler Line was severed. The 25th Army Tank Brigade would provide 1 CID's armoured support.[34] However, until all regiments in that brigade could move into position, the Three Rivers Tank Regiment would support the immediate right-hand flank attack carried out by 3rd Canadian Infantry Brigade.[35]

It would take approximately thirty-six hours for 1 CID to completely relieve 8th Indian Division, so Burns scheduled the renewed offensive for May 17. Meantime, 78th Division would pick up the pace. Burns left it to Major General Chris Vokes to deploy 1 CID.[36] Vokes visited Major General Dudley Russell early on May 15 to hammer out the details of the takeover. Russell told Vokes that the enemy consisted primarily of remnants of the 44th German Infantry Division and that, with Pignataro in his hands, the relief should proceed smoothly. Vokes agreed, saying he would bring his division across the Gari River bridges on successive nights by brigades. The 1st Canadian Infantry Brigade was already on the move and would cross that very night to relieve 19th Indian Infantry Brigade. The following night, 3rd Canadian Infantry Brigade would relieve 21st Indian Infantry Brigade. Until 3 CIB completed the relief in its sector, the two brigades would be under Russell's command to ensure better control. Once the relief was complete, Vokes would take command, retaining one of Russell's brigades until 2nd Canadian Infantry

Brigade crossed into the bridgehead on the night of May 17–18. Before the meeting ended, Russell gave Vokes "a glowing account of the superlative tank support which had been given his troops by the 1st Canadian Armoured Brigade."[37]

While his meeting with Russell was taking place, two of Vokes's staff officers, Major George Rennison and Lieutenant David Dickie were reconnoitering a forward site for divisional headquarters near the Gari River. When the men finished, they were to join Vokes at Russell's HQ. After waiting for several hours, an impatient Vokes decided to leave without the two men, but just as he prepared to depart it was reported that their Jeep had blown up on an antitank mine. Dickie and a lance corporal from the Provost Company were dead and Rennison and the driver badly injured. As part of Vokes's personal team, all four men were close to him. For a few minutes, he was badly shaken. Then Vokes quickly submerged his grief and got back to business. He later wrote: "Thirteen thousand officers and men of my division were waiting to enter the Liri Valley and embark on offensive operations which might result in death and injury to several thousand of them. My one and only aim was to direct them in such a way the casualties could be kept to a minimum.

"I had learned in the hard school of experience in battle, one could not afford to grieve for lost comrades. One had to adopt the philosophy a man's fate is written the day he is born, and no amount of dodging can avoid it. If one is destined to die or suffer injury in war one must accept it and not worry about it.

"Without this personal philosophy I could not have carried on as a soldier in command of troops, knowing full well when they entered battle under my command the inevitable result in human sacrifice. War is a dirty business at the best of times and the whole object in battle is kill or be killed."[38]

◆ ◆ ◆

About the same time that Vokes was masking his emotions, Corporal Gwilym Jones of the Three Rivers Regiment was on a mission to recover the body of a fallen comrade, Wally Burnett. Staggering with exhaustion and the effects of the morphine dose, he led the two Stuarts in his patrol to where his friend had reportedly been killed. The Gurkhas, Jones discovered, had already buried Burnett wrapped in a blanket and interred standing straight up in accordance with their customs. Jones got permission from their commander to dis-inter Burnett and move him to a graveyard for Canadian dead. Most of the Canadians were being interred communally in a series of German bunkers, but Jones wanted Burnett buried apart. When his group set to work with their shovels, the blades just bounced off the solid rock. They resorted to using hand grenades to shatter the rock. Finally the hole looked deep enough and Jones went to fetch the Three Rivers' padre to lead the burial ceremony.

Jones returned shortly with the padre, who bent down and checked Burnett's identity disks. "*Un juif,*" he declared and said he would not bury a Jew. Jones saw his men were both tired and angry, even though most were French-Canadian and, like the padre, Roman Catholic. A dark rage descended on him. Drawing his revolver, Jones pointed it at the priest's chest. "Padre, you bury him or we'll bury you," he snapped. The padre quickly got down to business.

At dawn, Jones was summoned into the presence of Lieutenant Colonel Caron. When he arrived, the regimental sergeant major was jumping around as if he were on a hot griddle and demanded to know what the hell Jones had done. Jones told him drily what had occurred and the RSM escorted him inside without further word. In Caron's office, nobody asked that he remove his black tanker's beret so Jones kept it on, realizing he had not yet been placed on a charge. The padre was present, standing next to Caron, and so was Major Grey, the second-in-command. Given all the rankers present, things looked pretty serious.

Caron was blunt. He asked what had happened. Jones didn't sug-arcoat anything. He told what he had done and how the padre had prompted his action. Caron gave no sign of his frame of mind. He just told Jones to return to his tank. But as Jones was leaving, he heard Caron say to the padre, "I want to talk to you." Within hours, the padre vanished and nobody knew his fate. The French Canadians awarded Jones a nickname he thought praiseworthy: *Le Maudit Gallois* or The Welsh Devil. And rather than being punished, Jones soon received a promotion to troop sergeant.[39]

10

IT IS STIFF FIGHTING

In the early afternoon of May 15, Allied traffic rather than the Germans most impeded 1st Canadian Infantry Brigade's relief of 8th Indian Division's 19th Infantry Brigade. The original plan had called for the brigade's trucks to cross the Gari River on various bridges and then advance along the "Speedway" to the front lines. The Speedway was an old railroad bed, long stripped of rails and ties and so named because it followed an almost perfectly straight course with virtually no grade change and was bordered on either side by high embankments that provided excellent cover.[1] When it was discovered that this route was currently being used by a thousand trucks from the Corps Expéditionnaire Français, Brigadier Dan Spry was told his battalions would have to march forward on foot. Hasty protestations got that order rescinded and a series of secondary tracks was reserved for 1 CIB's use.[2]

To accelerate the crossing, 1st Field Company of the Royal Canadian Engineers began frantically deploying an eighty-foot Bailey bridge across the river. Although work started at 1430 hours, the many mines dug into the riverbanks and approaches hampered the operation. Clearing the mines was stressful, but so too was the grim task of removing dozens of badly decomposed dead Americans from the bridge's approaches. Still, at 1600 hours, Quebec Bridge was open for traffic and engineers from XIII Corps shortly launched another bridge for Canadian use.[3] As the trucks loaded with Canadian infantry approached the bridges, the riverfront was screened by smoke created by generator teams and artillery shoots to prevent the Germans' realizing that I Canadian Corps was joining the offensive. Providing armoured support to the brigade was 142nd Regiment, Royal Armoured Corps.[4]

Incredible congestion slowed the column to a crawl and sometimes left it gridlocked altogether. It seemed every vehicle in the Eighth and Fifth armies jockeyed for position on the few available roads. Despite the increasing number of bridges erected across the Gari River, there were still too few to meet demand. The many German minefields further channelled traffic into a restricted number of lanes. Riding in a Jeep, Lieutenant Colonel Ian Johnston led the 48th Highlanders of Canada Regiment's column. Just across the Gari, he came upon the Jeep from Major George Rennison's reconnaissance party. It had been blown cleanly in half, the two sections cast up onto the verges. Johnston determined that the explosion had occurred when Rennison's driver had tried to turn around and inadvertently rolled the front wheels off the narrow track. Still, as a safety measure, he deployed pioneers ahead of the column to sweep the road for mines. Johnston was saddened to learn the identities of the two officers killed in the Jeep explosion. Both Rennison and Lieutenant David Dickie were 48th Highlanders who had been seconded to divisional staff.[5]

That evening, the regiments finally arrived at their forward assembly areas, dismounted, and marched on foot to positions immediately to the rear of 19th Indian Infantry Brigade's front lines. The Royal Canadian Regiment was digging in at 1830 hours, the rest of the brigade in place by 2200 hours.[6] On reporting to 8th Indian Division's Major General Dudley Russell, Spry was told that, in the morning, offensive action would continue across a divisional front, rather than, as earlier planned, the RCR carring out a battalion-wide offensive independent of the rest of the division. Obviously, Russell thought the Germans opposing the division were ripe for pushing back on a far broader front than originally envisioned. Spry decided he would deploy the RCR with its left flank braced against the Liri River and the Hastings and Prince Edward Regiment on the right, based around Pignataro, with 21st Indian Brigade on its right flank. The 48th Highlanders would be in reserve.[7]

"The morale of our own troops," noted Lieutenant Gordon Potts, the RCR Intelligence Officer, "was particularly high. . . . All ranks were imbued with the desire to close with the enemy and had complete confidence in their own arms and supporting arms and had gone through several exercises in the area of Lucera with 'B' Squadron 142 Suffolk Tank Regiment."[8]

While 1 CIB's journey forward kept somewhat to schedule, such was not the case for 1st Canadian Infantry Division's headquarters unit or 3rd Canadian Infantry Brigade. The divisional headquarters' convoy left a position north of the Volturno River area. Because of heavy traffic on Highway 6, the column followed a long arcing route using secondary roads that finally linked up to the highway about thirty miles east of Cassino. The divisional war diarist, Captain S.P. Lachance, wrote at day's end that the column was three hours behind schedule when, at 1730 hours, the British Provost Officer controlling entry onto Highway 6 gave permission to use the road. "You've a clear road now; the route is signed, and your people are watching for you," he said.

The column set off, Lachance wrote, "smoothly up Highway 6, were waved smoothly past Mignano junction, and would probably have moved smoothly into Cassino if the [officer] leading the convoy had not begun to recognize, with some trepidation, the topography of the fighting front. So the convoy turned itself laboriously around in a mercifully opportune field, and finally got back to the Mignano junction, where the correct turn was taken and the Speedway entered on. HQ signs were seen a few hundred yards up this route, and — we had almost lost hope — we had arrived. Why signs were not up at the Mignano junction remains a mystery. Camp and Provost attest to having put them there during the morning. So somebody for his own reasons must have taken them down."[9]

Divisional headquarters' first task was to arrange for 3 CIB to close on the Gari River so that it could move into the front lines the following night. The brigade was waiting in the Vairano area for transport. Soon after setting up in the new headquarters area adjacent to the Speedway, divisional staff received a report from a Royal Army Service Corps corporal commanding three platoons of XIII Corps's General Transport Company. The corporal said his transports had just finished dumping 1 CIB forward and was "supposed to get on to some other job, but could not remember just what." Lachance wrote that, "We were busy and could not take care of him at the time, but promised to find out from Corps and cautioned him to stand by." An hour later, Lachance learned that the corporal's transport was supposed to fetch 3 CIB. "All search for the little corporal was without avail; he had taken our neglect to heart, and gone away, taking his three platoons with him. So only by Corps managing to borrow another three platoons from XIII Corps (not without mutual recriminations) were we finally able to get this brigade up."[10]

◆ ◆ ◆

At 0700 hours on May 16, about 100 men in 'D' Company of the Royal Canadian Regiment walked through the front line of 19th Indian Infantry Brigade and advanced warily up a narrow dirt track bordering the Liri River. While the river itself wound through a series of oxbows in this sector, the road carved a slow, straight curve across the Cassino-Pignataro lateral road's southern extension and on to Pontecorvo six miles westward. This town was situated immediately behind the Hitler Line, and was believed to be strongly fortified.

RCR commander Lieutenant Colonel Bill Mathers's plan for the day was simple. 'D' Company would lead with 'B' Company in train immediately behind, then 'A' Company, followed by his tactical headquarters, and 'C' Company after that. Travelling up the centre of the road in single file and well back from the leading troops was 'B' Squadron of 142 Suffolk Tank Regiment.[11] The single-file formation Mathers used was designed for speed, as most of the men and the Shermans could stick to the road rather than beating a path through the fairly rugged countryside, which was a mixture of oak groves, vineyards, and wheat fields. No serious opposition was expected. Eighth Army intelligence staff thought the Germans must be withdrawing into the defensive works of the Hitler Line. Their reasoning was entirely logical, for the German right flank south of the Liri River to the coast had collapsed in the face of heavy fighting during the past two days. San Giorgio a Liri, a little village bordering the foothills of the Aurunci Mountains, had fallen to the Corps Expéditionnaire Français on May 14.

The village was approximately one mile west of the RCR start point and the Première Division de Marche d'Infanterie had jumped off from its shot-up buildings on May 15 and was making good progress along the southern bank of the Liri River.[12] The 71st and 94th Infantry divisions, tasked with defending the line facing the French divisions, having suffered heavy casualties were reeling back in disarray, unable to slow the French long enough to form a coherent line.[13] Every principle of military strategy mandated that a general withdrawal to the Hitler Line must be under way. The RCR should face only light rear-guard opposition.

In two hours, 'D' Company marched freely west from the start point to the Pignataro–San Giorgio a Liri road (the extension of the Cassino–Pignataro lateral road). Then, just as the company crossed the road, heavy machine-gun and mortar positions dug in on a facing low hill opened fire. The company commander reacted by sending the leading platoon to flank the position but it was stopped when six men, including the platoon's lieutenant, were wounded. When another 'D' Company platoon tried outflanking the German gunners from the opposite side, it was pinned down. Mathers decided he had best reorganize and work out a more considered attack.

The low hill where the Germans were dug in was identified as Point 59 on the regiment's tactical map. 'D' Company dug in where it had come under fire and 'B' Company took up an adjacent position on its right flank. 'A' Company set up immediately behind 'D' Company, while 'C' Company remained as the battalion reserve. Mortars and antitank guns were brought up and dug in among the infantrymen. Because of the continuing heavy fire, the companies were not all set up in their positions until about 1300 hours. By then, Mathers had hammered out his plan of attack in consultation with Major Easton, commander of 'B' Squadron of the Suffolk Tanks, and Captain Dick Dillon, commander of 'A' Company, which was to carry out the main assault on Point 59. Since the tanks needed time to get organized, the attack was set for 1700 hours.[14] The RCR were to have advanced to the southern bank of the Forme d'Aquino, a narrow stream that passed through the village of Aquino and then followed a southeasterly course to join the Liri River about one-third of the way between Pignataro and the Hitler Line. That was a distance of about three miles; they had covered less than a mile of that before being stopped at Point 59. The prospects for any further advance on May 16, other than possibly taking the hill, were few.

◆ ◆ ◆

By the time the RCR ran into trouble, the Hastings and Prince Edward Regiment was closing on Pignataro with the objective of passing through the 8th Indian Division troops and advancing on a line to the north of the RCR. Lieutenant Colonel Don Cameron, only recently promoted to command, had been advised that his regiment should expect to meet light resistance almost immediately after it passed through Pignataro. As the regiment entered the village, it found that, despite reports to the contrary, the Germans were still in possession of some of the rubble heaps that had once been houses and that the Indian troops were rooting them out in fierce fighting. A stonk of mortar fire struck 'A' Company. Two men were killed and two wounded.

Deciding that he needed to know what the Germans had out front of Pignataro, Cameron sent Intelligence Officer Lieutenant J.J. Nayler to consult with the Indian battalion commander. Nayler garnered little information. The Indian battalion had been too busy taking Pignataro to patrol west of the village. Cameron sent 'A' Company past Pignataro with simple instructions to just "exploit and try to contact the enemy."[15] The rest of the regiment followed. About 600 yards past Pignataro, 'A' Company literally bumped into the Germans at a narrow little crossroads. A short, fierce firefight ensued. The regiment was also coming under heavy mortar fire and several self-propelled guns were lurking threateningly behind the German lines. Cameron ordered his other companies to sidestep left and then south to bypass this determined concentration, and after four or five hours of heavy fighting was able to force the Germans to withdraw by chipping away at their right flank.[16] As the Germans retreated, they were forced to move across open ground and the Hasty P's called in artillery that, the regiment's war diarist reported, "did much damage." The regiment also bagged seven prisoners, who were identified as soldiers from 576th Grenadier Regiment. At dusk, the regiment had advanced a mere 1,000 yards beyond the village, but its casualties had been extremely light and nobody had been killed, so the troops considered the day's effort sufficient.[17]

♦ ♦ ♦

RCR's 'A' Company attacked Point 59 at 1700 hours, with No. 8 Platoon commanded by Lieutenant Jack Morgan on the left and No. 7 Platoon under Lieutenant Geoff Wright on the right. No. 9 Platoon remained in reserve. With the tankers battering the hill with .75-millimetre high explosives, the two attacking platoons charged up the gradual slope. When the Canadians reached the crest, the Germans retired and about fifty surrendered. Approximately the same number had been killed or wounded. 'A' Company was soon receiving heavy machine-gun, mortar, and self-propelled gunfire from a position on its left near the Liri River.[18] Morgan's more exposed platoon was particularly hard hit. When the lieutenant charged one of the machine guns, he was cut down and killed. Lance Corporal R.E. Deadman stood defiantly in the open, braced a 2-inch mortar on his hip and, ignoring the punishing recoil, hammered one self-propelled gun with repeated rounds until he knocked it out.

When 'C' Company attempted to reinforce 'A' Company, it was pinned down by heavy fire. Mathers ordered 'A' Company to withdraw from Point 59. As the men fell back, Private S. Johnston covered the withdrawal with measured bursts from his Bren gun and then scurried to join the rest of the company at its start position. The RCR had lost twelve dead and about twenty wounded. Even the companies back of the firefight had not escaped unscathed. 'D' Company lost one of its bravest, most aggressive men, on Point 59 — Sergeant R.J. Boone, who had joined the regiment in 1939. Also killed was Lieutenant H.D. Irving.[19] Wright was awarded a Military Cross and Deadman the Military Medal.[20] German shelling of the RCR position continued and several more casualties resulted. A six-pounder anti-tank gun and an ammunition truck bringing up supplies were both destroyed by direct hits. Mathers decided his men should dig in where they were rather than attempt to move up on the hill, which appeared still unoccupied by the enemy.

Both the RCR and Hasty P's sent out patrols to establish contact with each other and to determine how wide a gap existed between them. A small Hasty P patrol reported to the RCR that they had seen about 200 Germans falling back from Point 59.[21] An attempt to establish links with the French across the Liri River was forced back when the RCR patrol stumbled into a minefield. Two of the men were killed and the patrol leader, Lance Corporal Scott, was wounded.

The disposition of German forces in the area remained so uncertain that Lieutenant D.L. Lawrence, assigned as the RCR liaison officer to 1 CIB headquarters, drove his Jeep directly into a German machine-gun position while trying to reach the Hasty P's position. He was killed.[22] A short time after dusk, the 48th Highlanders of Canada's padre, Captain Stewart East, was searching for his battalion aboard an ambulance Jeep driven by Private Eddie Harrison. Stretcher-bearer Private Frank Murphy was also aboard. After bumping across country, the party found the road running up to Pontecorvo, but there was no sign of any Canadians and the padre wondered if they were too far west. Dismounting and going ahead on foot, East found a dead RCR officer sitting behind the wheel of a Jeep. The bullet holes in the man's body were still oozing blood. The padre realized he was behind enemy lines; otherwise the corpse would have been removed to a collection point.

Fetching the rest of his party, East and Murphy loaded the dead officer onto a stretcher and into the Jeep. Murphy made space for the body by sitting on the Jeep's hood and Harrison started turning around to head back toward the Canadian lines. Suddenly Murphy shouted, "Mines!" The Jeep was in the middle of a cluster of Teller antitank mines. After working their way slowly around these the party crept down the road at a pace that allowed Murphy to spot the detonators of other mines. After driving about half a mile, East's group suddenly came across the leading platoons of the Highlanders' 'B' Company, which had been ordered forward to plug the gap between the RCR and the Hasty P's. One of these platoons, seeking to contact the Hasty P's on the right, startled a machine-gunner from that regiment. The man ripped off a burst and Lieutenant Jock Mayne fell dead. That morning a letter had informed Mayne that he was the father of a baby girl born on April 22.[23]

♦ ♦ ♦

Although resistance had been unexpectedly strong, the two leading battalions had been sluggish, a point noted by General Sir Oliver

Leese. He informed Burns that the debut of I Canadian Corps in the Liri Valley battle had been inauspicious. Burns duly fired off a note to Vokes. Leese, Burns wrote, "is disappointed that no greater progress was made in the face of quite light opposition and is very urgent that a determined advance should be made tomorrow.

"The French have progressed very quickly as far as Esperia and your left flank is therefore quite secure. The weight of the enemy's reserves have been put in against 78 Division who are attacking tomorrow in conjunction with the Poles. According to the Army commander's information there is little immediately facing you to the west.

"Your task for tomorrow, the 17th, is to advance towards the Hitler Line and it is most important that you send your brigades forward with great determination."[24]

The French were about three miles further west than the Canadians, so it was true that 1 CIB's left flank was secure. To the north, British 78th Division had cracked through the Gustav Line immediately south of Cassino. The division's 12th Brigade was on the verge of severing Highway 6 west of the town, which would cut off the paratroopers defending Cassino. In the morning, the 78th would drive toward Aquino and Piedmonte, in an attempt to outflank Monte Cassino, II Polish Corps would assault the Abbey, and the 78th's 10th Infantry Brigade would clear the town of Cassino.[25] These attacks should, Leese thought, so stretch German reserves that the Canadians would face only an easily swept-aside screening force.

Intelligence staff at I Canadian Corps knew the Germans facing the Canadian front were a grab-bag of units commanded by the 2nd Battalion, 576th Grenadier Regiment of 305th Infantry Division. Present were other battalions from the 305th, three companies of 15th Panzer Grenadier Division's 115th Grenadier Regiment, three companies of 44th Infantry Division's 80th Engineer Battalion, two companies of 90th Panzer Grenadier Division's 190th Engineer Battalion, and a company of antitank gunners from 5th Mountain Division. All these units were considered tired and depleted by casualties. However, disturbingly, some prisoners taken during the day were members of the 361st Grenadier Regiment, 90th Panzer Grenadier Division — a division previously believed held in reserve well behind the front lines.

The Canadian Intelligence Officer also noted that things around Cassino were not normal. In his daily report, he wrote, "A fire burns on Monastery Hill [Monte Cassino], the enemy put down smoke at last light and has mortared the Continental Hotel [a major building in Cassino] — all very strange at this time." This action, he wrote, "may have been a covering for the withdrawal from the town, for Route 6 must be held if the Monastery force is to be got out." Contradicting Leese, he predicted the Canadians would face determined resistance, as the 90th deployed its infantry regiments and inherent three troops of assault guns, two troops of tanks, and various antitank companies across the Canadian front.[26]

◆ ◆ ◆

While the Canadian Intelligence Officer at I Canadian Corps speculated on a possible withdrawal of the 1st Parachute Division from Cassino and the abbey, Commander-in-Chief Southwest Generalfeldmarschall Albert Kesselring finally accepted the inevitability of surrendering these two remaining bastions of the Gustav Line. That evening, he discussed the situation by phone with Tenth Army commander Generaloberst Heinrich von Vietinghoff. "I consider withdrawal to the Senger position as necessary," Kesselring said.

Von Vietinghoff replied, "Then it will be necessary to begin the withdrawal north of the Liri. Tanks have broken through there."

"How far?"

Two miles northwest of Pignataro, von Vietinghoff said. There were another hundred tanks reportedly closing on Highway 6.

Kesselring sighed. "Then we have to give up Cassino." To which von Vietinghoff offered only one word. "Yes."[27]

Having made his decision, Kesselring had to get the withdrawal started. First Parachute Division was without question one of the most determined and well-led units in Italy. Its commander was General Richard Heidrich. Known as "Papa Heidrich" to his men, he bore a startling resemblance to Winston Churchill and shared the same taste for cigars. Heidrich was independent-minded and his troops would follow him anywhere. They had duly followed him into the hell of Cassino and Monte Cassino and had held those positions against overwhelming odds far longer than even Kesselring had truly expected. When Heidrich received orders to effect a withdrawal, he was not inclined to obey. Kesselring later wrote that "1st Parachute Division did not dream of surrendering 'its' Monte Cassino. In order to maintain contact with the 14th Panzer Corps I had personally to order these last, recalcitrant as they were, to retire, an example of the drawback of having strong personalities as subordinate commanders." Kesselring realized that the paratroops would obey his orders but that their withdrawal would be grudgingly slow, as they would not allow the Allies to consider them beaten. Such a withdrawal would force Kesselring to order XIV Panzer Corps defending the Liri Valley to "cling to the intermediate positions longer than seemed advisable in the tactical situation."[28]

◆ ◆ ◆

Having spent most of May 15 and 16 overcoming transportation shortages and fighting its way forward through seemingly endless traffic jams, 3rd Canadian Infantry Brigade finally approached the front lines. "Just as dusk was descending in the smoky battle scarred Liri Valley," wrote Carleton and York Regiment's war diarist, Major J.P. Ensor, "the men once again took their place in the line, relieving the short, tough, dusky fighters of a Maharatta battalion in the 8th Indian Division. . . . The ruined remains of Pignataro were a mile or two beyond and San Angelo a similar distance behind, but our task was clear: contain and destroy as great a force of the enemy as possible and push on to ROME.

"The first night in a new area is always weird and creates an uneasy feeling in one's mind. Our position as forward right battalion of the division hardly tended to ease matters, particularly with an enemy so active with artillery, mortars, Moaning Minnies, flares, and indiscriminate firing of MGs."[29]

About the same time Ensor recorded his impressions, the Royal 22e Regiment's war diarist wrote: "At about 1700 hours this evening Royal 22e Regiment arrives in an area just south of Cassino. The main defences of the German Gustav line in this sector have already been breached by Indian Troops from whom we are taking over. Our unit takes over from the 3rd Battalion, 15 Punjab Regiment. To our right are troops of the British 78th Division. Beyond them stands Monte Cassino, on top of which, one can just make out the outline of the Monastery, famed German bastion of the Gustav Line, still firmly and stubbornly held by enemy paratroops. On our left are units of 1st Canadian Infantry Brigade, and beyond them in the mountains there, is the French Expeditionary Corps, now well on its way toward the Hitler Line."[30]

The West Nova Scotia Regiment's war diarist recorded that heavy mortaring and shelling of the battlefield delayed the regiments in finding and relieving their 8th Indian counterparts. However, the relief was completed by 2100 hours. "Morale," he wrote, "was high and everyone in good spirits at the thought of really getting going again after the long weary winter months on the Ortona front."[31]

Vokes, having been urged to haste, wasted no time letting 3 CIB's regiments settle. He called an Orders Group at 2300 hours and issued orders for a dawn advance. Vokes told 3 CIB Brigadier Paul Bernatchez that at first light his three battalions would advance in leapfrog fashion from their position in front of Pignataro to a height of ground overlooking the Forme d'Aquino. Meanwhile, Spry's 1 CIB would press forward, with the 48th Highlanders passing from reserve into the attack between the RCR and Hasty P's. Supporting 3 CIB would be the Three Rivers Regiment of 1st Canadian Armoured Brigade, as the 51st Tank Regiment of the 25th Tank Brigade could not reach the battle area in time for the dawn attack.[32]

Unrecognized in Vokes's plan of attack was Spalla Bassa, an apparently insignificant physical feature. This small catchment stream flowed out of a gentle rise of land situated to the west and north of Pignataro. The stream followed an easterly arc from its source to where it drained into the Liri River, close to a blown bridge that had linked Pignataro to San Giorgio a Liri. At this time of year, the streambed was dry and in places it narrowed to little more than a deep ditch that a man could jump over. Elsewhere, however, it was relatively wide, deep, and steeply banked, so that it formed a natural tank barrier.[33] This feature was not as significant as the infamous "Gully" before Ortona that had cost 1 CID so many lives during the December fighting. Yet, although Spalla Bassa was more clearly marked on maps than had been The Gully, divisional intelligence staff completely overlooked the potential hazard it presented.

Such an oversight undoubtedly occurred in part because of the unreliability of the maps used in Italy, a problem that had plagued operations during the Moro River and Ortona battles. While the army drafted and released relevant maps prepared by the British War Office's Geographical Section, it used Italian military maps as a base. These maps were often in error. In this case, however, the stream was clearly indicated on Sheet 160 of the 1:100,000-scale map as only slightly less wide in most places than the more westerly Forme d'Aquino.[34] Even the maps prepared by Eighth Army for the specific use of the armoured formations showed Spalla Bassa clearly enough that its defensive features should have been appreciated. The Armoured Formation map — drawn to a scale of 1:50,000 — detailed the Liri Valley from the Gari River to a point west of Ceprano. In the area of this little creek, the map also indicated that the Germans had constructed on either side of its bank numerous antitank defences, with an especially heavy concentration situated in the area through which the 48th Highlanders would advance.[35]

The Canadians — particularly the 48th Highlanders and the Hasty P's — would go into the morning's attack with only the vaguest knowledge of the terrain or possible defences facing them. They would do so with little artillery support, and no engineers on hand to bridge the stream so that tanks could cross. There was no time for reconnaissance patrols to probe and test the German positions. On the right flank, 3 CIB was barely settled in and would attack at dawn. Meanwhile, 1 CIB was still licking its wounds from the day's fighting and trying to get its battalions into a consistent line that would enable the attack to proceed in the morning along a continuous front.

For his part, Leese expressed uneasy optimism for May 17 in a letter to his wife Margaret. "A good day in our battle — and tomorrow we have another big attack, which with a bit of luck, may lead to the capture of Cassino and the Monastery — it would be wonderful if this came off. This, together with our crossing of the [Gari], would be a great start for the new 8th Army. It is stiff fighting in the Liri Valley, as it is difficult country. He has plenty of troops and it is difficult to outflank him."[36] The new Eighth Army to which Leese referred was really not new, other than being engaged in battle for the first time with himself as army commander. In this and other letters written to his wife in early May, Leese made it clear that he feared this first major engagement might not end in a decisive Eighth Army victory that would confirm his ability and right to the command.

11

THE FOG
OF WAR

Lieutenant Colonel Jean Allard was honoured to command the Royal 22e Regiment, nicknamed the Van Doos. Today, the thirty-one-year-old officer knew the regiment would face its severest test since he had taken command at the end of December 1943. Allard, however, expected the day would go well because he believed his to be the finest regiment ever raised. One of three Permanent Force regiments in Italy, R22eR traced its roots back to World War I, when it had become the first all-francophone regiment in the Canadian army.

Although Québécois and commissioned in 1933, Allard had never previously served in a French-Canadian regiment. To understand how francophone soldiers differed from other Canadians under arms, he had spent hours with officers and common soldiers alike. They came, he noted, from "Gaspé, Acadia, the Lower St. Lawrence, the Saguenay, Quebec, Trois-Rivières, St. Maurice, Ottawa, Hull, Manitoba, Edmonton, and Montreal. Their backgrounds and education were different; all they had in common were their names and their language. Yet they all acted like brothers."

The Van Doos approached discipline differently from other

Commonwealth regiments. "The famous English 'spit and polish' made our boys laugh, although they applied it as well as their counterparts, but without the degree of seriousness they felt they saw in their English-speaking neighbours. If one of our men appeared to be slacking off a little too much, officers rarely shouted at him. We tended to use ridicule instead: the fellow would soon feel isolated and his 'regimental pride' would bring him back into line. . . . The language that best expressed this spirit was, of course, the French of Canada, as understood by the boy from the Gaspé and the Albertan alike."

Allard enjoyed commanding these men, "for their dedication and pride were written on their faces. The price of this pride in command was the loyalty that the men expected of their officers. We were perceived by the troops not as aristocrats or the rightful possessors of all wisdom and authority. Rather, the officers were chosen from among the men because they had the same spirit and the ability and courage to refuse meaningless adventures and to embark upon only those actions, regardless of the risks involved, in which they themselves were prepared to participate. This willingness on the part of the officers to share everything and to command by example created a unity of spirit which was the strength of the R22eR."[1]

Among his officers was twenty-nine-year-old Captain Pierre Potvin, who commanded 'B' Company. Potvin had grown up enchanted by the Van Doos, never missing a chance to watch when they paraded out of The Citadel in Quebec City. He had gobbled up everything there was to read about their history, particularly the battles in which they had fought during the Great War. Ypres, Mount Sorrel, the Somme, Ancre Heights, Vimy, Hill 70, Passchendaele, and Amiens were common tales to him. When the war broke out, Potvin enlisted, but as the R22e Regiment was Permanent Force and up to strength there was no place for him there. So he joined the Voltigeurs de Québec, rising to the rank of captain. The Voltigeurs, however, were detailed to guard armouries at home; Potvin wanted to see the sharp end. At the price of a demotion to subaltern rank, he gained acceptance into the Van Doos.

Joining the regiment in Britain, he laboured to prove himself worthy of a commission in a regular force regiment. He forfeited weekend leaves, using the time to pore over training pamphlets and books that would increase his knowledge and proficiency. Potvin trained his platoon equally hard, wanting them to be the best of the best. His diligence paid off when the platoon won a ten-mile race in full battle dress and bearing weapons. The platoon was rewarded with three days' leave in London. Potvin left the books behind and joined his men in the city.

In Sicily, Potvin had risen to command 'B' Company after its captain was wounded. He also won the Military Cross for carrying out a one-man charge against a German machine-gun position. Since then, he had led 'B' Company through many battles and was among the regiment's officers with the longest time served in action.[2]

At the Orders Group held at 1900 hours on May 16, Allard reported that the Van Doos would lead 3rd Canadian Infantry Brigade's morning assault, with 'D' Company under Major Ovila Garceau on the left and Captain Henri Tellier's 'A' Company on the right. 'B' and 'C' Company would follow. Because 'A' was expected to face stiffer opposition, Three Rivers Regiment's 'A' Squadron would support it with tanks. A fifteen-minute artillery barrage starting at 0630 hours would hammer the regiment's two objectives — two points of high ground halfway between the start line and the Forme d'Aquino. Once these objectives were taken, 'C' and 'B' companies would lead toward the next objective, another point of high ground closer to the river.[3] When this objective was secure, the West Nova Scotia Regiment would pass through. Eventually, the Carleton and York Regiment would leapfrog through the West Novas to maintain the momentum.[4]

◆ ◆ ◆

As the artillery fell silent at 0630 hours, the leading companies advanced across the Cassino-Pignataro road. Not far behind followed Potvin's 'B' Company and 'C' Company, commanded by Major Charles Bellavance. German fire was intense, but the standard pea-soup fog lying low upon the ground forced the enemy gunners to fire blind. The Van Doos ignored the fire. From a position near the attack's start point, Three Rivers Regiment Intelligence Officer Captain Horace Dugald Beach thought it "thrilling to see the battle-wise Van Doos march straight forward, spread out and half crouching. They never dug in — but the enemy did come out when presented with this array of marching men and rumbling tanks who never paused."[5]

While some Germans surrendered the moment the Canadians approached, many fought. Potvin passed two disabled Shermans; one stuck in mud, the other with a broken track. He could hear Garceau's 'D' Company tangling with some German machine guns, but from the sound he could tell the company was still moving up. Potvin's company reached 'D' Company's objective only to discover that Garceau's men had kept going rather than pausing to allow his company to leapfrog through. It was obvious that the Canadian attack had caught the Germans by surprise. The ground was cluttered with cooking pots containing warm food, as if the Germans had been just about to sit down to breakfast when the shelling started. Two Germans lay amid the debris, one with a profusely bleeding leg wound and the other with a hole in his abdomen from which a jet of blood shot every time he breathed. With the fog beginning to burn off, Potvin looked back toward the start line and saw Allard and Bernatchez standing on the balcony of a deserted house, observing the advance through binoculars. German shells were exploding around the house, but both men seemed oblivious to the danger. Potvin's men let out a cheer as they witnessed the "coolness of their chiefs under fire."[6]

On the hill's reverse slope, dead or wounded soldiers lay scattered about in weapon pits. Heavy machine guns, several Nebelwerfers, many rifles, and large stocks of ammunition lay abandoned on the field. With all the booty available, Potvin had to chide his men to leave things alone; this was no time for souvenir gathering. At any moment Potvin expected the 361st Grenadier Regiment's Panzer Grenadiers to counterattack. He could not afford to lose control of his men.

Potvin was surprised to encounter the tanks that were supposed to be supporting Tellier's 'A' Company. These had become separated from the infantry when they had to swing wide to get around a muddy ditch, where one had become stuck. The crews of the other two tanks agreed to accompany his men. Although 'A' and 'D' were still far ahead, the two following companies were bumping into numerous pockets of machine-gun and rifle positions bypassed by the leading troops. Once they left the hill behind, Potvin's men dropped back into thick fog. Supported by the tanks, he and his men mopped up points of resistance. In most cases, when the men and tanks suddenly erupted out of the fog into their midst the Germans fled and the Van Doos, firing from the hip, rushed on to prevent their stopping to form any organized defence.[7]

It was a chaotic, wild, charging battle that the officers barely controlled. Platoons and individual sections fought in isolation. Potvin found it difficult in the fog to maintain direction and retain contact with the tanks, resulting in "the battle-crazed infantry fighting like hell without tank support, while the tanks suffered the same fate, having to fight it out without infantry protection. In sum, not what the Book teaches. The Fog of War!" In the middle of this confusion, Potvin heard Tellier on the radio calling for his tanks. Having driven far ahead of the assigned objectives, 'A' Company was now pinned down in a murderous crossfire. Advancing in an arrowhead formation when it ran into the ambush, the platoons were badly separated and each now fought alone.

On the left, Lieutenant Alfred Letarte slowly advanced No. 8 Platoon forward until opposing fire suddenly escalated and a burst struck the officer and killed him. Sergeant J.P. LePage immediately took over the platoon and continued the advance. Meanwhile, No. 7 and No. 9 platoons also encountered stiff resistance. When No. 9 Platoon tried advancing up a narrow road, it ran into a strong enemy section guarding a crossroad and a wild hand-to-hand melee ensued. Lance Sergeant J.F. Blanchette and his platoon commander, Lieutenant L.A.R. Des Rosiers, leapfrogged from one point of cover to another to close on the enemy trench line. When they were only feet away, Des Rosiers and Blanchette plunged into the trench together and quickly knocked out two machine guns, capturing the crews. Des Rosiers, now aided by Corporal J.F. Appleby, rushed along the trench line while Blanchette took charge of the platoon and brought covering fire to bear. German resistance suddenly collapsed when Appleby knocked out another machine gun. No. 9 Platoon dug in and soon No. 7 Platoon, under Lieutenant R. Dusseault, set up on its right flank. In hard fighting, this platoon had suffered six casualties, but had a half dozen prisoners in tow.

When an attempt to establish contact with No. 8 Platoon was made, heavy mortar fire caught the small patrol in the open. Lance Corporal F.T.D. Viau was killed and three men were wounded. Company Sergeant Major B. Michaud, attempting to go to the aid of the wounded men, was himself wounded. Without tank support, it was obvious the rest of 'A' Company could not reach No. 8 Platoon and LePage could not withdraw his men from their embattled position.[8]

Back on the hill, Potvin had his map out and was frantically trying to figure out from Tellier's radio pleas where 'A' Company was so he could send the tanks to its relief. Just then, three wounded men from Tellier's company escorted about ten German prisoners into Potvin's position. Potvin later wrote that, "One volunteers to guide the lost tanks back to the company, despite his wounds! This brave lad, who seems not to give a darn about bullets and shells flying about, jumps on the rear deck of a tank and points out the direction to the tank commander. They are on their way to 'A' Company."[9] The time was 0830 hours and the tanks reached Tellier twelve minutes later. Tellier's men, supported by the tanks, quickly outflanked the German machine-gunners and at 0908 hours reported being in control of the situation. The company had suffered twenty-five casualties, almost one-quarter of its full strength.[10]

Potvin continued leading his company toward its assigned objective, coming across the body of Lieutenant Alfred Letarte of 'A' Company en route. Just past the dead officer, Potvin's leading platoon came under machine-gun fire. The Van Doos responded with a hail of small-arms fire and Lieutenant R.L. St.-Onge led his platoon out to one flank and struck the Germans from behind. About a dozen Panzer Grenadiers surrendered. When Potvin brought the rest of the company up, he found a dead German officer in the gun position. Lying beside his body was a briefcase containing maps and documents. Potvin closed the briefcase and carried it with him. When two soldiers from 'D' Company came back with several German prisoners, Potvin turned his company's prisoners and the briefcase over to them with instructions to see that the documents reached Allard. Soon 'B' Company was on its objective and the men started digging in. About ten minutes later, however, the sound of a German half-track personnel carrier was heard coming up a road toward them. St.-Onge's platoon opened fire on the approaching vehicle, while a two-man PIAT team slipped into brush at a bend in the road. When the half-track approached the team, they fired a round into its tracks. The vehicle spun around and crashed into the ditch. Two dazed Germans staggered out of the wreck and were taken prisoner.[11]

♦ ♦ ♦

With R22e Regiment's objectives now secured, the West Nova Scotia Regiment jumped through the Van Doos' positions, continuing 3 CIB's advance. As had been the case with the Van Doos, the West Novas' attack formation had 'A' and 'D' companies in the lead with 'B' and 'C' following close behind. Since Major W.C. Allan had been wounded when the regiment was caught by German counter-artillery fire just before the attack, command of 'B' Company had devolved to Lieutenant R.N. Knowles. As soon as the leading companies set out, they started accepting the surrender of German soldiers who came out of well-concealed holes yelling, "*Kamerad*, Tommy." A few small groups, mostly those dug into the shell-battered farmhouses, offered a fight, but they were overrun or blasted out of their positions by the tanks of 'C' Squadron, Three Rivers Regiment. Surrounding the small wheat fields were densely leafed trees in which the Germans had scattered snipers. These harassed the West Novas' advance, but failed to slow it. The main opposition the regiment faced was increasingly heavy mortar and artillery fire.[12]

Disrupting the advance far more than the Germans were the poor maps, which little reflected the actual terrain. What were supposed to be open fields were in reality choked by a maze of oak stands, olive groves, vineyards, and thickets of brambles. Maintaining a coherent line became impossible and companies were soon badly separated. 'D' Company's No. 16 Platoon on the far right flank drifted so far off course that it finally blundered into the left-hand flank of the British 78th Division.[13]

About 300 yards from the start line, the advancing troops bumped into the headwaters of Spalla Bassa. 'C' Squadron's tanks had been charging ahead so recklessly that several had already managed to sink into pockets of bog. Now several more plunged into the creek and were hopelessly mired. Only seven tanks eventually found a crossing and set off after the infantry, which had already disappeared into the thick brush beyond.[14]

Worried about the fate of 'D' Company, which seemed to have strayed far from its objective and might have even overshot it, West Novas commander Lieutenant Colonel Ron Waterman ordered the regiment's scouts and snipers under Captain D.I. Rice to find it. He sent the carrier platoon under Lieutenant C.H. Smith, meanwhile, to secure the small knoll that was 'D' Company's objective. Leaving their Bren carriers behind, the platoon advanced on foot up a rough cart track and reached the knoll without meeting resistance. On top of the objective stood several farm buildings, which the men rushed. Smith burst into one house with his revolver drawn and caught a machine-gun crew completely by surprise. He accepted their surrender, noting that one soldier was even in the middle of having a shave. Several other machine-gun teams were found in dugouts constructed under the buildings. These also surrendered without firing a shot. Rice's scouts and snipers came in a few minutes later, having seen nothing of the lost company.[15] Shortly thereafter, however, Captain J.K. (Dusty) Rhodes led the two 'D' Company platoons that were still with him onto the objective from the west. In their haste to keep pursuing the Germans, they had not only overshot their destination but had also charged into the middle of a friendly artillery barrage. Luckily the barrage, intended to soften up the forward ground in preparation for the scheduled leapfrog by the Carleton and York Regiment, had failed to inflict any casualties on the hapless company.[16]

Although the West Novas' attack had been fairly confused, it had succeeded beyond 3 CIB commander Brigadier Paul Bernatchez's expectations. He noted that the regiment "went for the enemy like wildcats."[17] Showing almost careless disregard for their own safety, the men had rolled right over the German opposition. Many wounded soldiers refused to leave their units. A shell knocked Corporal D.K. Carroll unconscious and tore his uniform to tatters, but on waking up he calmly rejoined his platoon and continued the fight. Waterman boosted the élan of his men by roaring around on the battlefield in a Jeep equipped with a sandbagged floor to blunt the effect of any mine he might encounter. Driving the Jeep himself, Waterman raced back and forth between companies, urging them on and helping the commanders determine their bearings. Minutes after 'A' Company reached its objective, Waterman pulled up in his Jeep with Bernatchez in the passenger seat. As German machine-gun fire zipped over their heads, the two officers calmly consulted a map to determine if this was the spot from which the Carleton and York Regiment should continue the brigade attack.[18]

At 1700 hours, the Carleton and York Regiment passed through the West Novas with orders to reach the eastern bank of the Forme d'Aquino and establish a bridgehead on the other side. Supporting the regiment was Three Rivers' 'B' Squadron. By this time, the opposing Panzer Grenadiers were so disorganized and worn down by casualties and men captured that they offered only the slightest resistance, most just melting away as the Canadians approached. By 1900 hours, the three leading companies were on their objectives overlooking the deep gully of the Forme d'Aquino in which a shallow flow of water moved sluggishly. Carleton and York commander Lieutenant Colonel Dick Danby ordered 'C' and 'D' companies to get across the gully and establish a firm bridgehead on the other side. Under cover of darkness, the two companies descended into the gully, splashed across the stream, and climbed the other bank. After moving a short distance forward, they dug in to wait for morning.[19]

In one day's determined fighting, 3 CIB had punched a hole almost six miles into the German line. Things had not, however, gone equally well for either 1st Canadian Infantry Brigade on its left or 78th British Division on the right. Both lagged well behind 3 CIB, leaving its flanks exposed.

♦ ♦ ♦

On 3 CIB's left flank, 1 CIB had attacked with a two-battalion-wide advance. The 48th Highlanders of Canada were on the left, with the Hastings and Prince Edward Regiment on the right. The Hasty P's jumped off at 0800 hours with 'C' Company leading, followed in line by 'B' Company, the battalion headquarters, 'A' Company, and 'D' Company. Problems with radio communications between the companies and commander Lieutenant Colonel Don Cameron resulted in 'D' Company's losing its way and straying off to the right. It eventually blundered into the 48th Highlanders and remained on that battalion's right flank for the rest of the day.

'C' Company, commanded by Captain R.A. Danude, advanced aggressively, brushing aside the light resistance it met, and was soon well ahead of the rest of the battalion. When Danude's company reached the edge of the gully through which Spalla Bassa flowed, he paused to let everyone else catch up. 'B' Company arrived and crossed the gully to anchor a position on the opposite side, but immediately German fire struck both its flanks and front. 'C' Company, which by now had also crossed the gully, came under intense fire in precisely the same manner. The Hasty P's faced a dense, deep stand of trees. What the regiment would soon dub "The Battle of the Woods" was under way and it was as sharp an action as the Ontario men had ever fought.

The firefight broke out at 1000 hours and continued unabated for the next four hours, with the regiment winning only minimal gains against determined and well-positioned machine-gun and small-arms opposition. Mortar fire was heavy and frighteningly accurate. When Lieutenant N.J. Duder's platoon from 'C' Company tried to close on several machine-gun positions, he was shot in the shoulder and arm. Captain Danude radioed Cameron that 'C' Company was in imminent danger of being cut off from the rest of the battalion. Meanwhile, Major F.J. Hammond's 'B' Company was forced to go to ground, neither able to move to 'C' Company's assistance nor with-draw. Cameron ordered Danude to pull his people back to the eastern side of Spalla Bassa and consolidate there. He then advanced 'A' Company up on its flank and established his battalion headquarters immediately behind that company. The persistent mortaring had killed four men and shrapnel had wounded Lieutenant B.A.C. Caldwell of 'B' Company.[20]

At 1400 hours, mortar and artillery fire was brought down on the German positions despite 'B' Company's being intermingled with them. Before the concentration arrived, Hammond ordered his men to dig in deep so that only a direct hit on a slit trench might inflict friendly casualties. The firing had the desired effect. Hammond told Cameron on the radio that his men were fine and he could see German troops running to the rear. Hammond's men gave chase. By 1700 hours, he reported that the Panzer Grenadiers had completely evacuated the position. Two hours later, the rest of the battalion was over the gully and digging in for the night. The price for winning a crossing over Spalla Bassa was high. The Hasty P's had lost seven men killed and thirty wounded. They captured six prisoners and killed about thirty Germans.[21]

Cameron believed the regiment could have performed better had it had more training in close-quarters combat and had there been "more aggressiveness on the part of junior leaders." He said: "There is always a hesitancy on the part of our infantryman when fired on, particularly by an MG34 or 42 to lie doggo and do nothing about it and for some time Jerry happened to have the initiative. Such fire must be returned with interest — and promptly. It shuts him off, then men are more easily encouraged to 'Close with him.'"[22]

While the Hasty P's were engaged in the Battle of the Woods, the 48th Highlanders had faced a stiff fight too. From the outset, the Highlanders' plan was mired in confusion. Having moved forward in darkness to fill a gap between the Hasty P's and the Royal Canadian Regiment on the brigade's left flank, the Highlanders had only the sketchiest sense of where the front line was situated and had never managed to contact the RCR. When Brigadier Dan Spry issued written instructions after midnight to Highlanders commander Lieutenant Colonel Ian Johnston that his battalion was to advance on the left of the Hasty P's, Johnston was uncertain whether he could implement the order without risking a friendly-fire situation between his battalion and the RCR. At 0300 hours, Johnston asked for clarification, but confirmation of his orders did not arrive until 0700 hours. The attack was consequently delayed, not getting under way until a half-hour after the Hasty P's moved out.

Still worrying about the location of the RCR, Johnston personally took the lead, moving cautiously forward. Finally, he encountered an RCR scout who reported that the battalion had moved during the night to a position behind his own regiment. The Highlanders were already in enemy territory. On the spot, Johnston quickly threw together an operational plan that called for 'D' Company to lead, followed by 'C' Company, then 'A', and finally 'B.' Each company had support from either a troop of British Churchills or Shermans. Johnston placed his regimental tactical headquarters immediately behind the leading company.

Major Jim Counsell's 'D' Company set off with two platoons out front, moving up opposite sides of the road running from the Pignataro–San Giorgio a Liri lateral to Pontecorvo. To their right, a low ridge overlooked the advancing troops and Johnston had warned Major Ed Rawlings of 'C' Company to be prepared to sweep up onto this ridge at the first sign of any German activity there. All progressed smoothly until 'D' Company, which was passing through a field of two-foot-high grain, came under fire from machine guns positioned inside two houses bracketing the road. The two leading platoons attacked, the men plunging off the road and then slithering forward in a crouch through the grain. Lieutenant Norm Ballard, a divinity student before the war, rushed No. 16 Platoon toward the house on the left side of the road. In a quick fight, they captured two antitank guns and one armoured fighting vehicle, killed nine Germans, and took thirty prisoners. On the right side of the road, No. 17 Platoon under Lieutenant Doug Snively overran another two antitank guns, killed eight Panzer Grenadiers, and captured another seven. Both platoons pressed on despite having lost radio contact with Counsell and their supporting tanks.

Meanwhile, Johnston had joined Counsell and 'D' Company's reserve platoon in the shelter of a small gully. The two officers waited there for word on the outcome of the battle for the houses. For their part, the tankers of 'C' Squadron 142nd Royal Tank Regiment had lost sight of the Canadians the moment they dived into the grain and could establish radio contact with neither the platoon commanders nor Counsell.

The squadron of tanks moved out on the right side of the road and advanced on its own toward the houses, but tumbled into a German position missed by Snively's platoon during its charge. The first the tankers knew of their danger was when a Panzer Grenadier popped up out of the grain and threw a grenade into the open turret of the commander's tank. The explosion wounded the troop commander and jammed the turret in place. The Churchill hastily turned around and the entire squadron fled for safety.

Seeing the retreating tanks, Johnston ordered Counsell to take his reserve platoon and catch up to the rest of his men. He then sent 'C' Company to take out the Germans who had ambushed the tanks and clear the ridge overlooking the road. The German ambush position proved a formidable one, with Panzer Grenadiers dug in on the high ground on either side of a narrow gully through which Spalla Bassa flowed. As usual, the Grenadiers were well equipped with MG42 machine guns. Rawlings decided to move his men up the right side. Somehow his intentions were misconstrued by the tank troop supporting him. It crossed the narrow stream at a low point and set off up the left-hand slope.[23] With 152-millimetre-thick frontal armour, the Churchills weighed thirty-nine tons and had a lumbering top speed of just 15.5 miles per hour. Although ponderous, they were not particularly well gunned, mounting only a 6-pounder gun and two machine guns.[24] Moving through the tall grain without an advance screen of infantry, the tanks were terribly vulnerable and the Panzer Grenadiers fell on them ferociously.[25] In seconds, all three were knocked out by direct hits to the more thinly armoured sides from a Faustpatrone, a new German antitank rocket launcher that fired a 5.5-pound projectile capable of penetrating armour 140 millimetres thick at a range of less than thirty yards.[26] The troop commander was killed.

Meanwhile, Rawlings's men were blocked by machine-gun and rifle fire. Seeing the tanks in trouble on the left-hand side of Spalla Bassa, the company hastily withdrew, crossed the gully, and scrambled to their aid. Arriving too late to save the tanks, Rawlings could do nothing in the face of the gunfire directed at his company but order his men to dig in. He reported back to Johnston that without more tanks there was no way the company was going to get up on the ridge.

Everywhere on the Highlanders' front, the Panzer Grenadiers were wreaking havoc with the new Faustpatrones. When 'A' Company advanced to support 'D' Company, it took three more tanks with it. Once again, poor communications resulted in that troop's wandering off on its own and two were promptly knocked out, but the other tank managed to get through.

Having rushed over to Rawlings's embattled company, Johnston realized that until the ridge was cleared, further advance up the road would leave his men dangerously exposed to attack from the right flank. He sent 'B' Company and another tank troop up the right side of the gully and 'C' Company up the left side. This time, the attack succeeded. 'B' Company gained the ridge and sent a patrol to two houses that soon proved to contain stout German defensive positions. Captain Jack Wilson, commander of 'B' Company, decided to break up the house on the right with artillery while his men and the tanks cleared the left house. The tankers, wary of Faustpatrones, refused to close to a distance closer than 400 yards from the house. Wilson spent a fruitless ninety minutes vexed by poor radio contact with the supporting artillery regiment trying to score a hit on the house.[27] Finally he said: "To hell with the artillery, we'll go under cover fire of the tanks even if they can't hit the houses."[28]

Wilson figured his men could come at the left-hand house from an angle that would screen it from any fire issued by the Germans concentrated in the house to the right. In the rapidly failing light, his men went forward, the attack supported by a large volley of machine-gun and high-explosive fire from the tanks. At first, the opposition seemed to be only about two or three heavy machine guns, dug in under the house. But as the soldiers drew nearer, they moved into a hornet's nest of light machine–gun fire that drove them to ground. With the infantry now between the tanks and the German position in the house, the British tankers could offer no further assistance. Nervous that the approaching darkness would serve to conceal tank-killer teams armed with the deadly rocket launchers, the tanks fled. When it became dark enough, 'B' Company followed their example, falling back to a position on the ridgeline.

As night closed in, 'A' and 'D' companies reached their objective on the eastern bank of the Forme d'Aquino. They were joined by the lost company from the Hastings and Prince Edward Regiment, which had been fighting its own private, unplanned battle throughout the day just to the right of the Highlanders. 'D' Company of the Hasty P's had taken twenty-five prisoners during its journey but had lost one man killed and another seriously wounded.[29]

Concerned that the Panzer Grenadiers would counterattack, Johnston rushed antitank guns and mortars up to support the three companies. They arrived just in time, for, at 2200 hours, tracked vehicles were heard coming down the road toward a bridge crossing the stream that had not been blown by the retreating Germans. One of the 6-pounder antitank guns, commanded by Sergeant Robert James Shaw, was quickly shifted to cover the road and the 2-inch mortar team started popping flares into the sky. Under the flare light, Shaw saw what looked to be three enemy tanks or self-propelled guns (SPGs) coming up the road with a thirty-strong platoon of infantry in support. He was relieved to realize the vehicles were open-roofed, fixed-position .75-millimetre guns mounted on tracks and surrounded by a light armoured body, rather than the more heavily armoured tanks.

When the lead vehicle reached the narrow, wooden bridge, it paused on the entry ramp. The commander appeared to be belatedly realizing that the rickety bridge would not support the weight of his SPG. When the second gun promptly stood on the commander's tail, blocking any quick withdrawal, Shaw opened fire.[30] The shell struck the second SPG's fuel tank. The vehicle burst into flames and its ammunition started cooking off in massive explosions. This left the lead gun trapped by a smoking wreck behind and a worthless bridge in front. Shaw fired on the leading SPG and missed. Both surviving SPGs started firing back and shells cracked overhead as Shaw adjusted his aim, but missed again. Undeterred, he punched out a third shot that wrecked the leading SPG. The crew bailed out, but was cut down by Bren gun fire.[31] While the third SPG withdrew to cover, from which it began firing on the Canadian position, the infantry rushed 'D' Company's flank. Counsell let them get into the stream and then his men showered the Germans with Type 36 grenades. The counterattack crumbled.[32] Shaw was awarded the Military Medal for his bravery.

Despite the ferocity of the day's fighting, the regiment's casualties were remarkably light: eight killed and eleven wounded, with no losses among the officers.[33] More important, even with all the confusion between the infantry and the tankers during the fight to cross the Spalla Bassa, the regiment had reached the Forme d'Aquino and was well positioned to renew the fight in the morning.

◆ ◆ ◆

Back at 1st Canadian Infantry Division headquarters, Major General Chris Vokes was little impressed by the day's performance. "The forward progress of both brigades was too slow for my liking," he later wrote. "Granted the enemy resistance was stubborn but he was very thin on the ground and in many cases his small pockets of resistance should have been more quickly liquidated. Much of the sluggishness in the forward infantry was due to inexperience in the assault as for many of the officers and men who had joined the division as reinforcements during the winter it was their first experience of offensive action. It had to improve and I instructed both Spry and Bernatchez to see to it."[34]

He suggested that wherever possible the brigade should advance with two battalions out front and one in reserve to "reinforce the soft spots. Thereby they would have an opportunity to envelop any pockets of resistance encountered." Although 2nd Canadian Infantry Brigade was now across the Gari River, Vokes decided neither to have it relieve one of the forward brigades nor to commit it in order to shorten the front the brigades faced. Rather, Vokes intended "to maintain this brigade in reserve as long as possible and to employ it in the assault against the Hitler Line should a prepared, deliberate attack to breach it become necessary."[35]

Elsewhere on the battle front, events had gone well for the Eighth Army on May 17. The Poles had attacked Monte Cassino and were well ensconced on the lower slopes and in several strategic points close to the abbey itself that left the bastion nearly encircled. Expectations ran high that the abbey would fall in the morning. The British 78th Division had also fared well, advancing two miles west of Cassino on the southern flank of Highway 6. The town of Cassino was now no longer militarily significant, although there were still some pockets of fanatical paratroopers dug into strongpoints who appeared determined to fight to the death. However, I Canadian Corps intelligence staff reported that the British had taken prisoners from No. 3 and No. 4 companies of the 4th Paratroop Regiment, indicating that the "Cassino force is already on its way out. Certainly 4 Para Regiment's position in the town is precarious, and it must extricate itself tonight or be completely cut off." Counterattacks directed at Polish positions on the slopes of Monte Cassino immediately overlooking the town must, believed the intelligence officers, "have as their object the keeping open of a route of withdrawal for the parachutists in the town. Their daring in remaining is remarkable, but even parachutists must realize that 'to stand fast and hold their ground,' though the wish of Heidrich, in this situation would be folly. Tomorrow should see both 3 Para Regiment down from the hills northwest of the town and 4 Para Regiment clear of the town itself."[36]

It was apparent the Germans now had no option but to fall back to the Hitler Line, and intelligence staff saw no sign that reinforcements had arrived from the north to bolster the defensive force available to defend it. Instead, only the weary units currently falling back from the shattered Gustav Line appeared available and that "left no complete formation to man the Hitler Line." A battle group drawn from the Anzio bridgehead was the most available source for immediate reinforcement of the new line and Canadian intelligence officers pegged 29th Panzer Grenadier Division as the likely candidate. If 1st Canadian Infantry Division and 78th Division could advance fast enough, they might bounce the line before the disorganized Germans could harden their defences. This was the hope for the morrow.

THREE

THE HITLER LINE

12

DON'T LET IT GET
YOU DOWN, CHUM

Creating enough space in 3rd Canadian Infantry Brigade's front line to mount a two-battalion-wide attack meant the Royal 22e Regiment had to conduct a three-mile night march north to come up alongside the Carleton and York Regiment. The troops marched toward a small vale, the western edge of which would form the start line for the morning attack. 'B' Company commander Captain Pierre Potvin noted that his men, though dirty and exhausted, groused little about spending the night on the move. En route, the regiment brushed aside scattered pockets of German resistance, but suffered no casualties.

The men were hungry as well as weary, having received no rations since yesterday's attack. At 0500 hours on May 18, a wireless message instructed the troops to break into emergency rations. A popular joke held that the biscuits were "hard enough to break the tracks of a tank." Potvin was not surprised to find that many of the chocolate bars were mysteriously missing from the men's packs. "Tough luck," he told those who said their bars had somehow been lost.

Fortunately for everyone, a few minutes after the order to delve into the emergency rations was received, another rescinded that instruction and reported that Major Fernand Trudeau had slipped two ration-laden Jeeps into a column that was supposed to bring only ammunition forward. Each man received two cheese sandwiches, a tin of bully beef, and some hardtack that was somewhat softer than the emergency-ration version. Potvin thought the ration "not a hell of a lot for men who have trudged all day and were shortly to go into the attack."[1]

Not long before dawn, the R22eR reached the vale and took up a position astride a sunken, dusty road overlooked from the west by the high ground that was its first objective. Brigadier Paul Bernatchez came up at 0600 hours to discuss the day's plan with Lieutenant Colonel Jean Allard. As the two officers were talking, German small-arms fire started kicking up dirt around them and the soldiers in their respective entourages dived for cover. Bernatchez and Allard never budged. The brigadier snapped, "Get that nonsense stopped, will you." Allard glanced over his shoulder toward Potvin crouching nearby. "See to it, Pot, will you." Potvin rushed one of his 'B' Company platoons toward the grove concealing the German snipers, who promptly ran off.[2]

Of concern to Allard and Bernatchez was how the regiment would cross the Forme d'Aquino. According to the maps, it widened significantly in front of the regiment's planned line of advance. Finally, after ordering the regiment to start moving generally in the direction of the river, Allard climbed into his Jeep. With his driver, Private Denis, and batman, Private Bujold, he set off to find a river crossing.[3] Fearing his commander was going too far in disregarding personal danger, Potvin hurriedly loaded a couple of men from his platoon into another Jeep and took off in pursuit. Soon the small reconnaissance party was more than a mile ahead of the regiment, both Jeeps leaving a thick cloud of dust in their wake. Peering through the dust and knowing it marked their position to any enemy observation, Potvin was alarmed to recognize the silhouette of an armoured scout car coming down an intersecting track toward them. There was no way he and two infantrymen armed with rifles could win a fight against an armoured car. Potvin sighed with relief when he saw that the armoured car was Canadian and the head and shoulders sticking out of the open turret were none other than Bernatchez's. The brigadier, too, sought a river crossing.

The now reinforced reconnaissance party hurried on to the river, which at this point was about thirty feet wide and ten feet deep. Three-foot-high vertical banks rose up from the water's edge. Potvin realized the river formed "a definite obstacle for vehicles, and likely the infantry as well." The officers stared in frustration at the river, knowing it could seriously delay the regiment's advance to the Hitler Line if they had to wait for a bridge to be constructed. "Meanwhile," Potvin stewed, "the Germans would surely put this time to good use, getting ready for us when we did get across. We could expect to fight them on the river banks and that must mean 'curtains' for many brave men."

Allard told the party to split up and "find a crossing place, a ford where the water is not deep, a foot bridge, or something to support at least an infantry crossing."[4] Allard's Jeep went one way and Potvin's the other. Bernatchez, seeing Allard had matters in hand, returned to 3 CIB headquarters. Soon Allard was on the radio reporting that he had found a small flour mill that straddled the river. Potvin raced to meet him. A wooden shack with high doors stood astride a narrowing in the stream. Approaching the shack from either side was a deeply rutted track, indicating that it had been used as a local farm crossing. The plank floor appeared strong enough to bear military vehicle weight. If the doors were torn off the building, Allard thought Jeeps towing antitank guns and hauling four-inch mortars could get through. Potvin was amazed the Germans had not blown up the building.

Several Italian farmers emerged, seemingly from thin air, to report that there were no Germans on the opposite bank. They also said that the shack was not booby-trapped, information soon corroborated by the regiment's pioneers. While the pioneers started ripping off the doors and improving the approaches to the shack, Allard's group crossed the bridge on foot. The lieutenant colonel wanted to see if the area was indeed clear of Germans. Encountering no opposition, Allard set up his headquarters in a small cluster of houses on top of a low rise. At 1500 hours, the regiment was all across the river and formed up around the houses.

Returning to 'B' Company, Potvin led the regiment's advance. Under the scorching sun, the men sweated beneath the weight of their gear and from tension as they moved through groves and across small wheat fields. The sudden crack of gunfire or explosion of shells that they feared did not materialize.[5] By 1640 hours, the Van Doos were in an olive grove, looking down on the Hitler Line about one mile away. From this distance, it appeared as no more than a thick tangle of barbed wire following an irregular path across the width of the Liri Valley. Allard ordered his weary troops to dig in for the night.[6]

The smooth advance indicated the Germans were surrendering the terrain in front of the Hitler Line. A radio bulletin from I Canadian Corps headquarters told Allard that the Corps Expéditionnaire Français had punched through the Hitler Line's less heavily fortified section in the southern mountains and was now behind it. High command thought this would force the Germans to abandon the entire line. In the morning, 1st Canadian Infantry Division's regiments were to reconnoitre the facing sections of the Hitler Line in force and, if possible, break through. Allard thought high command was being too optimistic and insufficiently pragmatic. The front was too calm for his taste. He believed the Germans were inside the Hitler Line in force and lying ready to pounce on the unwary. In their place, Allard would never surrender such fortified positions without a serious fight — turned flank or not. He unhappily learned that the only support allotted for the morning would be a single artillery battery and one British tank squadron.[7]

Like the Van Doos, the other regiments of 1 CID had enjoyed relatively easy advances against only light opposition. Once crossings of the Forme d'Aquino had been constructed by the division's engineering parties, tanks were able to support the infantry. By nightfall, both 1st and 3rd Canadian Infantry brigades stood about one mile from the Hitler Line.

Only the 48th Highlanders of Canada had tripped any opposition. At 1500 hours, Lieutenant Dave Duncan and two men were far ahead of the leading company and moving single file through tall stands of grain. Duncan led, followed by Private Leo Halstall, while Private H.E. Creswell played tail-end Charlie. Suddenly seeing a German soldier sleeping soundly in the tall grain, Creswell shouted a challenge to alert Duncan and Halstall to the danger and then covered the Panzer Grenadier with his rifle. Literally from under Duncan and Halstall's feet and completely surrounding them, about forty soldiers in German field grey jumped to their feet with guns at the ready. Creswell could do nothing to help Duncan and Halstall, so he grabbed his prisoner and fled. Duncan and Halstall were led off in the other direction to spend the rest of the war in a prisoner-of-war camp.[8]

♦ ♦ ♦

Although each day's battle resulted in a few Canadians' being taken prisoner, the number of Germans captured was much higher. May 18 alone netted 1 CIB about 200 prisoners. Major General Chris Vokes was pleased by the number of prisoners taken and "was well satisfied with the progress of both brigades as there was none of the tactical sluggishness, which had been apparent on the previous two days."[9] He visited both Bernatchez and 1 CIB's Brigadier Dan Spry at their respective headquarters, telling them to "close up to the enemy wire during the night and mount a series of probing attacks on the morrow." Vokes hoped to establish a lodgement inside the Hitler Line that could be expanded into a full-blown breakout. Failing that, the probes should yield vital information about the fortifications and enemy strength that would help his staff mount a more carefully planned attack. So far, intelligence on the Hitler Line was woefully inadequate.

Vokes ended up having to search out Bernatchez's headquarters and finally found it in a house apparently ahead of his own leading infantry regiments. He could see the ruined village of Aquino, a corner pin of the Hitler Line, just off to the north. As he was giving Bernatchez instructions, an artillery bombardment rained down around the house, forcing the two officers to cower under "the doubtful shelter provided by a six-foot folding army table. It was most unpleasant for about ten minutes. Fortunately no one was hurt or equipment damaged."

"As soon as quiet was restored," Vokes "gave poor Bernatchez a piece of my mind. I told him I found no fault with aggressive brigadiers siting their headquarters well forward, but to do so in full view of the enemy was not only foolhardy but errant stupidity, especially when there was concealment nearby, and he was to locate his headquarters there immediately." Vokes thought Bernatchez would prove a first-class infantry brigadier if he could just stop feeling he had to prove his courage at every step. However, this was the man's first major engagement as a brigadier so allowances could be made.

Given his performance in the past two days, Vokes thought Bernatchez was learning fast.

Back at his far more safely positioned headquarters, Vokes settled down in his caravan to puzzle out a plan for breaching the Hitler Line. Failing unexpected success by the morning's probing attacks, 1 CID would have to put in a deliberate set-piece attack. This would mean inevitable delay, something that would please neither Lieutenant General Tommy Burns nor General Sir Oliver Leese. But how much time would he actually need?

Vokes envisioned 2nd Canadian Infantry Brigade carrying out the attack, with 25th Royal Tank Brigade alongside. In support, he wanted every artillery gun that Eighth Army could provide to smother the fortifications under a blanket of fire. Drafting a major artillery-firing plan required at least forty-eight hours. Seventy-two hours would be better because Vokes wanted a creeping barrage, which entailed precise timing and coordination with the advancing troops. Also necessary was a day to patrol the line to determine the best ground for an attack. From the map, it appeared the right flank most suited tank operations, but this had to be confirmed by close-up reconnaissance. Vokes hoped to get that information tomorrow, meaning that the earliest he could begin issuing the orders necessary to launch a set-piece attack would be May 20. If Burns and Leese agreed to a forty-eight-hour or seventy-two-hour planning period, the actual attack would then proceed late on May 22 or early May 23. That would still mean a hasty staff work schedule and one that would exhaust everyone and might well overlook obvious complications.

◆ ◆ ◆

On May 18, Leese believed the Canadians might not have to fight at all for the Hitler Line. Not only had the Corps Expéditionnaire Français turned the line on the left-hand flank, but XIII Corps's British 78th Division had made remarkable progress on the right flank. By evening, the 78th was closing on the Aquino airport, just east of the village standing behind the Hitler Line's wire. Although a hasty attack that night toward Aquino was repulsed, a renewed attack in the morning was likely to succeed. Once Aquino fell, both of the Hitler Line's flanks would be turned. In that scenario, to continue to try to defend the line would leave the Germans facing encirclement.

First Canadian Corps's intelligence staff was much pleased by the day's developments. "Today has been a good day," one officer wrote. "The paratroopers were forced to evacuate Cassino, but they almost left it too late. Many prisoners were put in the bag, and others fought to a bloody finish. The Polish flag was raised over the monastery late in the morning, and the mopping up of the area continued for the rest of the day."[10]

From Royal Canadian Regiment's rear-area headquarters, Major Strome Galloway had jubilantly watched through his binoculars as the Poles attacked Monte Cassino. From such a distance, the Polish troops had looked like hundreds of ants rushing up the steep slope, some appearing to crawl on their hands and knees over the white rocky ground. At 1020 hours, a horde of men leading the charge plunged through the holes that had been punched in the massive walls surrounding the abbey ruins. The flag appeared at the highest point amid the rubble just a few minutes later.[11] The Poles paid a high price for the abbey. Lying dead on the surrounding slopes and heights were 860 men. A further 2,924 had been wounded.[12]

Shortly after the Poles raised their victory flag over the abbey, Leese visited General Wladyslaw Anders at his headquarters. In a letter to his wife Margaret, he wrote, "we drank sweet champagne. . . . It was terrific. The success has made up for all their casualties — and the Polish flag flies proudly on the Monastery.

"A victory and an advance are a great tonic. I thank God very much for allowing me a victory in my first Army battle."[13]

CBC Radio correspondent Peter Stursberg soon sweated his way up the steep mountainside to the abbey, passing along the way a blanket of corpses left during the many battles. The Germans still occasionally shelled the slope and the Polish officers guiding Stursberg and the other journalists advised them not to bunch together, for that might attract deliberate enemy attention. Stursberg later wrote: "It was not the sight of the dead, the swollen, glaucous faces, the stary eyes, that turned our stomachs but the stench." He did not mention the smell in his recorded broadcast. Instead, he said: "I have never seen such a grisly sight as I saw. There were the dead that had stormed and taken this fortress. . . . And there were the dead that had tried to take it months ago. I almost stumbled over a head that had almost mummified. The horrible thing about these battlefields above Cassino was that the men who fought there lived with the dead around them."

Stursberg climbed over the broken outer wall and entered the abbey. In a crypt, he found two gaunt monks and some ragged civilians who had hidden there throughout the months of fighting.[14] Hundreds of other civilians had sought protection in the abbey and been trapped inside, having to seek shelter in its cellars and crypts. How many civilians were buried in its rubble would never be determined.

Shortly after Cassino's fall, Canadian war artist Captain Charles Comfort drove into the town en route to corps headquarters. Although he had painted the rubble of Ortona, what he saw here was far worse. "For sheer horror and utter devastation," he wrote, "I had not set eyes on its equal. The terraced structure of the streets might be discerned, if one searched for structure in that formless heap of calcined stone, but it resembled rather some imagined landscape on the moon. It had ceased to be terrestrial, it was like some lidless, blind eye, glaring back at the sun with empty lifeless inertia.

"The town in itself was completely silent. Swallows darted aimlessly about, their plaintive shriek the only sound other than the roll of gunfire and the clatter of armour. Unburied dead, protruding from rubble or huddled grotesquely in cellars, still made a grisly spectacle. The heavy stench of corruption hung about in dense patches near the pile of debris that was once the Hotel des Roches. In the flats, near the Rapido [Gari] River, the lands flooded by the enemy bristled with shattered tree stumps, the stagnant surface dull with a heavy brownish algae. Streets were no longer streets, simply tiresome mountains of broken masonry, in some instances reaching to second-storey levels. . . . What had been gardens were whittled to the ground, thick stumps of palm torn and gashed, vines uprooted, unidentifiable trees chopped and shattered into kindling. The ground everywhere was strewn with shell fragments, spent casings, and a litter of German equipment. In a most depressed state of mind, I set up my equipment and sketched what was left of the town."[15]

Aware of the abbey's significance as "one of the oldest seats of learning in Christendom, where the lamp had burned through the darkest ages," Comfort wondered why "so great a monument should have been destroyed by our generation. . . . No doubt there had been very real provocation but in eliminating a military problem, western culture had lost a great monument of art, and an institution which had contributed vitally to its life for nearly fourteen hundred years."[16]

♦ ♦ ♦

Few on the sharp end mourned the destroyed historical treasure. Since the Canadians had first set eyes on the abbey, the place had seemed a malevolent presence that monitored their every move, like a sniper staring through a scope at a target. From that great shattered white ruin, firing orders had directed deadly artillery fire their way. Thousands of Allied soldiers had been killed or wounded attempting to wrest Monte Cassino from the Germans. Ontario Tank Regiment Chaplain Waldo Smith thought the abbey seemed "invested almost with a personality. It had become a symbol. To Germans also it had become such."[17] Smith was personally disheartened. Not a young man, the chaplain had found the past week of his tank regiment's battle at the Gari River terribly trying. He was exhausted and sometimes feverish. Smith realized that, even for chaplains, war was a young man's game. When the Ontario Regiment had withdrawn to the east bank of the Gari for a rest and refit on May 16, Smith visited the senior Canadian chaplain, Jock Logan-Vencta, at corps headquarters. He told Logan-Vencta that regimental morale and cohesion were good and he thought it would "do no harm if I stepped out and a younger man should be able to do a better job than I had prospect of doing." Logan-Vencta agreed to replace Smith in a week. As the regiment was expected to remain out of the line, Smith could use the week to prepare the troops for his departure, as there was no doubt how respected the chaplain was in the eyes of the tankers he had served since the Sicily invasion.

On May 18, Smith spent the day catching up on next-of-kin letters and was just finishing up when a warning order came down from regimental headquarters that the Ontario Tanks would move again toward the sound of the guns that night. The 78th British Infantry Division needed tank support and 1st Canadian Armoured Brigade had drawn the duty; the Ontario and Calgary regiments would move back across the river and support the division's drive toward Aquino the next morning. Smith knew the tanks needed repairs, particularly work on the radios, and also that his men were worn out. He saw one man, standing next to a tank, letting forth a long stream of expletives. Smith walked over and put his hands on the man's shoulders. "Don't let it get you down, chum! We know how you feel," he said. The man's worried, angry expression softened into a tired grin. They both laughed off his distress.[18]

Rushing ahead of the Calgary Tank Regiment in a Jeep, Lieutenant Jim Quinn of 'A' Squadron mired in a morass of traffic all trying to go west from the Gari River into the heart of the Liri Valley. He was looking for 11th British Infantry Brigade, the unit the Calgary tankers were assigned to support. Harried provost officers trying to sort out the tangle of trucks, tanks, Jeeps, towed guns, and other vehicles all jockeying for position repeatedly directed his Jeep onto muddy, twisting cart tracks. It took hours for him to find the infantry brigade's headquarters to the east of Aquino Airport. Inside, confusion reigned. Rumours abounded that the Germans had abandoned Aquino and were fleeing back to Rome. Plans were drafted and scrapped. New plans were cobbled together and then sent to the shredder to be replaced by another vague scheme. Quinn finally found out where the regiment was to set up its forward tank assembly area. The advance party, of which he was a member, did what they could to smooth the way for the regiment's arrival. At 0500 hours, the Shermans rolled into the assembly area.[19]

The nighttime journey was the worst Chaplain Smith had ever witnessed. "Our tanks led off across country along what may well have been a suitable track for them, but what heavy tanks do to a track through the fields does not always make easy driving for a Jeep. Barbed wire was everywhere. The dust raised by the tanks added to the obscurity of the night and we soon ceased to recognize any shape as part of our regiment." When British 26th Armoured Brigade tanks bullied into the column and a section of self-propelled guns also squeezed into the line, Smith feared the little Jeep would get crushed under somebody's tracks. Finding another lane in use only by trucks, Smith's driver took that route. This track proved so crowded and cut up with ruts, however, that the chaplain finally decided to pull over and proceed in daylight.[20]

The confusion inherent in a night move almost left behind twenty-one-year-old Lieutenant C. Malcolm Sullivan, who was commanding No. 3 Troop of the Ontarios' 'A' Squadron. Earlier, his tank had been manoeuvring through an olive grove to reach its position in the regimental line. Unseen branches had started scraping the turret. Sullivan ducked into the turret, while steadying himself with one hand gripping the hatch's outer rim. A branch caught his exposed right index finger, painfully twisted it 180 degrees, and broke the skin at the knuckle. One of his crewmen snapped the finger somewhat straight and Sullivan walked back to the Medical Dressing Station. Here, a Medical Officer reset and fixed the finger rigidly into place by taping it between two metal splints. Fearing the column would leave without him, Sullivan ran back to his tank. "Like so many volunteers," he later wrote, "it never occurred to me that I could escape danger if I didn't hurry back. There is an indefinable urge to rejoin your regimental and troop family." Sullivan got back just in time. Although his finger proved awkward and painful, he was able to handle the microphone and that meant he could do his squadron commander's job. After a torturous drive through the night, made worse every time he bumped his finger, the Ontario tankers "harboured in a softwood copse just south of the small *Aeroporto D'Aquino.*"[21]

◆ ◆ ◆

Ontario commander Lieutenant Colonel Bob Purves received his orders at an Orders Group held at the headquarters of the Royal East Kent Regiment (nicknamed the 5th Buffs). The whole plan sounded terribly rushed. "The gist of the plan was that the 26th Armoured Brigade would plunge through Aquino, and exploit the gain with a wide armoured sweep behind the German lines. In the event that exploitation was not very successful, the Ontarios were to support the 36th British Infantry Brigade in securing the bridgehead through the gap that the armoured brigade created. The two phases of the attack were to be prosecuted at the same time so that all of the attacking forces might take advantage of the barrage. It was stipulated, however, that the 26th Brigade tanks were to pass forward first."[22]

Purves returned to the assembly area and called a "rather dismal orders group in the back room of a farmhouse." The squadron commanders were all red-eyed and worn-looking, as was Purves. Everyone "squinted painfully at their maps in the dim candlelight, while the raw damp of a foggy night seeped coldly through the room." 'B' Squadron's Major D.H. McIndoe was to support the 5th

Buffs' drive directly into Aquino, while Major Harry Millen's 'A' Squadron moved to the north end of the airport and protected the right flank. Along with the 6th Royal West Kent Regiment, 'C' Squadron would be in reserve. The 8th Argyll and Sutherland Highlanders would protect the left flank.[23]

Throughout the night, there had been periods of drizzle. At 0500 hours on May 19, the tanks rolled toward battle through a thick fog that cloaked the valley. Ahead, the flash of the barrage's exploding shells could be seen through the murk. The Ontario Tanks moved west along an axis paralleling the road and running past the airport toward Aquino. 'B' Squadron and the 5th Buffs advanced warily up the road's left-hand side. Across the road, 'A' Squadron headed for the northern end of the airport. The fog soon proved so thick that the lead platoons were unable to distinguish landmarks, let alone detect signs of the enemy. A halt was called until 0700 hours to allow the sun time to burn off some of the fog, despite the fact that this largely nullified the effect of the barrage.[24]

At 0700 hours, 'A' Squadron's Shermans rolled out of a line of trees into the airport's open grounds. Sullivan felt nakedly exposed, resigned to the forthcoming danger, and mostly "too busy to be afraid." But it was not just fear for themselves that haunted young officers. More threatening, sometimes even paralyzing, was the fear of failure; the fear that a bad order would cause the death of men or misunderstanding an order from the squadron commander would lead to a terrible defeat. With experience, something Sullivan had, this fear lessened, but it never disappeared. Today, 'A' Squadron's immediate task was to give the Buffs covering fire and take on any targets detected in the vicinity of the railroad and Highway 6. These two major transportation links running from Naples to Rome paralleled each other immediately north of the airport, with the railroad being closest and the highway little more than a hundred yards beyond. The tanks advanced to the dubious cover offered by two hangars previously bombed into nothing more than metal frameworks. The tanks spread out to watch for signs of enemy positions.[25]

One troop of 'B' Squadron followed the Buffs toward the cemetery, situated between the village and the airport. Undoubtedly, this would be strongly defended with positions dug in around and inside of the tombs, crypts, and graves. At 0745 hours, a concealed antitank gun knocked out one Sherman. The infantry, engaged by numerous machine guns, were pinned down on the edge of the cemetery.[26]

Meanwhile, another troop of 'B' Squadron, commanded by Lieutenant Keith D. McCord, followed a company of Buffs through the cover of vineyards toward the village's outskirts. About 300 yards from Aquino's edge, an antitank gun opened fire from the left. The tanks quickly spun their turrets and blasted the gun apart. Suddenly, all three tanks were struck one after the other by a camouflaged .88-millimetre antitank gun firing at point-blank range from inside a concrete and steel pillbox positioned in the vines directly ahead of them.[27] Although each tank was holed at least twice by the deadly accurate fire, the crews stuck to their guns, exchanging shot for shot until fires started breaking out inside. The men bailed out, all escaping except for Jack Phillips, who was never seen again. He was believed to have either perished in the tank or to have been taken prisoner.[28]

Seeing 'B' Squadron's trouble, Major Millen sent a troop of 'A' Squadron across the railway to Highway 6 with orders to enter the town from the northwest. He hoped this might allow the troop to cut off German outposts there and loosen things up so that the infantry could enter Aquino. The troop commander drove his tank up the bank to get astride the railroad and came under immediate antitank fire. He hastily withdrew. Another 'A' Squadron troop tried to get over the railroad further east, but the commander's tank was hit and knocked out. 'C' Squadron, meanwhile, moved up behind 'A' Squadron to provide covering fire and to protect the forward squadron's right flank.[29]

Disaster struck the infantry regiment when a direct mortar strike blew up the Bren carrier carrying its commanding officer and entire signals section. The Ontario Tankers could no longer communicate with the infantry companies by radio. With no idea what any infantry was doing, other than those each tanker could personally see, their gunnery posed as great a danger to the British troops as to the Germans.

At 0930 hours, antitank guns knocked out two 'B' Squadron tanks and Captain J.I. Nichol was wounded.[30] In 'C' Squadron, Lieutenant J. Symons's tank caught fire and he was severely burned.[31] When 'C' Squadron moved a tank troop under Lieutenant J.A. Cameron across the railway, two of its tanks, including the commander's, were struck by antitank gun fire and burst into flames.[32] As the tank carrying Corporal Pete Andrew brewed, he bailed out along with all but the co-driver. This man froze with fear and could not bring himself to move. Instead he remained in his seat, screaming. Andrew jumped back into the burning Sherman and dragged the terrified and helpless man to safety. Afterwards, he said, "I didn't want to go back. But if I hadn't, I'd have heard that boy squeal the rest of my life."[33] When Corporal Cecil Jones's tank was knocked out, he almost led his crew into the German lines. Realizing his mistake, he got them turned around in time. To reach their own lines, however, they had to crawl through a series of mud-filled ditches.

In 'A' Squadron, Sullivan was parked next to Major Millen's tank. The entire battle had become a fiasco. There was virtually no forward movement any more. German shells were exploding all around and snipers were trying to shoot the tank commanders whenever they looked out of their turrets. A shell went off beside Millen's tank and he was wounded in the head and paralyzed.[34] Captain Bud Hawkins took over command of 'A' Squadron. After trying unsuccessfully to renew the advance, the Ontario Regiment received orders to hold its ground. This meant most of the tanks had to remain in very exposed positions. The supporting artillery dropped smoke shells, particularly on the northern flank, to provide concealment. When these started thinning out dangerously, Sergeant Ken Braithwaite and Trooper Kelly Turcott jumped into a Bren carrier and raced at breakneck speed around the fringe of the airport hurling out smoke canisters in their wake.[35]

The 5th Buffs had by now withdrawn behind the airport. In an apparent attempt to maintain protection of the regiment's right flank, 'C' Squadron's tanks moved in single file across the airport to where Sullivan's tanks were holding by the ruined barracks. Sullivan and his troop watched "wide-eyed as they drove past us, without stopping or communicating with us. They circled the hangars and retraced their path, still in single file, disappearing in the woods from which they had come."[36] What exactly the manoeuvre had been intended to achieve remained a puzzle to the tankers in the other squadrons.

◆ ◆ ◆

The terrific fight at Aquino generated a flood of infantry casualties, who all fell back to the eastern edge of the airport. Ontario Regiment Chaplain Waldo Smith and his driver, Trooper C. Westover, helped the wounded British soldiers. Smith sent Westover back to the Regimental Aid Post with a couple of wounded men, thinking he was getting the man away from the danger posed by the constantly exploding shells and mortar rounds. The driver set off with his pipe clenched in his mouth at a jaunty angle. Suddenly, a stonk of German Nebelwerfer fire threw up dust all around the Jeep, completely obscuring it from view. Smith was sure his driver was dead, but a little later Westover returned with an undamaged Jeep to report that the wounded had been safely delivered.[37]

Westover continued to shuttle wounded to the rear throughout the day, making more trips than anyone could count and personally evacuating about 180 casualties. At one point, the quartermaster, Captain Harrold, found Westover weeping with exhaustion, hunger, and despair from all he had seen. He could offer the young soldier no comfort other than a few moments of gentle sympathy. For his part, Smith was determined to get as far forward as possible to help the wounded who could not walk back on their own. He had Westover drive toward where he believed the front lines were, but a British military policeman tried to turn him back, telling him that the area ahead was under constant German fire. Smith told Westover, "Drive on! I'm on the Lord's side!" Westover obeyed, but a few minutes later said in a diffident voice, "It's okay for you, Padre. You're on the Lord's side; but whose side am I on?" Smith agreed to return to the dubious safety of the shell-torn airport.[38]

Smith was dismayed to see the tanks of 26th Armoured Brigade still milling about aimlessly, "raising dust and drawing fire. The shelling was incessant. It appeared to me that the enemy had us in the centre of a two-hundred-yard bracket both in traverse and range. I kept waiting for him to split that bracket and wipe us out. The odd mortar fell among us and caused some wounds but nobody was killed."[39]

The 26th's attack had never materialized; it had crumbled in the first minutes of the morning. Consequently, from the outset, the Buffs and the Ontario tankers had been engaged in a futile battle. At dusk, they retreated south of the airport and harboured behind the protection of regiments of 36th British Infantry Brigade. The Ontario

Regiment had lost thirteen tanks, twelve to antitank fire and one to a mine. That was almost one-third of their entire combat strength. Considering the number of tanks that had burned, human casualties were remarkably light. Only five men had been wounded and one was missing.[40] Every tank in the fighting squadrons had been struck by at least one antitank round. Sullivan's tank had been hit twice by armour-piercing shot, but each round had struck the angled glacis and veered off.[41] The infantry and tanks had destroyed the German positions east of the Forme d'Aquino. In the melee, the two squadrons had knocked out a German tank, a self-propelled gun, and numerous antitank guns.[42]

Smith collapsed into a slit trench and slept soundly through most of the night. At one point, he was shaken awake by a trooper wanting to borrow the Jeep to evacuate a wounded man. Smith agreed and fell back to sleep. In the morning, he woke to a feeling of deep shame, realizing he had not checked the wounded man's condition. That was his job and he had failed. This realization left him shaken and more acutely aware that he should be relieved "before further lapses of that kind should make me indifferent."[43]

In the aftermath of battle, Sullivan found 'C' Squadron's commander, the officer who had led the bizarre single-file column around the edge of the airport, "sitting on the edge of a ditch with his head in his hands. He had been replaced and it occurred to me that *the Fear* had claimed another victim."[44]

13

WHERE ARE YOU GOING
LIKE THAT, LITTLE POT?

Although 1st Canadian Infantry Division's May 19 reconnaissance in force against the Hitler Line was to be conducted on a two-brigade front, the availability of a single artillery regiment for the operation relegated one brigade to a diversionary role, while the other tried for a breakthrough. The Royal Canadian Horse Artillery guns were to fire a five-minute concentration in front of 3rd Canadian Infantry Brigade's Royal 22e Regiment and Carleton and York Regiment immediately prior to their crossing the start line at 0630 hours.[1] On 3 CIB's left flank, 1 CIB's 48th Highlanders and the Hastings and Prince Edward Regiment were to occupy a low ridgeline about a thousand yards from the Hitler Line and, if possible, probe the German wire with patrols. South of the 1st Canadian Infantry Brigade regiments, the Princess Louise Dragoons Guards' reconnaissance regiment would sweep through the pocket lying between the road approaching Pontecorvo from the east and the northern bank of the Liri River to mop up any remaining German elements there.[2]

Despite relatively heavy mortar fire, the two 1 CIB regiments reached their assigned positions by early morning. The 48th Highlanders sent a patrol of four scouts to the edge of the wire. Arriving undetected, the small patrol measured the width of the barbed-wire barrier, examined the depth of an antitank ditch, counted the number of mines emplaced in the forward lines, and discovered several narrow gaps in the wire. Still unopposed, the intrepid team measured the dimensions of several concrete pillboxes and counted the number of machine-gun and antitank positions along a carefully delineated length of line. This accomplished, they slipped through a gap in the wire to check out how several houses were used as defensive points.[3] By the time the scouts withdrew to safety, they had assembled a detailed picture of one section of the Hitler Line, a vital piece of intelligence for those developing the Canadian set-piece attack plan.

The Princess Louise Dragoon Guards conducted their sweep with 'B' and 'C' squadrons leading and 'A' Squadron in reserve. The reconnaissance regiments were equipped with four-wheeled armoured cars, mostly Fox 1 and Otter Mark 1 models.

Shortly after setting out, the PLDG squadrons engaged elements of the Hochlund Deutschmeister Division's Replacement Battalion, supported by several tanks and antitank guns. One 'B' Squadron Otter was quickly knocked out. Throughout the day, the Guardsmen fought through terrain so close that they seldom detected German positions until being fired upon. By day's end, the PLDG had lost two men killed and six wounded. They had, however, cleared their assigned area of operations to a point paralleling that of 1 CIB's front line.[4]

◆ ◆ ◆

The two regiments from 3 CIB got off on schedule, right on the heels of the artillery concentration. Royal 22e Regiment had 'A' Company out on the right and 'D' Company to the left. A troop of British Churchill tanks supported each company.[5] To the left of the Van Doos, the Carleton and York Regiment also advanced in a two-company-forward formation with 'A' and 'C' companies leading. As usual, thick morning fog obscured the ground. First objectives were quickly reached against resistance limited to desultory sniping, which evaporated when the Canadians closed on a sniper's position, usually situated in the tops of the scrub oaks scattered in groves among the small grain fields.

When the Carleton and York companies reached the first objective, however, concentrated German small-arms fire and mortar and artillery bombardments caught them in the open. Most of the day's casualties of eight killed and twenty-one wounded happened within minutes of the regiment's coming under this fire.[6] Determined to keep the attack going, Lieutenant Colonel Dick Danby ordered 'B' and 'D' companies to leapfrog past 'A' and 'C' and carry on despite the heavy fire. 'B' Squadron of the 51st Royal Tank Regiment was in support.[7] Once clear of the open ground of the first objective, infantry casualties became light, but sniper fire took a toll on the tank commanders, sitting head and shoulders out of the turret hatches to better spot enemy positions in the dense woods.[8]

Reaching the east slope of a low ridge about 800 yards from the Hitler Line's barbed wire, Danby ordered 'B' Company to halt just short of the summit while Major Rowland Horsey's 'D' Company and the tanks crossed over and descended the gradual slope to probe the defences. Just as 'D' Company was heading for the summit, 3 CIB commander Brigadier Paul Bernatchez ordered the Carleton and York Regiment to halt and assume a holding position on the ridge's east slope. The Van Doos, Bernatchez said, had met stiff opposition and, with only one regiment of artillery available, he was dedicating all guns to their support. Danby and his men were to sit tight until R22eR's situation stabilized.[9]

The Van Doos had run into heavy fire about 800 yards from the wire, just after Lieutenant Colonel Jean Allard had switched Captain Pierre Potvin's 'B' Company and Major Charles Bellavance's 'C' Company into the lead. Allard ordered this change so that 'A' and 'D' companies would be close behind the two leading companies, ready "to provide back-up support and even expand rapidly on the penetration which 'B' and 'C' companies were now preparing to effect." He hoped to get inside the Hitler Line defences before the fog burned off.[10] Potvin and Bellavance's objective was a height of land to the immediate west of the Pontecorvo-Aquino road, itself about one-third of a mile west of the Hitler Line.

As Potvin's company moved through 'D' Company, he saw its commander, Major Ovila Garceau, leaning nonchalantly against the door of a house. "Where are you going like that, Little Pot?" Garceau asked in his customary slow drawl. Trying to mimic his good friend's casual demeanour, Potvin replied, "We're off to kill some *Tedeschi*."[11]

With the Carleton and York Regiment halted behind the Van Doos' current position and no sign of anybody from the British 78th Division on the right, both regimental flanks were badly exposed. Suddenly, all the companies started taking small-arms fire from the surrounding woods. The men dropped down into the cover of the grain field in which they had been forming for the renewed advance. Potvin and the other company commanders realized that their men were now caught in a dangerous salient. If they were not to withdraw, they must attack. But Allard still did not give the order.[12]

Some of Potvin's men returned fire, despite the lack of obvious targets. Knowing they might need all their ammunition later, Potvin told his men to cease fire. He considered sending a fighting patrol into the woods to clear the Germans, but rejected the idea — he would probably end up with those men tangled in a firefight that would be hard to break off and that could throw the entire attack off balance. Finally, Potvin ran over to his assigned tank troop commander's Churchill and asked him to machine-gun the Germans. Once the tank raked the tree line with its machine guns and then fired a high-explosive round into it, the German fire abruptly ceased.

At 0935 hours — about thirty minutes after the men had first formed up in the grain field — the attack order came. Potvin's company set off with his three tanks in support, but he soon realized that 'C' Company was not moving. "Bellavance's radio must be out," he thought. Seeing Lieutenant Claude Gagnon nearby, Potvin shouted that the attack was on and to tell his commander. When Gagnon was unable to raise Bellavance by radio, he waved his own platoon forward. As this platoon joined Potvin's advance, the rest of 'C' Company rose up out of the grain and followed.

Potvin led his men directly toward a small wood from which much of the harassing German small-arms fire had emanated. The troops ran forward eagerly, firing from the hip and yelling in French, "Let's get those Germans!" As his men closed on the wood, the Germans scattered. A good number of German dead were left behind, testimony to the effectiveness of the earlier tank fire. As his men chased after the Germans, 'B' Company started to become disorganized. Potvin had to move quickly to regain control and get the men moving toward the objective, rather than engaging in a melee with the fleeing Germans.

Breaking out of the thin patch of woods, 'B' Company entered another wheat field. This time the grain was shoulder high. Potvin could hardly see any of his men. Reaching a small rise, he looked about frantically, able only to see men's helmets "floating on a sea of wheat." The captain could find his way only by taking compass readings. He shouted course changes to his invisible men and they in turn passed the corrections along the line. Looking behind him, Potvin saw that the tanks were just coming around the edge of the woods and were at least 500 yards back. "Some close support," he muttered. Still, the field was completely level, so they should soon catch up.

Men hidden in the tall grain were calling for stretcher-bearers. The steady sniper and machine-gun fire was taking its toll. Increasingly heavy artillery, mortar, and Nebelwerfer concentrations were wounding others. With bayonets fixed, the sweat-lathered infantrymen pressed on stoically through the intensifying fire from unseen positions. Potvin realized his company was now "entering the main defences of the Hitler Line, which at this particular place looked like a giant horseshoe with its arms turned toward us, as though to invite us into its killing ground." On the right, 'C' Company had disappeared in the grain. Potvin had no idea whether his company attacked alone or with Bellavance's company still on line. The tanks had also disappeared. As the enemy fire escalated, the air filled with dust thrown up by exploding artillery and mortar rounds. Adding to the chaos was the acrid smell of gunpowder and the deafening racket of gunfire and explosions. The Van Doos pressed on, firing from the hip at Germans crouching in slit trenches. Other Germans ran away, zigzagging wildly to avoid being hit. Most escaped; a few fell dead or wounded. 'B' Company started taking fire from behind, as snipers who had remained hidden in the scattered trees while the Van Doos passed now opened up.

Leading his small headquarters section up a cart track that cut through the wheat field, Potvin realized he was ahead of the company's two forward platoons when the section came up abruptly against barbed wire. From right behind the wire, a machine-gun position started firing, driving his section to ground. Hoping to find a route for attacking the gun, Potvin crawled up a small hillock. About thirty yards away from him was the concrete pillbox housing the gun position. Potvin heard both Lieutenant Audrin and Company Sergeant Major R. Drapeau shouting at him to take cover.

Audrin spotted a German light machine–gunner slipping into a trench about ten yards to the right and pointed the man out to one of his Bren gunners. The gunner, just a few feet from Potvin, emptied a thirty-round magazine into the German. Potvin called to Audrin to move men past the dead German's position and outflank the main machine-gun position. The Bren gunner said he would go with Audrin, but he needed fresh magazines. Potvin gestured to a man nearby to throw him a magazine, so he could in turn toss it to the gunner. As the soldier pitched the magazine over, a bullet struck Potvin's shoulder and passed out the other side. Potvin felt as if he had "been hit by a giant fist." Although he felt dizzy, there was no evident blood. "Must have just been the magazine hitting me," he thought.

The German machine gun was still chattering away. Ten feet from Potvin, Corporal Cloutier was hit in the forehead by a round and dropped dead. Potvin was sickened and enraged. Cloutier was old guard. He had been in 'B' Company in England and had landed with Potvin in Sicily. If the damned tanks would come up, he could send one to crush the gun under its tracks. Looking over his shoulder, however, he saw that the tanks were about a thousand yards back and that two of the three were burning. The three tanks supporting 'C' Company were holding a position near the surviving tank of his own support group, so he tried to reach them on the radio to ask for assistance. The set was broken. He fired a green flare. This signal indicated that a machine gun was holding up the advance and that tanks should assist. The tanks did not budge. A red flare indicating an antitank gun drew no response. 'B' Company would have to win or lose its fight alone, Potvin decided.

Already the troops were breaking up the visible resistance. While No. 10 Platoon's 2-inch mortar team bombarded the pillbox with rounds, Lieutenant Audrin and a platoon section tried to get through the wire and close on the position. Potvin went to assist with another section drawn from Lieutenant R.L. St.-Onge's platoon. Suddenly, the fog that had blanketed the battlefield lifted. With growing horror, Potvin saw that his company was directly in the centre of a semi-circle of German emplacements. Gun flashes erupted all around the Canadians as the Germans saw their exposed prey. A bullet slammed into Potvin's left hip and exited his back close to the spine. The impact threw him into the air and his knees snapped up just under his chin so that he landed on the ground in a fetal position. He was unable to rise because of excruciating pain each time he tried to move. At his side, the captain's radio operator desperately tried to get the set working so he could call for help. Potvin shouted to Audrin to hold his position and keep the Germans busy while he sent St.-Onge's platoon to establish a holding position on the right flank.

Lying on the ground in the tall wheat, Potvin could see little of how the manoeuvre was proceeding or whether it was succeeding at all. He threw his map case to Audrin and told him to take control of the company. Audrin started crawling toward St.-Onge. Artillery shells exploded all over the company's tenuous position, and "a storm of fire and steel swallowed us. The ground shook as if we were near an erupting volcano." Potvin could see that some men were breaking. If the men panicked and ran, Potvin knew the Germans could wipe out the entire company. Picking out those who looked on the edge of cracking, Potvin harshly reminded them to do their duty. Crawling painfully toward the nearest soldiers, he was hit in the left forearm by another bullet — his third wound. Seconds later, a piece of shrapnel from an exploding shell slashed a deep, long gash into his arm just above the bullet wound.

Company Sergeant Major Garceau and stretcher-bearer Private Gagnon rushed over and tried to staunch the flow of blood running from the four wounds. To reassure his men, Potvin sang "Alouette." Although a bullet broke Audrin's wrist, the young officer continued directing the company's resistance. St.-Onge meanwhile led a rush against the pillbox. As he was about to throw a grenade, the lieutenant was struck by a bullet. He fell to the ground, the live grenade landing alongside him. When it exploded, St.-Onge was killed. Sergeant Gérard Poitras of Chicoutimi took over his platoon.[13] As Audrin's wounds were now too painful for him to lead the company effectively, CSM Drapeau assumed command. Minutes later he, too, was wounded.

Royal Canadian Horse Artillery Forward Observation Officer Captain Keith Saunders, was also caught in the crossfire. Seeing that all the infantry officers were either dead or wounded, the artillery officer took charge, assisted by sergeants L. Couturier and Fernand Trembley. They tried to slowly shift the forward platoons to a strongpoint established 200 yards back by the reserve platoon. Despite managing to shoot some snipers out of trees and knocking out one machine-gun position, 'B' Company remained completely pinned down by heavy German fire from all sides. There was no way the surrounded company could break out on its own, even if it abandoned the eighteen wounded men.[14]

At 1200 hours, Allard drove his Jeep up to 'C' Company's headquarters section. Bellavance's company was behind and to the right of the cut-off 'B' Company. Allard saw that all his companies were under "heavy fire and suffering heavy casualties. Guns, mortars, machine guns, and snipers, all that the German could muster, seemed to be centred on the four rifle companies. Before them one could plainly see the barbed wire and the pill boxes in the enemy lines."[15]

'C' Company's position was little better than 'B' Company's. Lieutenant Claude Gagnon's platoon was pinned down and Lieutenant Roger Piché was down with a bullet in his arm. Allard called for artillery fire against the German positions, but was told all the artillery was either out of range or now committed to the 78th Division's drive toward Aquino. He refused the offered 4.2-inch mortars, fearing their less-than-accurate fire would hit his own exposed men. The situation, Allard decided, was hopeless. The attack must be broken off or his regiment would be wiped out inside the salient trap. Ordering smoke fired on the German positions, Allard jumped into his Jeep and drove toward 3 CIB headquarters to get permission for a retreat. At 'A' Company, he told Captain Henri Tellier to coordinate a withdrawal plan with Major Ovila Garceau and to be ready to move on Allard's order. Just outside 'A' Company's position, a burst of machine-gun fire shattered Allard's windshield. His driver, Private Denis, was wounded, but Allard was not even scratched. He dived into a ditch and headed for the rear on foot, leaving his bodyguard, Private Geonais, to tend the wounded driver.

Geonais, however, managed to start the Jeep, even though it was under constant fire from the German machine gun. Crouching next to the driver's side, he slowly guided the bullet-riddled vehicle down the road until it was out of the German gunner's range. Then he jumped in and caught up with Allard. Denis was still alive, somehow not having been hit by the many bullets that struck the Jeep during its extraction under fire. Allard took the wheel and raced to the rear, where he dropped Denis at an aid station before hurrying on to see

Bernatchez. At 1300 hours, he asked Bernatchez for permission to order a withdrawal. Bernatchez immediately sought authorization from Vokes.

While Allard anxiously waited, Bernatchez argued with Vokes. Allard realized that the divisional commander was proving difficult to convince, even though men had to be dying with every minute's delay.[16] When 'C' Company came up on the brigade radio pleading for permission to withdraw, Allard could only tell them to "take up a good position and wait for orders."[17] Finally, Vokes acquiesced. Allard rushed from 3 CIB headquarters back to his companies. Along the way, a report came in that five of the six tanks were knocked out. At 1405 hours, Allard burst into regimental headquarters and passed the order to the forward companies to undertake a fighting withdrawal. He told Major Garceau of 'D' Company to assume command of 'B' Company and bring both units out together. Bellavance radioed that he had twenty-five wounded, including one officer. 'C' Company broke off contact with the Germans and cleared out from behind 'B' Company. Garceau then sent a platoon forward to link up with 'B' Company.[18]

Inside 'B' Company's perimeter, the situation was chaotic as the men prepared for what would be a hazardous breakout under fire. Although also wounded, Drapeau was trying to convince Potvin to agree to be evacuated and he had two stretcher-bearers ready to load the wounded officer. A small party of walking wounded was going to slip through the corridor that Garceau's platoon had opened up between 'D' and 'B' companies. Drapeau wanted to send Potvin out with the wounded men. Potvin refused to consider the idea. "I go out with the company," he said, "not before." The captain still believed that, if his company were reinforced and supported by tanks, a break in the Hitler Line could be effected. With the radios all out of action, Potvin was unaware that 'D' Company was establishing contact with his company not to continue the offensive but rather to enable a withdrawal.[19]

Lieutenant Harry Pope coordinated the company's effort to get its wounded out to 'D' Company's lines. He made three trips carrying a wounded man on his back to safety each time. After the third trip, he set off to return to 'C' Company's lines and disappeared. (Taken prisoner, Pope would later escape with four other men and cross into Allied lines in late June.) From 'D' Company's perimeter, the many wounded in both companies were being evacuated by men carrying them out on their backs or in the regimental Jeeps, whose drivers bravely charged through enemy fire to reach the wounded troops. Driver C.A. Robitaille made several trips through intense German fire, bringing back two to three men each time. Although he had mounted a Red Cross flag on the Jeep, the German fire directed his way never slackened. A shell killed two stretcher-bearers who were carrying a wounded man to safety.[20]

When the shelling eased for a moment, Potvin struggled to his feet to see what was happening. A bullet slammed into his right wrist, breaking it. The bullet whirled him around and threw him to the ground. Regaining his senses a few minutes later, he found himself alone. It seemed his men had withdrawn while he lay there dazed. Even the dead had been carried away and Potvin realized that somehow he had been overlooked, probably because the impact of the last bullet had tumbled him into a small hole.[21]

◆ ◆ ◆

At 1450 hours, 'D' Company had established a sufficiently strong link with 'B' Company to enable Potvin's embattled troops to withdraw into the forward positions of Garceau's leading platoons. The men went slowly, the remnants of platoon sections leapfrogging back through each other so that when one section moved, the other was behind it and able to provide protective fire. When 'B' Company passed through 'D' Company, Garceau ordered his men to start falling back. The entire manoeuvre was carried out under heavy German gunfire and constant mortar and artillery bombardment. At 1540, the two companies passed Allard's tactical headquarters. He assumed that those who were going to escape from the deadly salient in which the regiment had spent an eleven-hour ordeal had done so.

Out of an initial strength of just under 400 men, the regiment had suffered 57 casualties. Allard was sickened that his "regiment had been the victim of the recklessness of High Command, which had sent it on a dubious mission on the basis of relatively limited information and without artillery support to surprise the defenders." Divisional staff, he thought, had not "shown much imagination in assuming that the Germans would abandon such well-built fortifications, which enabled them to contain the advance of the Eighth Army with minimum forces." Allard later wrote that he was "left with a bad taste in my mouth about the whole affair. I looked on those who had analysed the intelligence reports as ill-advised bureaucrats. And after this event I retained serious doubts about the competence of commanders who had blindly made the decision to hurl us, without preparation, against lines supposed to be abandoned shortly anyway. My friend and comrade Paul Bernatchez, who had reluctantly transmitted the order, silently shared the same opinion. He was as deeply affected as I by the losses his former regiment had suffered, losses that were to contribute very little to the eventual victory."[22]

Allard sent a prearranged signal to Bernatchez, who then directed a heavy artillery concentration into the salient to break up any German counterattack that might be forming to strike the Royal 22e Regiment while it was on the move. The regiment was to withdraw behind the West Nova Scotia Regiment, which had established a position alongside the Carleton and York Regiment.[23]

Out in the salient, Potvin heard German voices approaching. Despite the wounds to his arms, shoulder, wrist, and hip, he crawled about twenty yards away from their line of approach. Potvin was "exhausted, covered in sweat and blood, but determined to regain the Canadian lines and not to be captured." Surrender was unthinkable. As he started crawling, a burst of submachine-gun fire from a German Schmeisser kicked dirt up around him. Potvin rolled into a wagon rut and played dead. It was impossible for him to tell whether the fire had been intentional or just random searching fire.

Suddenly, shells and mortar bombs started exploding all around, sending great gouts of soil and flame firing into the air. The heavy hammering of Vickers machine guns told Potvin that the fire came from his own side. He imagined his good friend Major Rolly Yelle of the Saskatoon Light Infantry Regiment, which provided 3 CIB with heavy machine gun and 4.2-inch mortar support, directing the fire and almost laughed. "How ironic," he thought, "that, having escaped from the Germans so far, I am killed by our own fire, directed by my friend." A heavy feeling that he recognized as the result of blood loss settled over his brain. Although he struggled against it, Potvin passed out.

An hour later, he regained consciousness. His thirst was terrible, and his water bottle lost. Plucking some green grass, he chewed on it with the hope of extracting some coolness and moisture. The sun, however, had dried it and he was left with nothing but "the taste of dust on my lips." He stared up at the intense blue sky and prayed "to the Virgin Mary as only a miserable, wounded soldier might." Potvin was shortly convinced that his prayers were directly answered, for a light rain started falling. The drops striking his sunburned face felt refreshing, but his feeble attempts to catch enough water in his hands for a drink failed. He chewed on the rough fabric of his rain-drenched uniform. The small amount of water gained this way left him surprisingly refreshed.

Nearby, Potvin could hear Germans moving through the grain. Periodically, they fired bursts from their submachine guns, as if they were either finishing off wounded soldiers or hoping to flush out any who, like him, might be in hiding. Confused about their intentions, Potvin crawled away from their line of movement. A look at his watch told him that darkness was still some hours away. If he could remain hidden until nightfall, he might still reach the Canadian lines and survive this hellish day.

◆ ◆ ◆

May 19 had not developed the way Lieutenant General Tommy Burns had envisioned. The I Canadian Corps commander had truly expected the Van Doos to break through the Hitler Line and open a gap through which a flying column from 5th Canadian Armoured Division could plunge. Even at 1400 hours, as Allard was initiating the regiment's withdrawal, Burns and Major General Bert Hoffmeister were conferring about the breakthrough force. Hoffmeister told Burns that the Irish Regiment of Canada, the tanks of the British Columbia Dragoon Guards, a battery of ten self-propelled antitank guns, and a squadron of the Governor General's Horse Guards reconnaissance regiment were ready and waiting. Burns advised him to maintain sufficient flexibility in his dispositions to allow for a quick shift of the force to other parts of the Liri Valley should 1st Canadian Infantry Brigade or elements of XIII Corps near Aquino open a hole before 3rd Canadian Infantry Brigade. Burns actually hoped that a breakout might come in the south near Pontecorvo, so that 5 CAD could swing northward in a wide arc to link up with XIII Corps advancing south from Aquino. Between them, the two forces could then surround and destroy the German divisions forming up along the Hitler Line.

Such optimistic plans were dashed, however, when Burns returned to his headquarters and phoned Eighth Army commander General Sir Oliver Leese. By now, Leese knew there would be no breakthrough at Aquino and that the R22eR attack had ended in a bloody repulse. He told Burns "to plan for a set attack in about forty-eight hours time and to institute the necessary preparations."[24]

In a letter to his wife, Leese wrote that May 19 had been: "A disappointing day — all along the line we have come up against strong defences."[25] Leese was not terribly surprised by the failed attacks, for such hastily thrown–together affairs were always gambles. Eighth Army would now proceed with the type of offensive for which it was noted and with which it was most experienced — a carefully planned set-piece assault carried out with methodical precision.

The intelligence staff at I Canadian Corps headquarters chose to explain the setback as the logical outcome of probing the Hitler Line "in strength," rather than a failed breakthrough. One staff officer described the German defenders as "a hotch-potch of units, which, given time to sort themselves out, would probably remain on the line as long as we permitted them to do so. So far the enemy, failing to appreciate the weight of our attack, has committed his immediately available reserves and more strategic reserves piece by piece, rather than mount a counterattack on a divisional level. Not once has he reinforced any sector by a group larger than regimental size. This indecision has produced the picture as we now know it: reserves put in anywhere the thin line was weakening resulting in the variety of units identified, under the command of the formation HQ into whose sector they were committed." Leese predicted that, lacking a division-sized reserve, the Germans would now try to regroup into more organized lines of resistance. "Consequently, the momentum which has been lost for a time must be regained before the enemy has a breather to carry out the regrouping and reorganizing of which he is now badly in need."[26]

Once it became obvious that the attack must fail, Vokes personally reconnoitred the Hitler Line from the safety of the overlooking low ridge occupied by his forward regiments. The front faced by 1st Canadian Infantry Division stretched approximately 4,500 yards from a point on the north where the Forme d'Aquino passed through the German line to the Liri River on the south. From the maps, Vokes knew the right front had no natural features that would impede armoured movement. On the left, however, a steep ravine ran from the Liri River to a point where it petered out about midway across the Canadian front. Mindful of the debacle presented by The Gully during the Ortona battle, Vokes wanted to avoid attacking across this ravine. He knew the entire front was riddled with antitank minefields, but believed a creeping barrage should detonate enough of these to enable the tanks to get through. If this failed, he surmised, "the tanks must take their chances as prior mine clearance of lanes through known minefields was not possible under these circumstances." Vokes decided his divisional attack would strike against the right flank.

Back at divisional headquarters, Vokes received a call from Burns. The corps commander ordered a morning meeting to discuss the divisional commander's plan. Burns promised that Brigadier E.C. (Johnny) Plow, the corps's senior gunnery officer, would help Vokes's staff develop an artillery fire plan. Leese, Burns reported, wanted the attack launched no later than May 22 and had guaranteed that the Canadians would be able to call on all the artillery at Eighth Army's disposal.

Vokes and his staff had a plan sketched out by midnight. If Burns approved it in the morning, Vokes could issue the necessary orders immediately and believed everything would be ready to go sometime between 1000 hours on May 22 and 1000 hours on May 23. Thinking a night attack inadvisable and wanting to start before noon in hopes the battle would be concluded before nightfall, Vokes would request a start time of 0600 hours on May 23.

Vokes still hoped that the set-piece attack might prove unnecessary. There was a good chance that the French on the left flank might get far enough west to so threaten the Germans in the Liri Valley with encirclement that they would withdraw. He also intended to keep 1 CIB probing hard against Pontecorvo's defences in hopes that a breach might be made. If this happened, Vokes would immediately shove the fresh 2nd Canadian Infantry Brigade through, "instead of employing it in what promised to be a costly frontal assault."[27]

◆ ◆ ◆

As darkness fell, Captain Pierre Potvin struggled painfully to start walking toward the Canadian lines. Every movement was sheer agony and he could barely turn onto his side, let alone stand. It was difficult to keep focused on the task at hand. Visions of his parents passed through his mind. He thought of all the friends and family he would never see again. Death would come to him here alone. He would bleed to death, dying slowly without food or water. The more he dwelt on his family, the stronger Potvin felt. After a short prayer, he summoned every ounce of courage and resolve that he had left and pulled himself to his feet in the chest-high grain. About a hundred yards away, he saw a German soldier standing next to a motorcycle propped against a scrub oak. Beyond the German, a self-propelled gun was moving slowly forward, its commander shouting orders loudly to the crew as if he had no fear of being overheard. Potvin wondered why Garceau would allow the Germans to set up so close to his company perimeter without fighting back. Realizing he was exposed, Potvin cautiously lay down again and waited another hour for things to settle down.

While he was waiting, the captain heard rustling nearby in the grain. Someone was coming toward him. Drawing his heavy Colt .45 pistol, Potvin could barely hold the weapon in both hands. Pain shooting out from his broken right wrist made him grind his teeth. Whenever he moved the fingers of his left hand to improve his grip on the gun, blood gushed from the wounds in that arm. Would he even be able to pull the trigger?

Peering hard into the gathering darkness, Potvin saw a man crawling through the grain about ten feet away and with a wave of relief realized he wore khaki and a Van Doos shoulder patch. The other man was Private Réné Casavant from 'B' Company. His leg was broken, but he could move more quickly than Potvin by dragging himself along on his arms. Potvin could only crawl very slowly, in almost snakelike fashion, and so forced himself to stand. Finding he could walk, if only at a shuffle, Potvin set off at what he figured was about the pace of a turtle. Yet it was faster than Casavant could crawl. Knowing the two would inevitably become separated in the dark, Potvin told the private that if he kept going on the cart track it would lead to 'D' Company's perimeter. The captain then set off at his own pace. He promised to send a stretcher-bearer once he reached the company lines.

Potvin's clothes were in tatters. The left sleeve of his tunic had been cut up to bandage his wounds and the remnants flapped loose, threatening to snag on branches. Because of the bandages he had wrapped around his right wrist, he was unable to grip the flapping pieces strongly enough to tear them away. His suspenders had been cut when his men were treating the exit wound in his back, so Potvin was in constant peril of his pants falling around his ankles to trip him. When he tried to take the pants off, he was unable to remove his puttees, into which the cuffs were stuck. So he returned to shuffling along, clinging to the waist of his pants with one hand.

After midnight, Potvin reached what he believed was 'D' Company's sector. Ahead lay nothing but devastation, visible in the light cast by several smouldering Sherman tanks. Bodies hung from the turrets and others lay stiffly beside the scorched vehicles. All were terribly burned. Infantry weapons and equipment were strewn about and Potvin saw several R22eR insignias on some of the equipment. He could not believe Garceau's company would have left, so kept casting about for some sign of troopers hiding in slit trenches. Finally, he was within paces of the house where he had talked to Garceau during the advance. "Where are you going like that, Little Pot?" Garceau had asked. "Where have you gone, my friend?" Potvin wondered.

After waiting fruitlessly for Casavant to arrive, Potvin decided to continue along the track. But a tree knocked over by artillery soon blocked his path. Its thick foliage and heavy branches were impossible to climb over in his condition. Off in the darkness, an Italian Breda machine gun chattered, a sign that Germans were about. Dizzy and increasingly delirious, Potvin thought of returning to the little house and looking for some food and water there. He staggered back and pawed around in the cupboards, drawers, and among the equipment scattered on the floor. Finding some old nuts, he bit into them, but they crumbled between his teeth into dust. Dust to dust, nothing but dust, all was dust. Exhausted, he crawled into a corner under some collapsed ceiling beams and plunged into unconsciousness.[28]

14

OPERATION
CHESTERFIELD

At 0900 hours on May 20, Lieutenant General Tommy Burns attended a conference at Eighth Army General Sir Oliver Leese's headquarters to discuss the set-piece plan for attacking the Hitler Line. Leese confirmed that the Canadians would make the break-through, while XIII Corps maintained pressure in the Aquino area. To avoid diluting the supporting arms, Lieutenant General Sir Sydney Kirkman's corps would seek only to tie down the 1st Parachute Division elements at Aquino. The Canadians would have priority call on all air force and artillery assets available to the Eighth Army, the latter numbering between 500 and 600 guns.[1] Air support would be provided primarily by 239 (Fighter-Bomber) Wing, Desert Air Force.[2]

Controlling traffic on the extremely limited number of roads in the Liri Valley remained a serious problem. There was particular competition between the Canadians and XIII Corps over Highway 6, which provided "the only practicable route" for reaching both 1st Canadian Infantry Division's right flank and XIII Corps's left-flank division. Despite the fact that the Canadians were to carry out the offensive, Leese designated Highway 6 the sole preserve of XIII Corps. This left the Canadians with only secondary, mostly unpaved, roads or local farm tracks to link the rear area to the front lines. Burns offered no protest.[3]

Burns called Major General Chris Vokes and told him to report immediately for a briefing at corps headquarters, two miles east of the Gari River.[4] Seething, Vokes and his driver drove through bumper-to-bumper traffic on the heavily congested roads. For days, the weather had been dry, making dust a continual problem, but the previous night had brought rain and a steady drizzle persisted. The moment Italian soil met water, slippery, mushy mud resulted. With the roof up on the Jeep and the wipers ineffectually scraping away at the muddy spray, Vokes faced the same poor visibility plaguing the many Royal Canadian Army Service Corps drivers on the tracks and dirt roads linking 1 CID to the rear. When his driver pulled out on Highway 6 to make better time, the Jeep was caught in a two-way traffic jam. Vokes noticed that most of these were XIII Corps's vehicles. The ten-mile trip took three hours.

When Vokes stormed into Burns's office, he was met by an equally angry lieutenant general who demanded to know what had taken him so long. Burns said he and his staff had been waiting for hours to begin the meeting. Vokes shot back that he wanted to know whether "any son of a bitch on his staff was aware the only road forward was jammed by trucks nose to arse." Had Burns granted XIII Corps authority to monopolize the route with no form of control? Whatever the case, Vokes said, "someone's ears should be burned off."

Venting his frustrations to the fullest, Vokes kept rolling. He told Burns that "it was customary for corps commanders to go forward to the HQ of divisional commanders whose troops were in contact with the enemy, and not to call them to the rear." By the time Vokes gave his presentation and spent another three hours returning to the front, he said, the better part of the day would be shot before he issued even one order necessary to get the attack plan under way. When Vokes finished his tirade, Burns merely scowled hard at him and strode in silence toward the briefing room. Vokes was sure that the rapport he had tried to build with his grim-faced superior was now completely broken, but he was unapologetic. He had "served under too many experienced British corps commanders to put up with an incompetent and inexperienced one, even though he was a Canadian."5

In the meeting room, Vokes found not only Burns's staff and 5th Canadian Armoured Division's Major General Bert Hoffmeister present, but also Eighth Army Chief of Staff Major General George Walsh and other Eighth Army luminaries. In a one-hour oral presentation, Vokes described his plan. Second Canadian Infantry Brigade, supported by two 25th Royal Tank Brigade regiments, would carry out the attack. It would be a two-phase operation. In Phase One, two regiments of infantry supported by tanks would assault on a 2,000-yard front and sever the Aquino-Pontecorvo road. This would constitute the penetration of the Hitler Line main defences. In Phase Two, the left forward regiment and the reserve regiment, supported by all surviving tanks, would advance further west and capture the ridge lying between the Aquino-Pontecorvo road and the road running from Pontecorvo to Highway 6. A two-mile-deep, 2,000-yard-wide penetration of the German line would have been achieved by day's end.

During each phase, the infantry and tanks would advance behind a rolling barrage provided by all Eighth Army 25-pounders with the fire lifting 100 yards every five minutes. As soon as possible, Vokes wanted all available medium and heavy artillery regiments to start hammering designated targets. This harassment would continue until the attack was launched.

Vokes said he needed between forty-eight and seventy-two hours to prepare, mostly because of the complex artillery plan and the need to bring sufficient ammunition up to the gun positions. Putting the knife into Burns a little, Vokes said that he could not possibly get back to his headquarters until 1600 hours to start issuing the necessary oral orders, so an attack beginning at 0600 hours on May 23 was hurried but feasible.

Although confident of his plan, Vokes was concerned about XIII Corps's undertaking no significant operations at Aquino. The 2 CIB regiment on the attack's right flank, Vokes pointed out, would be dangerously exposed to fire from the town and the defences anchored around it. These positions overlooked the proposed route of his attack, so their fire could rip into his flank. The only apparent solutions Vokes saw were to widen the artillery plan to constantly suppress the Aquino-area positions, or for the 78th Division to attack

Aquino with sufficient determination to keep the Germans occupied throughout the Canadian breakthrough. Walsh and Burns assured him that XIII Corps would have the 78th do its part. Burns then approved Vokes's plan.

As predicted, Vokes was not back at his headquarters until 1600 hours. He glared around his desk at the stacks of papers, most emanating from corps headquarters, and issued his first order. Divisional war diarist Captain S.P. Lachance wrote: "The GOC [General Officer Commanding] has laid down that in future all miscellaneous paper for his attention will be retained in 'G' Branch on a file. Any important information will be passed to him by word of mouth. Other information will be passed to him in quiet spells by the duty officer taking the file down to him, telling him what the contents are, and letting him see anything he is interested in. The reason for this is of course that the GOC is more than a little busy these days, and the amount of paper . . . is fantastic."[6]

Having tried to minimize the impact of Burns's continual paper barrage, Vokes set to work on what was now designated Operation Chesterfield. Just as he did so, however, Burns phoned to say that Leese wanted changes. Generally, Burns said in a follow-up written memo, Leese "thinks the scheme is sound, but from his experience of breaching the sort of defended line that you are tackling, feels we are not using enough infantry, and the front is not quite wide enough. He feels very strongly that you should use two brigades up — either three or four battalions in the line as you see fit." The front should be expanded to 2,500 yards with the barrage extending 500 yards further on either side. Another tank regiment would be provided.

"I am sorry not to have raised this point before," Burns wrote, "as your planning and preparations may have gone ahead on the other idea. But on thinking it over and hearing the Army Commander's reason (and he has great experience in this type of battle), I am sure he is right. . . . The Army Commander emphasized that in this kind of battle things seldom go as well as one expects, and unless you have considerable depth, there is danger of the breakthrough failing."[7]

Vokes altered his plan to accord with Leese's recommendations. Even as he did so, however, Vokes continued to press 1st Canadian Infantry Brigade commander Brigadier Dan Spry to break through in the Pontecorvo area. If by 1200 hours on May 22, the brigade looked likely to succeed, Vokes would drive 2 CIB through 1 CIB. This, he was certain, would be the best way to crack the Hitler Line, encircle the German defenders, and minimize his own casualties.

To retain enough flexibility to permit a quick shift of 2 CIB, Vokes held it back from the front lines. He ordered 3 CIB to hold its current positions across the entire front, which included the ground through which 2 CIB was to attack. Although Vokes's orders meant that both brigades would be realigning and moving battalions forward less than eighteen hours before launching a complex offensive, neither brigade commander objected.[8] The chance that Spry might succeed at Pontecorvo and spare the division the price of a frontal offensive tantalized them all.

♦ ♦ ♦

The Canadians faced a daunting task. Although the Hitler Line did not benefit from a natural obstacle, such as the Gari River had given the Gustav Line, the Todt labour units had compensated by constructing an interlocking web of manmade fortifications and obstacles. The line was formally designated a *Sicherungs-hauptkampflinie* (Main Defensive Battle Line) by German high command.[9] Only three such lines existed in Italy: the Gustav Line, now severed; the Hitler Line; and the Gothic Line running from Pisa to Rimini. Once the Hitler Line was broken, there would be little chance the Germans could halt the Allied advance short of the Gothic Line.

Construction work had proceeded for five months under the watchful eye of Allied aerial reconnaissance. Thousands of photographs had been taken and scrutinized by intelligence specialists. Appreciations were drafted and redrafted as new information developed. By May 20, Eighth Army intelligence staff had a fair picture of the extent of fortifications and the strength of the German forces manning them.

While the Hitler Line was not fixed on a natural obstacle, it did use natural terrain to advantage. On the northern flank, it anchored into the mountains adjacent to Aquino. From Aquino, the line followed a slight rise in the ground running south to Pontecorvo, where the Liri River ran west to east and served to anchor that end of the line. It was believed that Aquino and Pontecorvo were heavily fortified, but that shortages of materials might have delayed full completion of this work.[10] Between the Liri River and the point where the Forme d'Aquino passed through the Hitler Line just south of Aquino, the fortifications had an average depth of 900 yards. In front of the line, the ground was generally level for a distance of 1,000 yards. Lacking sufficient time to clear the scrub oak from this area, there were many pockets of natural cover that approached the barbed-wire line. The tall grain that had sprouted up provided natural cover for attacking forces and limited German fields of fire.[11]

The woods and tall grain were, of course, also obstacles to the offence, providing ample camouflage for the placing of snipers, machine-gunners, and antitank guns out front of the line — a tactic used to good effect against the Royal 22e Regiment's assault. That attack had also run into a carefully prepared U-shaped killing ground that used the smallest advantage of height to bring fire against an attacker from three sides. Such positions were difficult to detect by aerial reconnaissance and the deliberately deceptive lack of obstacles offered in front of the horseshoe's mouth served to suck attackers into a narrow area that could be saturated with small-arms and presighted artillery and mortar fire.

Fronting the entire line was a nineteen-foot-wide apron of barbed wire into which a mixture of German and Italian mines had been laced. The ground inside the wire was overgrown with tall grass that made spotting mines difficult. More mines were scattered in front of the wire and immediately behind. Intelligence staff believed that mine-laying operations had not begun until May 11, when it became apparent that the Gustav Line might be breached. Done in haste, many mines — particularly the larger antitank varieties — were visible to the naked eye. All too many, however, were properly concealed. The mines numbered in the thousands and dense fields of them crisscrossed any obvious tank approach.[12] Because of the high grass and grain fields, aerial reconnaissance could not spot major minefields so that these could be avoided in the attack plan.[13] As well, every night more mines were being sown. On the nights of May 18–19 and 19–20 alone, 3,000 fresh Teller and Italian antitank mines had been added to the deadly mix.[14]

Zigzagging across the wire band was an antitank ditch created by setting off explosive charges at nineteen-foot intervals across the width of the entire valley. Because of the precise spacing of the charges, the ditch was really a series of overlapping craters that varied in depth from eight feet to fifteen feet and in width from fifteen to thirty feet, depending on their proximity to the centre of the explosion. Aerial observation revealed that the tendency of Italian soil to crumble into any adjoining depression and for those to become waterlogged had seriously plagued attempts to make the ditch an effective tank obstacle.[15] It was believed the tanks could wallow through, although when they reared to go up the side facing the Germans, their undercarriages would be momentarily exposed to antitank fire.[16]

From aerial reconnaissance and examination of the fortifications used at the Gustav Line, intelligence staff knew that many camouflaged concrete and steel pillboxes existed, housing antitank guns and machine guns. Most were impossible to locate, because the structures were so deeply buried that the embrasures housing the gun ports rose no more than three or four feet above ground level. Intelligence officers were baffled by one camouflaged structure that appeared on photos as a forty-nine-foot-by-forty-nine-foot square of concrete. On May 12, Eighth Army staff designated it a prototype defensive structure. Four similar structures were also noted. The staff could only surmise that "they are possibly large dugouts."[17]

◆ ◆ ◆

The large concrete structures were actually *Panzerturms* and they were masterfully camouflaged. Each Panzerturm was a fabricated steel-and-concrete shelter dug into the ground and mounted with the turret from a disabled Panther Mark V tank. Most were constructed on the site of a destroyed building. The building's rubble provided additional protective cover and camouflage. The turret was painted to match its immediate surrounding and camouflage nets made of wire interwoven with bamboo grass were arrayed over the position's entry points. Depressing the long distinctive barrel of the .75-millimetre gun between two rows of sandbags rendered it invisible from the air. Aerial photos revealed only regular-shaped, light-toned squares that lacked any visible detail. When detected at all, intelligence staff could do no better than label them "concrete structure." The form of defensive weapon housed was unknown.[18]

Camouflage was given priority in the German engineering work, even at the cost of completing fewer positions. But there was no shortage of fortified works. Tenth Army planners knew that any Allied attempt to breach the line must involve a combined infantry and tank force. If the tanks were destroyed, infantry penetrations could be contained and even repelled by counterattacks. Therefore the Germans focused on developing an impenetrable antitank screen. The Panzerturms were the centrepiece of this screen, with nine in the Canadian sector. Each turret could rotate through a 360-degree field of fire and had a maximum range of about 1,200 yards. Sited 150 to 200 yards behind or to the flank of each Panther gun were two to three towed .75- or .50-millimetre antitank guns that could support and protect the main gun from flanking fire. Dug in around this array of antitank weapons were heavy and light machine-gun pillboxes and open infantry trenches. Other antitank guns were scattered along the length of the line and self-propelled guns were so positioned that they could quickly move wherever an attack materialized. These latter included .88-millimetre guns mounted on Mark IV tank bodies, which the Allies called Hornets, 5-centimetre guns fitted onto the chassis of Mark IIIs, and .75-millimetre guns mounted on either the chassis of a Mark III or the back of an armoured half-track. In all, there were sixty-two mobile antitank guns, of which twenty-five were self-propelled guns.[19]

To prevent Allied infantry from closing on the Panzerturms, the surrounding ground was overlapped by well-emplaced machine-gun positions. Most were housed in concrete or steel pillboxes, log-roofed gun pits, or inside pits dug under houses. Ten heavily armoured pillboxes, each housing a two-man machine-gun team, were positioned between fifty and seventy-five yards behind the wire. One hundred yards back of the pillboxes stood a row of open-topped concrete gun emplacements for other machine-gun teams. The further the Allies came inside the Hitler Line defences, the more numerous the German positions became, forming a maze of weapon pits and pillboxes that could lay down a blanket of interlocking fire from all directions. The concrete emplacements were ringed by a metal track to which a machine gun was fitted, enabling the gunner to quickly swivel the weapon to face in any direction.

Because the number of German troops available to defend the line was quite limited, emphasis was placed on arming most with machine guns — weapons the Panzer Grenadiers and paratroopers were well versed in using. There were relatively few men left to serve as riflemen and it was intended that most of these would act as snipers, hiding in the trees and engaging Allied infantry as they approached the wire and minefields. Narrow gaps, amply covered by machine-gun emplacements that could fire directly down the gap's length, were left in the wire for back-and-forth infantry movement.[20]

A manpower shortage was the biggest German handicap. The two most effective German divisional commanders in Italy — 1st Parachute Division's General Richard Heidrich and 90th Panzer Grenadiers' Generalleutnant Ernst-Günther Baade — shared responsibility for this area. Both generals, and their divisions, were well known to the Canadians, who had fought them in Sicily and during the bloody battle of Ortona in December 1943. Baade was a flamboyant and highly competent cavalryman, with a penchant for wearing Scottish kilts. Since the paratroopers were arrayed along the section of line guarding Aquino, the Panzer Grenadiers would bear the burden of meeting the Canadian offensive.

The 90th Panzer Grenadiers were not the crack division they had once been. Although there were still many veterans who had spent almost five years of continual campaigning, the division had a large share of relatively new recruits. Morale was low, but the battalions were far from broken in spirit. The division was, however, seriously depleted. On May 20, the division had deployed from north to south: 200 men in the 361st Regiment's 2nd Battalion and 200 in its 3rd Battalion, 150 men in the 576th Regiment's 1st Battalion and 125 in its 2nd Battalion. Positioned immediately to the north of Pontecorvo were about 360 men in the 44th Field Replacement Battalion, which had a large contingent of foreign soldiers of very limited reliability. Inside Pontecorvo itself was a force of engineers drawn from the 334th Engineer Battalion and the 190th Engineer Battalion, numbering no more than 250. At best, Baade's force had 1,285 infantry trying to hold a 5,500-yard-long front.[21] Complicating matters even more for Baade, his small force was being relentlessly ground down by casualties resulting from the need to engage the daily Canadian probing attacks and reconnaissance patrols. As each day whittled his force away, Baade received virtually no reinforcements.

What provided Baade with a significant advantage was the

strength of his supporting arms and the defensive works inside which his men were positioned. He expected to meet a full-scale infantry-cum-tank offensive that would fall somewhere in the centre of his line. Accordingly, that was where he positioned his strongest and most seasoned regiment, the 576th. It was to Baade's advantage if the Canadians delayed their offensive in order to mount the set-piece operation of which Eighth Army was so fond. Time was his greatest ally. With time, he might receive more reinforcements, dig more infantry trenches, lay more mines, and clear better fields of fire through the grain fields. His men had started occupying the Hitler Line in strength on May 18 and needed about four more days to organize the best possible resistance.[22]

While Baade was going to get the time he needed, he would not be reinforced. Although Commander-in-Chief Southwest Generalfeldmarschall Albert Kesselring had ordered Fourteenth Army, containing the Anzio beachhead, to transfer the 26th Panzer Grenadier Division to Tenth Army command on May 20, he had done so in order to deploy it against the advancing French corps.[23] Kesselring had little to offer Baade. The general would have to do his best with what men he had. Despite the weakness of his forces in Italy, Kesselring remained confident that his generals could hold the Hitler Line. As Generalleutnant Fritz Wentzell, Tenth Army's Chief of Staff, later wrote, Kesselring's headquarters staff "persisted in their idea of defence of gradually wearing down the attackers as it had done in the previous battles of Cassino and the battle of the Sangro."[24]

◆ ◆ ◆

Kesselring was not the only one harking back to the winter battles for inspiration. Vokes, too, kept thinking of opportunities won and lost during 1 CID's advance from the Moro River to Ortona. In the end, it had been a flanking operation by 3rd Canadian Infantry Brigade that had carried his regiments past The Gully. The prospect of 1 CIB doing so at Pontecorvo, so that Operation Chesterfield need not be mounted, obsessed him.

Another piece of intelligence encouraged him in this hope. A Pole, impressed into the 44th Field Replacement Battalion and taken prisoner by the Princess Louise Dragoon Guards, reported that the defences around Pontecorvo were incomplete. Although a deep canal crossed in front of the town, the Pole assured his interrogators that tanks could easily cross over. Once Pontecorvo was taken, nothing could stop a tank advance westward on the Pontecorvo–San Giovanni road.[25]

This and other intelligence reaffirmed Vokes's certainty that Pontecorvo was the weak link. From the maps, it appeared that if 1 CIB moved at least one regiment across the Liri River and advanced along the south bank that had been cleared by the French, he could mount an amphibious attack across the river into Pontecorvo itself. With other regiments, backed by tanks, assaulting across the canal at the same time, the Germans defending the town should be easily overwhelmed.

Vokes ordered Brigadier Dan Spry to investigate the possibility of such an attack. Although dubious, Spry agreed. He selected Royal Canadian Regiment commander Lieutenant Colonel Bill Mathers and the RCR company commanders to go with him. If the plan proved feasible, it would fall to the RCR to carry out the river crossing.[26] To give Spry more resources, Vokes placed the normally independent Princess Louise Dragoon Guards reconnaissance regiment under his command. By the time Vokes called it a night on May 20, he had reason to be pleased. His staff was working out the full details for Operation Chesterfield and he had an alternative flanking assault in the works that promised a quicker and less costly conclusion.[27]

◆ ◆ ◆

About the time Vokes finished issuing instructions to Spry on May 20, R22eR Captain Pierre Potvin was painfully crawling toward the woods from which the regiments had attacked. Weak from loss of blood, Potvin knew if he did not find help very soon he would die. The likelihood of his living through another night was slight.

Since being wakened at dawn that morning by the hammering of a German machine gun, Potvin had narrowly escaped capture several times. He vaguely remembered seeing German troops moving through the house during the night, but not finding him hidden under the collapsed roof beams. Whether the memories were real or hallucinatory dreams, he knew not. In the morning, the house was wrapped in the inevitable fog. Digging in his pockets, Potvin had discovered his compass gone, leaving him with no idea which direction led toward the Canadian lines. He would have to wait until the fog lifted before moving.

Searching the house, he found a room where a stack of Van Doos' haversacks leaned against one wall. All were blood encrusted and many blood-soaked bandages were scattered across the floor. 'C' Company must have used the room as a first-aid post. Despite the bandages wrapping his broken right wrist and the pain shooting through his left arm from the wounds there, Potvin wrestled several packs open. In one, he discovered half a stale cheese sandwich and a dreg of red wine in a water bottle. He wolfed both down.

Just as he drained the wine, several shots were fired close to the house. Potvin squeezed into the cover afforded by some large wine casks. German voices came from the room where he had spent the night. Then one infantryman entered the room where Potvin crouched. The man kicked a few of the haversacks, conducting a desultory search. Potvin thought that if the German paused, he must surely hear his breathing. After a few minutes, the German left, but the party stuck around the house for another hour before wandering off. From the haversacks, Potvin removed a gas cape and spread it out on the floor under the raised wine casks. Then he lay down to wait for the fog to lift. Swarms of flies descended on him, crawling over his bloody bandages. The feel, sight, and sound of the insects blanketing his wounds and his bloody and tattered uniform were almost unbearable. He gritted his teeth and endured.

About noon, he left the house. The sun was shining. His only directional guide was a shaky memory of Major Ovila Garceau standing in the doorway of the house as Potvin passed. If his memory was correct, the door had opened toward his line of approach. Fearful of being spotted by the Germans, he crawled slowly in what he hoped was the right direction. To his left, the sound of tanks moving about could be heard, but whether they were Allied or German he could not tell. Potvin carried on, taking, as his strength failed, increasingly longer rests between ever shorter periods of slow crawling. Nearing the end of his reserves, he heard men coming through the brush under the scrub oaks. Peering into the dim light, he saw a flash of khaki and through parched lips croaked as loudly as he could: "Van Doo here. Twenty-second." Staggering to his feet, he moved toward the figures and saw them cautiously approaching with rifles at the ready.

A Carleton and York patrol gathered around him. They placed him on a stretcher and hurriedly carried him back to the lines. One man told him it was about 1900 hours. Potvin muttered that he had then been in no man's land for almost thirty hours. Hearing this, men on every side pressed water bottles and bits of rations his way. Potvin felt like weeping with gratitude. An overwhelming sense of the comradeship that exists among fighting soldiers washed over him.

Once inside Canadian lines, Potvin was transferred to the R22eR Regimental Aid Post. He learned there that the regiment had given him up for dead. Nobody had seen any sign of Private Réné Casavant, whom Potvin had briefly encountered during his trek across no man's land. A patrol was immediately mounted, however, to look for him. At dawn, when the patrol discovered a blood-covered bandage, it pressed on and Casavant was recovered. The two men were loaded into an ambulance and taken to a field dressing station. As a nurse cut away his tunic, Potvin asked her to detach his shoulder badges and place them in the bag with his other personal effects. A Medical Officer quipped, "I think these Van Doos think of their regiment even when they are dead." Potvin laughed, but thought it might be true. He also wondered how long it would be before he returned to 'B' Company. That he would return was, in his mind, not even a question.[28]

15

IT'S SHEER
MURDER

Like so many towns in the Liri Valley, Pontecorvo traced its lineage to the Roman Empire and a period two centuries before the birth of Christ. Set on a hill rising about 300 feet above the valley floor, it had been built with war in mind. Pontecorvo was bordered immediately to the south by the Liri River and to the east by the narrow San Martino River. In modern times, a canal had been created in the river in front of the town to prevent flooding. A bend in the Liri River provided some protection to the town's western flank. The hill upon which Pontecorvo stood was steeply sloped on all but the northwestern edge, where a road climbed up to enter the town square. Terraces for gardens created a series of almost sheer steps connected by switchback paths. A path of this kind ran up every side of the hill.

German engineers had positioned the Hitler Line's main defensive works about 2,000 yards in front of the canal. These defences were roughly equivalent in strength and design to those found elsewhere along the line. The barbed-wire field was a bit narrower, about nine feet, but mines were densely laid in front of and behind the wire. There was no doubt that the ancient, pale-grey stone buildings and church bordering the slope on the eastern side had been fortified and housed machine-gun positions. Given the advantage of their height, these positions could bring murderous fire down on any attack against the forward line.

Many buildings in Pontecorvo had been reduced to rubble. The rest had suffered bomb and shell damage. In past weeks, Pontecorvo had been bombed forty-seven times. The number would have been higher, but 239 (Fighter-Bomber) Wing, Desert Air Force command refused requests by 1st Canadian Infantry Brigade for indiscriminate bombing of the town. The air wing commanders had learned from Cassino that bombing a town into ruin only made it more defensible. Instead, they told the army commanders that they would bomb targets in towns only if "they were described with a six-figure map reference."[1]

Such map references had been provided on May 20 by 1 CIB headquarters when it called for bomb runs against pinpointed targets on the southeastern side of Pontecorvo. From these positions, German machine guns and mortars were engaging a French force that was trying to pass the town on the southern side of the Liri River. At the same time, 1 CIB requested the bombing of buildings identified as German barracks northeast of the town and of the town's clock tower, believed to house an observation post.[2] At 1300 hours, twenty-two Kittyhawk bombers swooped down and unleashed their bomb loads with deadly accuracy. Simultaneously, Canadian artillery hit Pontecorvo with a five-hour-long bombardment. Opposition to the French advance ceased soon after the artillery-bomber operation began.[3] The artillery was less precise than the bombers and much of the town was reduced to a smoldering ruin by dawn of May 21. The clock tower, having been knocked to pieces by a direct bomb hit, no longer dominated the skyline.

Long before, most of Pontecorvo's civilian population had fled. Nearby farms and country homes had also been abandoned. While some refugees had gone west toward Rome, the majority had taken to the northern mountains. Thousands of Liri Valley refugees crossed the Apennines into Abruzzo province on the Adriatic side. Few would ever return, for there was little to come back to in a land devastated by months of war. The Liri Valley, more than anywhere on the World War II western front, resembled the band of Belgium and northern

France inside which Germans and Allies had fought the better part of the previous war. As eking a life out of no man's land in Flanders had been impossible, so too was it nearly impossible to survive in the Liri Valley. For weeks, those residents who stayed remained hunkered in the shelter of basements and caves dug into hillsides or the banks of rivers. They were hungry, generally dirty, lice-infested, often sick. Explosions, shrapnel, or bullets injured many, particularly children. Of eighty-nine civilians treated by Canadian medical personnel during one short period, thirty-five were treated for wounds inflicted by military weapons.[4]

It was not unusual for the Canadians in the Liri Valley to find dead civilians when they entered a home. Relatively common also was the sight of civilians harvesting vegetables and grain, even when an area was under shellfire or known to be laced with mines. It was a dangerous practice for people who had no idea how to detect a mine's deadly presence, and many of these desperate harvesters were killed or maimed.[5] Sometimes people materialized out of the morning fog and wandered past the Canadians like black-clothed ghosts, heading who knew where. When the sun was out and the soft, warm light touched the land, the Liri Valley presented an enthrallingly beautiful landscape with its sharp-featured surrounding hills, red poppies intermixed with yellow stands of grain, rusty-leafed oak trees, and lush green vineyards. But a closer look revealed that hardly a tree had not been splintered by shell blast or shrapnel and the leaves were turning reddish because of this damage. And almost always, the civilians encountered were living with personal tragedy. Three Rivers Regiment's Charles Prieur thought Italy probably the most beautiful land in the world, but he was haunted by the memory of an Italian woman walking across a field toward him. She carried a young boy in her arms. The boy had lost a leg to a mine and the Medical Officers did what they could for him, as they did for any injured civilian who was brought to the aid stations. But there was nothing that could make him whole again.[6]

During the heat of battle, it was convenient to try to forget about the possible presence of civilians on the battlefield. Better not to worry about whether somebody other than Germans might occupy a house or cower in the dubious safety of a village's church, both of which were likely targets for artillery or aerial bombardment.

Looking up at Pontecorvo, so imposing on its hill, and yet seemingly deserted, the Canadians in 1 CIB gave little thought to whether there might be civilians in its buildings. They cheered the planes making bomb runs on the town and were heartened by the artillery shells exploding there.

The troops of the brigade's three regiments spent a lot of time looking toward Pontecorvo and reminding themselves that a direct attack against its formidable position would not be necessary. All had heard the news that the other two brigades would breach the Hitler Line and had no idea that Vokes hoped to avoid launching Operation Chesterfield by having their brigade crack through the German defences here.[7] The men in the three regiments of 1 CIB were happy to spend most of May 21 resting and cleaning their gear and weapons. Some patrols reached the wire's edge. Others sought to clear hard points of resistance east of the Hitler Line, but it was largely an appreciated day of relative quiet.

Not that the battlefield was silent. The Germans kept everyone on edge with sporadic shelling and mortaring. To the southwest, the French advance continued. Around noon, 1 CIB headquarters received an urgent appeal for the Canadians to bring artillery to bear against fifty German tanks massing on the north side of the river. It appeared the German armour was preparing to cross and attack the French, who had no artillery within range.[8] With the French providing map references, 2nd Field Regiment, Royal Canadian Artillery fired five missions designated "Mike" targets, which meant that all the regiment's 25-pounders were brought to bear. Soon the medium and heavy gun regiments backed up the 25-pounders and hundreds of high-explosive rounds rained down on the German tankers.[9] After forty-five minutes of concentrated shelling, the French reported that the tanks were dispersing and trying to hide in the small oak groves. Several tanks were reported to be burning.

The Germans were not finished, however. Once more, the tanks emerged from the woods to attempt a river crossing. A squadron of Kittyhawk bombers was called in while the Canadian gunners adjusted their guns to bring "Mike" fire against the road junctions the tanks had to cross. When the planes finished their bomb runs, the guns fired. Each time a squadron of bombers swooped in, the guns ceased shooting to avoid hitting the planes. The German attack broke up under this continual pressure. Aerial reconnaissance reported six burning tanks and intelligence estimated that at least ten had been destroyed.[10]

◆ ◆ ◆

While the Canadian gunners were helping the French repel the German armoured counterattack, 1 CIB Brigadier Dan Spry and a party of Royal Canadian Regiment officers crossed the river in an inflatable rubber boat. They sought to determine whether Major General Chris Vokes's idea of launching a one-regiment amphibious attack across the river into Pontecorvo was feasible. The party consisted of Spry, RCR commander Lieutenant Colonel Bill Mathers, the commanders of Mathers's infantry companies, and the regiment's artillery officer.[11]

Nothing Spry saw convinced him the attack was possible. Both riverbanks were steep and approximately twelve feet high. To carry out the attack, the RCR would first have to cross the river in inflatable rubber boats far enough to the east of the Hitler Line that they would avoid being seen. They would then have to carry the boats to a crossing point opposite Pontecorvo. In full view of the enemy, the regiment would have to scramble down the far bank, paddle across the thirty-foot-wide river, climb the opposite steep bank, and crawl up the 300-foot terraced hill to fight their way into the town. Of course, the Germans would be raking the troops with machine-gun and mortar fire every inch of the way. Spry thought the plan crazy, but he consented to Mathers' conducting a more thorough reconnaissance.[12]

Accompanied by some French officers, Mathers reconnoitred the river's edge opposite Pontecorvo. He then returned to French Brigade headquarters and briefed his waiting commanders: Captain Dick Dillon, Major Sandy Mitchell, Major Rick Forgrave, and Captain D.W. Rose. Mathers enthusiastically described how the attack could be executed. The company commanders listened in stunned silence. The men then returned to the regiment, while Mathers set off on an even more thorough reconnaissance mission.[13]

The moment the four officers reached regimental headquarters, Mitchell took them to see Second-in-Command Major Strome Galloway. Before the war, Mitchell had been a sergeant who had worked his way up through the ranks. A tough, no-nonsense soldier, he knew his business and hated wasting lives unnecessarily.

Mitchell spelled out Mathers's scheme. Dillon told Galloway, "It'll be a suicide." Galloway agreed. "We'll go see the brigade commander," he said. At brigade headquarters, Mitchell no sooner started describing Mathers's plan than Spry gestured him to stop. "That's all nonsense," he said. There was a new plan, approved by Vokes, and the river operation was dead.[14]

Vokes was still determined that 1 CIB would break through at Pontecorvo. During the day, the Princess Louise Dragoon Guards reconnaissance regiment had been patrolling aggressively in the pocket between the river and the east-west road approaching the town. They had swept up twenty-two prisoners and killed about an equal number in exchange for two of their own killed and nine wounded. Vokes took a look at the prisoners and decided "they were a very scruffy lot . . . pleased to be out of the war and volunteered the information their fellows . . . were ready and eager to surrender the moment opportunity afforded." This, Vokes later wrote, "convinced me even more there was a good possibility the 1st Brigade attacks might well succeed in breaching the defences."

When Spry reported that the river-crossing plan was impossible, Vokes ordered a head-on, one-regiment-strong assault against Pontecorvo. Vokes thought that Spry was not driving his brigade hard enough. Given the poor quality of the defenders at Pontecorvo, he believed Spry should have broken through. The day before he had placed the Princess Louise Dragoon Guards under Spry's control, but he now returned it to independent status. Vokes arranged for a troop of 142nd Royal Tank Regiment to support the PLDG in a drive right along the river's edge to Pontecorvo. This, he thought, would take some pressure off 1 CIB's attack and, given that "the unit was very aggressive in spirit and skillful in action, would certainly make a dint in the enemy defences."[15]

Spry called an Orders Group of his regimental commanders for 2230 hours. Believing Vokes's information to be inaccurate, he issued his orders reluctantly. Intelligence reports from I Canadian Corps headquarters indicated that there were about 1,200 men facing his brigade, while divisional intelligence said that it was only 700. Either way, a regiment-wide attack would field no more than 400 infantrymen. With two companies out front, there would be just 200 men on the attack's leading edge. Spry didn't think that outnumbered men attacking a massive fortification were likely to succeed, no matter what the quality of the defenders.

Attacking on a one-regiment front was a gamble at the best of times and one that Spry had seen repeatedly chopped to pieces by well-entrenched Panzer Grenadiers and parachutists during the Moro River–Ortona fighting. That the opposition this time was supposedly second-rate did little to minimize the fact that the 44th Field Replacement Battalion occupied superior ground and defences. Any attack against Pontecorvo faced significant obstacles. An attack cobbled together in such haste promised disaster.

Listening to the slight brigadier describe the attack plan, Lieutenant Colonel Ian Johnston hardly believed it. His 48th Highlanders of Canada were to punch through the Hitler Line alone and conduct a right hook to a point of high ground just to the north of Pontecorvo, designated Point 106. This position dominated the Pontecorvo-Aquino road. Once the Highlanders were on the objective, the Hastings and Prince Edward Regiment and the Royal Canadian Regiment would join the attack. These regiments would widen the breach, with the Hasty P's broadening the front to the north of Point 106 and the RCR driving into Pontecorvo from the northeast. As Spry continued, Johnston remained silent. He pointedly ignored the nervous glances cast his way by his subordinate officers. It was obvious they were waiting for him to bring this madness to an abrupt stop. The time for the attack was set at 0630 hours on May 22. As it was already past midnight, this left the regiment about four hours to prepare and then move to the start line.

Briefing over, the 48th Highlanders quietly left the room, save Johnston who remained stonily silent until he and Spry were alone. Johnston quietly, but firmly, told Spry that such an attack, prepared in haste, would fail and yield only heavy casualties. If he was ordered to proceed, Johnston wished to be relieved of command. He would not lead his regiment to its death.

Spry was sympathetic. He explained, however, that corps and even army command had endorsed the attack. There was little that could be done about the short timeframe. Johnston told Spry he understood all this, but that unless he had more time to prepare he would not order the regiment into battle. Somebody else would have to do that.

The brigadier did not want to lose one of his most capable regimental commanders because of a plan that he also thought poorly conceived. He called Vokes.[16] When Vokes came to the phone, Spry asked for a delay to noon. A heated argument ensued, but Vokes finally compromised and agreed to the attack's starting at 1000 hours.

Hanging up the phone, Vokes could barely contain his disappointment. Noon was the agreed point at which the 2nd and 3rd brigades would begin moving toward their assigned start points for Operation Chesterfield. If the Highlanders did not achieve a breakthrough in the first two hours of their attack, it would be too late to exploit any success gained there. Operation Chesterfield was almost inevitable.[17]

♦ ♦ ♦

Johnston arrived back at the battered Italian farmhouse that served as the regiment's tactical headquarters at 0130 hours on May 22. He found his officers, awaiting his return, all asleep on the floor. Hurriedly he woke them and told them the attack was a go.[18] Before the attack started, sappers from a company of the Royal Canadian Engineers would cut three gaps in the wire and clear the mines in front of and behind them to create tank lanes for the supporting 25th Royal Tank Brigade.[19]

Artillery support was to consist of twelve concentrations called in as required. However, the artillery trace that marked targets on the maps was not ready until 0300 hours. Only one copy was provided, meaning that regimental staff must quickly draw others and these would not be ready until after the 0600 final coordination conference. There would be little time for the company commanders to familiarize themselves with the preplotted firing points that the artillery could easily bring their guns to bear on if necessary. The other bad news regarding the artillery support was that, due to the haste with which the operation was being put together, the Highlanders would have only one Forward Observation Officer from 2nd Field Regiment.

At 0400 hours, an engineering officer from the Royal Canadian Engineers' 1st Field Company showed up with two sappers and a mine detector. Johnston sent an infantry patrol out with the team to cover their efforts to clear the gaps, but it was obviously too small a sapper party to do much good. Fortunately, sappers from 2 RCE Field Company had earlier that evening swept a road that ran up to the German wire, and a gap in the wire existed nearby. The sapper officer returned at 0500 hours from his mission. He told Johnston there were no mines in front of one of the points in the wire that was to have been cleared for a tank lane, and that the wire there was in such poor shape that it presented no obstacle to either infantry or tanks. But this gap was north of the road and he could not say if there were mines on the other side of the wire.

It was a haggard group of officers who reported to the 0600 meeting. They learned that the sappers from the tank regiment who were to have built crossings over the antitank ditch had never shown up. Johnston was concerned that if the regiment and the tanks attacked against the three points where gaps were originally to have been created, some or all of the companies might find their routes blocked by mines. He didn't want tanks and infantry, undoubtedly under fire, having to move across some minefield to find another way through the wire. The only solution was for the tanks to use the road, which also crossed the antitank ditch. As the gap found by the engineering officer was near the road, one tank troop could break off with an infantry company, shortly before the tanks reached the wire, to pass through it.

Johnston assigned 'D' Company to advance on the right and 'B' on the left, each supported by a tank troop. 'A' and 'C' companies would follow closely. The regiment's tactical headquarters section would remain on a height of land overlooking the battlefield. From here, Major Don Mackenzie — Johnston's second-in-command — would direct artillery fire as needed. This would to some extent reduce the operational handicap posed by having only one FOO. Johnston would travel immediately ahead of 'C' Company with a small "rover" party consisting of a radioman and a couple of riflemen. Briefing finished, the officers returned to their companies, where they had yet to give the platoon officers their final briefing. These officers in turn would brief the section leaders, who then had to explain the general nature of the attack to the troops.[20]

At 0940 hours, the tank liaison officer, Major A.H.S. Moser, told Johnston that the tank regiment had just received orders "to hold up until further orders." He said that Vokes had told the commander of the 25th Royal Tank Brigade that a reconnaissance by three tanks in line should be made up the road before the rest of the tanks were committed to the action. The tanks in 'C' Squadron had also not reached their forming-up point and it was obvious the attack would not be ready to proceed as scheduled at 1000 hours. Johnston radioed Spry and explained the situation. Spry knew nothing of orders for any reconnaissance preparatory to the attack and soon verified with Vokes's headquarters that no such suggestion had emanated from there. He told Johnston to get the attack under way at 1030 hours. When Johnston explained this to Moser, he agreed to proceed with the original plan and drop the reconnaissance idea.

As the second hands of the commanders' watches swept past 1030, Johnston blew his whistle and the platoon commanders followed suit. The soldiers had been standing quietly for thirty minutes as the attack finally came together. Now they trotted across wide-open terrain toward the German wire about a thousand yards away. Major Jim Counsell's 'D' Company and Captain Jack Wilson's 'B' Company led, with the tanks close behind and 'C' and 'A' companies bringing up the rear. The temperature was already cracking eighty degrees Fahrenheit and sweat poured off the running men. Their bodies were tense with expectation, waiting for the German machine guns and mortars to open up. Then, remarkably, the lead companies were at the wire and not a shot had been fired. The tanks were still coming up, but everything seemed to be going like clockwork.[21]

They entered the wire. In places, men could step over one wire apron or jump across it, but more often than not they had to snake over, under, or through the rusty strands. Barbs caught in uniforms, snagged on gear, tore flesh. They had been seen by now and the Germans were starting to rake the barbed-wire position with machine-gun fire. Yet it was a mistake for a man to hurry and try to fight his way through. That only ensured that more barbs grabbed him and, as he struggled, cut more deeply.[22]

Suddenly, from a position behind the wire the powerful thump of a .75-millimetre gun fired. A Sherman exploded. Two more shots pounded out from the hidden position and two more Shermans were knocked out. A troop of Churchills positioned behind the Highlanders was able to identify the source of the fire — a Panzerturm. The Churchills shelled the gun turret, as did a 17-pounder antitank gun stationed on a height of land in the section of line held by the Hasty P's. One of the gunners scored a lucky hit that silenced the gun.[23]

'D' and 'B' companies got through the wire and started crossing the antitank ditch. Machine-gun fire was coming their way from several directions. No. 17 Platoon commander Lieutenant Doug Snively jumped down into the ditch. In front of him, a redheaded private was just going over the top when a bullet hit him, throwing him back on top of Snively. The officer rolled the dead man aside, climbed out of the ditch, and pressed on. The Highlanders threw themselves into a network of German machine-gun positions and started working their way through. Initially, they threw grenades into the gun slits of the concrete and steel pillboxes, but soon realized the positions were empty. Most of the Germans who had been manning the guns moments before had fled.[24] Ten surrendered.

The entire regiment was now inside the wire and past the antitank ditch, holding a position about 300 yards wide on either side of the road and 400 yards deep. Although exposed to fire from the ridge to the north and from Pontecorvo, the position was relatively good for defence. Cover was provided by a number of scraggly oaks and poplars, and a few shallow gullies and ditches that could be used for shelters. Johnston established his forward headquarters in one of the concrete pillboxes.[25] To their left, the regiment discovered a squadron of the Princess Louise Dragoon Guards reconnaissance regiment. 'A' Squadron had crashed boldly through the line shortly before the Highlanders' attack. The squadron had rounded up about sixty prisoners and claimed "the distinction of being the first unit in the Eighth Army to penetrate the Hitler Line," wrote the PLDG's jubilant war diarist at day's end.[26] Johnston quickly incorporated this squadron into his defensive line.

As the men dug in, the Germans saturated the position with mortar, Nebelwerfer, and artillery fire. From his observation point, Major Mackenzie spotted the rapid six-at-a-time flashes that betrayed the presence of Nebelwerfers. He quickly plastered them with artillery concentrations and three launchers were destroyed. This relieved some of the pressure on the Highlanders. To the immediate north of their position, however, was a low ridge — the ridge they were to follow toward Point 106 — and German machine guns positioned there were kicking bullets up all through the area.

The tanks were still unable to get forward. To try moving up without the tanks would result in heavy casualties, but to remain in this small bridgehead for long without tank support would be equally costly. Johnston looked back anxiously toward the tanks and saw that they were hung up in a minefield on the road, which the engineers had failed to detect.

Complicating things was the wreck of a Canadian water truck blocking the centre of the road right where it crossed the antitank ditch. The truck was from the 3rd Field Regiment, Royal Canadian Artillery. It had been destroyed by a mine on the night of May 20 when its driver got lost and took the wrong road en route to the Liri River to load up with water. The front of the truck had been sheared off when the mine exploded. The driver, Gunner A. Stanyer, and his helper, Gunner Ernie Buss, had initially escaped injury. But as they tried to return to Canadian lines, Stanyer had been shot in the shoulder by a sniper. Buss had been forced to leave him in a ditch and flee for his life through a hail of bullets. He made it back safely and some hours later a patrol sent out by the PLDG had rescued Stanyer.[27]

In the current action, a Churchill trying to push past the wreck had struck an antitank box mine and been immobilized. This left the road completely blocked. Sappers from the tank brigade's engineering company examined the ditch and declared that tanks could cross it safely if the heavier Churchills led and crumbled the banks to enable the Shermans to cross behind. The Churchills rolled off the road and started toward the ditch only to run afoul of a wide swath of well-concealed antitank mines. None made it through; all that tried were knocked out in a succession of explosions.[28] Casualties among the tankers were high, with only two officers surviving. Major Moser, the squadron commander, was badly wounded, as was the other surviving officer.[29]

For ninety minutes, the Highlanders had waited in their narrow bridgehead for the tanks. Now, Johnston knew they would have to do the job alone. They certainly could not stay where they were. At about 1300 hours, he ordered Major John Clarke's 'A' Company and Major Ed Rawlings's 'C' Company to head north toward the ridge and Point 106. 'D' Company would follow behind, mopping up points of resistance bypassed by the leading companies. 'B' Company would hold the bridgehead until the RCR came up to occupy the position once the Highlanders reached Point 106.

◆ ◆ ◆

As the 48th switched back to the offensive, I Canadian Corps commander Lieutenant General Tommy Burns watched the action from an observation point west of the Liri River on Monte San Maria, a mountain overlooking Pontecorvo. He had moved there in the early morning and been led to the observation point by General de Larminat of the French Corps. His vantage point was about a thousand yards from the road on which the tanks supporting the Highlanders were moving. Through binoculars, he had watched the tanks going into the attack. Occasionally, he would see one or two Highlanders ducking through the tall grass or emerging from a ditch, but was not surprised that most of the Glamour Boys, as the Toronto-raised militia unit was nicknamed, slithered toward the wire without being seen — infantry lived longer when invisible. Then the Panzerturm ripped into the tanks and Burns watched grimly as they burned.

By noon, with the tanks mired in the minefield fronting the antitank ditch and the infantry apparently pinned down, Burns had seen enough. An hour before Johnston attacked the northern ridge, the corps commander abandoned hope and returned to corps headquarters. Operation Chesterfield must, he decided, proceed.

From the outset, Burns had been lukewarm toward Vokes's Pontecorvo-area attack. He felt it would mean "that attention would be distracted from the preparations for the three-battalion attack on the front running south from the Forme d'Aquino." The best it would achieve was a limited breakthrough that would end up with 1 CIB being sucked into a street fight for Pontecorvo. Burns noted that "fighting to clear a town that was resolutely defended could be a long and hard business — as many examples from World War I and the experience of Ortona more recently had shown."[30] Reaching corps headquarters by afternoon, Burns phoned Vokes. Shift everything to the three-battalion attack against the north end of the Hitler Line, he said.

Vokes waffled. Things on the 1 CIB front were not as bad as the events Burns had witnessed. Since Burns had left his observation post, the Highlanders had made progress. Now, Burns hesitated. The clock was running. The 2nd and 3rd brigades were still not moving to their starting points for Operation Chesterfield. Could the Highlanders succeed or not? Burns thought not, but about the time he might have closed Vokes down General Leese phoned to say that the 1 CIB operation should continue. "It would be valuable in any case,

whether the enemy was intending to evacuate the line or to stay,"
Leese said. However, even as he told Burns to let Vokes continue,
Leese "cautioned against getting too involved in this subsidiary oper-
ation in prejudice of the main Chesterfield Operation."[31]

According to the original ad hoc plan developed as an alternative
to Operation Chesterfield, if 1 CIB had not achieved a major breakthrough by noon on May 22, the other divisional brigades would
move to their Operation Chesterfield assembly points. Once that
process started, any success achieved by 1 CIB would be moot, as the
other brigades could not realign in time to exploit the situation.
Vokes, Burns, and Leese were all pausing, hoping for a miracle that
only one regiment could win — the 48th Highlanders of Canada.

♦ ♦ ♦

The moment the Highlanders left their position opposite the antitank
ditch, they entered a perfectly flat wheat field overlooked from two
sides by the fifty- to seventy-foot-high ridge. Crouching, Major Clarke
and Major Rawlings led their companies forward at a run. The men
were hunched as low as they could manage and still run, praying the
tall grain would conceal them. From the crest of the ridge, German
machine-gunners sprayed the field with bullets and brought heavy
direct fire to bear on any flash of khaki.

It took only a few minutes for the German gunners to hit 'C'
Company with such weight of fire that the men could only throw
themselves down and hug the ground. Rawlings, hoping to reach the
antitank ditch and use it to advance safely on the ridge, ordered
them to crawl to the east. That plan was quickly abandoned when
the first men entering the ditch drew fire from two steel-and-concrete
two-man pillboxes positioned so the machine-gunners could fire
down the ditch's length. Sergeant Edsell Allen, who had been in the
lead, was killed by a burst of fire.

With no choice but to stay in the open, Rawlings spread his men
out across a wide front of the field and led them forward. They tried
to advance, but it was soon obvious that the German gunners would
wipe out the company long before it reached the ridge's forward
slope. Realizing the attack was futile, Rawlings signalled for his men
to go to ground and dig in where they were.

On the left flank, 'A' Company met heavy fire coming from the ridge and from three houses bordering a narrow track that led to the ridge. Several MG42s and many rifles fired from the windows and doors of the houses. Major John Clarke and the leading platoons hit the ground. "It's sheer murder to raise our heads," Clarke yelled into his radio.

The tall young officer also knew there was no alternative but to raise their heads. They were too exposed to stay where they were. By platoons, the company tried jumping ahead. Each platoon moved only a few feet at a time before the German fire started to become too accurate. While that platoon burrowed into the ground, the one opposite set off to play the deadly game. Clarke realized the forward platoons could not do this for very long before the Germans would anticipate their next moves. They were not going to reach either the houses or a low spur off the ridge that he had been aiming for. Looking behind, he saw that the reserve platoon was taking little fire. Because of earlier casualties, a mere corporal, Richard A. Riley, commanded it. Clarke ordered Riley to conduct a left-flank rush on the houses.

With barely twenty men, Riley led a wild charge toward the houses. They closed on the buildings so quickly that the Germans inside had no time to react and shift their fire to meet the threat. The Highlanders poured grenades and bullets through the windows and doors, then burst inside and quickly killed, captured, or drove off the defending Germans.

From the houses, Riley and his platoon attacked the spur leading to the top of the ridge. Free of the fire coming from the houses, the other platoons joined the advance. The machine guns and mortars on the ridge, however, soon halted all of 'A' Company's platoons short of the spur, except for Riley's. Having dug in frantically atop the spur, they managed to fend off two determined counterattacks. Despite repeated efforts, Clarke and the other platoons could not reach Riley's position.

Johnston saw that the attack was collapsing. There was no sense in throwing 'D' Company into the maw, for it had no room to manoeuvre and would just end up pinned down like 'A' and 'C' companies. There was nothing for it but to tell Rawlings and Clarke to hold where they were until nightfall. They would then disengage and fall back to the bridgehead, where the rest of the regiment was organizing to meet counterattacks. Having won a toehold inside the Hitler Line, Johnston was determined to keep it.

Several men in 'A' Company had been wounded during its belea-
guered advance and at least four were scattered through the tall
grain, too badly wounded to make it back to the bridgehead on their
own. Knowing these men might die during the night if they went
unrecovered, stretcher-bearer Private Alfred Glendinning undertook
a personal mission to bring them in. The distance across open
ground back to the bridgehead, where a forward aid post had been
established, was about 400 yards. He and another man made two
trips, carrying a wounded soldier out on a stretcher each time. On
every journey, the grain field was swept by heavy machine-gun fire
and subjected to random mortaring. Glendinning made two more
trips to the front lines, both times carrying a wounded man out
on his back. Returning to 'A' Company once again, he was wounded
en route. Exhausted and bleeding, the private stumbled to the aid
station.[32]

Just before nightfall, a troop of Shermans from 'C' Squadron of
the 142nd Royal Tank Regiment managed to negotiate through the
mines to cross the ditch and enter the bridgehead. They arrived too
late to affect the outcome of the day's fighting, but Johnston hoped
they would prove valuable in the morning. At 0600 hours, he planned
to resume the offensive on Point 106. His attack would go in at the
same time that 2 CIB and 3 CIB kicked off the main Operation
Chesterfield assault. Johnston thought that the two attacks would
serve to take pressure off each other and increase the likelihood of
one or both of them succeeding. The commander of 'C' Squadron
promised to get the rest of the mixed Sherman and Churchill force
into the bridgehead before morning.

When night closed in, the survivors of 'A' and 'C' companies crept
out of their slit trenches and cautiously returned to the bridgehead
perimeter. The Highlanders had paid a high blood-price for the tenuous position they held inside the Hitler Line: nine killed and
thirty-three wounded.[33]

♦ ♦ ♦

Commander-in-Chief Southwest Generalfeldmarschall Albert Kesselring telephoned Tenth Army commander Generaloberst Heinrich von
Vietinghoff late on the evening of May 22 to congratulate him on the
90th Panzer Grenadier Division's determined stand against Johnston's

attack. He asked von Vietinghoff "to convey my full appreciation to the troops of Baade and Heidrich."

Vietinghoff said, "There was not much action today on Heidrich's front, but Baade fought brilliantly."

"Yes, in their case one could cry with admiration; in the case of others from rage."[34] Kesselring referred to the 26th Panzer Division, which he had detached from Fourteenth Army at Anzio on May 19. This division was to have shored up the defence facing the Corps Expéditionnaire Français, south of the Liri River. He had assumed that the 26th Panzers "could reach a position of considerable natural strength by the morning of 20 May and would thus be able to close the gap." That position was 1,542-foot-high Monte Leucio — a mountain that stood alone on the valley floor, less than one mile south of the Liri River and about three miles west of Pontecorvo. If the French could be stopped east of that natural obstacle, the crumbling German southern flank might be restored.

To Kesselring's dismay, Fourteenth Army's commander General-oberst Eberhard von Mackensen disobeyed. He delayed issuing the 26th Panzers' movement orders while simultaneously engaging in an argument with Kesselring about the wisdom of removing his last reserves. Kesselring sympathized, but told von Mackensen that his army encircling the Anzio beachhead was in danger of being struck from behind by the U.S. Fifth Army. Blocking the French advance might rescue the situation, but doing so would only be possible if the 26th Panzer Division were shifted.

Arriving at the 26th Panzer Division's new headquarters on May 21, Kesselring realized that it had "come up too late and had offered a fight in unprepared positions — with calamitous consequences. . . . An excellent defensive zone had been thrown away and the enemy handed an almost impregnable position." With Monte Leucio now firmly in French hands, Kesselring thought that the "whole situation had thus become more difficult, but it was not yet irreparable." He ordered von Mackensen to take units from the Anzio beachhead and close the gap opening on the southern flank of the Liri River. Ever optimistic, Kesselring maintained that the Allied drive from the east toward Anzio and Rome could be checked. All that was required was for everyone to fight with sufficient coordination and determination.[35]

As he arrayed his meagre force to meet the inevitable major offensive that was sure to come next morning, Generalleutnant Ernst-Günther Baade, commander of the 90th Panzer Grenadiers, faced a rapidly deteriorating situation. The fighting since May 20 had cost him almost 20 percent of his total infantry strength. There were no reserves to draw on. Instead, he had to ask 1st Parachute Division's General Richard Heidrich to lengthen his line 985 feet to the south, so Baade could slide all his units south to shore up the crumbling 44th Field Replacement Battalion. As a result of casualties, only 875 infantry defended the line facing the 1st Canadian Infantry Division on the night of May 22. A fifty-man-strong company of the 2nd Battalion of the 3rd Parachute Regiment held the most northerly sector. The sector most likely to be attacked was held by two battalions of the 361st Regiment, each fielding only 150 men — a reduction in strength of about 25 percent owing to casualties. North of Pontecorvo, the 576th Regiment had two battalions with a total remaining strength of 325, compared to 375 on May 20. Hardest hit by the fighting of May 22 was the 44th Field Replacement Battalion, which had been chopped from 360 to 150 by casualties and desertions.

Added to the infantry strength, of course, were the men serving in the supporting artillery, Nebelwerfer, antitank gun, Panzerturm, tank, and engineering units. These could fill a partial infantry role, if necessary, and their firepower gave the line the punch that would determine whether or not it could be held. In terms of raw numbers, these units added another 400 to 500 men to the German strength. Like their counterparts in the infantry, however, the supporting arms had also suffered heavy casualties since May 20. At least one had possibly been eliminated. This was the platoon from the 190th Engineer Battalion that had been positioned in front of Pontecorvo. On the evening of May 22, I Canadian Corps intelligence staff reported it as "wiped out in toto."[36] It was a thin line of Germans that prepared to meet the Canadian onslaught.

16

THE HARDEST THING
TO WATCH

They were three unhappy, even angry men. But each knew that there was nothing to do but soldier on. Lieutenant colonels Rowan Coleman, Sydney Thomson, and Cameron Ware believed that with Operation Chesterfield they risked sending their men into a slaughterhouse. The planning, they knew, was not primarily at fault. In fact, some of the planning had been brilliantly executed. They were certainly going in with the full support of the Eighth Army's artillery and there would be excellent air support on hand. There would be no shortage of bombs and shells hammering down when the 2nd Canadian Infantry Brigade marched toward the Hitler Line. There would be tanks, too. All in all, they would be undertaking a classic Eighth Army set-piece attack with all stops pulled out to ensure success. Or so they were promised.

But how the hell did a brigade's regimental commanders plan and execute a major attack when, one day before, it still remained unclear whether the operation was on or off? The brigade was supposed to move toward the start-line positions at noon on May 22 and prepare for the attack to begin at 0600 hours on May 23. Noon came with no orders. Instead, Major General Chris Vokes kept telling Brigadier Graeme Gibson to keep his regiments in readiness for a sudden shift south to exploit through 1st Canadian Infantry Brigade. Never noted for demonstrating personal initiative, Gibson did as directed. That left his regimental commanders to prowl their respective headquarters and hope a decision was made soon that stuck.

Lieutenant Colonel Cameron Ware, commander of the Princess Patricia's Canadian Light Infantry, spent the day drafting one plan and then shelving it in favour of another. First, he was to carry out the attack on the right flank against the Hitler Line. Then Gibson phoned and said Ware should prepare to march south to charge through a breach there. An hour later, the phone jangled and the old plan was reinstated, only to have the 1 CIB scheme resurrected thirty minutes later.[1] The same thing was happening at the headquarters of the Seaforth Highlanders of Canada and the Loyal Edmonton Regiment, where Lieutenant Colonel Syd Thomson and Lieutenant Colonel Rowan Coleman respectively duplicated Ware's efforts and grew increasingly frustrated and worried.

For all intents and purposes, nobody from 2 CIB had seen the ground on either flank. If they went with the left option, this mattered less because they would be punching through an existing breach in the line. There they would just go hell-bent for leather as far as possible. But on the right, the Hitler Line was an unknown bastion. There had been no opportunity for reconnaissance patrols to test the strength of the German wire or to probe into the defensive line behind. No points had been identified for tanks to break through and the engineers had been unable to lift mines to clear the way for either the armour or the infantry. Only the start line had been taped, so they knew precisely from where to begin the attack.

Finally, the right-flank attack was confirmed at 1600 hours. This left the three regiments only fourteen hours to conduct whatever preparations they could in the way of mine clearing and personal reconnaissance of the line. Like his counterparts, Syd Thomson still knew little about what opposition his Seaforths would face. He had received conflicting reports on which enemy units held the line and there was much uncertainty about their dispositions. Somehow the intelligence revealing that the line was held by the tough 90th Panzer Grenadiers never filtered down to his level. The only sure knowledge Thomson had was the width and height of the barbed-wire field. He also knew that beyond the field were many weapon pits and slit trenches, but what these contained was uncertain. This uncertainty also existed with regard to the disposition of antitank weapons. Worse, "it was at this time believed that the enemy intended to make only a delaying action and that a stubborn resistance would not be encountered."[2]

During the day, Thomson, Coleman, and Ware crossed paths or had opportunities to discuss the developments by phone. They shared their uneasiness about the manner in which the final preparations were coming together and the brigadier's seemingly laissez-faire attitude. The three men were veteran infantry officers who had worked their way up to regimental command positions after serving as company-level combat officers. Ware was the most experienced. The thirty-year-old officer had joined the militia as a boy soldier of fourteen in 1927 and entered Royal Military College in 1931. Upon graduation, he had joined the PPCLI. The beginning of the war found him already a captain and he soon earned major's crowns. Since becoming a PPCLI officer, Ware's dream had been to command the regiment. That dream was realized during the Sicily campaign when, on August 9, 1943, then 2 CIB Brigadier Chris Vokes sacked PPCLI commander Lieutenant Colonel Bob Lindsay and gave Ware the regiment. Since then, he had led it with great competence, winning a Military Cross during the fierce fighting in the Moro River phase of the Ortona Battle at a hamlet called Villa Rogatti.[3]

Whereas Ware's military path had always been directed toward membership in the club of Permanent Force officers, Thomson had never envisioned becoming an officer. Born on November 14, 1914, in Salmon Arm, British Columbia, Thomson had joined the local Rocky Mountain Rangers militia unit in 1931 as a private. Among other jobs, Thomson used to thin apple trees for a family whose son, Ed Turner, was scheduled to report for officer training days before war broke out in 1939. With the apple harvest in full swing, Turner was lifting a box full of fruit and badly strained his back — an injury that caused permanent damage. Thomson by this time was a sergeant, so he was called up instead of Turner to attend the officers-training course. With the outbreak of war, the Rocky Mountain Rangers served primarily as a feeder-regiment to the Seaforths, so Thomson was transferred into that regiment along with a number of other men from the Okanagan and Shuswap valleys. When the Seaforths hit the beach in Sicily, Thomson was a company commander. He was wounded on the first day, but returned to duty five weeks later. During the march up the Italian boot, a sharp fight at a crossroads named Decarta won him a Military Cross. When Bert Hoffmeister was promoted to command of 2 CIB, Thomson took over the regiment in time to lead it through the December 1943 fighting. For his bravery during the Ortona street battle, Thomson won the Distinguished Service Order.[4] He also proved himself tremendously popular with the rank-and-file Seaforths.

Coleman was new to regimental command, having only been promoted to lieutenant colonel's rank on May 5 and assigned to command the Edmontons. The son of Canadian Pacific Railway president D.C. Coleman, he had served with distinction as a PPCLI company commander during the Sicily campaign. On July 22, 1943, Coleman had won the Military Cross for leading a flying column of troops riding on the backs of tanks that burst into Leonforte and relieved the embattled Loyal Edmonton Regiment, caught in a bloody house-to-house battle for the ancient hilltop town. Coleman's appointment had come as a surprise to the Edmonton regiment, which believed Major Jim Stone had earned the command as reward for his brilliant performance in the Ortona street battle. However, Stone was considered insufficiently trained at regimental command level and, consequently, he departed on May 5 to attend a Unit Commanders' course in Britain.[5]

Operation Chesterfield's attack plan called for the PPCLI and Seaforths to lead the assault, with the PPCLI on the brigade's right flank opposite Aquino. Once the PPCLI reached its objectives, the Edmontons would pass through and widen the breach sufficiently to enable 5th Canadian Armoured Division to drive its combined tank-and-infantry regiments west toward Rome. Coleman and Ware were, therefore, mutually concerned about the terrain through which their regiments would move.

Both commanders thought there were too many unknown factors at play on the right flank. On their immediate right flank, the Forme d'Aquino followed a gentle northwest curve before turning sharply toward Aquino about 500 yards behind the Hitler Line's wire. A deep gully through which the river ran precluded any tank operations north of it and also protected them from German armoured counter-attack from that direction. But it also greatly narrowed the good tank country within their line of advance, so that between the PPCLI's right flank and its left-hand boundary with the Seaforths there was only a front of about 150 yards suited to armour.[6]

This meant that tank and infantry coordination must be very tight to ensure that the tanks had adequate protection while still retaining room to manoeuvre. To effect this, Ware met with Lieutenant Colonel Holton of the 51st Royal Tank Regiment. Since the Germans were shelling the tank harbour at the time, the two officers conducted their planning session lying under a Churchill tank where its body and tracks provided some shelter. The PPCLI and 51st RTR commanders had trained together from May 8–11 near Lucera, in preparation for a combined operation against the Hitler Line. They had developed a good rapport during that training operation. Ware and Holton hammered out five report lines between their forming-up point and the wire, which corresponded to tactical features in intervals of about 300 yards. They would follow the barrage forward in bounds from one point to another.

As Ware and his Intelligence Officer walked back through the West Nova Scotia Regiment's lines en route to their regimental head-quarters, an anxious-looking PPCLI adjutant, Captain R.G.M. Gammell, met them. Operation Chesterfield was definitely on, he told Ware, but 51st RTR was being sent elsewhere. The North Irish Horse would instead provide 2 CIB's tank support. It was a regiment unknown to 2 CIB. 'A' Squadron would support the PPCLI. Ware rushed to the Irish regiment's harbour and briefed its commander on his and Holton's plan. He also arranged for 'A' Squadron's troop commanders to confer with his own infantry company commanders. This way, at least everyone should know who was whom and the tankers might understand some basic elements of the plan.[7]

Ware was dismayed to learn that the 51st RTR was being shifted to provide two squadrons of tanks to support the Carleton and York Regiment's attack on Operation Chesterfield's left flank. Its remaining squadrons would stand in reserve, ready to move up with the Edmontons. He was completely baffled as to why the 51st RTR was given this task rather than the North Irish Horse, for the Carleton and

York Regiment had worked with neither armoured regiment in the past. There was, however, nothing to be done about it. Orders regarding which tank regiment went where came down from Eighth Army headquarters and, once issued, were sacrosanct.[8]

The regiments of 2 CIB moved toward forming-up positions at 1715 hours and by 1930 hours most were in place. As they moved in, the West Nova Scotia Regiment, which had been holding this sector of the line, side-slipped to the south to a position in reserve behind the Carleton and York Regiment. This placed the three regiments tasked with the initial assault in a continuous line, with the PPCLI on the extreme northern flank, the Seaforths in the centre, and the Carleton and York Regiment on the southern flank. The Edmontons were in reserve immediately behind the PPCLI. Before midnight, the tank squadrons joined their assigned infantry regiments. The infantry hunkered down in slit trenches. Some tried to sleep; others went over their weapons one more time and then repeated the process. Letters were written, prayers offered.

Ware and Coleman were still trying to limit the degree of danger into which their regiments would march at dawn. The ground to the north of the Forme d'Aquino was slightly higher than that through which the two regiments would be advancing. Operation Chesterfield called for the 78th Division to conduct a feint into this area to prevent the 1st Parachute Division from bringing flanking fire against the PPCLI and Edmontons. If that feint failed to develop or did not soak off the German fire, the two Canadian regiments would face a deadly situation. Nothing Ware or Coleman had seen so far reassured them that their right flank was secure.

Finally, the two officers decided they had to discuss the matter with their brigadier. They wanted an assurance that the paratroopers around Aquino would be suppressed, either by artillery high-explosive rounds or by smokescreens. Then it would matter less whether the 78th Division succeeded with its feint.[9] The two men arrived at Gibson's headquarters just after midnight to find the brigadier already in bed and not wishing to be disturbed. When they pressed the matter, "a sleepy voice informed the officers that no further changes could be made."[10]

While Ware and Coleman returned from brigade headquarters, small patrols of infantry and engineers slipped toward the German wire. One, led by the Royal Canadian Engineers Lieutenant Kenyon, consisted of a combined force of sappers and Seaforth Highlander riflemen, who were soon lying in the grass near a clutch of Germans sitting around a fire. They crawled past the Germans toward a house and spotted two immobilized British tanks next to it that had been knocked out during the failed Royal 22e Regiment attack of May 19. Several Germans were moving around in the vicinity of the house, precluding any investigation of the field stretching out west of it. Alternately crawling or moving forward in a crouch, the men made slow progress. It was difficult for Lance Sergeant Lloyd, armed with the mine detector, to work efficiently. When they did manage to sweep the ground, there was no sign of any mines.

As they moved through a hedge and into the last stretch of open country running up to the wire, they heard German tanks rumbling up and down the Pontecorvo-Aquino road and along an intersecting road that crossed through the wire to pass their position. That was going to have to be good enough. Kenyon "assumed that these roads would be safe for the advance of our own tanks" and the men warily withdrew. The best they had ascertained was that no obvious obstacles or minefields would hold up the tanks.[11]

◆ ◆ ◆

"Tomorrow I hope and pray that the Canadians will break the Adolf Hitler line," Eighth Army commander General Sir Oliver Leese wrote to his wife late on May 22. "Then we shall have finished with organized lines for a bit — they are expensive to deal with."[12]

To I Canadian Corps Lieutenant General Tommy Burns he sent a message to distribute to the troops on his behalf. "I am confident," Leese wrote, "that you will add the name of the Adolf Hitler Line to those epics of Canadian battle history — Sanctuary Wood; Vimy; Ortona. Good luck to you all."[13] Burns added no words of his own to the message. He had no interest in boosting morale through laudatory messages. The men would do their duty, just as he did. That would determine whether tomorrow's battle became a national battlefield icon or a tragic footnote. Many would die, even more would be wounded, and he would not be troubled by guilt for having sent them into harm's way. Burns believed that "a soldier who has reached the rank of general and commands a fighting formation is probably a fighter by nature. If he has no stomach for fighting he will not long remain in his post. . . . A general has spent most of his life training himself for the moment when he must make decisions — especially the decision to attack and destroy the enemy when the occasion is favourable. He has done it in the various tactical exercises, which have prepared him for the real thing. So he will take the action which he has been trained to take, his mind will be concentrated on victory, and he will hope that casualties will be few." If the general has done his job properly, no more need be said. That job, Burns was certain, was "to strain every nerve to ensure that the action is planned and prepared to give the very best chance for success, success without paying a heavy price in blood."[14]

As the evening progressed, 1st Canadian Infantry Division commander Major General Chris Vokes grew increasingly uneasy about 2 CIB's right flank. In the afternoon, he had set up shop in a new divisional tactical headquarters positioned in a recently abandoned enemy dugout burrowed into the side of a sand hill. This put him within a 500-yard radius of all the brigades that would be involved in the attack and provided his chief divisional gunnery officer, Brigadier Bill Ziegler, with excellent line and radio communications to both the infantry and artillery regiments that would be providing supporting fire. The tall, bespectacled Calgary native was chiefly responsible for the attack's intricately complex artillery program. He was also a neophyte, who had never before put together anything like it. Since the warning order for Operation Chesterfield had been issued, Ziegler and his staff had been housed in the dugout. They worked straight through, with no breaks, little sleep, barely time for the occasional bite to eat. By the time the guns spoke just before dawn, Ziegler would have been awake for seventy-two hours.

What he was putting together was possibly the most complex artillery program to date in the history of the war on the western front. The program involved a series of massive concentrations on selected targets, which had to dovetail with a creeping barrage moving 100 yards every five minutes during the attack's first phase and then 100 yards every three minutes in the second phase. Also tossed into the soup, but directed at specific targets, was a steady harassing fire of 1,000 shells every hour that had started with lesser rates of fire two days earlier. When German mortar and artillery positions were identified, they were logged in, assigned a map reference, and sub-jected to counter-battery fire. The same treatment was visited upon suspected supply routes, depots, and headquarters. Mistakes could be costly and Ziegler worked hard to eliminate them. A wrong map reference could bring friendly fire down on the advancing infantry and tanks, so every reference was checked and double-checked. Sufficient munitions had to be available on the gun lines and, under the guise of the harassing fire, the guns had to be registered on the tar-gets that each would take under fire during the attack. In all, 810 guns were available. Of these, 76 medium and heavy guns were tasked exclusively with counter-battery fire missions and 52 guns and mor-tars were assigned to counter mortar fire. That left 682 guns of all types for the divisional supporting fire plan.[15]

Additionally, 239 Wing, Desert Air Force would be in support. This wing had six squadrons with a total combined strength of 72 Kittyhawk and Mustang bombers. If needed, the full resources of 12 Tactical Air Command and all other DAF wings had been promised. The new tactical deployment of planes into "cab ranks" whereby six aircraft circled over the battlefield, ready to sweep down on targets as reported to them, would be available twice during the day. Each cab rank would be on hand for two to three hours.[16]

That evening, Vokes added a new complication to Ziegler's artillery recipe by raising his fears about the right flank. If the 78th Division did its job, the danger would be minimal. But Vokes knew there was the risk that "the commander of that division and indeed his corps commander might both interpret the meaning of a 'strong pressure' to . . . making faces only." If this proved the case, Vokes asked Ziegler, could he quickly bring "an overwhelming weight of medium and heavy gun fire on the enemy defences around Aquino?" Ziegler said that as long as the PPCLI could quickly provide targeting infor-mation, he could bring enough guns to bear without jeopardizing the overall plan.

Vokes's other concern was how to change the firing plan once the attack started. Currently, the first phase of the assault should see the three regiments on their objectives at about 0715 hours, having overrun a front about 2,500 yards wide. They were then to have one hour to mop up resistance, move the Edmontons up on the right, consolidate and reform into a coherent line, and begin the next phase. Realistically, would that be enough time? Could Ziegler delay the start of the second barrage? Ziegler thought about it a minute and then said that if he had thirty minutes' warning he could switch the start time. He needed that long because of the sheer number of 25-pounder gun regiments involved that must be contacted and rescheduled.

Pleased with Ziegler's confidence, Vokes realized there was nothing more he could do to improve the morning's odds. As he turned in at midnight for five hours' sleep, Vokes pondered the message he had sent the troops earlier. It was short and to the point and one they had heard from him before: "Kick the bastards in the crotch." Never one for "clever, mealy-mouthed phrases," Vokes believed "this was a message the troops could understand, and I hoped they would apply it literally."[17]

Vokes would have been surprised to learn that not many of his troops were much impressed with the major general's messages or his speeches. The PPCLI's war diarist, commenting on a speech Vokes had delivered to 2 CIB on May 4 at Guardiaregia wrote: "At about this point the General's talk was rudely interrupted by the loud braying of a mule, much to everyone's amusement." Vokes had rallied quickly, though, and gone on to chastise the infantry for not using their rifles enough during combat. During the Moro River fight, he said, more 25-pounder rounds had been fired than .303-calibre bullets. He then said that if any of them wanted a guaranteed ticket home, all they had to do was win a Victoria Cross. He would then see they immediately got a trip to Canada. In the forthcoming offensive, Vokes concluded: "Some of us are lucky and some of us are not. The high degree of training of the Canadian soldier has included the art of self preservation and those who apply that training will be lucky."[18] Throughout the speech, Vokes's language was peppered with obscenities and vulgar images.

Present that day was Seaforth chaplain Major Roy Durnford. "Watched speech. No inspiration, ending in the obscene. None of the men enjoyed it, indeed all are mad. What an opportunity missed! And how wide of the mark he was to assume that soldiers have heads of sawdust, bodies like oxen and a mind below their belt," he wrote in his diary.

During a service on Saturday, May 20, Durnford's sermon advised the men: "Don't try to fight a war on two fronts — fears within and fears without. Commend yourself to God and do your duty as it lies before you. Let God carry the responsibility of your survival. He alone can in any case since no officer, however clever, can control the forces pitted against you in every detail. But with God all things are possible, and if it is His will and purpose for you, you will survive." After the sermon, several men individually came to thank him and to say that his words helped prepare them for the trial ahead.

One section sergeant said he was anxious because his men were new and untried, making his job difficult and more dangerous. "My mother says, 'Read Psalm 91,'" the sergeant said. "I have, but I find it hard to believe."

The psalm, Durnford reminded the soldier, told man to put his trust in God, to let Him be both fortress and refuge. "You can't get God to help you if you insist on keeping the controls in your own hands," Durnford said. He later wrote of the time spent that day counselling the soldiers, including the sergeant: "I have rarely, if ever, spent a more profitable time or have I been more conscious of help given and help received."[19]

During the night of May 22, Durnford spent his time with the men helping them prepare spiritually and mentally for the morning battle. Already the harassing fire of the artillery was rising to a terrific crescendo that went on relentlessly all night. German shells arced back in retaliation, throwing up gouts of dirt and spraying shrapnel throughout the position. Durnford offered a word of comfort here, a short prayer there, a gentle press of a hand on a shoulder to one man, or a light joke to another. They were his men and he knew many well, had marched with them since the war's beginning. After the men had gathered their gear and weapons, formed into their companies, and set off toward the start line, Durnford was left alone with his diary. "My boys move in tonight," he wrote. "I see them off. How can one ever forget the scene? New boys with fears and nerves and anxiety hidden under quick smiles and quick seriousness. Old campaigners with far away look. It is the hardest thing to watch without breaking into tears."[20]

17

THOSE WERE
FINE BOYS

A thick haze hung over the Liri Valley as dawn broke on May 23. It was a cool morning with afternoon rain forecast. On the right flank of the Hitler Line, 2nd Canadian Infantry Brigade waited 200 yards behind the start line. This was to decrease the odds of the men being hit by artillery rounds that might fall short when the massive barrage began. Breakfast was a slice of Spam and four pieces of hardtack washed down with water.[1] Company commanders glanced at their maps and noted once more the codenames that they were to report by radio each time they crossed one of the designated points set 300 yards apart. January, February, March, April, Aboukir. Aboukir was the Aquino-Pontecorvo lateral road. When the leading companies hit the road, Phase One would conclude. Then, after a sixty-minute reorganization, came a renewed drive to cut the road running from Pontecorvo to Highway 6. This was code-named Caporetto.[2]

At precisely 0558 hours, the gently undulating ground extending from the start line to the Hitler Line's front wire erupted as the barrage opened with terrific force. Fifteen hundred rounds a minute slammed down. "The steady pounding of guns, the roar of tanks moving forward, made a terrific din," wrote the Princess Patricia's Canadian Light Infantry war diarist. The regiment's companies were organized with 'C' right and 'A' left. These two companies would lead the advance to Aboukir. Then 'B' Company would pass through, followed by the Loyal Edmonton Regiment. 'D' Company was in reserve. 'A' Squadron of the North Irish Horse supported the leading companies.[3] The PPCLI was seriously understrength. Each company numbered only 60 to 70 men, including officers, instead of the designated strength of 125. Lack of reinforcements, sickness, and men lost to injuries and wounds suffered while forming up for the battle had sapped away existing strength. Such was the case throughout 1st Canadian Infantry Division's other regiments and, indeed, the entire corps.

On the right flank, Major W. "Bucko" Watson, the veteran PPCLI commander of 'A' Company, led his men toward the start line. Along the way, Watson encountered Loyal Edmonton Regiment commander Lieutenant Colonel Rowan Coleman, who had come forward to see his old regiment march into battle. Coleman wore a soft hat instead of a helmet. Casually smoking his pipe, the ex-PPCLI officer greeted each man he knew with a pleasant word of encouragement. Watson said cheerily, "See you on the objective."[4]

Left of the PPCLI, the Seaforth Highlanders of Canada had 'A' and 'D' companies leading, with 'B' and 'C' companies behind. 'B' Squadron of the North Irish Horse supported the front two companies while 'C' Squadron stood alongside the rear companies.[5]

Within minutes of crossing the start line, an intense German artillery and mortar counter-barrage caught 2 CIB in the open. Whenever the Germans saw a creeping barrage approaching, it meant undoubtedly that infantry would, as doctrine dictated, be "leaning into the barrage" immediately behind. So they dropped a counter-barrage immediately to the rear of the Allied barrage, normally throwing the attack into confusion and causing heavy casualties.

When the first counter-barrage rounds came in, PPCLI's 'A' Company started taking casualties as it was moving through a small grove. Exploding mortar and artillery rounds shattered the trees, sending splinters of wood whistling through the air to pierce flesh. German machine guns opened up from positions that had been reported cleared by patrols the previous night, but the creeping barrage rolled over the gunners and silenced them.[6] At 0620 hours, 'A'

Company and 'C' Company both passed January. Eighteen minutes later, Watson's radio operator reported that 'A' Company was at February. No word came from 'C' Company. Its radio signaller had paused to make a minor adjustment to his No. 18 radio set. When he looked up, the rest of the company was lost in the smoke and fog. He blundered on in search of the company, but never found it.[7]

Bursting out of the woods, Watson saw the wire through the haze. While in the woods, his company had ceased moving in extended order. The men entered the grain field by platoon sections, each section zigzagging in single file to keep from presenting clear targets to the increasingly numerous machine guns. Casualties mounted. One section was cut down to only five men. Nobody stopped to help the wounded; the job was to reach the objective. To pause in the open to help a fallen man would only result in more casualties and the company's destruction.[8]

Just in front of the wire, Watson's men hit a minefield thick with S-mines. The mines tore off feet, mangled legs. Some wounded men landed on detonators of other mines that gutted stomachs, shredded arms, and tore open chests.[9] No. 7 Platoon climbed over what turned out to be a paltry wire field without trouble. Watson had just finished reporting that his men were in the wire, but casualties were heavy when a bullet hit the radio and knocked it out of action. On the opposite flank, 'C' Company had also reached the wire, but here it was a greater obstacle. No. 13 Platoon used pliers to cut a path. Men tripped mines inside the wire field and were killed or wounded. Some of the wounded became hopelessly tangled in barbs, trapped in twisted positions from which they were unable to free themselves. The dead also hung from barbs. Machine-gun bullets and shrapnel ricocheted off the wire with a screeching sound or thudded into the bodies of the corpses and living alike.[10]

The tanks had been left behind entirely by the leading companies. With their radios out, neither company commander was able to contact the tank troop commanders. As Watson managed to get two platoons, each numbering about twelve men, through the wire, he was unable to see how far back the tanks were. He had not seen them since entering the woods at the beginning of the attack. Any moment, he expected 'B' Company to come up in support, but as he advanced into a maze of German pillboxes and other concrete-and-steel gun emplacements, it seemed the remnants of his company were completely isolated. Knowing their own men were safe inside the concrete positions, the Germans dropped artillery and mortar fire on his company and more men fell. Exerting control was virtually impossible.[11]

On the right flank, 'C' Company was in similar dire straits. Lieutenant R.D. Browne-Clayton, commanding No. 14 Platoon, lost many men during the advance to the wire. Inside the Hitler Line, the well-concealed machine-gun emplacements exacted a heavy toll. Browne-Clayton knocked one out by throwing a grenade through the gun slit, but moments later he was hit by two bullets. He collected several men too badly wounded to walk and led them to the shelter of a shell crater. There the small group remained until being taken prisoner in the late afternoon.[12]*

As Acting Sergeant Roy Douglas Edkins ran past a Panzerturm, he sustained multiple shrapnel wounds from an exploding mortar round. He continued leading his 'C' Company platoon forward until being wounded again. Turning command over to a corporal, he refused evacuation and instead stalked a German sniper holding up the advance. Edkins closed on the camouflaged gun pit that concealed the man and took him prisoner. He then escorted the German to the Canadian lines before seeking medical treatment. His action won him the Military Medal.[13]

Meanwhile, Corporal Frederick William Snell's platoon was torn up in the minefield. Everyone senior to Snell was dead, so he took charge. Noticing movement in a tree ahead of him, Snell set off alone to investigate. Discovering three snipers, he raised his Thompson submachine gun and blasted them out of the tree with one long burst of fire. Snell was subsequently awarded the Distinguished Conduct Medal.[14]

◆ ◆ ◆

With no idea of what was going on up front, Lieutenant Colonel Cameron Ware moved his tactical headquarters to February, hoping to visually determine the battle's progress. What little he saw was

---

*Browne-Clayton, like many other Canadian prisoners taken during the course of May 23–24, was soon liberated and by July 2, 1944, he was recovering from his wounds in a Canadian hospital.

disheartening. The tanks were unable to get forward. Every time they tried, more were knocked out by mines or antitank guns. When one tank finally managed to get through the woods and into the clearing in front of the wire, a Panzerturm immediately blasted it into a wreck. At February, several tanks were burning and their ammunition exploding. The resulting shrapnel and flaming metal flying through the air added to the danger the tactical HQ faced from sporadic German shelling and sniper fire.

The PPCLI pioneer platoon worked frantically to clear the road for the tanks. Corporal R. Armstrong and his pioneer section lifted about seventy-five mines while being fired upon by machine guns. Heavy casualties soon forced them to abandon the effort. As there seemed to be innumerable box mines that the detectors couldn't find, their mine-lifting effort was mainly for naught.

The tankers did their utmost to push forward and paid the price in blood. When an antitank gun or mine immobilized one tank, its crew kept the gun firing until the tank finally caught on fire. A Panther tank engaged a Sherman knocked out by a mine. During the short firefight, the Sherman was struck eight times before it finally started burning and the crew grudgingly evacuated. The tankers scooped up rifles from dead infantry and fought alongside the PPCLI. Another tank, trying to edge past a minefield by hugging the slope running into the Forme d'Aquino, tumbled over and over into the narrow stream. Landing right side up, the tank clawed its way back up the slope and returned to the battle despite the crew's being badly battered by the accident. In all, 'A' Squadron lost ten of eighteen tanks. Most of the others were damaged.[15]

While the tanks tried gallantly to support 'A' and 'C' companies, 'B' Company was holding back at February. Before going forward, Captain A.M. Campbell wanted to establish some contact with the leading companies so he could link up with them. Runners were sent out, but either never returned or staggered back wounded without having reached either company. Ware told Campbell to try to advance anyway. The company was being chopped up where it was and would do more good forward. From reports of the walking wounded filtering back toward the field hospital, he had the impression that the two companies had some sections on Aboukir. If that were true, they must badly need support.[16]

Ware's tactical headquarters was taking a lot of mortar and artillery fire, resulting in casualties. Fragments from a mortar bomb that struck a nearby building killed Captain R. Shelton, the Forward Observation Officer for the 3rd Field Regiment, Royal Canadian Artillery. Then Major G. Rankin, representing the commanding officer of the 3rd Field Regiment, was shot in the leg.[17]

During the move up to February, Lieutenant Donald Gower had become separated from Ware's party. As the commander of the antitank gun platoon, Gower was to stay with Ware until it was determined where and how the guns should be deployed. Reaching the edge of the woods and seeing wire up ahead, Gower realized he had gone too far and began retracing his steps. Whenever a stonk of German shells or mortar rounds struck nearby, he took cover behind one of the knocked-out tanks, crowding in with the other infantry gathered there for protection. Once, when the shelling eased, Gower asked the man lying next to him if he had seen Ware. Getting no response, Gower shook him and only then realized that the man had been killed seconds earlier by flying shrapnel.

Pressing on, Gower found some more men huddled behind a tank. As he started asking them about Ware, another massive counter-barrage crashed down and everyone piled under the tank for cover. Suddenly the tank, which the infantry had thought derelict, fired up its engine and pivoted. Men clawed their way out from under the tank, rolling this way and that to avoid the grinding tracks. Gower found himself alone under the tank, scrabbling to escape. Reaching under to grab his hand, a soldier dragged him clear.[18]

It was obvious that the PPCLI attack was collapsing. Learning that the Seaforths were having better luck on the left flank of the brigade's attack, Ware tried to advise 2 CIB commander Brigadier Graeme Gibson to pass the Loyal Edmonton Regiment through that regiment instead of his own. He was unable to establish radio contact with brigade headquarters, however, and doubted that Gibson would agree to the change anyway. The brigade commander seemed always averse to spontaneity.[19]

Accordingly, at 0845 hours, ninety minutes behind schedule, Lieutenant Colonel Rowan Coleman waved his regiment forward. In the woods, the Edmontons found the rear elements of the PPCLI dug in at February. 'A' Company led, with 'C' immediately behind, followed by Coleman and his tactical headquarters, then 'D' Company. 'B' Company hung back in reserve. As 'A' Company burst out of the woods into the grain field, its commander, Captain P.G. Wright, was wounded in the head by a mortar fragment. He staggered forward, but another exploding mortar bomb severely wounded him in the lower body. Seeing the company wavering in the face of heavy casualties, Coleman rushed up and told Lieutenant W.B. Langston to take over.

Mortar, artillery, and machine-gun fire was increasing. Snipers hidden in the upper branches of nearby trees were also shooting at them. About twenty feet short of the wire, the fire became so intense that the company was forced to ground. Trying to rally the men, Coleman was shot in the leg and hand. Lying in a ditch, Coleman ordered another charge. Lieutenants Langston and B.P. Lange led two sections into the wire. They became mired in antipersonnel mines and were struck by intense machine-gun fire. With both lieutenants wounded, the sections were pinned down. They added more bodies to the tangle left earlier by the PPCLI.[20] One machine gun was firing on the Edmontons from just a few feet away. Private Douglas Robb calmly raised his rifle and shot the gunner dead.[21] When Lieutenant G.L. Sherman attempted to organize the bridgehead inside the wire, he was struck three times by sniper fire and killed.

Private Edmund Andrew Kidd found himself the only company stretcher-bearer who was neither dead nor wounded. While tending to one casualty, he was struck by mortar fragments. Ignoring his injuries, Kidd dressed the wounds of two more men and then started crawling forward to help others. With bullets and shrapnel snapping all around him, Kidd tended and evacuated six more men to safety. He remained with the wounded until his own condition became so critical that he was ordered to report to the Regimental Aid Post. He won a Military Medal.

Coleman, too, refused evacuation. Instead, he set up a forward tactical headquarters in the ditch where he lay wounded. The only tanks that were up near the wire were three disabled by mines, but still possessing operational machine guns. At 1100 hours, a Mark V Panther tank appeared about 500 yards ahead of 'A' Company and engaged the three helpless tanks. In minutes, they were burning.

When Major Archie MacDonald came up to the rear regimental headquarters, Coleman handed command to him. MacDonald started up to Coleman's position, stopping to compare notes with Ware en route. Both MacDonald and Ware recognized that much of the fire cutting their two regiments to pieces came from Aquino. MacDonald, who had a functioning radio, called for smoke to be fired along this flank. After leaving Ware's headquarters, MacDonald had to run across a field to reach Coleman. Just as he started out, a sniper bullet hit him in the heel. MacDonald radioed Coleman with a report on the situation and provided the location of Ware's headquarters, suggesting Coleman withdraw there. He then limped to regimental headquarters and relinquished command to Major F.H. McDougall.

By noon, 'A' Company, now commanded by the wounded Lange, extricated its forward sections from the wire and formed a circular defensive position in the open, just in front of the wire. Coleman, meanwhile, tried to crawl with his tactical headquarters back to a small gully, but he soon became too exhausted to continue. The headquarters staff carried him out to the safety of the gully, where they evacuated him by Jeep to the Regimental Aid Post.[22]

While the Edmonton attack ran out of steam, the two leading companies of the PPCLI were still well inside the wire. The only officer left standing in 'A' Company was its commander, Major "Bucko" Watson. With him were just five men, one of them a lance corporal. They paused next to a derelict German tank, so Watson could attempt to gather together more of his company. Men were spread out all over the battleground, moving about in ones and twos. Some were going forward, others backward. Many were wounded and having difficulty moving in any direction.

Suddenly, the supposedly derelict tank fired its main gun toward the Canadian lines. With no weapons capable of knocking it out, Watson and his party scampered away before the crew realized their presence. In the confusion, Watson and the lance corporal became separated from the others. Then the lance corporal was killed. Watson, himself twice wounded, carried on toward the objective. He reached it alone and could find no trace of his men.[23] Some scattered elements had, however, reached the Aquino-Pontecorvo road. Bits and pieces of PPCLI-marked equipment and gear were strewn around. Whether the men who lost the stuff had been taken prisoner or had withdrawn, Watson had no idea. Suffering from loss of blood and exhaustion himself, he was too weak to return to the wire. Watson crawled into a large shell hole, where he stayed until he was found the following day by a PPCLI patrol.[24]

♦ ♦ ♦

At divisional headquarters, the reports coming in from 2 CIB proved that the promised feint by the 78th Division in front of Aquino had failed to materialize. Yet shortly before noon, Major General Chris Vokes received a telephone call from the 78th Division's commander asking that he refrain from directing any artillery fire toward Aquino, "as his troops were about to enter the village." Vokes didn't believe a word of this. If that were true, why was 2 CIB taking so much fire on its right flank? He sent a liaison officer to determine the exact position of the 78th's most forward troops. The officer soon returned to say they were at least 1,000 yards from the Hitler Line and not moving. Vokes told artillery Brigadier Bill Ziegler that he needed him "to bring down on the enemy defences about Aquino a concentration of fire from all the heavy and medium artillery regiments within range of the target."[25]

Because he had no specific targets, Ziegler decided to throw everything he could into the general vicinity of Aquino. He called the commander of I Canadian Corps's artillery, Brigadier E.C. Plow, at 1227 hours and requested a "William" target designation for Aquino. This was a request that all divisional, corps, and army artillery regiments within range bring their guns to bear. Plow pulled out the stops. Thirty-three minutes later, the guns were ready. Precisely at 1300 hours, 668 guns from nineteen field, nine medium, and two heavy regiments, as well as several other batteries, fired. In little more than a minute, 3,509 rounds amounting to a total weight of ninety-two tons of shells crashed down on Aquino. The fire from that flank lessened significantly thereafter.[26] Ziegler's "William" target was the first time in World War II that all the guns of an entire army had been directed against a single compact target area.[27]

♦ ♦ ♦

Even though the Seaforth Highlanders of Canada were screened from much of the Aquino fire, their attack had also run into trouble the moment it kicked off. The same counter-barrage that had caught the PPCLI also fell upon the Seaforths.

As the men had formed up on the start line, twenty-four-year-old

Sergeant Harry Rankin pondered what it meant to go into an attack outfitted as a human bomb. Rankin and several other pioneers had been assigned to a section armed with either bangalore torpedoes or beehive bombs. Several such sections were to rush up to the wire ahead of the infantry platoons. Those men armed with bangalore torpedoes, which were long pipes filled with explosives, would thrust them deep into the wire. When the torpedoes were ignited, they would rip holes in the barbed wire through which the infantry could then pass. The pioneers carrying beehive bombs were to lead the way. Weighing about five pounds and consisting of plastic explosive crammed into a beehive-shaped metal casing, the bombs were to be placed on top of concrete pillboxes and the fuses lit. The bomb, whose shape focused the force of the exploding charge, should rip a hole in the pillbox and kill the Germans inside. At least that was the plan some officer had dreamed up. Rankin was dubious because nobody knew how thick the concrete was or whether it would be possible to get on top of one without getting killed.

Standing next to him on the start line was a nineteen-year-old private, who was the batman for a new officer, Lieutenant Don S. McLaughlin. Rankin, who had enlisted in 1939 at the same age as this boy, kept forgetting his name. It was hard to remember names of soldiers who were new and the lieutenant and his batman had just arrived on May 14. There was a tendency for the old hands to avoid learning the names of new men or getting to know them well, because so many didn't last long. The boy was nervous, fear etched all over his face. It was painfully obvious that he had no idea what was going on. Rankin said, "Stick with me. Follow me. You'll be okay." The whistles blew and the leading companies, accompanied by the pioneer assault sections, rushed forward.

Rankin had the beehive strapped across the small of his back with some mercury-fulminate igniters and short lengths of fuse stuffed in a front pocket. If any shrapnel hit the bomb or the igniters, Rankin figured they would never find a piece of him to bury. Explosions burst all around. Suddenly, something hit him hard between the shoulder blades. He was on the ground, then back on his feet. Blood poured from a batch of shrapnel punctures across the top of his back. The young batman lay dead in a pool of blood.

Stumbling toward the rear, Rankin passed a young Canadian with one leg severed at the hip and the stump was lying in a two-inch-deep pool of blood. The man's eyes were open and sightless. Rankin thought how easily it could have been him lying there dead rather than walking out with a wound that would heal.

In No. 7 Platoon of 'A' Company, Corporal Charles Monroe Johnson led one of the platoon's three sections. Johnson was an American from Tennessee. He had enlisted in the Canadian army in 1940 because it seemed the United States was going to steer clear of the war against fascism and he thought that wrong. Lieutenant Don McLaughlin was in charge of the platoon, but had made it clear that he was just along for the ride. Sergeant Jim Needham, who had been with the regiment since December 1939, was in charge. Johnson liked that. The last thing anyone needed in a tough battle was a new lieutenant who thought he knew it all. That sort of attitude got lieutenants killed quickly and usually a lot of good men died too.

There would obviously be a fair amount of dying this day. The cacophony of noise buffeting Johnson was terrific. He had never seen such heavy German fire. The machine guns firing at them were drowned out by the sounds of shells and mortar rounds exploding, both their own and the Germans'. Only the flicker of tracers arcing through the air, almost lazily, told Johnson they were taking machine-gun fire. The platoon advanced with rifles at high port across their chests to keep them out of the dew-wet wheat. Johnson saw a figure in the top of an olive tree ahead of him and fired at it from the hip. Several other men did the same. Nobody stopped to see if the shots killed the German sniper. Their orders were to stop for nothing, to get through the wire and take out the emplacements behind.

"Get through this barrage, get through this barrage, get through this barrage," Johnson repeated. He fired at another sniper in a tree out front of No. 9 Platoon and then saw the man brought down by a burst from a Thompson. The momentary distraction almost caused him to tumble into a slit trench in which two dead Germans lay in a pool of coagulating blood. To the left, a German suddenly stood up. Johnson thought he was raising his hands to surrender, but a Seaforth shot him too quickly for anyone to be sure. Directly ahead, a German stood up and fired a long burst with a light machine gun toward No. 9 Platoon. Every man in No. 7 Platoon cracked off a couple of rounds from the hip and the German folded in on himself. Without a second thought, Johnson stepped on his blood-covered head as he walked past. The number of Seaforths that were going down every minute did not leave him feeling merciful to the enemy.

Seeing three Germans suddenly bolt from a slit trench toward the wire line, Johnson took a bead with the butt of his rifle pressed into his shoulder. He snapped off the last three rounds in his clip, and one after the other the Germans crumpled. Slamming a new clip into the Lee Enfield, he resumed walking forward with the rifle at high port. Next thing, he was lying on his back, rifle still across his chest. Bewildered as to how he had fallen, Johnson stood up and looked about for his section. They were lost in the smoke. But they had been there just a split second before, he thought, how could they have disappeared? He walked forward, calling out, "Where is everybody? Where is everybody?" Stumbling over a dead German, he suddenly saw Private T. Seibert on his hands and knees. He had a gaping wound in his back and was calling out, "Am I hit?"

"You bet you are," Johnson said. The wound was about seven inches long and the man's ribs were showing. Johnson bound the wound with a shell dressing. Seibert pointed at his leg. "Where did you get that?" Looking down, Johnson saw that a big chunk of his left thigh was missing just below the hipbone. The pants and underwear there had been torn away and the skin for about six inches around the hole was black with powder burns. He applied a field dressing and flopped down next to Seibert.

A few minutes later, Corporal Bob Peebles hobbled up with a wound in his knee and lay down beside Johnson with his face about a foot away. Even then, the explosions were so loud it was hard to hear each other. Finally, after a shell exploded just feet away from the wounded men, Peebles said he would go for help and hobbled off. Time passed and nobody came, so Johnson left too. Finding a house filled with captured Germans and wounded Seaforths, Johnson crowded in and joined them. Seibert was eventually brought in as well and treated for his wounds.[28]

Up front, Johnson's company was taking terrible casualties. The new lieutenant, McLaughlin, was dead; so, too, was Sergeant Needham. Lieutenant Don Tuck "caught a sizeable chunk of shrapnel through the open collar" and had to hand off command to Corporal E.S. Weston. They still had not reached the barbed wire and already 'A' Company had no lieutenants left and few sergeants. 'A' Company's commander Major John McLean was unhurt, but he was having trouble keeping track of the whereabouts of his platoons.[29] McLean told Sergeant Rod McGowan, commanding No. 8 Platoon, to hold his men in front of the wire until he found out what had happened to the two already inside. He found Weston and learned that the two platoons had "generally broken up." McLean fetched No. 8 Platoon. When they were about fifty yards past the wire, McLean thought he saw a German machine-gun post on a facing low ridge.

He also encountered a platoon from 'D' Company commanded by Lieutenant T.E. Woolley on his right. The two platoons linked up under McLean's command and attacked the German position, which turned out to be a large bunker. After a short fight, the Germans inside surrendered and were sent back toward the Canadian lines. McLean pushed on with his platoon and Woolley took his unit back toward the right flank to try to find his company. At about 0700 hours, McLean and No. 8 Platoon reached the Aquino-Pontecorvo road. The major got on the radio and reported he was at Aboukir. McLean urged Lieutenant Colonel Syd Thomson to send up reserves, for he had too few men to hold the objective. Thomson replied that there were no reserves, but that he would try to get tanks through. While the platoon dug in, McLean and Weston went forward to find the rest of 'A' Company, which appeared to have overshot the objective.

Crossing the road, McLean looked south toward Pontecorvo and saw what looked to be two companies of the Carleton and York Regiment moving past the road toward the second objective — the Pontecorvo–Highway 6 road. Finding no sign of the missing platoons, McLean and Weston started back. They were just coming up to the road when three German tanks rolled toward them. Weston and McLean dived into an empty German slit trench, hoping the tanks had failed to spot them. A moment later, one of the tanks opened up with its main gun and a shell struck close to the trench. Knocked out, McLean awakened later to see Weston dead beside him. The major was in considerable pain. Two Seaforth privates appeared and half dragged, half walked him to the shelter of some trees on the east side of the wire. Burning tanks were scattered across the field approaching the wire. He later wrote: "The scene was one of mass devastation, burning tanks, wounded men, shell holes, continual firing."[30]

◆ ◆ ◆

At 0800 hours, 'B' Squadron of the North Irish Horse was right at the wire. Squadron commander Major G.P. Russell's leading tank was only thirty yards from a concealed Panzerturm when it opened fire. In seconds, Russell's tank and four others were ablaze. Russell was seriously wounded. The dust and smoke were so thick that the tank commanders were unable to see the gun firing at them. One after another, the tanks were picked off by the Panzerturm or by other anti-tank guns. The Panzerturm knocked out thirteen tanks before a North Irish Horse Churchill managed to destroy it with an armour-piercing round that penetrated the concrete base and detonated the gun's ammunition.[31] In all, the regiment lost forty-one of fifty-eight tanks.[32]

Initially, some of the Seaforths would have been just as happy to not be supported by the tanks. Warned that Germans armed with sticky bombs might jump out of the trees onto the tanks and blow them up, one troop behind 'D' Company raked the treetops ahead of it with machine-gun fire as it rolled along. Seeing that his company was being hit from behind by heavy machine-gun fire, Major L.M. McBride looked back and saw with horror that, as the tanks wallowed in and out of ditches and small gullies, each downward pitch directed bullets toward his men. To escape this danger, 'D' Company scattered and by the time McBride reached the wire it was spread from "hell to breakfast." Some ended up fighting alongside 'A' Company; others drifted into the PPCLI sector and fought there.

McBride and his headquarters section entered a wire area heavily laced with mines. McBride carefully picked his way along by stepping over the wire onto what looked like hard, undisturbed ground. His runner, Private Herbert Johnson, was cautiously following McBride's footsteps. It looked as if they would all get through safely when there was a tremendous explosion. McBride woke up on the ground in front of the wire, apparently thrown there by the blast. Johnson was dead. So too was Private Vic Warner, a forty-year-old radio signaller nick-named Pop because he was the oldest man in the Seaforths' signal section. McBride's other signaller had a bad shrapnel gash in his cheek. The major helped him reach a nearby ditch.

McBride then continued searching for his company but found only a lost PPCLI private. Carrying on together, the men entered an open field and were immediately fired upon by a machine gun. Ahead of him, McBride heard the heavy thumping of .75-millimetre or .88-millimetre guns and knew he had stumbled across concealed tanks or antitank guns. He was trying to figure out what to do next when something struck him in the left eye. When he came to, McBride saw several Germans looking down on him. One of them bandaged his eye and they loaded him into an ambulance, which, moments later, was hit by a shell. McBride received light shrapnel wounds to his left shoulder and leg and was knocked unconscious. His next conscious moment found him in a German operating room in Rome. Once the operation was finished, he was loaded onto a German Red Cross train going north. McBride would spend the rest of the war as a prisoner-of-war.[33]

Back at regimental headquarters, Thomson was having a terrible time following the course of the battle. He had no radio communications with most of the companies and was barely in contact with brigade. Half the time, the designated channels were clogged with unidentifiable voices and proper radio protocol was seldom followed. As noon approached, Thomson received a report that 'C' Company, commanded by Captain John Joseph Conway, was lagging on the left flank. Unable to establish radio contact with the captain, Thomson set off in his Jeep to check things out. When he got close to the company, Thomson left the Jeep and went up to the company headquarters section on foot. While he helped Conway reorient his attack, a soldier came up with two dead chickens. "You might as well have these," he said to the regimental commander. Thomson went back to the Jeep and tossed the chickens in the back next to his bedroll before driving away.

Regimental headquarters was in a stone house set on the reverse slope of a low hill. Although the Germans were unable to observe the house, they were routinely mortaring and shelling the area. Pulling up near the house, Thomson heard the whistle of incoming mortar rounds and dived into a storage room. One round struck the back of the Jeep, spewing chicken guts and blood all over. A door to Thomson's left opened and one of his runners looked out on the scene with a horror-stricken expression. "God, they got the old bastard finally," he muttered. Thomson stuck his head out the adjacent door. "No, not yet," he said.[34]

After Thomson had left, 'C' Company renewed its attack despite heavy casualties and the loss of most platoon commanders. Seeing one of his forward platoons pinned down by a German machine-gunner, Conway and four HQ section men moved up on the gunner's flank. As one of the men started to throw a grenade at the German, he fumbled it. Conway scooped the grenade off the ground to throw it away, but the grenade exploded and tore his right hand off. Since the explosion's full force was absorbed by Conway's hand, nobody else was injured. Ignoring the bleeding stump, Conway led an attack that destroyed the machine-gun position. Conway was awarded the Military Cross for his unhesitating action with the grenade.[35]

◆ ◆ ◆

Despite the terrible casualties, the attack continued, with 'C' and 'B' companies gathering up the remnants of the leading companies and driving through to Aboukir. At 1230 hours, about 100 Seaforths reached the Aquino-Pontecorvo road. As the senior surviving officer, 'B' Company's Major Jim Allan organized them into a single company over which he took command. His actions during the rest of the day resulted in his being awarded the Distinguished Service Order. Like the two leading companies, 'B' and 'C' had been shredded while breaching the wire. Allan had lost 20 percent of his men getting into the forward reaches of the Hitler Line. More fell as the company fought through to the road.[36]

'C' Company had suffered similar losses. No. 14 Platoon had been caught in a tremendous mortar barrage only 200 yards from the start line. The platoon commander was killed and just eight men remained unhurt. Company Sergeant Major Joe M. Duddle took over. The eight men had gone only a short distance when a stonk of Nebelwerfer rounds bracketed them. When the smoke cleared, Duddle was alone, so he began a one-man advance through the wire that carried him to where fifteen men had gathered under command of Lieutenant W.R. Artindale. Duddle and Artindale broke the group into two sections and crossed the Aquino-Pontecorvo road to occupy some half-ruined buildings 200 yards beyond. Soon the buildings were being shelled and raked by a heavy machine gun. Artindale returned to the road and found Allan, who told him to bring the group back. When Duddle got the order, he called out to the others. Only six responded.

Duddle quickly searched the buildings, finding several dead, no wounded, and others missing, probably taken prisoner. Duddle led the survivors to the road.[37]

While Duddle and Artindale were out west of the road, Allan and his ad hoc force had been knocking out nearby German positions. Near where the Seaforths had come up on the road, Allan spotted a Panzerturm. In front of it was a sunken track filled with fallen trees and fortified with slit trenches and dug-in machine guns. A small party of Seaforths crept down a gully that allowed them to outflank the Panzerturm and kill its crew with small-arms fire. They then dispatched the Germans in the sunken track.

Having knocked out this position, Allan gathered in the remnants of all the companies that had reached the road. He found that the regiment now effectively numbered only about fifty men. Of these, two were officers — Artindale and Lieutenant T.E. Woolley. Both were wounded, Woolley quite seriously.[38]

At about 1500 hours, Allan finished organizing the group in a defensive position anchored on a German trench eight feet long by two feet wide and some surrounding slit trenches, but almost immediately German tanks started firing into their position with machine guns. There was so much dust and smoke the Seaforths were unable to see the tanks. Eventually, using binoculars, Artindale sighted the tanks on both sides of the road several hundred yards north of their position. Allan told Duddle to take a PIAT team composed of Privates K.J. Gustafson and E.M. Richardson and see if they could sort the tanks out. Gustafson, the PIAT gunner, had only two bombs left. The three men crawled toward the tanks, which, as they drew closer, they could see through a gap in a hedge. Realizing a frontal shot would fail to penetrate the Panthers' armour, Duddle and the men circled through the high grass to come up behind the tanks. As they came to an opening in the field, Duddle saw a tank standing there that had not previously been detected. Richardson crouched down and Gustafson stabilized the awkward shoulder-fired weapon on his back. This enabled Gustafson to get the weapon higher than the top of the wheat, so he had a clear line of fire. Gustafson sighted the weapon on the tank and then lowered the butt of the launcher, took off his spectacles, wiped them with a handkerchief, replaced them, lifted the butt again and fired both bombs one after the other, disabling the tank. The three men then fled through a hail of small-arms fire back to the Seaforths' position.[39]

Allan, whose radio had been disabled by a damaged antenna, managed to restore the unit to life by fashioning an antenna out of some German aerial wire he found. He asked Thomson for 6-pounder antitank guns, PIAT bombs, and, most important, reinforcements. Thomson knew the ground was too rugged to move antitank guns over and he had no reinforcements. There was only one glimmer of hope. On the left flank, the Carleton and York Regiment had punched through to the Aquino-Pontecorvo road and were moving toward the second objective. Thomson asked 2 CIB Brigadier Gibson to direct some tanks behind that regiment and up the road to Allan's position. Gibson refused, as this sector was now part of a planned major break-through by the rest of the 3rd Canadian Infantry Brigade regiments.[40]

Thomson decided to move up and set up a tactical headquarters in Allan's position. That way, he could establish a radio link to call in artillery support to protect the surviving elements of his companies. He, Intelligence Officer Lieutenant R.K. Swinton, and a radio signaller started out in a turretless Stuart tank, but it soon lost a track on a mine. They switched to a Jeep, but got stuck in a ditch. Continuing on foot, they came under artillery fire and the signaller was killed. The radio was also knocked out. Pressing on, the two officers came across a bunker filled with Germans who, Thomson was thankful to discover, wanted to surrender. He told them to stay put and that someone would eventually take them in.

At Allan's position, some of the wounded were being gathered together to make a break for the Canadian lines. Lieutenant Woolley, although badly wounded, led this party back to safety. Duddle, meanwhile, learned at about 1600 hours that two Seaforth sections were pinned down by fire 200 yards to the right of the main group. He crawled over and found that some of the dozen men were too badly wounded to walk. Duddle cobbled together several stretchers from bits and pieces of wood, gas capes, and webbing belts. They were preparing to pull out at 1700 hours when three German tanks materialized northeast of them. Duddle and some of the other men quickly dragged the wounded on stretchers into a hollow where they were hidden from the tankers. He then watched in despair as the tanks charged the main Seaforths' position.[41]

The three tanks rolled in from the right at the same time that two others struck from the left. They proceeded to hammer the helpless Seaforths with .75-millimetre main gun and machine-gun fire. There was nowhere to run. After a few minutes, the tanks ceased firing and German infantry swept through the position, rounding up the wounded and a few unhurt survivors who had no choice but to surrender. Among these was Lieutenant Artindale. Allan, who had been hit in the leg and buttocks by machine-gun bullets, was covered in blood and playing dead. The Germans missed him.

Several others also managed to avoid being rounded up in the infantry sweep. When the tanks and infantry withdrew, these slowly emerged. Allan found he had twelve men left. Most were wounded. Duddle's group was still in the little hollow across the road and off to the right. There were also a couple of groups of two to three men hiding in nearby holes. Allan and his men held on as night closed in, but it was obvious the position was untenable. With his leg stiffening badly, Allan could no longer effectively exercise command. At 1830 hours, he ordered the men to withdraw toward the Regimental Aid Post situated in the Seaforths' tactical headquarters.

On the way back through the Hitler Line, the men met no Germans. It seemed apparent that those positions not destroyed during the attack had been abandoned.[42] Coming in behind Allan's small group was Duddle's. Once through the wire, Duddle and his party came across a number of wounded North Irish Horse tankers. Most were terribly burned. Most of the tankers could walk out under their own steam, but Duddle carried out one who was practically blind. The CSM's small party finally arrived at regimental HQ at 1930 hours. Duddle, who would win a Distinguished Conduct Medal for his ceaseless courage during this day, turned around ninety minutes later and led a stretcher-party search for more wounded. Unable to locate Allan's defensive position in the dark, they managed to rescue one wounded Seaforth in a slit trench and several more tankers.[43]

While Allan and Duddle had been withdrawing, Thomson and Swinton had finally arrived at the abandoned position. All they found were dead Seaforths. Looking at the bodies and the equipment scattered in the ditch, Thomson realized they had been overrun by tanks. A second later a machine gun started firing at them from 200 yards away. The flash of the gun illuminated the silhouette of a tank.

Thomson and Swinton dived into the ditch, then crawled back toward the safety of the Canadian lines. En route, they stopped at the bunker and picked up the Germans, who had not wavered in their eagerness to surrender.

♦ ♦ ♦

Although the battle was unquestionably a disaster for 2 CIB, the Germans were having a hard time as well. In the mid-afternoon, Ware contacted Gibson by radio to report that neither his regiment nor the Edmontons were capable of continuing the advance. Gibson responded: "Hold on, good work. Will do all we can for you, and send up more tanks. Looking at the broader picture the news is excellent. German transport is streaming up the road north westwards and the Adolf Hitler Line has been breached all along its length."[44]

Despite that promising news, Ware was increasingly concerned that the Germans might counterattack and easily wipe out the remnants of the two regiments. He told Lieutenant Donald Gower to bring up the antitank guns. Having done an earlier reconnaissance, the lieutenant knew the area was so confined that he only called up half the guns. Soon the big tow trucks arrived, each pulling a gun, and Gower directed them into the preselected sites. The men unhooked the guns and wheeled them into position, dragged the ammunition off the trucks, and then the vehicles tore back to safety. The area was still being heavily shelled, and a few minutes later a massive 105-millimetre shell smacked into the ground, buried itself under one of the guns and promptly exploded. The gun was wrecked, but its crew was unhurt.

As Gower and his antitank platoon started digging in, it began to rain. Gower and Sergeant Norman McCowan found a dead Patricia in a slit trench. The man had been killed after digging down only about six inches. They picked the body up, placed it on the parapet, and dug deeper with bayonets, knives, and their hands. Working frantically, they got down to about five feet before either felt that the trench provided sufficient protection. The bottom of the trench filled with rainwater. When one bout of shells fell near their position, Gower lay in the trench bottom with McCowan on top of him. The cold water made him shiver. McCowan said, "I don't know what you're shaking for, I'm on top."[45]

Nearby, Ware was also shaking, but less from fear than an over-whelming sorrow. The battle had broken him. He knew that. The regiment he loved was virtually destroyed and the decisions that a commanding officer must make without hesitation were too heavy a burden to bear. "You can command for so long," he later said, "and really when you start wondering if you should send 'Bucko Watson,' who you don't want killed, or Charlie McDonald, who you don't want killed either, it's too long."[46] A quick tally taken of the compa-nies determined that the regiment's initial fighting strength of 287 men was reduced to only 77.[47]

From the messages Ware had sent Gibson toward the end of the day, the brigade commander sensed Ware's mental state. As evening drew in, he sent the PPCLI's second-in-command, Major D.H. Rosser, to relieve him and pulled Ware back to brigade headquarters for a rest.[48] Captain Howard Mitchell of the Saskatoon Light Infantry was nearby when Ware came in. Gibson went over to the PPCLI com-mander and praised his performance and that of his regiment. Ware's eyes were glazed over with tears. "Those were fine boys. They are gone. I haven't anybody left. They are all gone."[49]

The 2 CIB regiments had suffered terribly. The first casualty fig-ures reported were worse than proved the case, but the reality was awful enough. The final butcher's bill for the PPCLI was 3 officers and 55 other ranks killed, 5 officers and 157 other ranks wounded, and 2 officers and 25 other ranks missing.[50] The Loyal Edmontons had lost 2 officers and 48 other ranks dead, 5 officers and 120 other ranks wounded.[51] Of the Seaforths, 3 officers and 49 other ranks died, 7 offi-cers and 99 other ranks were wounded, and 2 officers and 50 other ranks had been taken prisoner. The 210 casualties this regiment suf-fered on May 23 were its heaviest toll in any single day of battle during the war.[52] The same was true for the other regiments. Taken together, 2 CIB's ordeal was unequalled in a day of combat by any other brigade during the course of the Italian campaign.[53]

♦ ♦ ♦

The Regimental Aid Posts and all the hospitals back down the Canadian line had never dealt with such fearful casualty rates, but good advance planning paid off and the quality of care never suf-fered. When it became obvious that casualties were going to be higher than normal, Nos. 5 and 9 Field Ambulances moved their advanced dressing stations closer to the front, reducing the time lag that congested traffic conditions threatened to create. Soon No. 5 Field Ambulance, which was tasked to 2 CIB, found that the rate of casualties exceeded its resources, and some wounded were evacuated through the advanced dressing stations of the 5th Canadian Armoured Division. By the afternoon, "four field surgical units, two auxiliary surgical teams, and two field transfusion units were working at full capacity in the joint advanced surgical centre. Nursing sisters had also been brought forward from the hospitals, and were being employed in the post-operative care of patients."54

Seaforths chaplain Major Roy Durnford was horrified by the rate of wounded pouring into the Regimental Aid Post. The RAP was situated in a barn next to the tactical headquarters. Soon the house from which Thomson was trying to coordinate the battle also had to be used to hold the wounded. Durnford watched the surreal scene of "maps, signals, anxious officers battered and war weary" weaving about among the wounded. The shelling was continual, but the major casualties from it were German prisoners told to stand outside the RAP because nobody had time to figure out how to move them further to the rear. To Durnford, the Germans were "dull and dopey or nervous and excitable. Pale, dirty and utterly exhausted they stagger down the line."

Durnford concentrated on the wounded Canadians. One of the first things Durnford always did during a battle was build a small open fire near the RAP on which he boiled up gallons of tea and thin soup to nourish the wounded. This time there was never enough. "The boys keep coming in. Some bomb happy, some terribly broken and shell-shocked, some with limbs torn off and some almost gleefully with light wounds. . . . North Irish Horse tank boys went in with us. They were wonderful. Their casualties were heavy. Ours are extremely severe." Staring around the RAP bursting with wounded and knowing how many Seaforths had perished in the Hitler Line, Durnford knew that May 23 had "been our best and worst day."55

18

AN HONOUR
TO DIE

While 2nd Canadian Infantry Brigade was being torn asunder on May 23, the remaining two formations of 1st Canadian Infantry Division were cracking the Hitler Line open — no regiment more successfully than the one from New Brunswick. The Carleton and York Regiment had attacked on the immediate left flank of the Seaforth Highlanders of Canada. Far enough south to be largely unscathed by the flanking fire from Aquino, the regiment enjoyed another major advantage over those of 2 CIB. While that brigade had been held back through May 22, not knowing whether it was to attack on the division's extreme left or right flank, the New Brunswickers had conducted a diversionary action against the line intended to relieve pressure on 1st Canadian Infantry Brigade's assault on Pontecorvo.

It had fallen to 'D' Company to carry out the hastily organized attack on May 22, ordered only an hour and a half before it was to start. 'B' Squadron of the 51st Royal Tank Regiment supported the company.[1] Just before the attack, regimental adjutant Captain Don Smith had passed through 'D' Company's ranks and paused to talk with his old friend, Lieutenant Donald W. Moffett, a platoon commander. As the two men parted, Moffett said with great finality, "Well, goodbye Smitty." Smith knew then that he would never see Moffett again, for few lived long after such premonitions of death.[2]

The attack began ten minutes behind schedule at 1010 hours. With the Royal Canadian Horse Artillery heavily shelling the German defences, 'D' Company commander Major Rowland Horsey led his men to the wire without meeting any opposition. He then sent No. 16 and No. 18 platoons fifty yards beyond the wire. As these platoons passed through the wire, they came under heavy machine-gun fire from the front and both flanks. Moffett was killed by one of the first bursts and the other platoon commander, Lieutenant William McGrath, received a head wound.[3] Horsey, who had gone forward with the two leading platoons, saw a German trying to shoot some of his men with a machine gun. Shouldering his Lee Enfield, Horsey's third shot killed the German.[4]

One section of No. 18 Platoon, under Lance Corporal Aubrey Ward, was cut off by a German tank. The men hid out for about thirty minutes in a shell crater until the tank moved off. Then they withdrew through the wire, carrying out two wounded men.[5] Another section of five men in No. 16 Platoon found itself surrounded and forced to surrender. The Germans told the men to hand over their equipment and weapons. Section leader Corporal Bannister slipped his wire cutters back to a man sitting immediately against the wire. When the Germans turned their backs, the soldier cut a hole in the wire. The men then waited for a chance to make a break for it, which came when some 51st RTR tanks approached their position and distracted the Germans. The men slipped through the wire and fled to safety under covering fire provided by the tankers.[6]

'D' Company's attack went so well that 3rd Canadian Infantry Brigade commander Brigadier Paul Bernatchez thought if the rest of the Carleton and York Regiment joined it, they could break the Hitler Line wide open a day ahead of schedule. However, by this time it was evident that 1 CIB's assault on Pontecorvo was faltering and Major General Chris Vokes knew he could ill afford to risk Operation Chesterfield with yet another hurriedly conceived and executed attack. He ordered the New Brunswickers to pull back.[7]

It had been a costly operation. 'D' Company lost one officer killed and one wounded. Twenty-two other ranks were wounded and one killed. Six tanks were also knocked out. However, the Carleton and York Regiment had amassed a great deal of intelligence on the nature of the German defences. The location of many antitank gun and machine-gun positions was now known and several gaps had been cut into the wire to serve as lanes for the major attack in the morning. This enabled Lieutenant Colonel Dick Danby to develop a plan of attack worked out to the last detail, something that the regiments in 2 CIB — having been unable even to reconnoitre their section of the attack line — could not do.[8]

♦ ♦ ♦

At 0600 hours on May 23, the Carleton and York Regiment spearheaded 3 CIB's assault. The brigade plan was simple. The New Brunswick regiment would punch through to the Aquino-Pontecorvo road, code-named Aboukir. Then the West Nova Scotia Regiment would pass through and advance to a height of land overlooking the San Martino River. Operation Chesterfield called for the true breakthrough to come in 2 CIB's sector, so once the West Novas were on their objective, 3 CIB's part in the offensive would be concluded. The Royal 22e Regiment was acting as the divisional reserve, ready to move to the assistance of 2 CIB if necessary.[9]

The two leading Carleton and York companies — 'B' on the left and 'A' on the right — leaned on the barrage. But that failed to stop a counter-barrage by German artillery, mortars, and Nebelwerfers. Captain James Crook had barely taken 'A' Company across the start line when he was killed. Lieutenant H.J. Haining took over. With casualties mounting in 'A' Company, Major Rowland Horsey moved up with his much-reduced 'D' Company to bolster the leading company and unite the two under his command.

The two companies were to have breached the wire and reached Aboukir in seventy minutes. In fact, it took Major Burt Kennedy's 'B' Company five minutes more than that. A few minutes later, Horsey reported that the composite company had arrived.[10] The fighting had been stiff the entire way. Had Horsey not rushed to bolster 'A' Company with his own, the attack might have faltered. Horsey's Company Sergeant Major Earle Upton played a pivotal role in keeping 'D' Company's headquarters section organized. He also brought up the reserve platoons at the critical moment when its extra weight served to overwhelm the German defenders.

When his section commander had been killed, 'A' Company's Private Samuel Dow took over and led the men into the wire. The section got separated from the rest of the company when it dodged incoming mortar fire and was forced to ground by a German .88-millimetre antitank gun emplacement that stood about 300 yards ahead. Armed with a PIAT, Dow crawled to a position 50 yards from the gun. Although scoring three direct hits on the concrete emplacement, he failed to knock the gun out. However, his fire marked the weapon's position for the tanks. They blasted the gun position to pieces. Dow was, however, mortally wounded.[11]

Behind the Carleton and York Regiment, the 51st Royal Tank Regiment was caught in a fierce tank battle as several German tanks and self-propelled guns came up on the right flank to add the weight of their guns to the many antitank guns and Panzerturms engaging the British tankers. When both squadron commanders were wounded, the commander of the tank regiment rushed up to assume command. It took until 1000 hours for the British tanks to drive the German armour off and knock out most of the antitank gun emplacements. Losses among the tankers were heavy.[12]

While the tank battle raged, the New Brunswickers consolidated their hold at Aboukir. 'B' Company dug in on the left, 'D' and 'A' companies on the right, and 'C' Company lay in support. The Bren carrier company came up to protect the main breach in the wire. No sooner was everyone settled in than a German tank ground up to a position just fifty yards from 'B' Company's front. When Danby sent the antitank platoon, under Captain L.A. Watling, forward to strengthen the regiment's position, the tank retreated.[13]

Germans were surrendering all along the regimental front and others who had been bypassed earlier were also giving up. The scout platoon roved behind the wire rounding up or killing snipers, while Horsey's men sent prisoners to the rear in batches of twenty to forty at a time. Effective opposition against the Carleton and York Regiment had ceased. Although still taking significant amounts of German artillery and mortar fire, the regiment had successfully completed its mission of breaching the Hitler Line. The way was clear for the West Nova Scotia Regiment to pass through and begin the next phase.[14]

◆ ◆ ◆

That phase of the offensive was to have begun when 2 CIB and 3 CIB had established a three-regiment-wide front along the Aquino-Pontecorvo road. Only then was the second half of the massive barrage to begin. By noon, it was clear things were badly awry. Although 2 CIB's Seaforth Highlanders of Canada had reached the road, they had been devastated in the process. The Princess Patricia's Canadian Light Infantry and the Loyal Edmonton Regiment had no prospect of breaking through.

Vokes faced a dilemma. Currently, the West Nova Scotia Regiment was waiting in badly exposed ground for an order to pass through the Carleton and York Regiment. That advance was to have gone in behind a barrage that was now indefinitely postponed because of 2 CIB's situation. The only success Vokes had was that won by the New Brunswick regiment. Now he had to decide how best to exploit it.[15]

Throughout the morning, Vokes had sought news of progress on the 2 CIB front. But Brigadier Graeme Gibson had little to tell him and Vokes was having difficulty keeping calm. Communications between Gibson and the regimental commanders were badly disrupted. Vokes had told Gibson to "get a clear picture of the situation employing every means at his disposal." He told the brigadier to go out personally if need be to gather a situation report.

Eventually, Gibson, having sent a staff officer forward, reported the debacle his brigade had met. Vokes realized that he must either use the ground won by the Carleton and York Regiment or fail. Accordingly, Vokes decided to continue with the original plan for 3 CIB, but to supplement it by having the Royal 22e Regiment exploit through the West Nova Scotia Regiment. This regiment would drive across the Pontecorvo–Highway 6 road. By having the Van Doos hook to the right during their drive, he could open a path for 5th Canadian Armoured Division almost identical to that originally planned. By 1300 hours, Vokes had ordered Bernatchez to attack at 1700 hours with the postponed second phase of the artillery program to begin minutes before. As the 51st RTR had taken so many casualties during the Carleton and York attack and while waiting for the West Novas to go in, Vokes had to bring in the Three Rivers Regiment from 1st Canadian Armoured Brigade to support the attack. This regiment had been hanging in reserve, should it be needed.

The Three Rivers tanks and the R22eR were Vokes's last reserves. If this attack failed, Operation Chesterfield was finished. Vokes impressed this point on Bernatchez. Time was of the essence, he said, but he did not want to "have the attack go off half cocked."

Shortly after Bernatchez departed, I Canadian Corps commander Lieutenant General Tommy Burns arrived. Vokes thought the corps commander seemed "rather depressed by the picture" he painted of the battle's course. As it was Burns's first offensive battle as corps commander, Vokes thought his reaction understandable. Vokes himself was optimistic that the 3 CIB attack would succeed. He was also encouraged by the progress 1st Canadian Infantry Brigade had made at Pontecorvo. He expected this brigade to "have cleared the enemy out of their sector of the Hitler Line before dark."

Vokes's major concern was that the Germans would counterattack the Carleton and York Regiment. If they mounted a determined operation, it could seriously disrupt the planned attack. Vokes impatiently paced around his headquarters, waiting to hear that Bernatchez's men were ready. At 1610 hours, he got word that they were in position. Vokes decided to move the attack time up from 1700 hours to 1650. Even ten minutes might mean the difference between an attack going in clear or being blocked by a German counterattack. Vokes was profoundly aware that the second phase of Operation Chesterfield was now getting under way a full eight and one-half hours behind schedule. Such a delay, he later wrote, "seldom happens in peacetime training, and officers without battlefield training find it hard to understand. Those who study this battle will be critical of the delay and will no doubt believe I should have exploited the success of 3rd Brigade much earlier."[16]

Vokes could hardly have moved more quickly. No clear picture existed of what was happening on the 2 CIB front until shortly before noon. Perhaps if Gibson had sent staff forward earlier, or conducted a personal reconnaissance, he would have realized that his regiments were too badly shredded to fulfill their assigned task. He did neither. By the time 2 CIB's situation was clearly understood at divisional headquarters, the armour that was to have supported the West Nova

Scotia attack had been so badly shot up at its start line that it had to be reinforced and rearmed.[17]

♦ ♦ ♦

The West Nova Scotia Regiment and supporting 51st RTR squadrons had formed up in an extremely exposed position close to the German lines in expectation that their phase of the attack would soon begin. When the Carleton and York Regiment reported its success in reaching Aboukir just five minutes behind schedule, it was 0715 hours. The Nova Scotians and British tankers geared up for an imminent advance.

No order came. The German shelling of the area, heavy from the outset, steadily increased. More deadly for the tankers was the persistent and frighteningly accurate antitank fire from behind the German wire. The well-sited Panzerturms and a number of .88-millimetre gun emplacements were able to range in on the tanks, but their own positions were masked by the terrain and the dust and smoke raised by the Canadian barrage.

Hours passed and the situation remained unchanged. No orders came to either withdraw or advance. At 1030 hours, West Novas commander Lieutenant Colonel Ron Waterman told the infantry to dig in. Already, the regiment had had a number of men killed or wounded. Several Churchills were burning in every company area. Two hours later, it started to rain, but the German fire only intensified. More tanks burst into flames, more casualties were quickly evacuated. The West Novas' war diarist scribbled, "Everyone is getting a bit worried, no news, what can be holding up the attack?"[18]

'A' Company commander Major John Millard was running from one disabled tank to another trying to find the commander of the squadron assigned to his unit. Each Churchill was fitted with a buzzer on its back that infantrymen could use to signal the tankers inside. When the tankers heard the buzzer, the commander opened the top hatch and tossed a headphone set on a wire down to the infantryman to allow communication over the racket of exploding shells and whining bullets. After going through this process several times, Millard learned that the squadron commander, Major Hare, had already lost two tanks and had moved to one named *Champion*.

Millard found *Champion* and pushed the button. Repeated attempts brought no response. Seeing the hatch was open, he climbed up on the turret to shout inside. A shell had struck *Champion* and the interior was a shambles. Millard was backing away when Hare called to him from another tank. The infantry commander asked Hare how his squadron was faring. Hare said he had only five of eighteen tanks left and these had scattered. If and when the attack order came, Hare said, he would try rounding them up.

Twenty minutes later, Hare tracked Millard down. The major was in a badly battered tank that barely ran. Hare said grimly that the squadron was literally destroyed; only a handful of the Churchills were even repairable. A desert campaign veteran, Hare told Millard, "I've seen some rough goes but this is the worst. My whole squadron's had it. I'm going up with a tommy-gun to fight with the Carleton and Yorks!" Thompson in hand, he took off for the German wire.

Millard headed back toward 'A' Company's headquarters section to radio a report to Waterman. He ran across a small field that was blanketed by shell holes. More than a dozen tank wrecks were strewn about. Half were burning. One exploded, the turret flipping off and landing upside down on the ground. The driver and the commander crawled out of the escape hatches of one burning hulk. Both men were ablaze. The commander staggered toward Millard, his eyes seeming to plead for help. Millard started toward him, but the tank blew up, the blast hurling the man twenty-five yards through the air. Millard crawled over to him, but he was dead.

The driver was still alive, tumbling over and over in the grass. A soldier grabbed him and beat out the flames on his clothes with bare hands. His coveralls were charred to a crisp, his burns dreadful. The man swore repeatedly, offering no other complaint and showing no visible sign of fear or pain. Millard and a couple of infantrymen helped him to the Regimental Aid Post. On his way back, Millard met West Novas Captain A.H. Maclean. The captain had half the flesh on one arm torn away by shrapnel, but had come to ask Millard if there were enough tanks left for the attack. Millard told him no and then radioed Waterman. The regimental commander said he should wait. "We waited and waited," Millard later said.[19]

What they waited for was new tanks. The Three Rivers Regiment was on its way, but could not reach the area until 1630 hours at the earliest. The regiment had been holding behind 2 CIB's lines in anticipation of supporting the Royal 22e Regiment. Now they had to shift southward across rough ground. At the same time, the R22eR was also coming. 'A' Squadron was to support the West Novas, 'C' Squadron the Van Doos. Neither tank squadron was at full strength. Like the 51st RTR, they had been ordered to form up perilously close to the German front lines and had paid accordingly.

Three Rivers Intelligence Officer Lieutenant Horace Dugald Beach had thought the spot where 'A' Squadron had formed up was "not too good a one tactically." Both 'A' and 'C' had been positioned on a rise where they enjoyed a superlative view of the battleground and could watch the North Irish Horse tanks brewing up one after the other as they approached the Hitler Line in support of the PPCLI and Seaforths. The position also exposed their tanks to the same deadly combination of Panzerturm and .88-millimetre antitank gunfire. Armour-piercing shot, he noted, "was flying around as thick as the HE and mortars. Suddenly, 'BLAP' and 'A' Squadron's tanks were going up in flames. They were committed before they could bat an eyelash, on our side of the Start Line Major R.C. Yelland's tank and Corporal O'Brien's tank went up in flames. Lieutenant Homer-Dixon jumped from his tank and with a fire extinguisher tried to put out the flames and rescue the crew of 3 Baker. He was sniped in the back. 'A' Squadron moved back slightly and pulled over to the left."[20]

Captain D.C. Whiteford took over 'A' Squadron and led its remaining tanks over to the West Novas. They arrived with just three minutes to complete the marrying-up process before going into the attack at 1650 hours.[21] As the Canadian Shermans rolled past the still smoking wrecks of the Churchills, the West Novas dispensed with all training procedure for coordinating actions with tanks. The infantry just waved the tanks forward, climbed out of their slit trenches, and started running toward the German wire. As one officer put it, "Our plan was clear enough — to get forward out of that hell hole." The companies were terribly depleted. Millard's 'A' Company went into the attack with only 55 men. Five days previously, it had numbered 107. The West Novas had 'A' and 'B' companies forward, with 'C' and 'D' following 200 yards back. Leaning into a barrage that preceded them almost to where the Carleton and York Regiment waited on the Aquino-Pontecorvo Road, they found many holes torn in the wire by shells.[22]

With the tanks having difficulty keeping up, the West Novas reached the Carleton and York position and kept on without pause. "Good luck, West Novas!" the New Brunswick men yelled. The charge continued until the West Novas came up to the steep gully through which the San Martino River flowed. Here, Waterman called a halt to let the tanks catch up, but the regiment also caught the Panzer Grenadiers frantically trying to man fighting positions dug into the reverse slope. The West Novas cut them apart with small-arms fire and many Germans surrendered.[23]

When the Three Rivers tanks came up, they found the gully too steep to cross. Whiteford told Waterman that the tankers would have to reconnoitre for a crossing point.[24] The West Novas commander feared losing momentum so sent the infantry on alone. With the rain now a downpour, 'A' and 'B' companies led the way across the gully. They bypassed pockets of resistance, driving hard for the road above the San Martino River and leaving it to the following companies to mop up. The speed of the attack overwhelmed the Germans. The war diarist wrote, "Jerry prisoners and dead everywhere, they are completely demoralized at the speed of the attack but the shelling and mortaring is still intense. Before reaching the Pontecorvo Road the advance has been so rapid that the enemy counter barrage is dropping behind the reserve companies. 'B' Company reports Caporetto Code word for final objective, less than three-quarters of an hour after passing the start line. Seconds later 'A' Company report the same. The CO is so surprised he cannot at first believe it."[25]

The road proved to be little more than a narrow one-lane gravel track following a low wooded ridge that overlooked the gully of San Martino River. The West Novas crossed the road and dug in on the other side, with 'B' Company forming the right flank in the protection of some trees and shrubs. 'A' Company set up on a small spur rising above the road, 'C' moved to the southwest end of the ridge where some farmhouses were located, and 'D' dropped down into a sector of fields amid another cluster of farmhouses about a thousand yards north of Pontecorvo.

No sooner had the companies dug in than the Germans counterattacked with tanks and infantry. The West Novas faced a dicey few minutes, for they had been told that the 48th Highlanders of Canada, from 1st Canadian Infantry Brigade, were on their left flank. Seeing

a strong German force coming up the road from that direction, 'D'.
Company commander Captain J.K. (Dusty) Rhodes radioed Waterman
for artillery support. Waterman said, "I can't give you artillery fire
on that position — the Highlanders are there."

"Then, sir, they're wearing damned funny helmets!"

"Very well, Dusty — but on your head be it."

"For God's sake, not on my head, sir. On theirs!"

"Roger." Waterman signed off.[26] Artillery fire crashed down minutes later and broke the German counterattack from that direction,
but not before a 'D' Company section had been overrun in a large
house situated on the left flank.

Elsewhere, the Germans struck with equally determined counterattacks supported by tanks. As a tank approached 'C' Company, its
men braced for a mauling. The commander, however, opened his
turret, scanned the ridge with binoculars, and dropped promptly out
of sight when one of the Bren gunners fired a burst at him. Everyone
sighed with relief as the tank withdrew.

From his position on the spur looking west from the ridge, 'A'
Company's Major Millard saw Panzer Grenadiers massing with tanks
in the valley below. All he had to meet the tanks were a few PIATs.
Millard withdrew his company from its exposed position to one
astride the road, where the company's 6-pounder antitank gun platoon
was scheduled to set up once it arrived. Meanwhile, Royal Canadian
Horse Artillery Forward Observation Officer Captain Robinson
directed a concentration of 25-pounder gunfire on the German
forming-up point, successfully scattering them.

At dusk, 'A' Company was still digging in when a German soldier
rose up out of the tall wheat and started blazing away with a
Schmeisser submachine gun at the company headquarters section.
His first targets were Millard and three other men, who were having
a huddled conference in the open. Millard was unscathed but the
other three, including RCHA FOO Robinson, were hit.

Everyone dived for cover as more Germans opened fire from the
southeast side of the road. It soon became evident that the Germans
had infiltrated behind 'D' Company's rear to attack the centre of the
regiment. Most of the men in 'A' Company were surprised in the
process of digging in. Only a few sentries were armed; the others had
put down their guns in favour of shovels and bayonets. As the attack

struck from behind, the sentries had been caught looking the wrong way and were cut down by the advancing Germans. In minutes, the majority of 'A' Company was forced to surrender.

Despite the gunfire coming from the right of 'A' Company, the German commander curiously decided that the captured West Novas were the only Canadians in the sector. He formed his men up behind the prisoners and marched them north up the road. Minutes later, a Bren gun team on the left flank of 'B' Company was astonished to see about twenty-five West Novas approaching their position with hands raised in surrender. Behind the prisoners followed a closely grouped bunch of Germans. Privates Walter Peach and R.L. Hall swung their Bren gun to face the approaching group and fired a burst over the heads of the Canadians. This had the desired effect as the West Novas hit the dirt, leaving the Germans exposed to a long burst from the Bren. The Germans returned fire equally quickly and the two men were killed. They had bought enough time, however, for the rest of 'B' Company to bring up weapons, and a fierce volley of fire tore into the Germans. All were killed or wounded. Not a man in the sur-rendered element of 'A' Company had been scratched.

Not all of 'A' Company had been captured. Millard, a lieutenant, and eight other men were holding out in a farmhouse and some slit trenches against more Germans who had infiltrated the West Novas' position. Wounds incapacitated the RCHA FOO and another man in this group, and the other eight were hard pressed to repel repeated attacks. Elsewhere, the battle was equally desperate. 'D' Company was almost overrun by two Mark IVs supported by infantry. Just as darkness fell, the tanks were driven off by PIAT fire. Only one PIAT round remained when the German tank disengaged. 'C' Company was virtually surrounded. 'B' Company and the former prisoners of 'A' Company were in similar straits. With his radio batteries weak-ening and no spares on hand, Millard contacted Waterman and said he was on the verge of being overrun.[27]

While the West Novas' situation worsened, the Three Rivers tank squadrons continued seeking a way to cross the gully. Lieutenant N.H. Bier ran half a mile north and discovered a point where the tanks could probably cross. He led the two tank squadrons to the position and they skidded down a steep bank, wallowed through the mud at the bottom, and clawed a path up the other slope.[28]

With the tanks now across the gully, Waterman scraped the barrel for infantry reinforcements. Headquarters personnel and the platoon of scouts and snipers were rushed to link up with the tanks. The Bren carrier platoon under Lieutenant C.H. Smith went to relieve Millard's little group. Numbering only eighteen men, the platoon managed to break through to Millard and, small though it was, its presence stabilized resistance there. While the fighting around the West Novas remained stiff throughout the night, the situation slowly improved. By 0100 hours on May 24, it was apparent the regiment would survive until dawn. The companies, however, had lost between 20 and 60 percent of their effective strengths.

◆ ◆ ◆

As the West Nova Scotia Regiment had reached the Pontecorvo–Highway 6 road, the Royal 22e Regiment had broken off from its follow-on position, turning sharply right to reach the road on the objective point originally assigned to the Seaforth Highlanders of Canada. The regiment tenaciously fought its way through heavy defences with Major Ovila Garceau's 'D' Company on the left and Major Charles Bellavance's 'C' Company on the right. Captain Henri Tellier's 'A' Company followed. When the regiment wheeled to the right, Garceau's company stayed back of the main German fortifications and made directly for the objective, while Bellavance, supported by Tellier, began the slow work of clearing the German fortified positions.[29]

Garceau, an old-guard regimental mainstay, appeared completely unfazed by the persistent German artillery and mortar fire. He and two platoon commanders strolled ahead of the company, as if walking in a park. When they reached the San Martino gully, Garceau called a halt. He stood in the middle of the road, joking with his lieutenants, who sat on the verge. Garceau tried lighting a cigarette, but it was raining too hard. Suddenly a shell struck the middle of the road and shrapnel tore into Garceau's abdomen. As the lieutenants rushed to his side, Garceau looked up and made a joke. He continued laughing and joking as they wrapped him in a shell dressing and arranged his evacuation.[30]

Lieutenant Colonel Jean Allard and RCHA Major George Mitchell were bouncing along in the R22eR commander's Jeep between the two advancing companies. From a fortified house came the sharp thump of an .88-millimetre gun. The round hissed directly between

Allard and Mitchell. The two officers and two corporals accompanying them dived out of the Jeep and scrambled to cover. Travelling with Allard's party was a 17-pound gun crewed by members of the 1st Anti-tank Regiment, Royal Canadian Artillery. This crew swiftly unhooked their weapon from its carrier and brought it to bear. The German gun was destroyed as the Canadian gunners put accurate fire through the gun port that the enemy had cut in the stone wall.

When Allard returned to the Jeep, he heard on the radio that Garceau lay wounded in a nearby house. He hurried over to check on his childhood friend, who, like Allard, hailed from Trois Rivières. Even as Allard walked into the house and saw Garceau lying on the floor with a gaping wound in his abdomen, he knew the man was dying. Allard did not ask what had happened; that did not matter. Garceau, still lucid, said, "You know, Jean, old buddy, it's an honour to die for the Van Doos. Tell my mother I died happy and say goodbye to her for me. Say hello to Jos Trudeau for me." Allard and some others gently laid Garceau on a stretcher and sent him back to hospital, but he died on arrival. The Van Doos commander thought sadly that Garceau "had given his all, like thousands of other Canadians before him, in a war far from home, a war that would go on without him."[31]

But the Canadians had breached the Hitler Line. Allard found his companies had moved well west of the main fortifications and were pressing northward, ever widening the opening. 'D' Company, now commanded by Captain Vaugeois of the reconnaissance platoon, anchored the left flank near the West Nova Scotia line. 'C' Company moved up the Aquino-Pontecorvo road and found a lost platoon from the PPCLI there. And 1,500 yards to the northwest of where Allard established his regimental command post, Captain Tellier's 'A' Company was ensconced on the Pontecorvo–Highway 6 road. It was a victory that had come at a terrible price, for since crossing the Gari River on May 13 the regiment had suffered more than 200 casualties. Twenty-eight men were dead. Given the heavy artillery fire falling on the Canadian positions, Allard knew more of his men would not be alive to greet the morning.[32]

◆ ◆ ◆

The more-than-one-mile-wide breach opened by 3 CIB was a stunning achievement, particularly from an attack hastily thrown together to pluck victory out of potential disaster. South of the line of 3 CIB's attack, the 1st Canadian Infantry Brigade had also broken through the Hitler Line, albeit on a much narrower front.

Because all available artillery had initially been supporting Operation Chesterfield on the northern flank, the offensive conducted by 1 CIB was limited to continuing the 48th Highlanders of Canada's drive toward Point 106, the previous day's objective. Since the Princess Louise Dragoon Guards had established a bridgehead through to the isolated Highlanders during the night of May 22, a fresh squadron of tanks from the 142nd Regiment Royal Armoured Corps reached the regiment's forming-up point at 0645 hours. The Highlanders attacked at 0800 hours on May 23 with 'D' Company on the left and 'B' Company on the right, each supported by a tank troop. In a replay of the day before, the advancing troops immediately faced withering fire from the ridgeline. But yesterday there had been no Allied tanks. Today, they smothered the ridge with main gunfire, enabling the two companies to reach the road running along the foot of the ridgeline and to capture the houses there.[33]

'D' Company paid a heavy cost for the houses. Two platoons were badly cut up. Among the dead was Lieutenant Doug Snively. 'B' Company had also been shredded.[34] The two companies reorganized and 'B' Company commander Captain Jack Wilson radioed Lieutenant Colonel Ian Johnston to suggest that the drive to the ridgeline proceed with 'D' Company leading and the battered 'B' Company tagging close behind, ready to pass through once 'D' reached the crest. Johnston said, "Try it, Jack, and good luck."

Major Jim Counsell led 'D' Company up the slope into a storm of German fire that cut down men and brewed up Churchills. Just short of the crest, the one remaining tank was knocked out by a Faustpatrone rocket launcher. Counsell concluded that it would be suicide for the remaining men to venture up onto the crest without armoured support or reinforcements. Appreciating the situation, 'B' Company's Wilson, bleeding badly from a head wound, veered his men left to form up alongside Counsell's men. The supporting tanks died one after the other and then a mortar round killed Wilson.[35]

Johnston fed Major John Clarke's 'A' Company into the battle, but halfway up the slope before his company was driven to ground. 'C' Company remained in reserve, as there was no room on the slope for it to deploy. Clarke radioed back that trying to continue the attack in daylight would be futile. He suggested they hold in place and renew the attack under night's cover. Johnston agreed, but he already suspected the attack would not be necessary. Minutes earlier, the Hastings and Prince Edward Regiment had broken into the Hitler Line to the north and were already driving directly toward Point 106.[36]

◆ ◆ ◆

1 CIB Brigadier Dan Spry had ordered the Hasty P's into action at 1240 hours. He told commander Lieutenant Colonel Don Cameron that the Highlanders were "fairly cut-up and that it was vital that the battalion should move forward and contact their right forward company." Cameron held a hasty Orders Group, where he said that, "although the opposition would be strong, it was to be understood that it would be taken."[37] Cameron not only wanted to make contact with the Highlanders, but he wanted Point 106. To this effect, he ordered 'D' Company to attack on the left front and break through to the Highlanders. 'B' Company, meanwhile, would drive for Point 106. 'C' Company would provide covering fire from the front of the German wire and 'A' Company was in reserve.

At 1400 hours, 'D' Company jumped off into strong German machine-gun fire from several stone buildings. But the Plough Jockeys, as the regiment was nicknamed, were so determined to succeed, Cameron later wrote, that in "an outstanding display of initiative and courage, [they] stormed forward, and took their objective, destroying many enemy and taking numerous prisoners." One platoon hooked up with the Highlanders, while the rest mopped up positions in front of the Highlanders' front line.

Having held 'B' Company back until he knew whether 'D' Company would reach the Highlanders, Cameron unleashed it at 1500 hours. The men drove forward quickly, but once through the wire were forced to take cover by heavy machine-gun fire. A supporting troop of tanks was called up and its fire made short work of the German gunners. After that, 'B' Company moved easily to a position just short of Point 106, from which at 1700 hours 'A' Company moved toward the little hill. The company met only slight resistance from an enemy already in retreat. After a few minutes' fighting, the Hasty P's were on top of the hill and consolidating. The day's battle cost the regiment thirty casualties, of which eight had been killed. They took 300 prisoners.[38] "No one ever doubted that the job couldn't and wouldn't be done," the regiment's war diarist wrote.[39]

As the Hasty P's secured Point 106, the Royal Canadian Regiment entered the bridgehead from which the Highlanders had launched their morning attack and probed toward Pontecorvo. By nightfall, they were positioned to attack the town in the morning. To their south, the Princess Louise Dragoon Guards had tried to open a way between the town and the Liri River and advance to the Melfa River. However, when the regiment's armoured cars ran into a wide minefield in front of Pontecorvo, the advance ground to a halt.[40]

Several armoured cars were knocked out in the minefield, including one in which Trooper Bill Pasfield served as the gunner. Pasfield's head was injured in the blast. Although shaky and groggy, the trooper got the other, more seriously injured men in the car out and dragged them to safety. Then, seeing that the lead armoured car was pinned down by Germans threatening to overrun it, Pasfield ran back to his own car and brought its machine gun to bear against the enemy. His accurate fire forced the Germans to break off the attack, enabling the armoured car to escape safely from the minefield.[41]

◆ ◆ ◆

The breaches cut in the Hitler Line by 1 CIB and 3 CIB ended any hope of that front's containing Eighth Army's advance. Already German forces were streaming west, surviving units desperately trying to beat the Canadians in a race to the Melfa River. About five miles west of the Hitler Line, the Melfa drained out of the northern mountains and followed a winding path across the breadth of the Liri Valley to a junction with the Liri River. Behind its western bank, the Germans hoped to form another defensive line.

First Canadian Infantry Division had paid a high price to break the Hitler Line. After the one-day fight, 47 officers and 832 other ranks were dead or wounded, more than half from 2 CIB. In addition, 7 officers and 70 men from other Canadian units were casualties.[42]

The Germans defending the line were virtually annihilated. By last light, 1 CID had captured 15 officers and 547 other ranks. Canadian intelligence estimated that 500 Germans were dead. One intelligence officer wrote: "Of the infantry involved in the attack hardly any escaped. Of the supporting arms over 50 percent were killed or captured. Twenty-five percent of the PWs captured were from staffs and supporting arms. Presumably this is true of the killed too."[43]

The Canadians were not exaggerating German losses. As early as 1130 hours on May 23, Tenth Army Chief of Staff Generalmajor Fritz Wentzell learned from 90th Panzer Grenadier commander Generalleutnant Ernst-Günther Baade that 1st Battalion and 2nd Battalion of the 361st Grenadier Regiment "must be considered destroyed." Later it was reported that one battalion of the 1st Parachute Division and two companies of the 5th Mountain Division sent to strengthen the endangered line "were wiped out."

The Tenth Army war diarist wrote that "north of Pontecorvo the enemy obtains a rather deep penetration. Based on the situation as a whole, a fighting withdrawal to the 'C' position is under consideration."[44] The 'C' line was the last defensive bastion that the Germans had created south of Rome. It was officially called the Caesar Line, but was a last-ditch effort that lacked the heavy fortifications of the Hitler Line and enjoyed none of the terrain advantages of the Gustav Line. Running from the coast west of Velletri on the Alban Hills' southern slopes, the Caesar Line's main defences were strung across the Valmontone Gap between the Alban Hills and the Prenestini Mountains. Through this gap, Highway 6 ran west into Rome.[45] The Caesar Line lay about fifty miles west of the Hitler Line. Even as Commander-in-Chief Southwest Generalfeldmarschall Albert Kesselring considered withdrawal to it, he was determined that the ground between would not be surrendered easily to the Allies. Every advantageous point would be defended to the last moment.

The Canadians knew this would be the German strategy. That is why Burns's plan called for an immediate, powerful drive by 5th Canadian Armoured Division out of the breach created by 1 CID. The application of overwhelming force at devastating speed was essential to prevent the Germans' organizing a series of defensive lines that could slow or even block the Allied advance. At nightfall, as the reports came into 1 CID's headquarters that the Hitler Line was broken, Major General Chris Vokes turned to his counterpart, Bert Hoffmeister. Vokes looked hard at his friend and said, "Bert, this is the best that we can do. I hope there's a hole. Good luck to you."[46]

19

A GRUESOME
TASK

With the torch of battle handed to 5th Canadian Armoured Division, the officers and men of 1st Canadian Infantry Division began the grim task of reorganizing, sweeping the Hitler Line for remaining pockets of resistance, and burying their dead. Everyone was exhausted, physically and emotionally. May 23 was the worst day that any of the division's old campaigners had experienced. Even the fighting at the Moro River and Ortona paled by comparison.

Left Out of Battle on May 23, Loyal Edmonton Regiment Captain John Dougan led a fighting patrol through the wire the next morning. Everywhere Dougan looked, dead Canadians hung in the wire; torn bodies and body parts lay scattered on the ground. Had he not been LOB it seemed likely that he, too, would have perished. The practice of holding a few experienced officers and men back from each battle to serve as a nucleus around which a destroyed regiment could rebuild was now being put into effect by the devastated 2nd Canadian Infantry Brigade. A part of Dougan was ashamed to think that, while the regiment had been torn to shreds, he and other LOB officers had calmly enjoyed a card game of Red Dog, with Dougan losing about $100 in bets.

The deeper Dougan's patrol went into the Hitler Line defences, the more nightmarish the scene. Here were troops from the Princess Patricia's Canadian Light Infantry. Whole sections, even platoons, lay in twisted piles in front of concrete pillboxes. Some, obviously trying to force a way in to kill the defending Germans, had been killed at the rear entrances to the pillboxes. Dougan looked back across the wire at the wrecked North Irish Horse tanks. Eleven tanks stood in single file astride a lane that had been cleared through the minefield. It looked as if the Panzerturm that had destroyed these tanks had first knocked out the front and rear tanks, pinning the others helplessly between. Then the gunners had knocked out the rest. The Panzerturm had finally been destroyed by one of the British tanks. Its turret had been blasted so that it now lay atop the emplacement, the long, .75-millimetre gun barrel thrusting toward the sky. Finding that the only Germans present were those who were as dead as the Canadians among whom they lay, Dougan led his patrol back to regimental headquarters.[1]

◆ ◆ ◆

In the late afternoon of May 23, Major General Chris Vokes pondered the costs of the battle and how these might have been lessened. He was deeply depressed by the casualty rate suffered by 2 CIB, for he had personally led that brigade from the invasion of Sicily to the capture of Campobasso in southern Italy. He later wrote: "Obviously whatever blame for it must rest on my shoulders as the brigade was launched into the battle according to the plan devised by me." He felt that the fault lay with his not having ensured that the brigade's right flank was screened from the German defenders dug in around Aquino. Some responsibility for that, Vokes thought, rested with I Canadian Corps commander Lieutenant General Tommy Burns. The order given to the 78th Division facing Aquino had been to the effect that the British were to apply frontal pressure throughout the day. Vokes felt that the order's wording, as drafted by Burns, had been vague and should have been more clearly defined. Lack of clarity, he surmised, resulted from Burns's inexperience. He also thought that the part of the valley bordered by the mountains to the north and the

Liri River to the south was simply too narrow for two corps to operate effectively side by side. Had only one corps conducted operations across its width, it would have been easier to ensure that Aquino was properly screened. That it was not owed to shabby work at the Canadian Corps's headquarters staff level. This, he maintained, would never have happened if 1 CID still served under a British corps commander.[2]

Burns thought that Vokes had done a commendable job on May 23. When the 3rd Canadian Infantry Brigade opened the breach in the line, Vokes had phoned Burns and said, "This is the proudest day of my life!" That seemed entirely appropriate to Burns. He thought the general had every reason to be "proud of the brilliant and gallant fighting of the men he commanded, and of the will and resource he himself had shown on that historic day."[3] However, he did not believe the heavy casualties suffered by 2 CIB resulted from the flanking fire. Rather, he thought the fault lay with the brigade's inability to properly reconnoitre its front because it had been held back on May 22 in case 1st Canadian Infantry Brigade broke the Hitler Line near Pontecorvo.[4]

His general staff commander, Brigadier G.A. (Nick) McCarter, disagreed. He thought the flanking fire had definitely been a contributing factor. But the order passed to the 78th Division's parent corps, XIII Corps, had only instructed the division "to deceive the enemy into thinking the main attack would be along Highway 6." He later wrote: "In my opinion that is a very unsatisfactory type of order, if any really effective assistance was required or expected for 1 Canadian Division. In view of the strenuous fighting XIII Corps had experienced in the early stage of the battle, I suggest it should not be too surprising if they took advantage of a poor order, or a nebulous one, and were not particularly energetic on 23 May."

"It should be noted," he added, "that had XIII Corps been ordered to 'attack in force,' the artillery of XIII Corps, and some Army artillery, would not have been available for support of 1 Canadian Division. You can't have it both ways." McCarter thought the biggest culprit had ultimately been the weather. The onset of rain in the afternoon had curtailed air operations and limited the ability of artillery observation officers to locate German strongpoints and direct fire against them. He also believed that Burns persistently failed to keep his general staff properly informed of decisions he reached during consultations with his divisional commanders. This led to the issuing of fuzzy orders, such as the one Burns drafted for XIII Corps regarding operations in front of Aquino. Many problems the corps had faced in moving its troops and supplies efficiently from one part of the front to another, McCarter wrote, "came about because corps commanders made the original decisions and did not let staffs know details — certainly in our case."[5]

Eighth Army commander Lieutenant General Sir Oliver Leese was elated by developments. He wrote a lengthy personal note to Vokes. "I would like to write this letter to thank and congratulate you and all ranks of your great Division on your breach of the Adolf Hitler Line," he wrote. "This line was vaunted to the world as an impregnable position. One has only to visit the defences for a short time to realise the immense amount of work and ingenuity that have been put into their layout and construction.

"Your attack was extremely well laid on, very well supported and brilliantly executed. Your infantry attacked with that same dash and determination that I have grown always to expect in them since your first operations with me in Sicily. Your action played a decisive part of our initial victory. The Adolf Hitler Line will always be a worthy battle honour in the annals of the 1st Canadian Division."[6]

◆ ◆ ◆

Few of the men who had actually fought the battle gave much thought to its place in history. Most were simply too exhausted. Probably none more so than the division's chief gunnery officer, Brigadier Bill Ziegler. By nightfall of May 23, Ziegler was so tired that he could barely stand. Yet he was too jumpy and tense to consider sleep. He kept working, personally overseeing details normally left to staff. Receiving a summons from Vokes, Ziegler went reluctantly. Since assuming his duties with the division early in the new year, Ziegler and the gruff divisional commander had often clashed. Was he in for one of Vokes's legendary tongue-lashings?

When Ziegler entered Vokes's office, however, the major general slapped a bottle of rye in front of the gunnery officer. Placing a water tumbler on the desk next to the bottle, Vokes told Ziegler to pour himself a drink. Ziegler dribbled a small amount into the glass.

Vokes scowled. "Goddammit, I said, 'Pour yourself a drink!'" Ziegler added a bit more. "Goddammit, Ziegler, don't you understand English? *Pour yourself a drink!*" Filling the tumbler to the brim satisfied Vokes. The major general grinned, came around to sit on his desk next to Ziegler, and said gently, "Now drink it." Ziegler did and immediately passed out.

When he regained consciousness, Ziegler felt alert and refreshed. He realized that Vokes had known he was unable to stop and would have gone on trying to run the artillery operations until he dropped. So he had arranged for Ziegler's deputy to take over and then implemented a surefire method of putting the gunnery officer to sleep. From that moment on, the two men were fast friends.[7]

Ziegler was disinclined to enter into the after-battle analysis. He thought the answer was simple enough. Take about 20,000 soldiers, toss them into a complex frontal assault, and, no matter how good they are, you are going to have mistakes that result in casualties. The division, he believed, was "bloody good." In the end, the final acid test was simply who won and who lost. The division had won the ground.[8]

◆ ◆ ◆

On the morning of May 24, a small part of the Hitler Line was yet to be won. That ground was Pontecorvo, sitting on its hilltop. The job fell to the Royal Canadian Regiment. Since the town was heavily fortified, everyone feared another bloody Ortona-like battle. At first light, 'D' Company and 'A' Company reached the western approach into Pontecorvo, sweeping through the former German barracks at the base of the road that ran up in a series of sharp turns into the town. In the process, the two companies rounded up about seventy German prisoners, who seemed happy to surrender.[9]

A 'C' Company platoon under command of Lieutenant J.L. Davis and the regiment's scout platoon, commanded by Lieutenant Bill Rich, probed toward the town, the two officers sharing credit for being the first Canadian soldiers to enter Pontecorvo proper. While the 'C' Company platoon explored the outskirts, however, Rich and his platoon daringly pushed straight into the heart of the town. At 0630 hours, Rich, having met no resistance, climbed into the church bell tower. That this tower had been used as an observation post throughout the battle was known, so it had come to symbolize the German occupation of the Hitler Line. Rich grabbed the ropes and started ringing the bells. Their joyous tolling served as an audible signal that the Hitler Line was breached from one end of the Canadian line to the other.[10]

The Canadian breakthrough at the Hitler Line was not the only evidence on May 23 that the stalemate between the Germans and Allies on the western Italian coast was beginning to favour the Allied forces. May 23 also marked the beginning of a major breakout from the Anzio beachhead by General Lucien Truscott's VI U.S. Corps. That action kicked off with a powerful assault northward toward Valmontone, precisely half an hour after the Canadians began Operation Chesterfield. Caught completely by surprise, Fourteenth Army's commander Generaloberst Eberhard von Mackensen could do little to contain the Americans. By the end of the day, their advance threatened the entire German right flank.

Commander-in-Chief Southwest Generalfeldmarschall Albert Kesselring telephoned Tenth Army commander Generaloberst Heinrich von Vietinghoff that evening. "Contrary to all expectations," he said, "things do not look good on Mackensen's front."[11] Kesselring was disillusioned with von Mackensen's performance. It seemed to him that the general had completely misread where Truscott would direct his breakout and consequently had very little strength in the northern sector.

By breaking out where it had, Truscott's corps was taking a decided risk. Instead of driving eastward to link up with the advancing elements of the U.S. Fifth Army, Truscott's 3rd U.S. Infantry Division and the other units involved in the breakout (including the combined Canadian-American First Special Service Force) pushed northward away from the main Allied force. This meant they plunged into a pocket with their flanks exposed on either side, a weakness Kesselring was anxious to exploit. But Truscott also forced a gap between Fourteenth Army's divisions. That gap did not immediately concern Kesselring. He felt a single German battalion could easily close it, containing Truscott's breakout. As the gap continued to widen on May 24, Kesselring became increasingly alarmed. His conversations with von Mackensen did little to defuse his concern. The general seemed to have no idea how to contain the Americans.

Indeed, Kesselring thought the man paralyzed, with the result that his divisions remained fixed in place rather than moving to meet the Americans.[12]

Ultimately, the German defence, both around the Anzio beachhead and in front of the main Allied forces advancing from the east, collapsed because of a sheer deficiency of numbers. There were not enough German divisions to hold the line and those that were available were too reduced by casualties to contain the two Allied armies. On the Canadian left flank, the Corps Expéditionnaire Français smashed a wide wedge through the German lines. This put the French ahead of every other corps in the Allied advance. Generalmajor Fritz Wentzell, Tenth Army's Chief of Staff, credited the French advance as the decisive factor in the collapse of both the Gustav and Hitler lines. This, he later wrote, was not a reflection on the quality of the French troops, but rather arising simply from the fact that the French had struck the German line in the Aurunci Mountains, where they were weakest. Because of the threat posed, Wentzell added, all available reserves had to be assigned to that sector. Had even one division been available to reinforce the Hitler Line on May 23, Wentzell believed the Canadian offensive might have been defeated. "However, the German defence was soon worn down by the weight of armour and artillery employed by the enemy, and on the 24th of May the Corps had to begin to withdraw, in the first instance behind the sector of the River Melfa."[13]

◆ ◆ ◆

German attempts to explain their defeat at the Hitler Line would not have impressed the Canadians who had fought and bled on May 23. They had met fierce resistance and had overcome it at a terrible cost. Lance Corporal Jack Haley, a signaller currently attached to the Loyal Edmonton Regiment, thought, "My god, I've never seen anything like this." The battlefield carnage he looked on was "something awful. There were all these dead people with Canadian flashes. There must have been about three hundred bodies, including the North Irish Horse." Haley had never seen so many corpses in one place. "There was nothing but destroyed tanks all burned out and shell holes and debris all around. Bodies were hanging in the wire." Until recently, Haley had served with the PPCLI and had been a Seaforth prior to becoming a radio signaller. Wherever he went in the line, Haley recognized bodies.[14]

Another radio signaller, Lieutenant Wilf Gildersleeve, walked up into the wire and found Pop Warner hanging there. The forty-year-old signaller still had his headphones on and was standing upright so that his antenna ticked in the breeze. Gildersleeve heard the radio chirping with messages passing back and forth. He unwound the man from the wire and laid him on the ground. Then he carried on, looking for the other dead signallers. Out of six to eight signallers per company, most were dead or missing. Their antenna marked them for the German snipers and machine-gunners, who knew that killing a signaller and knocking out his radio rendered the Canadians incapable of calling in accurate artillery fire or bringing up reinforcements.

Accompanying Gildersleeve was the Seaforth Highlanders of Canada commander, Lieutenant Colonel Syd Thomson, and some of his staff. As they walked through the shattered fortifications and the corpses of Germans and Canadians that were strewn everywhere across the ground, a flock of chickens ran under their feet. The chickens were nesting among the pillboxes and had obviously been providing the Germans with an endless bounty of eggs. Some of the men poked amid the ruins and came away with a decent harvest. The chickens, too, were made short work of. Everyone was hungry, making the evening stew all the tastier.[15]

Gathering in the dead was a dreadful task; even grimmer was the burying of men who only hours before had lived and been friends. Seaforth Chaplain Major Roy Durnford worked to exhaustion bringing in bodies. "The battlefield is a carnage," he wrote in his diary. "We have to bury our own dead in a central cemetery. The job is unfair and awful. I will kick like a mule over this. Boys re-group a tattered remnant."[16]

Among those detailed to burying the dead was Seaforth Sergeant Bill Worton. A section leader in the Seaforth mortar platoon, Worton had spent May 23 hurrying up and then waiting. The whole day had been nothing but confusion for the mortarmen while they waited for an order to either go forward or retreat. Shells and mortar rounds had burst all around. Private Lou Street was hit in the chest by shrapnel and died in Sergeant Al Girling's arms. German artillery and mortar fire hammered into the trees where the mortar platoon was and nobody had a clue what was going on up front. Worton and Lance Corporal Gordie Winning had crowded into the cover of a tree and prayed for the best. As they hunkered there, Private L.P. Gamba walked by. "Got a Canada," he said. "Got hit in the knee."

Winning said, "Well, get the hell out of here fast. It's getting deadly here." Gamba staggered off and was never seen again. As the men gathered in the dead on May 24, Gamba was not among them. Yet he had never reached the Regimental Aid Post. Like a number of other soldiers, Gamba was designated Missing in Action.[17]*

When Lieutenant Colonel Syd Thomson had headed by on his way to the front, Worton stopped him. "What the hell is the point of us being here?" he demanded. "Either we go forward or do something because our trucks are going to get it."

Thomson said, "You're going to have to abandon your trucks. Because you're going to have to go back and we don't want to lose our mortar people." The platoon broke the mortars down, hefted the heavy parts onto their shoulders, and trudged to the rear. Left behind were the trucks, the ammunition, and, most important to Worton, 4,000 cigarettes he had hoarded in his vehicle.

In the battle's aftermath, Worton dug a grave on a height of land overlooking the field where the Edmontons were also burying their dead. The men dug a grave and then waited wearily for a body to be brought up. Because so few had survived, almost every remaining Seaforth took part. Durnford accompanied each corpse to its resting place, said a few words, and then the men shovelled in the dirt. Before each man was rolled into the grave, the chaplain gathered up his jacket, pay book, and identity disk. Everyone was sweating in the heat, and Worton noticed that a sergeant nicknamed "Piss" Willy had thrown his jacket on the ground. Durnford picked it up and started to note the man's name in his book. Worton yelled, "Hey, Willy, you're going back in a box if you don't watch out." He then told Durnford

---

*Years later, Victor de Petrillo, who as a young Italian boy had an eye torn out by shrapnel near Cassino and had been treated at a Canadian field hospital and later immigrated to Canada, sought to find Seaforth Highlanders missing from the official roster. He eventually found Gamba's grave in a Commonwealth cemetery some distance from the Hitler Line battlefield and brought a photograph of the headstone back to the Seaforths, finally resolving the fate of this "lost soldier."

that Sergeant Willy was still alive and kicking just over there with a shovel in his hands.

As the men toiled on in the hot sun, a terrible cry came from where the Edmontons were working. A wounded soldier spiked on morphine had been digging a grave and the next body dropped in front of him for burial was that of his brother.[18]

Elsewhere near the graveyards that 1 CID dug that terrible day, a Royal Canadian Horse Artillery gun troop stood next to their vehicles waiting for bulldozers to clear a path through the rubble below Pontecorvo. Sergeant Victor Bulger watched a burial party of 48th Highlanders of Canada unload blanket-wrapped bodies and drop them into graves. One of his gunners, Trooper Jim Brady, had recently heard that his younger nineteen-year-old brother had joined the Highlanders. "As if drawn by a hidden fear, he inspected several of the new temporary graves and found to his shock and sorrow, that his brother's 'I' Tag was nailed to a makeshift cross. He was naturally devastated and inconsolable and it really shook our whole sub-section." Bulger photographed the grave and did his best to try to calm his comrade, but everyone in the gun troop was saddened for the next few days by this tragedy. The worst of it was that Brady remained convinced that had he known his brother was in Italy he could have somehow claimed him to the artillery unit and got him out of the Poor Bloody Infantry, which always paid the greatest cost in combat.[19]

Owing to persistent sniper fire from fanatics who refused to surrender and continuing artillery and mortar harassing fire, it was necessary to use Bren carriers to collect many of the corpses. The collection parties had walked behind the armoured sides of the carriers for protection and piled the bodies on the back. Durnford had never been involved in such a "gruesome task." He had also registered his complaint about the regiment's having to recover and bury its own dead, but divisional staff offered no apology.

On May 25, he wrote, "we go back to cemetery, bury forty-two in the dark. Bodies keep coming in and lay, mute testimony to awful victory. The cemetery is filling fast. Work goes on at a fast and furious pace. The opening ceremony is for tomorrow at 10:00 a.m. I go to bed but not to sleep."[20]

Eventually, all the graves were finished and Durnford held a funeral ceremony for 2 CIB on May 26. Lance Corporal Jack Haley was among the men who gathered. The sheer number of rugged wooden crosses again struck him. Haley had been at Ortona, serving alongside the PPCLI, and had seen the graves there. There were many more this time. It was heartbreaking to see so many young men killed. The only thing that made any sense to Haley was the work of the Medical Officers and stretcher-bearers. They were still piecing people back together and even now bringing lost soldiers in from the battlefield. Haley was starting to think that, if he lived, perhaps he should train as a doctor. High hopes for a boy from a Depression-broken railroad family, but a light of a dream that glimmered nonetheless.[21]

The next day, Durnford wrote, "Service is impressive. Order and solemnity marks the occasion. Upwards of 500 there. Band also and pipe Major. More burials. Graham Fisher is killed. Poor Graham. God rest his soul. We finish our task and commit all to God. We pack up and go back to 'B' Echelon. Tomorrow I with a party of six will tour battlefield for last time in search of dead. . . . Brigadier Gibson, Vokes, and the Brigadier of the Armoured Division all spoke to me at the service and expressed their pleasure at the dignified service. The stricken look on the faces of the lads who search for their pal's grave. God, grant that this may soon be over."

The next day, however, Durnford continued his terrible duty. Even with the funeral ceremony over, there were more bodies left to recover. It seemed to Durnford that he wandered for bleak days through hell. He saw "men sitting up in their tanks with faces toward the enemy but sightless eyes and charred bodies bullet ridden or wracked with shell fragments. It is impossible to describe the inside of a tank after an explosion in which all ammo bursts and everything is torn to bits and shreds and jagged steel. . . . I buried a man in a ditch — an arty man. Also a German by the roadside. . . . We bury Russell. Back to Pioneers busy painting crosses. We take 15 and plant them."[22]

FOUR

THE
PURSUIT

20

PUNCH

At 1730 hours on May 23, I Canadian Corps commander Lieutenant General Tommy Burns authorized 5th Canadian Armoured Division to begin the breakout from the Hitler Line. Major General Bert Hoffmeister signalled his units that Punch, the codename for Operation Chesterfield's second phase, was on. Punch entailed seizing two objectives, each involving a five-mile advance. The first was a bridge-head across the Melfa River; the second was Ceprano, a major junction point on Highway 6. Hoffmeister assigned the first task to 5th Canadian Armoured Brigade, under command of Brigadier Desmond Smith. From the Melfa River, the 11th Canadian Infantry Brigade, under Brigadier Eric Snow, would drive through to Ceprano.[1] After capturing Ceprano, the armoured brigade would continue the pursuit of what should, by then, be a German army on the run.[2]

Because Hoffmeister's units had to shift from their original departure points south to the gap created by 3rd Canadian Infantry Brigade, the breakout started slowly. The narrow tracks were greasy with mud and choked by congestion. The 25th Royal Tank Regiment was withdrawing to rearm and refuel and the Canadians jockeyed with them for space on the roads. At 2030 hours on May 23, Hoffmeister reported to Burns that his leading elements could not possibly cross the start line until first light.[3]

Brigadier Smith had briefed his commanders on the plan for the breakout at a mid-afternoon Orders Group. Because the brigade's operational area was confined to a narrow front ranging from the north bank of the Liri River to the Naples-Rome main railroad, Smith could put only one armoured regiment, supported by an infantry regiment, out front at a time. There were simply not enough good roads in the area to support more than that. Complicating matters further, the Germans still held the ground around Aquino, meaning that the brigade's right flank would be exposed to enemy action throughout its advance to the Melfa River.

To address these problems, Smith broke his brigade and supporting forces into two strong striking groups and a reserve group. Rather than try to advance in such a manner that his flanks were always protected, Smith planned to quickly leapfrog one strike group past the other so that the Germans would not have the time to gather a force on his flanks before the brigade was already at the Melfa. The first strike group was designated Vokes Force, after the commander of the British Columbia Dragoons. Lieutenant Colonel Fred Vokes was the younger brother of 1st Canadian Infantry Division's commander. A Permanent Force officer, he had served in the Lord Strathcona's Horse Regiment before assuming command of the Dragoons. Like his older brother, Vokes was a loud, profane, hard-driving officer, more inclined by nature to frontal assaults than subtle manoeuvres. Vokes's Dragoons were to drive from the Hitler Line to a large farm — Mancini Farm — astride a road that ran west from the Pontecorvo–Highway 6 lateral straight to the Melfa River. At Mancini Farm, the B.C. Dragoons would establish a firm base capable of withstanding counterattacks. From here, the second strike force — Griffin Force, after Lord Strathcona's Horse Regiment's commander Lieutenant Colonel Phillip George Griffin — would advance to secure a bridgehead on the Melfa River.

The tankers in both forces would be accompanied by infantry and antitank guns. Supporting the B.C. Dragoons would be the Irish Regiment of Canada, temporarily lifted from 11th Canadian Infantry Brigade and assigned to Smith. 'A' Company of the motorized

Westminster Regiment and two of its scout platoons would back up the Strathconas. Both forces would have a self-propelled battery from the 4th Anti-tank Regiment, Royal Canadian Artillery, a detachment from the Royal Canadian Engineers' 10th Field Squadron, and a section of the 7th Light Field Ambulance to evacuate the wounded. As the Irish Regiment lacked adequate transport, two companies were provided with Bren carriers and the other two companies were to ride on the tanks.[4]

In reserve was the 8th Princess Louise's (New Brunswick) Hussars Regiment, the rest of the Westminster Regiment, and the self-propelled guns of the 8th Canadian Field Regiment. When Griffin Force established the bridgehead over the Melfa, this reserve group would back up 11 CIB's drive to Ceprano. Corps artillery would be available as needed.[5]

To guard Smith's flanks somewhat, Hoffmeister had instructed the division's reconnaissance regiment, the Governor General's Horse Guards, to deploy squadrons on either side of the armoured brigade. The Guards were equipped mostly with Sherman tanks and some armoured scout cars. Two squadrons would conduct an arcing sweep to the right in order to block any counterattack from Aquino toward Mancini. Meanwhile, another GGHG squadron would screen the left flank.

Like all the armoured regiments in the 5th Division, this was the Guards' first action. The Guards were nicknamed the GeeGees, but, because of their initials, they also styled themselves as "God's Gift to Hungry Girls" and "Good God, How Gorgeous!" Although the Guards traced their lineage back to 1822, they had never fought as a regiment. Rather, in both the Boer War and World War I, the Guards had served as a feeder unit to regiments in active service.

"At last the day has arrived," wrote the regiment's war diarist. "Four long years lie behind us. . . . Four long years with a single purpose — to hit the Hun where it hurts. As the hour approaches, there is a thrill that runs through all of us. The machine is tense and ready for battle. Months of training stand behind us and we are confident that the task will not find us wanting.

"This is a great, historic moment. For the first time in their long and varied history, the Governor General's Horse Guards stand as a Regiment, ready to give battle. Whatever may befall before this day is over, we are sure, that the honour and traditions of this unit are in the best of hands. From the Colonel to the newest trooper, sitting tense in his tank and jesting with his comrades, we shall add a chapter to its story, that will rank with the finest, in the annals of our predecessors."[6]

The Guards had to remain patient. Their tanks could not move until Vokes Force shoved off. Jump-off time was 0650 hours and the B.C. Dragoons started rolling toward the San Martino River, the eastern bank of which was to be the start line, at 0530 hours. The tanks trundled through a thick ground mist on this cold, damp morning. The regiment reached San Martino on schedule only to find that the engineers, driven off by German artillery fire, had failed to bridge the gully. The Shermans could not cross here without a bridge.

Lieutenant Ron Jewell and his B.C. Dragoons reconnaissance troop started searching for a viable crossing. Dawn was rapidly approaching and Fred Vokes wanted to be across the river before the growing morning light made the tanks targets for any antitank guns dug in on the opposite bank. Although hampered by mist, Jewell found a crossing about a mile north of Pontecorvo. Racing back to the regiment, Jewell contacted Lieutenant Neil Hockin, commander of 'C' Squadron's lead troop. The reconnaissance officer led Hockin's tanks through the mist to the crossing point, while all the other squadrons followed along.[7]

While Jewell guided the tankers toward the crossing point, the engineers brought up a bulldozer to cut a grade into the gully and up the other side that could be negotiated by armour. Finally, at 0757 hours, the leading tanks started over.[8] Once out of the gully, the tankers assumed their predesignated battle formation, with 'B' Squadron on the left, 'C' Squadron to the right, and 'A' Squadron in the rear. The companies of the Irish Regiment of Canada were either bouncing along beside the tanks in Bren carriers or riding on the Shermans.

Their maps had shown the ground between the San Martino and Melfa rivers as mostly open fields or clearings broken by scattered trees. What they found was a maze of meandering tracks cutting through thick groves and across small pockets of cultivated fields. Keeping direction was complicated by the fact that most of the distinctive land features were either screened by foliage or entirely concealed by the clouds of dust and smoke "hanging over the valley like a white sea mist. The troop leader, feeling his way towards an almost invisible foe, had thus to make his own decisions. On a small scale, he must fight his own battle. On his training, intelligence, and guts the success of the whole operation must ultimately depend."[9]

◆ ◆ ◆

'C' Squadron Lieutenant Neil Hockin at first thought everything was going according to the numbers as his three tanks rolled west from the start line and bumped into lines of German infantry still retreating from Pontecorvo. The tankers slashed into them with machine guns, but then had to break off the pursuit to turn northward toward their designated line of advance. Minutes later, Hockin, who prided himself on his map-reading ability, was lost. The map bore no resemblance to anything around him. There were also no distinguishing features to use for orientation; just clusters of dense groves, vineyards, and small grain fields randomly scattered about.

Coming across a group of Royal 22e Regiment troops dug in around some tanks of the Three Rivers Regiment, Hockin dismounted to ask directions. The infantry major looked at Hockin's map but could offer no help. "My friend," he told Hockin, "we have been here for twelve hours and have fought a first class battle — but where I am — I do not know."[10]

Equally troublesome was the problem of maintaining contact between the tanks and the infantry. Sergeant William Kurbis, in 'A' Squadron's No. 1 Troop, was in reserve behind the two lead squadrons when he saw the Irish on the back of one of the tanks ahead jump off. Kurbis thought the soldiers feared being knocked off by low-hanging tree branches under which the tank was passing. He stood up higher in the turret, intending to assure the men on the back that they had nothing to fear. There was a sharp ringing in his ears and then Kurbis noticed that bullets were bouncing off the turret around him and he was alone out there. He ducked inside the turret to escape from the snipers, while the infantry scattered into the woods to winkle the Germans out of their holes.[11] From that point on, infantry and tanks fought separate battles to reach the Mancini Farm objective.

Despite the confusion regarding their whereabouts, the B.C. Dragoons drove toward their first objective with relative ease. While the infantry had to fight it out with pockets of German snipers and machine guns, the tanks faced virtually no resistance. Even the German infantry seemed in disarray. Corporal G.T. Dodd, a gunner in 'C' Squadron, realized that they were meeting only remnants of German regiments. The men "were scattered, poorly organized, and suffering from concussion. They wandered about, neither surrendering nor fighting effectively. Most were machine-gunned, but a few were taken prisoner, riding unhappily, further into battle, on the back decks of two Shermans."[12] With the Irish Regiment left behind, controlling prisoners was a problem. Unless the Germans clearly demonstrated their intention to surrender, the Canadian tankers hit them with machine-gun fire. There was really no alternative, since they could not expose the flanks and rear of their tanks to infantry that might be armed with Faustpatrones or other antitank weapons.

By 1030 hours, the tanks had reached the midpoint objective en route to Mancini Farm. They continued grinding toward the farm itself, which lay only 2,000 yards farther west. Not only were the tanks advancing without infantry support but they lacked the previous cover on their right flank by two squadrons of the Governor General's Horse Guards. These squadrons had cut sharply to the right, driving on a parallel line north that followed the Pontecorvo–Highway 6 road, in order to isolate Aquino. The manoeuvre was intended to loosen the German hold there, enabling the 78th Division of XIII Corps to capture the town. It left the Dragoons with a badly exposed flank that immediately drew fire from artillery and hidden antitank positions. The German resistance, however, failed to significantly slow the advance.[13]

'C' Squadron of the Governor General's Horse Guards had initially got off to a confused start that left the right flank of the Dragoons — unknown to them — unprotected from the moment they crossed the San Martino River. Originally, the GeeGees' squadrons were to have followed through behind the Dragoons. With the original crossing point unavailable, however, the commander of 'C' Squadron, Major George Allan Burton, had requested permission to bypass the stream, whose headwaters originated out of a modest height of land halfway between Pontecorvo and Aquino, by going directly north and behind the stream's headwaters. Permission granted, 'C' Squadron raced off.

They soon came upon a clutch of wrecked 25th Royal Tank Regiment tanks and a smoking German Mark IV. The leading tanks

radioed back to Burton that they were seeing a lot of suspicious camouflaged objects and taking sniper fire. German artillery and mortar
fire was also increasingly heavy. Suddenly, Sergeant Sewel in No. 4
Troop realized that one of the camouflaged objects was actually
a hidden .88-millimetre gun and reported this to his troop leader,
Lieutenant Murphy. Rushing his tank up on Sewel's left, Murphy
plunged into a pocket of mud. With the .88 firing their way, but still
not finding the range, Sewel hooked a line onto Murphy's tank and
dragged his commander to firm ground. The two tanks then scuttled
back about a hundred yards to a hull-down position, from which
they fired several rounds at the German gun. The shells bounced
harmlessly off the concrete emplacement.

What would have become a deadly stalemate between the
squadron and the virtually impregnable gun position was broken by
a report that the engineers had managed to bridge the stream at the
original crossing point. 'C' Squadron disengaged and retreated to
the crossing. They arrived to find 'B' Squadron also in the process of
crossing the stream and a traffic jam slowed the advance to a crawl,
with each squadron competing for position and the provost officers
doing little to coordinate or calm things. 'C' Squadron then headed
north again with two troops out front and two behind. All around
the advancing tanks, German artillery and mortar shells exploded.

As the squadron approached a low height of land called Massa di
Falco, southwest of Aquino, No. 2 Troop commander Lieutenant
Gaskin spotted Germans rushing to man a .75-millimetre antitank
gun located at the side of a house about 900 yards ahead. Gaskin's
Sherman was alone, his sergeant having become lost and the two
Stuarts that were also part of his troop stuck back at the crossing.
Gaskin radioed Burton, asking for permission to fire. Burton gave
him an immediate affirmative. Firing his machine guns, Gaskin
charged the German gun, whose crew fled for the farmhouse. Gaskin
smashed his tank right over the gun. When the Germans broke for
some nearby woods, the assistant driver took them under fire with
his machine gun and Gaskin stood up in the turret blazing away with
a Thompson. Three of the Germans fell dead and the remainder surrendered. "They came crawling back on their knees, hands in the air
and weeping profusely," wrote the regiment's war diarist. "While Mr.
Gaskin was giving his attention to the prisoners attempting to look as

ferocious as possible, with a Tommy gun in one hand and a grenade in the other, shells began bursting at the rear of his tank. In no time at all the seven prisoners were scrambling wildly over the tank, attempting to enter the turret. Swinging with his Tommy gun Mr. Gaskin cleared them off, and sent them back to the farmhouse while he reorganized his troop." Unable to identify the source of the fire, he then withdrew.

No. 4 Troop was actually the source of the fire, more precisely Lieutenant Murphy's tank. Murphy was unaware that Gaskin was already at the farmhouse and soon he was also blasting away at his own Sergeant Sewel's tank. The Irish sergeant complained over the radio, "Yer firin' at me. Toimes is hard enough as it is." Somehow his comment served to break the tension the combat neophytes had been experiencing. Everyone settled down and stopped making so many mistakes.[14]

Meanwhile, 'B' Squadron banged into its first resistance from pockets of German infantry bypassed by the Dragoons and the Irish Regiment. They slogged forward through almost constant harassing fire from small arms. Various infantry positions were overrun and they destroyed an .88-millimetre gun position by calling down artillery fire on its position. The GeeGees' baptism of fire on May 24 was remarkably light, with only one man dead — a tank driver in 'B' Squadron who was killed when his tank received a direct hit from an antitank gun.[15]

◆ ◆ ◆

While 5th Canadian Armoured Division was moving toward Mancini Farm, 1st Canadian Infantry Division also had a regiment moving toward the Melfa River. In planning the breakout from the Hitler Line, Lieutenant General Burns had been concerned that 5 CAD's assault would prove too narrowly concentrated to force a general German withdrawal to the western bank of the Melfa. He therefore ordered Chris Vokes to create a mobile strike force, similar to that employed by Hoffmeister's division, that would push up the road paralleling the Liri River and secure a second crossing over the Melfa River.

Vokes, still justifiably enamoured of the performance of the Princess Louise Dragoon Guards, gave it the task. To give the armoured car regiment more punch, he had a squadron of the armoured car reconnaissance regiment — the Royal Canadian Dragoons — that was attached directly to I Canadian Corps headquarters and also two squadrons of Three Rivers Regiment from 1st Canadian Armoured Brigade, released to his command. Designated Adams Force, after the PLDG's commander Lieutenant Colonel Fred Dean Adams, the unit also included one regiment of 3rd Canadian Infantry Brigade. Vokes left it to that brigade's commander, Brigadier Paul Bernatchez, to assign a specific regiment to the duty. Bernatchez opted for the Carleton and York Regiment, which, despite being the first regiment to successfully breach the Hitler Line, had suffered fewer casualties than either the West Nova Scotia Regiment or the Royal 22e Regiment.[16]

'B' Squadron of the PLDGs was to lead Adams Force's advance beyond Pontecorvo, but the morning of May 24 saw the armoured car squadron sitting impatiently on the outskirts of the town waiting for engineers to fill in massive shell craters that blanketed the road. It took until 0935 hours for the engineers to bring a bulldozer up and the work was not finished until 1115. Even then, forward progress was slow because the Germans had blocked the road with mines and with fallen trees that the armoured cars could not get over. In the lead, Sergeant Gordon McGregor was suitably prepared for the task of clearing both obstacles. The twenty-three-year-old from Kamloops, B.C., had been a logger before his enlistment. Originally enlisting with the Rocky Mountain Rangers, he had been fed into the Seaforth Highlanders of Canada. Shortly before reporting for service, however, McGregor had severed a tendon in his ankle with a chainsaw blade. The injury made it difficult for him to march more than about ten miles at a time without pain. Not good for an infantryman, so McGregor was allowed a transfer to the PLDG, enabling him to ride into war.

McGregor spent more than two hours outside his armoured car personally carrying out the removal of the log barriers and jerking German antitank mines. Snipers kept taking potshots at the sergeant, but that day he led a charmed life. Hooked to the front of his armoured car was a long cable that he had used many times previously for pulling mines. A standard German trick was to bury one Teller antitank mine under another. Lifting the one on top detonated the one below. To avoid being blown up by such a trap, the PLDG troopers would hook the top mine to a long cable, return to the safety of their armoured car, and pull the top mine clear. Both mines then exploded harmlessly. The method worked as well as always and was also ideal for dragging the three-foot-high log barriers apart. For his work under fire, McGregor was Mentioned in Despatches.[17]

Meanwhile, the Carleton and York Regiment had moved up in troop carriers along with the Three Rivers Regiment's tank squadrons. Traffic bottlenecks and obstacles on the roads soon meant that 'D' and 'C' companies had to dismount from their trucks and "revert to the familiar foot-slogging method of advancing." Neither the infantry nor the armoured regiment squadrons saw any fighting, but both had paused here and there to round up Germans bypassed earlier by the PLDGs.[18] Mostly, the PLDG had faced only persistent sniper fire and sporadic attempts by Germans manning heavy machine guns to slow their advance.

On the PLDG right, 'C' and 'D' squadrons of the Royal Canadian Dragoons finally disentangled their armoured cars from the rubble-filled streets and minefield barriers of Pontecorvo at about 1400 hours. 'C' Squadron leader Major Veitch knew he was leading his armoured cars into one of the most confused military situations possible. "Operations in the rear of a strong line which has been broken are nightmarish," the regiment's commander, Lieutenant Colonel K.D. Landell, later wrote. "No one knows anything for certain and it is the unexpected which generally happens. Supply trucks join a column and find that they are in an enemy convoy. Infantrymen form up for the attack and discover that the objective is held by their own troops. Medical orderlies, on their way to the rear with wounded, pass through strongly held enemy positions and wave greetings, thinking that they are in their own reserve areas. Men are captured and in ten minutes accept the surrender of their captors. And above all the fear, exhaustion, and lack of information rises ever an insistent demand for speed, speed and more speed — deep into the rear of the enemy, to strike at his supplies, spread confusion wider and wider, turn his retreat into a rout and prevent him from forming another line."[19]

The men of 'C' Squadron entered this nightmare immediately outside of Pontecorvo when they came upon a blazing German truck. Sprawled about the wreck were eleven Germans, killed by their own artillery fire. Nebelwerfer fire straddled the road as they plunged forward. The situation soon became confused as lead cars raced on alone, while those behind paused to round up surrendering Germans.

At one point, the lead cars roared up on a group of Germans sitting outside their trenches smoking and chatting. Seeing the approaching Canadians, the Germans dived back into their holes to man machine guns. As the armoured cars raked the resisting Germans with deadly fire, just 100 yards away another group of Germans crawled through the grain signalling frantically that they wanted to surrender.

When Major Veitch climbed out of his armoured car to speak with one of his troop commanders, he was startled to turn around and find "three Germans, still armed, standing patiently at attention not six feet away, waiting to give themselves up." And all the time during the advance, Veitch's headset rang with the voice of Adams saying, "Speed it up! Speed it up!" Finally, at dusk, the RCD squadrons reached a little gully about two miles short of the Melfa River and were ordered to hold there for the night. As they started to consolidate, they nearly got into a firefight with the Carleton and York Regiment, which had come up on the gully from the south and mistook the armoured cars for Germans.[20]

With dusk approaching, McGregor was still leading the PLDG advance when he noticed a party of Germans stringing wire across the road. His troop opened fire and drove the Germans off, killing several. Next they spotted a clutch of Germans rushing toward a .75-millimetre antitank and cut them down.[21] At 2025 hours, McGregor rounded a corner and was waved down by a badly wounded German soldier. McGregor's crew jumped out and used three field dressings to stem the man's bleeding. He was discovered to be an impressed Czechoslovakian. As one of the men in the troop was also Czech, a quick interrogation followed. The prisoner told the Canadians that there were three antitank guns lying in ambush around the next corner.

McGregor's troop loaded up and careered around the corner at top speed, ripping into the German antitank gunners with their machine guns and the troop commander's .37-millimetre cannon. Seconds later, it was over. The antitank gunners were either impressed Czechs or Poles and all were killed. Only a seriously wounded German sergeant, charged with keeping the others at their post, was taken prisoner.[22]

Adams Force ceased its advance at 2105 hours. Planning started immediately for a drive in force toward the Melfa River to begin at first light on May 25.[23]

◆ ◆ ◆

By noon on May 24, the B.C. Dragoons were closing on Mancini Farm, having skirmished their way through light opposition the entire way. 'B' Squadron's No. 4 Troop commander, Lieutenant Nigel Taylor, had seen little determined resistance during the day. Taylor had enlisted as a trooper on August 9, 1940, and worked his way up through the ranks to lieutenant in September 1943. Upon completing officer training, Taylor assumed it would be ages before he was called from the reinforcement pool to the Dragoons. Accordingly, he married his English sweetheart and then headed to Scotland for a honeymoon. Upon his return to the reinforcement depot, Taylor received orders to report immediately to the Dragoons. He boarded a boat shortly thereafter for Italy.

On this, his first day of battle, things appeared to be going well. It seemed almost too easy. The squadron was rounding up prisoners and machine-gunning any Germans who had the temerity to resist. When Taylor spotted a house that seemed to fit the perfect profile for concealing an antitank gun, he ordered it knocked down. All it took was one high-explosive shell fixed with a 25-second delayed-action fuse. The shell punched a hole through the exterior sandstone brick wall and the following explosion inside caused the building to collapse.[24]

As Taylor rumbled happily along, his commander, Acting Major David Kinloch, was starting to think that 'B' Squadron had wandered in the maze of tracks off to the left of the objective. Indeed, it seemed likely that the troop had entirely overshot it. He ordered Taylor, whose tanks were on the squadron's left flank, to look for a ground feature over that way. If Taylor found it, Kinloch would be able to get his bearings. Taylor set off with the troop commanded by Lieutenant Howard Williams following, so that there were six tanks in his group.

Taylor never found the landmark. Instead, he found an enormous German tank that he quickly, and wrongly, assumed was a Tiger. What he had bumped into was a Panther, which fortunately had its gun pointing off in a right angle from the line of Taylor's approaching wedge of tanks. The Panther commander must have seen Taylor at the same time, because the huge machine started backing up on the road. Taylor told his gunner, Trooper Cecil D. Shears, that the range was a thousand yards. Shears, who was a crack shot, blasted off two armour-piercing rounds. Slamming into the less heavily armoured side, the rounds finished the Panther off.

Shears said, "I got him, sir." These were the last words he uttered, for suddenly two antitank guns that had been flanking the Panther opened up on Taylor's Sherman. Taylor cried, "Smoke!" to the loader and "Reverse!" to the driver, but as the words left his lips an armour-piercing round struck the periscope, penetrated the turret to kill Shears, and ricocheted upward to tear Taylor's cupola off as the round exited the tank. Had Taylor not been ducking to make sure the loader got the smoke round into the gun, the escaping round would likely have beheaded him. As it was, his helmet was forced down so hard by the concussion that it temporarily paralyzed him from the waist down.[25] Taylor's loader, Trooper Ferguson, and driver Trooper K.R. Anderson hefted the badly injured officer out of the tank. They carried him to the safety of a nearby ditch just "as it became a flamer and blew up."[26]

The German antitank guns kept on firing, knocking out another No. 4 Troop tank with a round that killed the crew commander, Corporal E.D. Shumaker, and his loader. The remaining tank in the troop, commanded by Sergeant W.J. Range, returned fire and destroyed both German guns. The tally in an engagement that lasted mere seconds was two Shermans destroyed for one Panther and two .75-millimetre antitank guns.

Taylor, who ended up with a metal plate in his skull but recovered from the paralysis, lay in a ditch watching his tank burn spectacularly and thought vaguely about how this would likely be his one and only battle. Lying beside him, Trooper A.E. Olsen had a more immediate concern. "Christ, my smokes!" the man shouted. He then crawled over to the wreck, reached up through the open escape hatch in its bottom, jerked out a box containing 1,000 cigarettes, and scurried back to safety with bits of the tank singing through the air around him as ammunition inside cooked off.[27]

Kinloch's tank, meanwhile, was stuck in mud. This left him unable to do anything to help his two embattled troops but follow the course of their sharp fight over the radio.[28] What he heard marked the first Allied tank-versus-tank fight between Shermans and Panthers. Although the Germans in the Italian theatre had received their first Panther unit — the 1st Panzer Battalion, 4th Panzer Regiment

— in early 1944, Commander-in-Chief Southwest Generalfeldmarschall
Albert Kesselring had so jealously husbanded them that he refused
to allow the new tanks into action. Only on May 15, after persistent
entreaty from Tenth Army commander Generaloberst Heinrich von
Vietinghoff, did Kesselring send one Panther company as reinforcement. It was a Panther from this company that Taylor had engaged.[29]
Although not a decisive victory, the fact that Taylor's gunner had managed to quickly destroy the German tank proved that the Sherman
could, if circumstances were favourable, best the more heavily gunned
and armoured Panthers.

While Kinloch's squadron had drifted off course, 'C' Squadron
under Major Jack Turnley and the Stuart Honey tanks of the reconnaissance troop reached Mancini Farm together at 1220 hours. They
found the Germans dug in and a short, sharp firefight ensued.[30] A
shot from a self-propelled gun struck Sergeant G. Thompson's tank,
causing it to burst into flames. The badly burned sergeant managed
to bail out along with the driver, Trooper J. Briscoe. Realizing that
another crew member, Trooper A.M. Johns, was trapped inside the
tank, Briscoe ran back to the burning wreck and managed to pull him
out. One of the Honeys was also destroyed along with one man killed
and four wounded. The Canadian tankers prevailed, however, as the
Germans fled, surrendered, or were killed.[31]

Vokes began consolidating his hold on the farm, deploying his
other squadrons and the self-propelled guns of the 98th Anti-tank
Battery into positions around the farm buildings. As the Irish Regiment
had not yet arrived, the reconnaissance squadron dismounted and,
along with some other tankers serving as infantry, swept the buildings and mopped up various German strongpoints that were still
resisting. This done, they dug in to form a defensive ring around the
tanks and await the Irish. They also awaited Griffin Force, which had
been ordered by Smith to leapfrog through Vokes Force and press on
to the Melfa River.

21

Our Somewhat
Weary Shoulders

Throughout the morning of May 24, Lieutenant Edward J. Perkins and his Lord Strathcona's Horse reconnaissance troop doggedly followed Vokes Force until it reached Mancini Farm. Perkins's troop travelled in Stuart tanks from which the turrets had been removed, so that they were open-topped. For firepower, each five-man crew had a mounted .50-calibre and .30-calibre Browning machine gun, a Bren gun, a PIAT launcher, and four Thompson submachine guns. An assortment of prepared explosive charges and boxes of grenades bolstered the crew's gunpower. Perkins believed that the crew's combined firepower per man was "as large as any force in the army."

Normally, his troop consisted of eleven Stuarts. However, six had been taken away and manned by engineers accompanying Griffin Force. Then, crossing the start line in late morning, Perkins's Honey broke down. He and his crew replaced the crew in one of the others, so he now had only twenty men in four Honeys. Perkins's task was deceptively simple. The moment the B.C. Dragoons consolidated around Mancini Farm, he was to charge the remaining 4,000 yards to the Melfa River. Once there, his tiny force would seize a crossing and hold it until the Strathcona's tanks and the supporting Westminster Regiment infantry arrived to consolidate and expand the bridgehead.

During the planning phase, Perkins and Strathcona's commander Lieutenant Colonel Phillip Griffin had examined countless aerial photographs of the Melfa River. They had identified two possible crossing points. The first and best was obviously the main crossing still being used by the Germans. Since, logically, the Germans would defend this route heavily, requiring it to extricate their retreating forces from the east bank of the river, Griffin told Perkins to secure the less viable crossing. A short distance to the north of the main crossing point, the meandering river narrowed between two wider flood plains at this spot.

At 1340 hours, Perkins led his little troop past the Dragoons, rolling straight up the centre line marked for Griffin Force's advance.[1] Following a short distance behind the reconnaissance troop was 'A' Squadron of the Strathconas. In trail behind this squadron were, respectively, Griffin and his regimental headquarters team, 'A' Company of the Westminsters in their armoured White scout cars, and the Anti-tank Battery with its M-10 "tank destroyers." To the right of this column, Lord Strathcona's 'B' Squadron was deployed abreast of the regimental HQ unit and 'C' Squadron held a similar position on the left flank.[2] Each flanking squadron was accompanied by a scout platoon of Westminsters in Bren carriers. The country was close, crisscrossed by narrow gullies. Dense brush and groves of trees limited visibility. Perkins found the map next to useless, but his aerial photographs enabled him to keep his bearings.

About a thousand yards beyond Mancini Farm, Perkins spotted a German half-track with a crew of seven Germans standing around it. The Canadians opened up with their machine guns, killing five outright and sending the two survivors running for cover. When he was approximately a thousand yards from the Melfa, a Panther tank cut across Perkins's path from the right flank. The German tank was about 300 yards ahead of the reconnaissance troop, moving at top speed, with the crew commander standing out of the turret hatch. Perkins ripped off a burst with the .50-calibre and saw the German slump forward out of his cupola. The death of their commander seemed to stun the Panther crew. Knowing that his Honeys were no match in a firefight with the Panther, Perkins led his troop in a dash past the German tank. Two more tanks appeared through the foliage on his left. Hearing on the radio that a troop of 'A' Squadron had flushed the German tanks, he left them to the Shermans. Perkins discovered that he was now down to only three Honeys, the fourth having taken a wrong turn somewhere.

Closing on the river, Perkins saw movement in a farmhouse. The crews of the three Honeys blazed away at the building and a white flag appeared after a few seconds' firing. Eight 1st Parachute Division soldiers came out with their hands up. Although not wanting to be distracted with prisoners, Perkins paused long enough to await the arrival of a Westminster section to take the Germans off his hands. Then he pushed on to the river, arriving on its bank at 1500 hours.

Parking beneath some trees, Perkins and Sergeant Clifford Macey dismounted to reconnoitre the crossing point. Macey had been riding shotgun with Perkins during the advance. About seventy-five yards to the right of their position, Perkins found a kind of ledge running down to the riverbed. Although steep, he figured the tanks could negotiate it. The riverbed was about fifty yards wide at this point, so tanks or men crossing would be exposed to fire for only a minute or so. As the previous two days had brought heavy rains, the river had filled most of its flood plain. The riverbanks were riddled with slit trenches and other fighting positions. Given the amount of equipment lying around, Perkins realized the Germans had pulled out in a hurry.

He and Macey descended into the streambed. As they started up the opposite bank, a German machine gun chattered. The gunner was firing at Perkins's troop on the other side of the stream and one man was hit in the shoulder. Macey and Perkins scrambled up the slope and wriggled into some cover. They had just crawled into the brush when they came under friendly fire from a Sherman tank's machine gun. Neither was injured by it, but Perkins found "the experience nerve-wracking, not only because the fire was close, but because we did not know how soon it would be followed by a high explosive round from the .75. Fortunately the squadron leader saw what was happening and ordered the tank to stop."[3]

Although Perkins was sure the Honeys could get down into the riverbed, he knew they would have difficulty getting up the opposite bank. Still, he thought some rough engineering work would make it possible. While two men armed with Brens took up protective positions on the riverbank, the other thirteen developed the crossing. They used explosives to blow away a portion of bank that posed an obstruction. Then they dragged some fallen tree trunks over to construct a quasi-retaining wall and filled the gaps between the trunks with dirt. Working fiercely with picks and shovels, the men carved out a ramp braced by the retaining wall. Perkins prodded the men to ever greater haste, knowing that sooner or later the Germans would cotton on to what the Canadians were up to and bring them under fire. Macey was a literal tower of strength, encouraging the men to greater effort with a stream of curses, while wielding shovel and pick with immense energy.

Once the crossing seemed adequate, Perkins had the Honeys brought over. All made it and were soon hidden in hull-down positions on the river's edge. To the left of their position was an apparently occupied house. Perkins decided it needed capturing. Accompanied by Macey and three other men, Perkins moved alongside the riverbank to a position screened from the house by its courtyard wall. Perkins rushed through the courtyard, kicked in the back door, and found himself standing behind eight paratroopers all looking out windows and loopholes toward the main crossing point. "Drop it!" Perkins yelled and raised his Thompson. The Germans spun as one to face him. They were big men, and heavily armed. Perkins had gone in alone. The Strathcona officer was itching to open fire, but aware that a shootout at such close quarters would almost certainly end in his being killed or wounded, no matter how many of them he got first. The tension broke as one German dropped his rifle and the others followed suit. Perkins had single-handedly bagged an officer, a sergeant, and six other ranks. This and a string of subsequent heroics during the course of the ensuing day would win the officer a Distinguished Service Order and immediate battlefield promotion to captain. Macey would win the Distinguished Conduct Medal.

Since the newly won farmhouse offered a good defensive position and dominated the river crossing, Perkins moved his Honeys there and set them up, hull down, to the right of the building. Two men manned the machine guns in each Stuart. The rest, armed with the Brens, Thompsons, and PIATs, formed a perimeter. One trooper escorted the prisoners back to Griffin Force, while Macey crossed the river to guide 'A' Squadron over. That left Perkins and twelve men to hold the bridgehead. The entire action since their arrival at the river's edge had taken only about thirty minutes.

Perkins knew the Germans were starting to recover from their surprise when a sniper began firing from a tree about 150 yards off. He was a remarkably poor shot but, finding him "very annoying," the lieutenant took a PIAT and fired two rounds into the tree. The second round exploded in the branches, the sniper's rifle hit the ground, and the German visibly "slumped across a branch like a bag of grain." The position quiet once again, Perkins settled in to await arrival of the Westminsters and Lord Strathcona's Sherman tanks.[4]

◆ ◆ ◆

Behind Perkins's reconnaissance troop, the Strathconas had enjoyed a largely uneventful advance until they closed to within a few hundred yards of the Melfa River. The leading troop of 'A' Squadron under Lieutenant R.A. Gartke reached the river in the late afternoon, but the remaining troops "encountered heavy opposition and a very hot battle developed" just as the squadron came astride a crossroads code-named Benedictine.[5] A mixed bag of Panthers, Mark IVs, and self-propelled guns struck 'A' Squadron's left flank. Thick vegetation made it impossible for the squadron commander, Major G.L. Symms, to exercise effective control over his subunits. Instead, each 'A' Squadron troop fought alone. Sometimes a troop itself broke up and individual tanks had to fight in isolation. In quick succession, Symms and Captain J.B. Windsor were wounded when their tanks were knocked out.

During its approach, 'C' Squadron's two leading troops had become confused by the terrain and were widely separated. One troop got entangled with 'B' Squadron on the right flank and the other swung far off to the south before realizing its error and heading back toward Benedictine Crossroads.[6] As the 'C' Squadron troops came toward the crossroads from their varying directions of approach, the tankers could hear a sharp battle under way. Soon they spotted tanks and antitank guns all over in the brush and started blasting away frantically. After some minutes, the tankers realized they were engaging not only real targets but also an array of well-camouflaged dummy positions.[7] When these drew fire, they betrayed the shooting tanks' locations to well-concealed German units. The results were deadly. Squadron commander Major J. Smith was wounded, but refused to relinquish command. Captain R.G. Grimes was killed and Captain L.S. Payne wounded within minutes of the squadron entering into the melee.

All around the crossroads and to the south of it, Canadian and German tanks and self-propelled guns were burning. Others dodged from position to position, hammering away at enemy targets. It soon became clear, however, that the Germans were not so much seeking to destroy the advancing Canadian tanks as to check their advance in order to allow a withdrawal of men and equipment across the main crossing point and another crossing near Highway 6.[8]

On the western bank of the river, Perkins's small force clung precariously to its bridgehead. Shortly before the tank battle began, two Panthers and a self-propelled gun mounting an .88-millimetre gun appeared about 400 yards to the left of the farmhouse. The German guns began shooting at the building with a slow rate of heavy explosive fire, but its stout walls withstood the battering. When 'A' Squadron's lead troop showed up at the riverbank, the guns shifted their fire to greet them. Several 'A' Squadron tanks were quickly reduced to flaming wrecks. Perkins could see that the Canadian tankers were unable to locate the source of the fire that was killing them. Perkins ran down and splashed across the river, then jumped onto Captain Whittle's tank and tried pointing out targets to him. He then moved to Lieutenant Angus MacKinnon's tank and repeated the effort. Neither tanker was able to hit the Germans, either because they failed to identify the targets or the range was too long. Realizing he could not help the tankers, Perkins ran back to his men on the opposite side of the river. He found that Macey had also returned — the latter realizing that 'A' Squadron would be unable to reinforce the reconnaissance troop until the tank battle concluded. Whittle's tank was soon destroyed by the German self-propelled gun and the officer badly wounded. Lieutenant Gartke assumed command of the squadron.

About 150 yards left of the bridgehead was a house sheltering a German heavy machine gun. Perkins saw approximately twenty German infantrymen massing there, and assumed they were preparing a counterattack. Hoping to deceive the Germans into thinking there were more Canadians in the bridgehead than was true, Perkins ordered a heavy rate of fire directed at the house. He particularly shot it up with the .50-calibre machine guns. Meanwhile, the German tanks and self-propelled gun had returned to firing at his position. Most of their shots, however, whistled past about fifty yards overhead to explode harmlessly in the distance. Perkins was holding, but he knew that if the Germans put in a coordinated attack his little force would be snuffed out in no time. He desperately needed reinforcement by the Westminsters and radioed Griffin to that effect at 1600 hours. Griffin gave Perkins permission to withdraw, but the lieutenant replied that as they had so far succeeded in bluffing the Germans as to their strength, he would hold on a little while longer.[9]

'A' Company of the Westminsters, under command of thirty-two-year-old Major John Mahony, who would earn a Victoria Cross this day, was frantically trying to reach Perkins. The company's White scout cars, however, were incapable of easily negotiating the rough track followed by the tanks. The Bren carriers in which the scout platoons travelled proved little more manoeuvrable. Irrigation ditches, tree stumps, and fallen trees presented impassable obstacles until they were cleared or filled in. Several times, Mahony had to lead the cars off the road and bushwhack across fields. "At those times," Mahony — a prewar correspondent for the Vancouver *Province* — later wrote, "it became a nightmare of pulling our cumbersome White scout cars out of one drainage ditch after another."[10]

The company's mortar truck, loaded to the brim with 3-inch mortar bombs, took a direct hit from shell fire "and proceeded to put on a good 4th of July display, with mortar bombs exploding in every direction." Finally, about half a mile from the river, a burning Sherman tank sitting in the centre of the road hopelessly blocked the Westminsters' armoured cars. Mahony ordered the men to gather all the weapons and ammunition they could carry and follow him on foot to the river. At 1645 hours, an increasingly worried Perkins radioed Griffin. "Any sign of flatfeet?" Griffin responded, "They are coming up now — are near Benedictine."[11] Fifteen minutes later, Mahony and one platoon of 'A' Company reached the Melfa River.[12]

◆ ◆ ◆

The Strathcona Regiment's baptism of fire was proving to be the largest tank battle that Canadian forces had fought. They were learning tough lessons that resulted in men killed or terribly wounded by burns. During the planning for Operation Punch, brigade headquarters had issued an order for the tanks to carry more main-gun ammunition than could be stored inside the protected shell-storage bins. The reasoning had been that the regiments were going to be so far out front that ammunition replenishment might not be possible before they exhausted all the shells on board. Twenty-four-year-old Lieutenant John Francis Burton of No. 4 Troop in 'B' Squadron had .75-millimetre shells stacked on the floor of the turret and all over the tank like so much cordwood. The crew could barely move for all the shells.

Burton, seeing one tank after another blowing up on the regiment's left flank, realized this extra ammunition was more a hazard than a necessity. Another problem was that the men had been trained to stay in their tanks and fight to the last round, even when the tank was hit by enemy shells. Burton realized the better part of valour was to bail out the moment a shell struck the tank. If it failed to burn up, fine and good — crawl in and go back to war.

At 1645 hours, Burton spotted German movement near Highway 6 and requested permission to advance and engage targets of opportunity. His squadron commander, Major Bill Milroy, agreed. Burton's troop headed toward the highway and soon happened on a battery of Oerlikon multi-barrelled anti-aircraft guns standing in a field. His tanks and the guns exchanged a rapid flurry of fire before the Germans decided they were outgunned and fled, leaving their weapons behind to be casually knocked to pieces by the tankers. The whole fight was over in seconds, but it seemed to Burton that time slowed down and that he had been in action for hours. Worrying that they might have seriously drained the ammunition stocks, he asked, "How many rounds did we use?" His loader said, "Twelve or thirteen." They had barely used up one stack of the extra ammunition and come nowhere near to digging into their normal stock of seventy-five rounds.

Burton had another immediate response to his first combat, an urgent and simultaneous desire to urinate and to eat something. His men shared these urges, so they hastily broke open the emergency chocolate ration and handed it around, while one after the other urinated into one of the spent shell casings. Burton was wearing gloves when he took the casing and started relieving himself. He let out a shriek as his penis brushed the side of the shell and was seared by its still nearly red-hot casing. "I asked for a cool shell casing," he snapped. "It's the coolest shell casing we got," the crewman replied peevishly.[13]

By the time Burton's troop rejoined the regiment, the tank battle was over. It had lasted slightly less than ninety minutes. His squadron had suffered no tank losses, but 'A' Squadron had lost nine tanks, 'C' seven and the regimental headquarters one. Two officers were dead, seven wounded. Twenty other ranks had been killed and another twenty-seven wounded. The regimental HQ tank had been knocked out going to the aid of Westminsters under fire from a self-propelled gun. Second-in-command Major George J. Wattsford managed to destroy the gun, but lost his own tank in the process and was wounded. Milroy took over as second-in-command.[14]

The regiment had given better than it had received. Counted as captured or destroyed were seven Panthers, four Mark IVs, nine self-propelled guns, five antitank guns, one field gun, five Nebelwerfers, four multi-barrelled anti-aircraft guns, twenty-one motor vehicles, and three motorcycles. Twenty-two prisoners of war had been taken, and thirty-six Germans were known to be dead.

With night falling, the battered tank squadrons huddled together to form an all-round defensive position at Benedictine Crossroads. Since the Westminsters were all being committed to holding the Melfa River bridgehead, the tankers set out personal weapons and dug slit trenches in order to defend their tanks from possible infantry counterattack. The Germans, recovering quickly from being thrown across the river, started shelling the position soon after it was set up. Some enemy infantry and armoured vehicles still lurked in the vicinity of the Melfa's eastern bank. The ferocious fight had exhausted everyone, but it was obvious the Strathconas would have to stand to throughout the night.[15]

◆ ◆ ◆

Inside the bridgehead, the situation remained precarious even following the Westminsters' arrival just after 1700 hours. The first platoons across were No. 4 under Lieutenant Ross Douglas on the left and No. 3 on the right, commanded by Lieutenant Heber Smith. Mahony was right behind, but as he started down the bank toward the river the major caught his foot on a vine and fell headfirst into the chilly water. He dangled there a moment, struggling to keep

his Thompson dry while extricating himself. This much amused
Lieutenant Ken Harrison and No. 2 Platoon, as they came up behind
the major and helped free him from the vines.[16]

There was nothing funny after that. German fire was thick and
furious. The men splashed through the river and ran through a
gauntlet of fire ripping across the width of the riverbed. Private Dan
Nikiforuk of No. 4 Platoon plunged into waist-deep water. Water
spouted up around him and the others as they sloshed across the river.
One Westminster was shot dead during the crossing. On the other
side, Mahony and Perkins hammered out a quick battle plan. Mahony
sent No. 3 Platoon out on the right, where there were no houses and
the going should be less opposed. Then he set off to help Douglas
and No. 4 Platoon go after the houses that formed the backbone of
German resistance against Perkins's left flank. A No. 4 Platoon runner
intercepted Mahony and reported that one section was pinned down
between the Canadians and the German-held houses.

Running up, Mahony saw the men lying face down in the open.
Moving toward them, he came under fire from a Panther jutting its
front end and main gun out of the inside of a house about 300 yards
away. Mahony realized his Westminsters were trapped by the tank
and could only "lie still and hope the folds in the ground would conceal them." The tank, meanwhile, was trying to pick them off with
its co-axial machine gun. Doubling back to Perkins's Honeys, Mahony
scooped up a handful of smoke grenades and threw these as close to
the men as possible. Once the smoke thickened, he yelled for them
to bug out. Two men failed to move, although one seemed to be
clawing at the ground and trying to get up. Perkins and Mahony ran
to help. One soldier was dead; the other wounded. They brought the
wounded man in, escaping unscathed through a hail of machine-gun
fire from the tank. While this was going on, Douglas had jumped the
houses with the remainder of his platoon and cleared them of
Germans, several men being wounded in the process. They sent back
about twenty prisoners.[17]

Several German tanks were prowling around the Canadian
perimeter and at least two .88-millimetre self-propelled guns alternately hammered the thin bridgehead and directed fire across the river
toward the Strathcona's tanks. Independently, two groups of the
Westminsters and Strathconas in the bridgehead decided to tackle

the SPGs with PIATs. Strathcona's Trooper Jacob Kippenstain Funk headed out under covering fire laid down by two Westminsters manning Bren guns. His target was the SPG that had been tormenting the reconnaissance troops for hours. The trooper crawled along below the crest of the riverbank until he was about 150 yards from the SPG. He fired one round that exploded prematurely when it struck some branches in a tree. Funk left the riverbank and crawled to within 100 yards of the German vehicle. His second round was high, the third low. Firing his fourth and final round, he scored a hit on the suspension and the crew bailed out. The Bren gunners cut down one man and the rest fled. Funk was awarded the Military Medal for his efforts. The Panthers, which had been operating in tandem with the SPG, hastily retreated about 800 yards to the rear, where their fire posed little threat.[18]

Mahony and Westminster Corporal J.A. Thrasher stalked the other .88-millimetre SPG. Mahony provided covering fire while Thrasher manned the PIAT. His first round fell thirty yards short, but the SPG crew failed to notice the explosion. Mahony and Thrasher crept closer. This time, the PIAT bomb hit the left track, spurring the crew to bail out. No. 2 Platoon opened fire on the escaping crew, and cut down a couple of the men. Mahony and Lieutenant Harrison — nicknamed Killer — both ripped away with their Thompsons in what Mahony later called "a pretty poor display of marksmanship when we missed two of them who just ran about fifty yards past us."[19]

Not everyone was engaged in heroics. Nikiforuk's section was grouped near the river's edge on the left flank and trying to dig slit trenches. Bullets and shrapnel snapped overhead. Exploding shells and mortar bombs threw up great clods of dirt, brush, smoke, and flame. The ground was hard and laced with tree roots from the poplars and other trees bordering the river. Nikiforuk was carrying a small round explosive dubbed the No. 25 antitank grenade, which was three inches high by six inches wide. Useless against modern German tanks, the grenades were used by the Westminsters to help loosen hard ground for digging. He dug the grenade in a bit, stretched out the built-in fuse and lit it. After waiting several minutes for the explosion, Nikiforuk gave up on the explosive charge. He wrenched it out of the ground and flung it disgustedly off into the bush, only belatedly realizing that the grenade might well have exploded and torn off his fingers. Nikiforuk dug with his bayonet, more for something to do than in expectation of carving out a useable slit trench. Everyone in his section was watching nervously for signs of a counterattack. There were supposed to be eleven men in his section, but personnel shortages had resulted in its going into battle just six strong. It had been this way since the Westminsters arrived in Italy. Most of the time it was just a nuisance being understrength, but in combat it made one feel mighty alone and vulnerable.

Nikiforuk saw Mahony and noticed the officer had a head wound, but was going on as if it were nothing more than a scratch. His already considerable respect for Mahony heightened to new levels. It surprised him, however, that Mahony was proving such a lion under fire. He didn't seem the type. The officer was a quiet, unassuming guy — not Nikiforuk's normal image of a natural leader or hero.[20] Mahony seemed to be everywhere at once, dodging from platoon to platoon to offer encouragement or help a platoon or section leader meet a local crisis. Crises abounded.

Lieutenant Heber Smith was wounded and evacuated. Sergeant S.R. White took over, radioing Mahony with a report that No. 3 Platoon was taking a lot of fire and suffering heavy casualties. White was a veteran of World War I and known throughout the regiment as a tough old sweat. Mahony figured he could hold if reinforced with a section from No. 2 Platoon. He got the men over to White and the situation eased, but it was clear the infusion of men had purchased only momentary relief.

The arrival of two Bren carriers from Lieutenant Bill Delaney's No. 1 Platoon, which had managed to cross the river with a section of men aboard, only boosted the total fighting strength in the bridgehead to about sixty men. Some of these, like Mahony himself, were wounded but refusing evacuation. Mahony withdrew the sections of No. 4 Platoon holding the houses on the left and shrank his perimeter down to a narrow, horseshoe-shaped front.

From beyond the left flank came the ominous clanking and squeaking sound of tanks closing on the Canadian position. Mahony had a momentary lifting of spirits. These might be Lord Strathcona's tanks. Then he thought of all the burning Shermans on the opposite bank and acknowledged that the tanks were more likely German.[21] He had nothing with which to fight Panthers or even Mark IVs.

Desperate, he ran over to Perkins and asked him to deploy his Honeys out front. Perkins refused; the German tanks would just chop his Honeys to pieces. All he could do was keep the Honeys hidden from sight with their engines running to give the illusion that there were actually some tanks with .75-millimetre guns lurking inside the Canadian perimeter. Refusing Mahony's request was difficult, but Perkins believed it necessary.[22]

Mahony went out on the left flank to try to identify the tanks. A thick cloud of chemical smoke lay over the ground outside the perimeter, obscuring them from view. This made Mahony increasingly sure that the tanks were German and a counterattack was being set up. Still, he tried radioing the Strathconas for a report, but was unable to establish contact. Mahony spread the word through the platoons to prepare to meet a tank and infantry counterattack. The men were to hold fire until he gave permission, so they did not betray their positions prematurely.

If they could hold just a little longer, help might arrive. Westminster commander Lieutenant Colonel Gordon Corbould had radioed that the rest of the regiment was closing on the river. 'C' Company should cross within the hour. Breaking contact with Corbould, Mahony received a call from Sergeant White. The old veteran reported that his platoon was now so cut up that he really doubted it could hold much longer. Mahony told him "to sit tight, as Charlie Company was coming over soon." White responded, "Wilco." The sergeant did not bother reporting that he had taken a machine-gun burst in the stomach and was lying with the radio, incapable of any other movement. No. 3 Platoon was in shreds, but the survivors stuck grimly to their positions.

One of the forward positions reported that there were tanks forming up about half a mile off. Mahony doubled over and saw four German tanks lining up in extended order in front of a house about 800 yards from the bridgehead. Three were Panthers, the other possibly a self-propelled gun. Fifty infantrymen were milling about behind the tanks. Mahony figured they would strike right at the centre of the bridgehead, hitting his tiny company headquarters section head on. He told everyone to hold fire and ordered the platoons on the flanks to "hold their ground regardless of what happened to company headquarters."[23]

The Canadians had one card left to play — the illusion that they had antitank guns in their perimeter. Perkins drew the three Honeys up in hull-down positions facing the front. By the time the attack started, Perkins counted almost a hundred infantry accompanying the three Panthers — more than enough to easily overwhelm the couple of dozen Canadians facing them. The tanks approached slowly, careful not to outpace the infantry.

Perkins's reconnaissance troops were manning the machine guns inside the Honeys, with the extra men either armed with two PIATs or Thompson submachine guns. When the tanks were 400 yards off, Perkins told the men to open up with everything they had. The Strathconas and Westminsters in the headquarters section raked the approaching tanks and infantry, while the two PIAT teams punched bombs out toward the tanks. These initially fell about a hundred yards short, but Perkins had no expectation of actually destroying the Panthers. He just wanted the tankers to think the explosions were from antitank rounds.

The Panthers started shooting high explosives at the bridgehead, but the shots were high and the only damage was two aerials clipped off Honeys.[24] Mahony was blasting away with his Thompson, the tracers dropping well short of the approaching enemy. Only the Brownings were finding the range. Mahony saw their tracers bouncing harmlessly off the tanks, but the intensity of the fire drove the German infantry to ground.[25] When the tanks closed to within 200 yards, the PIAT rounds started exploding around them but no hits were scored. Then, just as Perkins and Mahony thought the jig was up and they were to be overrun, the three Panthers swerved to the right and retreated. The infantry had already withdrawn.

Minutes later, the tanks reappeared, probing toward No. 3 Platoon. Again, the tanks fired high-explosive rounds that passed over the heads of the troops facing them. Some of these shells, however, crashed down near Perkins's Honeys just as he was climbing in to man a .50-calibre Browning. The blast knocked down the last operative radio aerial. A fragment of shrapnel scratched Perkins's cheek and left him slightly dazed by concussion.[26]

White radioed Mahony to say the tanks were going to overrun him. Mahony rushed a handful of men over from the company headquarters section, knowing they were all too few to do much. In the gathering darkness, however, the German tanks failed to locate No. 3

Platoon and drove down the bank into the riverbed. After milling about for a few minutes, they started to withdraw. One Panther paused a few yards from the slit trench of Private John Culling of Swift Current, Saskatchewan. The hatch opened and the tank commander stood up, apparently seeking a better vantage. Culling rose up out of his slit trench and threw a Type 36 grenade onto the tank. The blast killed the commander. His body slumped into a sitting position inside the turret. Aiming for the open hatch, Culling quickly threw another grenade onto the turret. The grenade circled around the turret rim like a basketball on a hoop, and dropped inside. After it exploded, three members of the crew bailed out. Culling cut two down with his Bren gun and the survivor surrendered. For his actions, Culling was awarded a Military Medal. So, too, for his refusal to relinquish command and be evacuated was Sergeant White.[27]

◆ ◆ ◆

Mahony was dismayed to learn that 'C' and 'B' companies of the Westminsters had run into opposition from some German remnants on the opposite side of the Melfa. Combined with their resistance and the heavy shellfire that was pounding the convoy, the advance had slowed to a crawl. They were still coming on, but Corbould expected it would be yet another hour before 'C' Company crossed. One White scout car coming up to Benedictine, with Lieutenant R.E. Ketcheson and nine scouts and snipers aboard, took four direct hits in rapid succession from a hidden self-propelled gun positioned about a hundred yards from the crossroads. Six of the men, including Ketcheson, were killed, and the other four badly wounded.

Seeing that both his advancing companies were meeting stiff resistance on the eastern side of the river, Corbould rerouted 'C' Company to bring it up directly across from 'A' Company's perimeter. This way, the company could pass into the lines there and expand the bridgehead from inside, rather than by moving into unsecured ground on 'A' Company's left flank.[28]

While 'C' Company moved to the crossing point, the men in the bridgehead were carrying out the more badly wounded soldiers on their backs. All the stretchers had been used up long before. Mahony ordered the bridgehead shrunk once again so that 'A' Company pulled in to a point where it was holding a "small, but tight" position that had previously contained only the company headquarters section and Perkins's Honeys. Based on the house that Perkins had captured early in the fighting, it had narrow flanking lines extending back to the riverbed. The Germans by now had the bridgehead ranged in for punishment from their artillery, mortars, and Nebelwerfers. Concentrations of fire constantly plastered the position. "Each shelling," Mahony later reported, "brought more reports of casualties in our rapidly diminishing little band."

The ground was rock hard, making it difficult to carve out holes for protection from the shrapnel flying through the air. Having either exhausted all the little antitank grenades or, like Nikiforuk, having thrown them away, the men resorted to tossing Type 36 grenades down where they wanted a trench and loosening the ground with its explosion. Then they set to work with bayonets and a few shovels and picks to dig a useable hole.[29]

At 2100 hours, 'C' Company's leading platoons crossed the river and entered the bridgehead. As the company commander, Major Ian Douglas, came up, Mahony was struck by the realization that today was a national holiday in Canada recognizing the birth of Queen Victoria. "What a way to spend the 24th of May!" he said.[30] Douglas and Mahony quickly agreed that the reinforcements should thicken up the bridgehead defence rather than try to expand the position in the dark.[31] Among those in 'C' Company was Sergeant Ron Hurley, the Okanagan-born running athlete who had acted as Douglas's guide on International Ridge. Hurley was hunkered down below the crest of the riverbed, waiting for instructions on where to set his section. Mahony arrived. He had a big, blood-soaked bandage wrapped around his head like a turban. Hurley identified himself as the section sergeant. Mahony said, "Be careful, there are Jerry tanks over there and they're going to come back." His platoon commander, Lieutenant Art Miller, then showed Hurley where to fit the section into the Westminster line on one of the flanks. The men lay down behind rocks, bushes, and trees to anxiously await the German tanks. Occasionally, small knots of German infantry tried to probe the line. Each time, the men hit them with rifle and Bren gun fire, causing a quick withdrawal. German flares periodically washed the position with a garish light. Hurley could see the corpses scattered through the underbrush. Although some wore field grey, all too many wore khaki.[32]

Throughout the night, the Westminsters' 6-pounder antitank platoon wrestled one gun at a time down the eastern bank of the river, carried it through the water, and then dragged it into the embattled bridgehead. It was slow, back-breaking work that took almost two hours per gun. All the time, Mahony kept expecting the Germans to overrun the bridgehead with tanks before the 6-pounders could get set up. But they never came. By first light, the Westminsters had three antitank guns and ammunition across the Melfa.

At midnight, Corbould had personally inspected the bridgehead. He decided that it was too narrow to hold both its present strength and 'B' Company, too. Not that there was much left to 'B' Company. In its attempts to cross the river north of 'A' Company's perimeter, the company had been badly cut up. It now mustered only forty-five men. The entire regiment would break out of the bridgehead in the morning, Corbould told Mahony. They would not, however, move off alone. On their left, using the main German crossing, the Irish Regiment of Canada, which had spent the day marching up from Mancini Farm, would attack at first light. Mahony was greatly relieved, believing that the infantry regiment "would take the heavy burden off our somewhat weary shoulders."

When Corbould left for the eastern bank of the river, Mahony began feeling the effects of the day. He was exhausted, but too keyed up to rest. The major was also cold. During the day, the temperature had hovered in the high eighties, so he had not noticed that his uniform was still soaking wet from his headfirst plunge into the Melfa. Now, the cool night air seeped into him. He started to dig a slit trench to warm up, but was soon prowling the lines instead. Mahony passed on the good news of the impending morning relief. The morale of the Westminsters and the small reconnaissance troop of Strathconas inspired him. After a day of nearly continual close-quarters fighting, "they were still joking and laughing about some of the humorous and exciting incidents of the day. When a Canadian infantryman can't crack a joke," he decided, "then things are pretty bad."[33]

22

BE VERY,
VERY CAREFUL

At first light on May 25, the Irish Regiment of Canada failed to relieve the embattled Westminsters on the Melfa River's western bank. Westminster commander Lieutenant Colonel Gordon Corbould informed Major John Mahony that the Irish attack would be delayed an hour to 0630. The weary defenders hung on, thankful that the Germans seemed equally worn out by the previous day's fighting.

At about 0600 hours, however, Mahony was alerted to a threat of German infantry closing on the perimeter. He arrived at the position in time to see fifteen Germans rise out of the tall grass 400 yards off and then run diagonally across the Canadian front line. Mahony shouted, "Fire!" The Germans went to ground under an immediate hail of rifle and Bren gun fire. Several rounds from a 2-inch mortar and a PIAT also hit the spot where the infantrymen had disappeared into the grain. This appeared to convince them to keep a healthy distance from the Canadians.

Offering no explanation, Corbould reported there would be another hour-long delay. Across the river, the Irish could be heard noisily forming up. Shouted orders and a great deal of crashing about in the woods betrayed the fact they were massing for an attack. Apparently the Germans heard the racket, too, for artillery and mortar fire blasted the woods and a heavy machine gun in a building near the Westminsters ripped the tree line with long bursts.

Mahony decided to tackle the machine gun. He gathered up a small section of men, including Sergeant Ron Hurley, from Lieutenant Art Miller's 'C' Company platoon. In addition to rifles, the party carried three Brens and a PIAT. Scout platoon commander Lieutenant Bill Delaney came along for the ride.[1] Hurley's section included a private named Lou Schachter from Winnipeg, one of those sad-sack soldiers seemingly incapable of staying clean and cursed with a cadaver's pallor. Shaken by the previous fighting, Schachter said to Hurley, "What am I going to do? What happens if I get scared?"

"Schachter, don't worry," Hurley replied. "You'll be fine."[2]

Mahony's assault party worked through brush along the riverbank to close on the half-destroyed farmhouse. Artillery fire had smashed a gaping hole in one wall. Mahony planned to fire PIAT rounds through the hole to smoke out the German machine-gunner.[3]

The German machine gun was still hammering away with long, steady bursts. Seeing an overturned ox cart on the farmyard's edge, Hurley decided to put a Bren gunner under it to cover their left flank. That seemed good duty for the frightened Schachter. "Gotta be careful," he said to the private. "Anything comes up there, fire at it, because it won't be us."[4]

Once everyone was in position, the PIAT man popped two bombs through the hole. Out tumbled two Germans, one carrying the machine gun, the other with the gun's tripod strapped to his back. A volley of fire dropped the tripod man, but the other ducked around the corner. Mahony thought the German had made a clean escape until he heard one sharp rifle crack and someone shout, "I got the bastard." Mahony recognized Lieutenant Bill Delaney's voice and knew the German was a goner. "For some reason," Mahony later said, "Bill was one of those unusual soldiers who really hated the Germans. Bill was a ruthless fighter, but a swell fellow and a first class soldier."[5]

With the machine gun disposed of, the party started returning to the Westminsters' perimeter. They were almost home when Lieutenant Miller asked Hurley, "Where's Schachter?"

"Jesus Christ, I left him." The sergeant ran back to the farm wagon and found Schachter lying there, anxiously staring off to the left as directed. "Where have you been?" he sobbed.

"Sorry we're late," Hurley replied. With Schachter in tow, he scampered back to the perimeter.[6]

♦ ♦ ♦

The Irish Regiment of Canada was still delayed. In their forming-up area, things were chaotic. The companies were drawing heavy enemy fire, particularly from multi-barrelled Nebelwerfers. Men were being wounded and killed for no good reason, because the regiment was ready to go. Instead, the commander, Lieutenant Colonel Bobby Clark, repeatedly told his company officers to hold their positions. They waited for supporting tanks — tanks from a regiment that, as yet, had no idea it was to fight that day.

Above 5th Canadian Armoured Division's regimental level, confusion in command reigned during the early hours of May 25. According to plan, 11th Canadian Infantry Brigade was to cross into the bridgehead won by Griffin Force and push on to Ceprano. No change in that order had been issued during the evening of May 24. Brigadier Eric Snow accordingly moved the Perth Regiment of Canada and the Cape Breton Highlanders behind the Irish Regiment that night. The divisional commander, Major General Bert Hoffmeister, told Snow the 8th New Brunswick Hussars armoured regiment would support his attack. Snow's first objective was a low ridge paralleling a road running from the Liri River north to Highway 6. The road stood about a thousand yards west of the Melfa River. The brigade's leading companies would pause there, Hoffmeister said, until everything behind them was "completely firmed and tidy."

Because of the limited number of crossings, Snow planned to force the river with one regiment — the Cape Breton Highlanders, supported by a squadron of Hussars. Once the Highlanders were across, the Perths would follow and the Irish move up in reserve so that a two-regiment-wide front was established on the objective. Snow, a seasoned Permanent Force veteran, visited Clark's headquarters to discuss the Irish role in the action. Clark advised him that Hoffmeister had "issued orders for the Irish to attack across the Melfa with the Westminster Regiment on the right and supported by a squadron of B.C. Dragoons." Snow realized his operational plan was significantly compromised by this unexpected development. He now had to swing the Highlanders and Perths 1,000 yards south and carry out a two-battalion attack without a reserve regiment. Existing artillery support plans must be scrapped and reissued. All this meant delays. Snow knew it would be a mad scramble to get the attack off on schedule at 1200 hours.[7]

Hoffmeister was exercising divisional control from a highly mobile tactical headquarters that consisted of his tank and a large armoured command vehicle. He felt that his orders were being precisely issued and delivered through a line of communications routed to his divisional headquarters in the rear and then down the brigade and regimental links. The system allowed him to rove the battle front and gather a personal appreciation of developments while maintaining communications with divisional staff and brigade and regimental commanders. "Organization, delegation, and communication" were Hoffmeister's three watchwords.[8]

The system of communication, however, functioned poorly at best. Snow only learned of the revised plan from Clark. Nor did the orders to the B.C. Dragoons to detach a tank squadron to support the Irish attack get transmitted during the night. It was only at about 1000 hours that Lieutenant Colonel Fred Vokes received orders from 5th Canadian Armoured Brigade's Brigadier Desmond Smith to detach a squadron with the urgent mission of supporting the Westminster Regiment. Vokes understood that the Lord Strathcona's Horse had suffered too many casualties to back up the Westminsters. No mention of the Irish Regiment was made.[9]

Vokes gave the job to Major Jack Turnley's 'C' Squadron. Like Vokes, Turnley was a Permanent Force Lord Strathcona's Horse veteran. Although he had only joined the Dragoons a few weeks earlier, he had earned six months' combat experience while posted to the British 5th Lancers armoured regiment during the North African campaign. Vokes urged Turnley to make haste.[10]

Turnley came running into the squadron section as Sergeant H.A. (Butch) Smitheram and his men were brewing some tea. "I want an O Group as fast as you can get to my tank," he shouted excitedly to the troop commanders. Five minutes later, Lieutenant Jock MacKinnon, commander of Smitheram's No. 3 Troop, strode back with word that the troop had five minutes to move out. MacKinnon took two of the five minutes to give a cursory briefing. The Westminsters, he said, were going to be counterattacked at any moment by massed infantry and Tiger tanks. The Dragoons must crash through to the bridgehead and break up the massing German armour. There was no information on enemy positions, suspected gun emplacements, or strength.[11]

While the tankers scrambled to their Shermans, Turnley raced ahead in his headquarters tank and conducted a hasty reconnaissance of the river with the Strathcona's commander, Lieutenant Colonel Phillip Griffin. During the night, an engineering team had graded a rough ramp on either side of the river that looked passable to tanks. Beyond the river, however, the ground levelled out into an open grain field. With no idea where the Germans had antitank weapons or tanks positioned, the Dragoons would be charging into a highly dangerous situation. Normally, such an attack would be preceded by reconnaissance to determine enemy positions. Then, artillery or air bombardment would suppress these positions while the tanks closed to engage the Germans. There was no time for such niceties. The Westminsters might be overwhelmed while all the preparatory work was under way.

Turnley advised the approaching troop commanders that, because of the confused situation, they were not to push more than 1,000 yards beyond the Melfa. Their marking point for the outward boundary was to be wherever they came into contact with railroad tracks that angled across the valley from the southwest to connect with the Rome-Naples mainline, just before it crossed the Melfa and entered Roccasecca Station.[12]

None of the Westminsters in the bridgehead had any idea that their position was in such peril. Nor had they called for tank support, believing it was already arranged. Certainly Mahony, who commanded the bridgehead, no longer feared an overwhelming counterattack. Indeed, the regiment was preparing to shift to the offensive, with 'C' Company driving out from the bridgehead in concert with the Irish, whenever the latter deigned to cross the river. 'B' Company would then cross the river immediately and come up on 'C' Company's right flank. The Westminsters within the bridgehead were in bad shape, but they were confident of expanding their hold on the Melfa's western shore. Their biggest problem was German artillery that had their position tightly registered.[13] One particularly heavy mid-morning concentration wounded lieutenants Bill Delaney and Ross Douglas, along with several other ranks. Sergeant "Pop" Becker and one man from 'C' Company's mortar section were killed. Sergeant Angus Kreiger lost his right hand. Mahony caught two pieces of shrapnel in a leg. He soldiered on despite the wounds.[14]

As the Dragoons approached the Melfa, Turnley ordered them into a line for the crossing. No. 4 Troop led, under twenty-four-year-old Lieutenant Stephen Coppinger. Lieutenant Neil Hockin's No. 2 Troop followed. The other two troops and the two-tank-strong regimental headquarters section would make a display along the river's edge to draw fire away from the crossing tanks. Once the first two troops were out of the riverbed, the rest of the squadron would cross.[15] Hockin was rolling into battle with a new troop. Both Sergeant Edmund Singbeil and Corporal Larsen had arrived with their tank crews only that morning from the reinforcement depot. Other than his own crew, Hockin didn't know any of the men. They had to net their radios into his during the run toward the river.[16]

Because of the hasty departure, some co-drivers were outside their tanks, clinging to the hulls, frantically tugging the muzzle covers off the main .75-millimetre guns even as the Shermans approached the river.[17] Coppinger had only recently taken command of Troop No. 4, making him a bit of an unknown entity to his men. He led, with Sergeant R.A.C. Davis immediately behind, and Corporal Patterson bringing up the rear. No. 4 Troop rolled past some wrecked, still smouldering Strathcona tanks on the river's edge. Davis was nervous. Like all of the 5th Canadian Armoured Brigade tanks, his brimmed with extra ammunition whose presence scared the crew. The loader had been muttering that if the tank got hit he was probably going to be trapped because of the extra shells. Coppinger was unable to put the troop into the picture about what they were doing. There were no maps, no clear objective, and no tactical plan except a vague order to find and repel German armour. It was a crazy way to fight.

◆ ◆ ◆

Coppinger's tanks skidded down the rough ramp cut by the bulldozer and struck the water with a mighty splash. After churning across the sand and gravel bed, the tanks paused at the base of the ramp leading up the opposite bank.[18] It was coming up to noon. The three tanks were met by Mahony, who explained that just beyond the bank was an open field with dense woods on the opposite side and on the flanks. He told the tankers to wait until the Westminsters got organized and then the two forces could advance together. As Coppinger was talking on his radio to Turnley, Mahony grabbed the phone attached to the rear of Davis's tank and reiterated his instructions. "Sergeant," he said, "the troop should remain here until we can regroup and carry on our part of the attack."

Through his earphones, Davis heard Coppinger describing to Turnley the lay of the land as reported by Mahony. Turnley, who had a speech impediment that tended to make him sound somewhat like Elmer Fudd, said, "Push on, boy. But be very, very careful."[19] Turnley added that Coppinger was to secure the woods on the other side of the field. This plan "didn't seem like a good idea," to the lieutenant, but he "was too young to even dream of questioning an order."[20] Waving his arm dramatically, like a cavalry officer signalling a charge, Coppinger led his troop up onto the plain. His tank was in the centre and slightly ahead of the others, so that the three tanks assumed the conventional arrowhead formation. No. 2 Troop formed on their right, with Hockin on the arrowhead's tip. Before them lay 1,000 yards of wide open ground that was as flat as a billiard table and utterly devoid of hollows or other positions that could form hull-down shelters. Everything was surprisingly quiet; only a few German shells were exploding here and there near the riverbank. In the distance, Hockin saw the railroad line. He didn't like the tactical situation or the topography, but thought there was nothing that could be done about things.[21] He described the ground to Turnley, but the order to advance held.[22] "We came to fight a war," Hockin later wrote, "and now the chips were down and it was either go or accept the consequences."

Coppinger dutifully led his troop forward. Hockin held back slightly inside a thin screen of trees bordering the river in order to provide covering fire. A hundred yards out from the woods, Davis looked across to Corporal Patterson's tank and saw it was burning in the aftermath of a direct armour-piercing shell hit. Davis's tank was hit a moment later and the driver reported that the engine was dead. Davis ordered the crew to abandon it. They scrambled out and hid in

△ Supplying 11th Canadian Infantry Brigade regiments stationed on International Ridge in April 1944 was only possible by mules. A supply column sets off from the rear area supply depot toward the ridge.
— STRATHY SMITH, NAC, PA-166756

◁ On March 3, 1944, Lieutenant General Harry Crerar (right) turned command of I Canadian Corps over to Lieutenant General Tommy Burns (left). — ALEXANDER MACKENZIE STIRTON, NAC, PA-132784

▽ Westminster Regiment Private W. Sutherland (left) and Cape Breton Highlanders Regiment Private V.A. Keddy repack comporations for transport to International Ridge.
— STRATHY SMITH, NAC, PA-151177

▷ Major General Chris Vokes treats personnel of the Hastings and Prince Edward Regiment to one of his trademark speeches peppered with bombast and profanity, May 13, 1944.

— C.E. NYE, NAC, PA-132770

△ By the time the Canadians arrived in the Liri Valley area in late April, the town of Cassino had been destroyed by repeated aerial and artillery bombardment. In the background, above the town, is the ruin of a medieval-era castle.

— W.H. AGNEW, NAC, PA-136204

▷ General Sir Oliver Leese (seated in car) faced his first major test as British Eighth Army commander during the May fighting in the Liri Valley.

— STRATHY SMITH, NAC, PA-131420

◁ In late April, I Canadian Corps undertook a major move over the Apennine Mountains to Italy's west coast to participate in Operation Diadem. The roads through the mountains were ill-suited to handle large amounts of military traffic.
— STRATHY SMITH, NAC, PA-140132

▷ To prevent the Germans defending the Gustav Line from realizing that a major offensive was imminent, positions were thoroughly camouflaged. The headquarters of 3rd Field Regiment, Royal Canadian Artillery, for example, was dug into a hillside and screened with sandbags in such a way that from the air it would appear to be part of the natural landscape.
— J. ERNEST DEGUIRE, NAC, PA-140133

◁ Operation Nunton — a major radio and communications network deception scheme carried out by I Canadian Corps — deceived the Germans into thinking that the Canadians were preparing an amphibious operation against the German rear rather than joining the direct assault up the Liri Valley.
— J. ERNEST DEGUIRE, NAC, PA-143895

△△Heavy mortars of I Canadian Corps added
the weight of their firepower to the massive
barrage of May 11–12 against the Gustav Line.
— C.E. Nye, NAC, PA-116819

△Daybreak found the Canadian artillery still
firing in support of the attacking British infantry
regiments and 1st Canadian Armoured Brigade.
Here, a Canadian self-propelled gun loader casts
a shell casing overboard immediately after firing.
— Alexander Mackenzie Stirton, NAC, PA-139892

▷Major Strome Galloway realized early in 1944
that not being a Permanent Force officer would
deny him the possibility of ever commanding
the Royal Canadian Regiment.
— Photo courtesy of Strome Galloway

◁ A Sherman tank of the 1st Canadian Armoured Brigade crosses a Bailey bridge over the Gari River on May 12. The smoke canisters in the foreground screen the bridge from German observation.
— ALEXANDER MACKENZIE STIRTON, NAC, PA-173362

△ A bulldozer of the Royal Canadian Engineers' Field Park Company improves the approach to a Gari River bridge crossing.
— ALEXANDER MACKENZIE STIRTON, NAC, PA-142069

◁ The shattered ruin of the village of San Angelo looks down upon the hastily erected London Bridge spanning the Gari River.
— ALEXANDER MACKENZIE STIRTON, NAC, PA-193898

△ A 1st Canadian Armoured
Brigade Sherman advances toward
a Gari River crossing point on May 11.
— ALEXANDER MACKENZIE STIRTON, NAC, PA-139890

▷ A German soldier emerges from
the ruins of a village across the
Gari River to surrender.
— ALEXANDER MACKENZIE STIRTON, NAC, PA-167301

▽ 1st Canadian Armoured Brigade
vehicles and tanks wait for orders to
cross a Gari River Bailey bridge that
is being concealed from enemy
observation by a heavy smoke screen.
— ALEXANDER MACKENZIE STIRTON, NAC, PA-177098

◁ Canadian infantrymen advance into the open countryside beyond the Gari River, supported by artillery concentrations directed against the facing ridgeline.
— G. BARRY GILROY, NAC, PA-141698

▷ Men of the Carleton and York Regiment advance beyond Pignataro on May 16.
— ALEXANDER MACKENZIE STIRTON, NAC, PA-166753

◁ Intense German shelling sends a group of Canadians scrambling for cover.
— ALEXANDER MACKENZIE STIRTON, NAC, PA-136205

▷ Despite the overall dry conditions, the poor tracks that Canadian regiments had to use to advance up the Liri Valley quickly broke up under heavy motorized traffic.
— STRATHY SMITH, NAC, PA-140208

▷ Major General Bert Hoffmeister believed he could exercise better divisional control from a highly mobile tactical headquarters that consisted of his tank *Vancouver* and a large armoured command vehicle (visible to left). Here, Hoffmeister is shown looking out of the turret hatch on May 26, 1944.
— Strathy Smith, NAC, PA-201346

△ Major General Bert Hoffmeister briefs 5th Canadian Armoured Division personnel on their role in the planned breakout from the Hitler Line toward Rome.
— Strathy Smith, NAC, PA-189920

▷ Six snipers from the Royal 22e Regiment move into the field on May 23, the day of the major offensive against the Hitler Line.
— W.R. Agnew, NAC, PA-117835

a nearby ditch. The Germans were now firing at the tanks with mortars and artillery. When his tank failed to burn, Davis ran for it. Just as he got there, another armour-piercing round slammed into its hull. The concussion blew him off his feet and shell fragments peppered his hand and arm.[23]

In the same instant, a shell ripped through the right-hand side of Coppinger's tank, spraying the interior with cordite and propellant charge. His radio operator–loader died instantly. The blast threw Coppinger into a pool of flames on the floor. He saw his gunner tumbling out of the turret hatch. Clawing his way up, Coppinger followed him. The driver and co-driver also managed to escape, although everyone's clothes were ablaze. They rolled on the ground and tore off bits and pieces of uniform to extinguish the flames. Coppinger was in agony.[24]

Davis ran over to him, who was screaming the name of a sergeant from some former unit in which he had served. When his present sergeant calmed him down a little, Coppinger told Davis to gather the rest of the troop together and lead them back to the river. Because of his severe facial burns, Coppinger was virtually blind. Davis pulled his own gloves off and put them on the lieutenant's charred hands. Then he got him down on his hands and knees, pointed him in the right direction, and told him to crawl to the river. He and the other men in the troop crawled along behind.[25] At the river, Coppinger staggered into the water. The cool liquid washing over his burns felt so good that he had to resist the temptation to lie down in the river and drift off to sleep.[26]

Just as Coppinger's troop was knocked out, Hockin had started leading No. 2 Troop out into the field. He ordered his driver to stop immediately, believing his tank still sufficiently covered by trees. A sharp wham shuddering through the tank told him otherwise. The driver reported that the warning light had come on, indicating an engine fire and that he had turned on the fire extinguishers mounted inside the engine compartment. Hockin called Turnley to say his tank was hit and told the crew to get out. He could smell gasoline and engine parts burning and knew the extinguishers had failed to smother the fire.

Jumping out of his tank, Hockin thought he saw the antitank gun that was killing the Dragoons out on the right flank. He ran to where his sergeant's tank stood about fifty feet behind his own burning Sherman. Scrambling up on the turret, Hockin rapped Singbeil on the helmet to get his attention. Singbeil had spotted the same German gun and was traversing his gun to bring it under fire. The antitank gun won the race and a round slammed hard into the tank. With only one foot securely placed on the back deck and the rest of his body sprawled across the turret, the concussion ripped so severely through Hockin's body that it broke a bone in his foot and chucked him off the tank. As he gathered himself up, he saw the last tank in the troop burst into flames. Singbeil and his crew all suffered burn wounds, as did the men bailing out of the other tank.*

Hobbling on his broken foot, Hockin led his troop back to the river. Standing on the Melfa's shore, he watched in dismay as the remaining two Dragoon troops started across. Hockin tried to signal them, wanting to warn them of the danger. They rolled on, either ignoring or having failed to see him. When the tanks moved up into an area that was less exposed than that utilized by No. 2 and No. 4 troops, Hockin thought they might be safe.

As he gathered up some of the wounded men in the river bottom, Hockin asked which troop they were from. One man said that he, Hockin, was their lieutenant. Hockin knew now that he would never get to know most of these men. He led them across the river to the Westminsters' Regimental Aid Post.[27]

◆ ◆ ◆

While No. 4 and No. 2 troops were being butchered, the other Dragoon troopers had listened helplessly to their radio traffic. Sergeant Butch Smitheram in No. 3 Troop heard somebody yell, "Sunray [standard radio term for a unit commander] has been hit and his tank is on fire!" Turnley came up, saying, "Very well, push on to your objec-

---

*Singbeil would die several months later from burn-related complications just two weeks after being returned to Canada and hospitalized in Vancouver. Coppinger, however, was fortunate enough to come under the care of a doctor in Caserta who was a leading specialist in burn injuries. His treatment, which involved extensive use of blood transfusions and constant, regularly changed, wet dressings on the burns, resulted in the lieutenant's recovering not only from his first-, second-, and third-degree burns but suffering no scarring. Coppinger would return to active duty in the Calgary Regiment later in 1944.

tive, but be very, very careful." Another tank was reported hit, then another, then the man speaking trailed off "into a bedlam of screams as his own tank was hit while he was on the air."

Turnley ordered the remaining two troops forward, crossing as well with his squadron headquarters section. No. 3 Troop was on the right flank and No. 1 on the left, with the two headquarters tanks in the centre and slightly behind. When Smitheram's tank came out of the riverbed onto the open ground, he saw the burning wrecks of the first two troops. No. 3 Troop assumed an arrowhead formation and halted in some cover. The men sat there for twenty minutes. A heavy artillery piece was dropping shells nearby. Each time a shell landed, the concussion brought tears to Smitheram's eyes and he felt as if someone had punched him in the nose with a boxing glove. When the shells started creeping closer, Smitheram edged his Sherman further to the right to avoid the line of fire. A massive explosion tore up the ground in front of him and then another shell struck just behind. Smitheram realized he was being bracketed and the next round would likely hit him. He moved the Sherman again to the shelter of a large oak tree that stood next to a knocked-out German half-track mounting an .88-millimetre gun.

Smitheram dismounted to check out the German vehicle. The corpse of a young blond soldier was hanging half out of the door on the driver's side. Blood had run out of the man's nose and mouth and dried over his face. Smitheram rolled him onto the ground and searched the cab. The radio was still on and he could hear Germans chattering away to each other, but had no idea what was being said.

On the return trip, Smitheram encountered a Canadian infantryman "coming back down the flat with his rifle slung and his steel helmet hanging on the back of his head. He was talking and crying." Smitheram asked how far away his platoon was, but the man stumbled on toward the riverbank without stopping or responding.

Back aboard his Sherman, Smitheram learned it had developed battery trouble. The electrical system was out. The engine wouldn't start and there was barely any juice for the radio. Unable to move, he decided to fire some shots at a house about 400 yards away that appeared to be sheltering German snipers. While his gunner banged away at the target, Smitheram scanned the vicinity and spotted a half-track mounted with a short-barrelled .88 that sat among several others knocked out earlier. This one moved. Looking closer, Smitheram saw a driver and another German sitting in the front seat. They were staring toward his tank. The vehicle advanced through some tall wheat and then rolled up on a small rise with its gun pointed directly toward Smitheram. The sergeant reported his sighting to Lieutenant MacKinnon. The troop commander said he was unable to see the vehicle. Then the radio died.

Smitheram ran over to MacKinnon's tank and tried pointing out the half-track, but the officer still couldn't find it among all the foliage and tall grain. Running back to his own tank, Smitheram had his gunner use the manual traverse crank to bring his gun to bear on the half-track. Earlier, the gunner had loaded a high-explosive round. When they tried to switch it for armour-piercing, the case pulled free, leaving the HE shell jammed in the breech. Now the only option was to carefully fit the case back on the shell, fire it, and quickly reload with armour-piercing.

The high explosive landed short and before the AP shell could be loaded, the half-track started backing up over a hill. The AP round missed, but the half-track disappeared behind the hill for good. Smitheram's driver had been working on the battery and reported that he had managed to tape some melted wires back together, restoring power. Just as well, for Smitheram spotted what he thought was a Tiger tank off to the right. Knowing his Sherman's .75-millimetre gun was useless against the other's armour, he ran back to where a 4th Canadian Anti-tank Regiment self-propelled 13-pounder gun had just come across the Melfa. The powerful weapon, noted as the latest thing in Allied tank destroyers, rolled up and fired three shots at the German tank. The latter retreated into the smoke and dust that were increasingly obscuring visibility over the entire area. Smitheram returned to his tank.

The Dragoons continued holding in place, frustrated that the deteriorating visibility made it difficult to provide effective support to the infantry, which were somewhere out front driving toward the railroad objective.[28] Because of the uncertainty regarding the position of the German guns that had knocked out the first two Dragoon troops, Turnley had abandoned the plan to cross the open field. The infantry were carrying the battle forward largely alone, with only 'B' Troop of the 4th Anti-tank Regiment's 98th Anti-tank Battery in support. That battery had been assigned to back up the Irish Regiment of Canada in the absence of any available tank squadrons.[29]

♦ ♦ ♦

Finally crossing the Melfa River, the Irish Regiment's 'A' and 'C' companies led, followed by the other two companies and the anti-tank regiment's self-propelled guns. The regiment's war diarist later wrote that the "battlefield of the Melfa vied with the Hitler Line in its fury. Burning tanks . . . littered the field and everywhere enemy shells were bursting, directed at our tanks and SP Guns. Our return fire disintegrated houses in a cloud of smoke and masonry and the enemy could be seen fleeing from their posts."[30] Shortly after crossing the river, one of the SPGs took a direct hit, resulting in four crew casualties. The battery commander, who was aboard this vehicle, was the only one uninjured. The three remaining SPGs got through the rest of the battle without significant damage or casualties.[31] At about 1330 hours, the Irish were on the objective. They dug in and sweated through the rest of the day under intense German shelling.[32]

On the Irish right flank, the Westminsters had jumped off in concert with the Irish's crossing of the Melfa. Lieutenant Edward Perkins and his plucky troop of Strathconas fired the last of their .50-calibre Browning machine-gun ammunition over the heads of the advancing Westminsters to provide some covering fire. Then Perkins ordered the three Honeys withdrawn to the Strathcona's harbour. They crossed back over the Melfa at 1215 hours. It had been, Perkins wrote, "an extremely eventful twenty-four hours."[33]

The Westminsters had gone into the attack with 'B' Company on the right and 'C' Company on the left. They measured their pace to match that of the Irish Regiment, so that the Canadians maintained a fairly continuous line as they pushed across the open ground. A four-company-wide advance was almost unknown in World War II, more reminiscent of the Great War. Soldiers in 'C' Company were even more reminded of the World War I scenes they had read about as they walked through a wide field of grain mixed with vivid red poppies.

Five minutes out from the start line, 'C' Company's headquarters section saw an entire platoon of Germans suddenly materialize out of the grain. The Germans started marching toward them with their hands in the air. One German had a fine pair of Zeiss binoculars hanging on a strap from his neck. The company signaller said, "Those are mine." He plucked the binoculars from around the German's neck and carried on without pausing, leaving the Germans to surrender to someone else.

When the Westminsters were 900 yards out, they started taking artillery fire. They were still about 600 yards from the low ridge and railroad line that was the objective. Sergeant Ron Hurley of 'C' Company saw men start to fall with shrapnel wounds. Then one man in his section took a direct hit from a mortar bomb and disappeared in a spray of gore. Two other men, fresh reinforcements who had arrived only a few days before, were killed by another direct hit. One of them was almost decapitated and his face mangled.

The Westminsters had now reached the objective and were trying to dig in. Hurley and others tried using the No. 25 antitank grenades to loosen the hardpan soil without success. The explosives barely raised a puff of dirt. They retrieved some picks and shovels from some knocked-out German tanks standing nearby and started hacking at the ground.

Their bodies ran with sweat raised by their exertions, fear, and the sizzling sun that beat down upon their exposed position. There was nothing the Westminsters could do to improve their situation. They just had to lie there on the open ground and take the shelling. Hurley was amazed at how much ammunition the Germans had. Shells seemed to fall like raindrops. The constant danger grated on his nerves. He kept wondering when he "was going to get smoked like those other guys." Occasionally, he would take a pull from his water bottle. As always, this was filled with *vino bianco*. Hurley avoided Italian water, fearing dysentery. He would avoid it even more after today. Just before the attack, he had watched in disgust as a Canadian water truck rolled up to the edge of the Melfa. The water crew had chucked a filtering system that looked like a child's toy swimming pool into the river and started pumping water up into the tank. Floating around the filter system were German corpses and several dead horses. Hurley figured it unlikely the little water purification tablets they were supposed to add to their water bottles could disinfect all the contagion lurking in water gathered like that. Wine was safer. Most of his men felt the same.

As the terrible day dragged on, officers tried to organize parties to evacuate the wounded, but everyone was afraid to volunteer. Going back over the killing ground of the field while carrying or helping wounded men to walk seemed suicidal. For seven hours, the Westminsters and the Irish Regiment held their ground under the pounding of the German artillery, mortars, tanks, and self-propelled guns. Finally, with darkness closing in, the German fire slackened and the men heard the roaring of engines from enemy positions.[34]

Just before dark, one of the Westminsters in the rear, Ted Boyer, risked exposing himself to German fire by driving a White scout car up to the forward position. Hurley and some of the other men hurriedly loaded nineteen dead and wounded on board. Among them was the nearly decapitated soldier, whose identity discs were missing.

Boyer looked at the body and said that, given the grubby condition and the pallor of the skin, it had to be Private Lou Schachter. He then drove back to the river with his load and duly reported to the chaplain that Schachter was dead.

With unusual speed and efficiency, a telegram reporting the private's death was dispatched to Schachter's family within hours. No sooner had it been sent, however, than Boyer bumped into Schachter returning from the front lines. "God, that's not you," Boyer gasped. Schachter was devastated to hear that his family had been wrongly notified of his demise, so distraught in fact that he had to be taken out of the lines. The unit never saw him again.[35]

During their fierce two-day battle, the Westminsters had suffered about 100 casualties, of which 20 were fatalities. They had accounted for between 50 and 100 Germans killed and more than 100 captured.[36] More important, the regiment had secured a bridgehead across the Melfa River that threw the German defensive plan into disarray.

♦ ♦ ♦

At midday on May 25, Commander-in-Chief Southwest Generalfeldmarschall Albert Kesselring phoned Tenth Army commander Generaloberst Heinrich von Vietinghoff and stated that the Battle of Rome was at "a decisive stage. . . . The main goal must be to paralyze the offensive spirit of the enemy by the infliction of very heavy casualties. This can only be done by fanatical defence of the main lines."

Kesselring specifically forbade "the withdrawal of any division and the giving up of any strongpoint without my prior explicit consent."[37] Kesselring's Chief of Staff, General der Kavallerie Siegfried Westphal, also rang von Vietinghoff. "The Führer absolutely demands that any withdrawal be carried out step by step with the consent of Army Group. If at all possible, no withdrawal is to be made without the personal concurrence of the Führer."[38]

Von Vietinghoff duly called up LI Mountain Corps commander General Valentin Feurstein to say, "I would like to emphasize that according to the Führer's orders the Melfa Line must be held for several days. An early withdrawal is out of the question. Enemy elements that have crossed the river must be thrown back."[39] Feurstein was amazed that his commander could be so blind as to think a counterattack could throw the Canadians back across the Melfa. The 90th Panzer Grenadiers had been so reduced by casualties that the 200th Grenadier Regiment numbered only 300 men and the 361st Grenadier Regiment a mere 100.

"I report as a matter of duty that we will not bring back many men if we have to hold at all costs," Feurstein said stiffly.

"We must accept that risk; Army Group has given explicit orders to hold the line for several days."

"I report to the Generaloberst that the enemy has already crossed the Melfa in two places and that no forces are available to rectify the situation," Feurstein replied.

Von Vietinghoff went back to Kesselring in the early morning hours of May 26 and the two had a long, painful discussion in which they tried to balance reality against Hitler's delusional orders. The Tenth Army commander wanted a retreat back along Highway 6, with a new line formed somewhere behind Ceprano that could be used to stall the Canadian advance. Kesselring, normally so calm, exploded: "It is the Führer's explicit order and also my belief that we must bleed the enemy to exhaustion by hard fighting. You have always been so optimistic; why has your attitude changed?"[40]

The Tenth Army commander's attitude was only rational. Increasingly, his LI Mountain Corps and the XIV Panzer Corps were at risk. He feared that the Americans breaking out of the Anzio beachhead and the Corps Expéditionnaire Français's rapid advance on the Canadian left flank could soon cut them off. Von Vietinghoff's

Chief of Staff, Generalmajor Fritz Wentzell, was even more outspoken. He declared, "We have to get out of here as fast as we can or we shall lose the whole XIV Panzer Corps!"[41]

Finally Kesselring saw the light, mainly because a rapidly developing crisis on the Fourteenth Army's front left him no option but to consider withdrawal. On May 25, the VI U.S. Corps, breaking out of the Anzio beachhead, overran two German divisions, captured Cisterna, and ended the day midway between Anzio and Valmontone. Americans from the main divisions of Fifth Army advancing up the coastline toward Anzio also linked up with the beachhead's southern flank. This brought to an end the encirclement of VI Corps inside the Anzio beachhead. It also left the Fourteenth Army and the far right divisions of Tenth Army holding a long, badly fragmented, curving line that was impossible to defend. Should the Americans reach Valmontone and sever Highway 6 before XIV Panzer Corps was able to slip west and escape, it might be encircled and destroyed.

Kesselring finally won Hitler's agreement to a redeployment that would see the northern wing of Fourteenth Army holding firm between Velletri and the sea. The south wing of this army would then move into a blocking position in front of Cisterna. Tenth Army would meanwhile fall back, conducting a slow, determined delaying action against the Eighth Army as a general withdrawal was conducted to the Caesar Line, anchored on the Alban Hills. Kesselring's orders to his commanders stated that their immediate objective was not "to reach the Caesar Line soon. Rather, whilst stubbornly holding the sectors designated from time to time," they must "inflict such heavy casualties on the enemy that his fighting potentiality will be broken even before the Caesar Line is reached."[42] The Germans planned to bleed Eighth Army, particularly the Canadians, to a point where the Allied advance might falter and die through attrition.

◆ ◆ ◆

As night fell on the weary Canadians holding the lines west of the Melfa River, the thought that casualties might break them seemed not improbable. The Westminster Regiment had lost approximately a quarter of its fighting strength. Among the Irish Regiment, casualties had totalled ten other ranks killed, and three officers and thirty-two other ranks wounded.

At 1630 hours, Brigadier Snow finally managed to get his other two infantry regiments moving across the Melfa. The Cape Breton Highlanders led the way, supported by the 8th New Brunswick Hussars. The tankers had 'C' Squadron leading, followed by the regimental headquarters section, then 'A' and 'B' squadrons. 'C' Squadron had advanced only a few hundred yards into the open on the west side of the river when it became tangled in a duel with some antitank guns. Three tanks were knocked out, but they managed to destroy the three .75-millimetre antitank guns and an SPG.[43] Remarkably, only three men were wounded. One of these died later in hospital.[44]

The infantry were not so fortunate. About a thousand yards from the river, the leading 'A' and 'B' companies "encountered terrific mortar fire from SP guns."[45] 'B' Company commander Major Tony MacLachlan was hit in the chest and leg by shrapnel. He doggedly led his men to the objective before agreeing to evacuation. His act earned him a Military Cross. The commander of 'A' Company, Captain C.M. Archibald, was killed as that company moved onto the objective. He was one of six Highlanders to die reaching the objective, which was to be the jumping-off point for their forthcoming advance. The Perth Regiment of Canada got through to its objective on the Highlanders' left flank with only three other ranks wounded.[46]

South of the 5th Canadian Armoured Division's operations, the 1st Canadian Infantry Division had continued its advance toward the Melfa. 'D' Company of the Carleton and York Regiment had won the bridgehead early in the day. The regiment had then advanced with 'D' Company leading, followed by 'C', 'B,' and 'A' with two troops of Three Rivers Regiment tanks. The West Nova Scotia Regiment then passed through the Carleton and York Regiment and established a forward position as the jumping-off point for a follow-on attack toward the Isoletta Reservoir. Shelling of the Melfa River crossing caused such casualties that the Carleton and York troops named the crossing point "Death Valley." The regiment, already badly depleted by casualties resulting from breaking the Hitler Line, suffered five other ranks killed and two officers and eighteen other ranks wounded. The regimental war diarist wrote: "Positions were firmly established by last light in spite of depleted state of the companies."[47]

For the badly battered 'C' Squadron of the B.C. Dragoons still in place at the bridgehead on the west side of the Melfa River, the day ended with a heart-stopper when German artillery smothered the forward area with a massive smoke barrage. The sun was sinking in the west, making it extremely difficult for the men in their tanks to see any German tanks or gun positions. Their radios crackled with warnings passed back and forth to be on the lookout for signs of a counterattack. Corporal G.T. Dodd, serving in Major Jack Turnley's headquarters' tank, noted that the "tension was very high." Nothing happened. Instead, the smoke was masking a general withdrawal of German armour. 'C' Squadron's battle was over. Soon they got word to withdraw to the east side of the Melfa and rejoin the regiment.[48]

Back in the harbour, Sergeant Butch Smitheram was in a cold fury. He thought the entire battle a stupid disaster. That opinion had only hardened when Turnley ordered one of the headquarters tanks to move to some high ground to gather an appreciation of what German positions might be visible from there. As the tank crested the top of the hill, it was hit. The tank commander's body flew "out of the tank like an old pair of overalls, all limp and floppy." That evening, Turnley gathered the survivors around and called the roll. Many men were missing.[49]

The squadron had lost seven of fourteen tanks. Three men were dead, nine wounded, and fourteen missing. Turnley made the mistake of citing the action as a victory. After the meeting ended, Smitheram went up to Turnley and asked if the commander had been "trying for a DSO or something." The two men had a hot and heavy argument, during which Smitheram called his commander "Blood and Guts Turnley" to his face. The major demanded to know if Smitheram wanted a transfer. "Yes," Smitheram said. He had had enough of Turnley and had no better opinion of Lieutenant Colonel Fred Vokes. Smitheram thought both men vainglorious and ignorant. Turnley paraded Smitheram in front of Vokes, who gave the sergeant a stern dressing down. Smitheram asked for a transfer to the Calgary Tank Regiment, but Vokes assigned him to regimental headquarters.[50]

When Vokes finished with Smitheram, he called an Orders Group to discuss actions for the morning. On May 23, Major George Carrington Smith had returned to the regiment to resume command of 'B' Squadron. As the regiment was moving into battle right then, Smith remained in reserve and the squadron's present commander, twenty-nine-year-old Acting Major David Kinloch, led it into action. When the fighting was over, Kinloch reverted to being a captain and resumed command of one of the squadron's troops. This back-and-forth movement in rank had become so common for the Vernon, B.C., orchardist and prewar militiaman that he had two battle-dress tunics — one fitted with the three pips of a captain and the other with major's crowns. Each morning, Kinloch sent his batman over to regimental headquarters to find out whether he was to be a captain or an acting major that day.

Kinloch wore his captain's uniform as the officers left the meeting and walked along a hedgerow in single file toward their squadrons. Throughout the meeting, the area had been receiving sporadic shelling. Captain George Baker was leading the file, followed by Major Gerry Eastman, then Major George Smith, and lastly Kinloch. Hearing the whoosh of incoming Nebelwerfer fire, Kinloch dived between the bogies on the tracks of a tank and into a pit sheltering its crew. Six massive explosions rocked the tank. Kinloch crawled out into the thinning smoke and dust to see Smith, Eastman, and Baker being carried off on stretchers. Although relatively minor, their wounds would keep them all out of action for at least a few days. Kinloch walked back to his tank, retrieved the uniform with crowns and was reanointed an acting major.[51]

23

A Bit of
a Black Eye

In the predawn hours of May 26, the men of the 11th Canadian Infantry Brigade's three regiments ate hard rations from their packs. Heavy traffic congestion in the rear area of 5th Canadian Armoured Division prevented the regimental cooks' bringing a hot breakfast forward. The same congestion was becoming a routine nightmare in the narrow Liri Valley as the two Eighth Army corps competed for routes forward. They followed the maze of dirt tracks and narrow gravel roads that, other than Highway 6, were the only viable paths. The bad roads reduced the divisional artillery regiments to a crawl toward positions from which they could support the advance and also delayed the trucks bearing fuel and munitions to the 8th New Brunswick Hussars. Tanks rolled toward battle with fuel tanks that were little more than half-full.[1] Brigadier Eric Snow's orders were to drive his brigade and supporting tank regiment around the northern shore of the Isoletta Reservoir to effect a crossing of the upper Liri River near Ceprano. This entailed traversing a distance of about four and a half miles.[2]

Everyone knew a hard day lay ahead. The maps told the story

with unexpected accuracy. Once across the railroad, the regiments would enter ground covered in thick scrub. Tank movement would be "restricted to tracks" clear to the reservoir. Countless little streams snaked across the line of advance and irrigation ditches were plentiful. This was ideal ground for a delayed withdrawal, something at which the Germans were masterful.

The Cape Breton Highlanders moved out first at 0700 hours, with 'C' Company on the right and 'D' on the left. Behind was regimental headquarters, followed by 'A' Company on the right and 'B' on the left. The Perth Regiment was left of the Highlanders, with 'D' Company left and 'B' Company right. Each regiment had a squadron of the 8th New Brunswick Hussars — 'A' Squadron with the Highlanders and 'B' Squadron with the Perths.

Perth Regiment Private Stan Scislowski, serving in No. 18 Platoon of Major Sammy Ridge's 'D' Company, marched through shin-deep grain. At first it was a walk in the park, "no small-arms fire, no mortars, no shells." Only the Highlanders, momentarily confused, fired on the men appearing on their left — a situation quickly corrected without injuries. Scislowski later wrote: "The way things were going thus far, it looked very much like the Germans had picked up and skedaddled across the Liri River. . . . Our momentary reverie, however, evaporated in the express-train rush of enemy shells slamming into the wheat all around us."[3] Scislowski dived into an irrigation ditch he was following and crawled like crazy about fifty yards forward. Then, hearing the German shells landing well behind him, the private jumped up and sprinted another 200 yards ahead. The move toward the source of artillery was reflexive — a response to training. Scislowski was surprised to find himself alone, none of his mates having followed.

Shells were exploding all around the platoon. "There won't be a damned one of my guys alive after that," he thought. When the shelling stopped, however, he was relieved to see his friends popping up out of the grain and coming on. In fact, nobody had been killed and just a couple had suffered superficial wounds.

It suddenly struck Scislowski, with a surge of pride, that for the last fifteen or twenty minutes he had been the "point man in the whole damn Canadian Corps on this beautiful spring day, May 26, 1944. The only people ahead of me on that battlefield were guys wearing field-grey — the Jerries. So there I was, standing all alone, waiting for the rest of the corps to catch up to me, feeling like an all-conquering hero."

Scislowski sat down on a mound of dirt, calmly took out an over-seas edition of the *Windsor Star*, and started reading the comics page. He was just digging into "L'il Abner" when a machine gun ripped up dirt about five feet away. Scislowski tossed the paper and rolled into a ditch just in time to avoid a burst that tore across the ground where he had been sitting. Then he heard the clanking of tank tracks and a New Brunswick Hussars tank rolled out of the brush. Scislowski realized the tankers had nearly killed him, thinking he was a German. One of the men was perched on the turret, waving a Thompson at him to stand with hands raised. As he rose up out of the trench, the soldier relaxed at the sight of his uniform and Tommy helmet. "What in bloody hell are you doing up this far?" the man shouted. Not waiting for an answer, he jumped back into the tank without apology and the Sherman rumbled off. Scislowski's platoon came up moments later. "What the hell kept you guys so long?" the still-shaken private demanded. "Did you expect me to fight the war alone?" Everyone ignored him and just trudged on.[4]

On the brigade's right flank, the Cape Breton Highlanders met heavier resistance than the Perths. They faced heavy machine-gun and sniper fire twenty minutes beyond the start line. Forced to ground, the infantry hid while the Hussars knocked out German positions in some farmhouses and bunkers.[5] The Hussars in Major P.M. Blanchet's 'A' Squadron easily erased the German resistance points with machine-gun or main-gun fire. When the advance renewed, however, the Shermans were reduced to a crawl. While the infantry proceeded alone, the Hussars warily advanced in single file down tracks rife with antitank mines and booby traps. Engineers, riding in Honeys, came forward to clear obstacles. They also built diversions across seemingly endless streams and irrigation ditches. The engineers and tankers were routinely subjected to German small-arms fire from the railroad embankment that formed an unnatural ridge cutting across the line of advance. Finally, at 1430 hours, Blanchet's tankers and the Highlanders succeeded in clearing the Germans off the embankment.[6]

Just beyond the railroad, the Highlanders encountered signs of a hasty German retreat. Among scattered bodies were some food sup-plies, which "disappeared in a big hurry," noted the regiment's war diarist. "A lot of the boys also got a change of socks, which was more than welcome."[7]

'B' Squadron, commanded by Major Howard Keirstead, had an even more difficult time getting across a series of streams that cut across its line of advance. Only the ingenuity of the engineers, who used explosives to blast ramps into the banks, enabled the armour to keep pace with the Perth infantry.

Shortly before noon, the combined force reached the reservoir. It proved to be nothing more than a giant mud flat cut in the middle by the river. The Germans had blown the dam that also served as a bridge across the southeastern edge. In the distance, the Canadians could see the rooftops of Ceprano. Bright red tiles glowed in the sunshine.

Scislowski's company marched up a dirt road paralleling the reservoir. They passed two horses killed by artillery fire, still har-nessed to a wagon loaded with ammunition boxes. Just beyond the dead animals, Scislowski passed Sergeant Pete McRorie returning from a reconnaissance patrol. Scislowski greeted him, but before the heavily built sergeant could reply he stepped on the detonator of a Teller antitank mine. McRorie's lower body disappeared in a shower of blood and body parts.

Concussion walloped Scislowski in the back and flung him in a swan dive face-first into the road. His mouth full of gravel and dirt, and momentarily disoriented, Scislowski stared in horror at McRorie's "body lying in the middle of the road — a welter of blood, guts, and bone." He felt himself on the edge of cracking apart. Then there was an almost audible click in his brain, followed by calm. "Glad it's not me," he thought.

Two massive explosions caught his attention in time to see two Hussar tanks disabled by Teller mines. Everyone in Scislowski's pla-toon lay on the ground, afraid to move for fear of tripping mines. The private was the second man in the lead section "and it took some guts to get up and go on." Go on the Perths did, crossing the railroad embankment and entering the two-mile-stretch of open terrain leading to Ceprano.[8]

◆ ◆ ◆

Brigadier Eric Snow thought the country reminiscent of "bush country in Africa." Given the density of ground cover, the poor tracks, and the presence of so many mines and booby traps, the 11 CIB commander considered the sluggish pace unavoidable. Major General Bert Hoffmeister disagreed. He hovered at Snow's shoulder, urging the brigadier to "get on, that the advance was much too slow and that something must be done." The divisional commander's temper flared considerably at 1430 hours when the supporting Hussar squadrons ran low on fuel. On the right flank, the Cape Breton Highlanders had just passed 'A' and 'B' companies into the lead. Lieutenant Colonel Jim Weir ordered his men to form a defensive position around the tanks and dig in until the Hussars could pull back for refuelling. Perth commander Lieutenant Colonel J.S. Lind halted his regiment's advance to avoid outrunning the Highlanders. When this situation was reported to Snow, Hoffmeister ordered the "battalions to get going at once. The Perths got going within thirty minutes, but it was nearly two hours before the CBH got going again," Snow later wrote.[9]

Hoffmeister was exasperated by Snow's apparent failure to exert command. The major general had spent the morning searching for Snow and failed to find him at either his brigade or tactical headquarters. Instead, the brigadier and a few staff officers were discovered at the end of a dusty road that formed a "bit of a cul-de-sac, without adequate knowledge of what was going on and in no position to control the battle." Hoffmeister decided then and there to get rid of Snow. If he could have fired Snow on the spot, he would have. Instead, Hoffmeister hovered close by, taking personal control of the brigade's operations.[10]

As Hoffmeister steamed and fretted, the Hussars conducted a devious smuggling operation to bring badly needed fuel and ammunition up to their leading tank squadrons. Early in the morning, the tank regiment had been given permission by 11 CIB staff to send only five resupply vehicles across the Melfa because of heavy traffic behind the front lines. Knowing this was totally insufficient, rear-echelon staff smuggled thirteen more trucks into the convoys of other regiments. By 1030 hours, ten lorries bearing ammunition and eight loaded with fuel were across the river, able to rendezvous with the tanks when they needed resupply.

When the tanks hit the refuel or stall point, they withdrew to designated rendezvous points. 'B' Squadron arrived at 1430 hours and was ready to go back into action at 1600. A small hill, however, combined with dense foliage and confused tracks, prevented 'A' Squadron from marrying up with the supply convoy and this squadron's refuelling and rearmament were not completed until 1845 hours.[11]

Lieutenant Sted Henderson of 'A' Squadron was just leaving the resupply area when a German soldier popped out of brush and threw a stick grenade into his open turret. The grenade landed on the tank floor, was scooped up by the driver and handed up to Henderson, who threw the charge out seconds before it exploded. Without pausing to engage the German, the tankers rejoined the still slowly advancing Highlanders.[12]

Because of the resupply delay, the Highlanders did not renew their advance until 1900 hours. This was fully four and a half hours after the Hussars had run out of fuel, rather than the two hours that Snow believed had passed before they returned to the offensive. His confusion derived from the fact that some of the regiment had moved off two hours earlier without the tanks. At 1630 hours, 'A' and 'B' companies had led off for 500 yards and then for no apparent reason huddled down to await return of the Hussars. When 'A' Squadron caught up, Weir called a thirty-minute Orders Group to clarify an already well-determined plan of advance.

Finally the regiment started moving again, but it was quickly engaged by German snipers firing from an overlooking hill. The tankers killed several and drove off the rest with machine-gun fire and the infantry then filtered forward apprehensively.[13] Snow was abandoning hope that the brigade might reach Ceprano before night-fall. The brigadier set a low ridge about two miles east of the river as the final objective. Once there, the two regiments were to dig in for the night.[14]

While the Highlanders dithered, the Perth Regiment had returned to the offensive, practically reaching the ridge objective before Snow's order arrived. The Perth advance had been uneventful, more bothered by the sweltering heat and lack of streams for refilling empty water bottles than by German action. The Hussars' 'B' Squadron Shermans, however, had banged into an antitank ambush as they swept aside a German machine-gunner pestering the Perths. A German gun sheared the suspension off the right side of Lieutenant Jim Jones's Sherman. Stopped dead in its tracks, the tank was a sitting duck. Many a tank crew would have bailed out then and there, especially as the tank was out of armour-piercing shot. Instead, Jones and his men stuck to their guns. They fired high-explosive rounds at a persistent muzzle flash coming from a thicket. To their surprise, a huge Panther tank exploded in flames as the result of a direct hit from their gun. That spelled the end of the ambush, as the other German armour fled.[15]

'D' Company was in the middle of a wide meadow when the order came to halt. "What the hell are we stopping here for!" Scislowski groused. "Nobody's shooting at us. Shit, we might as well keep going." The Germans were running, he figured, and the Canadians should deny them opportunity to regroup. "What a way to fight a war," he thought, "sitting here in the hot sun, fingers up our ass, while Jerry's up ahead somewhere probably building himself another Hitler Line."[16]

Snow hesitated out of fear of tripping a counterattack. He wanted his brigade and the Hussars circled in a tight group capable of all-round defence. With the British still on the east side of the Melfa and only two companies of the Westminster Regiment and a squadron of the Governor General's Horse Guards linking his regiment back to the rest of the division, Snow fretted that his brigade held "a rather precarious position."[17]

Curiously, Snow forgot the presence of Adams Force, composed of 3rd Canadian Infantry Brigade's West Nova Scotia and Carleton and York regiments and the Princess Louise Dragoon Guards armoured car regiment. They had also crossed the Melfa that morning and driven to the blown bridge on the eastern end of the reservoir without meeting significant resistance. Unable to get armoured cars across the Liri River, 'C' Squadron of the PLDGs sent a foot patrol out. The troops waded across the stream and advanced two miles west to the southern shore of the Sacco River, where they found a 120-foot-span bridge blown out. Wading this stream, the men advanced a further 500 yards toward the Ceprano railroad station and dug in for the night — becoming Eighth Army's most advanced unit.[18]

♦ ♦ ♦

When Hoffmeister heard Snow's report, he countermanded the brigadier's orders and told him to get on to Ceprano. Snow "ordered the Irish to send two companies out of the fortress and secure the crossing if these were not strongly held by the enemy, and to reconnoitre the whole line of the river for possible crossings."[19]

Whatever the precise wording of his orders, Lieutenant Colonel Bobby Clark, understanding that he was to send one company forward from the ridge to the Liri River, gave the duty to 'D' Company.[20] He also dispatched Lieutenant G.J. Wood and five men, including Royal Canadian Engineer Lieutenant Y. Young, to determine whether Ceprano was defended and to check two main bridges crossing the Liri River near the town.

Passing through the Canadian lines at 2200 hours on May 26, Wood's party reached the Liri River at 0430 hours. They found both bridges blown and determined that Ceprano was probably unoccupied. Wood tried radioing a report to Clark, but an intervening ridgeline blocked the transmission. Leaving the four other ranks near the river's edge, the two officers returned on foot to report. While they were gone, the four soldiers intercepted a German truck and killed the driver. Apparently deciding the shots that had killed the driver betrayed their presence in no man's land, the four men got in the truck and hightailed it north on Highway 6 in an attempt to reach the advancing Eighth Army lines. Promptly meeting a German-manned roadblock, they were taken prisoner. Two escaped captivity six days later.

By first light on May 27, 'D' Company was on its objective — a low rise overlooking Ceprano from 500 yards back of the Liri River. A narrow gravel track cut along the base of the ridge. This road, extending in front of the Melfa River and paralleling the Liri River's eastern bank to Ceprano, was designated Highway 82. It crossed the Liri just north of town to intersect Highway 6.[21]

The Liri River followed a tightly snaking path out of the northern mountains for about four miles before passing Ceprano. Another ancient Roman town, Ceprano was built on a narrow height of land protected on three fronts by a bend in the river. Lieutenant Wood's reconnaissance had determined that here the river was about a hundred feet wide and ran swift and deep. With all bridge crossings destroyed, Snow decided to cross the infantry in boats. Once his regiments secured Ceprano, he would raft over antitank guns, mortars, and Vickers medium machine guns to consolidate the Canadian hold. During the night, engineers would throw a Bailey bridge over the river to get tanks over.[22]

At 0600 hours, Snow held an Orders Group at the Perth Regiment's headquarters. The Perths were to put two companies more than 1,000 yards downstream from the town. Once these companies established a strong bridgehead, the remaining Perth companies were to occupy Ceprano. The Cape Breton Highlanders would then cross the river and come up beside the Perths to cut the lateral road running from Ceprano south to Ceprano Station.[23] Snow was uncertain about the whereabouts of his Irish Regiment and fearful of hitting them with friendly fire. Accordingly, he advised 8th New Brunswick Hussars commander Lieutenant Colonel George Robinson that Irish patrols were across the river — probably inside Ceprano. Robinson's squadrons were "not to fire upon the town under any circumstances and not to fire on anything until it had fired upon the tanks."[24]

At 0730 hours, the Hussars' 'B' Squadron with the Perths' 'B' Company aboard rolled toward the Liri River. Once 'B' Company commander Major Harold Snelgrove reported his men secure in the woods bordering the river and beginning the crossing, 'D' Company would follow on foot. As the tanks closed on the river, the Germans started mortaring. The infantry scuttled for cover. Most of the fire originated from positions on the Canadians' badly exposed right flank. The Perths pressed on through flying shrapnel and explosive blasts to the river's edge. Snelgrove had been told that trucks carrying the assault boats would meet his company at the river, but soon learned the trucks were delayed.

An initial order that Snelgrove's men should swim the river was rescinded when the major reported that the current was too swift and the water too deep for wading. The flurry of German mortar fire had petered out by this time and the Hussars, with nothing to do but sit in their tanks because of the standing order not to engage targets across the river, received permission from Major Howard Keirstead to stretch their legs. They stood around smoking and chatting, some even sitting down and brewing tea. One tanker noticed that the Perths were hastily digging slit trenches. A warning light went off in his head just as a stonk of German artillery rained down on the knots of tankers. For forty-five minutes the shelling continued, so heavily that the men were unable to seek refuge in their tanks. When the fire lifted, five Hussars were dead and eight wounded. Among those killed were Keirstead's gunner and radio operator.[25] Keirstead moved his squadron away from the river to a sheltered rise that provided a spectacular view of Ceprano and beyond the town for about 3,000 yards. Still shaken by the loss of his men, the major watched help-lessly as German vehicles streamed west out of Ceprano on Highway 6 while his orders prevented his firing on them.

At 0950 hours, an Irish patrol approached his tanks. They said that no Irish troops had crossed the river, no Canadians were in Ceprano, and they had no idea whether Germans occupied the town. Soon Keirstead noticed a half-track just west of Ceprano painted with the Red Cross symbol. Accompanying the vehicle was a file of infantry. Knowing it was impossible for there to be any Canadian vehicles across the river, the major sought permission to fire on the infantry. Leaving the vehicle unscathed would still honour the Geneva Convention rules. Permission was refused.[26]

◆ ◆ ◆

Although their reasons were different, both Hussars and Perths spent a wasted and frustrating early morning. While the Perths' 'B' Company waited for the promised boats, 'D' Company sat in the open meadow it had occupied the previous evening, sweating under a hot sun. Scislowski had no idea why the company had not moved. He easily imagined the Germans across the river frantically improving posi-tions while everyone sat on their hands.

With growing curiosity, Scislowski watched a Lynx scout car roar up the road toward the regiment's position in a cloud of dust. Soon he recognized one of its passengers as Major General Bert Hoffmeister. Pulling up forty feet from Scislowski's slit trench, Hoffmeister started scanning the terrain around Ceprano through his field glasses. Scislowski was certain the divisional commander had come up to "the sharp end to see what the hell the bloody hold up was." He wished, however, the officer would leave before his scout car drew fire from the German artillery that undoubtedly had the valley bottom under observation from the many surrounding hills. Sure enough, a few minutes later mortar rounds howled down. "The first salvo dropped short of the scout car, close enough though, to give even the bravest a good scare. But damn it, Hoffmeister didn't so much as blink an eye — just stood there with those big glasses scanning the terrain ahead." Hunkering in his hole, Scislowski asked nobody in particular, "Why doesn't the son of a bitch get the hell outta here before he gets us all killed?"[27] No sooner was the question uttered than the scout car wheeled about and sped off.

Scislowski imagined flying orders. The Perths' commander would be blasted for not getting his men moving, Snow would get a rocket for being so slow. This was pretty much the case. Within half an hour of Hoffmeister's visit to the front, boats were being manhandled from the trucks to the shoreline and 'B' Company started paddling across by platoons. Mortar fire was heavy throughout the crossing and several boats were hit. Others capsized in the fast-running current, but the men tossed into the water managed to reach the other side safely despite the weight of their equipment.

The crossing effort was well under way when 'D' Company reached the river. A few minutes later, the trucks bearing the rest of the boats arrived. These proved so riddled with shrapnel that only one was serviceable. The crossing effort slowed dramatically as an entire regiment waited its turn to cross in the tiny vessel.[28]

'B' Company was finally across by mid-morning and Snelgrove led his men into the town. Because Ceprano was a major junction for Highway 6, it had been subjected to much artillery and aerial bombardment. Most buildings were badly damaged or entirely destroyed. Rubble from collapsed walls and roofs choked the streets. Shell and bomb craters added to the overall destruction. Snelgrove's men were amazed to meet only sporadic small-arms fire from no more than a rearguard screening force attempting to delay the Canadian advance. The Perths quickly cleared the town. By 1400 hours, the entire Perth Regiment was across the Liri River. 'B' Company was on the right, to the west of Ceprano, and 'D' Company was on the left. 'C' Company, commanded by Major T.H. White, took position immediately behind.

The three companies were being heavily shelled and raked by heavy machine-gun fire from a ridge to the west designated as Point 119. White was ordered to take the ridge. His company was to be supported by a section of 'D' Company moving forward on the right. As the 'D' Company section closed on a large villa, machine guns fired out of windows and doorways. White directed two sections from No. 13 Platoon to come up on the flank and support the 'D' Company element. Despite heavy opposition, the combined force managed to press up close to the house, killing several of the defending Panzer Grenadiers and taking some prisoners along the way.

German fire lulled. A moment later, two Panzer Grenadiers appeared in the main doorway. Although one was waving a white flag, both men were fully armed. A soldier shouted, "Are you surrendering?" The answer was a burst of fire from their guns, followed by the men ducking back inside. The firefight resumed.[29]

Finally, with dusk falling and the sound of heavy vehicles approaching, White retreated because he had no weapons with which to meet an armoured attack. Brigadier Snow advised White that no further attempt to secure the ridge should be made until the Cape Breton Highlanders crossed the river and could protect the regiment's left flank from counterattack.[30]

◆ ◆ ◆

While the Perths had been advancing, the Cape Breton Highlanders spent the day waiting for Lieutenant Colonel Jim Weir to issue orders. At 1100 hours at an Orders Group, he outlined the regiment's river crossing. The rifle companies would cross in single file, followed by regimental headquarters and then the support platoons. Everyone hunkered in slit trenches awaiting orders. And there they waited, occasionally being potted at by German artillery and mortars that caused several casualties.

At 1615 hours, the regiment still waited, with no indication of haste on Weir's part despite his having been ordered by Snow in the mid-morning to get under way as soon as possible. Although also given to a leisurely pace, this was finally too much for Snow. He called Weir to brigade headquarters and "granted" him a seventy-two-hour rest.[31] Major Boyd Somerville assumed command in his absence and quickly got the regiment marching. By now, the little boat used by the Perths was no longer serviceable. Instead, there was a raft that could carry one platoon at a time.

The raft had been built by pioneers of the 4th Canadian Anti-tank Regiment's 49th Anti-tank Battery for ferrying their guns across the Liri River. At first, the rafting operation was harassed by a German machine-gun position and two snipers dug in on the opposite shore. After four guns had been floated across, with each crossing drawing fire, Acting Sergeant Hamish Munro of 'F' Troop decided to clear off the problem. Commandeering a 6-pounder antitank gun from the Perth Regiment, Munro brought the gun to bear and knocked the machine gun out of action — earning a Military Medal. By 1800 hours, the antitankers had seven 17-pounder guns across the Liri River and turned the raft over to the Highlanders.[32]

The Highlanders started crossing at 1910. 'B' Company was over by 2055 hours. Three hours later, all the regiment's rifle companies were west of the Liri River and digging in on the Perths' left flank.[33] Perths commander Lieutenant Colonel Lind had originally been under orders from Snow to continue the attack against Point 119 once the Highlanders were in position. However, now that it was dark, he asked Snow for permission to wait for daylight. The men, he said, had gone with virtually no sleep for forty-eight hours and also had been subsisting on nothing but hard rations and tea. Snow "entirely agreed and issued orders for the further advance at first light."[34]

◆ ◆ ◆

During their two-day advance from the Melfa River to Ceprano, the Canadians had been engaging the 26th Panzer Division, commanded by Generalleutnant Smilo, Baron von Lüttwitz. Having taken a heavy battering from the French corps on the Canadian left, this division was too depleted to effectively meet 11 CIB's offensive. The immediate Ceprano area contained only the 150-man-strong 26th Panzer Battalion and a similarly weakened battalion of the 1027th Panzer Grenadier Regiment. Still trying to stem the advancing French tide, von Lüttwitz panicked when the Perth Regiment fought its way into Ceprano. His report to Tenth Army commander Generaloberst Heinrich von Vietinghoff was despairing. "Numerous tanks in assembly positions on the east bank of the Liri indicate that after dark, and when the bridges are ready, the enemy will cross the river with the intention of carrying out an armoured breakthrough along the Via Casilina [Highway 6] on 28 May."[35]

Lacking sufficient armour to block a breakthrough, von Lüttwitz asked for and received permission from von Vietinghoff to withdraw five miles to positions west of Pofi, where the terrain was better suited to defence. At dawn, rearguard units of 26th Panzer Division anxiously awaited the approaching armoured onslaught and were confused when no tanks appeared. Instead, the Perths and Cape Breton Highlanders plodded off at first light for Point 119, finding the Germans had retreated from this objective during the night. Moving forward only a few hundred yards beyond Point 119, the Perth Regiment established a defensive strongpoint straddling Highway 6 northwest of Ceprano. The Highlanders formed up on the Perths' left flank. Lacking any armoured support, the two regiments dug in.[36]

Although the two regiments were on the objective assigned by Hoffmeister for the outer limit of the brigade's May 28 advance, the major general was angered by the attack's execution. He called Snow "to say that he was most displeased that Point 119 feature had not been captured the night before and that there was no excuse whatever for not capturing it." The much-hectored Snow did not defend his actions and continued consolidating his brigade's grip around Ceprano.[37]

The Germans, seeing the infantry pause and not knowing what delayed the expected armoured advance, assumed the many antitank mines they had left in their wake were exacting a hefty toll on the Canadian tankers. It was not mines, however, that stalled the 5th Canadian Armoured Brigade's regiments. What kept them was the lack of a bridge over the Liri River.[38]

Confused staff work at all levels of 5th Canadian Armoured Division's upper command had significantly delayed construction of the bridge. Although Snow had planned to use a Bailey bridge to transfer his transportation and support vehicles across the Liri River, he had neglected to advise the acting commander of 10th Field Squadron, Royal Canadian Engineers — the sapper unit assigned to support his brigade — of his May 27 attack. This meant it was well into the day before the engineers knew that they should build a bridge. The lack of engineers anywhere near the Liri River had apparently been noted by Hoffmeister during his personal reconnaissance, for he alerted the divisional engineering commander, Lieutenant Colonel Jack Christian, of the situation about midday. Christian immediately went to the river and organized four reconnaissance parties. One, led by Lieutenant G.L. Williamson of 1st

Field Squadron, found a suitable site near where the Perths had made their one-boat crossing, which had previously been used by the Germans as a ferry crossing. The river here was 120 feet wide, with 20-foot banks that were nearly vertical on both sides. Bridging such a span required a bridge that was stronger than normal and close to the maximum span possible. After Williamson's crossing point was approved for use, the lieutenant returned to the river to make more detailed measurements. Taken prisoner by a German patrol while doing measurements on the other side, the lieutenant never returned from his mission. This meant another delay.

First Field Squadron commander Major R.B. Cameron started organizing his bridging team, but was delayed by mixed orders that had the job on, then off, then back on again "as an insurance." What bridge 5 CAD intended to use in its place was never clear to the engineers. Only one route was open to the Liri River's western bank and that was a looping one that ran south of the Isoletta Reservoir and then followed narrow tracks to a crossing of the Sacco River on the Ceprano Station–Ceprano lateral road south of the station. This route was designated for 1st Canadian Infantry Division use and the two bridges required there had just been completed.

Finally, work began at 2330 hours with completion scheduled for 0900 on May 28. The site was registered by the enemy and subjected to random artillery and mortar fire. This was typical, for German engineers could determine crossing sites and rate their likely priority for suitability as well as any other sappers. Construction appeared to proceed smoothly, however, and by morning the bridge was almost complete. Then came trouble. "Perhaps," the engineering corps's historian later wrote, "fatigue, over-eagerness to make good time, and inexperience on operations all contributed to a degree of carelessness." Whatever the reasons, "as the bridge was pushed across the gap, the launching nose hit the far bank and buckled." The entire bridge came apart and sank into the river. A fresh troop from 10th Squadron was rushed to the site and began the job over. The second bridge was finally completed at 1730 hours.[39] Christian wrote after the event: "This delay caused a change in the Army plan, and has given us a bit of a black eye."[40]

Indeed, the delay and confusion that resulted in the slow start of construction had stalled the entire Eighth Army advance. No bridges existed north of Ceprano for XIII Corps to cross the Liri River. A vast traffic jam built up along Highway 6 and all paralleling roads and tracks as 5 CAD and the 78th British Infantry Division lined up to await the bridge's completion. Until the bridge was finished, the British were unable to advance to the right of the 11 CIB's flank and provide the much sought-after, and so rarely found, protection this division was supposed to have provided for the Canadian advance up the entire Liri Valley.[41]

Finally, I Canadian Corps commander Lieutenant General Tommy Burns realized that the tankers of 5 CAB could get to Ceprano via the bridges recently completed in the 1st Canadian Infantry Division sector. "I was not quick enough to appreciate the point that while no tank crossing was available on the right, there was a crossing on the left. There had been a lack of reports on the situation on the front of the 5th Armoured Division. I should have gone up to see for myself how things were when the slowdown became apparent."[42]

The lack of reports on May 28 from 5 CAD to corps headquarters was not unique. Burns's general staff commander, Brigadier Nick McCarter, had been grousing in his diary for days about the ineffectual work being done by 5 CAD's headquarters staff. Hoffmeister, roving with his smaller tactical HQ group, had paid scant attention to the broader picture of logistics needed to keep an entire division of almost 20,000 men operating. He left those details to his staff and they were proving woefully incapable. On May 25, McCarter, well aware of the problem, wrote: "It is a hopeless task to try and get any information out of HQ 5 Canadian Division. They are behaving like complete amateurs in many ways. We have to badger them continually about sending back information and even that seldom produces results. If only they would be systematic it would not throw such a strain on them. 5 Div have also been bad about using other people's routes and not sticking reasonably close to own axis. The staff work in that Div has been lousy."[43]

As a result of the delayed communications, it was not until midafternoon that Burns directed Hoffmeister to use the left-flank bridges to get an armoured regiment across the Liri River. Brigadier Desmond Smith, commander of 5th Canadian Armoured Brigade, had been waiting with a strike force comprising the B.C. Dragoons, two companies of the Westminster motorized infantry regiment, and two batteries of self-propelled guns from 4th Canadian Anti-tank Regiment to drive through to Pofi. Now the Dragoons set off on a long trek to a new start position north of the Sacco River and west of Ceprano, arriving there finally at 2100 hours.[44]

When the first bridge collapsed, Snow resorted to rafting the entire Irish Regiment across the Liri River. Once the bridge was finally able to handle traffic, he won priority call on its use to shift the brigade's transport and other supporting elements over to Ceprano. As the first vehicles started up the road past the bridge toward Ceprano, antitank mines began exploding. The Irish Regiment also found themselves afoul of anti-personnel mines as they walked out from the river crossing point.[45] Four Irish Regiment soldiers were killed, the first losses the regiment had experienced from mines.[46]

Once Snow had his brigade firmly ensconced on the western bank of the Liri, he was pleased to receive a call from Hoffmeister to the effect that 11 CIB would "probably remain in present position for about thirty-six hours before moving on." Snow conveyed the happy news to his regimental commanders, who passed it down the line. The expectation was that 5 CAB would move through the infantry brigade and carry the advance 1,000 yards beyond Pofi without need of 11 CIB's support.

24

PUSH ON

Wearing his tunic bearing major's crowns, David Kinloch had arrived at the forming-up point south of Ceprano well ahead of the British Columbia Dragoon squadrons. He and the other squadron commanders had not much liked the look of the ground they were to cross in the morning. This they made clear at an Orders Group called by Lieutenant Colonel Fred Vokes at 2000 hours on May 28. Kinloch had another more immediate worry — while all the other tank squadrons had arrived, his 'B' Squadron was still on the road, apparently lost.[1]

Vokes's briefing confirmed their fears. The ground from Ceprano to Pofi was extremely close and heavily vegetated. Narrow streams running through steeply banked gullies, irrigation ditches, sunken roads, countless twisting tracks and trails, and repeated ridge-backed hills that cut across at right angles to the line of advance rendered the terrain virtually impassable for tanks. Vokes had accordingly been directed by 5th Canadian Armoured Brigade commander Brigadier Desmond Smith to break the armoured regiment into two columns that could "take advantage of any possible route forward which might be found." Tanks operating alone in such country would invite disaster, so each column was to be supported by a Westminster Regiment company. A battery of 4th Anti-tank Regiment's self-propelled guns would accompany the columns.[2]

Kinloch's squadron would lead the right column with the Westminsters' 'C' Company in support. This lead element would be followed by 'A' and 'B' Troops of the 4th Anti-tank Regiment's 98th Battery, Vokes's regimental headquarters troop, 'A' Squadron, and two bridging tanks to provide crossings as needed. 'C' Squadron, with 'B' Company of the Westminsters and the 98th Battery's 'C' Troop, would comprise the left column.[3] The objective was a north-south ridge midway between Pofi and Arnara. Pofi, a typical Italian hilltop village, was to be secured en route.[4] Major Ian Douglas, commander of the Westminsters' 'C' Company, expressed concern that the White scout cars might be unable to keep up with the tanks and even prove incapable of negotiating the terrain at all. "What happens then?" he asked.

"You get off and bloody walk!" Vokes snapped.[5] It was imperative that the infantry keep up with the tanks, he said, while the tanks must not outpace the infantry.[6]

Meeting over, Kinloch returned to the empty space where his tanks were supposed to harbour. A section from the reconnaissance troop was out searching the main roads for the missing tanks, but had so far been unsuccessful. Finally, in the early morning hours, the squadron rumbled in. Kinloch's second-in-command, Captain Bill Malkin, described a nightmarish journey along roads choked with other traffic that finally brought the squadron to a checkpoint manned by British provost officers. The provost officer, confusing them with a retiring British division, had pointed them south instead of north to the reservoir. Soon intermingled with British trucks, Jeeps, and tanks, Malkin realized the mistake, but it had taken hours to unsnarl his tanks from the column and turn them in the right direction. He had been very happy to encounter the reconnaissance Honeys and follow them into the regiment's tank harbour. With the eastern skyline already brightening, Kinloch briefed his weary tankers.

Kinloch was pleased with his team, particularly since Captain Barney Finestone had just rejoined the regiment and been posted to his squadron to serve as battle captain. This was a position of pivotal importance to armoured regiments. The battle captain's chief task was to monitor the regiment's radio communications, maintaining a continuous link between the squadron commander, up forward with the squadron's fighting troops, and the regimental commander. It was a tough job at the best of times and in the close Italian terrain, where the always troublesome radio sets were prone to interference, the job was even more complicated. Then there was the sheer patience a B.C. Dragoon battle captain had to show when being constantly hectored by Vokes with orders or demands for information.[7]

Dawn of May 29 heralded another dry, sweltering day. The two columns advanced at 0500 hours and immediately encountered delays caused by the terrain and presence of antitank and antipersonnel mines dug into the tracks or scattered across many of the small fields. After about a mile, Kinloch's squadron came to the Fornelli River, a tributary of the Sacco River. The bridge had been blown and a delay ensued while one of the bridging tanks was brought up. It was 0620 hours before the column lurched off again.[8]

Both columns were subjected to sporadic shelling. The Sherman used by the B.C. Dragoons' regimental HQ troop commander, Lieutenant Gordon Lyle Mortenson, was damaged by an exploding shell. Taking command of another Sherman, Mortenson advanced only fifty yards before a mine tore off its track. Unable to raise the regiment's second-in-command, Major Ira Secord, on the radio, Mortenson walked over to the major's tank. Standing in front of the Sherman, he waved his arms and shouted to try to catch Secord's eye. Talking on his radio, Secord failed to see the officer and ordered his driver to advance. The tank ground forward, bashed into Mortenson and drove right over him. Fortunately, he fell between the tracks. Although shaken, he was unhurt.[9]

The right-hand column, stretched out in single file, straggled onward as the lead troop paused to clear one obstacle after another. The Westminsters, as predicted by Major Douglas, were having a terrifically hard time keeping up with the tanks. Scout cars were becoming mired in ditches, high-centred on stumps, logs, and rocks, and even tipping over into gullies when chunks of the roads fell away. Some sections were left to follow on foot and others found alternative routes that the cars could negotiate, while most continued to doggedly follow Kinloch's tanks.

B.C. Dragoons' 'C' Squadron on the left flank made only slightly better progress, while facing much the same terrain and the presence of mines and other obstacles barring paths. Ahead of the main column, Honeys from the reconnaissance troop and Bren carriers from the Westminsters' scout platoon raced up and down the many tracks to find the best forward route. The scouts also probed for pockets of German resistance, but so far none had been located. It appeared the Germans had withdrawn from east of Pofi. Finally, the Westminsters' 'B' Company got permission to advance ahead of the tanks and test the German defence of the town. The infantry drove off in their White scout cars, leaving the tanks behind.[10]

At 0840 hours, the right-hand column reached the Meringo River, another Sacco tributary. Typically, the bridge had been destroyed. Where the bridge had been, the river was too wide and the banks too steep for the remaining bridging tank to deploy.[11] Kinloch halted the column at the river's edge while the reconnaissance troop searched for a crossing point. Stuck back in the column, Vokes was unable to see the extent of the problem. He kept carping at Kinloch via Captain Finestone. Whether short or long, his messages were all of a type. "Push on!" or "Why the hell are you not pushing on?" Patient detailing of the situation brought only temporary silence from the rear. Fifteen minutes or so later, it was "Push on!" or "Why the hell are you not pushing on?" all over again.

Kinloch wanted to push on. The last thing he wanted was to have his squadron milling about for hours on the grassy shoreline of Meringo River under sporadic German shelling and mortaring. But there was no damn crossing. Finally, at 1515 hours, the reconnaissance troop discovered a crossing point that would suffice and the column moved. Once there, the tankers kept their engines running. This, combined with the heavy radio traffic plugging the radio net and the static that garbled transmissions, made it difficult for Kinloch to send or receive communications. Despite having his headphones on to monitor the radio, the major became aware of a commotion near the side of his tank. Looking down, he saw Finestone lying on a stretcher and being loaded onto a Jeep ambulance. Unable to raise Kinloch on the radio, he had run over to the major's tank to pass on Vokes's latest urgent message personally. Just as he reached Kinloch's tank, an exploding shell had riddled his back with shrapnel. Kinloch thought the message, never to be delivered, had probably instructed him to "Push on as soon as the bridge is in place." Now his battle captain was badly wounded, probably for no good reason.[12]

♦ ♦ ♦

Meanwhile, the Westminsters in 'B' Company had reached the outskirts of Pofi by 0900 hours. The scout platoon, riding Bren carriers, was just coming up to the railroad station at the bottom of the town's hill when several machine guns fired in their direction. When the scouts veered off the railroad tracks they were following, one Bren carrier hit a mine. Despite the fact that the Westminsters routinely reinforced the carrier floors with heavy bags of sand to provide protection from exploding mines, the explosion killed Sergeant Tony Finlayson and wounded two of his men.[13]

The scouts quickly knocked out the machine guns, which had been manned by fifteen Germans, apparently Pofi's entire defence. As the platoon went up the hill road into the town centre, an urgent message ordered it to pull back because the town was about to be shelled. Agreeing with his scout commander that the Germans had abandoned Pofi, the commander of 'B' Company tried to get the artillery fire mission on Pofi cancelled. There seemed little to be gained by subjecting the town to yet another pounding. The major's attempts to stop the shelling were futile, however. Once the concentration lifted, the major again pushed his company toward the town. As the platoons entered the streets and moved past the mostly wrecked buildings, another urgent warning to pull back was received. This time a cab rank of American dive-bombers was en route. Once again the major tried to stop the bombing mission, but was "informed it was impossible." He led his men back to a position well outside the town. The American Thunderbolt dive-bombers struck at 1420 hours. When the dive-bombers finally broke off their pointless attack, 'B' Company received orders to forget about Pofi and head directly for the ridgeline objective beyond.[14] The town itself would be secured by 11th Canadian Infantry Brigade, which was coming up behind the armoured brigade to take over the advance.

Having belatedly recognized that the ground from Ceprano through Pofi to Frosinone was unsuitable for tank operations, Major General Bert Hoffmeister had decided that his infantry brigade should again spearhead 5th Canadian Armoured Division's advance. This decision dovetailed with one made the previous day by Lieutenant General Tommy Burns. He had issued orders for 1st Canadian Infantry Division to gradually take over the advance from 5 CAD. To prevent the pursuit's being broken off by a major reorganization, the hand-off would be undertaken one brigade at a time. May 30 was to be the final day that 5 CAD led the advance.[15]

The dive-bombing raid against Pofi proved to some Canadians that air support was a mixed blessing. Not only did the bombers attack an undefended town but some flew wildly off course and bombed the leading troop of B.C. Dragoons' 'C' Squadron. Sergeant Butch Smitheram, yet to be formally transferred from Major Jack Turnley's 'C' Squadron to regimental headquarters after his outburst over the Melfa battle, was shocked to see several Thunderbolts flashing down toward the Shermans. Fortunately, the bombing was erratic. Only one bomb came close, striking the road with a deafening explosion right in front of one Sherman. The tank's driver slammed the Sherman into reverse, going back so fast that he lost control and overturned the machine into a ditch. One crewman was trapped underneath the tank. Once the Thunderbolts broke off, the merely bruised trooper was dug out.[16]

'C' Squadron moved slowly over the rough ground, bypassing Pofi and heading toward its ridgeline objective. Breakdowns, stuck tanks, and those knocked out by mines reduced the squadron to only four tanks by the time it wound up a narrow road onto the objective.[17] As they came up on the hill, a machine gun dug into a root cellar opened up. Smitheram raked the cellar with his machine gun. The Germans fired back, then abandoned their gun and made a break for it. A burst from Smitheram's gun dropped one of the four. The others ran back and scooped him up. Then they fled. Impressed by their bravery in returning for their fallen comrade, Smitheram's tank crew let them go.[18]

◆ ◆ ◆

'B' Squadron, meanwhile, struggled on — grateful that the Germans offered only some shelling by way of resistance. Kinloch found the battle with the terrain hard enough. The heat was terrible and the men sweltered inside the Shermans, which were forever becoming stuck and having to be dragged out of mud or holes by other tanks.

Sometimes the men had to root out stumps or rocks that managed to hang them up. And all the time Vokes harangued Kinloch with his battle cry of "Push on. Push on." With Finestone wounded, Captain Bill Malkin was serving as the squadron battle captain and Kinloch could tell that the constant berating was starting to grind on the man's nerves.

Kinloch finally called a halt so that he could do a wireless check and determine the location of all his tanks. Some had thrown tracks and been abandoned along the trail. He paused in the grassy backyard of a small farmhouse. Once the check was over, Kinloch walked over to the farm's well and drew up a bucket "of wonderful, fresh cool water."

Back aboard the tank, the major decided that perhaps his leading troop commander had been overcautious in his pace. Kinloch ordered him to pull off the road and took over the lead with his squadron headquarters tanks. Perhaps if he personally led the advance, he could keep Vokes happy.

As the sun dropped toward the horizon, 'B' Squadron broke out into relatively open country to the northwest of Pofi, with a level road bordering the left-hand edge of a narrow valley. Ahead, Kinloch thought he saw the objective. The artillery regiments had established designated reference points for potential strongpoints of resistance, as well as the various objectives. Forward Observation Officer Captain Jack Handley was riding in a tank immediately behind Kinloch. With little to do for want of targets, Handley had been helping Kinloch by serving as his map navigator. Now, Kinloch asked him to have an air-burst dropped on the objective coordinates. The shell went off right where it was supposed to, confirming his location.

Normally, when faced with such open ground as the squadron was poised to enter, Kinloch would have brought up infantry to cover his flanks and gone ahead with two tank troops deployed in arrowhead formations. Instead, still responding to the endless "Push on, push on" pressure created by Vokes, Kinloch led his tanks into the open, "like a bunch of ducks in a shooting gallery."

Thinking he should report to Vokes, he called back on the radio for Handley to give him a map reference for his current position. Receiving no response, Kinloch looked over his shoulder and saw a headless body sitting in the turret where Handley should have been. Suddenly, a shell exploded fifty yards ahead of Kinloch's tank, followed by another fifty yards behind. "Driver advance, hard left!" he yelled. The tank slewed sideways into a large pit and became stuck. Over the radio, someone shouted, "Fire smoke!" Smoke shells rained around Kinloch's Sherman, screening it from view of the German gunners. Kinloch ordered his crew to bail out. Then, after collecting his mapboard, code ciphers, orders, and gear, he started easing out of the turret. Just as he swung clear of it, Kinloch looked back inside and saw a Browning .50-calibre ammunition box fall and strike the solenoid switch that fired the main gun. A horrendous blast and concussion pounded him as the gun fired an antipersonnel round into the ground nearby. Nearly deafened, Kinloch did not want to think what would have happened had the round been high explosive.

During the confusion, the scout platoon of the Westminsters' 'C' Company had come up in its Bren carriers. Kinloch shifted to his second-in-command's tank and sent No. 1 Troop forward with the Bren carriers, following normal tactics. He came behind with the remnants of squadron headquarters, reaching the objective at 1915 hours. One lone German, who had been left behind, defended the position. Someone shot him.[19]

Kinloch was saddened to learn that a sniper had killed Lieutenant Ron Jewell of the reconnaissance troop at the farm where Kinloch had taken his refreshing drink from the well. The officer had gone into the farmhouse to check it and been shot in the back. When his driver, Trooper A.V. Harris, came over to investigate the shot, he too had been killed by a burst of machine-gun fire.[20]

Only five 'B' Squadron tanks reached the objective; 'C' Squadron had arrived with just four. Vokes's regimental headquarters had also lost three tanks. Only 'A' Squadron, which had been following in reserve, arrived intact. Five 'B' Squadron tanks had been lost to enemy fire. The rest of the tanks "were bogged down, stuck on banks, rocks, tree stumps."[21]

The Westminsters had fared no better. At the end of the day, wrote the regiment's war diarist, "bits and pieces of the regiment were all over the country side, numerous vehicles being suspended over cliffs or jammed in sunken roads. . . . The day certainly brought out the point, the Higher Command cannot expect the motor battalion to cover the same ground as the tanks equipped as we now are without sustaining heavy vehicle casualties."[22]

◆ ◆ ◆

At 1030 hours on May 29, Brigadier Snow had ordered the Perth Regiment to saddle up and occupy Pofi. The regiment was standing around ready to move two hours later, when Hoffmeister contacted Snow and made the operation a brigade-strong show. Since the Perths were already organized, Snow decided they would lead the march from Ceprano and take up a final position to the right of Pofi. The Cape Breton Highlanders would occupy Pofi itself, while the Irish Regiment of Canada secured the ground south of the town.

Although transport was available for the move out of Ceprano, Highway 6 was jammed with British transport from the 78th Division. The Perths, therefore, trudged off on foot.[23] After marching about a mile, however, the regiment received orders to hold up and wait for its transport, which was being shunted into the bridge traffic. Private Stan Scislowski and his mates in 'D' Company's No. 18 Platoon gathered tomatoes and potatoes from a nearby garden and took the opportunity to whip up a stew. Using a mortar ammunition box for a pot, they mixed the fresh contents together with compo-ration cans of bully beef, meat and vegetables, and steak and kidney pie. The trucks rolled up just as the men finished their feast. The Perths climbed aboard the Dodge three-ton trucks and rolled toward Pofi.[24]

Eleven CIB's advance went smoothly enough for the Perths and the Highlanders, for there were trucks to transport them. The Irish Regiment, however, had recently had its transport recalled by divisional headquarters to help with an artillery move. The trucks could neither be found nor replaced, so the Irish shouldered their packs and hurriedly marched forward.[25]

Arriving in front of Pofi at 1600 hours, the Perths disembarked and prepared to clear the town. 'D' Company drew the duty and two platoons swept through it easily. A few snipers were quickly killed, driven off, or taken prisoner. The Perths pressed on toward their objective 1,000 yards northwest of the town and reached it shortly before 1800 hours. They were just settling in when orders arrived that they were to carry on in the morning to capture Arnara.[26]

The new plan was for the Perth Regiment and the Cape Breton Highlanders to advance two miles beyond Pofi to secure the high ground in front of Arnara. The 5th Canadian Armoured Brigade would jump off from the position held by the B.C. Dragoons and pass by Arnara to capture three high points respectively code-named "Tom," "Dick," and "Harry." The three 11 CIB regiments were then to move up and consolidate the Canadian hold on these features, which would serve as start-line points for 2nd Canadian Infantry Brigade of 1st Canadian Infantry Division, which would take over the advance.[27]

Back at brigade headquarters, Hoffmeister and Snow were having another argument. Snow did not think his regiments could reach their start positions for the move by first light — the time dictated by Hoffmeister for their jumping off. To do so would also mean his men would have to proceed without opportunity for either rest or food. Hoffmeister told Snow "that was ridiculous and of course they'd be in position long before first light."

Snow raced to Pofi, where he gave the regimental commanders their new instructions.[28] They were to be ready to move for Tom, Dick, and Harry at 0500 hours on May 30. The Perth Regiment proved Snow overly pessimistic, arriving at its start point for the move on Arnara at midnight. Leaving one company behind in Pofi, the Cape Breton Highlanders concluded their move by 0130 hours, as did the foot-weary Irish Regiment. The day's advance for 11 CIB had been remarkably easy, with only two Perths wounded and no casualties in the other regiments.[29]

From his position on the hill looking out on Arnara, Scislowski could see the town on a height of land only slightly lower than the one he currently occupied. A narrow valley lay between the two hills. Like all the country west of Ceprano, this valley was choked with vegetation and terrain obstacles. As Scislowski stretched out to grab a few hours' sleep, he hoped "the advance on the town would be as bloodless an action as that of Pofi."

It proved even better. At 0430 hours, 'C' Company slipped into the town through the darkness and found it entirely evacuated except for one German, who was quickly captured. By 0900 hours, the rest of the regiment had crossed the valley and was spread out around Arnara. When 'D' Company passed through, Scislowski walked "straight into the arms of a deliriously happy crowd of Arnara's citizens. . . . A most exhilarating feeling it was too, to look on these people lavishing gratitude and adulation as we marched by." The private felt a hero as the reception provided "an incalculable lift to the human spirit. Arnara was ours, without a shot. What a joy! What relief that it had been so easy!"[30] For the Perth Regiment, the Battle of the Liri Valley was over. The regiment proceeded to enjoy what was essentially a furlough in Arnara.

◆ ◆ ◆

For other regiments of I Canadian Corps, the fighting was not yet done. But everyone recognized that the campaign for Rome was winding down. There was no doubt that the Germans were on the run; the grand design of forming a last-ditch defensive bastion on the Caesar Line had been no more than wild fancy in the face of the Allied advance. The juggernaut of a U.S. Fifth Army reunited after VI Corps's breakout from the Anzio beachhead and Eighth Army's gathering strength, as the ever sluggish XIII Corps finally drew up alongside I Canadian Corps, overwhelmed the Germans. Demolished in the May 11–25 Liri Valley fighting, there was nothing Tenth Army could put in the way of Eighth Army's advance that would do more than delay the inevitable end.

Delay, however, was what mattered. Tenth Army fought a desperate rearguard action to enable itself and Fourteenth Army to extricate divisions from a trap that could end in destruction of the German forces in Italy. In this action, they had an unexpected ally — General Mark Clark of U.S. Fifth Army. General Harold Alexander's Operation Diadem had not been mounted just to liberate Rome. He had sought to destroy Generalfeldmarschall Albert Kesselring's armies in Italy. Clark had always had his eyes set more on being first into Rome than on decisively finishing off the Germans. Early on May 30, following a refusal from Alexander to allow Fifth Army to sideslip the French corps — currently driving westward through the Lepini Mountains — north of Highway 6 to free up space for a general American drive toward Rome, Clark decided he was in a race with the British. The American general's orders had been to drive hard to the southern flank of the Alban Hills and Valmontone, creating a roadblock on Highway 6 that could check the retreat by Tenth Army and some divisions of Fourteenth Army on the only available modern road.[31] Instead, as early as May 25, Clark decided to shift the axis of his advance so that VI Corps marched south of the Alban

Hills directly toward Rome. Hence a gap was created through which the retreating Germans were allowed to escape, badly depleted but able — as they had proven themselves so capable in the past — to rebuild their divisions and fight again.[32]

In a May 30 diary entry, Clark justified his decision: "Eighth Army had done little fighting." He determined to squeeze the Corps Expéditionnaire Français eastward to create a situation by which this corps "by right of eminent domain will 'slop over' into Eighth Army area, usurp Route 6, and put him [Marshal Alphonse-Pierre Juin] on my north headed for Rome."[33]

Alexander well understood Clark's scheme, but was powerless to stop his American subordinate. The British High Commissioner for Italy, Harold Macmillan, saw Alexander hours after Clark's intentions had become obvious. He noted that Alexander's eye was twitching as it did before battle and he asked what was wrong. "What is right?" Alexander barked. He told Macmillan what Clark was doing. When the High Commissioner asked why Alexander did not insist that Clark conform to his orders, he shot back, "Why do you talk nonsense? How can I give orders?"[34]

The uneasy alliance between Americans and British in Italy was never more apparent or fractured. Both knew that the opening of a new front in Western Europe was imminent. Any day, Operation Overlord must overshadow events in Italy. Clark was determined to be the liberator of Rome before the first Allied soldiers splashed ashore on the beaches of France and he had precious few days to make it happen.

For his part, Eighth Army commander General Sir Oliver Leese was ambivalent about Rome and disinclined to compete with Clark for the prize. On May 30, he wrote his wife: "I hear that [Clark] stated . . . he would get to Rome in five days. I understand that they have everything prepared for a 5th Army Triumph with [Clark] as the Jeanne D'Arc of his era. Well, I can only hope he can do it. It will save a lot of trouble and lives — but if he can't, it will mean a big battle for us both — and then I shall race him to it."

Later, he added that Clark was "making desperate efforts to get Rome on his own. I only hope he will do so, and we can then go north on our own business — but I'm so afraid he'll bungle it like Cassino — and then we shall have to clear it up. I believe it would have been much better if he would wait for us to help — but he is now terrified that we might get to Rome first, which is the last thing we now want to do. I only hope it will not warp his military decisions."[35]

Clark's military decision-making was already badly warped by his obsession with Rome. Nothing the Canadians driving up the ever narrowing valley toward Rome could do would rescue the situation. They continued punching into the centre of the deliberately slow withdrawal by Tenth Army's veteran divisions, which still enjoyed the great tactical defensive advantage of rugged terrain. Even as the width of their front was increasingly encroached on from the right by XIII Corps and on the left by the intentional "slop" of the French Corps, so that room for manoeuvre was ever more restricted, the Canadians fought on.

◆ ◆ ◆

First light of May 30 found two regiments of the 5th Canadian Armoured Brigade moving toward Frosinone, a provincial capital and key junction point at which Highway 6 intersected with a north-south lateral highway, with links through the mountains to the Adriatic. A short distance into the mountains, this road intersected with Via Prenestina, an alternative route from the east to Rome. The capture of Frosinone would hinder German attempts to shunt some of the retreating army inland to take advantage of this line of retreat. Eighth Army's intention was to channel the retreating Germans onto Highway 6 and subsidiary roads in the hope that the Americans would still sever this route at Valmontone to trap and eliminate some enemy divisions.

The 8th New Brunswick Hussars attempted to dodge the choked terrain that had so hindered the B.C. Dragoon advance by following a road running from Pofi southwest to Ceccano and then looping back via a road from that town to Frosinone. The ground was riddled with streams. All the bridge and culvert crossings had been blown. Lieutenant Herb Snell's reconnaissance troop discovered that retrieved Teller antitank mines and Italian box mines could be used to blast down streambanks to create passable diversions.[36] At 0900 hours, they hit the Arnara River, halfway to Ceccano. This was too great a barrier for Snell's crude demolitions. A bridging tank was brought forward, but it was almost 1230 before the column was under way again.

Snell had been ordered to find a faster route north to Frosinone than would be possible if they had to go all the way into Ceccano, but he came up dry. The Hussars continued toward Ceccano until coming to a "point where many mines were found on the road and verges." At 1800 hours, the first Shermans started creeping over ground that the engineers and reconnaissance troops thought was now clear. Two tanks were damaged as mines exploded under their tracks. The Hussars withdrew to a defensible point of high ground and dug in for the night. On May 31, the regiment advanced only slightly farther before being ordered at 1030 hours to stand down. Events on the Canadian right flank had rendered the attempt to reach Frosinone by the long leftward march no longer necessary.[37]

♦ ♦ ♦

The Lord Strathcona's Horse had spent an equally frustrating morning on May 30 trying to take a more direct route past Arnara toward Frosinone. "At this time the situation was very vague," the war diarist recorded, "the CBH were understood to be in the vicinity, the GGHG on the high ground to our right but the situation on the left was completely obscure." German shells followed them. Finally, a Cape Breton patrol was encountered. They reported seeing enemy tanks in the area.[38] After wallowing across narrow streams and irrigation ditches, the Shermans rolled up onto a hogback ridge barely wider than the narrow road with almost sheer cliffs falling away on either flank. The Shermans were completely exposed to any lurking German tanks or antitank guns.

A sweaty, anxious advance followed, worsened when unidentified guns started firing on the column from a ridge 2,000 yards to the west. An 'A' Squadron tank was hit and burned. This left 'A' and 'C' squadrons blocked on the ridgeline, unable to creep around the burning tank or to push it off the road. The Strathconas' commander, Lieutenant Colonel Phillip Griffin, ordered the tanks in these squadrons to wheel about and fire on the German-held ridge with high explosives and smoke while the leading 'B' Squadron moved off the exposed ground and occupied a small, unmarked village. This fire seemed to quiet down the Germans, although some desultory shelling from that quarter continued throughout the day.

Griffin went ahead on foot to find out what was happening to his leading squadron and the reconnaissance troop. Along the way, he encountered the Cape Breton Highlanders acting commander, Major Boyd Somerville, using a church as an observation point. Somerville said that his infantry had been driven off the ridge earlier by the German shelling. The infantry officer had also observed German tanks at the crossroads where the road they were following met Highway 6. Commandeering one of the Honeys from the reconnaissance unit to use as a command vehicle, Griffin ordered Captain Jock Usher to get his 'B' Squadron up to the crossroads.

With the remaining Honeys in the reconnaissance troop leading the way, Usher's tanks lumbered up to where a huge crater had been blasted into the road on a tight curve at the bottom of a steep little hill. The Honeys had no trouble slipping past it, but the first Sherman got ditched in the hole. When others tried creeping off the road, they mired in holes and ditches.

Captain Edward Perkins, of Melfa River fame, took his Honeys up to the crossroads, which the Strathconas were now calling Torrice, after a small nearby village. He radioed that there were indeed German tanks around. Griffin told Perkins to send back some guides who could lead 'B' Squadron into good fighting positions from which to engage the German tanks. While the guides returned on foot, Perkins tangled with some enemy infantry and drove them off with .50-calibre Browning machine-gun fire. He then formed a defensive circle with the Honeys and dismounted reconnaissance troops to await the tanks. Although wounded, Perkins stayed with the troop for another six hours before agreeing to evacuation. The Germans were bringing artillery fire to bear on the reconnaissance troop, so Perkins retaliated by directing artillery against any target he saw.

Lieutenant D.P. Ramsay's No. 2 Troop was first to get around the crater and head for Perkins's position. The troop was down to only two Shermans, the other having earlier broken down. They had just crossed an open stretch of road and were passing a burning Honey that had been knocked out during Perkins's advance when a German tank fired on Sergeant A. Zeal's Sherman, which burst into flames. The two flaming tanks now nearly blocked the road. Ramsay carried on alone, reaching Torrice Crossroads at 1530 hours. Parking just south of Highway 6, Ramsay and co-driver Trooper A. Scott dismounted to find a good fighting position. As they started across the highway, the two men heard a throaty engine roar and saw a Panther tank backing up onto the road about 200 yards east of their position. Scott, having already crossed the road, hid in a small concrete hut while Ramsay ran back to the tank. The Sherman crept up to a corner in the road and halted when the gunner could just see down Highway 6 toward the Panther, now rolling west toward their position. The gunner blasted the Panther's heavy frontal armour with fifteen .75-millimetre armour-piercing rounds. Neither slowing nor returning fire, the Panther kept coming. When it was only fifty yards off, a shot broke a track. This made the tank slew slightly sideways and Ramsay's gunner got a shot into the thinner side armour, bringing it to a halt mere feet from the Sherman. As the Germans bailed out, Scott scrambled from his shelter and cut them down with his Thompson submachine gun.

Returning to the job of finding a position for the tank, Ramsay was standing on the side of the road when a German Mark IV sped past in the direction of Rome without giving the lieutenant a second glance. Ramsay jumped into his tank and ordered it backed up a slope so he could get above the highway. As the tank went up the bank, a German machine gun put a short burst directly into Scott's open hatch. The bullets ricocheted into the turret and struck both Ramsay and his radio operator in the legs. Ramsay fainted from loss of blood just as the tank backed over a mine. With the driver keeping the brakes engaged to prevent the disabled tank from rolling back down the hill, Scott and the gunner evacuated the two wounded men. The driver then bailed out as the tank slid to the bottom of the hill and came to rest.

While Ramsay's crew fought its action at Torrice Crossroads, Lieutenant J.W. Black's No. 1 Troop approached the open gap where Zeal's tank had been knocked out. Sergeant Clifford Macey of the reconnaissance troop, who had won a Distinguished Conduct Medal for his part in the Melfa battle, met the lieutenant. Having lost one tank in mud, Black had only his corporal's tank behind him. Macey jumped onto Black's tank and pointed out suspected gun positions in the woods. He told Black to make his crossing as fast as possible. Black was almost up to the two burning tanks when a shell hit his Sherman and killed him. The addition of a third wrecked tank blocked the road entirely. Without crossing the gap, Corporal J.B.

Matthews set up in a covered position from which he was able to see Highway 6. As Macey and other reconnaissance troops pointed out targets, Matthews brought them under fire, changing position as needed to get a better firing angle. One Panther and a self-propelled gun were confirmed kills and he also assisted in knocking out another Panther and a Mark IV tank engaged by other troops of 'B' Squadron that had formed up alongside his tank. Matthews was awarded the Distinguished Conduct Medal.

The Strathconas were under constant artillery and tank fire during this action. Griffin was running around on foot, helping the tankers target German tanks trying to escape westward. A high-explosive shell exploded near him. A piece of shrapnel sliced deep near his left eye while sand and gravel kicked up by the blast penetrated his face, neck, chest, and arms. Covered in blood, Griffin walked to Perkins's position by the road and was given first-aid treatment.

As darkness approached, the battle quieted down and no more German armour or vehicles attempted to get past the tanks' position. Griffin was evacuated to the church being used by Highlander Major Somerville as an observation point. Here he found three brigadiers gathered: 5 CAB's Desmond Smith, 11 CIB's Eric Snow, and 2 CIB's Graeme Gibson. The latter's brigade was preparing to take over the advance that night, with the Loyal Edmonton Regiment leading. The tankers were to pass into reserve in the morning. During the fight at the crossroads, the Strathconas had had one officer killed and 3 wounded; 6 other ranks were killed, 4 more would die of wounds, and another 11 were wounded. One Honey and four Shermans had been destroyed in exchange for three Panthers, one Mark IV, one self-propelled gun, two half-tracked vehicles, a number of trucks, two motorcycles and their riders, and an unknown number of German infantry killed.[39]

25

VIVA
IL CANADESE

There were many new faces in the 2nd Canadian Infantry Brigade regiments as they marched toward the sound of the guns on May 30. Since it mauling at the Hitler Line, the brigade had been heavily reinforced to regain combat strength. On May 25, for example, the Seaforth Highlanders of Canada received eight new officers and 208 other ranks.[1] Some were returning after recovering from wounds, sickness, or completing assigned training duties. Most, however, were raw recruits fresh from training bases in Canada or Britain. On May 27, Major Jim Stone returned from training in Britain to take over acting command of the Loyal Edmonton Regiment. He was still settling into this role when 2 CIB commander Brigadier Graeme Gibson advised him early on May 30 that the Eddies would spearhead the Canadian advance on Frosinone.

The brigade plan was for the Edmontons to pass through the Cape Breton Highlanders and advance to the high ground code-named Harry, which the Cape Bretoners had failed to reach. On the Edmontons' left, the Princess Patricia's Canadian Light Infantry would pass through the Irish Regiment of Canada, which was holding the height of land code-named Dick. Meeting no opposition, the Edmontons reached Harry in just forty-five minutes. 'A' and 'B' companies pressed straight on to another height of land two miles from Frosinone. Again, they met no resistance and were in position by 2220 hours. Ten minutes after arriving on the objective, Stone sent a four-man patrol toward Frosinone to determine whether it was occupied.[2]

On the left flank, the PPCLI was less fortunate. The regiment had spent a difficult day getting to Dick because heavy traffic on Highway 6 had log-jammed its trucks. Finally, Lieutenant Colonel Cameron Ware ordered the regiment to dismount and march cross-country. There was no time to dispatch food rations, so the men carried only water bottles and hard rations.[3] They arrived at the Irish position after a six-hour trek and immediately continued on with 'B' Company leading. Crossing a patch of open high ground, the company came under mortar, machine-gun, and small-arms fire. 'B' Company went to ground and all attempts by Ware to get other companies around the German flanks were blocked by heavy fire.

At nightfall, the PPCLI leapfrogged forward by companies to find the enemy gone. They scooped up a few prisoners on the way and were soon anchored on the Edmontons' left flank. All except for Major P.D. Crofton's 'D' Company, which had become separated in the thick brush and was missing. The men in the other companies settled in for the night with grumbling stomachs and the knowledge that no rations would reach them until Frosinone was taken and their transport rejoined them.

In the morning, Ware sent six scouts out to locate Crofton's company. Finally, Sergeant T. Inverarity of the scout platoon brought the major, who had only joined the regiment on May 26, and his men in from the woods. Ware then set off after the Edmontons.[4]

During the night, that regiment's four-man patrol into Frosinone had failed to return. Stone consequently moved 'D' Company to just outside the town and then had it probe the defences with a fighting patrol. The patrol found only rearguard troops scattered in the town, but a short firefight ensued in which the commander, Lieutenant E.M. Simms, was killed. With the company only five days, this had been his first combat. The rest of the company followed the patrol into the streets and swept it clear, scooping up five Germans, but finding no sign of the lost patrol. Stone could only surmise that the patrol had been captured. Except for the Germans taken prisoner, the regiment's war diarist wrote, "the city was empty and in ruin."[5]

While the Edmontons secured Frosinone, the PPCLI enjoyed "a pleasant march through cultivated fields, orchards, and vineyards. Many were so hungry they pulled up potatoes and ate them raw." Upon reaching the day's objective about 1,000 yards south of Frosinone, the PPCLI dug in on both sides of Highway 6 without having fired a shot during the advance. When a patrol went into Frosinone, however, one of the scouts, Private H.A. McDonald, was wounded by light machine–gun fire. Whether the fire originated from Germans, however, was undetermined. The regiment's intelligence section also went into the town to search for a badly needed type-writer. They returned to report that Frosinone "had been completely gutted of all furniture or equipment of any kind. Apart from bomb and shell fire damage, everything breakable had been deliberately and needlessly smashed by the Germans."

At noon on May 31, the Seaforth Highlanders of Canada moved through the PPCLI position to secure the main crossroads. Severing that junction would block the major route north into the mountains from use by the retreating Germans. Behind the Seaforths came the quartermaster trucks, bringing food to end the PPCLI's thirty-six-hour fast. The Canadian vehicles were followed later by several German trucks that, depending on the belligerence of the passengers, the PPCLI either shot up or captured.[6]

The Seaforths had been on the move forward since 0400 hours, initially by truck. Faced with clogged roads, however, they had soon unloaded north of Arnara and marched on a mule track to the PPCLI position. Seaforths commander Lieutenant Colonel Syd Thomson had been warned that the Germans would put up a stiff fight for the road crossing. However, "it became evident that the main body of the Germans had withdrawn from the area, leaving only delaying parties and one task force which included some Panther tanks."[7]

At 1445 hours, the Seaforths started a left-hand flanking manoeuvre to get behind Frosinone and cut the road junction. 'B' Company moved across open country to a disused railway. Following the railway, the company came out on Highway 6, just west of the junction. When Captain O.H. Mace led his men up to the road, they came under fire from tanks and machine guns. Six men were hit, three fatally. While

Mace spread his platoons out so that they dominated the road, mortars began pounding their line.

'C' Company, meanwhile, had paralleled 'B' Company's line of advance by following the road that cut laterally across Highway 6 en route to the mountains to the north. As it skirted the edge of Frosinone, mortar fire injured seven men. When 'A' Company passed through 'B' Company's line to seize a height of ground on the other side the ground was quickly taken. Highway 6 was now well covered by Seaforth rifles and machine guns.[8]

The regiment began reaping a bountiful harvest of German vehicles trying to escape toward Rome. By nightfall, they had knocked out or captured four enemy Jeeps, two trucks, and one motorcycle. Four Germans were dead, 3 wounded, and 17 captured. The Seaforths' casualties were 3 killed and 16 wounded.[9]

◆ ◆ ◆

From where Frosinone stood atop a 300-foot summit, the next objectives lay straight up Highway 6. Seven miles northwest, the town of Ferentino perched on top of a 500-foot-high pinnacle-shaped feature that rose out of the surrounding plain. Three miles east of Ferentino was 850-foot-high Monte Radicino. The assigned 1st Canadian Infantry Brigade drew the task of seizing Ferentino and 2 CIB Monte Radicino.

Brigadier Dan Spry detailed the capture of Ferentino to the Royal Canadian Regiment, preceded by 'C' Squadron of the Princess Louise Dragoon Guards. Much to the relief of the RCR's rank and file, Lieutenant Colonel Bill Mathers had been assigned to run a training centre at Avellino. He handed over command to Lieutenant Colonel Jim Ritchie at noon on May 31. The regiment's second-in-command, Major Strome Galloway, had not for a moment dreamed that he would get the regiment. Nor was he surprised to see an old-guard Permanent Force officer show up from rear-area administrative duties to assume command.[10]

Across the valley, preparing for the assault on Monte Radicino, Major Jim Stone felt bitter at learning that the Loyal Edmonton Regiment would not remain his. Stone's tenure was to be short-lived, with another officer to assume command on June 6.[11] Extremely popular throughout the regiment, Stone would lead it through one more fight, then revert to second-in-command. At 1130 hours on June 1, the Eddies crossed the start line and marched toward the mountain. In support was a squadron of the British North Irish Horse Armoured Regiment. 'D' Company was on the right and 'A' on the left. A blown bridge over a wide irrigation ditch named Fosso Terravalle delayed the advance. It took Lieutenant R. Hayter and his pioneer platoon thirty minutes of frantic work with shovels and explosives to create a diversion for the tanks. Although the diversion was passable, another hour and fifteen minutes slipped by as the fourteen tanks in the squadron struggled, one after the other, over the crossing.

At 1440 hours, the regiment assaulted the mountain. 'D' Company made the charge and was soon consolidated in a clearing just below the rocky summit. No opposition was met. A fighting patrol was sent to the summit, which proved undefended. Moving across the mountain's left flank, 'B' Company engaged an MG42 machine-gun position at 1500 hours. Several Germans were killed in the short, sharp engagement and three were captured.

On the right flank, 'C' Company and a troop of tanks went to secure a small, isolated hill. A large convent had been cut out of the rock at the base. As the Edmontons closed on the structure, which looked like a massive cave with several doors and windows, a machine gun fired from a doorway and wounded two men. The company went to ground and put patrols out on the flanks. One of these took four prisoners, who were immediately sent back to brigade headquarters for interrogation. The prisoners reported that 200 men, supported by four heavy mortars, held the convent. Their orders were to fight a delaying action until dark and then withdraw. One of the prisoners volunteered to help direct artillery fire on the position. Although the Edmontons felt nothing but contempt for this traitor, they used his services to good effect as, under his supervision, tanks, medium artillery, 4.2-inch mortars, and 3-inch mortars all pounded the convent. Nevertheless, the defenders continued to hold out. Finally, at 2200 hours, 'C' Company rushed the convent only to find that the Germans had beat a hasty retreat minutes earlier. Several German corpses were found and eighteen prisoners rounded up. The Edmontons had suffered two men killed and four wounded. By 0100 hours on June 2, the small hill was secure.[12]

While the Edmontons were seizing Monte Radicino, the RCR and

PLDG moved on Ferentino. In the late afternoon, as the force approached the base of the hill on which the hamlet perched, German artillery fired from positions inside the town. Both the troops in the armoured cars and the infantry were delicately picking routes through a dense blanket of mines and booby traps that covered the wide-open ground, so hastening to cover was not an option. RCR Intelligence Officer Lieutenant Gordon Potts was amazed that nobody was hit, particularly as "there were between 800 and 900 men moving across the valley."[13] One PLDG trooper, R.K. McCrae was, however, mortally wounded during a brief engagement between 'B' Squadron and a German gun position.[14] The force reached the base of the hill and dug in for the night.

After dark, scout platoon commander Lieutenant Bill Rich — the bell-ringer of Pontecorvo — sent three patrols up the hill into the hamlet. They reported that the Germans had left only a screening force.[15] At dawn, Major Sandy Mitchell took 'B' Company forward, with 'D' Company following closely behind. A smattering of German infantry fired off a few quick shots, then fled, except for seven who took the opportunity to surrender. Another German was plucked out of a bed he was sharing with a woman.

With the possible exception of the German's lover, the towns-people were wildly excited by the Canadians' arrival. As Lieutenant Colonel Ritchie strode into Ferentino, which had been badly battered by aerial bombardments over the past few days, a girl ran up, kissed his hand, and presented him with a red rose.

The Canadians were given little pause to celebrate the hamlet's capture. Orders came at 1400 hours to march another ten miles and seize the next hilltop village, Anagni. Initially, Captain D.W. Rose's 'D' Company proceeded straight up Highway 6 before swinging off to the right on a lateral road leading to the town. No reconnaissance to test the strength of its defences had been possible. As the Canadians pushed forward, they came under sporadic gunfire from small pockets of Germans, but these were easily swept aside. Night found the RCR on the lateral road facing Anagni. "At 0500 hours," Lieutenant Potts later wrote, "the leading company was punching through one side of the town and the Germans were going hell-bent out of the other. . . . By 0800 hours the whole regiment was sitting astride the centre of the town. Again the populace gave us a great welcome and Colonel

Ritchie was accorded the honour of receiving an egg which half an hour later broke in his pocket.

"The Germans had been sent scuttling out of Anagni before they had time to do much looting. The case was quite different in the town of Ferentino, which they had systematically cleaned out. In Anagni the food situation seemed easy and we had roast chicken for lunch today accompanied by music by the daughter of the house."[16] Anagni marked the end of the RCR advance.

The Canadian advance continued, however, in the form of a five-Jeep patrol by the Princess Louise Dragoon Guards toward the village of Colleferro, ten miles up Highway 6 from Anagni. Arriving in the village at 1600 hours on June 3, they established contact with a Corps Expéditionnaire Français company that had earlier occupied the town. With the French cutting across the Canadian front to drive up Highway 6 to Rome, I Canadian Corps operations abruptly ended. They were only thirty miles from the centre of Rome. At noon on June 4, Fifth Army's General Mark Clark paraded into the largely undefended city, fulfilling his vision of himself as Rome's liberator.

About the same time, the RCR held its Sunday service in Anagni's small auditorium. Ritchie then paraded the regiment down the narrow central thoroughfare lined by the traditional two- and three-storey Italian houses and shops. From the overlooking windows and balconies, women showered the men with flowers. Roses of all colours soon blanketed the cobblestones. In the main square, Ritchie formed the regiment up to salute about 500 partisans, who had come in from the hills in the wake of the German retreat. The partisans marched past to the applause of the townspeople. As the partisan march past was concluding, Brigadier Dan Spry arrived. "Noting that he was of superior rank to the Commanding Officer of the RCR, the Partisan leader had his men march back into the square so that the brigadier could take the salute. The whole affair was most dramatic and colourful, and the square was draped with Italian flags and bunting in Savoy colours."[17]

Although Military Police hurriedly erected signs ten miles outside Rome that read "ROME OUT OF BOUNDS — TURN BACK NOW," there was a steady, unofficial flow of Canadians into the city. One of the first to enter Rome had been Seaforth Sergeant Bill Worton. On June 2, two days before Clark's triumphal march, Worton had

ridden into the city on the back of Corporal Gabe Kennedy's motorcycle. They found the city virtually deserted and saw no signs of
Germans. Worton and Kennedy went into a bar and bought liquor.
Then they purchased some new clothes at a shop, took in a few of
the famous sights, and rode back to the Highlanders' position with
the authorities none the wiser.[18]

◆ ◆ ◆

In the wake of every major campaign comes a period of assessment,
self-examination, and recrimination at every level in the chain of
command. Operation Diadem had achieved only a limited victory.
Although Rome was liberated, the German army in Italy had escaped
to fight another day. Casualties on both sides were high. The Fifth
and Eighth armies collectively suffered 43,746 casualties in exchange
for losses estimated at slightly more than 50,000 on the German side.
Of these, 24,334 were men taken prisoner. Total Canadian battle
casualties from May 11 to June 4 were 3,368: 789 killed, 2,463
wounded, and 116 missing. Hardest hit was 1st Canadian Infantry
Division, which suffered 1,964 casualties, including 487 killed.[19]

That division's losses reflected the fact that the majority of the
Canadian casualties had come at the Hitler Line. A narrow two-kilo-
metre front that invited concentrated German resistance, XIII Corps's
failure to distract the Germans at Aquino, an inflexible artillery fire
plan, Vokes's decision to hold 2 CIB back so that it had insufficient
time to reconnoitre its final line of attack were among the reasons
mustered by generals, staff officers, and line soldiers alike to explain
the casualties.[20] Each factor had contributed — the measure free to
be mixed as desired.

Then there was the perpetual traffic congestion that had badly
hindered Eighth Army's operations in the Liri Valley. The congestion
had combined with poor staff work, particularly by 5th Canadian
Armoured Division headquarters, to slow I Canadian Corps's advance
more than German resistance necessitated. Lieutenant General
Tommy Burns had been made sharply aware of this fact when Eighth
Army commander General Sir Oliver Leese had given him a "rocket"
regarding the slow advance west of the Melfa River.

In early June, Leese told Burns that 1st Canadian Infantry Division
was the best infantry division in Italy and that in time 5th Canadian

Armoured Division would undoubtedly emerge as the best armoured division. Leese said that he was, however, less impressed with I Canadians Corps's headquarters. Burns agreed and plans were made for making replacements. When Burns asked Leese straight out whether he was satisfied with his performance as corps commander, Leese dissembled by asking how Burns felt himself. Could he do the job? Burns replied that he could and had no doubts about that. In fact, Leese and Alexander did not believe Burns capable. They also did not believe that a Canadian corps possessed the staff competence to operate effectively and were consequently "loath to put a British or Indian Division under a headquarters in which [Leese] did not have full confidence."[21] Burns would spend much of the summer of 1944 fighting to keep his job. Several of his staff officers would be sacrificed, including his general staff commander, Brigadier Nick McCarter, and corps engineer, Brigadier A.B. Connelly.

Burns thought that Major General Bert Hoffmeister had performed excellently. Vokes, Burns said, "did very well," although he required direction and some prodding from Burns to perform his job properly.[22] For his part, Hoffmeister made good on his resolve to fire 11th Canadian Infantry Brigade commander Brigadier Eric Snow. On June 6, Hoffmeister recommended that Snow be given a "change of employment," preferably a posting to command of a basic training camp, a posting for which he "has had a great deal of experience . . . and has demonstrated that he is suitable." Hoffmeister's recommendation was written on the same day that he read a report submitted by Snow on the brigade's actions during the campaign.

Snow described that report as "outspoken and inclined to be critical of my commander as well as myself." He detailed the arguments that had flared between the two men and recorded the flow of changed and often contradictory orders issued by Hoffmeister. "It was terribly confusing to the junior officers to have plans changed as many times as they were during the campaign." The men, he argued, had felt they were being carelessly tossed about and there had been a resultant "loss of efficiency."

There was also implied criticism embedded in his comments regarding the exercise of command from tactical headquarters rather than main headquarters. Although addressing only himself and his regimental commanders, Snow's comments here could easily be extrapolated as applicable to Hoffmeister, who had spent much time roaming the battlefield in his highly mobile and pared-down tactical HQ, which relied on a tenuous radio communication link back to main headquarters. A brigade commander, Snow said, should remain at main headquarters rather than basing himself in a small tactical headquarters. Being away from main headquarters more "than five hours," he wrote, "means that neither my staff nor myself are thoroughly in the picture."

Finally, having often had Hoffmeister at his shoulder offering critical comment, he wrote, "under no circumstances must I nag or hound my battalion commanders while they are conducting their battle even though I am being pressed by my own commander. . . . To hound battalion commanders when they are doing their best and things are going well will only cause disorganization and perhaps adversely affect the results of the battle."[23]

The report brought a summons to divisional headquarters, where Hoffmeister told Snow it "was insubordinate and that he would not have [Snow] in the Division any longer." When Snow demanded the right to appeal to Burns, the corps commander backed Hoffmeister, telling Snow he could appeal the matter in England. Snow did so, but was unable to win reassignment back to combat command.[24]

◆ ◆ ◆

The same day that Hoffmeister fired Snow, the Allies struck the beaches of Normandy and opened a new front in northern Europe. Immediately, the Italian theatre was overshadowed to the point that many at home forgot that Canadians fought there at all. Soon, Allied soldiers in Italy started calling themselves D-Day Dodgers. Initially, this was considered a derogatory term assigned them by Britain's first female Member of Parliament, Lady Nancy Astor. Although Astor's role may be apocryphal, derogation soon developed into a mark of honour. The theme song, "We Are the D-Day Dodgers," sung to the tune of "Lili Marlene," followed.

On June 6, Royal Canadian Regiment's Major Galloway and the regimental adjutant drove a Jeep into Rome, ignoring the signs declaring it out of bounds. After driving around the Coliseum and pausing to have their picture taken in the Piazza di San Pietro, with the towering basilica in the background, they drove back to regimental headquarters. On entering his office, Galloway learned of the invasion. He turned to his orderly, Corporal Baker, who was typing up the regiment's casualty list for the battle. "Baker," Galloway said excitedly, "it's just come over the air that the 3rd [Canadian Infantry] Division is fighting on the beaches of Normandy." Without pausing in his typing, Baker responded, "It's about fucking time that those bastards did something, isn't it, sir?"[25]

Not all the Canadians had to sneak into Rome. The Royal 22e Regiment received a formal audience with Pope Pius XII on July 3. Among those in attendance was Captain Pierre Potvin, who because of his wounds had to wear his dress jacket draped like a cape over his shoulders. Lieutenant Colonel Jean Allard had personally fetched Potvin from his hospital bed in Caserta for the audience.[26] Most of the Van Doos were devout Catholics and accordingly were "all extremely moved at meeting the Pope, a frail, ascetic giant," wrote Allard. "After his kind words to us, in French, a special mass was said by our chaplain." Canadian ambassador Georges-Philéas Vanier briefly addressed the Van Doos outside the Basilica San Pietro.[27]

Two weeks before the papal audience, another group of Canadians entered Rome with great formality. These were "The Drums" of the Royal Canadian Regiment. Since October 1943, the regiment's pipes and drums, smuggled into Sicily during the invasion and thence into Italy, had been stored in Campobasso. With the regiment standing down for a few weeks, the instruments were brought forward. As Canadian leave parties to Rome then allowed each regiment to send a mere ten men at a time, the adjutant had restricted the band accordingly. Galloway, ever one to fiddle a rule, let them all go.[28]

And so it was on June 22 that twenty-three Canadians had entered Piazza di San Pietro. The drum major, thirteen buglers, and nine drummers — dressed in khaki drill, white webbing, full dress cords, and all other accoutrements of an infantry bugle corps — formed up in the centre of the ever crowded square under a brilliant blue sky. For forty-five minutes, Drum Major Sergeant T.W. Beales led them through a dazzling display of stationary playing and counter-marching. Hundreds of Italians gathered around shouting, "Bravo!" and "Viva il Canadese!" as Canadians and Italians together celebrated Rome's liberation.[29]

EPILOGUE

VALLEY OF LOSS

Fifty-six years gone by and the first months of a new century. I stand upon the rough stones of a path possibly set in place by Benedictine monks more than a thousand years ago. Two continuous deep grooves gouged into the stones by carts are proof of the path's antiquity. The path, once a main route up the east slope of Monte Cassino to the Benedictine Abbey, survives now as only a fragment. Most of it is undoubtedly buried beneath the bed of the aptly named Via Serpentina, which switchbacks up the steep slope so tightly that its asphalt base and the concrete retaining walls shoring it up leave scant space for archaeological remnants or even vegetation.

Several hundred metres upslope, the reconstructed Benedictine Abbey stands majestically atop Monte Cassino's summit. The architectural plans for the abbey were removed to Rome, along with its artworks and library, before the bombs and shells reduced the structure to a half-million-cubic-metre rubble pile. On February 15, 1945, one year after its destruction, new foundation stone was set down for its rebuilding. Nineteen years later, the Marshall Plan–supported rebuilding was completed and Pope Paul VI consecrated it. All the treasures and archival documents were returned. The great paintings, carvings, and other artwork built into the abbey's walls, floors, doors, and ceilings were meticulously reproduced. The abbey is a perfect replica of its past self. Today, convoys of tour buses grind slowly up Via Serpentina in long lines and tourists throng through the abbey. Mostly they come to the abbey as a day trip out of Rome or Naples.

Few tourists pause to overnight in the modern town of Cassino. The buses, en route to or from the *autostrada* to the abbey, hasten by Cassino's western outskirts, carrying their passengers to lunch in some quainter, more "Italian" community. Unlike the abbey, Cassino was not reconstructed. It was instead built anew, shifted two kilometres so that it stands on the narrow valley plain through which the Gari River flows, rather than on the lower slopes of Monte Cassino. At first glance, Cassino seems stark, even grim. Most of the buildings are made of featureless concrete, streets are choked with cars, and sidewalks are narrow. There are few trattorias or *ristorantes*, but many pizzerias and cafés. There is also, outside the train station, a rusty Mark IV tank, its front end crawling up onto some large white stone rubble blocks, as if it still wants a fight. There is a similarly rusted, but not so aggressive, Sherman tank and antitank gun in the square outside city hall. Several stores sell black-and-white postcards that show the pleasant town Cassino once was. Some of the postcards are of the rubble after, and others capture scenes of soldiers locked in battle. In one, two American GIs lean toward each other. One is pointing dramatically toward the summit of Monte Cassino where exploding bombs throw debris and flame several hundred metres into the air above the ruins of the abbey. The photo was taken on February 15, 1944 — the day the abbey perished.

Although Cassino today bears no resemblance to the town it was before it became the most destroyed community in Italy during World War II, there are few of its former residents left to remember. Most of its current citizens did not have family here before the war. They came after, many as refugees from other war-torn parts of Italy. Finding a ruin, they reclaimed it, just as they made new lives for themselves.

I spend a week in Cassino, coming to see behind the plain façade a town and people that have their own unique charm and grace. The people are shy, even reticent at first when they hear I have come to write about the war. Gradually, however, they open up, becoming friendly and sincerely interested in my work. Ask if they know anyone who lived here or in the other towns of the Liri Valley during the war, though, and most can only shrug. It was a long time ago. They left. They were all killed. There was an uncle, but he is dead now. There is an old fellow in San Angelo, but nobody remembers his name. There is Federico Lamberti at the bookstore. And so there is.

Federico was nine in May 1944 and, although he had many uncles and aunts in Cassino, he lived in Atina, a smaller town set in the foothills north of Cassino. He was the fourth of five children. His father, Michael, also owned a bookshop. Michael Lamberti was born in England, hence the anglicized name, but his parents moved to Atina when he was a teenager. In December 1943, the Germans came and brought the war with them to the town. Federico's family fled to Arpino, east of Frosinone, but the war followed. So they walked into the mountains to a place north of Monte Cairo. Here they found a shepherd's hut and remained there until the fighting passed by. From their lofty perch, the family watched the month-long battle for the Liri Valley. Mostly, they followed the ebb and flow of the Allies' fortunes by where the artillery and aerial bombardments struck.

When the Allies advanced so far west that much of the valley was no longer subject to shelling or bombing, the Lambertis returned to Atina on June 2, 1944. They found 99 percent of the town demolished. That was significantly better than Cassino. There, every building had been destroyed. Nobody went near Cassino at the time, Federico says. There were too many mines and unexploded shells in the rubble and surrounding fields. Much of the ground had been flooded, transformed into malarial swamps. It was years before anyone started to rebuild Cassino. When they did, there were shortages of concrete and steel. Brick was impossible to find. Construction equipment was also in short supply.

Federico and I walk around Cassino and he points out sights that few tourists would ever hear of. There is the two-storey concrete commercial building that has a German tank serving as part of its foundation. The builders were unable to wrench the wreck out of the cellar in which it had been positioned, so they poured concrete over and around it and its steel became the footing for a section of their building. There is an overgrown and nearly collapsed tunnel at the base of Monte Cassino where a German railroad gun was hidden and trundled out periodically to fire massive shells toward the Allied line.

We drive in the chaotic Italian manner to San Angelo and Federico points out the position where Tony Kingsmill's Plymouth Bridge was put over the Gari River on the night of May 11–12. East of the river, there are wide-open fields, which in fall lie fallow and deeply ploughed, but by May will be thick with tall grain dotted with poppies.

Federico, a slight, intense, bespectacled, and chain-smoking man, has spent much of his life studying the battles for Cassino and the Liri Valley. He confesses, however, to knowing little about the Canadians' role. Plymouth Bridge he knows; that's about all. He never met a Canadian soldier until many years after the war, when a veteran came to his bookshop in Cassino. The man had worked on Plymouth Bridge and it is he who directed Federico to the site. No, he does not remember the man's name. It was not the bridge's architect, who never returned to the Liri Valley.

This is true of most of the Canadians who fought there. And those who have returned confess to passing through the Liri Valley quickly, usually without looking, in the manner of veterans, for remembered places of battle or positions of bivouacs. This is understandable. The Liri Valley of today, or even of twenty years ago, little resembles the place in which they fought and buried comrades. Where the Hitler Line was a massive Fiat auto-manufacturing plant has erased most traces of the fortifications. Many of the residents of Cassino work at the plant and it is the greatest source of the valley's surging prosperity. An ever-widening autostrada linking Naples to Rome slashes up the valley, and cloverleaf exits and entry ramps abound. Yet, not far from the autostrada, I see an old farmer bent to a plough being pulled by a large white ox. He prods it on with soft trills. The old and new in Italy seem always to reach some amiable form of accommodation.

The other towns in the Liri Valley, such as Pontecorvo, Ceprano, and Aquino, fared little better than Cassino. A few old churches survive and have been repaired, as have some other buildings. But there are few traces of battle in their streets. In Ortona and out in its surrounding countryside, I saw buildings still pocked and pitted from bullets and shrapnel. Some had roofs collapsed in the telltale manner caused by a direct hit from an artillery shell. Nothing like that here.

There remains one prominent reminder of the terrible fighting that went on in the Liri Valley — the graves of soldiers. On Monte Cassino, the Polish cemetery holds 1,000 graves, including that of General Wladyslaw Anders, who was interred here among his fallen comrades after his death in London in 1970. Anders, who, like his men, fought for a free Poland, lived out his life as an expatriate from a nation held under the Soviet fist. He believed that the western Allies betrayed the Polish soldiers who fought at their side in the expectation that Poland's national independence would be guaranteed. He was right in that.

North of Cassino, near the village of Caira, is a graveyard holding 20,057 dead Germans. Not all of these died in the Liri Valley. Many were brought here after the war from smaller graves scattered across Italy. At Venafro, on the other side of the valley, 3,414 French soldiers lie. The Americans interred their Cassino dead, alongside those who fell at Anzio, in Nettuno. There are 7,862 graves there and a memorial for 3,094 missing. Just south of Highway 6, outside Cassino, is the British and Commonwealth cemetery. It holds 4,266 graves with a memorial commemorating 4,054 missing. The Canadians are mostly buried together in one section of the cemetery. Between the ordered marble rows of tombstones grows carefully tended grass. Bright flowers are interspersed between the headstones. In the distance stands Monte Cassino, with the white monolithic structure of the abbey clearly visible.

The dates on the Canadian headstones retell the story of the battle fought. May 23 stands out. I find 138 headstones of men who died that day. Most served in the 2nd Canadian Infantry Brigade. A few headstones bear not one but several names. One entire Three Rivers Regiment tank crew shares the same grave — a stark reminder of what happens when a tank explodes and burns. The epitaphs on many headstones tell another tale, that of the struggle by families to come to terms with the deaths of men who were so young and so far away. Private Arthur Edgar Harris of Calgary was older than many. He died at thirty-one. His epitaph reads: "Died that fascism/Be destroyed/and that workers/might build a new world." Lance Corporal George Amos was also thirty-one and his family asked: "Went the day

well?/He died and never knew/well or ill/Freedom, he died for you."
Private John Wallace's headstone reads: "Sometime we'll meet/and
understand/Mother and Dad." He was twenty-seven on May 23
when he breathed his last breath. Trooper Cyril Fairhead's age is not
recorded on his headstone, but I find his epitaph deeply moving: "I
cannot say/and I will not say/That he is dead/He is just away."

Went the day well? A difficult question when one ponders the
course of the Liri Valley battle and Canada's role there. In the end, it
was a victory. But it was a victory won at a tragically high price in
men killed and men wounded. Could the price have been less?
Canadian historians and professional soldiers rarely debate this. Not
because the issue is unimportant; rather because the Battle of the Liri
Valley is undoubtedly the most forgotten of the large battles Canadians
fought in World War II. Ortona, a smaller battle, has recently emerged
from the darkness to capture some of its rightful place in the collec-
tive Canadian consciousness. The 1998 and 1999 Christmas dinner
reconciliation meetings of veteran German and Canadian soldiers at
Ortona played a role in renewing interest in that battle, but it is
unlikely that such an event will ever commemorate the Liri Valley
battle.

I find when talking to veterans of this battle, as was not true for
those who fought at Ortona, that the events of May are often poorly
remembered, if at all. Everything happened so quickly, they often
say. And the memories that stuck were hard ones to carry. The burials
of the dead after May 23. The cries of men as they burned inside
their Shermans. A man unexpectedly finding his brother's grave.
"The Hitler Line was the worst day of my life," says one veteran.
"Ortona was nothing compared to it. I never expected to live through
it." Another stares almost vacantly into space as he clearly and
vividly recounts lying on the bank of the Melfa River, while Major
John Mahony rushed back and forth through the bullets and shrapnel
during the Westminster Regiment's stand there. He ends the tale by
saying, "We lined twenty-three of our dead up on the river's edge the
next morning. It was heartbreaking to see."

In the Liri Valley battle, the Canadians in Italy lost the belief that
individually they had much of a future. The veterans, who came
ashore in Sicily and had fought through and survived Ortona, lost
many comrades in May 1944 — far more than at any other time in

past battles. It was harder after May to believe they would survive the inevitable coming battles. For 5th Canadian Armoured Division's regiments and the new recruits posted to the more seasoned regiments, the fighting in May was shocking. How could they hope to live through many more days like these? One man tells me that he joined his regiment on May 22. His first day in battle was at the Hitler Line and he was in the Edmonton regiment. It was weeks before he realized how extraordinarily terrible and unique that day's fighting had been.

When he learned finally that battles are interspersed with long periods of tedium, the man felt better able to cope and hoped, just maybe, he would live to the end of the war. Until then, he had expected, at any moment, to die. But he also knew that there was no end in sight and that there would be many more, and possibly even worse, battles. The road the Canadians marched in Italy was a long one. In May 1944, they were but halfway down it. When they marched out of the Liri Valley, few bothered to look back at the ruined land behind them. They marched toward an uncertain future and the Liri Valley battle slipped into obscurity, where it still remains.

APPENDIX A
EIGHTH ARMY ORDER
OF BATTLE

X Corps
(Lieutenant General Sir R.L. McCreery)

2nd New Zealand Infantry Division
24th Guards Brigade
12th South African Motor Brigade
Hermon Force
Corps of Italian Liberation
26th British Armoured Brigade
2nd Army Group Royal Artillery

XIII Corps
(Lieutenant General S.C. Kirkman)

6th British Armoured Division
4th British Infantry Division
78th British Infantry Division
8th Indian Infantry Division
1st Canadian Armoured Brigade
6th Army Group Royal Artillery
1st Canadian Army Group Royal
   Canadian Artillery

I Canadian Corps
(Lieutenant General E.L.M. Burns)

5th Canadian Armoured Division
1st Canadian Infantry Division
25th Royal Tank Brigade

II Polish Corps
(Lieutenant General W. Anders)

3rd Carpathian Infantry Division
5th Kresowa Infantry Division
2nd Polish Armoured Brigade
Army Group Polish Artillery

6th South African Armoured Division

11th African Armoured Brigade

12th Anti-Aircraft Brigade

Appendix B
Canadians at the Liri Valley
(Not all units listed)

1st Canadian Corps
1 Canadian Armoured Car Regiment
(Royal Canadian Dragoons)
7th Anti-Tank Regiment
No. 1 Army Group, RCA
1st Survey Regiment
11th Army Field Regiment
1st Medium Regiment
2nd Medium Regiment
5th Medium Regiment

1st Canadian Infantry Division
4th Reconnaissance Regiment
(Princess Louise Dragoon Guards)
The Royal Canadian Artillery:
1st Field Regiment
(Royal Canadian Horse Artillery)
2nd Field Regiment
3rd Field Regiment
1st Anti-tank Regiment
2nd Light Anti-Aircraft Regiment
Corps of Royal Canadian Engineers:
1st Field Company
3rd Field Company
4th Field Company
2nd Field Park Company
Brigade Support Group:
The Saskatoon Light Infantry
1st Canadian Infantry Brigade:
The Royal Canadian Regiment
(permanent force)
The Hastings and Prince Edward
Regiment
48th Highlanders of Canada Regiment

2nd Canadian Infantry Brigade:
Princess Patricia's Canadian Light
Infantry Regiment (permanent force)
Seaforth Highlanders of Canada
Regiment
Loyal Edmonton Regiment
3rd Canadian Infantry Brigade:
Royal 22e Regiment (permanent force)
Carleton and York Regiment
West Nova Scotia Regiment

5th Canadian Armoured Division
Motorized Troops
Westminster (Motorized) Regiment
Reconnaissance Troops
3rd Canadian Armoured
Reconnaissance Regiment
(Governor General's Horse Guards)
Brigade Support Group:
Princess Louise Fusiliers
The Royal Canadian Artillery:
17th Field Regiment
8th Field Regiment (Self-Propelled)
4th Anti-tank Regiment
5th Light Anti-tank Regiment
5th Canadian Armoured Brigade
2nd Canadian Armoured Regiment
(Lord Strathcona's Horse)
(permanent force)
5th Canadian Armoured Regiment
(8th Princess Louise New Brunswick
Hussars)
9th Canadian Armoured Regiment
(British Columbia Dragoons)

11th Canadian Infantry Brigade
Perth Regiment
Cape Breton Highlanders
Irish Regiment of Canada
Corps of Royal Canadian Engineers
1st Field Squadron
4th Field Park Squadron
10th Field Squadron

1st Canadian Armoured Brigade
11th Canadian Armoured Regiment
(Ontario Tanks)
12th Canadian Armoured Regiment
(Three Rivers Tanks)
14th Canadian Armoured Regiment
(Calgary Tanks)

APPENDIX C
CANADIAN INFANTRY BATTALION
(TYPICAL ORGANIZATION)

HQ Company
No. 1: Signals Platoon
No. 2: Administrative Platoon

Support Company
No. 3: Mortar Platoon (3 inch)
No. 4: Bren Carrier Platoon
No. 5: Assault Pioneer Platoon
No. 6: Antitank Platoon (6 pounder)

A Company
No. 7 Platoon
No. 8 Platoon
No. 9 Platoon

B Company
No. 10 Platoon
No. 11 Platoon
No. 12 Platoon

C Company
No. 13 Platoon
No. 14 Platoon
No. 15 Platoon

D Company
No. 16 Platoon
No. 17 Platoon
No. 18 Platoon

APPENDIX D
CANADIAN MILITARY ORDER OF RANK

Private (Pte.)
Gunner (artillery equivalent of private)
Trooper (armoured equivalent of private)
Lance Corporal (L/Cpl.)
Corporal (Cpl.)
Lance Sergeant (L/Sgt.)
Sergeant (Sgt.)
Company Sergeant Major (CSM)
Regimental Sergeant Major (RSM)
Lieutenant (Lt. or Lieut.)
Captain (Capt.)
Major (Maj.)
Lieutenant Colonel (Lt. Col.)
Colonel (Col.)
Brigadier (Brig.)
Major General (Maj. Gen.)
Lieutenant General (Lt. Gen.)
General (Gen.)

APPENDIX E
GERMAN MILITARY ORDER OF RANK

Because the German army and the Luftwaffe ground forces had a ranking system where rank also usually indicated the specific type of unit in which one served, only basic ranks are given here. The translations are roughly based on the Canadian ranking system, although there is no Canadian equivalent for many German ranks.

Schütze	Private, infantry
Grenadier	Private, infantry
Kanonier	Gunner
Panzerschütze	Tank crew member
Pionier	Sapper
Funker	Signaller
Gefreiter	Lance Corporal
Obergefreiter	Corporal
Unteroffizier	Lance Sergeant
Unterfeldwebel	Sergeant
Feldwebel	Company Sergeant Major
Oberfeldwebel	Battalion Sergeant Major
Leutnant	Second Lieutenant
Oberleutnant	Lieutenant
Hauptmann	Captain
Major	Major
Oberstleutnant	Lieutenant Colonel
Oberst	Colonel
Generalleutnant	Lieutenant General
Generalmajor	Major General
General der Artillerie	General of Artillery
General der Infanterie	General of Infantry
General der Kavallerie	General of Cavalry
General der Pioniere	General of Engineers
General der Panzertruppen	General of Armoured Troops
Generaloberst	Colonel General
Generalfeldmarschall	General Field Marshal
Oberbefehshaber Süd	Commander-in-Chief South

Appendix F
The Decorations

Many military decorations were won by soldiers in the Liri Valley Battle. The decoration system that Canada used in World War II, like most other aspects of its military organization and tradition, derived from Britain. A class-based system, most military decorations can be awarded either to officers or to "other ranks," but not both. The exception is the highest award, the Victoria Cross, which can be won by a soldier of any rank.

The decorations and qualifying ranks are:

Victoria Cross (VC)
Awarded for gallantry in the presence of the enemy. Instituted in 1856. Open to all ranks. The only award that can be granted for action in which the recipient was killed, other than Mentioned in Despatches — a less formal honour whereby an act of bravery was given specific credit in a formal report.

Distinguished Service Order (DSO)
Officers of all ranks, but more commonly awarded to officers with ranks of major or higher.

Military Cross (MC)
Officers with a rank below major and, rarely, warrant officers.

Distinguished Conduct Medal
Warrant officers and all lower ranks.

Military Medal
Warrant officers and all lower ranks.

GLOSSARY OF COMMON CANADIAN MILITARY TERMS AND WEAPONRY

ANTITANK GUNS
Canadian forces used two antitank guns. The six-pounder was the main anti-tank gun attached directly to infantry battalions. Each battalion had its own antitank platoon. This gun had a range of 1,000 yards and fired a six-pound shell. Also available were the seventeen-pounder antitank guns of the antitank regiments. This was basically an up-gunned version of the six-pounder. It had greater range and greater hitting power because of the seventeen-pound shell.

ARMOURED CARS
The Fox mounted a .50-calibre machine gun in the turret that the commander handled and a .30-calibre co-axial machine gun operated by the wireless man. Originally, the Otter had been fitted with only a .303 Bren gun on an anti-aircraft mount in the turret, but soon after landing in Italy the Guardsmen had replaced most of the Brens with .50-calibre Brownings. Both the Fox and Otter were lightly armoured, with the thickest armour not exceeding 15 millimetres. In favourable conditions, the drivers could coax a top speed of 45 miles per hour out of either model's six-cylinder gas engine. Each troop in a squadron had five armoured cars, manned by three men apiece.

BREN CARRIER
Also known as the universal carrier. A lightly armoured tracked vehicle capable of carrying four to six soldiers and their weapons. Provided no overhead protection, but was walled on all sides by armour. Top speed of thirty-five miles an hour. The Commonwealth forces battlefield workhorse, its open design enabled it to be used for carrying just about any kind of military gear used by infantry. Some were converted into weapons carriers and played a combat role by being fitted with Vickers .303 medium machine guns, Bren light machine guns, or two-inch mortars, or were used as the towing vehicle for six-pounder antitank guns.

BREN GUN
Standard light machine gun of Commonwealth forces. Fired .303 rifle ammunition held in thirty-round magazines. An excellent, although slow-firing, weapon. It had a range of about 500 yards and weighed twenty-two pounds.

BROWNING 9-MILLIMETRE AUTOMATIC

The standard pistol used by Canadian forces. Officers in the line rifle companies generally kept their pistols hidden or even threw them away to avoid being easily identified as officers by German snipers.

CIB

Canadian Infantry Brigade.

FAUSTPATRONE

A hand-held, disposable German antitank rocket launcher that proved quite effective against Western Allied armour. The first model Faustpatrone 1 (Fist-Cartridge) fired a 5.5-pound projectile capable of penetrating armour 140 millimetres thick at a range of less than thirty yards. Faustpatrone 2 was heavier and had a stronger punch against armour. The 6.39-pound charge fired by the new weapon could slice through armour 200 millimetres thick. The biggest flaw in both weapons was their effective range of only about 100 feet, which brought the soldier employing it perilously close to the target and any infantry that might be screening it. However, the Faustpatrone was simpler to use, lighter, and more powerful than the PIAT or the American bazooka, both of which were more cumbersome, non-disposable weapons. The Faustpatrone was soon nicknamed Panzerfaust (Tank Fist) by the soldiers using them and later, even more powerful models were officially designated as such.

FORWARD OBSERVATION OFFICER (FOO)

Artillery batteries had two officers, usually captains. During a battle, one officer remained with the guns to oversee their operation. The other, the FOO, accompanied the infantry regiment that was being supported. He was usually part of a three-man team that included the FOO, a radio signaller, and a Bren carrier driver. The FOO was in charge of calling for artillery support and directing the fire toward enemy targets that were threatening or holding up the infantry.

GUNNER

The artillery regiment equivalent to a private.

HE

High explosive.

HQ

Any form of headquarters.

JERRY

Common term for Germans. Also spelled Gerry. Canadians seldom if ever used the harsher term Kraut, favoured by American soldiers. *Tedeschi*, the Italian word for German, was also popular, and Canadians occasionally used the terms Hun or Boche.

LEE ENFIELD RIFLE, NO. 4, MARK 1

Standard rifle of Commonwealth forces. The Mark 1 was made in Canada for Canadian personnel. It fired .303 ammunition contained in five-round clips. Effective range was 900 yards, but most accurate when fired at ranges under 600 yards. A highly reliable, rugged weapon. Capable of being mounted with an 8-inch spike bayonet.

MG

Machine gun.

MO

Medical Officer.

MORTARS

The Canadians had three weights of mortars: 2-inch, 3-inch, and 4.2-inch. The latter was a heavy mortar operated by the Saskatoon Light Infantry in support of the infantry regiments. The 3-inch was operated by a mortar platoon attached to each battalion, while 2-inch mortars were carried directly into battle by a section attached to each company. A mortar lobs a bomb on what is usually a high trajectory toward a target. The bombs can be high-explosive, shrapnel, or phosphorous (smoke). Range and firepower varied according to the size of the gun. The bigger the mortar, the greater its range and firepower. The 3-inch could engage targets as close as 125 yards and as far away as 2,800 yards. Its bomb weighed ten pounds. The 4.2-inch fired bombs of twenty pounds and had a much greater range. The small 2-inch put out only a 2.5-pound bomb, but was extremely useful for laying smokescreens.

NBH

8th Princess Louise New Brunswick Hussars.

NCO

Non-Commissioned Officer. All Warrant Officers, sergeants, and corporals are considered non-commissioned officers. NCOs provide the leadership backbone of infantry platoons and armoured troops.

NEBELWERFER

A launcher system that fired either 15-centimetre or 21-centimetre rockets in a rapid, 10-second sequence. The most common launch carriage used in Italy resembled a two-wheeled artillery gun carriage, but was mounted with six tubes rather than a single gun. A Nebelwerfer crew could routinely load and fire a volley every 90 seconds, but to avoid injury from the significant exhaust backblast had to take shelter in a trench at least 15 feet from the weapon before firing. Maximum Nebelwerfer range varied according to launcher size. The 15-centimetre Nebelwerfer 41 had a maximum range of 6,900 metres, while the 21-centimetre Nebelwerfer 42 could reach 7,850 metres. Known as "Moaning Minnies" because of the loud howling noise the rockets emanated during flight, Nebelwerfers were quite inaccurate. But when a stonk landed near or on target, casualties were almost inevitable because of the concentration of explosive and large chunks of shrapnel created when the rocket casing shattered.

OPS ORDERS
Operational orders.

ORDERS GROUP (O GROUP)
A session at which the orders setting out the tactics to be used in a forthcoming action are given to participating commanders. Most actions entail multiple O Groups, starting at the highest level and descending downward. A brigade planning an attack, for example, will have its first O Group called by the brigadier. He and brigade HQ staff will brief regimental commanders and the commanders of included supporting arms (artillery, heavy mortars, etc.). Regimental commanders then brief the company commanders, who in turn brief platoon commanders, who pass the information down to individual sections. What will start as a broad-stroke tactical plan at the brigade level will, by the time it hits platoon and section stages, become a set of intensely specific tasks that must be accomplished for the overall attack to succeed. A process of filtering out nonessential detail occurs all down the line until the section leader will have little idea of the purpose of the tasks his section must achieve.

PIAT
Projector Infantry Antitank. The hand-held antitank weapon of Commonwealth forces, weighing thirty-two pounds and firing a two-and-a-half pound hollow-charge explosive bomb. Difficult to load, prone to mechanical failure, and complicated to operate, the PIAT was an unpopular weapon. Effective against German tanks only if fired against the thinner side and rear armour plate, or against the tracks.

PIONEERS
Engineering personnel who were members of an infantry battalion's pioneer company. Pioneers had a higher level of expertise with regard to handling explosives, laying charges, carrying out demolitions, and defusing enemy mines and booby traps than the average soldier.

RECCE
Abbreviation of reconnaissance. Recce units are reconnaissance units, such as the Princess Louise Dragoon Guards or Governor General's Horse Guards.

SAPPER
Explosive and engineering personnel in the Royal Canadian Engineers, equivalent to private in the infantry.

SHERMAN TANK

The standard tank used by Canadian forces was the Sherman M-4A2, usually called the M-4. It weighed just under thirty-five tons. The Sherman had a five-man crew, consisting of commander, gunner, loader, driver, and assistant driver. Its main armament was a 75-millimetre gun. Fixed into the front of the tank was also a .30-calibre machine gun, and a .50-calibre machine gun could quickly be mounted on top of the turret for use as an anti-aircraft weapon. The Sherman had a top speed of about 29 miles per hour and a maximum range without refuelling of 150 miles. Although the Sherman would undergo only slight modifications over the course of the war, it was generally considered inferior to most German tanks in firepower and armour. It also had a higher profile, which made it harder to get into a hull-down (protected) stance than German tanks.

SLI

Saskatoon Light Infantry Regiment. The more official, but less commonly used, abbreviation was Sask LI.

SPG

Self-Propelled Gun. A standard artillery piece mounted on a tracked body. Lacking a turret, it could only fire directly at targets by wheeling the entire vehicle to face it. They also had no overhead cover to protect the crew and so were more vulnerable than tanks. The Allies generally used SPGs as mobile artillery that operated close to, but behind, the front lines. In many cases, the tank-deficient Germans attempted to deploy SPGs in a tank role, but their open-top design and inability to turn quickly to face a new threat left them highly vulnerable to both tank and infantry attack.

START POINT (SP)

Also called the Start Line (SL) or Jumping Off Point, the spot where a unit of any size forms up immediately before going into an attack.

THOMPSON SUBMACHINE GUN

Fondly referred to as the Tommy Gun by those who carried it, the Thompson was a .45-calibre submachine gun. The favoured submachine gun of Canadian forces and the only American weapon they respected. The Thompson could fit either a box or drum-shaped magazine. The use of .45-calibre ammunition gave the gun tremendous stopping power.

TROOPER

The armoured corps equivalent to a private. Trooper harks back to the armour's cavalry heritage.

TWENTY-FIVE POUNDER

The workhorse artillery gun of Commonwealth forces. Incredibly durable and reliable, the twenty-five pounder was manned by a crew of six. It was generally used as a howitzer — firing high-explosive shells at a high angle — but could also fire armour-piercing shot at flat trajectories. Effective range of 12,500 yards. Weighed four tons.

TYPE 36 GRENADE

Standard grenade of Commonwealth forces. Its metal case was ribbed, leading to its being called the "pineapple." Each of the eighty ribs broke into a separate shrapnel piece upon exploding. This type of grenade was usually thrown overhand in a lobbing manner.

VICKERS .303 MACHINE GUN, MARK 1

Remarkably, the medium machine gun that the Canadians used throughout World War II was essentially the same gun Canadian forces had used in World War I. With a simple gas-assisted recoil system, the gun was water-cooled and fired belts of .303 ammunition. Its accurate range was 1,100 yards, but it could fling bursts much farther. At full automatic, the Vickers put out bursts of 10 to 20 rounds. Rate of fire varied from 60 rounds a minute to 250 rounds, depending on whether the gunner was using slow or rapid fire. The Vickers weighed in at 40 pounds. It had amazing endurance, seldom failing to operate in even the most adverse conditions.

Although an adequate weapon, the Vickers was outclassed in performance by its German counterpart. The MG42 was rated the best gun of its type in the world for years after the war. Introduced in 1942, it had a remarkable firing rate of 1,200 rounds a minute. The MG42 had another advantage over the Vickers. It was actually a light–machine gun, weighing only 25.35 pounds. When fired using a bipod, the gun had a light machine gun range of about 600 yards. On a tripod, the range more than doubled and the weapon proved effective as an anti-aircraft gun.

NOTES

CHAPTER 1 / MILITARY SINS

1 Ron Hurley, interview by author, Vancouver, BC, 4 Oct. 2000.

2 Major J.E. Oldfield, *The Westminsters' War Diary: An Unofficial History of The Westminster Regiment (Motor) in World War II* (New Westminster, BC: n.p., 1964), 66–67.

3 Ron Hurley interview.

4 Stan Scislowski, *Not All of Us Were Brave* (Toronto: Dundurn Press, 1997), 174–75.

5 Alex Morrison and Ted Slaney, *The Breed of Manly Men: The History of the Cape Breton Highlanders* (Toronto: The Canadian Institute of Strategic Studies, 1994), 174.

6 Oldfield, 68–69.

7 Eric Morris, *Circles of Hell: The War in Italy, 1943–1945* (New York: Crown Publishers, 1993), 259–64.

8 Albert Kesselring, *The Memoirs of Field-Marshal Kesselring*, Lynton Hudson (trans.) (London: William Kimber, 1953), 196–97.

9 Morris, 270.

10 Colonel J.H. Green, *Cassino 1944: The Battles of Cassino* (Cassino: Lamberti Editore, 1989), 5–7.

11 David Hapgood and David Richardson, *Monte Cassino* (New York: Congdon & Weed, 1984), 211.

12 Green, 5–6.

13 Morris, 281.

14 Hapgood and Richardson, 42–46.

15 Morris, 7.

16 Green, 5.

17 Ibid., 57.

18 Ibid.

19 Morris, 295.

20 Ibid., 299.

21 Field Marshal Harold Alexander, "The Allied Armies in Italy," National Archives of Canada, n.d., 1.

22 Morris, 16.

23 Ibid., 1.

24 G.W.L. Nicholson, *Canadians in Italy: 1939–1945*, vol. 2 (Ottawa: Queen's Printer, 1956), 388.

25 Ibid., 463.

26 Ibid., 463–65.

27 Alexander, 4–5.

28 Colonel C.P. Stacey, "Report No. 179 Historical Section Canadian Military Headquarters: Canadian Operations in the Liri Valley, May–June 1944," 12–13.

29 Fred Majdalany, *The Battle of Cassino* (Boston: Houghton Mifflin, 1957), 253–54.

30 Ibid., 253.

31 Morris, 318.

32 Kesselring, 191–92.

33 Ibid., 199–200.

34 Morris, 315.

35 Ibid., 319.

CHAPTER 2 / THE UNWANTED CANADIANS

1 G.W.L. Nicholson, *Canadians in Italy: 1943–1945*, vol. 2 (Ottawa: Queen's Printer, 1956), 341–48.

2 Ibid.

3 Ibid.

4 Daniel G. Dancocks, *The D-Day Dodgers: The Canadians in Italy, 1943–1945*. (Toronto: McClelland & Stewart, 1991), 18–19.

5 J.A. Granatstein, *The Generals: The Canadian Army's Senior Commanders in the Second World War* (Toronto: Stoddart Publishing, 1993), 102–3.

6 Ibid., 157–58.

7 Dominick Graham, *The Price of Command: A Biography of General Guy Simonds* (Toronto: Stoddart Publishing, 1993), 60–62.

8 Ibid., 109–10.

9 Ibid.

10 Ibid., 110–12.

11 Nigel Hamilton, *Master of the Battlefield: Monty's War Years, 1942–1944* (New York: McGraw-Hill, 1983), 150.

12 Ibid., 177.

13 Richard S. Malone, *A Portrait of War: 1939–1943* (Don Mills, ON: Collins Publishers, 1983), 196–97.

14 Ibid., 197–98.

15 Ibid., 214–15.

16 Ibid., 215.

17 Dancocks, 208.

18 Dan Nikiforuk, interview by author, Sidney, BC: 27 Dec. 2000.

19 W.B. Fraser, *Always a Strathcona* (Calgary: Comprint Publishing, 1976), 148.

20 Nicholson, 357–59.

21 Crerar Papers, MG30 E157, vol. 7, 958C.001 (D180), National Archives of Canada, 10 Dec. 1943.

22 Malone, 199–200.

23 Crerar Papers, 17 Dec. 1943.

24 Ibid., 21 Dec. 1943.

25 Hamilton, 476.

26 Vokes Papers, Royal Military College of Canada Massey Library, "The Adriatic Front — Winter 1944, n.p.

27 Ibid., 9.

28 Granatstein, 107.

29 Nicholson, 355.

30 Ibid., 357.

31 Ibid., 363.

32 Ibid., 364.

CHAPTER 3 / BAPTISM OF FIRE

1 Stanley Scislowski, *Not All of Us Were Brave* (Toronto: Dundurn Press, 1997), 104.

2 Ibid., 109.

3 Strome Galloway, interview by author, Ottawa, ON, 6 May 2000.

4 Vokes Papers, Royal Military College of Canada Massey Library, "The Adriatic Front — Winter 1944," n.p.

5 Ibid.

6 Ibid.

7 Major General George Kitching, *Mud and Green Fields: The Memoirs of Major General George Kitching* (Langley, BC: Battleline Books, 1985), 186–87.

8 Ibid., 183.

9 Scislowski, 112–13.

10 Ibid.

11 Ibid., 113–14.

12 G.W.L. Nicholson, *Canadians in Italy: 1943–1945*, vol. 2 (Ottawa: Queen's Printer, 1956), 367.

13 Ibid.

14 Donald Creighton, interview by author, Vancouver, BC: 4 Oct. 2000.

15 Nicholson, 367.

16 Scislowski, 114–15.

17 Ibid., 114–16.

18 Nicholson, 371.

19 Ibid., 368–69.

20 Scislowski, 117.

21 Kitching, 187.

22 Charles Prieur, "Chronicles of The Three-Rivers Regiment (Tank) at War: Period 1939–1945" (unpub. MS, n.d., possession of the author), 144.

23 Scislowski, 118–19.

24 Nicholson, 369–70.

25 Alex Morrison and Ted Slaney, *The Breed of Manly Men: The History of the Cape Breton Highlanders* (Toronto: The Canadian Institute of Strategic Studies, 1994), 144–45.

26 Kitching, 188–89.

27 Nicholson, 370–71.

28 Prieur, 146.

29 Galloway interview.

30 Scislowski, 130–31.

31 Vokes, n.p.

32 Captain J.W. Spurr, "Report No. 111B Historical Section Canadian Military Headquarters: Situation of the Canadian Military Forces Overseas, Spring 1944," Department of National Defence, n.d., n.p.

33 Nicholson, 375–79.

34 Daniel G. Dancocks, *The D-Day Dodgers: The Canadians in Italy, 1943–1945* (Toronto: McClelland & Stewart, 1991), 213.

35 Vokes, n.p.

36 Don Smith, correspondence with author, 15 Aug. 2000.

37 Strome Galloway, *Sicily to the Siegfried Line: Being Some Random Memories and a Diary of 1944–1945* (Kitchener, ON: Arnold Press, n.d.), 11–12.

CHAPTER 4 / FRUSTRATED AMBITIONS

1 G.W.L. Nicholson, *Canadians in Italy: 1943–1945*, vol. 2 (Ottawa: Queen's Printer, 1956), 380.

2 Chris Vokes, *Vokes: My Story* (Ottawa: Gallery, 1985), 147.

3 Daniel G. Dancocks, *The D-Day Dodgers: The Canadians in Italy, 1943–1945* (Toronto: McClelland & Stewart, 1991), 212.

4 Vokes, *Vokes: My Story*, 147.

5 Vokes Papers, Royal Military College of Canada Massey Library, "The Adriatic Front — Winter 1944," n.p.

6 Nicholson, 378 ff.

7 Vokes papers, n.p.

8 Strome Galloway, *Sicily to the Siegfried Line: Being Some Random Memories and a Diary of 1944–1945* (Kitchener, ON: Arnold Press, n.d.), 13.

9 Captain J.W. Spurr, "Report No. 111B Historical Section Canadian Military Headquarters: Situation of the Canadian Military Forces Overseas, Spring 1944," Department of National Defence, n.d., n.p.

10 Ibid.

11 Bert Hoffmeister, interview by B. Greenhous and W. McAndrew transcript, Directorate of History, Department of National Defence, n.d., 78–79.

12 Spurr, n.p.

13 Strome Galloway, interview by author, Ottawa, 6 May 2000.

14 G.W. Stephen Brodsky, *God's Dodger* (Sidney, BC: Elysium Publishing, 1993), 203.

15 Galloway interview.

16 Ibid.

17 Lieutenant General E.L.M. Burns, *General Mud: Memoirs of Two World Wars* (Toronto: Clarke, Irwin, 1970), 133.

18 Ibid., ix–x.

19 J.A. Granatstein, *The Generals: The Canadian Army's Senior Commanders in the Second World War* (Toronto: Stoddart Publishing, 1993), 118–26.

20 Ibid., 132.

21 Dominick Graham and Shelford Bidwell, *Tug of War: The Battle for Italy, 1943–1945* (New York: St. Martin's Press, 1986), 254.

22 Ibid.

23 Bert Hoffmeister, interview by Greenhous and McAndrew transcript, 76.

24 Vokes papers, n.p.

25 Ibid.

26 Galloway interview.

27 Burns, 135–36.

28 Bert Hoffmeister, interview by Greenhous and McAndrew, 80.

29 Ibid., 79.

30 Ibid., 81–82.

CHAPTER 5 / DECEPTIONS

1 Colonel C.P. Stacey, "Report No. 179 Historical Section Canadian Military Headquarters: Canadian Operations in the Liri Valley," Department of National Defence, n.d., 15.

2 G.W.L. Nicholson, *Canadians in Italy: 1943–1945*, vol. 2 (Ottawa: Queen's Printer, 1956), 392.

3 Ibid.

4 Ibid.

5 Albert Kesselring, *The Memoirs of Field-Marshal Kesselring*, Lynton Hudson (trans.) (London: William Kimber, 1953), 198.

6 Field Marshal Harold Alexander, "The Allied Armies in Italy," vol. 3. National Archives of Canada, n.d., 9.

7 Ralph Bennett, *Ultra and Mediterranean Strategy: 1944–1945* (London: Hamish Hamilton, 1989), 276.

8 Stacey, 16.

9 Ibid., 15–16.

10 Alexander, 9.

11 Patrick D. Harrison, interview with author, Sidney, BC, 23 Aug. 2000.

12 Kim Beattie, *Dileas: History of the 48th Highlanders of Canada: 1929–1956* (Toronto: 48th Highlanders of Canada, 1957), 518.

13 Jim Quinn, "Gari River and the Gustav Line & Hitler Lines," *Onward II: The Informal History of the*

Calgary Regiment, 14th Canadian Armoured Regiment, Dick and Jessie Maltby (eds.) (Vancouver: 50/14 Veterans' Association, 1989), n.p.

14 Harrison interview.

15 Major G.D. Mitchell, *RCHA — Right of the Line: An Anecdotal History of the Royal Canadian Horse Artillery from 1871* (Ottawa: RCHA History Committee, 1986), 123.

16 Victor Bulger, correspondence with author, 6 Oct. 2000.

17 Ibid.

18 Brigadier E.A. McCusker, "Medical History of the War: 1 Canadian Corps, 1 April 1944–30 June 1944." RG24, Vol. 10779, National Archives of Canada, 9.

19 Bulger correspondence.

20 Harrison interview.

21 Alexander, 9.

22 Stacey, 19–20.

23 Ibid., 21.

24 Nicholson, 399.

25 W.G.F. Jackson, *Alexander of Tunis: As Military Commander* (London: B.T. Batsford, 1971, 282–83.

26 Martin Blumenson, *Mark Clark: The Last of the Great World War II Commanders* (New York: Congdon & Weed, 1984), 201–2.

27 Tony Foster, *Meeting of Generals* (Agincourt, ON: Methuen Publications, 1986), 418.

28 J.A. Granatstein, *The Generals: The Canadian Army's Senior Commanders in the Second World War* (Toronto: Stoddart Publishing, 1993), 133.

29 Lt. Gen. E.L.M. Burns, *General Mud: Memoirs of Two World Wars* (Toronto: Clarke, Irwin, 1970), 142–43.

30 1 Canadian Corps War Diary, May 1944, 1, National Archives of Canada.

31 1 Canadian Corps War Diary, May 1944, Appendix 1, Page 1, National Archives of Canada.

32 Tony Poulin, correspondence with author, 8 Sept. 2000.

33 Dan Nikiforuk, interview by author, Sidney, BC, 27 Dec. 2000.

34 1 Canadian Corps War Diary, May 1944, Appendix 1, p. 1.

35 Ibid.

36 Terry Copp and William McAndrew, *Battle Exhaustion* (Montreal: McGill-Queen's University Press, 1990), 77–78.

37 Vokes Papers, Royal Military College of Canada Massey Library, "The Adriatic Front — Winter 1944," n.p.

CHAPTER 6 / A JUST AND RIGHTEOUS CAUSE

1 Colonel C.P. Stacey, "Report No. 158 Historical Section Canadian Military Headquarters: Operations of the 1st Canadian Armoured Brigade in Italy: May 1944 to February 1945 — Part I, The Gustav and Hitler Lines," Department of National Defence, n.d., 7.

2 John Ellis, *Cassino: The Hollow Victory: The Battle for Rome, January–June 1944* (London: Andre Deutsch, 1984), 67–68.

3 G.W.L. Nicholson, *Canadians in Italy: 1943–1945*, vol. 2 (Ottawa: Queen's Printer, 1956), 395.

4 Ellis, 68–69.

5 Nicholson, 396.

6 Ellis, 68–69.

7 Three Rivers Regiment (12 CAR) War Diary, May 1944, Sheet No. 24, National Archives of Canada.

8 Ibid., Sheets No. 25–26.

9 Ibid., Sheet No. 26.

10 Stacey, 7–10.

11 Gwilym Jones, *To the Green Fields Beyond: A Soldier's Story* (Burnstown, ON: General Store Publishing, 1993), 80.

12 Ibid.

13 Three Rivers Regiment (12 CAR) War Diary, Sheets No. 28–29.

14 Ibid., Sheet No. 29.

15 Dominick Graham and Shelford Bidwell, *Tug of War: The Battle for Italy, 1943–1945* (New York: St. Martin's Press, 1986), 258–59.

16 Colonel C.P. Stacey, "Report No. 179 Historical Section Canadian Military Headquarters: Canadian Operations in the Liri Valley," Department of National Defence, 25 July 1947, 23.

17 Ellis, 280.

18 Ralph Bennett, *Ultra and Mediterranean Strategy: 1944–1945* (London: Hamish Hamilton, 1989), 277.

19 Ellis, 279–80.

20 Bennett, 277–78.

21 Ellis, 282 ff.

22 Ibid., 280.

23 Bennett, 277 ff.

24 Ellis, 281.

25 Ibid.

26 Nicholson, 393.

27 Graham and Bidwell, 265.

28 Nicholson, 398–99.

29 G.S. Branch HQ I Canadian Corps War Diary, May 1944, Appendix A, Intelligence Summary No. 52, National Archives of Canada, n.p.

30 Stephen E. Ambrose, *D–Day, June 6, 1944: The Climactic Battle of World War II* (New York: Simon & Schuster, 1994), 35.

31 Fritz Illi, interview by Major Michael Boire, Sinsheim, Germany, 19 Feb. 1999.

32 John Ellis, *Brute Force: Allied Strategy and Tactics in the Second World War* (London: Andre Deutsch, 1990), 325.

33 Graham and Bidwell, 269.

34 Ellis, 294.

35 Victor Bulger, correspondence with author, 6 Oct. 2000.

36 Major G.D. Mitchell, *RCHA — Right*

of the Line: An Anecdotal History of the Royal Canadian Horse Artillery from 1871 (Ottawa: RCHA History Committee, 1986), 124.

37 Bulger correspondence.

38 Peter Stursberg, CBC Radio broadcast, 11 May 1944, CBC Radio Archives.

39 Strome Galloway, interview by author, Ottawa, 6 May 2000.

40 Patrick Harrison, interview by author, Sidney, BC, 23 Aug. 2000.

41 Bulger correspondence.

42 Mitchell, 124.

43 Peter Stursberg, CBC Radio broadcast, 13 May 1944, CBC Radio Archives.

CHAPTER 7 / AN UNHOLY BALLS-UP

1 John Ellis, *Cassino: The Hollow Victory: The Battle for Rome, January–June 1944* (London: Andre Deutsch, 1984), 293–97.

2 Dominick Graham and Shelford Bidwell, *Tug of War: The Battle for Italy, 1943–1945* (New York: St. Martin's Press, 1986), 275.

3 G.W.L. Nicholson, *Canadians in Italy: 1943–1945*, vol. 2 (Ottawa: Queen's Printer, 1956), 402.

4 Ellis, 293.

5 Fred Majdalany, *The Battle of Cassino* (Boston: Houghton Mifflin, 1957), 77.

6 Ellis, 296–98.

7 Fred Ritchie, correspondence with author, Oct. 2000.

8 Ibid.

9 Colonel C.P. Stacey, "Report No. 158 Historical Section Canadian Military Headquarters: Operations of the 1st Canadian Armoured Brigade in Italy: May 1944 to February 1945 — Part I, The Gustav and Hitler Lines," Department of National Defence, n.d., 10.

10 Cyril Neroutsos, "Background to the Kingsmill Bridge," *Onward II: The Informal History of the Calgary Regiment, 14th Canadian Armoured*

Regiment, Dick and Jessie Maltby (eds.) (Vancouver: 50/14 Veterans' Association, 1989), n.p.

11 Tony Kingsmill, correspondence with author, 22 Jan. 2001.

12 Ibid.

13 Neroutsos, n.p.

14 Ian Seymour, "A Bridge Too Soon — For the Germans, That Is," *Onward II: The Informal History of the Calgary Regiment, 14th Canadian Armoured Regiment*, Dick and Jessie Maltby (eds.) (Vancouver: 50/14 Veterans' Association, 1989), n.p.

15 Kingsmill correspondence with author.

16 Tony Kingsmill, telephone interview with author, 26 Jan. 2001.

17 Kingsmill correspondence.

18 Stan Kanik, interview by author, Sidney, BC, 9 Aug. 2000.

19 Seymour, *Onward II*, n.p.

20 Stacey, 12.

21 Seymour, *Onward II*, n.p.

22 Ibid.

23 Gwilym Jones, *To the Green Fields Beyond: A Soldier's Story* (Burnstown, ON: General Store Publishing, 1993), 83.

24 11th Canadian Armoured Regiment War Diary, May 1944, National Archives of Canada, 4.

25 Al Cawsey, "The Gary River and Beyond," *Onward II: The Informal History of the Calgary Regiment, 14th Canadian Armoured Regiment*, Dick and Jessie Maltby (eds.) (Vancouver: 50/14 Veterans' Association, 1989), n.p.

26 11th Canadian Armoured Regiment War Diary.

27 Cawsey, n.p.

28 Kanik interview.

29 Jim Quinn, "Gari River and the Gustav & Hitler Lines," *Onward II: The Informal History of the Calgary Regiment, 14th Canadian Armoured*

Regiment, Dick and Jessie Maltby (eds.) (Vancouver: 50/14 Veterans' Association, 1989), n.p.

30 Ian Seymour, "A Bridge Too Soon," *Esprit de Corps*, n.d., 56.

31 Seymour, *Onward II*, n.p.

32 Kingsmill correspondence.

33 Seymour, *Onward II*, n.p.

34 Quinn, *Onward II*, n.p.

35 Graham and Bidwell, 278.

36 Eric Morris, *Circles of Hell: The War in Italy, 1943–1945* (New York: Crown Publishers Inc., 1993), 322.

37 Ibid., 216.

38 Major G.D. Mitchell, *RCHA — Right of the Line: An Anecdotal History of the Royal Canadian Horse Artillery from 1871* (Ottawa: RCHA History Committee, 1986), 124–25.

39 Ibid., 323.

40 Ibid.

41 Graham and Bidwell, 281.

CHAPTER 8 / A MOST SATISFACTORY DAY

1 G.W.L. Nicholson, *Canadians in Italy: 1943–1945*, vol. 2 (Ottawa: Queen's Printer, 1956), 404.

2 Colonel C.P. Stacey, "Report No. 179 Historical Section Canadian Military Headquarters: Canadian Operations in the Liri Valley," Department of National Defence, n.d., 24.

3 Ralph Bennett, *Ultra and Mediterranean Strategy: 1944–1945* (London: Hamish Hamilton, 1989), 282–83.

4 Albert Kesselring, *The Memoirs of Field-Marshal Kesselring*, Lynton Hudson (trans.) (London: William Kimber, 1953), 200.

5 Bennett, 283–84.

6 Nicholson, 404.

7 GS Branch HQ I Canadian Corps War Diary, May 1944, Appendix A, Intelligence Summary No. 51, National Archives of Canada, n.p.

8 John Ellis, *Cassino: The Hollow Victory: The Battle for Rome, January–June 1944* (London: Andre Deutsch, 1984), 310–11.

9 Jim Quinn, "Gari River and the Gustav & Hitler Lines," *Onward II: The Informal History of the Calgary Regiment, 14th Canadian Armoured Regiment*, Dick and Jessie Maltby (eds.) (Vancouver: 50/14 Veterans' Association, 1989), n.p.

10 Stan Kanik, interview by author, Sidney, BC, 9 Aug. 2000.

11 Quinn.

12 Fred Ritchie, correspondence with author, Oct. 2000.

13 Capt. R.T. Currelly, "Report on Operations of 14 CAR (Calgary Regiment) for the period of 10 May to 28 May 1944," Ottawa: Directorate of History, Department of National Defence, Aug. 31, 1944, 3–4.

14 Ritchie correspondence.

15 11th Canadian Armoured Regiment (Ontario) War Diary, May 1944, National Archives of Canada, p. 5.

16 Colonel C.P. Stacey, "Report No. 158 Historical Section Canadian Military Headquarters: Operations of the 1st Canadian Armoured Brigade in Italy: May 1944 to February 1945 — Part I, The Gustav and Hitler Lines," Department of National Defence, n.d., 14.

17 Stan Kanik interview.

18 Nicholson, 405.

19 Ibid., 6.

20 Peter Stursberg, CBC Radio broadcast, 18 May 1944, CBC Radio Archives.

21 Capt. Lex Schragg, *History of the Ontario Regiment: 1866–1951* (n.p., n.d.), 203.

22 N.a., "Account of Recent Operations by 11th Canadian Armoured Regiment (Ontario Regiment): The Breaking of the Gustav Line," Ottawa: Directorate of History,

Department of National Defence, n.d., 4.

23 Stursberg, 18 May 1944.

24 Schragg, 204.

25 Colonel C.P. Stacey, "Report No. 179," 25.

26 Ritchie interview.

27 Ibid.

28 14th Canadian Armoured Regiment (Calgary Tanks) War Diary, National Archives of Canada, n.p.

29 Colonel C.P. Stacey, "Report No. 158," 15.

30 14th Canadian Armoured Regiment War Diary.

31 Stacey, ibid.

32 Headquarters, 1st Canadian Armoured Brigade War Diary, May 1944, National Archives of Canada, 17–19.

33 Stan Kanik interview and Donald Reid, correspondence with author, 25 Oct. 2000.

34 Stan Kanik interview.

35 Bryan Perrett, *Tank Warfare* (London: Arms and Armour Press, 1990), 105–34.

36 Steve J. Coppinger, interview by Tom Torrie, 11 Aug. 1987, University of Victoria Special Collections.

37 Perrett, 105–34.

38 Lieutenant General E.L.M. Burns, *General Mud: Memoirs of Two World Wars* (Toronto: Clarke, Irwin, 1970), 140–41.

39 John Ellis, *Brute Force: Allied Strategy and Tactics in the Second World War* (London: Andre Deutsch, 1990), 325.

40 Bennett, 280–82.

41 Dominick Graham and Shelford Bidwell, *Tug of War: The Battle for Italy, 1943–1945* (New York: St. Martin's Press, 1986), 280.

42 Eric Morris, *Circles of Hell: The War in Italy, 1943–1945* (New York: Crown Publishers, 1993), 321–23.

43 Graham and Bidwell, 277.

CHAPTER 9 / ONE COULD NOT AFFORD TO GRIEVE

1 Gwilym Jones, *To the Green Fields Beyond: A Soldier's Story* (Burnstown, ON: General Store Publishing, 1993), 87–88.

2 G. W. L. Nicholson, *Canadians in Italy: 1943–1945*, vol. 2 (Ottawa: Queen's Printer, 1956), 405–6.

3 Horace Dugald Beach, interview by Chris D. Main, 15, 19, 24 May 1978, University of Victoria Special Collections.

4 12th Canadian Armoured Regiment (Three Rivers Regiment) War Diary, May 1944, Sheet No. 34, National Archives of Canada.

5 Ibid.

6 Colonel C.P. Stacey, "Report No. 158 Historical Section Canadian Military Headquarters: Operations of the 1st Canadian Armoured Brigade in Italy: May 1944 to February 1945 — Part I, The Gustav and Hitler Lines," Department of National Defence, n.d., 16.

7 12th Canadian Armoured Regiment War Diary, Sheet No. 35.

8 Beach interview.

9 12th Canadian Armoured Regiment War Diary, ibid.

10 Beach interview.

11 Ibid.

12 Colonel C.P. Stacey, 17.

13 Capt. Lex Schregg, *History of the Ontario Regiment: 1866–1951* (n.p., n.d.), 205.

14 Stacey, ibid., 16.

15 12th Canadian Armoured Regiment War Diary, Sheet No. 35.

16 Colonel C.P. Stacey, "Report No. 179 Historical Section Canadian Military Headquarters: Canadian Operations in the Liri Valley," Department of National Defence, n.d., 26.

17 Albert Kesselring, *The Memoirs of Field-Marshal Kesselring*, Lynton

Hudson (trans.) (London: William Kimber and Co., 1953), 200.

18 GS Branch HQ I Canadian Corps War Diary, May 1944, Appendix A, Intelligence Summary No. 53, National Archives of Canada, 1–2.

19 14th Canadian Armoured Regiment (Calgary Tank Regiment) War Diary, National Archives of Canada, n.p.

20 Stan Kanik, interview by author, Sidney, BC, 9 Aug. 2000.

21 Ibid.

22 Jim Quinn, "Gari River and the Gustav & Hitler Lines," *Onward II: The Informal History of the Calgary Regiment, 14th Canadian Armoured Regiment*, Dick and Jessie Maltby (eds.) (Vancouver: 50 / 14 Veterans' Association, 1989), n.p.

23 Kanik interview.

24 14th Canadian Armoured Regiment (Calgary Tank Regiment) War Diary.

25 Kanik interview.

26 14th Canadian Armoured Regiment (Calgary Tank Regiment) War Diary.

27 12th Canadian Armoured Regiment War Diary, Sheet No. 36.

28 11th Canadian Armoured Regiment (Ontario Tank Regiment) War Diary, National Archives of Canada, n.p.

29 12th Canadian Armoured Regiment War Diary, Sheet No. 37.

30 Jones, 85.

31 12th Canadian Armoured Regiment War Diary, ibid.

32 Dominick Graham and Shelford Bidwell, *Tug of War: The Battle for Italy, 1943–1945* (New York: St. Martin's Press, 1986), 282.

33 Lt. Gen. E.L.M. Burns, *General Mud: Memoirs of Two World Wars* (Toronto: Clarke, Irwin, 1970), 140.

34 Ibid., 144–45.

35 12th Canadian Armoured Regiment War Diary, Sheet No. 38.

36 Burns, 145.

37 Vokes Papers, Royal Military College of Canada Massey Library, "The Adriatic Front — Winter 1944, 36.

38 Ibid., 37.

39 Jones, 86–87.

CHAPTER 10 / IT IS STIFF FIGHTING

1 G.S. Branch, HQ 1st Canadian Infantry Division War Diary, May 1944, National Archives of Canada, n.p.

2 1st Canadian Infantry Brigade War Diary, May 1944, Sheet 4, National Archives of Canada.

3 Operations — Italy — Hitler Line, "Part III Engineers, 1 Canadian Infantry Division in the Liri Valley Battle," RG 24, Volume 10779, National Archives of Canada, 1.

4 1st Canadian Infantry Brigade War Diary, May 1944, Sheet 5.

5 48th Highlanders of Canada War Diary, May 1944, National Archives of Canada, n.p.

6 Royal Canadian Regiment War Diary, May 1944, National Archives of Canada, n.p.

7 1st Canadian Infantry Brigade War Diary, ibid.

8 Lieutenant G. Potts, "Battle Narrative: The Royal Canadian Regiment, 15 May 1944–24 May 1944," Department of National Defence, n.d., 1.

9 G.S. Branch, HQ 1st Canadian Infantry Division War Diary, May 1944, 10–11.

10 Ibid.

11 Royal Canadian Regiment War Diary, May 1944, n.p.

12 Dominick Graham and Shelford Bidwell, *Tug of War: The Battle for Italy, 1943–1945* (New York: St. Martin's Press, 1986), 284.

13 Colonel C.P. Stacey, "Report No. 179 Historical Section Canadian Military Headquarters: Canadian Operations in the Liri Valley,"

Department of National Defence, n.d., 26.

14 Royal Canadian Regiment War Diary, May 1944, n.p.

15 Hastings and Prince Edward War Diary, May 1944, National Archives of Canada, n.p.

16 1st Canadian Infantry Brigade War Diary, May 1944, Sheet 5.

17 Hastings and Prince Edward War Diary, ibid.

18 Stacey, 28.

19 Royal Canadian Regiment War Diary, May 1944, n.p.

20 Strome Galloway, *The General Who Never Was* (Belleville, ON: Mika Publishing, 1981), 200.

21 Stacey, 28.

22 Royal Canadian Regiment War Diary, ibid.

23 Kim Beattie, *Dileas: History of the 48th Highlanders of Canada, 1929–1956* (Toronto: 48th Highlanders of Canada, 1957), 519–20.

24 Stacey, 30.

25 Graham and Bidwell, 284–87.

26 G.S. Branch HQ I Canadian Corps War Diary, May 1944, Appendix A, Intelligence Summary No. 55, National Archives of Canada, n.p.

27 G.W.L. Nicholson, *Canadians in Italy: 1943–1945*, vol. 2 (Ottawa: Queen's Printer, 1956), 407.

28 Albert Kesselring, *The Memoirs of Field-Marshal Kesselring*, Lynton Hudson (trans.) (London: William Kimber, 1953), 202.

29 Stacey, 29.

30 Ibid.

31 War Diary West Nova Scotia Regiment, May 144, National Archives of Canada, n.p.

32 Ibid., 30.

33 Beattie, 525.

34 Cassino Map Sheet 160, Second Edition, 1943 Geographical Service, General Staff No. 4164. Copied from Carta Topigrafica 1/100,000 Sheet 160, 1927. Map in possession of the author.

35 Italy 1:50,000 Sheet No. 1, Atina, AFV Going Overprint, April 1944. Map in possession of the author.

36 Rowland Ryder, *Oliver Leese* (London: Hamish Hamilton, 1987), 168.

CHAPTER 11 / THE FOG OF WAR

1 Jean V. Allard, *The Memoirs of General Jean V. Allard* (Vancouver: University of British Columbia, 1988), 71–72.

2 Pierre Potvin, account in possession of the author, translated from French version published in *The Citadelle* (Tony Poulin, trans.), n.d., n.p.

3 Royal 22e Regiment War Diary, May 1944, National Archives of Canada, n.p.

4 3rd Canadian Infantry Brigade War Diary, May 1944, National Archives of Canada, n.p.

5 12th Canadian Armoured Regiment (Three Rivers) War Diary, May 1944, Sheet No. 39, National Archives of Canada.

6 Potvin account.

7 Ibid.

8 N.a., "History of Royal 22e Regiment from 17 May 1944 to 26 May 1944," Directorate of History, Department of National Defence, n.d., 1–2.

9 Potvin account.

10 Royal 22e Regiment War Diary, n.p.

11 Potvin account.

12 Thomas H. Raddall, *West Novas: A History of the West Nova Scotia Regiment* (n.p., 1947), 188.

13 West Nova Scotia Regiment War Diary, May 1944, National Archives of Canada, n.p.

14 12th Canadian Armoured Regiment War Diary, Sheet No. 39.

15 Raddall, 189.

16 West Nova Scotia Regiment War Diary, n.p.

17 3rd Canadian Infantry Brigade War Diary, n.p.

18 Raddall, 190.

19 N.a., "Regimental History Carleton and York Regiment," Directorate of History, Department of National Defence, n.d., 1.

20 Hastings and Prince Edward War Diary, May 1944, National Archives of Canada, n.p.

21 Lieutenant Colonel Don Cameron, Operations — Italy — Hitler Line, "Part V 1 Canadian Infantry Brigade in the Liri Valley Battle," RG 24, Volume 10779, National Archives of Canada, 3.

22 Lieutenant Colonel Don Cameron, The Hastings and Prince Edward Regiment Canadian Army Overseas, CMF, "The Battle of the Woods — Wed. 17 May 1944," Directorate of History, Department of National Defence, n.p.

23 Lieutenant Colonel Ian Johnston, 48th Highlanders of Canada, "The Liri Valley and the Adolf Hitler Line," Directorate of History, Department of National Defence, 1–2.

24 Bryan Perrett, *Tank Warfare* (London: Arms and Armour Press, 1990), 134–35.

25 Johnston, 2.

26 G.S. Branch HQ I Canadian Corps War Diary, May 1944, Appendix A, Intelligence Summary No. 58, National Archives of Canada, n.p.

27 Johnston, 3.

28 Kim Beattie, *Dileas: History of the 48th Highlanders of Canada, 1929–1956* (Toronto: 48th Highlanders of Canada, 1957), 532.

29 Hastings and Prince Edward War Diary, n.p.

30 Johnston, 3.

31 Beattie, 534–35.

32 Johnston, 3.

33 Ibid., 7.

34 Vokes Papers, Royal Military College of Canada Massey Library, n.p.

35 Ibid.

36 G.S. Branch HQ I Canadian Corps War Diary, May 1944, Appendix A, Intelligence Summary No. 56, National Archives of Canada, n.p.

CHAPTER 12 / DON'T LET IT GET YOU DOWN, CHUM

1 Pierre Potvin, account in possession of the author, translated from French version published in *The Citadelle* (Tony Poulin, trans.), n.d., n.p.

2 Ibid.

3 Jean V. Allard, *The Memoirs of General Jean V. Allard* (Vancouver: University of British Columbia, 1988), 74.

4 Potvin account.

5 Ibid.

6 Allard, 74.

7 Ibid., 74–75.

8 Lieutenant Colonel Ian Johnston, 48th Highlanders of Canada, "The Liri Valley and the Adolf Hitler Line," Directorate of History, Department of National Defence, 3.

9 Vokes Papers, Royal Military College of Canada Massey Library, n.p.

10 G.S. Branch HQ I Canadian Corps War Diary, May 1944, Appendix A, Intelligence Summary No. 57, National Archives of Canada, n.p.

11 Strome Galloway, interview by author, Ottawa, 6 May 2000.

12 Dominick Graham and Shelford Bidwell, *Tug of War: The Battle for Italy, 1943–1945* (New York: St. Martin's Press, 1986), 289.

13 Rowland Ryder, *Oliver Leese* (London: Hamish Hamilton, 1987), 170.

14 Peter Stursberg, *The Sound of War* (Toronto: University of Toronto Press, 1993), 167–68.

15 Charles Comfort, *Artist at War*

(Pender Island, BC: Remembrance Books, 1995), 135–36.

16 Ibid., 125–35.

17 Waldo E.L. Smith, *What Time the Tempest: An Army Chaplain's Story* (Toronto: Ryerson Press, 1953), 219–20.

18 Ibid., 238–39.

19 Jim Quinn, "Gari River and the Gustav & Hitler Lines," *Onward II: The Informal History of the Calgary Regiment, 14th Canadian Armoured Regiment*, Dick and Jessie Maltby (eds.) (Vancouver: 50/14 Veterans' Association, 1989), n.p.

20 Smith, 240.

21 C. Malcolm Sullivan, *3 Troop: A fighting unit of a Canadian Tank Squadron in wartime Italy and Holland, where Fear of Failure was finally overcome* (Saint John, NB: ImPresses, 1998), 73.

22 Capt. Lex Schregg, *History of the Ontario Regiment: 1866–1951* (n.p., n.d.), 208.

23 Ibid.

24 Ibid.

25 Sullivan, 74.

26 Schregg, 209.

27 Colonel C.P. Stacey, "Report No. 158 Historical Section Canadian Military Headquarters: Operations of the 1st Canadian Armoured Brigade in Italy: May 1944 to February 1945 — Part I, The Gustav and Hitler Lines," Department of National Defence, n.d., 22.

28 Schregg, 209.

29 Ibid., 209–10.

30 Ibid.

31 Stacey, 22.

32 "Account of Recent Operations by 11th Canadian Armoured Regiment (Ontario Regiment): The Breaking of the Gustav Line," Directorate of History, Department of National Defence, n.d., 7.

33 Schregg, 212.

34 Sullivan, 74.

35 Schregg, 212.

36 Ibid., 75.

37 Smith, 241–42.

38 Schregg, 211–12.

39 Smith, 241.

40 Stacey, 22.

41 Sullivan, 76.

42 "Account of Recent Operations by 11th Canadian Armoured Regiment (Ontario Regiment): The Breaking of the Gustav Line," 7.

43 Smith, 242.

44 Sullivan, 75.

CHAPTER 13 / WHERE ARE YOU GOING LIKE THAT, LITTLE POT?

1 N.a., Operations — Italy — Hitler Line, "Part VII, The Advance to and Breaching of the Adolf Hitler Line by 3 Canadian Infantry Brigade," RG 24, vol. 10779, National Archives of Canada, 1 June 1944, 3.

2 1st Canadian Infantry Brigade War Diary, May 1944, Sheet 7, National Archives of Canada.

3 48th Highlanders of Canada War Diary, May 1944, National Archives of Canada, n.p.

4 4th Canadian Reconnaissance Regiment (Princess Louise Dragoon Guards) War Diary, May 1944, National Archives of Canada, p. 4.

5 Jean V. Allard, *The Memoirs of General Jean V. Allard* (Vancouver: University of British Columbia, 1988), 71–75.

6 N.a., "Regimental History, Carleton and York Regiment," Directorate of History, Department of National Defence, n.d., 2.

7 Major J.P. Ensor, Carleton and York War Diary, May 1944, National Archives of Canada, n.p.

8 N.a., Operations — Italy — Hitler Line, "Part VII, The Advance to and

Breaching of the Adolf Hitler Line by 3 Canadian Infantry Brigade," 3.

9 Ibid.

10 Allard, 75.

11 Pierre Potvin, account in possession of the author, translated from French version published in *The Citadelle* (Tony Poulin, trans.), n.d., n.p.

12 Ibid.

13 Ibid.

14 Allard, 75.

15 N.a., "History of Royal 22e Regiment from 17 May 1944 to 26 May 1944," Directorate of History, Department of National Defence, 3.

16 Allard, 76.

17 Royal 22e Regiment War Diary, May 1944, National Archives of Canada, n.p.

18 Ibid.

19 Potvin account.

20 N.a., "History of Royal 22e Regiment from 17 May 1944 to 26 May 1944," 4.

21 Potvin account.

22 Allard, 76–77.

23 Royal 22e Regiment War Diary.

24 Lieutenant General E.L.M. Burns, I Canadian Corps War Diary, May 1944, National Archives of Canada, pp. 8–9.

25 Rowland Ryder, *Oliver Leese* (London: Hamish Hamilton, 1987), 170.

26 GS Branch, HQ I Canadian Corps War Diary, May 1944, Appendix A, Intelligence Summary No. 58, National Archives of Canada, n.p.

27 Vokes Papers, Royal Military College of Canada Massey Library, n.p.

28 Potvin account.

CHAPTER 14 / OPERATION CHESTERFIELD

1 Lieutenant General E.L.M. Burns, I Canadian Corps War Diary, May 1944, National Archives of Canada, p. 9.

2 N.a., "Report on Air Operations in Support of I CDN Corps, 11 May–4 June 1944," 8 June 1944, Directorate of History, Department of National Defence, 1.

3 Burns, I Canadian Corps War Diary, 9.

4 Ibid.

5 Vokes Papers, Royal Military College of Canada Massey Library, n.p.

6 GS Branch, HQ 1st Canadian Infantry Division War Diary, May 1944, National Archives of Canada, p. 15.

7 Colonel C.P. Stacey, "Report No. 179 Historical Section Canadian Military Headquarters: Canadian Operations in the Liri Valley," Department of National Defence, n.d., 40.

8 Vokes Papers.

9 John Ellis, *Cassino: The Hollow Victory: The Battle for Rome, January–June 1944* (London: Andre Deutsch, 1984), 389.

10 N.a., "Report Hitler Line Defences by GS, 1 Canadian Infantry Division," n.d., National Archives of Canada, 1.

11 Ibid.

12 Ibid.

13 GS Branch, HQ I Canadian Corps War Diary, May 1944, Appendix A, Intelligence Summary No. 54, National Archives of Canada, n.p.

14 G.W.L. Nicholson, *Canadians in Italy: 1943–1945*, vol. 2 (Ottawa: Queen's Printer, 1956), 416.

15 GS Branch, HQ I Canadian Corps War Diary, May 1944, Appendix A, Intelligence Summary No. 54.

16 N.a., "Report Hitler Line Defences by GS, 1 Canadian Infantry Division," 8.

17 GS Branch, HQ I Canadian Corps War Diary, May 1944, Appendix A, Intelligence Summary No. 54.

18 N.a., "Report Hitler Line Defences by GS, 1 Canadian Infantry Division," 10–14.

19 Ibid., 6–7.

20 Ibid., 5–10.

21 N.a., "The Enemy on the Adolf

Hitler Line: May 1944," n.d., National Archives of Canada, 4–5.

22 Ibid., 4.

23 Albert Kesselring, *The Memoirs of Field-Marshal Kesselring*, Lynton Hudson (trans.) (London: William Kimber, 1953), 202.

24 Stacey, 38.

25 GS Branch, HQ I Canadian Corps War Diary, May 1944, Appendix A, Intelligence Summary No. 58.

26 Royal Canadian Regiment War Diary, May 1944, National Archives of Canada, n.p.

27 Vokes Papers.

28 Pierre Potvin, account in possession of the author, translated from French version published in *The Citadelle* (Tony Poulin, trans.), n.d., n.p.

CHAPTER 15 / IT'S SHEER MURDER

1 N.a., "Report on Air Operations in Support of I CDN Corps, 11 May–4 June 1944," 8 June 1944, Directorate of History, Department of National Defence, 1.

2 Ibid.

3 1st Canadian Infantry Brigade War Diary, May 1944, Sheet 8, National Archives of Canada.

4 E.A. McCusker, "Medical History of the War: 1st Canadian Corps, 1 April 1944–30 June 1944," National Archives of Canada, 6–12.

5 Ibid., 5.

6 Charles Prieur, correspondence with author, 17 Aug. 2000.

7 Kim Beattie, *Dileas: History of the 48th Highlanders of Canada, 1929–1956* (Toronto: 48th Highlanders of Canada, 1957), 541.

8 1st Canadian Infantry Brigade War Diary, Sheet 8.

9 2nd Field Regiment, Royal Canadian Artillery War Diary, May 1944, National Archives of Canada, n.p.

10 1st Canadian Infantry Brigade War Diary, Sheet 8.

11 Ibid.

12 Daniel G. Dancocks, *D-Day Dodgers: The Canadians in Italy, 1943–1945* (Toronto: McClelland & Stewart, 1991), 248.

13 Strome Galloway, *A Regiment at War: The Story of the Royal Canadian Regiment, 1939–1945* (Royal Canadian Regiment, 1979), 139.

14 Strome Galloway, interview with author, Ottawa, 6 May 2000.

15 Vokes Papers, Royal Military College of Canada Massey Library, n.p.

16 Beattie, 543–45.

17 Vokes Papers.

18 48th Highlanders of Canada War Diary, May 1944, National Archives of Canada, n.p.

19 Ian Johnston, "48th Highlanders of Canada: The Liri Valley and the Adolf Hitler Line," Directorate of History, Department of National Defence, 4.

20 Ibid.

21 Ibid., 4–5.

22 Beattie, 556.

23 Johnston, 5.

24 Beattie, 557.

25 Johnston, 5.

26 Princess Louise Dragoon Guards War Diary, May 1944, National Archives of Canada, n.p.

27 3rd Field Regiment, RCA War Diary, May 1944, National Archives of Canada, n.p.

28 Johnston, 5.

29 Beattie, 559.

30 Lt. Gen. E.L.M. Burns, *General Mud: Memoirs of Two World Wars* (Toronto: Clarke, Irwin, 1970), 148.

31 Lt. Gen. E.L.M. Burns, I Canadian Corps War Diary, May 1944, National Archives of Canada, p. 10.

32 Beattie, 560–62.

33 Johnston, 6–7.

34 G.W.L. Nicholson, *Canadians in*

Italy: 1943–1945, vol. 2 (Ottawa: Queen's Printer, 1956), 414.

35 Albert Kesselring, *The Memoirs of Field-Marshal Kesselring*, Lynton Hudson (trans.) (London: William Kimber, 1953), 202.

36 N.a., "The Enemy on the Adolf Hitler Line: May 1944," n.d., National Archives of Canada, 5–6.

CHAPTER 16 / THE HARDEST THING TO WATCH

1 Cameron Ware, interview by Reginald Roy and William S. Thackray, 23 June, 25 June, and 10 July 1979 and 16 July 1980, University of Victoria Special Collections.

2 N.a., "Battle for the Liri Valley," Appendix to Seaforth Highlanders of Canada War Diary, May 1944, National Archives of Canada, n.p.

3 Ware interview.

4 Sydney Thomson, correspondence with author, Oct.1998; interview by author, 27 May 2000, Salmon Arm, BC.

5 G.R. Stevens, *A City Goes to War* (Brampton, ON: Charters, 1964), 289.

6 Princess Patricia's Canadian Light Infantry War Diary, May 1944, Appendix 15, "Battle of the Hitler Line," National Archives of Canada, June 1944, 2.

7 Ibid., 2–3.

8 Ware interview.

9 Ibid.

10 Stevens, 293.

11 "Account by Lieutenant Kenyon, RCE," 2 July 1944, Directorate of History, Department of National Defence, 1.

12 Rowland Ryder, *Oliver Leese* (London: Hamish Hamilton, 1987), 170.

13 G.W.L. Nicholson, *Canadians in Italy: 1943–1945*, vol. 2 (Ottawa: Queen's Printer, 1956), 414.

14 E.L.M. Burns, *General Mud: Memoirs of Two World Wars* (Toronto: Clarke, Irwin, 1970),149–50.

15 Brigadier Bill Ziegler, Operations — Italy — Hitler Line, "Part II Artillery 1 Canadian Infantry Division in the Liri Valley Battle," RG 24, vol. 10779, National Archives of Canada, 3–5.

16 N.a., "Report Hitler Line Defences by GS, 1 Canadian Infantry Division," n.d., National Archives of Canada, 5.

17 Vokes Papers, Royal Military College of Canada Massey Library, n.p.

18 PPCLI War Diary, Sheet 3.

19 Major Roy C.H. Durnford, diary, National Archives of Canada, 49.

20 Ibid., 54.

CHAPTER 17 / THOSE WERE FINE BOYS

1 Reginald Roy, *The Seaforth Highlanders of Canada, 1919–1965* (Vancouver: Evergreen Press, 1969), 292–93.

2 Princess Patricia's Canadian Light Infantry War Diary, May 1944, Sheet 18, National Archives of Canada.

3 Ibid.

4 Ibid.

5 Seaforth Highlanders of Canada War Diary, May 1944, National Archives of Canada, n.p.

6 N.a., "Major W. DeN. Watson, MC, interviewed at 14 General Hospital, 2 July 1944." Directorate of History, Department of National Defence, 1.

7 Princess Patricia's Canadian Light Infantry War Diary, May 1944, Appendix 15, "Battle of the Hitler Line," National Archives of Canada, June 1944, 3.

8 N.a., "Attack by 2 CIB on the Adolf Hitler Line, 23 May 1944," 10 July 1944, Directorate of History, Department of National Defence, 3.

9 N.a., "Major Watson interviewed at 14 General Hospital," 1.

10 N.a., "Attack by 2 CIB on the Adolf

Hitler Line, 23 May 1944," 10 July 1944, 4.

11 N.a., "Major Watson interviewed at 14 General Hospital," 1–2.

12 N.a., "Lieutenant Browne-Clayton, PPCLI, interviewed 15 Canadian General Hospital," 2 July 1944, Directorate of History, Department of National Defence, 1.

13 Arthur Bishop, *Courage on the Battlefield: Canada's Military Heritage, Vol. 2* (Toronto: McGraw Hill-Ryerson, 1993), 220–21.

14 Ibid., 221.

15 N.a., "Attack by 2 CIB on the Adolf Hitler Line, 23 May 1944," 5.

16 PPCLI War Diary, Sheet 20.

17 Ibid., Sheet 19.

18 Donald Gower, correspondence with author, 25 June 2000.

19 Cameron Ware, interview by Reginald Roy and William S. Thackray, 23 June, 25 June, and 10 July 1979 and 16 July 1980, University of Victoria Special Collections.

20 Loyal Edmonton Regiment War Diary, May 1944, National Archives of Canada, n.p.

21 G.R. Stevens, *A City Goes to War* (Brampton, ON: Charters, 1964), 294.

22 Loyal Edmonton Regiment War Diary, n.p.

23 Stevens, 161.

24 N.a., "Major Watson interviewed at 14 General Hospital," 1–2.

25 Vokes Papers, Royal Military College of Canada Massey Library, n.p.

26 "Report by CCRA 1 CDN Corps on Operations of Canadian Artillery in Italy, May–June 1944," n.d., Directorate of History, Department of National Defence, 23–24.

27 G.W.L. Nicholson, *The Gunners of Canada*, vol. 2 (Toronto: McClelland & Stewart, 1972), 204.

28 Charles Monroe Johnson, *Action*

With the Seaforths (New York: Vantage Press, 1954), 304–9.

29 Roy, 294–95.

30 Jack McLean, correspondence with Dr. Reginald Roy, n.d.

31 N.a., *The North Irish Horse, Battle Report: North Africa and Italy* (Belfast: W. and G. Baird, 1946), 33.

32 Seaforth Highlanders of Canada War Diary, n.p.

33 L.M. McBride, correspondence with Dr. Reginald Roy, 15 Feb. 1968.

34 Sydney Thomson, interview with author, 27 May 2000, Salmon Arm, BC.

35 Bishop, 223.

36 N.a., "Major Jim Allan, Seaforths of Canada, interviewed at 14 Canadian General Hospital 2 July 1944," Directorate of History, Department of National Defence, 1–2.

37 N.a., "CSM Duddle, Seaforth of Canada, interviewed 1 July 1944," Directorate of History, Department of National Defence, 1–2.

38 N.a., "Major Jim Allan interviewed at 14 Canadian General Hospital 2 July 1944," 2.

39 N.a., "CSM Duddle, interviewed 1 July 1944," 2–3.

40 Thomson interview.

41 N.a., "CSM Duddle, interviewed 1 July 1944," 3–4.

42 Roy, 305–6.

43 Ibid.

44 PPCLI War Diary, Sheet 21.

45 Gower correspondence.

46 Cameron Ware, interview by Reginald Roy and William S. Thackray.

47 Nicholson, 423.

48 PPCLI War Diary, Sheet 21.

49 Howard Mitchell, *My War: With the Saskatoon Light Infantry (M.G.), 1939–1945* (n.p., n.d.), 97.

50 G.R. Stevens, *Princess Patricia's Canadian Light Infantry, 1919–1957*, vol. 3 (Griesbach, AB: Historical

Committee of the Regiment, n.d.),
163.

51 Stevens, *A City Goes to War*, 296.

52 Roy, 310.

53 Nicholson, 423.

54 W.R. Freasby (ed.), *Official History
of the Canadian Medical Services,
1939–1945. Vol. 1: Organization and
Campaigns* (Ottawa: Queen's
Printer, 1956), 183.

55 Durnford, 54–55.

CHAPTER 18 / AN HONOUR TO DIE

1 Carleton and York War Diary, May
1944, National Archives of Canada,
p. 11.

2 Don Smith, correspondence with
author, 15 Aug. 2000.

3 Carleton and York War Diary, 11.

4 N.a., "Regimental History, Carleton
and York Regiment," n.d.,
Department of National Defence,
Directorate of History, 2–3.

5 Robert Tooley, *Invicta: The Carleton
and York Regiment in the Second
World War* (Fredericton, NB: New
Ireland Press, 1989), 238.

6 Ibid., 239.

7 Colonel C.P. Stacey, "Report No. 179
Historical Section Canadian
Military Headquarters: Canadian
Operations in the Liri Valley,"
Department of National Defence,
n.d., 44.

8 N.a., "Regimental History, Carleton
and York Regiment," 3.

9 3rd Canadian Infantry Brigade War
Diary, May 1944, National Archives
of Canada, pp. 4–5.

10 N.a., "Regimental History, Carleton
and York Regiment," 3.

11 Tooley, 242.

12 Stacey, 47.

13 N.a., "Regimental History, Carleton
and York Regiment," 4.

14 Stacey, 48.

15 Ibid., 50.

16 Vokes Papers, Royal Military College
of Canada Massey Library, n.p.

17 Stacey, 50.

18 West Nova Scotia War Diary, May
1944, National Archives of Canada,
p. 2.

19 Thomas H. Raddall, *West Novas: A
History of the West Nova Scotia
Regiment* (n.p., 1947), 193–94.

20 12th Canadian Armoured Regiment
(Three Rivers) War Diary, May 1944,
Sheets No. 45–46, National
Archives of Canada.

21 West Nova Scotia War Diary, 2.

22 Raddall, 195.

23 West Nova Scotia War Diary, 2.

24 12th Canadian Armoured Regiment
War Diary, Sheet No. 47.

25 West Nova Scotia War Diary, 2.

26 Raddall, 198.

27 Ibid., 200–2.

28 12th Canadian Armoured Regiment
War Diary, Sheet No. 47.

29 Jean V. Allard, *The Memoirs of
General Jean V. Allard* (Vancouver:
University of British Columbia,
1988), 78.

30 N.a., "History of Royal 22e Regiment
from 17 May 1944 to 26 May 1944,"
n.d., Directorate of History,
Department of National Defence, 5.

31 Allard, 78.

32 Ibid., 79.

33 Ian Johnston, "48th Highlanders of
Canada: The Liri Valley and the Adolf
Hitler Line," Directorate of History,
Department of National Defence, 6.

34 48th Highlanders of Canada War
Diary, May 1944, National Archives
of Canada, n.p.

35 Kim Beattie, *Dileas: History of the
48th Highlanders of Canada,
1929–1956* (Toronto: 48th
Highlanders of Canada, 1957),
570–74.

36 Johnston, 6.

37 Hastings and Prince Edward War

Diary, May 1944, National Archives of Canada, n.p.

38 Stacey, 54.

39 Hastings and Prince Edward War Diary, n.p.

40 Stacey, 54–55.

41 Arthur Bishop, *Courage on the Battlefield: Canada's Military Heritage, Vol. 2* (Toronto: McGraw-Hill Ryerson, 1993), 224.

42 G.W.L. Nicholson, *Canadians in Italy: 1943–1945*, vol. 2 (Ottawa: Queen's Printer, 1956), 425.

43 N.a., "The Enemy on the Adolf Hitler Line: May 1944," n.d., National Archives of Canada, 6.

44 Nicholson, 425–26.

45 Ibid., 397.

46 Bert Hoffmeister, interview by B. Greenhous and W. McAndrew transcript, Directorate of History, Department of National Defence, n.d., 87.

CHAPTER 19 / A GRUESOME TASK

1 John Dougan, interview by author, 9 Oct. 2000, Victoria BC.

2 Vokes Papers, Royal Military College of Canada Massey Library, n.p.

3 Lt. Gen. E.L.M. Burns, *General Mud: Memoirs of Two World Wars* (Toronto: Clarke, Irwin, 1970), 152.

4 Ibid., 149.

5 G.A. McCarter, correspondence with G.W.L. Nicholson, Deputy Director Historical Section General Staff, 3 Apr. 1951, 2–4.

6 Colonel C.P. Stacey, "Report No. 179 Historical Section Canadian Military Headquarters: Canadian Operations in the Liri Valley," Department of National Defence, n.d., 57.

7 Daniel G. Dancocks, *D-Day Dodgers: The Canadians in Italy, 1943–1945* (Toronto: McClelland & Stewart, 1991), 261.

8 Ibid., 263.

9 Royal Canadian Regiment War Diary, May 1944, National Archives of Canada, n.p.

10 Strome Galloway, *A Regiment at War: The Story of the Royal Canadian Regiment, 1939–1945* (n.p., n.d.), 139–40.

11 G.W.L. Nicholson, *Canadians in Italy: 1943–1945*, vol. 2 (Ottawa: Queen's Printer, 1956), 425.

12 Albert Kesselring, *The Memoirs of Field-Marshal Kesselring*, Lynton Hudson (trans.) (London: William Kimber, 1953), 202–3.

13 Stacey, 56–57.

14 Jack Haley, interview by author, 24 Aug. 2000, Victoria.

15 Wilf Gildersleeve, interviews by author, 14 Oct. 1998, 5 Oct. 2000, West Vancouver, BC.

16 Major Roy C.H. Durnford, diary, National Archives of Canada, 55.

17 Bill Worton, interview by author, 4 Oct. 2000, Vancouver, BC.

18 Ibid.

19 Victor Bulger, correspondence with author, 28 Nov. 2000.

20 Durnford, 56.

21 Haley interview.

22 Durnford, 56.

CHAPTER 20 / PUNCH

1 G.W.L. Nicholson, *Canadians in Italy: 1943–1945*, vol. 2 (Ottawa: Queen's Printer, 1956), 427.

2 Bill McAndrew, *Canadians and the Italian Campaign, 1943–1945* (Montreal: Éditions Art Global, 1996), 101.

3 I Canadian Corps War Diary, May 1944, National Archives of Canada, p. 12.

4 Nicholson, 427–28.

5 Colonel C.P. Stacey, "Report No. 179 Historical Section Canadian Military Headquarters: Canadian Operations in the Liri Valley,"

Department of National Defence, n.d., 59.

6 3rd Canadian Reconnaissance Regiment (Governor General's Horse Guards) War Diary, May 1944, National Archives of Canada, n.p.

7 Reginald Roy, *Sinews of Steel* (Toronto: Charters Publishing, 1965), 246.

8 N.a., "9th Canadian Armoured Regiment (British Columbia Dragoons): Report on Operations — 19 May 1944 to 29 May 1944," Directorate of History, Department of National Defence, 1.

9 "Comments by Major J.W. Eaton on the Battle of the Melfa Crossing," Reginald Roy Collection, University of Victoria, Special Collections, 2.

10 Roy, 247–48.

11 William Kurbis, correspondence with Reginald Roy, 26 July 1962, University of Victoria, Special Collections, 2–3.

12 G.T. Dodd, "Recollections of the Battle of the Melfa River," n.d., Reginald Roy Collection, University of Victoria, Special Collections, n.p.

13 Roy, *Sinews of Steel*, 249.

14 3rd Canadian Armoured Reconnaissance Regiment War Diary, n.p.

15 N.a., Governor General's Horse Guards, 1939–1945 (Toronto: Canadian Military Journal, 1954), 81–82.

16 Vokes Papers, Royal Military College of Canada Massey Library, n.p.

17 Gordon McGregor, interview by author, 3 Jan. 2001, Victoria, BC.

18 Carleton and York Regiment War Diary, May 1944, National Archives of Canada, 13.

19 K.D. Landell, *Royal Canadian Dragoons* (Montreal: The Regiment, 1946), 78–79.

20 Ibid., 79–80.

21 Lieutenant Colonel H.M. Jackson, *The Princess Louise Dragoon Guards: A History* (n.p., n.d.), 191.

22 McGregor interview.

23 Carleton and York War Diary, 13.

24 Nigel Taylor, correspondence with Reginald Roy, 15 July 1962, University of Victoria, Special Collections, 1–5.

25 Ibid.

26 Roy, 251.

27 Taylor correspondence, 5–6.

28 Roy, 250.

29 Nicholson, 429.

30 9th Canadian Armoured Regiment (British Columbia Dragoons) War Diary, May 1944, National Archives of Canada, n.p.

31 Roy, 251.

CHAPTER 21 / OUR SOMEWHAT WEARY SHOULDERS

1 Lieutenant E.J. Perkins, "Account of Action," n.d., Directorate of History, Department of National Defence, 1–3.

2 Lieutenant Colonel J.M. McAvity, *Lord Strathcona's Horse (Royal Canadians): A Record of Achievement* (Toronto: Brigdens, 1947), 69.

3 Perkins, 3–6.

4 Ibid.

5 N.a., "Report on Operations: 2nd Canadian Armoured Regiment Lord Strathcona's Horse (Royal Canadians) — 17 May to 31 May 1944," n.d., Directorate of History, Department of National Defence, 2.

6 2nd Canadian Armoured Regiment (Lord Strathcona's Horse) War Diary, May 1944, National Archives of Canada, p. 6.

7 McAvity, 74.

8 2nd Canadian Armoured Regiment War Diary, 7.

9 Perkins, 6–7.

10 Major John Mahony, "The Melfa Crossing," 1948, Directorate of History, Department of National Defence, 4.

11 McAvity, 75.

12 Westminster Regiment (Motorized) War Diary, May 1944, National Archives of Canada, n.p.

13 John Francis Burton, interview by Morgan Witzel, 12 Jan. 1984, University of Victoria Special Collections.

14 2nd Canadian Armoured Regiment War Diary, 7.

15 McAvity, 79.

16 Major J.E. Oldfield, *The Westminsters' War Diary: An Unofficial History of the Westminster Regiment (Motor) in World War II* (New Westminster, BC: n.p., 1964), 76.

17 Major John Mahony, "The Melfa Crossing," 5–6.

18 Perkins, 7–8.

19 Mahony, 6.

20 Dan Nikiforuk, interview by author, 27 Dec. 2000, Sidney, BC.

21 Mahony, 7.

22 Perkins, 8.

23 Mahony, 8.

24 Perkins, 9.

25 Mahony, 8–9.

26 Perkins, 9.

27 Mahony, 8–10.

28 Westminster War Diary, n.p.

29 Ibid.

30 Oldfield, 94–95.

31 Mahony, 11.

32 Ron Hurley, interview by author, 4 Oct. 2000, Vancouver, BC.

33 Mahony, 13.

CHAPTER 22 / BE VERY, VERY CAREFUL

1 Major John Mahony, "The Melfa Crossing," 1948, Directorate of History, Department of National Defence, 14.

2 Ron Hurley, interview by author, 4 Oct. 2000, Vancouver, BC.

3 Mahony, 14.

4 Ron Hurley interview.

5 Mahony, 14.

6 Ron Hurley interview.

7 Brigadier T.E. Snow, "11th Canadian Infantry Brigade: Report on the Battle of the Liri Valley," n.d., Directorate of History, Department of National Defence, 1–2.

8 Bert Hoffmeister, interview by B. Greenhous and W. McAndrew transcript, Directorate of History, Department of National Defence, n.d., 89–90.

9 N.a., "9th Canadian Armoured Regiment (British Columbia Dragoons): Report of Operations — 19 May 1944 to 29 May 1944," 7 June 1944, Directorate of History, Department of National Defence, 2.

10 Reginald Roy, *Sinews of Steel* (Toronto: Charters Publishing, 1965), 255.

11 H.A. Smitheram, correspondence with Dr. Reginald Roy, 29 May 1962, University of Victoria, Special Collections, 1–2.

12 Roy, 256–57.

13 Mahony, 14.

14 Major J.E. Oldfield, *The Westminsters' War Diary: An Unofficial History of the Westminster Regiment (Motor) in World War II* (New Westminster, BC: n.p., 1964), 92.

15 Roy, 257.

16 Neil Hockin, correspondence with Dr. Reginald Roy, 8 July 1962, University of Victoria, Special Collections, 7.

17 G.T. Dodd, correspondence with Dr. Reginald Roy, 16 July 1962, University of Victoria, Special Collections, 1.

18 Smitheram correspondence, 2.

19 R.A.C. Davis, correspondence with

Dr. Reginald Roy, 27 Sept. 1962, University of Victoria, Special Collections, 1–2.

20 Stephen J. Coppinger, interview by Tom Torrie, 11 Aug. 1987, University of Victoria, Special Collections.

21 Neil Hockin correspondence, 2–3.

22 Coppinger interview.

23 Davis correspondence, 3.

24 Coppinger interview.

25 Davis correspondence, 3.

26 Coppinger interview.

27 Hockin correspondence, 3–7.

28 Smitheram correspondence, 2–4.

29 N.a., "4th Canadian Anti-tank Regiment, RCA: General Report and Lessons Learned on Operations — 22 May 1944 to 31 May 1944," Directorate of History, Department of National Defence, n.p.

30 Irish Regiment of Canada War Diary, May 1944, National Archives of Canada, p. 16.

31 N.a., "4th Canadian Anti-tank Regiment, RCA," n.p.

32 Irish Regiment of Canada War Diary, 16.

33 Lieutenant E.J. Perkins, "Account of Action," n.d., Directorate of History, Department of National Defence, 12.

34 Ron Hurley interview.

35 Ibid.

36 Westminster War Diary, n.p.

37 G.W.L. Nicholson, *Canadians in Italy: 1943–1945*, vol. 2 (Ottawa: Queen's Printer, 1956), 436.

38 John Ellis, *Cassino: The Hollow Victory: The Battle for Rome January–June 1944* (London: Andre Deutsch, 1984), 421.

39 Nicholson, 436.

40 Ibid.

41 Dominick Graham and Shelford Bidwell, *Tug of War: The Battle for Italy, 1943–1945* (New York: St. Martin's Press, 1986), 337.

42 Nicholson, 437–38.

43 8th Princess Louise's New Brunswick Hussars War Diary, May 1944, National Archives of Canada, n.p.

44 Douglas How, *The 8th Hussars: A History of the Regiment* (Sussex, NB: Maritime Publishing, 1964), 216.

45 Cape Breton Highlanders War Diary, May 1944, National Archives of Canada, n.p.

46 The Perth Regiment of Canada War Diary, May 1944, National Archives of Canada, n.p.

47 Carleton and York Regiment War Diary, May 1944, National Archives of Canada, p. 14.

48 Dodd correspondence, 2.

49 Smitheram correspondence, 4–5.

50 Ibid., 1.

51 David Kinloch, correspondence with author, 30 Nov. 2000.

CHAPTER 23 / A BIT OF A BLACK EYE

1 Brigadier T.E. Snow, "11th Canadian Infantry Brigade: Report on the Battle of the Liri Valley," n.d., Directorate of History, Department of National Defence, 3.

2 Colonel C.P. Stacey, "Report No. 179 Historical Section Canadian Military Headquarters: Canadian Operations in the Liri Valley," Department of National Defence, n.d., 68.

3 Stanley Scislowski, *Not All of Us Were Brave* (Toronto: Dundurn Press, 1997), 203–5.

4 Ibid.

5 Cape Breton Highlanders of Canada War Diary, May 1944, National Archives of Canada, n.p.

6 Douglas How, *The 8th Hussars: A History of the Regiment* (Sussex, NB: Maritime Publishing, 1964), 217–18.

7 Cape Breton Highlanders of Canada War Diary, n.p.

8 Scislowski, 205–6.

9 Snow, 3.

10 Bert Hoffmeister, interview by B. Greenhous and W. McAndrew transcript, Directorate of History, Department of National Defence, n.d., 88.

11 N.a., "5 Canadian Armoured Regiment (8 NBH): Operations from Hitler Line to Ceprano, 24 May–31 May 1944," n.d., National Archives of Canada, 7–8.

12 How, 218.

13 Cape Breton Highlanders War Diary, n.p.

14 Snow, 3.

15 How, 219.

16 Scislowski, 207.

17 Snow, 3.

18 G.W.L. Nicholson, *Canadians in Italy: 1943–1945*, vol. 2 (Ottawa: Queen's Printer, 1956), 439–40.

19 Snow, 3.

20 N.a., "The Irish Regiment of Canada: Report on Operations — 17 May 1944 to 31 May 1944," n.d., Directorate of History, Department of National Defence, 2.

21 Irish Regiment of Canada War Diary, May 1944, National Archives of Canada, p. 17.

22 Snow, 4.

23 Stacey, 69.

24 Snow, 4.

25 How, 220–21.

26 N.a., "5 Canadian Armoured Regiment (8 NBH): Operations from Hitler Line to Ceprano, 24 May–31 May 1944," 9.

27 Scislowski, 208–9.

28 Ibid., 210.

29 N.a., "Report on Perth Operations: 24 May–30 May 1944, Appendix A," 22 June 1944, Directorate of History, Department of National Defence, n.p.

30 Snow, 4.

31 Cape Breton Highlanders of Canada War Diary, n.p.

32 N.a., "49th Anti-tank Battery, RCA: Report on Recent Operations — 21 June 1944," Directorate of History, Department of National Defence, 2.

33 Cape Breton Highlanders of Canada War Diary, n.p.

34 Snow, 4.

35 Nicholson, 440.

36 N.a., "49th Anti-tank Battery, RCA: Report on Perth Operations: 24 May–30 May 1944," 3.

37 Snow, 4–5.

38 Nicholson, 441.

39 Col. A.J. Kerry and Maj. W.A. McDill, *History of the Corps of Royal Canadian Engineers*, vol. 2 (Ottawa: The Military Engineers Association of Canada, 1966), 211–12.

40 Nicholson, 441.

41 Kerry and McDill, 212.

42 Lt. Gen. E.L.M. Burns, *General Mud: Memoirs of Two World Wars* (Toronto: Clarke, Irwin, 1970), 159.

43 G.A. McCarter, correspondence with G.W.L. Nicholson, Deputy Director Historical Section General Staff, 3 April 1951, 3.

44 9th Canadian Armoured Regiment (British Columbia Dragoons) War Diary, May 1944, National Archives of Canada, n.p.

45 Snow, 5.

46 N.a., "The Irish Regiment of Canada: Report on Operations, 17 May 1944 to 31 May 1944," 3.

CHAPTER 24 / PUSH ON

1 David Kinloch, correspondence with author, 22 Nov. 2000.

2 Brigadier Desmond Smith, "The Crossing of the Melfa and the Securing of a Bridgehead by 5 Canadian Armoured Brigade Group," in Canadian Operations in the Mediterranean Area: May 1944, Extracts from Memoranda (Series

20), n.d., National Archives of Canada, 11–12.

3 9th Canadian Armoured Regiment (British Columbia Dragoons) War Diary, May 1944, National Archives of Canada, n.p.

4 Reginald Roy, *Sinews of Steel* (Toronto: Charters Publishing, 1965), 269.

5 Kinloch correspondence, 22 Nov. 2000.

6 9th Canadian Armoured Regiment War Diary, n.p.

7 Kinloch correspondence, 22 Nov. 2000.

8 9th Canadian Armoured Regiment War Diary, n.p.

9 Kinloch correspondence, 22 Nov. 2000.

10 N.a., "The Westminster Regiment (Motor): Report on Operations, 24 May–30 May 1944," n.d. Directorate of History, Department of National Defence, n.p.

11 9th Canadian Armoured Regiment War Diary, n.p.

12 Kinloch correspondence, 22 Nov. 2000.

13 Major J.C. Oldfield, *The Westminsters' War Diary: An Unofficial History of the Westminster Regiment (Motor) in World War II* (New Westminster, BC: n.p., 1964), 99.

14 N.a., "The Westminster Regiment (Motor): Report on Operations, 24 May–30 May 1944," n.p.

15 G.W.L. Nicholson, *Canadians in Italy: 1943–1945*, vol. 2 (Ottawa: Queen's Printer, 1956), 444.

16 H.A. Smitheram, correspondence with Dr. Reginald Roy, 29 May 1962, University of Victoria, Special Collections, 5.

17 9th Armoured Regiment War Diary, n.p.

18 Smitheram correspondence, 5.

19 Kinloch correspondence, 22 Nov. 2000.

20 Roy, 271; Kinloch correspondence, 22 Nov. 2000.

21 N.a., "9th Canadian Armoured Regiment (British Columbia Dragoons): Report on Operations — 19 May 1944 to 29 May 1944," 7 June 1944, Directorate of History, Department of National Defence, 3.

22 The Westminster Regiment (Motorized) War Diary, May 1944, National Archives of Canada, n.p.

23 Brigadier T.E. Snow, "11th Canadian Infantry Brigade: Report on the Battle of the Liri Valley," n.d., Directorate of History, Department of National Defence, 5.

24 Stanley Scislowski, *Not All of Us Were Brave* (Toronto: Dundurn Press, 1997), 218.

25 Snow, 5.

26 N.a., "Report on Perth Operations: 24 May–30 May 1944," 22 June 1944, Directorate of History, Department of National Defence, n.p.

27 Colonel C.P. Stacey, "Report No. 179 Historical Section Canadian Military Headquarters: Canadian Operations in the Liri Valley," Department of National Defence, n.d., 72.

28 Snow, 5.

29 Stacey, 71.

30 Ibid., 220–21.

31 John Ellis, *Cassino: The Hollow Victory: The Battle for Rome, January–June 1944* (London: Andre Deutsch, 1984), 448–51.

32 Nicholson, 437.

33 Ellis, 448.

34 Ibid., 451.

35 Rowland Ryder, *Oliver Leese* (London: Hamish Hamilton, 1987), 171–72.

36 Douglas How, *The 8th Hussars: A History of the Regiment* (Sussex, NB: Maritime Publishing, 1964), 222.

37 8th Princess Louise's New Brunswick Hussars War Diary, May 1944, National Archives of Canada, n.p.

38 N.a., "Report on Operations: 2nd Canadian Armoured Regiment, Lord Strathcona's Horse (Royal Canadians) 17 May to 31 May 1944," Directorate of History, Department of National Defence, 3.

39 Lieutenant Colonel J.M. McAvity, *Lord Strathcona's Horse (Royal Canadians): A Record of Achievement* (Toronto: Brigdens, 1947), 90–94.

CHAPTER 25 / VIVA IL CANADESE

1 Seaforth Highlanders of Canada War Diary, May 1944, National Archives of Canada, n.p.

2 Loyal Edmonton War Diary, May 1944, National Archives of Canada, n.p.

3 G.R. Stevens, *Princess Patricia's Canadian Light Infantry, 1919–1957*, vol. 3 (Griesbach, AB: Historical Committee of the Regiment, n.d.), 165.

4 Princess Patricia's Canadian Light Infantry War Diary, May 1944, Sheet 27, National Archives of Canada.

5 Loyal Edmonton War Diary, n.p.

6 Princess Patricia's Canadian Light Infantry War Diary, Sheet 28.

7 N.a., "Report on Action of May 31 1944, Appendix 17 to Seaforth Highlanders of Canada War Diary," May 1944, National Archives of Canada, n.p.

8 Reginald Roy, *The Seaforth Highlanders of Canada, 1919–1965* (Vancouver: Evergreen Press, 1969), 315–16.

9 Seaforth Highlanders of Canada War Diary, n.p.

10 Strome Galloway, interview by author, 6 May 2000, Ottawa.

11 Jim Stone, interview by William S. Thackray, 13 and 20 May; 3, 10, and 17 June 1980, University of Victoria, Special Collections.

12 N.a., Operations — Italy — Hitler Line, "Part VI 2 Canadian Infantry Brigade in the Liri Valley Battle, Section V: Capture of Mt. Radicino," RG 24, Volume 10779, National Archives of Canada, n.d.

13 Lt. Col. Jim Ritchie, "Capture of Ferentino and Anagni by the RCR," Directorate of History, Department of National Defence, 1.

14 Lt. Col. H.M. Jackson, *The Princess Louise Dragoon Guards: A History* (Ottawa: The Regiment, 1952), 193.

15 G.R. Stevens, *The Royal Canadian Regiment: Vol. 2, 1933–1966* (London, ON: London Printing, 1967), 142.

16 Lt. G. Potts, "The Following Supplementary Narrative," attached to Lt. Col. Jim Ritchie, "Capture of Ferentino and Anagni by the RCR," Directorate of History, Department of National Defence, 2.

17 Strome Galloway, *A Regiment at War: The Story of the Royal Canadian Regiment, 1939–1945* (Royal Canadian Regiment, reprint 1979), 143.

18 Bill Worton, interview by author, 4 Oct. 2000, Vancouver, BC.

19 Colonel C.P. Stacey, "Report No. 179 Historical Section Canadian Military Headquarters: Canadian Operations in the Liri Valley, Appendix C," Department of National Defence, n.d., n.p.

20 Bill McAndrew, *Canadians and the Italian Campaign, 1943–1945* (Montreal: Éditions Art Global, 1996), 108.

21 Lt. Gen. E.L M. Burns, *General Mud: Memoirs of Two World Wars* (Toronto: Clarke, Irwin, 1970), 162–63.

22 Burns correspondence to Crerar, 7
July 1944, MG30 E157, vol. 7,
National Archives of Canada.

23 Brigadier T.E. Snow, "11th Canadian
Infantry Brigade: Report on the
Battle of the Liri Valley," n.d.,
Directorate of History, Department
of National Defence, 7–8.

24 Documents contained in MG30,
E157 GOC-in-C 5-0-3, vol. 1,
National Archives of Canada.

25 Galloway interview.

26 Pierre Potvin, account in possession
of the author, translated from French
version published in *The Citadelle*
(Tony Poulin, trans.), n.d., n.p.

27 Jean V. Allard, *The Memoirs of
General Jean V. Allard* (Vancouver:
University of British Columbia,
1988), 82.

28 Galloway interview.

29 Galloway, *A Regiment at War*, 146.

BIBLIOGRAPHY

BOOKS

Allard, Jean V. *The Memoirs of General Jean V. Allard*. Vancouver: University of British Columbia Press, 1988.

Beattie, Kim. *Dileas: History of the 48th Highlanders of Canada, 1929–1956*. Toronto: 48th Highlanders of Canada, 1957.

Bennett, Ralph. *Ultra and Mediterranean Strategy: 1944–1945*. London: Hamish Hamilton, 1989.

Bishop, Arthur. *Courage on the Battlefield: Canada's Military Heritage, Vol. 2*. Toronto: McGraw Hill-Ryerson, 1993.

Blumenson, Martin. *Mark Clark: The Last of the Great World War II Commanders*. New York: Congdon & Weed, 1984.

Boissonault, Charles-Marie. *Histoire du Royal 22e Régiment*. Québec: Éditions du Pélican, 1964.

Brodsky, Gabriel Wilfrid Stephen. *God's Dodger*. Sidney, BC: Elysium Publishing, 1993.

Burns, E.L.M. *General Mud: Memoirs of Two World Wars*. Toronto: Clarke, Irwin, 1970.
—— . *Manpower in the Canadian Army, 1939–1945*. Toronto: Clarke, Irwin, 1956.

Cederberg, Fred. *The Long Road Home: The Autobiography of a Canadian Soldier in Italy in World War II*. Toronto: Stoddart Publishing, 1985.

Comfort, Charles. *Artist at War*. Pender Island, BC: Remembrance Books, 1995.

Copp, Terry, and William McAndrew. *Battle Exhaustion*. Montreal: McGill-Queen's University Press, 1990.

Dancocks, Daniel G. *The D-Day Dodgers: The Canadians in Italy, 1943–1945*. Toronto: McClelland & Stewart, 1991.

Duquemin, Colin K. *Stick to the Guns: A Short History of the 10th Field Battery, Royal Regiment of Canadian Artillery, St. Catharines, Ontario*. St. Catharines, ON: Norman Enterprises, 1996.

Ellis, John. *Brute Force: Allied Strategy and Tactics in the Second World War*. London: Andre Deutsch, 1990.
—— . *Cassino: The Hollow Victory: The Battle for Rome, January–June 1944*. London: Andre Deutsch, 1984.

———. *The Sharp End of War: The Fighting Man in World War II*. London: David and Charles (Publishers), 1980.

Foster, Tony. *Meeting of Generals*. Agincourt, ON: Methuen Publications, 1986.

Fraser, W.B. *Always a Strathcona*. Calgary: Comprint Publishing, 1976.

Freasby, W.R. (ed.). *Official History of the Canadian Medical Services, 1939–1945, Vol. 1: Organization and Campaigns*. Ottawa: Queen's Printer, 1956.

———. *Official History of the Canadian Medical Services, 1939–1945, Vol. 2: Clinical Subjects*. Ottawa: Queen's Printer, 1953.

Galloway, Strome. *The General Who Never Was*. Belleville, ON: Mika Publishing, 1981.

———. *A Regiment at War: The Story of the Royal Canadian Regiment, 1939–1945*. Royal Canadian Regiment, reprint 1979.

———. *Sicily to the Siegfried Line: Being Some Random Memories and a Diary of 1944–1945*. Kitchener, ON: Arnold Press, n.d.

The Governor General's Horse Guards, 1939–1945. Toronto: Canadian Military Journal, 1954.

Graham, Dominick. *The Price of Command: A Biography of General Guy Simonds*. Toronto: Stoddart Publishing, 1993.

———, and Shelford Bidwell. *Tug of War: The Battle for Italy, 1943–1945*. New York: St. Martin's Press, 1986.

Granatstein, J.A. *The Generals: The Canadian Army's Senior Commanders in the Second World War*. Toronto: Stoddart Publishing, 1993.

Green, J.H. *Cassino 1944: The Battles of Cassino*. Cassino: Lamberti Editore, 1989.

Hamilton, Nigel. *Master of the Battlefield: Monty's War Years, 1942–1944*. New York: McGraw-Hill, 1983.

Hapgood, David, and David Richardson. *Monte Cassino*. New York: Congdon Weed, 1984.

History of 17th Field Regiment, Royal Canadian Artillery: 5th Canadian Armoured Division. Groningen, Holland: J. Niemeijer's Co., 1946.

How, Douglas. *The 8th Hussars: A History of the Regiment*. Sussex, NB: Maritime Publishing, 1964.

Hurley, Ron. *Ritorno in Italia: Thirty Years After*. New Westminster, BC: n.p., 1976.

Jackson, H.M. *The Princess Louise Dragoon Guards: A History*. Ottawa: The Regiment, 1952.

———. *The Royal Regiment of Artillery, Ottawa, 1855–1952*. n.p., 1952.

Jackson, W.G.F. *Alexander of Tunis: As Military Commander*. London: B.T. Batsford, 1971.

Johnson, Charles Monroe. *Action With the Seaforths*. New York: Vantage Press, 1954.

[Johnston, Stafford.] *The Fighting Perths: The story of the first century in the life of a Canadian county regiment*. Stratford, ON: Perth Regiment Veterans' Assoc., 1964.

Jones, Gwilym. *To the Green Fields Beyond: A Soldier's Story*. Burnstown, ON: General Store Publishing, 1993.

Kerry, Col. A.J., and Maj. W.A. McDill. *History of the Corps of Royal Canadian Engineers*. Vol. 2. Ottawa: The Military Engineers Assoc. of Canada, 1966.

Kesselring, Albert. Lynton Hudson (trans) *The Memoirs of Field-Marshal Kesselring*. London: William Kimber, 1953.

Kitching, George. *Mud and Green Fields: The Memoirs of Major General George Kitching*. Langley, BC: Battleline Books, 1986.

Landell, K.D. *Royal Canadian Dragoons*. Montreal: The Regiment, 1946.

McAndrew, Bill. *Canadians and the Italian Campaign, 1943–1945*. Montreal: Éditions Art Global, 1996.

McAvity, J.M. *Lord Strathcona's Horse (Royal Canadians): A Record of Achievement*. Toronto: Brigdens, 1947.

McDougall, Robert L. *A Narrative of War: From the Beaches of Sicily to the Hitler Line With the Seaforth Highlanders of Canada*. Ottawa: Golden Dog Press, 1996.

Majdalany, Fred. *The Battle of Cassino*. Boston: Houghton Mifflin, 1957.

Malone, Richard S. *A Portrait of War: 1939–1943*. Don Mills, ON: Collins Publishers, 1983.

Maltby, Dick, and Jessie Maltby (eds.). *Onward I: The Informal History of the Calgary Regiment, 14th Canadian Armoured Regiment*. Vancouver: 50/14 Veterans' Assoc., 1989.

——— . *Onward II: The Informal History of the Calgary Regiment, 14th Canadian Armoured Regiment*. Vancouver: 5/14 Veterans' Assoc., 1989.

Mitchell, G.D. *RCHA — Right of the Line: An Anecdotal History of the Royal Canadian Horse Artillery from 1871*. Ottawa: RCHA History Committee, 1986.

Mitchell, Howard. *My War: With the Saskatoon Light Infantry (M.G.), 1939–1945*. N.p., n.d.

Morris, Eric. *Circles of Hell: The War in Italy, 1943–1945*. New York: Crown Publishers, 1993.

Morrison, Alex, and Ted Slaney. *The Breed of Manly Men: The History of the Cape Breton Highlanders*. Toronto: The Canadian Institute of Strategic Studies, 1994.

Mowat, Farley. *The Regiment*. 2nd ed. Toronto: McClelland & Stewart, 1973.

Nicholson, G.W.L. *The Canadians in Italy: 1939–1945*. Vol. 2. Ottawa: Queen's Printer, 1956.

——— . *The Gunners of Canada*. Vol. 2. Toronto: McClelland & Stewart, 1972.

The North Irish Horse, Battle Report: North Africa and Italy. Belfast: W. and G. Baird, 1946.

Oldfield, J.E. *The Westminsters' War Diary: An Unofficial History of the Westminster Regiment (Motor) in World War II*. New Westminster, BC: n.p., 1964.

Perrett, Bryan. *Tank Warfare*. London: Arms and Armour Press, 1990.

——— . *Through Mud and Blood: Infantry/Tank Operations in World War II*. London: Robert Hale and Co., 1975.

Quayle, J.T.B. *In Action: A Personal Account of the Italian and Netherlands Campaigns of WW II*. Abbotsford, BC: Blue Stone Publishers, 1997.

Raddall, Thomas H. *West Novas: A History of the West Nova Scotia Regiment*. N.p., 1947.

Rowland, David Parsons. *The Padre*. Scarborough, ON: Consolidated Amethyst Communications, 1982.

Roy, Reginald H. *The Seaforth Highlanders of Canada, 1919–1965*. Vancouver: Evergreen Press, 1969.

——— . *Sinews of Steel*. Toronto: Charters Publishing, 1965.

Ryder, Rowland. *Oliver Leese*. London: Hamish Hamilton, 1987.

Schragg, Lex. *History of the Ontario Regiment: 1866–1951*. N.p., n.d.

Scislowski, Stan. *Not All of Us Were Brave*. Toronto: Dundurn Press, 1997.

Smith, Waldo E.L. *What Time the Tempest: An Army Chaplain's Story*. Toronto: Ryerson Press, 1953.

Stevens, G.R. *A City Goes to War*. Brampton, ON: Charters Publishing, 1964.

——. *Princess Patricia's Canadian Light Infantry, 1919–1957*. Vol. 3. Griesbach, AB: Historical Committee of the Regiment, n.d.

——. *The Royal Canadian Regiment. Vol. 2, 1933–1966*. London, ON: London Printing, 1967.

Stursberg, Peter. *The Sound of War*. Toronto: University of Toronto Press, 1993.

Sullivan, C. Malcolm. *3 Troop: A fighting unit of a Canadian Tank Squadron in wartime Italy and Holland, where Fear of Failure was finally overcome*. Saint John, NB: ImPresses, 1998.

Tooley, Robert. *Invicta: The Carleton and York Regiment in the Second World War*. Fredericton, NB: New Ireland Press, 1989.

Vokes, Chris. *Vokes: My Story*. Ottawa: Gallery, 1985.

Wallace, John F. *Dragons of Steel: Canadian Armour in Two World Wars*. Burstown, ON: General Store Publishing, 1995.

Westphal, Siegfried. *The German Army in the West*. London: Cassell and Co., 1951.

Wood, Gordon. *The Story of the Irish Regiment of Canada, 1939–1945*. Heerenveen, Holland: Hepkema, 1945.

UNPUBLISHED MATERIALS

Account of Recent Operations by 11th Canadian Armoured Regiment (Ontario Regiment): The Breaking of the Gustav Line. 141.4A11.013(D1). Department of National Defence, Directorate of History.

Allan, J.C. (Major). "Major J.C. Allan, Seaforths of Canada, interviewed at 14 Cdn. Gen. Hosp. 2 July 1944." 145.255.011. Department of National Defence, Directorate of History.

Alexander, Harold Rupert Leofric George (Field Marshal). The Allied Armies in Italy, Vol. 3. MG27 III AI, Vol. 6.

Attack by 2 CIB on the Adolf Hitler Line, 23 May 1944. 10 July 1944. RG24, Vol. 10982. DND Dir. of History.

Award of the Victoria Cross to Major John Keefer Mahony, The Westminster Regiment (Motor). 713.013(D2). Department of National Defence, Directorate of History.

Battle of the Hitler Line: Part Played by the Princess Patricia's Canadian Light Infantry. 10 June 1944. War Diary Appendix, Princess Patricia's Canadian Light Infantry. RG24, Vol. 15157. National Archives of Canada.

Browne-Clayton (Lieutenant). "Lieut. Browne-Clayton, PPCLI, interviewed in 15 Cdn. Gen. Hosp. 2 July 1944." 145.2P7.011 (D3). Department of National Defence, Directorate of History.

Burns, E.L.M. (Lieutenant General). Canadian Operations in the Mediterranean Area, May–June 1944: Extracts from Memoranda (Series 23). The Liri Valley Battle: 1 CDN Corps Narrative of Events; The Set Piece Attack: Lessons from the Breakthrough of the Hitler Line; and The Pursuit from the Melfa to Anagni: Lessons. Department of National Defence, Directorate of History.

Cameron, D.C. (Lieutenant Colonel). The Hastings and Prince Edward Regiment Canadian Army Overseas, CMF, The Battle of the Woods — Wed. 17 May 1944 and Assault on the Adolf Hitler Line — 23 May 1944. 145.2H1.013(D2) Department of National Defence, Directorate of History.

Canadian Operations in the Mediterranean Area, May 1944: Extracts from Memoranda (Series 20). RG24, Vol. 2782. National Archives of Canada.

Canadian Operations in the Mediterranean Area, May 1944: Extracts from War Diaries and Memoranda (Series 21); Extract from Report of 3rd Canadian Armoured Recce Regiment (Governor General's Horse Guards) on Operations 24–30 May 1944. Department of National Defence, Directorate of History.

Canadian Operations in the Mediterranean Area, May 1944: Extracts from War Diaries and Memoranda (Series 22). Department of National Defence, Directorate of History.

Canadian Operations in the Mediterranean Area, May–June 1944: Extracts from War Diaries and Memoranda (Series 26). Department of National Defence, Directorate of History.

Cape Breton Highlanders War Diary, May 1944. RG24, Vol. 15047. National Archives of Canada.

Capture of Ferentino and Anagni by the RCR and Battle Narrative, the Royal Canadian Regiment, 15 May–24 May 1944. 145.2R13.011(D1). Department of National Defence, Directorate of History.

Carleton and York Regiment War Diary, May 1944. RG24, Vol. 15050. National Archives of Canada.

The Crossing of the Melfa and the Securing of a Bridgehead by 5th Canadian Armoured Brigade (Report by Commander 5 CDN ARMD BDE). RG24, Vol. 10991. National Archives of Canada.

Currelly, R.T. (Captain). Report No. 158, Historical Officer Canadian Military Headquarters: Operations of the 1st Canadian Armoured Brigade in Italy, May 1944 to February 1945. 27 September 1946. Department of National Defence, Directorate of History.

——. Report on Activities of 1st Canadian Armoured Brigade for period of 11 May to 30 May 1944. 15 August 1944. RG24, Vol. 10990. National Archives of Canada.

——. Report on Operations of the 11th CAR (Ontario Regiment) from 11 May to 30 May 1944. 14 July 1944. 141.4A11.013(D1). Department of National Defence, Directorate of History.

——. Report on Operations of 14th CAR (Calgary Regiment) for the period 10 May to 28 May 1944. 31 August 1944. 141.4A14.013(D1). Department of National Defence, Directorate of History.

——. Report on Operations of 12th CAR (Three Rivers Regiment) for the period of 1 April to 6 May 1944 and 11 May to 26 May 1944. 31 July 1944. 141.4A12.013 Department of National Defence, Directorate of History.

Duddle, J. M. (Company Sergeant Major). "CSM Duddle, Seaforth of Canada, interviewed 1 July, 1944." 145.255.011 Department of National Defence, Directorate of History.

Durnford, Roy C.H. Diary of Major Roy Durnford, Chaplain (Padre), the Seaforth Highlanders of Canada. June 1943 – June 1945. National Archives of Canada.

Eaton, J.W. Comments by Major J.W. Eaton on the Battle of the Melfa Crossing. Department of National Defence, Directorate of History.

8th Canadian Field Regiment (Self-Propelled). Royal Canadian Artillery War Diary, May 1944. RG24, Vol. 14451. National Archives of Canada.

8th Princess Louise's New Brunswick Hussars War Diary, May 1944. RG24, Vol. 14208. National Archives of Canada.

The 11th Canadian Armoured Regiment. Infantry and Tank Cooperation in the Attack. 23 August 1944. 141.4A11.013(D1). Department of National Defence, Directorate of History.

11th Canadian Armoured Regiment (Ontario) War Diary, May 1944. RG24, Vol. 14238. National Archives of Canada.

11th Canadian Infantry Brigade (Headquarters) War Diary, May 1944. RG24, Vol. 14159. National Archives of Canada.

Enemy Defences: The Adolf Hitler Line. 8 May 1944. 124.4F3(D17). Department of National Defence, Directorate of History.

The Enemy on the Adolf Hitler Line, May 1944. RG24, Vol. 10883. National Archives of Canada.

5th Canadian Armoured Division (GS Headquarters) War Diary. May 1944. RG24, Vol. 13796. National Archives of Canada.

5th Canadian Armoured Regiment (8 NBH). Operations from Hitler Line to Ceccano, 24 May–31 May 1944. RG24. National Archives of Canada.

5th Canadian Armoured Regiment (8 NBH). Report on Operations 24 May–31 May 1944. 10 June 1944. 141.4A5011(D1). Department of National Defence, Directorate of History.

1st Canadian Armoured Brigade War Diary, May 1944. RG24, Vol. 14034. National Archives of Canada.

1st Canadian Armoured Regiment (Royal Canadian Dragoons) War Diary, May 1944. RG24, Vol. 14188.

1st Canadian Corps War Diary (General E.L.M. Burns), May 1944. RG24, Vol. 17507. National Archives of Canada.

1st Canadian Corps War Diary (GS Branch Headquarters), May 1944. RG24, Vol. 13687. National Archives of Canada.

1st Canadian Field Regiment (Royal Canadian Horse Artillery), May 1944. RG24, Vol. 14409. National Archives of Canada.

1st Canadian Infantry Brigade (Headquarters) War Diary, May 1944. RG24, Vol. 14076. National Archives of Canada.

1st Canadian Infantry Division War Diary (GS Branch), May 1944. RG24, Vol. 13728. National Archives of Canada.

1st Light Anti-Aircraft Regiment War Diary, May 1944. RG24, Vol. 14587. National Archives of Canada.

48th Highlanders of Canada Regiment War Diary, May 1944. RG24, Vol. 15297. National Archives of Canada.

14th Canadian Armoured Regiment (Calgary Tanks) War Diary, May 1944. RG24, Vol. 14244. National Archives of Canada.

4th Canadian Anti-tank Regiment War Diary, May 1944. RG24, Vol. 14565. National Archives of Canada.

4th Canadian Armoured Reconnaissance Regiment (Princess Louise Dragoon Guards) War Diary, May 1944. RG24, Vol. 14205. National Archives of Canada.

Fraser (Major) and Lieutenant Kenyon. Royal Canadian Engineers (3 Field Company) Report on Engineers accompanying of 2 CIB patrols in front of Hitler Line. 143.3F011(D1) Department of National Defence, Directorate of History.

Hastings and Prince Edward Regiment War Diary, May 1944. RG24, Vol. 15073. National Archives of Canada.

History of Royal 22e Regiment from 17 May 44 to 25 May 44. 145.2R19011(D1). Department of National Defence, Directorate of History.

Hughes (Captain). Account by Brigadier T.G. Gibson, commander 2 CIB, 27 May 1944. RG24, Vol. 10982. National Archives of Canada.

———. Account by Lt. Col. R.L. Purvis, OC, 11th CAR, and Capt. J.L. Slinger, IO, 11th CAR. 24 May 1944. 141.4A11.013(D1). Department of National Defence, Directorate of History.

Infantry Battalion in an Infiltration Role. RG24, Vol. 10779. National Archives of Canada.

Irish Regiment of Canada War Diary, May 1944. RG24, Vol. 15086. National Archives of Canada.

Italian Campaign — Sicily and Southern Italy, July 1943–April 1945. Condensed from an Official Historical Sketch prepared by the Canadian Army Historical Section. N.a., n.d., n.p. Department of National Defence, Directorate of History.

Johnston, Ian (Lieutenant Colonel). 48th Highlanders of Canada: The Liri Valley and the Adolf Hitler Line. 145.2H3013(D1). Department of National Defence, Directorate of History.

Landell, K.D. (Lieutenant Colonel). Military 1 CACR (Royal Canadian Dragoons) Report on Ops 23 May to 2 June inclusive. 15 June 1944. 140.4A1(D1). Department of National Defence, Directorate of History.

Leese, Oliver (General). Message to the Troops. RG24, Vol. 10888. National Archives of Canada.

Loyal Edmonton Regiment War Diary, May 1944. RG24, Vol. 15114. National Archives of Canada.

McCarter, Nick (Brigadier). Letters Regarding Liri Valley Operations. RG24, Vol. 10779.

McCusker, E.A. (Brigadier). Medical History of the War: 1st Canadian Corps, 1 April 1944–30 June 1944. RG24, Vol. 10779. National Archives of Canada.

Mahony, J.K. (Lieutenant Colonel). The Melfa Crossing: Address recorded by Lieutenant Colonel J.K. Mahony (VC) for delivery at Regimental Dinner, Westminster Regiment, 1948. 145.2W1011(D3). Department of National Defence, Directorate of History.

9th Canadian Armoured Regiment (British Columbia Dragoons) War Diary, May 1944. RG24, Vol. 14229.

Operations — Italy — Hitler Line. RG24, Vol. 10779. File: 234C1.013(D3). National Archives of Canada.

Perkins, E.J. (Lieutenant). Account of Action. 141.4A2011(D2). Department of National Defence, Directorate of History.

Perth Regiment of Canada War Diary, May 1944. RG24, Vol. 15136. National Archives of Canada.

Potvin, Pierre, account in possession of the author, translated from French version published in *The Citadelle* (Tony Poulin, trans.).

Prieur, Charles. Chronicles of the Three Rivers Regiment (Tank) at War: Period 1939–1945. Unpublished manuscript.

Princess Patricia's Canadian Light Infantry War Diary, May 1944. RG24, Vol. 15157. National Archives of Canada.

The Pursuit Battle and Capture of Frosinone. RG24, Vol. 10982. National Archives of Canada.

Regimental History Carleton and York Regiment. 145.2C6.011(D1). Department of National Defence, Directorate of History.

Report on Air Operations in Support of 1 CDN Corps, 11 May–4 June 1944. 8 June 1944. Department of National Defence, Directorate of History.

Report by CCRA 1 CDN Corps on Operations of Canadian Artillery in Italy, May–June 1944. 142.2013(D1). Department of National Defence, Directorate of History.

Report Hitler Line Defences by GS, 1 CDN Infantry Div. RG24, Vol. 10888. National Archives of Canada.

Royal Canadian Regiment War Diary, May 1944, RG24, Vol. 15210. National Archives of Canada.

Royal 22e Regiment War Diary, May 1944, RG24, Vol. 15329. National Archives of Canada.

Seaforth Highlanders of Canada War Diary, May 1944, RG24, Vol. 15256. National Archives of Canada.

2nd Canadian Armoured Regiment (Lord Strathcona's Horse) War Diary, May 1944. RG24, Vol. 14192. National Archives of Canada.

2nd Canadian Infantry Brigade (Headquarters) War Diary, May 1944. RG24, Vol. 14079. National Archives of Canada.

2nd Field Regiment, Royal Canadian Artillery War Diary, May 1944. RG24, Vol. 14419. National Archives of Canada.

The "Set-Piece" Attack: Lessons From the Breakthrough of the Hitler Line. RG24, Vol. 10779. National Archives of Canada.

17th Field Regiment, Royal Canadian Artillery War Diary, May 1944. RG24, Vol. 14528. National Archives of Canada.

Snow, T.E. (Acting Brigadier). Report on the Battle of the Liri Valley. Department of National Defence, Directorate of History.

——. Statement in Protest Against Adverse Report on A/Brigadier T.E. Snow. MG30, Vol. E-157. National Archives of Canada.

Spurr, J.W. (Captain). Report No. 111B Historical Section Canadian Military Headquarters: Situation of the Canadian Military Forces Overseas, Spring 1944. 19 April 1944. Department of National Defence, Directorate of History.

Stacey, C.P. (Lieutenant Colonel). Report No. 179 Historical Section Canadian Military Headquarters: Canadian Operations in the Liri Valley, May–June 1944. 25 July 1947. Department of National Defence, Directorate of History.

——. Report No. 141 Historical Section Canadian Military Headquarters: Situation of the Canadian Military Forces Overseas, Progress in Equipment (January–December 1944). 18 July 1945. Department of National Defence, Directorate of History.

——. Report No. 122 Historical Officer Canadian Military Headquarters: Situation of the Canadian Military Forces Overseas, Spring 1944: Growth of the

Canadian Army Overseas, October 1943–May 1944. 29 August 1944. Department of National Defence, Directorate of History.

———. Report No. 113 Historical Officer Canadian Military Headquarters: Situation of the Canadian Military Forces Overseas, Winter 1943–1944: I. 25 January 1944. Department of National Defence, Directorate of History.

Stursberg, Peter. Broadcasts from 12 May 1944 to 13 July 1944. CBC Radio Archives, Toronto.

3rd Canadian Field Regiment, Royal Canadian Artillery War Diary, May 1944. RG24, Vol. 14435. National Archives of Canada.

3rd Canadian Infantry Brigade (Headquarters) War Diary, May 1944. RG24, Vol. 14084. National Archives of Canada.

3rd Canadian Reconnaissance Regiment (Governor General's Horse Guards) War Diary, May 1944. RG24, Vol. 14199. National Archives of Canada.

12th Canadian Armoured Regiment (Three Rivers Regiment) War Diary, May 1944. RG24, Vol. 18207. National Archives of Canada.

Vokes, Chris (Major General). Canadian Operations in the Mediterranean Area, July–September 1944: Extracts from War Diaries and Memoranda (Series 27). 20 July 1944. Department of National Defence, Directorate of History.

Vokes, Chris. "The Adriatic Front — Winter 1944." Vokes Papers, Royal Military College of Canada Massey Library.

Watson, W. deN. (Major). "Major W. deN. Watson PPCLI (MC) interviewed at 14 Gen. Hosp. 2 July, 1944." 145.2P7011(D3). Department of National Defence, Directorate of History.

Westminster Regiment (Motor) War Diary, May 1944. RG24, Vol. 15283. National Archives of Canada.

West Nova Scotia Regiment Diary, 16–26 May 1944 Inclusive. 145.2W2011(D1). Department of National Defence, Directorate of History.

INTERVIEWS AND CORRESPONDENCE

Beach, Horace Dugald. 1978. Interview by Chris Main. Victoria, BC 15, 19, 24 May. University of Victoria Special Collections.

Brown, Ted. 2000. Correspondence with author. 30 July.

Bulger, Victor. 2000. Correspondence with author. 6 October.

Burton, John Francis. 1984. Interview by Morgan Witzel. Victoria, BC 12 January. University of Victoria Special Collections.

Coppinger, Stephen. 1987. Interview by Tom Torrie. Victoria, BC 11 August. University of Victoria Special Collections.

Creighton, Donald. 2000. Interview by author. Richmond, BC 4 October.

Davis, R.A.C. N.d. Memo to Dr. Reginald Roy, Reginald Roy Papers. University of Victoria Special Collections.

Dodd, G.T. 1962. Memo to Dr. Reginald Roy, Reginald Roy Papers. 16 July. University of Victoria Special Collections.

Dougan, John Alpine. 2000. Interview by author. Victoria, BC 9 October.

———. Interview by Ken MacLeod. Victoria, BC N.d.

Galloway, Strome. 2000. Interview by author. Ottawa. 6 May.

Gildersleeve, Wilf. 2000. Interview by author. West Vancouver, BC 5 October.

Gower, Don. 2000. Correspondence with author. 25 June.

Haley, Jack. 2000. Interview by author. Victoria, BC 24 August.

Harrison, Patrick. 2000. Interview by author. Victoria, BC 23 August.

Hockin, Neil. 1962. Memo to Dr. Reginald Roy, Reginald Roy Papers. 8 July. University of Victoria Special Collections.

Hoffmeister, Bert M. N.d. Interview by B. Greenhous and W. McAndrew. Department of National Defence, Directorate of History.

Hurley, Ron. 2000. Interview by author. Vancouver, BC 4 October.

Illi, Fritz. 1999. Interview by Michael Boire. Zuffenhausen, Germany. 20 February.

Kanik, Stan. 2000. Interview by author. Sidney, BC 9 August.

Kennedy, Earle. 2000. Correspondence with author. 1, 19 July; 17 August.

Kingsmill, Tony. 2001. Correspondence with author. 22 January.

Kinloch, David. 2000. Correspondence with author. 22, 30 November.

Kurbis, Bill. 1962. Memo to Dr. Reginald Roy, Reginald Roy Papers. 26 July. University of Victoria Special Collections.

Lamberti, Federico. 2000. Interview by author. Cassino, Italy. 1 November.

Logan, Rodman. 2000. Correspondence with author. 28 June.

McBride, L.M. N.d. Memo to Dr. Reginald Roy, Reginald Roy Papers. University of Victoria Special Collections.

McGregor, Gordon. 2001. Interview by author. Victoria, BC 3 January.

McLean, John. N.d. Memo to Dr. Reginald Roy, Reginald Roy Papers. University of Victoria Special Collections.

Maltby, Richard Gosse. 1984. Interview by Morgen Witzel. Victoria, BC 18 January. University of Victoria Special Collections.

Milroy, W.A. 2000. Correspondence with author. 5 September.

Nikiforuk, Dan. Interview by author. Sidney, BC 27 December.

Rankin, Harry. 2000. Interview by author. Vancouver, BC 15 October.

Reid, Donald. 2000. Correspondence with author. October and 6 December.

Reynolds, Garnet. 2000. Correspondence with author. October.

Ritchie, Fred. 2000. Correspondence with author. 25 September.

Smith, Don. 2000. Correspondence with author. 15 August.

Smitheram, H.A. 1962. Memo to Dr. Reginald Roy, Reginald Roy Papers. 29 May. University of Victoria Special Collections.

Stone, James Riley. 1980. Interview by William S. Thackray. Victoria, BC 13, 20 May; 3, 10, 17 June. University of Victoria Special Collections.

Taylor, Nigel. 1962. Memo to Dr. Reginald Roy, Reginald Roy Papers. 15 July. University of Victoria Special Collections.

Tellier, Henri. 2000. Correspondence with author. 18 July; 22 August; 23 September.

Thomas, Sydney. 2000. Interview with author. Salmon Arm, BC 27 May.

Tuck, Don. 1967. Memo to Dr. Reginald Roy, Reginald Roy Papers. 22 November. University of Victoria Special Collections.

Ware, Cameron. 1979. Interview by Reginald Roy. Victoria, BC 23, 25 June; 10 July. University of Victoria Special Collections.

Worton, Bill. 2000. Interview by author. Vancouver, BC 4 October.

GENERAL INDEX

Index of Formations, Units, and Corps